W9-AZO-037

LET'S GO

■ THE RESOURCE FOR THE INDEPENDENT TRAVELER

"The guides are aimed not only at young budget travelers but at the indepedent traveler; a sort of streetwise cookbook for traveling alone."

—The New York Times

"Unbeatable; good sight-seeing advice; up-to-date info on restaurants, hotels, and inns; a commitment to money-saving travel; and a wry style that brightens nearly every page."

—The Washington Post

"Lighthearted and sophisticated, informative and fun to read. [Let's Go] helps the novice traveler navigate like a knowledgeable old hand."

—Atlanta Journal-Constitution

"A world-wise traveling companion—always ready with friendly advice and helpful hints, all sprinkled with a bit of wit."

—The Philadelphia Inquirer

■ THE BEST TRAVEL BARGAINS IN YOUR PRICE RANGE

"All the dirt, dirt cheap."

—People

"Anything you need to know about budget traveling is detailed in this book."

—The Chicago Sun-Times

"Let's Go follows the creed that you don't have to toss your life's savings to the wind to travel—unless you want to."

—The Salt Lake Tribune

■ REAL ADVICE FOR REAL EXPERIENCES

"The writers seem to have experienced every rooster-packed bus and lunar-surfaced mattress about which they write."

—The New York Times

"A guide should tell you what to expect from a destination. Here Let's Go shines."

—The Chicago Tribune

LET'S GO PUBLICATIONS

TRAVEL GUIDES

Alaska & the Pacific Northwest 2003
Australia 2003
Austria & Switzerland 2003
Britain & Ireland 2003
California 2003
Central America 8th edition
Chile 1st edition **NEW TITLE**
China 4th edition
Costa Rica 1st edition **NEW TITLE**
Eastern Europe 2003
Egypt 2nd edition
Europe 2003
France 2003
Germany 2003
Greece 2003
Hawaii 2003 **NEW TITLE**
India & Nepal 7th edition
Ireland 2003
Israel 4th edition
Italy 2003
Mexico 19th edition
Middle East 4th edition
New Zealand 6th edition
Peru, Ecuador & Bolivia 3rd edition
South Africa 5th edition
Southeast Asia 8th edition
Southwest USA 2003
Spain & Portugal 2003
Thailand 1st edition **NEW TITLE**
Turkey 5th edition
USA 2003
Western Europe 2003

CITY GUIDES

Amsterdam 2003
Barcelona 2003
Boston 2003
London 2003
New York City 2003
Paris 2003
Rome 2003
San Francisco 2003
Washington, D.C. 2003

MAP GUIDES

Amsterdam
Berlin
Boston
Chicago
Dublin
Florence
Hong Kong
London
Los Angeles
Madrid
New Orleans
New York City
Paris
Prague
Rome
San Francisco
Seattle
Sydney
Venice
Washington, D.C.

SOUTHWEST USA 2003

Co-Editors
Charles Elijah Ewing
Jakub Wrzesniewski

Researcher-Writers
Sheila Baynes
Robert Cacace
Dustin Lewis
Evan North
Jonathan Sherman

Eric Brown Map Editor
D. Cody Dydek Managing Editor
David Muehlke Typesetter

St. Martin's Press ⚞ New York

HELPING LET'S GO

If you want to share your discoveries, suggestions, or corrections, please drop us a line. We read every piece of correspondence, whether a postcard, a 10-page email, or a coconut. Please note that mail received after May 2003 may be too late for the 2004 book, but will be kept for future editions. **Address mail to:**

Let's Go: Southwest USA
67 Mount Auburn Street
Cambridge, MA 02138
USA

Visit Let's Go at **http://www.letsgo.com,** or send email to:

feedback@letsgo.com
Subject: "Let's Go: Southwest USA"

In addition to the invaluable travel advice our readers share with us, many are kind enough to offer their services as researchers or editors. Unfortunately, our charter enables us to employ only currently enrolled Harvard students.

CONTENTS

HOW TO USE THIS BOOK

ORGANIZATION. This book begins with an **Essentials** section. This contains important practical information that will help you plan your travels, travel your trip, and even get back in one piece. The chapters following detail the different destinations in the region starting with a special chapter on the Grand Canyon and then proceeding state by state. Here is where you'll access the invaluable information on the sights and hikes, the dives and honky-tonks, the hidden gems and big splurges that our crack team of ingenious researcher-writers have put together. The black tabs on the side of the book should help you navigate your way through it all.

PRICE RANGES AND RANKINGS. Our researchers list establishments in order of value from best to worst. Our absolute favorites are denoted by the Let's Go thumbs-up (**🖑**). Since the best value does not always mean the cheapest price, we have incorporated a system of price ranges in the guide. The table below lists how prices fall within each bracket.

SOUTHWEST USA	❶	❷	❸	❹	❺
ACCOMMODATIONS	Free-$20	$20-40	$40-60	$60-80	$80 and up
FOOD	$1-7	$7-11	$11-15	$15-18	$18 and up

PHONE CODES AND TELEPHONE NUMBERS. Area codes for each region appear opposite the name of the region and are denoted by the ☎ icon. Phone numbers in text are also preceded by the ☎ icon.

WHEN TO USE IT

TWO MONTHS BEFORE. The first chapter, **Discover Southwest USA,** contains highlights of the region that can help you plan your trip (see pp. 1). The **Essentials** (see p. 16) section contains practical information on planning a budget, making reservations, renewing a passport, and has other useful tips about traveling in the Southwest.

ONE MONTH BEFORE. Take care of insurance, and write down a list of emergency numbers and hotlines. Make a list of packing essentials (see **What to Buy,** p. 58) and shop for anything you are missing. Read through the coverage and make sure you understand the logistics of your itinerary (catching trains, ferries, etc.). Make any reservations if necessary.

2 WEEKS BEFORE. Leave an itinerary and a photocopy of important documents with someone at home. Take some time to peruse the **Life and Times** (see p. 7), which has info on history, culture, flora and fauna, recent political events, and more.

WHO WE ARE

A NEW LET'S GO FOR 2003

With a sleeker look and innovative new content, we have revamped the entire series to reflect more than ever the needs and interests of the independent traveler. Here are just some of the improvements you will notice when traveling with the new *Let's Go.*

MORE PRICE OPTIONS

Still the best resource for budget travelers, *Let's Go* recognizes that everyone needs the occassional indulgence. Our "Big Splurges" indicate establishments that are actually worth those extra pennies (pulas, pesos, or pounds), and price-level symbols (❶ ❷ ❸ ❹ ❺) allow you to quickly determine whether an accommodation or restaurant will break the bank. We may have diversified, but we'll never lose our budget focus—"Hidden Deals" reveal the best-kept travel secrets.

BEYOND THE TOURIST EXPERIENCE

Our Alternatives to Touism chapter offers ideas on immersing yourself in a new community through study, work, or volunteering.

AN INSIDER'S PERSPECTIVE

As always, every item is written and researched by our on-site writers. This year we have highlighted more viewpoints to help you gain an even more thorough understanding of the places you are visiting.

IN RECENT NEWS. *Let's Go* correspondents around the globe report back on current regional issues that may affect you as a traveler.

CONTRIBUTING WRITERS. Respected scholars and former *Let's Go* writers discuss topics on society and culture, going into greater depth than the usual guidebook summary.

THE LOCAL STORY. From the Parisian monk toting a cell phone to the Russian *babushka* confronting capitalism, *Let's Go* shares its revealing conversations with local personalities—a unique glimpse of what matters to real people.

FROM THE ROAD. Always helpful and sometimes downright hilarious, our researchers share useful insights on the typical (and atypical) travel experience.

SLIMMER SIZE

Don't be fooled by our new, smaller size. *Let's Go* is still packed with invaluable travel advice, but now it's easier to carry with a more compact design.

FORTY-THREE YEARS OF WISDOM

For over four decades *Let's Go* has provided the most up-to-date information on the hippest cafes, the most pristine beaches, and the best routes from border to border. It all started in 1960 when a few well-traveled students at Harvard University handed out a 20-page mimeographed pamphlet of their tips on budget travel to passengers on student charter flights to Europe. From humble beginnings, *Let's Go* has grown to cover six continents and *Let's Go: Europe* still reigns as the world's best-selling travel guide. This year we've beefed up our coverage of Latin America with *Let's Go: Costa Rica* and *Let's Go: Chile;* on the other side of the globe, we've added *Let's Go: Thailand* and *Let's Go: Hawaii.* Our new guides bring the total number of titles to 61, each infused with the spirit of adventure that travelers around the world have come to count on.

ACKNOWLEDGMENTS

LET'S GO

TEAM SOUTHWEST THANKS: The best team of RW's at Let's Go. Sheila, Cacace, Dusty, Evan and Sherm, you guys made our jobs easy. Eric, we would be only slightly less lost without you than without your maps. Cody, you came through in the clutch with vigor and style. Cali krew 2003 - more solid than GI Joe. West B for their funky fresh flavor. Nit, REL, Chairman Dubbinwells, and USA for East B solidarity. Michelle Bowman and Kevin Yip for ungrudging last-minute fixes. Prod, for giving our book the hot-rod finish to match its souped-up copy.

KUBA THANKS: Eli, for hiring my shiftless Polish self. Wansley, for the watch. Brenna, Scott and Megan for not evicting me, despite the mountain of coke cans. Mangela, Blaz, Clayton, Cain for trouble. Sue and Mike, for basketball. My former denizens, for "basketball." Alex Leichtbeer, for being queeb bee. Kwok, may you get what you want and happiness besides. Bowie, Spoon, PER brothers. GZ and BC command for keepin' it real. Julie, for more than I can say. This book is for North, Dusty, Cacace, Sherm, and Sheila and for workers everywhere. *Mama, Tata i Ania—sciskam was. Z wami wszystko, bez was nic.*

ELI THANKS: Kuba, for your diligence and Technocratic knowhow. The rw's, for making this book happen. The guys of 44 JFK for late nights and mischief. Digamma. My C-house coterie of ne'er-do-well's: Frank, Muldog, Ray, and Sean. Beef, Tommy, Brad, John Mark, Yarbrough, Kevin, Sammy and the rest of the guys from God's Country for always "bleeding Crimson and Cream." Devon, for being the most beautiful woman in the world; as always, you inspired me. Mom, Dad, AL, AN, UH, and the family, for love and support. Alex, for sharing the womb and looking out for me ever since.

ERIC THANKS: Team SW: bravo! Thanks also to Jerry and the Gang for 5-8-77, Seeders for jalapeño style, and K for everything else.

Co-Editors
Charles Elijah Ewing, Jakub Wrzesniewski
Managing Editor
D. Cody Dydek
Map Editor
Eric Brown

Publishing Director
Matthew Gibson
Editor-in-Chief
Brian R. Walsh
Production Manager
C. Winslow Clayton
Cartography Manager
Julie Stephens
Design Manager
Amy Cain
Editorial Managers
Christopher Blazejewski,
Abigail Burger, D. Cody Dydek,
Harriett Green, Angela Mi Young Hur,
Marla Kaplan, Celeste Ng
Financial Manager
Noah Askin
Marketing & Publicity Managers
Michelle Bowman, Adam M. Grant
New Media Managers
Jesse Tov, Kevin Yip
Online Manager
Amélie Cherlin
Personnel Managers
Alex Leichtman, Owen Robinson
Production Associates
Caleb Epps, David Muehlke
Network Administrators
Steven Aponte, Eduardo Montoya
Design Associate
Juice Fong
Financial Assistant
Suzanne Siu
Office Coordinators
Alex Ewing, Adam Kline,
Efrat Kussell

Director of Advertising Sales
Erik Patton
Senior Advertising Associates
Patrick Donovan, Barbara Eghan,
Fernanda Winthrop
Advertising Artwork Editor
Leif Holtzman
Cover Photo Research
Laura Wyss

President
Bradley J. Olson
General Manager
Robert B. Rombauer
Assistant General Manager
Anne E. Chisholm

RESEARCHER-WRITERS

Sheila Baynes   *Four Corners and surrounding region*

Working for her second consecutive year as a Let's Go Researcher-Writer, Sheila camped and climbed her way through the four corners region. Sheila brought to her work three years of experience as a wilderness survival instructor and an intense interest in environmental issues. Her enthusiasm for the Southwest is evident in every line she crafted.

Robert Cacace   *Nevada and the Grand Canyon*

Though he hails from New York City, Rob is a seasoned guest of one of the Southwest's top draws: Las Vegas. With an acute knowledge of this gritty scene under his belt, Rob employed his Southwestern instincts to draw out the the essential elements of Tahoe, Reno, and even the Grand Canyon. Even when thrust into the cowboy culture of the Ruby Mountains, this city slicker triumphed.

Dustin Lewis   *Arizona*

Apparently, children in Dusty Lewis's Colorado hometown are raised to be a little bit tougher. During his time in Arizona, the veteran traveler of the Southwest took on a mugger, numerous rattlesnakes, forest fires, and record drought. When not living at extremes, Dusty is a budding historian with a passion for all things Southwest.

Jonathan Sherman   *New Mexico, Texas*

Sherm's account of his first night in a New Meixco hostel provides a glimpse of his impassioned grasp of Southwestern flavor and budget travel: "Either I'm at the center of the world or its appendix." Jon's knowledge of both the history and myth of the region resulted in the development of a verve that seems almost indigenous to the Southwest.

Evan North   *Utah*

Evan's gusto for outdoor thrill-seeking and wry wit made him a true find for Team Southwest. Careening across Utah desert in a battle-scarred sedan, he captured both wild terrain and urban settings with flair and aplomb. Even after a mountain road automobile collison hurled him inches from disaster (See On the Edge, p. 252), his poise, creative voice, and sense of humor remained well intact.

Sara Clark   *Southern California Desert*

James Kearney   *Los Angeles*

Kevin Yip   *The Sierra Nevadas*

CONTRIBUTING WRITERS

Claudia Cyganowski graduated from Harvard University with a degree in Astronomy. She has participated in archeological field research in Southwestern Colorado and Copan, Honduras, and has researched the significance of astronomy and the calendar in classic Maya society as well as the Zapotec hieroglyphic writing system and other archaeological topics.

Ryan Hackney was the Editor of *Let's Go: Ireland 1996* and a Researcher-Writer for *Let's Go: Ireland 1995* and *Let's Go: Ecuador 1997*. He now lives in Texas, where he is pursuing a career as a novelist.

Mark Kirby attended rugged Deep Springs College, one of the few in the US that include mending fences on their curricula. His cowboy training gave him the skills to cover the Grand Canyon, Utah and northern Nevada for Let's Go: Southwest USA 2002, the inaugural edition of the Southwest book. Although he's gone on to routes in New Zealand and the Pacific, he remains a dedicated Southwesterner, taking a balanced approach to the important issues of the region.

Southwest USA Maps Overview

NEVADA
pp. 193-237

UTAH
pp. 238-322

COLORADO
pp. 323-356

GRAND CANYON
pp. 66-85

CALIFORNIA
pp. 152-192

ARIZONA
pp. 86-151

NEW MEXICO
pp. 357-425

TEXAS
pp. 426-448

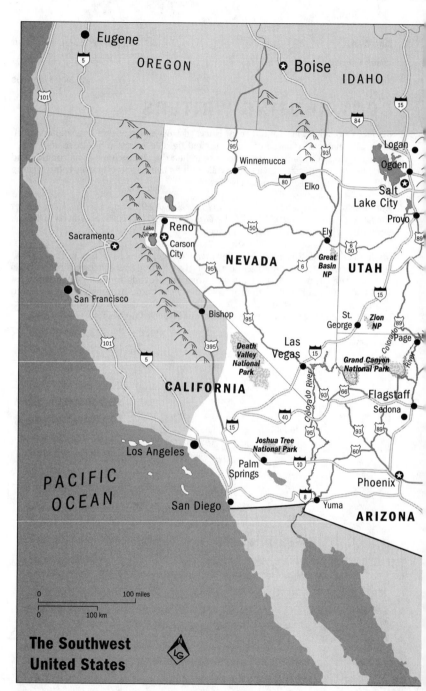

The Southwest
United States

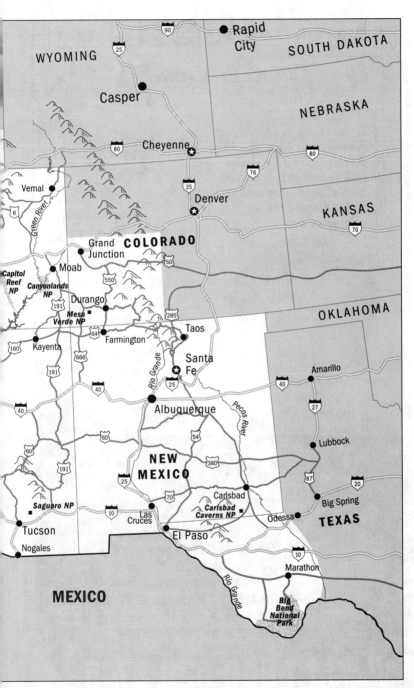

DISCOVER
SOUTHWEST USA

While the vastness of the Southwestern desert, the dramatically colored canvas of Arizona's red rock, sandstone, scrub brush, and pale sky, and the breathtaking vistas from Utah's mountains all invite contemplation, awe, and photo-ops, the opportunity for mild and extreme outdoor activities define a side of the region that Kodak cannot capture. Be it hiking at Canyonlands National Park, biking around Moab, bouldering at Hueco Tanks, river running on the Colorado, backpacking in the remote Gila Wilderness, or skiing the slopes of northern Utah, the rich and varied opportunities for outdoor adventure are unparalleled. At the same time, while the Southwest is best known for its dramatic landscape and recreational activities, its kaleidoscopic mix of cultures is just as intriguing. True to the eccentric spirit of the land, the Southwest can call itself home to hippies, cowboys and cowboys-at-heart, New Age spiritualists, Native Americans, Mexicans and Mexican-Americans, government scientists, aging conservatives, liberal outdoor junkies, transplanted suburban families, and droves of tourists who have all rambled their way there, to the real American desert.

ACTIVITIES AND ADRENALINE RUSHES

HIKING AND BACKPACKING (HIGH AND LOW). The sheer number of destinations and variety of terrain make hiking the Southwest a confusing proposition. The upside: if you know what you want, you can find it. In **Utah**, red-rock turrets and the amazing Narrows Trail of **Zion** (p. 291) contrast with astounding slickrock and the Turret Arch Trail found in **Arches** (p. 277). You can get off the beaten path in popular **national parks** by making a rim-to-rim trek through the **Grand Canyon** (p. 66) or by hiking **Death Valley** (p. 166) and its myriad washes in winter. The opportunity for long **backpacking** treks exists both in the well-trod **Pecos Wilderness**, NM (p. 376) and in the hidden **Great Basin National Park,** NV (p. 208). For a little of everything, **Big Bend** (p. 440) fits the bill, with great hikes both in the high Chisos Mountains and in the lowlands along the Río Grande. For more hiking and backpacking opportunities, see **In the Middle of Nowhere,** below.

MOUNTAIN BIKING. The secret's out. Everyone knows that **Moab** (p. 268) and its slickrock has the best mountain biking in the West. Of course, **Durango** (p. 328) is right behind, offering trails in the foothills and mountains north of town. Not as well-known are the singletrack trails near **Taos** (p. 380) and **Flagstaff**, especially around **Sedona** (p. 113).

ROCK CLIMBING. As with biking, adventurous travelers now know they can count on **Moab** (p. 268) for good climbing routes of varying difficulty, but the massive boulders of **Joshua Tree** (p. 179) offer the true climbing paradise, providing fodder for thousands of climbers at a time. **Hueco Tanks** (p. 433), **Black Canyon** (p. 354), and **Unaweep Canyon** (p. 353) round out the Southwest's best climbing spots.

DISCOVER

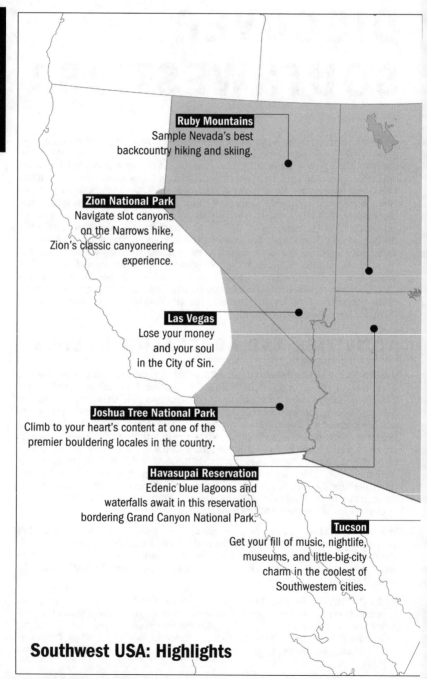

Ruby Mountains
Sample Nevada's best
backcountry hiking and skiing.

Zion National Park
Navigate slot canyons
on the Narrows hike,
Zion's classic canyoneering
experience.

Las Vegas
Lose your money
and your soul
in the City of Sin.

Joshua Tree National Park
Climb to your heart's content at one of the
premier bouldering locales in the country.

Havasupai Reservation
Edenic blue lagoons and
waterfalls await in this reservation
bordering Grand Canyon National Park.

Tucson
Get your fill of music, nightlife,
museums, and little-big-city
charm in the coolest of
Southwestern cities.

Southwest USA: Highlights

Canyonlands National Park
Hike the Needles, backpack in the Maze, and ride the rapids of the Green and Colorado Rivers in one of Utah's most awe-inspiring and least-visited parks.

Weminuche Wilderness
Explore remote backcountry trails along 50 miles of the Continental Divide in the San Juan Mountains.

Chaco Culture National Monument
Hike among the canyon's incredibly well-preserved Ancestral Puebloan ruins.

Truth or Consequences
Try the hot mineral baths in one of the coolest small towns in New Mexico.

Big Bend National Park
The Río Grande calls with hiking in Santa Eleña Canyon, and rafting on the Wild and Scenic River.

Chiricahua National Monument
Wander through sculpted volcanic formations at this peaceful "Wonderland of Rocks."

DISCOVER

RIVER RUNNING. The wild rivers that rage in the Southwest carve the region's canyons, but they also bear rafters, kayakers, and canoers down their rapids. The **Green River** in **Dinosaur National Monument** (p. 257) requires permits, but is among the area's most scenic rivers. The **Río Grande** provides entertaining rapids through **Taos Box** (p. 380), but peters out by the time it reaches **Big Bend** (p. 440). The **Colorado** runs near **Moab** (p. 268) and through the **Grand Canyon** (p. 66).

SKIING. Even before it received the Olympic nod, the **Salt Lake City** area claimed to have the greatest snow on earth. The best skiing is located near **Park City** (p. 248) and **Ogden** (p. 251). In southwestern Colorado, both **Telluride** (p. 336), **Purgatory** (p. 340), and **Silverton** (p. 334) have first-rate slopes. **Taos Ski Valley** (p. 388) is strictly for experts, boasting some of the region's most difficult terrain.

SPELUNKING. If you've had just about enough of the Southwest's summer sun beating down on you, the region's **subterranean wonders** will cool you off and stun you will their intricate beauty. **Carlsbad Caverns** (p. 421) is the most developed of the lot; **Lehman Cave** (p. 208) is the least-visited. Other regional caves include **Timpanogos Cave** (p. 250) and **Kartchner Caverns** (p. 138).

SCINTILLATING SCENERY. Though experiencing many of the Southwest's wonders require hiking boots or crampons, other regional highlights involve merely snapping a few photos and taking in the impressive view. The granddaddy of all views, the **Grand Canyon** won't disappoint, but if you are looking for less-crowded canyon rim vistas, you might check out **Canyon de Chelly** (p. 123) or **Black Canyon of the Gunnison** (p. 354). Other canyon wonders include the falls of **Havasupai Reservation** (p. 75) and the hoodoos of **Bryce Canyon** (p. 300). Rounding out the most spectacular photo-ops in the Southwest are the otherworldly volcanic pillars of **Chiricahua** (p. 150) and the tufa formations of **Pyramid Lake** (p. 229).

IN THE MIDDLE OF NOWHERE

If you are looking for a large piece of unspoiled land on which to play modern-day adventurer or to fulfill your extreme backcountry urges, the Southwest is the best place south of Alaska to find vast tracts of unspoiled wilderness.

Though the Southwest's **deserts** should not be explored without precaution, a backcountry trip into arid climes will appeal to solitude-seeking travelers and stringent ascetics. **Grand Staircase-Escalante National Monument** (p. 308) offers almost two million acres of sandstone narrows and sedimentary stair-steps down toward Lake Powell. The **Black Rock Desert** (p. 230) features the **Burning Man Festival** (p. 232), immense stretches of playa, and some of the most remote canyons and mountains in the nation. To the southwest, **Mojave National Preserve** (p. 177) is bisected by railroad tracks and marked by occasional dirt roads, but the park's cinder cones and sand dunes are set amid large chunks of desert wilderness. On the Mexican border, **Organ Pipe National Monument** (p. 141) presents visitors with great winter biking set in stands of eponymous cacti. Finally, eastern Utah's vast **Canyonlands National Park** (p. 282) is only criss-crossed by the occasional four-wheel-drive road—a true backpacker's delight!

While the Southwest is known for its deserts, its **mountain wilderness** deserves equal attention. The scrubby **Guadalupe Mountains** (p. 433) make for an unknown, sparsely traveled desert in the sky. In the heavily developed Colorado Rockies, the **Weminuche Wilderness** in the San Juan Mountains (p. 333) is a haven of tranquility in strip-mall civilization. East of Salt Lake City, the **Uinta Wilderness** (p. 266) also provides an alternative to the heavily trafficked trails of the Wasatch Range. Finally, the **Ruby Mountains** (p. 233) compose a still-glaciated range of rugged peaks and alpine lakes, maybe the most rugged of the Southwest's alpine ranges.

ARCHAEOLOGY

Home to some of the oldest ancient cultures in North America, the Southwest offers great opportunities to examine and explore the remnants of these ancient cultures. One of the best sites is **Canyon de Chelly** (p. 123), home to indigenous peoples for almost five millennia. Another, **Chaco Culture National Historical Park** (p. 396), maintains the first great settlement of the Ancestral Puebloans, dating to the 9th century. Encompassing 33,000 acres of wilderness with 70 miles of trails, **Bandelier** (p. 375) features spectacular cliff dwellings and stone houses of the Ancestral Puebloans. **Mesa Verde** (p. 344) is the only national park set aside exclusively for archaeological remains and offers views of 13th-century Ancestral Puebloan cliff dwellings. In Utah, the **Nine-Mile Canyon** (p. 263) houses the world's most concentrated collection of prehistoric rock art, dating to the first century AD.

Several Southwestern locales serve not only as archaeological sites, but as sites of contemporary inhabitation. **Taos Pueblo** (p. 387) contains homes between 700 and 1000 years old and is the oldest continuously inhabited settlement in the US.

CITIES

TUCSON. Arguably the cosmopolitan center of Arizona, Tucson offers world-class museums, entertainment, a diverse population, and bustling nightlife. The local outdoors attractions of **Saguaro Park** and **Sabino Canyon** make easy daytrips, while longer treks lead to **Organ Pipe Cactus National Monument,** hikes in the **Coronado National Forest,** Mexican **border towns,** and the thriving small town of **Bisbee.**

ALBUQUERQUE. The **Sandía** and less well-known **Manzano Mountains** tower over the city to the west, seeming to watch over the historic buildings of **Old Town** and the city's delicious restaurants. These mountains offer plentiful hiking, biking, and skiing opportunities for the tourists who fly or drive into Albuquerque each day.

PHOENIX. The hub of all hubs, sprawling Phoenix provides the most convenient destination for all flights to the Southwest, and lying nearly equidistant between Flagstaff and Tucson, can easily be first stop on any journey in the state. Take the time to explore Phoenix's own gems before setting out: visit Frank Lloyd Wright's **Taliesin West,** drive the **Apache Trail,** and wander through the **Heard Museum.**

SANTA FE. Though the city's accommodations and food are pricey, hiking in the **Pecos Wilderness,** biking near **Los Alamos,** viewing **Bandelier's** dwellings, and visiting pueblos on the **High Road** provide sufficient escape from the city's glitz and glamor.

SALT LAKE CITY. Host to the 2002 Olympics, Salt Lake City has undergone a facelift over the past several years, and now, with premier **skiing and rock climbing** near **Park City,** a host of new ethnic restaurants, and an improving nightlife, SLC is ready to become a tourist city of a new-and-improved order. And remember, the **Uintas** and **Dinosaur National Monument** are only a hop, skip, and jump away.

LAS VEGAS. The gloriously overdone city of sin, filled with grandiosely outfitted gambling casinos and entertainment spectaculars, offers enough decadence for a lifetime. Balance out your time with the water sport paradise of **Lake Mead,** a visit to **Red Rocks,** and a tour of **Hoover Dam.**

WHEN TO GO

Most tourists and vacationers descend upon the Southwest's sights during the summer, when the Grand Canyon and other national parks strain to accommodate the influx of visitors. However, during the summer, some of the low desert sights along the southern periphery of the Southwest are simply too hot to enjoy. In the winter, ski season heats up and even the high deserts don a layer of sparkling white on their red-rock formations. Meanwhile, the low deserts along the Mexican border afford a mild refuge of year-round warmth. All things considered, the best time to catch the entire region at is best may well be spring, when the Grand Canyon is not yet packed, the low deserts sport blooming wildflowers, and the high deserts have already emerged from winter's snow and ice.

NATIONAL HOLIDAYS

DATE IN 2003	HOLIDAY
January 1	New Year's Day
January 20	Martin Luther King, Jr. Day
February 17	Presidents Day
April 20	Easter Sunday
May 26	Memorial Day
July 4	Independence Day
September 1	Labor Day
October 13	Columbus Day
November 11	Veterans Day
November 27	Thanksgiving
December 25	Christmas Day

FESTIVALS

MONTH	FESTIVAL
January	**National Cowboy Poetry and Music Festival,** Elko, NV (see p. 235)
February	**National Date Festival,** Indio, CA (see p. 191)
March	**Cowboy Poetry Festival,** Alpine, TX (see p. 437)
June	**Durango Shakespeare Festival,** Durango, CO (see p. 331)
	Telluride Bluegrass Festival, Telluride, CO (see p. 338)
	Utah Shakespeare Festival, Cedar City, UT (see p. 289)
July	**UFO Festival,** Roswell, NM (see p. 420)
	Artown Festival, Reno, NV (see p. 218)
August	**Jazz Celebration,** Telluride, CO (see p. 338)
	Indian Market, Santa Fe, NM (see p. 372)
	Basque Festival, Reno, NV (see p. 218)
September	**Telluride International Film Festival,** Telluride, CO (see p. 338)
	Blues and Brews Festival, Telluride, CO (see p. 338)
	International Bat Festival, Carlsbad, NM (see p. 424)
	Burning Man Festival, Black Rock Desert, NV (see p. 232)
	Marfa Lights Festival, Alpine, TX (see p. 437)
October	**Hot Air Balloon Rally,** Albuquerque, NM (see p. 362)
November	**49ers Encampment Festival,** Death Valley, CA (see p. 168)
	Festival of the Cranes, Truth or Consequences, NM (see p. 404)

LIFE AND TIMES

While the vastness of the Southwestern desert, the dramatically colored canvas of Arizona's red rock, sandstone, scrub brush, and pale sky, and the breathtaking vistas from Utah's mountains all invite contemplation, the opportunity for mild and extreme outdoor activities define a side of the region that Kodak cannot capture. Be it hiking at Canyonlands National Park, biking around Moab, bouldering at Hueco Tanks, river running on the Colorado, backpacking in the remote Gila Wilderness, or skiing the slopes of northern Utah, the rich opportunities for outdoor adventure are unparalleled. At the same time, while the Southwest is best known for its dramatic landscape and recreational activities, its kaleidoscopic mix of cultures is just as intriguing. True to the eccentric spirit of the land, the Southwest can call itself home to hippies, cowboys and cowboys-at-heart, New Age spiritualists, Native Americans, Mexicans and Mexican-Americans, government scientists, aging conservatives, liberal outdoor junkies, transplanted suburban families, and droves of tourists who have all rambled their way there, to the real American desert.

HISTORY

THE PRE-EUROPEAN SOUTHWEST

Archaeologists now estimate that the first Southwesterners were big game hunters who arrived in the Southwest at least 25,000 years ago, having crossed over from Asia along the Bering Strait. Knowledge of the earliest distinct culture was solidified in the 1930s, when the discovery of prehistoric spear points provided concrete evidence of the **Clovis** people, a society of hunters and gatherers who settled in the Southwest around 9500 BCE. Over the next several centuries, drastic environmental changes transformed the region into the desert land that we associate with the Southwest today. Evidence suggests that by 3500 BCE, the region's dwellers had capitalized on the warmer climate to begin agricultural civilizations.

Between 500 and 100 BCE, three major cultures emerged. From around 500-300 BCE, the **Mogollon** people arrived at the Arizona/New Mexico border and established what may have been the region's first true farming civilization. While the Mogollon culture seems to have died out around 1200 AD, it is likely that Mogollon people may have survived and to become the modern **Zuni.** The **Hohokam,** a second farming culture, migrated from modern-day Mexico around 300 BCE, and settled farther west in southern Arizona. With the help of highly advanced agricultural and technical innovations, they expanded their civilization into the Tucson Basin, the Phoenix area, and even to modern-day Flagstaff, peaking in prosperity between 1100 and 1200 CE. Finally, the **Ancestral Puebloans** emerged around 100 BCE in the Four Corners area, and moved from a foraging way of life to farming around 400 CE, adopting the pueblo pattern of living around 700 CE. The Ancestral Puebloans, formerly known as the **Anasazi,** flourished in the Great Pueblo Period, from 1100-1300 CE, before their mysterious decline in the 13th century. While the notion of the Anasazi "disappearance" is common, it is more likely that they migrated from the Four Corners region, and provided the ancestry of modern-day pueblo-inhabiting Native Americans, such as the Hopi.

The most recent additions to the civilizations of the Southwest prior to the arrival of Europeans were the nomadic tribes of the **Navajo** and the **Apache,** known in Navajo language as *Dineh*. The **Dineh,** originally inhabitants of the subarctic, most likely arrived in the Southwest around 1450. Tension immediately developed between the nomads and settled agricultural peoples. Though the Navajo subsequently developed a lifestyle that was relatively settled in comparison to the nomadic Apache, both civilizations remained at odds with the Pueblo Indians.

THE ERA OF THE SPANISH

After four survivors from a 1527 Spanish shipwreck off the coast of Florida spent nine years traveling west, ultimately arriving in the town of Culiacán in New Spain, they came with tales of the gold-filled **"Seven Cities of Cibola,"** otherwise known as the adobe pueblos of New Mexico. Fascinated by these tales, the Spanish government sent **Francisco Vásquez de Coronado** on a mission to conquer the land in 1540. Equipped with hundreds of soldiers and horses, Coronado made his way to Zuni territory on an expedition which marked the beginning of the Spanish era of the Southwest. However, the government of New Spain did not officially begin its period of colonization until the turn of the 17th century, at which point the influx of soldiers and horses came accompanied by fleets of priests on a mission to pacify and Christianize the Indians.

Although the Spanish occupation of the Southwest was based on the themes of assimilation and Christianization rather than that of annihilation that characterized the later Anglo-American presence, the relationship between Native tribes and Spanish settlers was less than peaceful. The Spanish encouraged active slave trade, brought disease, occupied native land, and often violently repressed the practice of indigenous religious beliefs. In return, Native American groups, including the Puebloans, the Apaches, and the Navajos, often offered determined resistance, as was seen especially in the **Pueblo Revolt** of 1680, when the Puebloans managed to drive the Spanish from Santa Fe for several years. Due to factionalism among the Puebloans, however, the Spanish were able to achieve reconquest in 1692, and maintained power for the next 125 years, until Mexico gained independence from Spain in 1821.

ANGLO EXPANSION

The US declared war on Mexico in May 1846, and three months later claimed New Mexico as American land. In 1848, the **Treaty of Guadalupe Hidalgo** ceded a large portion of Southwestern land to the US. Five years later, the **Gadsden Purchase** added the remaining portions of what is today known as Arizona and New Mexico. By 1853, Mexico had ceded the territories that would eventually make up southwestern Texas, Arizona, New Mexico, Utah, Nevada, and California.

The US encroached on Native lands and life in a manner unprecedented. Following Andrew Jackson's massive removal of Native tribes such as the Cherokee and Choctaw from the Southern United States to what is now Oklahoma in the 1830s, the 1850s saw the US government build **Fort Defiance** in Navajo land, forcing Navajos to negotiate for their own land and water. Anger over this and other encroachments led to the **Navajo-Apache Wars,** fought for the next 20 years between the respective tribes in Arizona and New Mexico and the Federal Government.

Between 1863 and 1864, in one of the most tragic and infamous events of American history, **Kit Carson** rounded up over 8000 Navajo and led them on the **Long Walk.** This "walk," a winter-long death march on which people starved and were shot for walking too slowly, ended at the concentration camp at Bosque Redondo, where many Navajo and Apache died. In 1868, the Navajo signed the **Treaty of Bosque Redondo** with the US government, through which they were allowed to return to their land and received a scant 10% of their original territory. In exchange, they agreed not to conduct war against the US, not to carry firearms, and to send their children to white schools, where they would be forced to learn English and assimilate to every aspect of white culture.

In part because the land the Navajo received was unfit for grazing and lacked suitable water sources, the treaty set off a new period of **Navajo-Hopi land disputes.** Since the Hopi did not participate in the wars, they were not included in the dubious terms of the treaty, and the lands that were designated as the Navajo Reservation land conflicted with the lands that the Hopi had called home for centuries. In 1882, the government set boundaries around a 2.5 million acre area enclosed in Navajo land for the Hopi Reservation.

While Native Americans struggled for rights to life and land, Anglo settlement in Arizona and New Mexico continued in full-force, and with it, the booming industries of mining and the railroad. Despite the fact that the region was becoming increasingly profitable and entrenched in the US economy, statehood for Arizona and New Mexico was put off for longer than any of the other states in the lower 48, largely as a result of the anti-Hispanic racism that prevailed in Congress and in the majority of American minds. Both states joined the Union in 1912.

TODAY

IN THE 20TH CENTURY

Throughout the 20th century, Native Americans struggled to defend their rights of access and ownership to the natural resources on their reservations, while the US government sought to reap the economic benefits of all Southwestern land.

MINING. While agriculture has always provided a backbone of Southwestern economies, the 20th century introduced mainlining as the other lifeline of the economy. Two years after oil was discovered on the Navajo Reservation in 1922, Congress passed the **Indian Oil Leasing Act,** which gave the states royalties from all oil produced on Indian lands. The barren land that had been granted the Navajos had proven valuable to US interests after all, and the discovery ushered in another century of struggle between the two groups. In 1937, **coal** and **natural gas** were also found on the Reservation, and the 1938 **Indian Lands Mining Act** gave the US Bureau of Indian Affairs broad powers over all the Reservation's natural resources. Huge mining projects were underway on indigenous land several years before Arizona Indians were even granted the right to vote in US elections, in 1948.

LAND RIGHTS. Land-use controversy is not, of course, limited to conflicts between the US government and Native Americans. Environmentalists concerned with the effects of mining and damming, and with the preservation of endangered species and habitats, have time and butted heads with locals who value the economic benefits of such projects and ideologically resent the government regulation of local land. Throughout the 20th century, several **Sagebrush Rebellions** arose throughout the Southwest as protests against federal land regulation, demanding more land for private use.

WATER RIGHTS. The struggle for ownership and access to water supplies is one that has taken center stage on many fronts. Not only do water rights provide fodder for the continual struggles of Native Americans seeking to gain and maintain control of the water on their lands, it has sparked ongoing controversy between private economic interests and environmentalists. Recently, farmers and fishermen have butted heads with preservationists who long to close off certain waterways in an effort to protect endangered species of fish and other wildlife.

LIFE AND TIMES

THE NUCLEAR AGE. The first atomic bomb was detonated at the **Trinity Site,** northwest of Alamogordo, New Mexico, on July 16, 1945. With wide-open spaces and a relatively sparse population, many areas of the Southwest seemed and continue to seem the perfect locales for nuclear power plants, and many Southwesterners embraced the local presence of atomic power for its jobs and revenue. At the same time, the environmental costs of nuclear research stations and power plants appear to be immense, and concerns over issues including **nuclear waste disposal** and **transport** have created constant controversy. In 1951, Nevada welcomed a Nuclear Test Site to the state, but today, many Nevadans are singing a different tune as places such as **Yucca Mountain** are being considered as possible depositories for highly radioactive nuclear waste.

OTHER WORLDS. In the 1950s, a remote tract of land on Groom Lake dubbed **Area 51** by the federal government became a symbol for alleged US government UFO cover-ups, after tales of **UFO sightings.** In 1947, an unidentified flying object allegedly crashed down in the town of **Roswell,** New Mexico, and was alledgedly subsequently snatched by the US government as part of an elaborate conspiracy to cover up the reality of extraterrestrial life and presence.

GO WEST, YOUNG MAN. A population boom has left New Mexico with more than three times as many residents as in 1940, and the Arizona population has multiplied by an astounding ten times in the same period. Over the last 25 years, Nevada has been the fastest growing state in the country, and the city of Las Vegas, born less than 100 years ago, now is home to over one million people. Recently, the 2002 Winter Olympics in Salt Lake City, drew unprecedented attention to Utah.

PEOPLE

DEMOGRAPHICS

The Southwest was the last of the continental United States acquired by the American government, and thus the last part of the United States exposed to Anglo colonization and development. This historical fact has very visible manifestations in the demography of the Southwest. Whereas in much of the United States Native peoples have been reduced to tiny proportions of the population, in the Southwest large-scale Native communities have survived into the present, maintaining their traditional pueblo culture and way of life.

Similarly, Mexico's stake in the region is visible in the population of the Southwest; to an extent greater than anywhere else in the United States, Spanish is very much a public language and Mexicans and Mexican-Americans form a sizeable portion of the community. Even within the Mexican-American community, however, diversity is the rule; some Mexican Americans are recent immigrants, while others' families have an older history in the area than the United States. Economically, some individuals and communities have thrived while others still struggle towards the American dream.

A similar diversity is visible in Anglo settlement in the Southwest. At roughly the same time as the Mormons were making their historic pilgrimage from the East and Midwest into Utah, a gold and silver rush created a culture with many outlaws and opportunists in the rest of the area. Cheap land and isolation soon brought more newcomers and increased the region's agricultural focus. The 20th century saw large scale migration of artists, new-age spiritualists, extreme sports enthusiasts, and other counter-culture supporters to the area. As it stands today, the Southwest is one of the most multi-faceted regions of a nation known for its diversity.

CULTURE

FOOD AND DRINK

Southwestern cuisine emerged from a blend of **Mexican, Spanish,** and **Native American** cooking. Therefore, while traveling in the Southwest will certainly bring you your fill of burritos, tacos, and enchiladas, these Mexican tortilla-based entrees will be offset with the **Three Sisters** of corn, beans, and squash, all traditionally grown by Southwestern tribes. When traveling through the reservation, be sure to try **Navajo fry bread,** not unlike the fried dough found at festivals and carnivals.

Most important, of course, are the **chiles.** More than the food of any other region of the country, Southwestern cuisine can be thought of synonymously with this one ingredient. The heat of a chili is measured in **Scoville Units.** While the bell pepper measures in with a rating of 0, the red habanero has been tested at 577,000 Scoville Units. The jalapeño pales in comparison, at about 5000. Be prepared to hear the same question over and over when ordering in Southwestern restaurants: red or green? This refers to the color of the chiles that will be used in your meal. A combination of the two can be referred to as "Christmas."

CUSTOMS AND ETIQUETTE

The standards for civil behavior in the Southwest are much the same as those for the rest of the country. Bargaining is futile, except with the purchase of real-estate and automobiles. Don't spit, or expel other bodily fluids, onto the street. Chew with your mouth closed. Keep your elbows off the table

UTAH. Utah is home to Mormons, comprising 73% of the total population of the state. The strength of the religion, and the honest devotion of its followers, make Utah a uniquely wholesome place, more so than the other Southwestern states, and especially moreso than California. Mormonism strictly forbids the consumption of alcohol, caffeine, nicotine, illicit drugs and premarital sex.

The Mormons will help you keep away from the firewater. The only liquor widely sold in Utah is watered down (3% alcohol by volume) beer, and only "private clubs" can serve liquor. Local entrepreneurs have found ways to stretch the definition of "private club," so regular bars exist, albeit with cover charges and bizarre entry rituals. Dress is more modest in Utah than in other parts of the country; revealing clothing will fetch disapproving grimaces. Mormons are scrupulous about clean language, especially respecting the Lord's name, so avoid profanity. The Sabbath is also treated more seriously in Utah than in other parts of the US, so expect stores to be closed on Sunday and people to be less willing to work or play.

NATIVE RESERVATIONS. Crossing into a Native American reservation entails more than just a change of administrative jurisdiction, but also a wholesale change of culture. In the Southwest especially, Native Americans have resisted encroachment by Anglo culture onto their reservations and have preserved a distinct society. Customs and social mores vary from people to people; be aware of which tribe's land you're visiting and learn what behavior is expected of you ahead of time. Generally speaking, it doesn't hurt to dress conservatively and to be reserved in speech and demeanor. Visitors to the Navajo reservation should expect people to be more withdrawn than their Anglo counterparts. Eye contact and chattiness are thought to be disrespectful, and many outsiders confuse Navajo politeness with standoffishness. Hopi tradition forbids the depiction of people in any medium; if you plan to visit the Hopi, leave your cameras and recorders behind.

THE ARTS

PAINTING AND PHOTOGRAPHY

In Taos in 1915, a group of artists led by **Joseph Sharp,** enchanted by the beauty of the region and determined to share the area and its art with the rest of the American public, decided to found the **Taos Society of Artists.** Though the group disbanded in 1927, their effort was not in vain. Ever since, Taos has been the site of a thriving artistic community that still feeds on the inspiring beauty of the area.

At about the same time as the Taos group was forming out West, **Georgia O'Keeffe** was studying and teaching art in New York City, an apprenticeship in form and in texture that would find its inspiration in New Mexico. Though she lived on the east coast for much of her married life, O'Keeffe became more and more infatuated with the Southwest, and she finally moved permanently after her husband (Alfred Stieglitz) died in 1946, spending the rest of days in Abiquiu, southwest of Taos. She claimed to take her inspiration from the pure colors and forms she found in the high desert, and certainly, her large (and largely suggestive) flower canvases are what most people associate with Southwestern art.

As O'Keeffe is known for her flowers, so **Ansel Adams** is known for his black-and-white landscape photography. Though Adams is probably most remembered for his photos of Yosemite National Park and the High Sierra, much of his work was actually within the boundaries of the Southwest. In the mid-1940s, the Guggenheim gave Adams his first grant photograph US national parks. Images of the Grand Canyon and a panorama of the Panamint Mountains from Badwater in Death Valley are among the Southwest images made famous by Adams.

NATIVE AMERICAN ART

The roots of modern Native American art lie in the in the early 19th century. Though interactions with the United States varied greatly among Native peoples, the Government's aggressive removal policies created an occasion for Native American tribes to define themselves in relation to white America as a means of cultural preservation. 19th century Native American art was largely created by members of a tribe for other members of the same tribe.

Early modern paintings were created in the late 1910's and 20's by two distinct groups: one led by **Carl Sweezy** and **Ernst Spybuck** and the **Kiowa Five,** a group of Kiowa artists from Oklahoma including Spenser Asah, Jack Hokeah, Stephen Mopope, Lois Smokey, Monroe Tsatoke, and James Auchiah, Sweezy and Spybuck helped bring Native American art to an appreciative international market. By the 1960s and 70s, artists like T.C. Cannon and Fritz Scholder pushed the genre in a more political direction, placing emphasis on individual pride in Native American cultural heritage.

Since the mid-80s, Native American painting has embraced many characteristics of postmodernism. Among the first Native American artists to utilize postmodern themes was **George Longfish,** whose highly political paintings, like other postmodern works, employ art as an occasion for moral performance that generally displays a resistance to cultural assimilation. Alongside modern developments in painting, traditional forms continue to thrive as a mainstay in Native American art, and both have gained an enormous following. The Southwest USA is an ideal region for viewing traditional and modern Native American art. Both the Heard Museum of Phoenix and the Museum of New Mexico in Santa Fe display large collections of Native American art, while numerous festivals in the Southwest are dedicated solely to showcasing the still growing genre.

ARCHITECTURE

In part because of his innovative work throughout the Southwest, **Frank Lloyd Wright** forever changed thinking about architecture both in America and, to a lesser extent, around the world. Wright believed that designs for living spaces should be more "organic," or representative of their surroundings. Wright designed several buildings in Phoenix, including the Biltmore, and he established Taliesin West, his school of architecture, on the outskirts of the city. **Paolo Soleri,** a follower of Wright's, studied at Taliesin West and established his own architectural project in Arizona called **Arcosanti** (see p. 120). About midway between Phoenix and Flagstaff, this planned community is Soleri's response to the fragmentation and isolation of modern America. He designed this communal townsite to blend in with the desert and to foster a better, healthier lifestyle.

LITERATURE

From frontier novels to naturalists' escapades to Native Americans' struggles, the literature of the Southwest is multi-faceted, layered with the experiences of different eras and cultures. These are just a few of the books integral to the development and flourishing of the regional canon:

James Fenimore Cooper, *The Pioneers* (1823). Widely considered the first American frontier novel, this is the first of Cooper's Leatherstocking series starring Natty Bumppo. Cooper is more famous for *The Last of the Mohicans*, a later book in this same series.

Mark Twain, *Roughing It* (1872). Between 1861 and 1866, Twain (a.k.a. Samuel Clemens) traveled west through Salt Lake City and the Nevada desert, all the way to San Francisco, documenting his personal experiences with the West Coast silver rush.

John Wesley Powell, *Canyons of the Colorado* (1875). A travelogue and adventure story of Powell's trips down the Green and Colorado Rivers from 1867 to 1875. This account and Powell's exploration was an inspiration to many latter-day Western writers, including Wallace Stegner and Edward Abbey.

Zane Grey, *Riders of the Purple Sage* (1912). Set in the Mormon country of southern Utah, the most popular of Grey's novels focuses on the life of Jane Withersteen, a beautiful, rich Western cattle heiress forced to make crucial decisions about her lifestyle and religion in the heat of a vicious town power struggle.

Louis L'Amour, *Hondo* (1953). L'Amour is the prolific modern-day master of the "Cowboys and Indians" genre, taking up the mantle of the Western novel. This novel and his many others go down smooth—no aftertaste.

Edward Abbey, *Desert Solitaire* (1968). Documenting his experience as a ranger in Arches National Park, Abbey's work revels in the stark desert landscape and struggles to redefine the relationship between man and nature on a personal level. Abbey's later novel, *The Monkey-Wrench Gang* (1975), is a comic yet fanciful novel about eco-terrorists and their run-ins with Western infrastructure.

Larry McMurtry, *Lonesome Dove* (1986). Follows the story of Gus and Call, two ranchers living in a small Texas border town. McMurtry skillfully captures the rich landscape and tenuous existence on the frontier.

Tony Hillerman, *Skinwalkers* (1986). Sergeant Jim Chee and Lieutenant Leaphorn are the crime-solving heroes of Hillerman's series of mystery thrillers. Along the way, Hillerman skillfully weaves into his plots a taste of Navajo culture and mysticism.

Terry Tempest Williams, *Refuge* (1991). An environmentalist-*cum*-lyricist, Williams tells the story of her mother's fight with cancer side-by-side with her account of the flooding of the Great Salt Lake, an event which threatened the lake's saline ecosystem.

LIFE AND TIMES

FILM

Nowhere does the region find its cinematic backbone as memorably as in **Westerns.** The genre's plot is commonly one of good and evil, featuring the stereotypically wild, untamed West as the playground for the surly, introspective loner, or the tough-talking vigilant defender of peace and civilization amid the chaos of barbaric Indians, sinister thieves, and corrupt local politicians. Westerns have existed since the earliest days of the silver screen, and have varied widely in terms of quality, budget, and prominence. Some of these most memorable include:

Stagecoach (1939). Considered a ground-breaking film that reinvented the genre of the Western and raised it out of the dubious "B" designation, this John Ford film depicts 9 stagecoach passengers, each forced to navigate dangerous adventures and reveal their true character, all against the backdrop of Monument Valley.

Gunfight at OK Corral (1957). Burt Lancaster and Kirk Douglas star in this movie that relives the legendary relationship between Wyatt Earp and Doc Holliday.

True Grit (1969). John Wayne received the Oscar for Best Actor for his role as a no-nonsense marshall in this movie based on the novel by Charles Portis.

Young Guns (1988). This popular and transparently Gen-X Western features Billy the Kid (Emilio Estevez) seeking adventure with his Wild West crew of outlaws. The 1990 sequel offers more of the same.

Tombstone (1993). Val Kilmer and Kurt Russell star in a more current interpretation of the Earp-Holliday duo and their southern Arizona hangout, Tombstone.

While Westerns take first place as the genre defining Southwestern film, many other films have employed the landscape of the Southwest as a canvas for tales of adventure, drama, and comedies alike.

Easy Rider (1969). Peter Fonda and Dennis Hopper star in this classic 1960s counter-culture road-tripping adventure.

The Milagro Beanfield War (1988). In this Robert Redford movie based on the novel by John Nichols, a New Mexican town supports a farmer who unintentionally irrigates his land with water owned by a rich entrepreneur.

Thelma and Louise (1991). This movie about two friends (Susan Sarandon and Geena Davis) on a weekend-getaway-*cum*-outlaw-adventure doubles nicely as a roadtripping movie featuring the great Southwest.

Leaving Las Vegas (1995). This tragic and disturbing romance starring Elizabeth Shue and Nicholas Cage captures the darker side of the glittering city.

Smoke Signals (1998). Two Navajo young men living in Idaho, Victor and Thomas Builds-the-fire, travel to Arizona to retrieve the remains of Arnold, who was Victor's father and the man who saved Thomas Builds-the-fire's life at early age. The two have very different visions of Arnold, which they debate along the way.

SPORTS AND RECREATION

While outdoor sports like hiking, mountain climbing and biking dominate the imagination of travelers to the Southwest and much of this book is devoted to exploring their function in the region, the Southwest offers a number of unique opportunities for viewing and occasionally participating in unique sports.

RODEO

Born from a fusion of Hispanic *vaquero* and American cowboy traditions, rodeo rose to popularity largely in the Southwest in the late 19th and early 20th centuries and continues to thrive throughout the region as a spectator sport. Thousands pour into arenas for weekly events on the **Professional Rodeo Cowboys Association** (PRCA) Tour to watch events like team roping, bareback riding, saddle bronc riding and a crowd favorite, bull riding. Each December, the PRCA holds its championship, the **Wrangler National Finals Rodeo,** in Las Vegas, and sponsors numerous other events across the Southwest, which are surprisingly accessible to fans in any budget range. For information about PRCA events visit www.prorodeo.com.

ADDITIONAL RESOURCES

GENERAL HISTORY
The following works provide a partial historical overview of Southwestern culture.

Donald Worster, *Dust Bowl: The Southern Plains in the 1930's* (1982). A history of the political, economic, and social ramifications of the nation's worst agricultural disaster, which forced many Americans to travel the deserts of the Southwest.

Marc Reisner, *Cadillac Desert* (1986). A jarring look at the no-holds-barred struggle for scarce water in the West. The author focuses on the story of L.A., the great Western water parasite.

Richard White, *'It's Your Misfortune and None of My Own': A New History of the American West* (1993). This is a history of the relationships between whites and Native Americans in the West by one of the foremost historians on the topic.

Robert S. McPherson, *The Northern Navajo Frontier, 1860-1900: Expansion Through Adversity* (2001). McPherson traces the success and failures of the Navajo in dealing with the Federal Government.

Steven G. Hyslop, *Bound for Santa Fe: The Road to New Mexico and the American Conquest, 1806-1848* (2002). Hyslop presents an in depth historical examination of the actions leading up to the Treaty Guadalupe Hidalgo.

TRAVEL NARRATIVES
As the home of Route 66, Las Vegas, Hollywood, and vast expanses of untouched land, the Southwest has proved an ideal setting travel narratives. Below are some of the premier works of this genre that employ the Southwest as a setting.

Woody Guthrie, *Bound for Glory* (1943). In this autobiographical work, the legendary American folk singer recounts his life and travels across the United States including numerous trips through the Southwest.

Jack Kerouac, *On the Road* (1957). One of America's first beatniks, Kerouac recalls his trips on Route 66 across the Southwest to California.

Hunter S. Thompson, *Fear and Loathing in Las Vegas* (1971). In this "new journalism" classic, Thompson explores Vegas and all of its decadence and depravity.

LIFE AND TIMES

ESSENTIALS

FACTS FOR THE TRAVELER

ENTRANCE REQUIREMENTS
Passport (p. 17). Required for citizens of all foreign countries except Canada.
Visa (p. 18). Visitors from most of Europe, Australia, and New Zealand can travel in the US for up to 90 days without a visa, although you may need to show a return plane ticket. Citizens of South Africa need a visa.
Inoculations: (p. 24).
Work Permit (p. 18). Required for all foreigners planning to work in the US.
Driving Permit (p. 43). Required for all those planning to drive.

EMBASSIES AND CONSULATES

US EMBASSIES AND CONSULATES ABROAD

Contact the nearest embassy or consulate to obtain information regarding visas and permits to the United States. Offices are only open limited hours, so call well before you depart. The US State Department provides contact information for US diplomatic missions on the Internet at http://foia.state.gov/keyofficers.asp. Foreign embassies in the US are located in Washington, D.C., but there are consulates in the Southwest that can be helpful in an emergency. For a more extensive list of embassies and consulates in the US, consult the web site www.embassy.org.

AUSTRALIA. Embassy and Consulate: Moonah Pl., Yarralumla **(Canberra),** ACT 2600 (☎02 6214 5600; fax 6273 3191; www.usembassy-australia.state.gov). **Other Consulates:** MLC Centre, Level 59, 19-29 Martin Pl., **Sydney,** NSW 2000 (☎02 9373 9200; fax 9373 9184); 553 St. Kilda Rd., **Melbourne,** VIC 3004 (☎03 9526 5900; fax 9525 0769); 16 St. George's Terr., 13th fl., **Perth,** WA 6000 (☎08 9202 1224; fax 9231 9444).

CANADA. Embassy and Consulate: 490 Sussex Dr., **Ottawa,** ON K1N 1G8 (☎613-238-5335; fax 688-3101; www.usembassycanada.gov). **Other Consulates:** 615 Macleod Trail SE, Room 1000, **Calgary,** AB T2G 4T8 (☎403-266-8962; fax 264-6630); 1969 Upper Water St., Purdy's Wharf Tower II, suite 904, **Halifax,** NS B3J 3R7 (☎902-429-2480; fax 423-6861); 1155 R. St-Alexandre, **Montréal,** QC H3B 3Z1 (mailing address: P.O. Box 65, Postal Station Desjardins, Montréal, QC H5B 1G1; ☎514-398-9695; fax 398-0702); 2 Place Terrasse Dufferin, B.P. 939, **Québec City,** QC G1R 4T9 (☎418-692-2095; fax 692-4640); 360 University Ave., **Toronto,** ON M5G 1S4 (☎416-595-1700; fax 595-0051); 1095 W. Pender St., 21st fl., **Vancouver,** BC V6E 2M6 (☎604-685-4311; fax 685-7175).

IRELAND. Embassy and Consulate: 42 Elgin Rd., Ballsbridge, **Dublin** 4 (☎01 668 8777 or 668 7122; fax 668 9946; www.usembassy.ie).

NEW ZEALAND. Embassy and Consulate: 29 Fitzherbert Terr. (or P.O. Box 1190), Thorndon, **Wellington** (☎04 462 6000; fax 478 1701; http://usembassy.org.nz). **Other Consulate:** 23 Customs St., Citibank Building, 3rd fl., **Auckland.**

SOUTH AFRICA. Embassy and Consulate: 877 Pretorius St., **Pretoria**, P.O. Box 9536, Pretoria 0001 (☎012 342 1048; fax 342-2244; http://usembassy.state.gov/pretoria). **Other Consulates:** Broadway Industries Center, Heerengracht, Foreshore, **Cape Town** (mailing address: P.O. Box 6773, Roggebaai, 8012; ☎021 421-4280; fax 425-3014); 303 West St., Old Mutual Building, 31st fl., **Durban** (☎031 305-7600; fax 305-7691); No. 1 River St., Killarney, **Johannesburg,** P.O. Box 1762, Houghton, 2041 (☎011 644-8000; fax 646-6916).

UK. Embassy and Consulate: 24 Grosvenor Sq., London W1A 1AE (☎020 7499 9000; fax 7495 5012; www.usembassy.org.uk). **Other Consulates**: Queen's House, 14 Queen St., Belfast, N. Ireland BT1 6EQ (☎01232 328 239; fax 248 482); 3 Regent Terr., Edinburgh, Scotland EH7 5BW (☎0131 556 8315; fax 557 6023).

CONSULAR SERVICES IN THE SOUTHWEST

Australia: 2049 Century Park E, 19th fl. of the Century Plaza Towers between Olympic Blvd. and Santa Monica Blvd., **Los Angeles,** CA 90067 (☎310-229-4800).

Canada: 550 S. Hope St., 9th fl., **Los Angeles,** CA 90071 (☎213-346-2700; fax 346-2767, ingls-td@dfait-maeci.gc.ca).

Ireland: Honorary Consul at 920 Schelbourne St., **Reno,** NV 89511 (☎/fax 775-853-4497; bbrady@nvbell.net).

New Zealand: 1379 N. Brookhurst Circle, Centerville, **Salt Lake City,** UT 84014 (☎801-296-2494; fax 296-1523).

South Africa: 6300 Wilshire Blvd., #600, **Los Angeles,** CA 90048 (☎323-651-0902).

UK: 11766 Wilshire Blvd., #400, **Los Angeles,** CA 90025 (☎310-481-0031).

DOCUMENTS AND FORMALITIES

PASSPORTS

REQUIREMENTS. All foreign visitors except Canadians need valid passports to enter the United States and to re-enter their own country. The US does not allow entrance if the holder's passport expires in under six months; returning home with an expired passport is often illegal, and may result in a fine. Canadians need to demonstrate proof of citizenship, such as a citizenship card or birth certificate.

NEW PASSPORTS. Citizens of Australia, Canada, Ireland, New Zealand, and the United Kingdom can apply for a passport at any post office, passport office, or court of law. Citizens of South Africa can apply for a passport at any Home Affairs office. Any applications must be filed well in advance of the departure date, although most passport offices offer rush services for a very steep fee.

PASSPORT MAINTENANCE. Be sure to photocopy the page of your passport with your photo, as well as your visas, traveler's check serial numbers, and any other important documents. Carry one set of copies in a safe place, apart from the originals, and leave another set at home. Consulates also recommend that you carry an expired passport or an official copy of your birth certificate in a part of your baggage separate from other documents. If you lose your passport, immediately notify the local police and the consulate of your home government. To expedite its replacement, it helps to have a photocopy. In some cases, a replacement may take weeks to process, and it may be valid only for a limited time. Any **visas** stamped in your old passport will be irretrievably lost. In an emergency, ask for **temporary traveling papers** that will permit you to re-enter your home country.

ESSENTIALS

VISAS, INVITATIONS, AND WORK PERMITS

VISAS. Citizens of South Africa and some other countries need a visa—a stamp, sticker, or insert in your passport specifying the purpose of your travel and the permitted duration of your stay—in addition to a valid passport for entrance to the US. See http://travel.state.gov/visa_services.html for more information. To obtain a visa, contact a US embassy or consulate.

Canadian citizens do not need to obtain a visa for admission to the US. Citizens of Australia, New Zealand, and most European countries can waive US visas through the **Visa Waiver Program.** Visitors qualify if they are traveling only for business or pleasure (*not* work or study), are staying for fewer than **90 days**, have proof of intent to leave (e.g. a return plane ticket), possess an I-94W form, and are traveling on particular air or sea carriers. See http://travel.state.gov/vwp.html for more information.

If you lose your I-94 form, you can replace it by filling out form I-102, although it's very unlikely that the form will be replaced within the time of your stay. The form is available at the nearest **Immigration and Naturalization Service (INS)** office (☎800-375-5283; www.ins.usdoj.gov), through the forms request line (☎800-870-3676), or online (www.ins.usdoj.gov/graphics/formsfee/forms/i-102.htm). **Visa extensions** are sometimes granted with a completed I-539 form; call the forms request line (☎800-870-3676) or get it online at www.ins.usdoj.gov/graphics/formsfee/forms/i-539.htm.

All travelers, except Canadians, planning a stay of more than 90 days also need to obtain a visa. Admission as a visitor does not include the right to work, which is authorized only by a **work permit.** Entering the US to study requires a special visa. For more information, see **Alternatives to Tourism,** p. 50.

IDENTIFICATION

When you travel, always carry two or more forms of identification with you, including at least one photo ID; a passport combined or a driver's license with birth certificate is usually adequate. Never carry all your ID together. Split them up in case of theft or loss, and keep photocopies of them in your bags and at home.

TEACHER, STUDENT AND YOUTH IDENTIFICATION. The **International Student Identity Card (ISIC),** the most widely accepted form of student ID, provides discounts on sights, accommodations, food, and transport; access to a 24hr. emergency helpline (in North America call 877-370-4742; elsewhere call US collect +1-715-345-0505); and insurance benefits for US cardholders (see **Insurance,** p. 26). The ISIC is preferable to an institution-specific card (such as a university ID) because it is more likely to be recognized and honored abroad. Applicants must be degree-seeking students of a secondary or post-secondary school and must be at least 12 years of age. Because of the proliferation of fake ISICs, some services (particularly airlines) require additional proof of student identity, such as a school ID or a letter signed by your registrar and stamped with your school seal.

The **International Teacher Identity Card (ITIC)** offers teachers the same insurance coverage and similar but limited discounts. For travelers who are 25 years old or under but are not students, the **International Youth Travel Card (IYTC;** formerly the **GO 25** Card) offers many of the same benefits as the ISIC.

Each of the cards costs $22 or equivalent. ISIC and ITIC cards are valid for roughly one and a half academic years; IYTC cards are valid for one year. Many student travel agencies (see p. 35) issue the cards, including STA Travel in Australia and New Zealand; Travel CUTS in Canada; usit in the Republic of Ireland and Northern Ireland; SASTS in South Africa; Campus Travel and STA Travel in the UK; and Council Travel and STA Travel in the US. For more information, contact the **International Student Travel Confederation (ISTC),** Herengracht 479, 1017 BS Amsterdam, The Netherlands (☎ +31 20 421 28 00; fax 421 28 10; www.istc.org).

CUSTOMS

Upon entering the US, you must declare certain items from abroad and pay a duty on the value of those articles that exceeds the US customs allowance. Note that goods and gifts purchased at duty-free shops abroad are not exempt from duty or sales tax at your point of return and thus must be declared as well; "duty-free" merely means that you need not pay a tax in the country of purchase. Upon returning, you must similarly declare all articles acquired abroad and pay a duty on the value of articles in excess of your home country's allowance.

MONEY

CURRENCY AND EXCHANGE

The currency chart below is based on August 2002 exchange rates between local currency and Australian dollars (AUS$), Canadian dollars (CDN$), Irish pounds (IR£), New Zealand dollars (NZ$), South African Rand (ZAR), British pounds (UK£), US dollars ($), and European Union euros (EUR€). Check the currency converter on financial web sites such as www.bloomberg.com and www.xe.com, or a large newspaper, for the latest exchange rates.

US DOLLARS ($)	
AUS$1 = US$0.54	US$1 = AUS$1.84
CDN$1 = US$0.64	US$1 = CDN$1.56
NZ$1 = US$0.47	US$1 = NZ$0.47
ZAR1 = US$0.09	US$1 = ZAR10.79
UK£1 = US$1.52	US$1 = UK£0.66
EUR€1 = US$0.97	US$1 = EUR€1.03

As a general rule, it's cheaper to convert money in the Southwest than at home. While currency exchange will probably be available in your arrival airport, it's wise to bring enough foreign currency to last for the first 24 to 72 hours of a trip. When changing money, try to go only to banks or other establishments that have at most a 5% margin between their buy and sell prices. Since you lose money with every transaction, **convert large sums but no more than you'll need.**

If you use traveler's checks or bills, carry some in small denominations (the equivalent of $50 or less) for times when you are forced to exchange money at poor rates, but bring a range of denominations since charges may be levied per check cashed. Store your money in a variety of forms; at any given time you should carry some cash, some traveler's checks, and an ATM and/or credit card.

TRAVELER'S CHECKS

Traveler's checks are one of the safest and least troublesome means of carrying funds. American Express and Visa are the most widely recognized brands. Many banks and agencies sell them for a small commission. Check issuers provide refunds if the checks are lost or stolen, and many provide additional services, such as toll-free refund hotlines, emergency message services, and stolen credit card assistance. They are readily accepted throughout the region. Ask about toll-free refund hotlines and the location of refund centers when purchasing checks, and always carry emergency cash.

ESSENTIALS

American Express: Checks available with commission at select banks and all AmEx offices. US residents can also purchase checks by phone (☎888-887-8986) or online (www.aexp.com). AAA (see p. 43) offers commission-free checks to its members. *Checks for Two* can be signed by either of 2 people traveling together. For purchase locations or more information contact AmEx's service centers: In the US and Canada 800-221-7282; in the UK 0800 521 313; in Australia 800 25 19 02; in New Zealand 0800 441 068; elsewhere US collect +1-801-964-6665.

Visa: Checks available (generally with commission) at banks worldwide. For the location of the nearest office, call Visa's service centers: in the US 800-227-6811; in the UK 0800 89 50 78; elsewhere UK collect +44 20 7937 8091.

Travelex/Thomas Cook: In the US and Canada call 800-287-7362; in the UK call 0800 62 21 01; elsewhere call UK collect +44 1733 31 89 50.

CREDIT, DEBIT, AND ATM CARDS

Where they are accepted, credit cards often offer superior exchange rates—up to 5% better than the retail rate used by banks and other currency exchange establishments. **MasterCard, Visa** and **American Express** are the most widely accepted, and the premium versions have a number of perks.

ATMs are found throughout the Southwest, and operate on most national exchange systems. ATMs get the same wholesale exchange rate as credit cards, but there is often a limit on the amount of money you can withdraw per day (around $500), and there is typically also a surcharge of $1-5 per withdrawal.

Debit cards are as convenient as credit cards but have a more immediate impact on your funds. A debit card can be used wherever its associated credit card company (usually Mastercard or Visa) is accepted, yet the money is withdrawn directly from the holder's checking account. The two major international money networks are **Cirrus** (to locate ATMs ☎800-424-7787 or www.mastercard.com) and **Visa/PLUS** (to locate ATMs ☎800-843-7587 or www.visa.com). Most ATMs charge a transaction fee that is paid to the bank that owns the ATM.

GETTING MONEY FROM HOME

If you run out of money while traveling, the easiest and cheapest solution is to have someone back home make a deposit to your credit card or cash (ATM) card. Failing that, consider one of the following options.

WIRING MONEY. It is possible to arrange a **bank money transfer,** which means asking a bank back home to wire money to a bank in the Southwest. This is the cheapest way to transfer cash, but it's also the slowest, usually taking several days or more. Money transfer services like **Western Union** are faster and more convenient than bank transfers—but also much pricier. Western Union has many locations worldwide. To find one, visit www.westernunion.com, or call in the US 800-325-6000, in Canada 800-235-0000, in the UK 0800 83 38 33, in Australia 800 501 500, in New Zealand 800 27 0000, in South Africa 0860 100031. To wire money within the US using a credit card (Visa, MasterCard, Discover), call 800-225-5227. Money transfer services are also available at **American Express** and **Thomas Cook** offices.

COSTS

The cost of your trip will vary considerably depending on where you go, how you travel, and where you stay. The single biggest cost of your trip will probably be your round-trip airfare to the Southwest (see p. 33). Renting a car will be another major expense, but may be a wise decision because many areas in the region are accessible only by car. Before you go, calculate a reasonable per-day budget to meet your needs. Don't forget to factor in emergency funds (at least $200).

STAYING ON A BUDGET. Accommodations start at about $12 per night in a hostel bed, while a basic sit-down meal costs about $8-10 depending on the region. If you stay in hostels and prepare your own food, you'll probably spend from $25-40 per person per day. Camping opportunities abound in the Southwest, and often provide the cheapest option, with prices ranging from free to as much as $20 for a tent site (see **The Great Outdoors,** p. 55, for more info on camping). A slightly more comfortable day (sleeping in hostels/guesthouses and the occasional budget hotel, eating one meal a day at a restaurant, going out at night) would run $45-65; for a luxurious day, the sky's the limit. Transportation costs will increase these figures. Gas prices have risen significantly in the US over the past year but still remain much lower than in Europe. A gallon of gas now costs about $1.45 per gallon (37¢ per liter), but prices vary widely according to state taxes.

TIPS FOR SAVING MONEY. Considering that saving just a few dollars a day over the course of your trip might pay for days or weeks of additional travel, the art of penny-pinching is well worth learning. Learn to take advantage of **freebies:** for example, museums will typically be free once a week or once a month, and cities often host free open-air concerts and/or cultural events (especially in the summer). Great hiking and biking can often be found for free, and if you're going to be visiting more than a few national parks, a **National Parks Pass** can easily save you $50 or even $100. Bring a sleepsack (see p. 58) to save on sheet charges in hostels, and do your **laundry** in the sink. You can split **accommodations** costs (in hotels and some hostels) with trustworthy fellow travelers; multi-bed rooms almost always work out cheaper per person than singles. Of course, with few exceptions, camping will always be the least expensive option, and you can quickly make up for the cost of a tent after a few weeks of traveling. Visits to the supermarket, in stead of the restaurant, can save you a bundle. With that said, don't go overboard with your budget obsession. Though staying within your budget is important, don't do so at the expense of your sanity or health.

TIPPING AND BARGAINING

In the US, it is customary to tip waitstaff and cab drivers 15-20%, but do so at your discretion. Tips are usually not included in restaurant bills. At the airport and in hotels, porters expect a tip of at least $1 per bag to carry your baggage. Unless you are at a flea market, bargaining is generally frowned upon and fruitless in the US.

TAXES

In the US, sales tax is similar to the European Value-Added Tax, but is generally not included in advertised prices. Southwestern sales taxes range 5-8% depending on the item and the place; in many states, groceries are not taxed.

SAFETY AND SECURITY

Although the vast majority of the Southwest is sparsely populated, the few urban areas are among the most crime-ridden in the nation. One should be particularly cautious when visiting Phoenix, Albuquerque, Las Cruces, El Paso, Gallup, Farmington, and towns outlying the Navajo Nation. However, the conscientious and common-sensical traveler should have no problems if abiding by a few basic guidelines. For info on outdoors safety, see **The Great Outdoors** section, p. 55.

EMERGENCY = 911. For emergencies in the US, dial **911.** This number is toll-free from all phones, including coin phones. In a very few remote communities, 911 may not work. If it does not, dial 0 for the operator and request to be connected with the appropriate emergency service. In national parks, it is usually best to call the **park warden** in case of emergency. *Let's Go* always lists emergency contact numbers where 911 is not applicable. If you are calling from a cellular phone, be sure to tell the 911 dispatcher your exact location. Due to the vagaries of cellular networks, you may not be connected to the closest call center.

BLENDING IN. Tourists are particularly vulnerable to crime because they often carry large amounts of cash and are not as street-savvy as locals. To avoid unwanted attention, try to blend in as much as possible: take your fashion cues from the locals, not from other tourists. The gawking camera-toter is a more obvious target than the low-profile traveler. Familiarize yourself with your surroundings before setting out. Also, carry yourself with confidence. If you are traveling alone, remember Little Red Riding Hood: be sure that someone at home knows your itinerary and *never admit that you're traveling alone.*

EXPLORING. Extra vigilance is always wise, but there is no need to panic when exploring a new city or region. Find out about **unsafe areas** from tourist offices, from the manager of your hotel or hostel, or from a local whom you trust. You may want to carry a **whistle** to attract attention. Whenever possible, *Let's Go* warns of unsafe neighborhoods and areas, but there are some good general tips to follow.

When walking at night, stick to busy, well-lit streets and avoid dark alleyways. Do not attempt to cross through parks, parking lots, or other large, deserted areas. Buildings in disrepair, vacant lots, and unpopulated areas are all bad signs. The distribution of people can reveal a great deal about the relative safety of the area; look for children playing, women walking in the open, and other signs of an active community. Keep in mind that a district can change character drastically between blocks. If you feel uncomfortable, leave as quickly and directly as you can, but don't allow fear to turn you into a hermit.

GETTING AROUND. Driving in the Southwest is generally safe, though desert driving requires some extra precautions. Always keep a few unopened gallons of bottled water in your trunk, in case your car overheats or you are stranded. For long drives in desolate areas, invest in a cellular phone and a roadside assistance program (see p. 41). It is a good idea to drive during the day, because you can get help faster if you run into trouble on the highways, and you can avoid trouble in the city streets at night. Avoid driving at midday and the early afternoon during the summer, however, as the temperatures can be hellish. For more info, see p. 41.

Public transportation across states (buses and trains) is generally safe. Occasionally, stations can be dangerous; *Let's Go* warns of these stations where applicable. If possible, avoid using public transportation late at night unless you are in a large group. **Taxis** are usually safe and reliable.

Let's Go does not recommend **hitchhiking** under any circumstances, particularly for women. Hitching is especially dangerous in the Southwest, with its vast lengths of remote and seldom-traveled highways—see **Getting Around,** p. 39, for more info.

SELF DEFENSE. There is no sure-fire set of precautions that will protect you from all of the situations you might encounter when you travel. A good self-defense course will give you more concrete ways to react to different types of aggression. **Impact, Prepare, and Model Mugging** can refer you to local self-defense courses in the US (☎ 800-345-5425). Workshops (2-3hr.) start at $50 and full courses run $350-500. Both women and men are welcome.

ESSENTIALS

FINANCIAL SECURITY

PROTECTING YOUR VALUABLES. Theft in the US is most rampant in big cities and at night. To prevent easy theft, don't keep all your valuables (money, important documents) in one place. **Photocopies** of important documents allow you to recover them in case they are lost or filched. Carry one copy separately and leave another copy at home. Label every piece of luggage both inside and out. *Don't put a wallet with money in your back pocket.* Never count your money in public and carry as little as possible—keep some aside in case of an emergency. If you carry a **purse,** buy one with a secure clasp. Secure packs with small combination padlocks which slip through the two zippers. A **money belt** is the best way to carry cash; you can buy one at most camping supply stores. A nylon, zippered pouch with a belt that sits inside the waist of your pants or skirt combines convenience and security. A **neck pouch** is equally safe, although far less accessible and discreet.

CON ARTISTS AND PICKPOCKETS. In large cities **con artists** often work in groups, and children are among the most effective. Beware of certain classics: sob stories that require money, rolls of bills "found" on the street, mustard spilled (or saliva spit) onto your shoulder to distract you while they snatch your bag. **Don't ever let your passport out of your sight,** especially near the Mexican border. Don't let your bags out of sight; never trust a new "friend" who offers to guard your bag while you are gone. Beware of **pickpockets** in city crowds, especially on public transportation. Also, be alert in public telephone booths: if you must say your calling card number, do so very quietly; if you punch it in, make sure no one can look over your shoulder.

ACCOMMODATIONS AND TRANSPORTATION. Never leave your belongings unattended; crime occurs in even the most demure-looking hostel or hotel. Bring your own **padlock** for hostel lockers, and don't ever store valuables in any locker.

Be particularly careful on **buses** and **trains;** horror stories abound about determined thieves who wait for travelers to fall asleep. Carry your backpack in front of you where you can see it. When traveling with others, sleep in alternate shifts. When alone, use good judgment in selecting a train compartment: never stay in an empty one, and use a lock to secure your pack to the luggage rack. Try to sleep on top bunks with your luggage stored above you (if not in bed with you), and keep important documents and other valuables on you. If traveling by **car,** don't leave valuables (such as jewelry or luggage) in it while you are away.

Drivers should take necessary precautions against **carjacking,** which has become one of the most frequent crimes committed in the US. Carjackers, who are usually armed, approach their victims in their vehicles and force them to turn over the automobile. Carjackers prey on cars parked on the side of the road and cars stopped at red lights. If you are going to pull over on the side of the road, keep your doors locked and windows up at all times, and do not pull over to help a car in the breakdown lane; call the police instead.

DRUGS AND ALCOHOL

In the Southwest, as in the rest of the US, the drinking age is a strictly enforced 21. **Never drink and drive**—you risk your own life and those of others, and getting caught results in imprisonment and fines. It is illegal to have an open bottle of alcohol inside a car even if you are not the driver. Non-prescription drugs of any sort are always illegal. If you carry prescription drugs, it is vital to have a copy of the prescriptions. Cigarette purchasers must be at least 18 years old with photo ID.

HEALTH

Common sense is the simplest prescription for good health while you travel. Luckily, the US has an excellent health-care system and travelers can usually be treated easily for injuries and health problems. Travelers complain most often about their gut and their feet, so take precautionary measures: drink lots of fluids to prevent dehydration and constipation, and wear sturdy, broken-in shoes and clean socks.

BEFORE YOU GO

In your **passport,** write the names of any people you wish to be contacted in case of a medical emergency, and list any allergies or medical conditions. Carry up-to-date, legible prescriptions or a statement from your doctor stating the medication's trade name, manufacturer, chemical name, and dosage. While traveling, be sure to keep all medication with you in your carry-on luggage. For tips on packing a basic **first-aid kit** and other health essentials, see p. 27.

IMMUNIZATIONS AND PRECAUTIONS

Travelers should make sure that the following vaccines are up to date: MMR (for measles, mumps, and rubella); DTaP or Td (for diptheria, tetanus, and pertussis); OPV (for polio); HbCV (for haemophilus influenza B); and HBV (for hepatitis B).

USEFUL ORGANIZATIONS AND PUBLICATIONS

The US **Centers for Disease Control and Prevention,** or **CDC** (☎877-394-8747; fax 888-232-3299; www.cdc.gov/travel), maintains an international travelers' hotline and an informative web site. The CDC's comprehensive booklet *Health Information for International Travel,* an annual rundown of disease, immunization, and general health advice, is free online or $25 via the Public Health Foundation (☎877-252-1200). Consult the appropriate government agency of your home country for consular information sheets on health, entry requirements, and other issues. For detailed information on travel health (and a list of travel clinics in the US) try the **International Travel Health Guide,** by Stuart Rose, MD ($20; www.travmed.com). For health info, contact the **American Red Cross** (☎800-564-1234; www.redcross.org).

MEDICAL ASSISTANCE ON THE ROAD

In case of medical emergency, dial **911** from any phone and an operator will send out paramedics, a fire brigade, or the police as needed. Emergency medical care is also readily available in the Southwest at any emergency room on a walk-in basis. If you do not have insurance, you will have to pay for emergency and other medical care (see **Insurance,** p. 26). **Non-emergency** care is available at any hospital or doctor for a fee. Appointments are required for non-emergency medical services.

Those with medical conditions (such as diabetes, allergies to antibiotics, epilepsy, heart conditions) may want to obtain a Medic Alert membership (first year $35, annually thereafter $20), which includes a stainless steel ID tag, among other benefits, including a 24hr. collect-call number. Contact the Medic Alert Foundation, 2323 Colorado Ave., Turlock, CA 95382 (☎888-633-4298; outside the US ☎+1-209-668-3333; www.medicalert.org).

ENVIRONMENTAL HAZARDS

Heat exhaustion and dehydration: Heat exhaustion can lead to fatigue, headaches, and wooziness. Avoid it by drinking plenty of fluids, eating salty foods, and avoiding dehydrating beverages. Continuous heat stress can eventually lead to heatstroke, characterized by a rising temperature, severe headache, and cessation of sweating. Victims should be cooled off with wet towels and taken to a doctor.

Sunburn: If you are planning on spending time near water, in the desert, or in the snow, you are at risk of getting burned, even through clouds. If you get sunburned, drink more fluids than usual and apply an aloe-based lotion.

Hypothermia and frostbite: A rapid drop in body temperature is the clearest sign of overexposure to cold. Victims may also shiver, feel exhausted, have poor coordination or slurred speech, hallucinate, or suffer amnesia. *Do not let hypothermia victims fall asleep.* To avoid hypothermia, keep dry, wear layers, and stay out of the wind. When the temperature is below freezing, watch out for frostbite. If skin turns white, waxy, and cold, do not rub the area. Drink warm beverages, get dry, and slowly warm the area with dry fabric or steady body contact until a doctor can be found.

High altitude: Allow your body a couple of days to adjust to less oxygen before exerting yourself. Note that alcohol is more potent and UV rays are stronger at high elevations.

INSECT-BORNE DISEASES

Many diseases are transmitted by insects—mainly mosquitoes, fleas, ticks, and lice. Be aware of insects in wet or forested areas, especially while hiking and camping; wear long pants and long sleeves, tuck your pants into your socks, and buy a mosquito net. Use insect repellents containing DEET and soak or spray your gear with permethrin (licensed in the US for use on clothing). To stop the itch after being bitten, try Calamine lotion or topical cortisones. Lyme Disease is a bacterial infection carried by ticks and marked by a circular bull's-eye rash of 2 in. or more. Later symptoms include fever, headache, fatigue, and aches and pains. Antibiotics are effective if administered early. Left untreated, Lyme can cause problems in joints, the heart, and the nervous system. Ticks, responsible for Lyme and other diseases, are a particular danger in the mountains—watch out for them while camping and hiking. If you find a tick attached to your skin, grasp the head with tweezers as close to your skin as possible and apply slow, steady traction. Removing a tick within 24 hours greatly reduces the risk of infection. Do not try to remove ticks by burning them or coating them with solvents.

FOOD- AND WATER-BORNE DISEASES

Generally, in the Southwest, the risk of food poisoning is fairly low, and can be further reduced by eating only at clean, respectable establishments. Visiting Mexico, further precautions are necessary, as the water is generally unreliable. When camping, bring water, or purify stream water by bringing it to a rolling boil or treating it with **iodine tablets;** note, however, that some parasites such as *giardia* have exteriors that resist iodine treatment, so boiling is more reliable. Always wash your hands before eating, or bring a quick-drying purifying liquid hand cleaner.

Traveler's diarrhea: Results from drinking untreated water or eating uncooked foods. Symptoms include nausea, bloating, and urgency. Try quick-energy, non-sugary foods with protein and carbohydrates to keep your strength up. Over-the-counter anti-diarrheals (e.g. Immodium) may counteract the problems. The most dangerous side effect is dehydration; drink lots of water. If you develop a fever or your symptoms don't go away after 4-5 days, consult a doctor.

Parasites: Microbes, tapeworms, etc. that hide in unsafe water and food. **Giardiasis,** for example, is acquired by drinking untreated water from streams or lakes. Symptoms include swollen glands or lymph nodes, fever, rashes or itchiness, and digestive problems. Boil water, wear shoes, and eat only cooked food.

OTHER INFECTIOUS DISEASES

Rabies: Transmitted through the saliva of infected animals; fatal if untreated. By the time symptoms (thirst and muscle spasms) appear, the disease is in its terminal stage. If you are bitten, wash the wound thoroughly, seek immediate medical care, and try to have the animal located. A rabies vaccine, which consists of 3 shots given over a 21-day period, is available but is only semi-effective.

Hepatitis B: A viral infection of the liver transmitted via bodily fluids or needle-sharing. Symptoms may not surface until years after infection. A 3-shot vaccination sequence is recommended for health-care workers, sexually active travelers, and anyone planning to seek medical treatment abroad; it must begin 6 months before traveling.

Hepatitis C: Like Hepatitis B, but the mode of transmission differs. IV drug users, those with regular exposure to blood, hemodialysis patients, and recipients of blood transfusions are at the highest risk, but the disease can also be spread through sexual contact or sharing items like razors and toothbrushes that may have traces of blood on them.

AIDS, HIV, AND STDS

For detailed information on **Acquired Immune Deficiency Syndrome (AIDS)** in the United States, call the **US Centers for Disease Control's** 24hr. hotline at 800-342-2437, or contact the **Joint United Nations Programme on HIV/AIDS (UNAIDS),** 20 av. Appia, CH-1211 Geneva 27, Switzerland (☎+41 22 791 3666; fax 791 4187).

Sexually transmitted diseases (STDs) such as gonorrhea, chlamydia, genital warts, syphilis, and herpes are easier to catch than HIV and can ruin your life. **Hepatitis B** and **C** can also be transmitted sexually (see p. 26). Though condoms may protect you from some STDs, oral or even tactile contact can lead to transmission. If you think you may have contracted an STD, see a doctor immediately.

WOMEN'S HEALTH

Women traveling in unsanitary conditions are vulnerable to **urinary tract** and **bladder infections,** common and very uncomfortable bacterial conditions that cause a burning sensation and painful (sometimes frequent) urination. Over-the-counter medicines can sometimes alleviate symptoms, but if they persist, see a doctor.

Vaginal yeast infections may flare up in hot and humid climates. Wearing loosely fitting trousers or a skirt and cotton underwear will help, as will over-the-counter remedies like Monostat or Gynelotrimin. Bring supplies from home if you are prone to infection, as they may be difficult to find on the road.

Since **tampons, pads,** and reliable **contraceptive devices** are sometimes hard to find when traveling, bring supplies with you.

INSURANCE

Travel insurance generally covers four basic areas: health problems, property loss, trip cancellation/interruption, and emergency evacuation. Although your regular insurance policies may well extend to travel-related accidents, you might consider purchasing travel insurance if the cost of potential trip cancellation/interruption is greater than you can absorb. Prices for travel insurance purchased separately generally run about $50 per week for full coverage, while trip cancellation/interruption may be purchased separately at a rate of about $5.50 per $100 of coverage.

Medical insurance (especially university policies) often covers costs incurred abroad; check with your provider. **Canadians** are protected by their home province's health insurance plan for up to 90 days after leaving the country; check with the provincial Ministry of Health or Health Plan Headquarters for details. **Home-**

owners' insurance (or your family's coverage) often covers theft during travel and loss of travel documents (passport, plane ticket, railpass, etc.) up to $500.

ISIC and **ITIC** cards (see p. 18) provide basic insurance benefits, including $100 per day of in-hospital sickness for up to 60 days, $3000 of accident-related medical reimbursement, and $25,000 for emergency medical transport. Cardholders have access to a toll-free 24hr. helpline (run by the insurance provider **TravelGuard**) for medical, legal, and financial emergencies (☎ 877-370-4742). **American Express** (☎ 800-528-4800) grants most cardholders automatic car rental insurance (collision and theft, but not liability) and ground travel accident coverage of $100,000 on flight purchases made with the card.

INSURANCE PROVIDERS. Council and **STA** (see p. 35) offer a range of plans that can supplement your basic coverage. Other private insurance providers in the US and Canada include: **Access America** (☎ 800-284-8300; www.accessamerica.com); **Berkely Group/Carefree Travel Insurance** (☎ 800-323-3149; www.berkely.com); **Globalcare Travel Insurance** (☎ 800-821-2488; www.globalcare-cocco.com); and **Travel Assistance International** (☎ 800-821-2828; www.travelassistance.com). Providers in the **UK** include **Columbus Direct** (☎ 020 7375 0011; www.columbusdirect.net). In **Australia,** try **AFTA** (☎ 02 9375 4955).

PACKING

Pack lightly: lay out only what you absolutely need, then take half the clothes and twice the money. If you plan to do a lot of hiking, see the section on **Camping,** p. 57.

LUGGAGE. If you plan to cover most of your itinerary by foot, a sturdy **frame backpack** is unbeatable. (For the basics on buying a pack, see p. 58.) Toting a **suitcase** or **trunk** is fine if you plan to live in one or two cities or can store things in your car, but otherwise can be burdensome. In addition to your main piece of luggage, a **daypack** (a small backpack or courier bag) is a must.

CLOTHING. For travel in alpine areas, pack layers of clothing—mornings and evenings tend to be cold year-round, while days can vary drastically. A sweater and light jacket or windbreaker may be necessary even in mid-summer. From late fall to early spring, be sure to bring a rain jacket (Gore-Tex® is both waterproof and breathable) or umbrella and a mid-weight jacket or heavy sweater. Wherever you go, **sturdy shoes** and **thick socks** can save your feet. **Flip-flops** or waterproof sandals are crucial for grubby hostel showers. You may also want to add one outfit beyond the jeans and t-shirt uniform, and maybe a nicer pair of shoes if you have the room.

CONVERTERS AND ADAPTERS. In the United States, electricity is 110V; 220/240V electrical appliances are not compatible with 110V current. Appliances from anywhere outside the US and Canada will need to be used with an **adapter** (which changes the shape of the plug) and a **converter** (which changes the voltage).

TOILETRIES. Toothbrushes, towels, cold-water soap, talcum powder (to keep feet dry), deodorant, razors, tampons, and condoms are all readily available. If you wear **contact lenses,** bring an extra pair as well as back-up glasses. Also bring a copy of your prescription in case you need emergency replacements.

FIRST-AID KIT. For a basic first-aid kit, pack: bandages, pain reliever, antibiotic cream, a thermometer, a Swiss army knife, tweezers, moleskin, decongestant, motion-sickness remedy, diarrhea or upset-stomach medication (Immodium or Pepto Bismol), an antihistamine, sunscreen, insect repellent, burn ointment, and a syringe for emergencies (get an explanatory letter from your doctor).

ESSENTIALS

FILM. Camera stores abound in the Southwest, offering many film and developing options. Less serious photographers may want to bring a **disposable camera** or two rather than an expensive permanent one. Despite disclaimers, airport security X-rays *can* fog film, so buy a lead-lined pouch at a camera store or ask security to hand-inspect it. Always pack film in your carry-on luggage, since higher-intensity X-rays are used on checked luggage.

OTHER USEFUL ITEMS. For safety purposes, you should bring a **money belt** and **padlock. Quick repairs** of torn garments can be done on the road with a needle and thread; also consider bringing electrical tape for patching tears. If you want to do laundry by hand, bring detergent, a small rubber ball to stop up the sink, and string for a makeshift clothes line. **Other things** that will come in handy: an umbrella; seal-able **plastic bags** (for damp clothes, soap, food, shampoo, and other spillables); an **alarm clock;** safety pins; rubber bands; a flashlight; earplugs; garbage bags; and a small **calculator.** For advice on outdoor gear, see **The Great Outdoors, p. 58.**

IMPORTANT DOCUMENTS. Don't forget your passport, traveler's checks, ATM and/or credit cards, and adequate ID (see p. 18). Also check that you have any of the following that you may need: a hosteling membership card (see p. 28); driver's license (see p. 18); travel insurance forms; and/or rail or bus pass (see p. 39).

ACCOMMODATIONS

HOSTELS

Hostels are generally laid out dorm-style, often with large single-sex rooms and bunk beds, although some do have private rooms. They sometimes have kitchens and utensils for your use, bike or moped rentals, storage areas, and laundry facilities. There can be drawbacks: some hostels close during certain daytime "lockout" hours, have a curfew, don't accept reservations, impose a maximum stay, or require that you do chores. In the Southwest, a bed in a hostel will average around $15-20. Many hostels require proof of foreign citizenship or international travel.

HOSTELLING INTERNATIONAL

Although many of the hostels in the Southwest are independently managed, it may be worth it to join a hosteling association for its services and the lower rates offered at member hostels. **Hostelling International-American Youth Hostels (HI-AYH)** is the largest of these associations. HI hostels are scattered throughout the Southwest, and may accept reservations for a nominal fee via the **International Booking Network** (US ☎ 800-909-4776, Australia ☎ 02 9261 1111, Canada ☎ 800-663-5777, England and Wales ☎ 01629 58 14 18, Northern Ireland ☎ 01232 32 47 33, Republic of Ireland ☎ 01 830 1766, NZ ☎ 03 379 9808, Scotland ☎ 08701 55 32 55; www.hostel-booking.com). Two comprehensive hosteling web sites are www.iyhf.org, which lists contact info for all national associations, and www.hostels.com/us.south-west.html, which has a listing of hostels in the Southwest and other resources.

Most HI-AYH hostels also honor **guest memberships**—you'll get a blank card with space for six validation stamps. Each night you'll pay a nonmember supplement (one-sixth the membership fee) and earn one guest stamp; get six stamps, and you're a member. Most student travel agencies (see p. 24) sell HI-AYH cards, as do all of the national hosteling organizations listed below. All prices listed below are valid for **one-year memberships** unless otherwise noted.

Australian Youth Hostels Association (AYHA), Level 3, 10 Mallett St., Camperdown, NSW 2050 (☎02 9565 1699; fax 9565 1325; www.yha.org.au). AUS$52, under 18 AUS$16.

Hostelling International-Canada (HI-C), 400-205 Catherine St., Ottawa, ON K2P 1C3 (☎800-663-5777; fax 237-7868; hihostels.ca). CDN$35, under 18 free.

An Óige (Irish Youth Hostel Association), 61 Mountjoy St., Dublin 7 (☎01 830 4555; fax 830 5808; anoige@iol.ie; www.irelandyha.org). €15, under 18 €7.50.

Youth Hostels Association of New Zealand (YHANZ), P.O. Box 436, 193 Cashel St., 3rd Fl., Union House, Christchurch 1 (☎03 379 9970; fax 365 4476; info@yha.org.nz; www.yha.org.nz). NZ$40, under 17 free.

Hostels Association of South Africa, 3rd fl., 73 St. George's House, P.O. Box 4402, Cape Town 8000 (☎021 424 2511; fax 424 4119; info@hisa.org.za; www.hisa.org.za). ZAR55, under 18 R30.

Scottish Youth Hostels Association (SYHA), 7 Glebe Crescent, Stirling FK8 2JA (☎01786 89 14 00; fax 89 13 33; www.syha.org.uk). UK£6.

Youth Hostels Association (England and Wales) Ltd., Trevelyan House, Dimple Rd., Matlock, Devonshire DE4 3YH (☎01629 59 26 00; fax 59 27 03). UK£13, under 18 UK£6.50, families UK£26.

Hostelling International Northern Ireland (HINI), 22-32 Donegall Rd., Belfast BT12 5JN, N. Ireland (☎02890 31 54 35; fax 43 96 99; info@hini.org.uk; www.hini.org.uk). UK£10, under 18 UK£6.

Hostelling International-American Youth Hostels (HI-AYH), 733 15th St. NW, #840, Washington, D.C. 20005 (☎202-783-6161; fax 783-6171; hiayhserv@hiayh.org; www.hiayh.org). $25, under 18 free.

OTHER TYPES OF ACCOMMODATIONS

HOTELS

HOTEL CHAIN	TELEPHONE	HOTEL CHAIN	TELEPHONE
Best Western	800-528-1234	La Quinta Inns	800-531-5900
Comfort Inns	800-221-2222	Motel 6	800-891-6161
Days Inn	800-325-2525	Ramada Inns	800-272-6232
Econo Lodge	800-446-6900	Red Carpet Inns	800-251-1962
Embassy Suites Hotels	800-362-2779	Select Inns	800-641-1000
Hampton Inns	800-426-7866	Sleep Inns	800-221-2222
Hilton Hotels	800-445-8667	Super 8 Motels	800-800-8000
Holiday Inns	800-465-4329	Travelodge	800-255-3050
Howard Johnson	800-654-2000	YMCA	800-922-9622

Hotel singles in the Southwest cost about $30-75 per night, and doubles are $45-100. You'll typically have a private bathroom and shower with hot water, although some cheaper places may offer shared restrooms. If you make reservations by mail, indicate your night of arrival and the number of nights you plan to stay. Not all hotels take reservations, and few accept traveler's checks in a foreign currency.

BED AND BREAKFASTS (B&BS)

For a cozy alternative to impersonal hotel rooms, B&Bs range from the acceptable to the sublime. Rooms in B&Bs generally cost $50-70 for a single and $70-90 for a double in the Southwest, but on holidays or in expensive locations (such as Jerome), prices can soar to over $300. For more info on B&Bs, see **Bed & Breakfast Inns Online,** P.O. Box 829, Madison, TN 37116 (☎615-868-1946; info@bbonline.com; www.bbonline.com), **InnFinder,** 6200 Gisholt Dr. #100, Madison, WI 53713 (☎608-285-6600; fax 285-6601; www.inncrawler.com), or **InnSite** (www.innsite.com).

UNIVERSITY DORMS

Many **colleges and universities** open their residence halls to travelers when school is not in session; some do so even during term-time. Getting a room may require some advanced planning, but rates tend to be low, and many offer free local calls.

YMCAS AND YWCAS

Young Men's Christian Association (YMCA) lodgings are usually cheaper than a hotel but more expensive than a hostel. Not all YMCA locations offer lodging; those that do are often located in urban downtowns. Many YMCAs accept women and families; some will not lodge those under 18 without parental permission. **Young Women's Christian Association (YWCA)** buildings offer similar services, but only accept women boarders. The Travel Y web site (www.travel-ys.com) offers on-line booking for free.

   YMCA of the USA, 101 North Wacker Drive, Chicago, IL 60606 (☎888-333-9622 or 800-872-9622; fax 312 977-9063; www.ymca.net). Provides a listing of the nearly 1000 Ys across the US and Canada. Offers info on prices, services available, and telephone numbers and addresses, but no reservation service.

   YWCA of the USA, Empire State Building, #301, 350 Fifth Ave., New York, NY 10118 (☎212-273-7800; fax 465-2281; www.ywca.org). Publishes a directory ($8) on YWCAs across the USA.

KEEPING IN TOUCH

BY MAIL

DOMESTIC RATES

First-class letters sent and received within the US take 1-3 days and cost 37¢; **Priority Mail** packages up to 1 lb. generally take 2 days and cost $3.85, up to 5 lb. $7.70. **All days specified denote business days.** For more details, see www.usps.com.

SENDING MAIL HOME FROM THE SOUTHWEST

Airmail is the best way to send mail from the United States; letters or packages sent by airmail generally take five to seven days to arrive. **Aerogrammes,** one form of airmail, are printed sheets that fold into envelopes and are available at post offices. Write *"par avion"* or "air mail" on the front. Most post offices will charge exorbitant fees or simply refuse to send aerogrammes with enclosures. Letters sent by regular airmail cost 60-80¢, packages up to 1 lb. run $12-16, and packages up to 5 lb. are $22-33. **Surface mail** is by far the cheapest and slowest way to send mail. It takes one to three months to cross the Atlantic and two to four to cross the Pacific—good for items you won't need to see for a while, such as souvenirs or other articles you've acquired along the way that are weighing down your pack.

SENDING MAIL TO THE SOUTHWEST

Mark envelopes "air mail" or *"par avion,"* or your letter or postcard will never arrive. In addition to the standard postage system, **Federal Express** (Australia ☎13 26 10, US and Canada ☎800-247-4747, New Zealand ☎0800 73 33 39, UK ☎0800 12 38 00; www.fedex.com) handles express mail services from most home countries to the United States, as well as within the country; for example, they can get a letter from New York to Los Angeles in 2 days for $9.95, and from London to New York in 2 days for UK£25.80.

RECEIVING MAIL IN THE SOUTHWEST

There are several ways to arrange pick-up of letters while you are abroad. Mail can be sent via General Delivery to almost any city or town in the Southwest with a post office. Address General Delivery letters as follows:

Jebediah BEAUREGARD

General Delivery

Flagstaff, AZ 86004 USA

The mail will go to a special desk in the central post office, unless you specify a post office by street address or postal code. Bring your passport or other photo ID for pick-up. If the clerks insist that there is nothing for you, have them check under your first name as well. Let's Go lists post offices in the Practical Information section for each city and most towns.

American Express's travel offices throughout the world offer a free Client Letter Service (mail held up to 30 days and forwarded upon request) for cardholders who contact them in advance. Some offices will offer these services to non-cardholders (especially AmEx Travelers Check holders), but call ahead to make sure.

BY TELEPHONE

CALLING HOME FROM THE SOUTHWEST

A **calling card** is probably your cheapest bet. Calls are billed collect or to your account. You can frequently call collect without even possessing a company's calling card just by calling their access number and following the instructions. To **call home with a calling card,** contact the operator for your service provider in the United States by dialing the given toll-free access number. You can often also make **direct international calls** from pay phones, but if you aren't using a calling card, you may need to drop your coins as quickly as your words. Where available, prepaid phone cards and occasionally major credit cards can be used for international calls, but they are less cost-effective (see **Placing International Calls,** p. 33).

Let's Go has recently partnered with **ekit.com** to provide a calling card that offers a number of services, including email and voice messaging. Before purchasing any calling card, always be sure to compare rates with other cards, and to make sure it serves your needs (a local phonecard is generally better for local calls, for instance). For more information, visit www.letsgo.ekit.com.

CALLING WITHIN THE SOUTHWEST

The simplest way to call within the country is to use a coin-operated phone; local calls in the Southwest cost 35¢. **Prepaid phone cards,** which carry a certain amount of phone time depending on the card's denomination, usually save time and money in the long run, although they often require a 25¢ surcharge from pay phones. These cards can be used to make international and domestic calls.

PLACING INTERNATIONAL CALLS. To call the US from home or to call home from the US, dial:

1. The **international dialing prefix.** To dial out of **Australia,** dial 0011; **Canada** or the **US,** 011; the **Republic of Ireland, New Zealand,** or the **UK,** 00; **South Africa,** 09.
2. The **country code** of the country you want to call. To call **Australia,** dial 61; **Canada** or the **US,** 1; the **Republic of Ireland,** 353; **New Zealand,** 64; **South Africa,** 27; the **UK,** 44.
3. The **city/area code.** *Let's Go* lists the city/area codes for cities and towns in the Southwest opposite the city or town name, next to a ☎.
4. The **local number.**

TIME DIFFERENCES

The majority of the Southwest is in **Mountain Standard Time,** including all of Utah, Colorado, and New Mexico. Arizona is an anomaly in the States, with the vast majority of the state not observing Daylight Savings Time. Therefore, while Arizona abides by Mountain Time during the winter months, in the summer it is on **Pacific Standard Time,** along with Nevada and California. The entire Navajo Nation is in Mountain Time year-round, so it is one hour off from the rest of Arizona in the summer. To add to the confusion, the Hopi Reservation, enclosed within the Navajo Nation, sticks with the rest of Arizona, spending half the year on Mountain Time and the other half on Pacific Time. For a visual clarification of this confusing system, look to the time zone map on the inside of the back cover of this book.

BY EMAIL AND INTERNET

Though in some places it's possible to forge a remote link with your home server, in most cases this is a much slower (and thus more expensive) option than taking advantage of free **web-based email accounts** (such as www.hotmail.com and www.yahoo.com). Travelers with laptops can call an Internet service provider via a **modem.** Long-distance phone cards specifically intended for such calls can defray normally high phone charges; check with your long-distance phone provider to see if it offers this option. Most Southwestern cities have public libraries with free Internet terminals. Establishments offering Internet access are listed in the Practical Information sections of major cities. **Cybercafe Guide** locates cybercafes throughout the United States (www.cyberiacafe.net/cyberia/guide/ccafe.htm).

GETTING TO THE SOUTHWEST

BY PLANE

AIRFARES

When it comes to airfare, a little effort can save you a bundle. If your plans are flexible enough to deal with the restrictions, courier fares are the cheapest. Tickets bought from consolidators and standby seating are also good deals, but last-minute specials, airfare wars, and charter flights often beat these fares. The key is to hunt around, be flexible, and persistently ask about discounts. Students, seniors, and those under 26 should never pay full price for a ticket.

DETAILS AND TIPS

Timing: International airfares to the US peak in the summer and over holiday weekends. Midweek (M-Th morning) round-trip flights run $40-50 cheaper than weekend flights, but the latter are generally less crowded and more likely to permit frequent-flier upgrades. Return-date flexibility is usually not an option; traveling with an "open return" ticket can be pricier than fixing a return date and paying later to change it.

Route: Round-trip flights are by far the cheapest; "open-jaw" (arriving in and departing from different cities) flights are pricier but reasonable alternatives. If the Southwest is only 1 stop on a more extensive globe-hop, consider a round-the-world (RTW) ticket. Tickets usually include at least 5 stops and are valid for about a year; prices range $1200-5000. Try **Northwest Airlines/KLM** (☎800-447-4747; www.nwa.com) or **Star Alliance**, a consortium of 14 airlines including United Airlines (☎800-241-6522; www.star-alliance.com). Cheap destinations in the Southwest include Phoenix, Albuquerque, and Salt Lake City. Many travelers choose to fly into L.A. and drive from there.

Boarding: Whenever flying internationally, pick up tickets for international flights well in advance of the departure date, and confirm by phone within 72hr. of departure. Most airlines require that passengers arrive at the airport at least 2hr. before departure. One carry-on item and 2 pieces of checked baggage are the norm.

BUDGET AND STUDENT TRAVEL AGENCIES

While knowledgeable agents specializing in flights to the Southwest can make your life easy and help you save, they may not spend the time to find you the lowest possible fare—they get paid on commission. Travelers holding **ISIC and IYTC cards** (see p. 18) qualify for big discounts from student travel agencies. Most flights from budget agencies are on major airlines, but in peak season some may sell seats on less reliable chartered aircraft.

usit world (www.usitworld.com). Over 50 **usit campus** branches in the UK, including 52 Grosvenor Gardens, **London** SW1W 0AG (☎0870 240 10 10); **Manchester** (☎0161 273 1880); and **Edinburgh** (☎0131 668 3303). Nearly 20 **usit NOW** offices in Ireland, including 19-21 Aston Quay, O'Connell Bridge, **Dublin** 2 (☎01 602 1600; www.usitnow.ie), and **Belfast** (☎02 890 327 111; www.usitnow.com). Offices also in Athens, Auckland, Brussels, Frankfurt, Johannesburg, Lisbon, Madrid, Paris, Sofia, and Warsaw.

Council Travel (www.counciltravel.com). Countless US offices, including branches in Atlanta, Boston, Chicago, L.A., New York, San Francisco, Seattle, and Washington, D.C. Check the web site or call 800-2-COUNCIL (226-8624) for the office nearest you. Also an office at 28A Poland St. (Oxford Circus), **London**, W1V 3DB UK, (☎020 7437 7767).

CTS Travel, 44 Goodge St., **London** W1T 2AD, UK (☎020 7636 0031; fax 7637 5328; ctsinfo@ctstravel.co.uk).

STA Travel, 7890 S. Hardy Dr., Suite 110, Tempe AZ 85284 (24hr. reservations and info ☎800-781-4040; www.sta-travel.com). A student and youth travel organization with over 150 offices worldwide, including US offices in Boston, Chicago, L.A., New York, San Francisco, Seattle, and Washington, D.C. Ticket booking, travel insurance, railpasses, and more. In the UK, walk-in office 11 Goodge St., **London** W1T 2PF, or call 020 7436 7779. In New Zealand, Shop 2B, 182 Queen St., **Auckland** (☎09 309 0458). In Australia, 366 Lygon St., **Carlton** (a suburb of Melbourne), VIC 3053 (☎03 9349 4344).

Travel CUTS (Canadian Universities Travel Services Limited), 187 College St., **Toronto,** ON M5T 1P7 (☎416-979-2406; fax 979-8167; www.travelcuts.com). 60 offices across Canada. Also in the UK, 295-A Regent St., **London** W1R 7YA (☎020 7255 1944).

ESSENTIALS

FLIGHT PLANNING ON THE INTERNET.
Many airline sites offer special deals on the web. Other sites do the legwork and compile the deals for you—try www.bestfares.com, www.flights.com, www.hot-deals.com, www.lowestfare.com, www.onetravel.com, and www.travelzoo.com.

StudentUniverse (www.studentuniverse.com), **STA** (www.sta-travel.com), **Council** (www.counciltravel.com), and **Orbitz.com** provide quotes on student tickets, while **Expedia** (www.expedia.com) and **Travelocity** (www.travelocity.com) offer full travel services. **Priceline** (www.priceline.com) allows you to specify a price, and obligates you to buy any ticket that meets or beats it; be prepared for antisocial hours and odd routes. **Skyauction** (www.skyauction.com) allows you to bid on both last-minute and advance-purchase tickets.

COMMERCIAL AIRLINES

The commercial airlines' lowest regular offer is the **APEX** (Advance Purchase Excursion) fare, which provides confirmed reservations and allows "open-jaw" tickets, coming with hefty cancellation and change penalties. Generally, reservations must be made seven to 21 days in advance, with seven- to 14-day minimum and up to 90-day maximum stay limits.

Although APEX fares are probably not the cheapest possible fares, they provide a sense of the average commercial price, against which you can measure other bargains. Many airlines offer **"e-fares,"** special, last-minute fares available over the Internet; check airline web sites for details. **STA Travel**'s website (www.sta-travel.com) is a pretty reliable web site offering deals for student travelers. Specials in newspapers may be cheaper but have more restrictions and fewer available seats.

NORTH AMERICAN CARRIERS

Air Tran (☎800-247-8726; www.airtran.com). A budget carrier which also offers the "X-Fares Standby Program" for 18- to 22-year-olds (☎888-493-2737).

America West (☎800-235-9292; www.americawest.com). Services the Western US.

American (☎800-433-7300; www.americanair.com). Offers "College SAAvers" fares for college students.

Continental (☎800-525-0280; www.flycontinental.com). Great deals for senior citizens in the "Freedom Club" (☎800-441-1135).

Northwest (☎800-225-2525; www.nwa.com). Travels to the Southwest.

Southwest (☎800-435-9792; www.iflyswa.com). Budget carrier with a friendly attitude.

TWA (☎800-221-2000; www.twa.com). Offers last minute email "TransWorld specials."

United (☎800-241-6522; www.ual.com). Another major US airline.

TRAVELING FROM THE UK AND IRELAND

Airfares from Britain and Ireland peak between June and September and near holidays. Expect round-trip fares from either London or Dublin to Los Angeles to range about $500-1500 and fares to New York and Boston (where you can pick up connecting flights to the Southwest) to be less ($300-$1100).

Peak-season rates generally take effect from mid-May to mid-September. If you can, take advantage of cheap off-season flights within Europe to reach an advantageous point of departure for North America. London is a major connecting point for budget flights to the US. New York is often the destination for such flights. Once in the States, you can catch a continental flight to make your way out West.

TRAVELING FROM AUSTRALIA AND NEW ZEALAND

Flights from Sydney to Los Angeles cost between $900-1200. Traveling from Auckland to Los Angeles is a tad cheaper ($700-1100). **Qantas** (☎ 13 13 13 or US ☎ 800-227-4500; www.qantas.com.au), **United** (see above), and **Air New Zealand** (☎ 0800 737 000 in New Zealand; ☎ 13 24 76 in Australia; www.airnewzealand.co.nz) fly to the US. Advance purchase fares from Australia have extremely tough restrictions. Many travelers from Australia and New Zealand take **Singapore Airlines** (☎ 02 93 500 100 in Australia; ☎ 0800 808 909 in New Zealand; www.singaporeair.com) or other East Asian carriers for the initial leg of their trip.

TRAVELING FROM SOUTH AFRICA

Traveling from either Cape Town or Johannesburg to New York will cost $900 to $1400. Most flights into the US will go through either Boston, New York, or Washington, D.C. Standard commercial carriers like Virgin Atlantic will probably offer the most convenient flights. **South African Airways** (www.saa.co.za), **American,** and **Northwest** connect South Africa with North America.

AIR COURIER FLIGHTS

Those who travel light should consider courier flights. Couriers help transport cargo on international flights by using their checked luggage space for freight. Generally, couriers must travel with carry-ons only and deal with complex flight restrictions. Most flights are round-trip only, with short fixed-length stays (usually one week) and a limit of one ticket per issue. Most of these flights also operate only out of major gateway cities, mostly in North America. Round-trip courier fares to the Southwest will vary greatly, but are generally cheaper than normal fares. Most flights leave from New York, Los Angeles, San Francisco, or Miami in the US; and from Montreal, Toronto, or Vancouver in Canada. Generally, you must be over 21 (in some cases 18). The most popular destinations usually require an advance reservation of about two weeks (you can usually book up to two months ahead). Super-discounted fares are common for "last-minute" flights (three to 14 days ahead).

STANDBY FLIGHTS

Traveling standby requires considerable flexibility in arrival and departure dates and cities. Companies dealing in standby flights sell vouchers rather than tickets, along with the promise to get to your destination (or near your destination) within a certain window of time (typically 1-5 days). Call the company with your specific window of time to hear your flight options and the probability that you will be able to board each flight. You can then decide which flights you want to try to make, show up at the appropriate airport at the appropriate time, present your voucher, and board if space is available. Vouchers can usually be bought for both one-way and round-trip travel. You may receive a monetary refund only if every available flight within your date range is full; if you opt not to take an available flight, you can only get credit toward future travel. Carefully read agreements with any company offering standby flights as fine print can leave you in a lurch.

TICKET CONSOLIDATORS

Ticket consolidators, or **"bucket shops,"** buy unsold tickets in bulk from commercial airlines and sell them at discounted rates. The best place to look is in the Sunday travel section of any major newspaper (such as *The New York Times*), where many bucket shops place tiny ads. Call quickly, as availability is typically extremely limited. Not all bucket shops are reliable, so insist on a receipt that gives full details of restrictions, refunds, and tickets, and pay by credit card (in

ESSENTIALS

spite of the 2-5% fee) so you can stop payment if you never receive your tickets. For more info, see www.travel-library.com/air-travel/consolidators.html.

CHARTER FLIGHTS

Charters are flights a tour operator contracts with an airline to fly extra loads of passengers during peak season. Charter flights fly less frequently than major airlines, make refunds particularly difficult, and are almost always fully booked. Schedules and itineraries may also change or be cancelled at the last moment (as late as 48 hours before the trip, and without a full refund), and check-in, boarding, and baggage claim are often much slower. However, they can also be cheaper.

Discount clubs and **fare brokers** offer members savings on last-minute charter and tour deals. Study contracts closely; you don't want to end up with an unwanted overnight layover. Try **Travelers Advantage,** Trumbull, CT (☎877-259-2691; www.travelersadvantage.com); the $70 annual fee includes discounts and cheap flight directories specializes in travel and tour packages.

BORDER CROSSINGS

It is possible to enter the Southwest overland from Mexico—indeed, thousands do every day, legally and otherwise. There are, however, a number of drawbacks to this approach. Due to high levels of drug smuggling and illegal immigration, the crossing procedure is long and involved. Waits can be unpleasant, and for most people, so can the lengthy searches. Border officials are likely to be less accommodating at the overland crossings, and proper documentation (especially if you could be mistaken for a Latin American national) is essential. The major crossings in the Southwest region are at El Paso, TX (see p. 426) and Nogales, AZ (see p. 143). A small, rarely-used crossing can be found in the Organ Pipe Cactus National Monument at Lukeville, AZ (see p. 141).

GETTING AROUND

BY TRAIN

Locomotion is still one of the cheapest (and most pleasant) ways to tour the Southwest, but keep in mind that discounted air travel may be cheaper, and much faster, than train travel. As with airlines, you can save money by purchasing your tickets as far in advance as possible, so plan ahead and make reservations early. It is essential to travel light on trains; not all stations will check your baggage.

AMTRAK

Amtrak is the only provider of passenger train service in the Southwest, via its Southwest Chief and Sunset Limited lines. (☎800-872-7245; www.amtrak.com. Albuquerque to L.A.: 15hr., $120; Albuquerque to Flagstaff: 4hr., $106; Tucson to L.A.: 12hr., $90.) The Southwest Chief line runs parallel to Rte. 66/I-40 and the Santa Fe railroad line, passing through Albuquerque (p. 357), Gallup (p. 398), Flagstaff (p. 103), and Williams (p. 103) on its way to Los Angeles. The Sunset Limited Line runs just north of the border, serving cities including San Antonio, El Paso, Tucson, and L.A. Train travel to Phoenix is arranged through a bus connection to Tucson. Cities on the Amtrak line have ticket offices, but tickets must be bought through an agent in some small towns. Amtrak's web site lists up-to-date schedules, fares, and arrival and departure info, and makes reservations. **Discounts** on full rail fares are given to senior citizens (10% off), students with a Student Advantage card (15% off; call 800-96-AMTRAK to purchase the $20 card), travelers with disabilities (15% off), children 2-15 accompanied by an adult (50% off), and children under 2 (free). Active-duty veterans may enroll in the Veterans Advantage program, which provides discounts from 15 to 50% for an annual fee of $20. Amtrak's "Rail SALE" allows travelers to save up to 90% on certain trips. Visit the web site for details and reservations. Amtrak also offers **special packages:**

Air-Rail Vacations: Amtrak and United Airlines allow you to travel in 1 direction by train and return by plane, or to fly to a distant point and return home by train. The train portion of the journey can last up to 30 days and include up to 3 stopovers. A multitude of variations are available (☎800-437-3441).

BY BUS

Buses offer the most frequent and complete service between the cities and towns of the Southwest. Often a bus is the only way to reach smaller locales without a car. In rural areas and across open spaces, however, bus lines tend to be sparse. *Russell's Official National Motor Coach Guide* (around $17, including postage) is an invaluable tool for constructing an itinerary. Updated each month, *Russell's Guide* has schedules of every bus route (including Greyhound) between any two towns in the US. Russell's also publishes semiannual *Supplements;* a Directory of Bus Lines and Bus Stations; and a series of maps ($8.40 each). Write to **Russell's Guides, Inc.,** P.O. Box 278, Cedar Rapids, IA 52406 (☎319-364-6138; fax 364-4853).

GREYHOUND

Greyhound (☎800-231-2222; www.greyhound.com) operates the largest number of routes in the US, though local bus companies may provide more extensive services within specific regions. Schedule info is available at any Greyhound terminal, on the web site, or by calling the 800 number. Reserve with a credit card over the phone at least 10 days in advance, and the ticket can be mailed anywhere in the US. Otherwise, reservations are available only up to 24hr. in advance. You can buy your ticket at the terminal, but arrive early.

If **boarding at a remote "flag stop,"** be sure you know exactly where the bus stops. You must call the nearest agency and let them know you'll be waiting and at what time. Catch the driver's attention by standing on the side of the road and flailing your arms wildly—better to be embarrassed than stranded. If a bus passes (usually because of overcrowding), a later, less-crowded bus should stop. Whatever you stow in compartments underneath the bus should be clearly marked; be sure to get a claim check for it and make sure your luggage is on the same bus as you.

Advance purchase fares: Reserving space far ahead of time ensures a lower fare, although expect a smaller discount during the busy summer months (June 5-Sept. 15). For tickets purchased more than 7 days in advance, the one-way fare anywhere in the US will not exceed $80, while the round-trip price is capped at $158 (June-Sept., the one-way cap is $89 and the round-trip $178). Fares are often reduced even more for 14-day or 21-day advance purchases on many popular routes; call the 800 number for up-to-the-date pricing, or consult the user-friendly web site.

Ameripass (☎888-454-7277). Allows adults unlimited travel for 7 days ($219), 15 days ($339), 30 days ($449), or 60 days ($629). Prices for students with a valid college ID and for senior citizens are slightly less: $197/$305/$404/$566. Children's passes are half the price of adults. The pass takes effect the first day used. Before purchasing an Ameripass, total up the separate bus fares between towns to make sure that the pass is really more economical, or at least worth the unlimited flexibility it provides. **TNM&O**

Coaches, Vermont Transit, Carolina Trailways, and **Valley Transit** are Greyhound sub-sidiaries, and as such will honor Ameripasses; actually, most bus companies in the US will do so, but check for specifics.

International Ameripass: For foreign visitors only. A 7-day pass is $204, 15-day pass $314, 30-day pass $424, 60-day pass $574. Call 888-454-7277 for info. International Ameripasses are not available at the terminal; they can be purchased in foreign countries at Greyhound-affiliated agencies; telephone numbers vary by country and are listed on the web site. Passes can also be ordered on the web site, or purchased in Greyhound's International Office, in Port Authority Bus Station, 625 Eighth Ave., New York, NY 10018 (☎212-971-0492 or 800-246-8572; fax 402-330-0919; intlameripass@greyhound.com). **Australia:** ☎04 934 2088. **New Zealand:** ☎09 479 65555. **South Africa:** ☎011 331 2911. **UK:** ☎01342 317 317.

BY CAR

Driving is undoubtedly the most convenient way of getting around the Southwest, and, depending on the amount of traveling you'll be doing, is probably also the cheapest and most enjoyable. Even for the US, the region is very sparsely populated and, unlike in New York or Boston, owning a car is generally the only option for residents. Since most cities and even many smaller towns, true to the Western-sprawl school of urban planning, cannot be explored without wheels, and since almost everyone has wheels, public transportation is often paid lax attention. Gas and car rentals are exceptionally cheap in the Southwest, and roads are wide, straight, and laid out logically—all the more reason to go by car if possible.

AUTOMOBILE CLUBS

Most automobile clubs offer free towing, emergency roadside assistance, travel-related discounts, and random goodies in exchange for a modest membership fee. Travelers should strongly consider membership if planning an extended roadtrip.

▨ **American Automobile Association/AAA** (emergency road service ☎800-AAA-HELP/222-4357; www.aaa.com). Offers free trip-planning services, road maps and guidebooks, 24hr. emergency road service anywhere in the US, free towing, and commission-free traveler's checks from American Express, with over 1000 offices scattered across the country. Discounts on Hertz car rental (5-20%), Amtrak tickets (10%), and various motel chains and theme parks. AAA has reciprocal agreements with auto associations in other countries which often provide you full benefits while in the US. Memberships vary depending on which branch you join, but range $50-60 for the first year and less for renewals and additional family members; call 800-564-6222 to sign up.

Mobil Auto Club, 200 N. Martingale Rd., Schaumbourg, IL 60174 (info ☎800-621-5581; emergency service 800-323-5880). Benefits include locksmith reimbursement, towing (free up to 10 mi.), roadside service, and car-rental discounts. $7 per month covers you and another driver.

ON THE ROAD

Tune up the car before you leave, make sure the tires are in good repair and have enough air, and get good maps. Rand McNally's Road Atlas, covering all of the US, is one of the best (available at bookstores and gas stations, $11). Research gas station availability before you set out, and carry some basic tools and **spare parts,** including a **spare tire** and **jack, jumper cables, extra oil, flares,** a **flashlight,** and **blankets** (in case you break down at night or in the winter). A **compass** and a **car manual** can also be very useful. Those traveling long undeveloped stretches of road may want to consider renting a **car phone** or purchasing a **cell phone** in case of a breakdown (although any cell provider's coverage is bound to be sporadic in much of the region, emergency calls can be made on whatever local service is available). When traveling in the summer or in the desert bring five gallons of **water** for drinking and for the radiator. In extremely hot weather, use the air conditioner with restraint; if you see the car's temperature gauge climbing, turn it off. Turning the heater on full blast will help cool the engine. If radiator fluid is steaming, turn off the car for 30min. Never pour water over the engine to cool it. Never lift a searing hot hood. In remote areas, remember to bring emergency food and water. If your car breaks down, wait for the police to assist you.

While driving, be sure to buckle up—seat belts are **required by law in the Southwest. Speed limits** on interstates throughout most of the Southwest are 70-75 m.p.h. Though the openness of the roads makes higher speeds relatively safe, a collision at such a high speed will always be serious. Also, local police and state troopers make frequent use of radar to catch speed demons, so be very attentive when zipping along the interstates. Slower **state and local highways** can be even more dangerous, especially those that are two-lane and allow passing on the left. Only attempt such a pass if there is absolute certainty that it can be pulled off.

Be sure to park your vehicle in a garage or well-traveled area, and use a steering wheel locking device in cities. **Sleeping in a car or van parked in the city is extremely dangerous**—even the most dedicated budget traveler should not consider it.

HOW TO NAVIGATE THE INTERSTATES

In the 1950s, President Dwight "Ike" Eisenhower envisioned a well-organized **interstate highway system.** His dream has been realized: there exists a comprehensive, well-maintained, efficient means of traveling between major cities and between states. Luckily for the traveler, the highways are named with an intuitive numbering system. Even-numbered interstates run east-west and odd ones run north-south, decreasing in number toward the south and the west. In the Southwest, the main interstates are I-40, running east-west through northern New Mexico and Arizona; I-10, running through southern Arizona and New Mexico, from El Paso, TX, to Tucson, Phoenix, and off to L.A.; I-25, which runs north-south through the center of New Mexico, through Albuquerque and Santa Fe, up to Denver, CO; and I-17, which connects Phoenix and Flagstaff. Three-digit numbers signify branches of other interstates (e.g., I-287 is a branch of I-87), which are often bypasses skirting around large cities. As for smaller highways, "U.S." (as in "U.S. 1") refers to US highways, while "Rte." (as in "Rte. 7") refers to state and local highways.

DANGERS FOR SOUTHWEST DRIVERS

While the Southwest has an excellent system of interstates and state highways, the region also boasts a number of unpaved and often unmapped roads. Attempting to drive these roads can be treacherous, particularly for vehicles not designed for off-road navigation. Roads that seem at first to be safe may turn rough, leaving drivers in a remote area with no means of transportation. On the whole, you should avoid seeking shortcuts or four-wheel-drive adventures on unmarked rural roads.

RENTING

Rental agencies fall into two categories: national companies with hundreds of branches, and local agencies serving a city or region. **National chains** usually allow cars to be picked up in one city and dropped off in another (for a hefty charge, sometimes in excess of $1000); occasional promotions linked to coastal inventory imbalances may cut the fee dramatically. By calling a toll-free number or using the agency's web site, you can reserve a reliable car anywhere in the country. Generally, major city branches carry the cheapest rates; of these, branches in the city itself have the lowest rates, with airport branches often tacking on surcharges. However, like airfares, car rental prices change constantly and often require scouting around for the best rate. Drawbacks include steep prices (a compact rents for about $35-45 per day, though often with significant weekly-rate reductions) and high minimum ages for rentals (usually 25). Most branches rent to ages 21-24 with an additional fee, but policies and prices vary from agency to agency. If you're 21 or older and have a major credit card in your name, you may be able to rent where the minimum age would otherwise rule you out. **Alamo** (☎ 800-327-9633; www.alamo.com) rents to ages 21-24 with a major credit card for an additional $20 per day, **Enterprise** (☎ 800-736-8222) rents to customers aged 21-24, often with no surcharge, and many **Dollar** (☎ 800-800-4000; www.dollar.com) and **Thrifty** (☎ 800-367-2277; www.thrifty.com) locations rent to under-25s for varying surcharges. **Rent-A-Wreck** (☎ 800-944-7501; www.rent-a-wreck.com) specializes in supplying vehicles that are past their prime for lower-than-average prices; a bare-bones compact less than 8 years old rents for $20-25; cars 3-5 years old average under $30.

Most rental packages offer unlimited mileage, although some allow you a certain number of miles free before the usual charge of 25-40¢ per mi. takes effect. Most quoted rates do not include gas or tax, so ask for the total cost before handing over the credit card; many large firms have added airport surcharges not covered by the designated fare. Return the car with a full tank unless you sign up for a fuel option plan that stipulates otherwise. When dealing with any car rental company, ask whether the price includes insurance against theft and collision. There may be an additional charge for a collision and damage waiver (CDW), which usually comes to about $12-15 per day. Some major credit cards (including Master-Card and American Express) will cover the CDW if you use their card to rent a car; call your credit card company or inquire at the rental agency for specifics.

BUYING

Adventures on Wheels, 42 Rte. 36, Middletown, NJ 07748 (☎ 732-583-8714 or 800-943-3579; info@wheels9.com; www.wheels9.com), sells travelers a motorhome, camper, minivan, station wagon, or compact car, organizes its registration and provides insurance, and guarantees they will buy it back after you have finished your travels. Cars with a buy-back guarantee start at $2500. Buy a camper for $6500, use it for six months, and sell it back for $3000-4000. The main office is in New York/New Jersey; there are other offices in Los Angeles, San Francisco, and Miami. Vehicles can be picked up at one office and dropped off at another.

DRIVING PERMITS

If you do not have a license issued by a US state or Canadian province or territory, you might want an International Driving Permit (IDP). While the US allows you to drive with a foreign license for up to a year, it may help with police if your license is written in English. You must carry your home license with your IDP at all times. You must be 18 to obtain an IDP, it is valid for a year, and it must be issued in the country in which your license originates. Contact these offices to apply:

Australia: Contact your local Royal Automobile Club (RAC) or the National Royal Motorist Association (NRMA) if in NSW or the ACT (☎ 08 9421 4444; www.rac.com.au/travel). Permits AUS$15.

Canada: Contact any Canadian Automobile Association (CAA) branch, or write to 1145 Hunt Club Rd., #200, Ottawa, ON K1V 0Y3 (☎613-247-0117; www.caa.ca/caainternet/travelservices/internationaldocumentation/idptravel.htm). Permits CDN$10.

Ireland: Contact the nearest Automobile Association (AA) office or write to the UK address below. Permits €5.08.

New Zealand: Contact your local Automobile Association (AA) or their main office at Auckland Central, 99 Albert St. (☎09 377 4660; www.nzaa.co.nz). Permits NZ$8.

South Africa: Contact the Travel Services Department of the Automobile Association of South Africa at P.O. Box 596, 2000 Johannesburg (☎011 799 1400; fax 799 1410; http://aasa.co.za). Permits ZAR28.50.

UK: To visit your local AA Shop, contact the **AA Headquarters** (☎0990 44 88 66), or write to: The Automobile Association, International Documents, Fanum House, Erskine, Renfrewshire PA8 6BW. To find the location nearest you that issues the IDP, call 0990 50 06 00 or visit www.theaa.co.uk/motoringandtravel/idp/index.asp. Permits UK£4.

CAR INSURANCE

Most credit cards cover standard insurance. If you rent, lease, or borrow a car, you will need a **green card,** or **International Insurance Certificate,** to certify that you have liability insurance and that it applies abroad. Green cards can be obtained at car rental agencies, car dealers (for those leasing cars), some travel agents, and some border crossings. Rental agencies may require you to purchase theft insurance in areas that they consider to have a high risk of auto theft.

BY TWO WHEELS

BY BICYCLE

Safe and secure cycling requires a quality helmet and lock. A good helmet costs about $40—much cheaper than critical head surgery. U-shaped **Kryptonite** or **Citadel** locks ($30-60) carry insurance against theft for one or two years if your bike is registered with the police. **Bike Nashbar,** P.O. Box 1455, Crab Orchard, WV 25827 (☎800-627-4227), will beat any nationally advertised in-stock price by 5¢, and ships anywhere in the US or Canada. Their techline (☎800-888-2710; open M-F 8am-6pm ET) fields questions about repairs and maintenance. Check out books like: *Best Bike Rides in Northern California,* by Kim Grob (Globe Pequot; $13); and *Mountain Bike! Southern California: A Guide to Classic Trails,* by David Story (Menasha Ridge; $16). For more info on bike trips, contact **Adventure Cycling Association,** P.O. Box 8308, Missoula, MT 59807 (☎800-755-2453; www.advcycling.org). It's a national, nonprofit organization that researches and maps long-distance routes and organizes bike tours (75-day Great Divide Expedition $2800, 6-9 day trip $650-800). Annual membership is $30 and includes access to route maps and a subscription to *Adventure Cyclist* magazine.

BY MOTORCYCLE

The wind-in-your-face thrill, burly leather, and revving crackle of a motorcycle engine unobscured by windows or upholstery has built up quite a cult following, but motorcycling is the most dangerous of roadtop activities. Of course, safety should be your primary concern. Helmets are required by law in the US. Those considering a long journey should contact the American Motorcyclist Association, 13515 Yarmouth Dr., Pickering, OH 43147 (☎800-262-5646; www.ama-cycle.org), the linchpin of US biker culture. A full membership ($39 per year) includes a subscription to the extremely informative *American Motorcyclist* magazine, discounts on insurance, rentals, and hotels, and a patch for your riding jacket.

BY THUMB

Let's Go urges you to consider the great risks and disadvantages of **hitchhiking** before thumbing it. Hitching means entrusting your life to a randomly selected person who happens to stop beside you on the road. While this may be comparatively safe in some areas of Europe, it is generally *not* so in the US, and especially not in the Southwest. We do not recommend it. We strongly urge you to find other means of transportation and to avoid situations where hitching is the only option.

SPECIFIC CONCERNS

WOMEN TRAVELERS

Women exploring on their own inevitably face some additional safety concerns, but it's easy to be adventurous without taking undue risks. If you are concerned, consider staying in hostels which offer single rooms that lock from the inside or in religious organizations with rooms for women only. Stick to centrally located accommodations and avoid solitary late-night treks or rides on public transit.

Always carry extra money for a phone call, bus, or taxi. **Hitchhiking** is never safe for lone women, or even for two women traveling together. When on overnight or long train rides, if there is no women-only compartment, choose one occupied by women or couples. Look as if you know where you're going and approach older women or couples for directions if you're lost or uncomfortable.

Generally, the less you look like a tourist, the better off you'll be. Dress conservatively, especially in rural areas. Trying to fit in can be effective, but dressing to the style of an obviously different culture may cause you to be ill at ease and a conspicuous target. Wearing a **wedding band** may help prevent unwanted overtures.

Your best answer to verbal harassment is no answer at all; feigning deafness, sitting motionless, and staring straight ahead at nothing in particular will do a world of good that reactions usually don't achieve. The extremely persistent can sometimes be dissuaded by a firm, loud, and very public "Go away!" Don't hesitate to seek out a police officer or a passerby if you are being harassed. Memorize the emergency numbers in places you visit, and consider carrying a whistle on your keychain. A self-defense course will both prepare you for a potential attack and improve your awareness of your surroundings.

For general information, contact the **National Organization for Women (NOW),** 733 15th St. NW, 2nd. Fl., Washington, D.C. 20005 (☎202-628-8669; www.now.org), which has branches across the US that can refer women travelers to rape crisis centers and counseling services.

TRAVELING ALONE

There are many benefits to traveling alone, including independence and more interaction with locals. On the other hand, any solo traveler is more vulnerable to harassment and theft. As a lone traveler, try not to stand out as a tourist, look confident, and be especially careful in deserted or very crowded areas. If questioned, never admit that you are traveling alone. Maintain regular contact with someone at home who knows your itinerary. For more tips, pick up *Traveling Solo,* by Eleanor Berman (Globe Pequot Press, $17) or subscribe to **Connecting: Solo Travel Network,** 689 Park Road, Unit 6, Gibsons, BC V0N 1V7, Canada (☎604-886-9099; www.cstn.org; membership $35). **Travel Companion Exchange,** P.O. Box 833, Amityville, NY 11701 (☎631-454-0880 or ☎800-392-1256; www.whytravelalone.com; $48), will link solo travelers with companions with similar travel interests.

OLDER TRAVELERS

Senior citizens are eligible for a wide range of discounts on transportation, museums, movies, theaters, concerts, restaurants, and accommodations. If you don't see a senior citizen price listed, ask, and you may be delightfully surprised. The books *No Problem! Worldwise Tips for Mature Adventurers*, by Janice Kenyon (Orca Book Publishers; $16), and *Unbelievably Good Deals and Great Adventures That You Absolutely Can't Get Unless You're Over 50*, by Joan Rattner Heilman (NTC/Contemporary Publishing; $13), are both excellent resources. For more information, contact one of the following organizations:

Elderhostel, 11 Ave. de Lafayette, Boston, MA 02111 (☎877-426-8056; www.elderhostel.org). Organizes 1- to 4-week "educational adventures" throughout the United States on varied subjects for those over 55.

The Mature Traveler, P.O. Box 15791, Sacramento, CA 95852 (☎800-460-6676). Deals, discounts, and travel packages for the over-50 traveler. Subscription $30.

Walking the World, P.O. Box 1186, Fort Collins, CO 80522 (☎800-340-9255; www.walkingtheworld.com). Organizes trips for over-50 travelers to the Southwest.

BISEXUAL, GAY, & LESBIAN TRAVELERS

Many areas of American cities are generally accepting of all sexualities, and thriving gay and lesbian communities can be found in most cosmopolitan areas in the Southwest. Many college towns are gay-friendly as well. Nevertheless, incidents of homophobia are all too prevalent. A vast spectrum of political and religious beliefs as well as a great range of urban and rural environments exist throughout the Southwest, so attitudes toward gay and lesbian travelers will vary greatly throughout the region. However, BGL travelers should feel confident and safe traveling in all parts of the Southwest. BGL travelers who experience harassment should immediately report incidents to the police.

FURTHER READING: BISEXUAL, GAY, AND LESBIAN.
Spartacus International Gay Guide 2001-2002. Bruno Gmünder Verlag ($33).
Damron Road Atlas, Damron's Accommodations, and *The Women's Traveller.*
Damron Travel Guides ($14-19). For more info, call 800-462-6654 or visit www.damron.com.
Ferrari Guides' Gay Travel A to Z, Ferrari Guides' Men's Travel in Your Pocket, and *Ferrari Guides' Inn Places.* Ferrari Publications ($16-20). Purchase the guides online at www.ferrariguides.com.
Gayellow Pages USA/Canada, Frances Green. Gayellow pages ($16). They also publish smaller regional editions. Online at www.gayellowpages.com.

TRAVELERS WITH DISABILITIES

Federal law dictates that all public buildings should be handicap-accessible, and recent laws governing building codes have made disabled access more the norm than the exception. However, traveling with a disability still requires planning and flexibility. Those with disabilities should inform airlines and hotels when making arrangements for travel; some time may be needed to prepare special accommodations. US Customs requires a certificate of immunization against rabies for **guide dogs** entering the country.

In the US, both Amtrak and major airlines will accommodate disabled passengers if notified at least 72 hours in advance. Hearing-impaired travelers may contact Amtrak using teletype printers (☎ 800-523-6590 or 654-5988). Greyhound buses will provide free travel for a companion; if you are without a fellow traveler, call Greyhound (☎ 800-752-4841) at least 48 hours, but no more than one week, before you plan to leave and they will make arrangements to assist you.

If you are planning to visit a national park or attraction in the US run by the National Park Service, obtain a free **Golden Access Passport,** which is available at all park entrances and from federal offices whose functions relate to land, forests, or wildlife. The Passport entitles disabled travelers and their families to free park admission and provides a 50% discount on all fees. Check out *Resource Directory for the Disabled*, by Richard Neil Shrout (Facts on File; $45). The following organizations and tour agencies should be helpful in planning your trip:

USEFUL ORGANIZATIONS

Mobility International USA (MIUSA), P.O. Box 10767, Eugene, OR 97440 (☎ 541-343-1284; www.miusa.org). Sells *A World of Options: A Guide to International Educational Exchange, Community Service, and Travel for Persons with Disabilities* ($35).

Society for Accessible Travel and Hospitality (SATH), 347 Fifth Ave., Suite 610, New York, NY 10016 (☎ 212-447-7284; www.sath.org). An advocacy group that publishes free online travel information and the travel magazine *Open World* ($18, free for members). Annual membership $45, students and seniors $30.

TOUR AGENCIES

Directions Unlimited, 123 Green Ln., Bedford Hills, NY 10507 (☎ 800-533-5343). Books individual and group vacations for the physically disabled; not an info service.

The Guided Tour Inc., 7900 Old York Rd., #114B, Elkins Park, PA 19027 (☎ 800-783-5841; www.guidedtour.com). Organizes travel programs for persons with developmental and physical challenges in the US.

MINORITY TRAVELERS

Racial and ethnic minorities sometimes face blatant and, more often, subtle discrimination and/or harassment. The best way to deal with such encounters is to remain calm and report individuals to a supervisor and establishments to the Better Business Bureau for the region (the operator will provide local listings); contact the police in extreme situations. *Let's Go* always welcomes reader input regarding discriminating establishments. In larger cities, African-Americans can usually consult chapters of the Urban League and the **National Association for the Advancement of Colored People,** or **NAACP** (www.naacp.org), for info on events of interest to African-Americans. Conflicts between Native Americans and Anglos from the first moment of European contact have lent the Southwest a history of interethnic tension. Travelers in the Southwest should be sensitive to these issues, particularly when traveling on reservation land (see **History,** p. 7).

TRAVELERS WITH CHILDREN

Family vacations often require that you slow your pace, and always require that you plan ahead. When deciding where to stay, remember the special needs of young children; if you pick a B&B or a small hotel, call ahead and make sure it's child-friendly. If you rent a car, make sure the company provides a car seat for young children. Be sure that your child carries some sort of ID in case he/she gets lost or in trouble, and arrange a meeting spot in case of separation.

Restaurants often have children's menus and discounts. Virtually all museums and tourist attractions also have a children's rate. Children under two generally fly for free or 10% of the adult airfare on domestic flights (this does not necessarily include a seat). Fares are usually discounted 25% for children from ages 2 to 11. For more information on traveling with children, consult the following books:

Backpacking with Babies and Small Children, Goldie Silverman. Wilderness Press ($10).

Adventuring with Children: An Inspirational Guide to World Travel and the Outdoors, Nan Jeffrey. Avalon House Publishing ($15).

Trouble Free Travel with Children, Vicki Lansky. Book Peddlers ($9).

DIETARY CONCERNS

Home of the bean burrito and other treats, the Southwest's culinary selections will easily fulfill vegetarian dietary requirements. The North American Vegetarian Society (☎518-568-7970; www.navs-online.org) publishes information about vegetarian travel, including *Transformative Adventures: a Guide to Vacations and Retreats* ($15), and the *Vegetarian Journal's Guide to Natural Food Restaurants in the US and Canada* ($12). For more information, consult *The Vegetarian Traveler: Where to Stay if You're Vegetarian, Vegan, or Environmentally Sensitive,* by Jed and Susan Civic (Larson Publications; $16).

Travelers who keep **kosher** should contact synagogues in larger cities for information on kosher restaurants. Your own synagogue or college Hillel should have access to lists of Jewish institutions across the nation. If you are strict in your observance, you may have to prepare your own food on the road. The *Jewish Travel Guide,* by Michael Zaidner (Vallentine Mitchell; $17), is an excellent resource, as is the online kosher restaurant database at www.shamash.org/kosher.

OTHER RESOURCES

Let's Go tries to cover all aspects of budget travel, but we can't put *everything* in our guides. Listed below are books and web sites that can serve as jumping-off points for your own research.

TRAVEL PUBLISHERS AND BOOKSTORES

Hippocrene Books, Inc., 171 Madison Ave., New York, NY 10016 (☎718-454-2366; www.hippocrenebooks.com). Publishes dictionaries and language learning guides.

Hunter Publishing, 470 W. Broadway, 2nd fl., Boston, MA 02127 (☎617-269-0700; www.hunterpublishing.com). Has an extensive catalog of travel guides.

Rand McNally, P.O. Box 7600, Chicago, IL 60680 (☎847-329-8100; www.randmcnally.com). Publishes road atlases.

Travel Books & Language Center, Inc., 4437 Wisconsin Ave. NW, Washington, D.C. 20016 (☎800-220-2665). Over 60,000 titles from around the world.

WORLD WIDE WEB

Almost every aspect of budget travel is accessible via the web. Within 10min. at the keyboard, you can make a reservation at a hostel, get advice from other travelers, or find out exactly how much a train from Amarillo to Los Angeles costs. Listed here are some budget travel sites to start off your surfing; other relevant web sites are listed throughout the book. Because web site turnover is high, use search engines (such as www.google.com) to strike out on your own.

ESSENTIALS

WWW.LETSGO.COM Our newly designed web site now features the full online content of all of our guides. In addition, trial versions of all nine City Guides are available for download on Palm OS™ PDAs. Our web site also contains our newsletter, links for photos and streaming video, online ordering of our titles, info about our books, and a travel forum buzzing with stories and tips.

Microsoft Expedia (www.expedia.msn.com) has everything you'd ever need to make travel plans on the web: compare flight fares, look at maps, make reservations. The free FareTracker sends you monthly mailings about the cheapest fares to any destination.

The CIA World Factbook (www.odci.gov/cia/publications/factbook/index.html) has tons of vital statistics on the US and the Southwest. Check it out for an overview of the American economy, and an explanation of the US system of government.

Shoestring Travel (www.stratpub.com), an alternative to Microsoft's monolithic site, is a budget travel e-zine with listings of home exchanges, links, and accommodations info.

City Net (www.city.net) dispenses info on renting a car, restaurants, hotel rates, and weather for a wide array of cities and regions across the US.

ESSENTIALS

ALTERNATIVES TO TOURISM

VISA INFORMATION
Visa. Visitors from most of Europe, Australia, and New Zealand can travel in the US for up to 90 days without a visa, although you may need to show a return plane ticket. Citizens of South Africa need a visa.
Work Permit. Required for all foreigners planning to work in the US.

Traveling from place to place around the world may be a memorable experience. But if you are looking for a more rewarding and complete way to see the world, you may want to consider Alternatives to Tourism. Working, volunteering, or studying for an extended period of time can be a better way to understand life in the Southwest. This chapter outlines some of the different ways to get to know a new place, whether you want to pay your way through, or just get the personal satisfaction that comes from studying and volunteering. In most cases, you will feel that you partook in a more meaningful and educational experience—something that the average budget traveler often misses out on.

All travelers planning a stay of more than 90 days (180 days for Canadians) need to obtain a visa. **The Center for International Business and Travel (CIBT),** 23201 New Mexico Ave. NW #210, Washington, D.C. 20016 (☎800-925-2428; www.cibt.com), or 6300 Wilshire Boulevard, Suite 1520, Los Angeles, CA 90048 (☎323-658-5100), secures "pleasure tourist" or B-2 visas to and from all possible countries for a variable service charge (6-month visa around $45). If you lose your I-94 form, you can replace it at the nearest **Immigration and Naturalization Service (INS)** office (☎800-375-5283; www.ins.usdoj.gov), although it's very unlikely that the form will be replaced within the time of your stay. Visa extensions are sometimes attainable with an I-539 form; call the forms request line (☎800-870-3676).

Foreign students who wish to study in the US must apply for either an M-1 visa (vocational studies) or an F-1 visa (for full-time students enrolled in an academic or language program). If English is not your native language, you will probably be required to take the Test of English as a Foreign Language (TOEFL), which is administered in many countries. The international students office at the institution you will be attending can give you more specifics. Contact **TOEFL/TSE Publications,** P.O. Box 6151, Princeton, NJ 08541 (☎609-771-7100; www.toefl.org).

If you are a foreigner, you need a **work permit** or "green card" to work in the United States. Your employer must obtain this document, usually by demonstrating that you have skills that locals lack. Friends in the Southwest can sometimes help expedite work permits or arrange work-for-accommodations exchanges. Obtaining a worker's visa may seem complex, but it's critical that you go through the proper channels, particularly in the Southwest, where sentiment against undocumented workers is strong.

STUDYING ABROAD

Study abroad programs range from basic language and culture courses to college-level classes, often for credit. In order to choose a program that best fits your needs, you will want to find out what kind of students participate in the program and what sort of accommodations are provided. In programs that have large groups of students who speak the same language, there is a trade-off. You may feel more comfortable in the community, but you will not have the same opportunity to practice a foreign language or to befriend other international students. For accommodations, dorm life provides a better opportunity to mingle with fellow students, but there is less of a chance to experience the local scene. If you live with a family, there is a potential to build lifelong friendships with natives and to experience day-to-day life in more depth, but conditions can vary greatly from family to family. Some good resources for finding programs that cater to your particular interests are www.studyabroad.com and the always helpful www.study-abroaddirectory.com, which have links to various semester abroad programs based on a variety of criteria, including desired location and focus of study.

PROGRAMS IN THE SOUTHWEST

In order to live the life of a real American college student, you'll have to drink Milwaukee's Best beer until you puke. Otherwise, consider a visiting student program lasting either a semester or a full year. The best method by far is to contact colleges and universities in your home country to see what kind of exchanges they have with those in the Southwest; college students can often receive credit for study abroad. A more complicated option for advanced English speakers is to enroll directly, full-time in an American institution. The Southwest hosts a number of reputable universities, among them the Universities of Utah, Arizona, and New Mexico, as well as the world-renowned UCLA. Apart from these, each state maintains a public state university system, and there are innumerable community, professional and technical colleges. Unfortunately, tuition costs are high in the United States and a full course of undergraduate study entails a four-year commitment.

LANGUAGE SCHOOLS

Unlike American universities, language schools are frequently independently-run international or local organizations or divisions of foreign universities that rarely offer college credit. Language schools are a good alternative to university study if you desire a deeper focus on the language or a slightly less rigorous courseload. These programs are also good for high school students who might not feel comfortable with older students in a university program. There are lots of language schools located in the Southwest's major cities. Some good programs include:

Eurocentres, 101 N. Union St., Suite 300, Alexandria, VA 22314 (☎703-684-1494; www.eurocentres.com), or in Europe, Head Office, Seestr. 247, CH-8038 Zurich, Switzerland (☎41 1 485 50 40; fax 481 61 24). Language programs for beginning to advanced students with homestays in the Southwestern US.

Nomen Global Language Center, 63 North 400 West, Provo, UT 84601 (☎801-375-7878; www.nomenglobal.com). $1510 for a 15-week course, $325 for a 2-week short course, with corresponding costs for shorter and longer programs. Housing can also be arranged; homestays $110, accommodation rentals $225-1000.

American Language Programs, 56 Hobbs Brook Rd., Weston, MA 02493 (☎781-888-1515; fax 894-3113; info@alp-online.com; www.alp-online.com). ALP runs programs in Phoenix that include homestay and intensive English training. $900-1080 per week (15-25hr.) for 1 person, $1600-1960 for 2 people.

Osako Sangyo University Los Angeles (OSULA) Education Center, 3921 Laurel Canyon Blvd., Los Angeles, CA 91604 (☎818-509-1484; www.osula.com). Offers intensive and general English classes in the suburbs of Los Angeles, in a residential college setting.

ARCHITECTURAL AND ARTS COLONIES

Attracted by the cheap land, the laid-back lifestyle and the relative isolation, a number of art and architectural colonies have flourished in the Southwest. Few generalizations can be made about them as a group; they vary greatly in size, in field and in organization. Some are *de facto* colleges, offering specialized training at the graduate level and beyond, while others are more informal affairs. Inquire about the possibility of getting college credit for your programs.

Arcosanti, HC 74 BOX 4136, Mayer, AZ 86333 (☎928-632-7135; tminus@arcosanti.org; www.arcosanti.org.) Founded by Frank Lloyd Wright disciple Paolo Soleri, who still lives here, Arcosanti is an experimental community based on Soleri's theories of architecture and urban organization. It hosts 5-week workshops ($950) in which participants help expand the settlement while learning about Soleri's project and developing their skills at construction and planning. For those with some background in construction or architecture, an expense-paid internship is available for a 3-month commitment.

Taliesin West, 12621 N. Frank Lloyd Wright Blvd., Scottsdale, AZ 85261 (☎480-860-2700; www.taliesin.edu). The Phoenix branch of the elite architectural school founded by Frank Lloyd Wright, Taliesin West offers a full course load of work leading to a Bachelor of Architectural Science or Master of Architecture degree. There are a small number of non-degree positions available. All slots are highly competitive.

Santa Fe Art Institute, 1600 St. Michael's Drive, NM 84505 (☎505-424-5050; fax 505-424-5051; info@sfai.org; www.sfai.org). A world-class artistic center, the Santa Fe Art Institute offers 1- and 2-week workshops ($1000-1800) giving participants the opportunity to work with professional resident artists in Santa Fe.

WORKING

There are two main schools of thought about working travelers. Some travelers want long-term jobs that allow them to get to know another part of the world in depth (such as teaching their native language or working in the tourist industry). Other travelers seek out short-term jobs to finance their travel. They usually seek employment in the service sector or in agriculture, working for a few weeks at a time to finance their journey. This section discusses both short-term and long-term opportunities for working in the Southwest. Make sure you understand the United States' **visa requirements** for foreign workers; see the box on p. 50.

Job seekers should look in the classified sections of major daily newspapers such as the *Arizona Republic* or the *Salt Lake Tribune*. Another option is to seek out temp agencies. It may be possible to volunteer in exchange for room and board in parts of the Southwest; such instances are noted in the guide.

LONG-TERM WORK

If you're planning on spending a substantial amount of time (more than three months) working in the Southwest, search for a job well in advance. International placement agencies are often the easiest way to find employment abroad. **Intern-**

ships, usually for college students, are a good way to segue into working abroad, although they are often unpaid or poorly paid (many say the experience, however, is well worth it). Be wary of advertisements or companies that claim the ability to get you a job abroad for a fee—often times the same listings are available online or in newspapers. It's best, if going through an organization, to use one that's somewhat reputable. Some good ones include:

Council Exchanges, 52 Poland St., London W1V 4JQ, UK (☎020 748 2000; www.councilexchanges.org.uk), has a jobs and internships database for US positions.

Camp Counselors USA, Green Dragon House, 64-70 High Street, Croydon CRO 9XN, UK (☎+44 020 8668 9051; www.workexperienceusa.com), places people aged 18-30 as counselors in summer camps in the US.

AU PAIR WORK

Au pairs are typically women, aged 18-27, who work as live-in nannies, caring for children and doing light housework in foreign countries in exchange for room, board, and a small spending allowance or stipend. Most former au pairs speak favorably of their experience, and of how it allowed them tMo really get to know the country without the high expenses of traveling. Drawbacks, however, often include long hours of constantly being on-duty, and the somewhat mediocre pay. In the United States, weekly salaries typically fall well below $200, with at least 45hr. of work expected. In the US, au pairs are expected to speak English and have at least 200 hours of childcare experience. Much of the au pair experience really does depend on the family you're placed with. The agencies below are a good starting point for looking for employment as an au pair.

Childcare International, Ltd., Trafalgar House, Grenville Pl., London NW7 3SA, UK (☎+44 020 8906 3116; fax 8906 3461; www.childint.co.uk).

InterExchange, 161 Sixth Ave., New York, NY 10013 (☎212-924-0446; fax 924-0575; www.interexchange.org or www.aupair.tripod.com).

International Educational Services, Calle Los Centelles 45-6-11, 46006 Valencia, Spain (☎+34 96 320 6491; fax 320 7832; US fax 707-281-0289; ies@ciberia.com; ww.ies.ciberia.com).

SHORT-TERM WORK

Traveling for long periods of time can get expensive; therefore, many travelers try their hand at odd jobs for a few weeks at a time to make some extra cash to carry them through another month or two of touring around. Many travelers defray the cost of their journey through occasional work. While this is a popular tactic, there are particular difficulties with it in the Southwest—the proximity of Mexico depresses wages, and competition for work is fierce, although well-spoken and educated travelers will have the upper hand over Mexican migrants. A common way to make some extra cash in the Southwest is agricultural work. Those who try agricultural labor should be prepared for a difficult and character-building experience. The high season for harvest is May to October. Another popular option is to work several hours a day at a hostel in exchange for free or discounted room and/or board. Most often, these short-term jobs are found by word of mouth, or simply by talking to the owner of a hostel or restaurant. Many places, especially due to the high turnover in the tourism industry, are always eager for help, even if only temporary. Random jobs (moving, working in cafes) can usually be found in bigger cities, like Phoenix and Albuquerque. Additionally, temp agencies can arrange for relatively short-term white-collar work (www.net-temps.com is a good place to start). *Let's Go* tries to list temporary jobs like these whenever possible; check the practical information sections in larger cities, or check out the list below for some of the available short-term jobs in popular destinations.

Willing Workers on Organic Farms (WWOOF), P.O. Box 2675, Lewes BN7 1RB, UK (www.phdcc.com/sites/wwoof; $20), allows you to receive room and board at organic farms in California (and other parts of the world) in exchange for help on the farm.

Travelers Earth Repair Network (TERN), P.O. Box 4469, Bellingham, WA 98227 (www.geocities.com/rainforest/4663/tern.html; $50, students $35), offers a network of room-and-board options for international travellers.

Kelly Services, 3030 N. 3rd St., Suite 1040, Phoenix, AZ 85012 (☎602-264-0717; fax 277-4188). **Other branches:** 480 East 400 St., Salt Lake City, UT 84111 (☎801-363-4460; fax 363-4899); 6000 Uptown Blvd. NE, Suite 120, Albuquerque, NM 87110 (☎505-883-6873; fax 881-2597). International temp service.

VOLUNTEERING

Volunteering can be one of the most fulfilling experiences you can have in life, especially if you combine it with the wonder of travel in a foreign land. Many volunteer services charge you a fee to participate in the program and to do work. These fees can be surprisingly hefty (although they frequently cover airfare and most, if not all, living expenses). Try to do research on a program before committing—talk to people who have previously participated and find out exactly what you're getting into, as living and working conditions can vary greatly. Different programs are geared toward different ages and levels of experience, so be sure to make sure that you are not taking on too much. The more informed you are and the more realistic expectations you have, the more enjoyable the program will be.

Most people choose to go through a parent organization that takes care of logistical details, and frequently provides a group environment and support system. In the Southwest's major cities, small organizations are often seeking eager volunteers.

Earthwatch, 3 Clocktower Pl. Suite 100, Box 75, Maynard, MA 01754 (☎978-461-0081 or 800-776-0188; www.earthwatch.org). Arranges 1- to 3-week programs in the United States and around the world to promote conservation of natural resources. Fees vary based on program location and duration; costs average $1700 plus airfare.

Heritage Resource Management Department of US Forest Service, P.O. Box 31315, Tucson, AZ 85751 (☎520-722-2716 or 800-281-9176; www.passportintime.com). Needs volunteers for archaeological surveys and recording oral histories within the parks.

Four Corners School of Outdoor Education, P.O. Box 1029, Monticello, UT 84535 (☎801-587-2156; fax 801-587-2193; fcs@igc.apc.org). Volunteers take part in wilderness excursions and archeological surveys throughout the Colorado plateau region. Camping accommodation is provided for the week-long programs.

Utah State Parks, P.O. Box 146001, Salt Lake City, UT 84114 (☎801-538-7220). Seeks volunteers for numerous outdoor functions, including trail construction and maintenance, campground supervision, and wilderness interpretation for the public.

Lubbock Lake Landmark, Museum of Texas Tech. University, Lubbock, TX 79409 (806-742-2481 or 742-1117; fax 806-742-1136; mxgi@ttacs.ttu.edu). 6-week to 3-month summer programs in which volunteers excavate landmarks and do lab and public education work. Volunteers cover travel expenses, but food and lodging are provided.

National Hispanic Cultural Center of New Mexico, 1701 4th St. SW, Santa Fe, NM 87102 (☎505-246-2261, ext. 142; fax 246-2613). Offers unpaid volunteer opportunities in all facets of the preservation, presentation, and research of Hispanic culture.

THE GREAT
OUTDOORS

This is what you came for. The scenery in the Southwest is unmatched and by far the single biggest attraction in the region. From Grand Canyon to Chaco Canyon, from the High Uinta Wilderness to the Gila Wilderness, the Southwest has vast tracts of public lands and innumerable recreation opportunities. However, enjoying your experience to the fullest requires forethought, preparation, and a little bit of knowledge about US federal lands.

PUBLIC LANDS IN THE SOUTHWEST

The different agendas of farmers, ranchers, miners, tourists, and environmental activists construct clear battle lines on the issues of land use and conservation, and as a result, the very concept of public land in the Southwest is a controversial issue. To appease a diverse citizenry and to fulfill the conservationist agendas of certain presidents, an intricate and confusing system of public land management has been created under the supervision of the Department of the Interior and the Department of Agriculture. The National Park System gets all of the glory and tourists, but lands managed by the National Forest Service, the Bureau of Land Management, and the Department of Fish and Wildlife are abundant in the Southwest and in many cases offer similar recreational opportunities. Although the traveler might not much care about the structure of these federal and state landholdings, the classifications are important in determining which organization to contact for more info on specific activities, permits, and restrictions.

NATIONAL PARKS AND MONUMENTS

National parks protect some of the most spectacular and most heavily touristed scenery in the Southwest. Though their primary stated purpose is preservation, the parks also host a variety of recreational activities, including ranger talks, guided hikes, marked trails, bus tours, and snowshoe expeditions. For info, contact individual parks or the **National Park Service,** Office of Public Inquiries, 1849 C St. NW #1013, Washington, D.C. 20240 (☎202-208-4747). The slick and informative webpage (www.nps.gov) lists info on all the parks, detailed maps, and fee and reservation data. The **National Park Foundation's** *Complete Guide to America's National Parks* is available at any major bookstore or on amazon.com; a guide to national parks is available online at www.nationalparks.org.

Entrance fees vary widely. The larger and more popular parks charge a $4-20 entry fee for cars and occasionally a $2-7 fee for pedestrians and cyclists. The **National Parks Pass** ($50), available at park entrances or on the National Parks Service web site, allows the pass-holder's party entry into all national parks for one year. For an additional $15, the Parks Service will affix a **Golden Eagle Passport** hologram to your card, which will allow you access to sites managed by the US Fish and Wildlife Service, the US Forest Service, and the Bureau of Land Management. US citizens or residents 62 and over qualify for the lifetime **Golden Age Passport** ($10 one-time fee), which entitles the holder's party to free park entry, a 50% discount on camping, and 50% reductions on various recreational fees. Persons eligible for federal benefits on account of disabilities can enjoy the same privileges with the **Golden Access Passport** (free). Golden Age and Golden Access Passports must be purchased at a park entrance with proof of age or federal eligibility. All passports (not the Parks Pass) are also valid at national monuments, forests, wildlife preserves, and other national recreation sites.

Most parks have both backcountry and developed **camping;** some welcome RVs, and a few offer grand lodges. At more popular parks, reservations are essential.

DAMN, THIS PARK IS CROWDED! (2000 VISITATION FIGURES IN VISITOR-DAYS)	
Lake Mead National Recreation Area	6,502,591
Grand Canyon National Park	5,729,121
Glen Canyon National Recreation Area	4,780,734
Zion National Park	1,369,481
Bryce Canyon National Park	750,100
Joshua Tree National Park	738,844
Death Valley National Park	728,482
Canyon de Chelly National Monument	718,361
Big Bend National Park	675,594
Canyonlands National Park	354,570

NATIONAL FORESTS

Often less accessible and less crowded, **US National Forests** (www.fs.fed.us) are a purist's alternative to parks. While some have recreation facilities, most are equipped only for primitive camping—pit toilets and no water are the norm. Entrance fees are seldom charged, and camping is generally free or less than $10. If you are interested in visiting and exploring a national forest, pick up *The Guide to Your National Forests* at any Forest Service branch, or call or write the main office (USDA Forest Service, P.O. Box 96090, Washington, D.C. 20090-6090; ☎202-205-8333). This booklet includes a list of all national forest addresses; request maps and other info directly from the forest(s) you plan to visit.

BUREAU OF LAND MANAGEMENT

The US Department of the Interior's **Bureau of Land Management (BLM)** oversees 270 million acres of land in the western US, with an especially strong presence in Nevada, Utah, and the rest of the desert Southwest. The Bureau's pride and joy is Grand Staircase-Escalante National Monument, a hybrid park holding national monument status, yet managed entirely by the BLM. The BLM differs from the Forest Service and the Park Service in that it generally aims for sustainable land use rather than conservation. In keeping with this goal, BLM lands offer a variety of recreation opportunities, including hiking, mountain biking, rock climbing, river running, and often ATV and snowmobile use. Unless otherwise posted, all public lands are open for recreational use. BLM campgrounds charge up to $10, but dispersed primitive camping on BLM land is generally permitted and always free. For more info, contact individual state offices:

Arizona State BLM Office, 222 N. Central Ave., Phoenix, AZ 85004 (☎602-417-9200; fax 602-417-9556; www.az.blm.gov).

California State BLM Office, 2800 Cottage Way, Suite W1834, Sacramento, CA 95825 (☎916-978-4400; fax 916-978-4416; www.ca.blm.gov).

Colorado State BLM Office, 2850 Youngfield St., Lakewood, CO 80215 (☎303-239-3600; fax 303-239-3933; www.co.blm.gov).

Nevada State BLM Office, 1340 Financial Blvd., Reno, NV 89502 (☎775-861-6400; fax 702-861-6606; www.nv.blm.gov).

New Mexico State BLM Office, 1474 Rodeo Rd., Santa Fe, NM 87505 (☎505-438-7400; fax 505-438-7582; www.nm.blm.gov).

Texas BLM Office, 801 S. Filmore St., Ste. 500, Amarillo, TX 79101-3545 (☎806-324-2617; fax 324-2633).

Utah State BLM Office, P.O. Box 45155, Salt Lake City, UT 84145-0155 (☎801-539-4001; fax 801-539-4013; www.ut.blm.gov).

WILDERNESS AREAS

The **Wilderness Act of 1964** established a federal system intended to provide the maximum level of preservation to incorporated parcels of land. As it stands now, there are over 105 million acres of protected wilderness in the US. These areas are administered by several different agencies, including the Park Service, the Forest Service, the Bureau of Land Management, and the US Fish and Wildlife Service. Though exceptions exist in some areas, mining, motorized vehicles (including bicycles), and permanent, man-made structures are generally prohibited. Wilderness areas dot the landscape of the Southwest. For more info on restrictions and permits in specific regions, contact the agency responsible for managing the area that interests you.

STATE PARKS

Though much of the spectacular scenery and recreation in the Southwest resides on federal land, **state parks** hold their own and some are as worthy of a visit as national parks and forests. Usually, the primary function of state parks is motorized recreation, which often means **all-terrain vehicle (ATV)** use and **boating**. In fact, a large percentage of state parks in the Southwest feature lakes and other bodies of water. Prices for camping at public sites are usually better than those at private campgrounds. Some parks may limit your stay and/or the number of people in your group. Crowds are rarely a problem, except at the most popular parks. For general info, contact:

Arizona State Parks, 1300 W. Washington St., Phoenix, AZ 85007 (☎602-542-4174; fax 602-542-4180; www.pr.state.az.us).

California State Parks, P.O. Box 942896, Sacramento, CA 94296 (☎916-653-6995; www.cal-parks.ca.gov).

Colorado State Parks, 1313 Sherman St., #618, Denver, CO 80203 (☎303-866-3437; fax 303-866-3206; www.parks.state.co.us).

Nevada Division of State Parks, 1300 S. Curry St., Carson City, NV 89703 (☎775-687-4384; fax 775-687-4117; www.state.nv.us/stparks).

New Mexico State Parks Division, P.O. Box 1147, Santa Fe, NM 87504 (☎888-667-2757; www.emnrd.state.nm.us/nmparks).

Texas Parks and Wildlife, 4200 Smith School Rd., Austin, TX 78744 (☎800-792-1112 or 512-389-4800; www.tpwd.state.tx.us).

Utah Division of Parks and Recreation, 1594 W. N. Temple, #116, Salt Lake City, UT 84114 (☎801-538-7220; http://parks.state.ut.us).

CAMPING

Camping is probably the most rewarding way to slash travel costs. Considering the sheer amount of public land available for camping in the southwestern United States, it may also be the most convenient option. Well-equipped campsites (usually including prepared tent sites, toilets, and potable water) go for $5-20 per night. In general, the more popular the park or forest, the better-equipped and the more

GREAT OUTDOORS

expensive the established campgrounds. Most campsites are first-come, first-served, though a few accept reservations, usually for a small fee (see below for more info). **Backcountry camping,** which lacks all amenities, is often free, but permits may be required in some national parks and may cost up to $20. Dispersed backcountry camping is usually inconvenient for those traveling by car, because it requires a long hike. For those sticking to the highways, the ubiquitous **Kampgrounds of America (KOA)** offer a ritzy kamping experience at a premium. All of the komforts of home add up to about $20-30 a night for a tent site. It is not legal or safe to camp on the side of the road, even on public lands; *Let's Go* lists areas where dispersed roadside camping is permitted.

RESERVATIONS PLEASE!!! Though many campgrounds, both in national forests and national parks, are first-come, first-served, making reservations can make travel much more relaxed and enjoyable. The **National Forest Service** takes reservations through the **National Recreation Reservation Center,** P.O. Box 550, Ballston Spa, NY 12020 (☎518-885-3639 or 877-444-6777; fax 518-884-9578; www.reserveusa.com). Camping reservations usually require a $9 service fee and are available for most forests, though they are often unnecessary except during high season at the more popular sites. You may write or call up to one year in advance. The **National Park Reservation Service** (☎800-365-2267 or 301-722-1257; http://reservations.nps.gov) takes reservations for campgrounds in Grand Canyon, Zion, Death Valley, and Joshua Tree National Parks. Campgrounds are reservable starting five months in advance. There is no additional fee for this service. Many **state park** campsites are also available for reservation. Check with individual state offices for more info.

EQUIPMENT

WHAT TO BUY...

Good camping equipment is both sturdy and light. It is also worth the investment, because a leaky tent or poorly fitting boots can be annoying, painful, and downright dangerous. Equipment is generally more expensive in Australia, New Zealand, and the UK than in North America.

Sleeping Bag: Most good sleeping bags are rated by "season," or the lowest outdoor temperature at which they will keep you warm ("summer" means 30-40°F at night and "four-season" or "winter" often means below 0°F). Sleeping bags are made either of down (warmer and lighter, but more expensive, and miserable when wet) or of synthetic material (heavier, more durable, and warmer when wet). Prices range from $80-210 for a summer synthetic to $250-500 for a good down winter bag. Because the climate of the Southwest is highly variable, do some research so as to buy exactly what you will need. **Sleeping bag pads,** including foam pads ($10-20) and air mattresses ($15-50), cushion your back and neck and insulate you from the ground. **Therm-A-Rest** self-inflating sleeping pads are part foam and part air-mattress and partially inflate when you unroll them, but cost $45-80. Bring a **"stuff sack"** lined with a plastic bag to store your sleeping bag.

Tent: The best tents are free-standing, with their own frames and suspension systems; they set up quickly but require staking in high winds. Low-profile dome tents are the best all-around; their internal space is almost entirely usable, which means little unnecessary bulk. Tent sizes can be somewhat misleading: 2 people *can* fit in a 2-person tent, but will find life more pleasant in a 4-person. If you're traveling by car, go for the bigger tent, but if you're hiking, stick with a smaller tent that weighs no more than 5-6 lbs. (2-3kg). Good 2-person tents start at $90, 4-person tents at $300. Seal the seams of your tent with waterproofer, and make sure it has a **rain fly**. Tent accessories include a **plastic groundcloth** and, for the luxurious, a **battery-operated lantern**.

Backpack: If you intend to do a lot of hiking, you should have a frame backpack. **Internal-frame packs** mold better to your back, keep a lower center of gravity, and can flex adequately to allow you to hike difficult trails that require a lot of bending and maneuvering. If your trip involves significant numbers of flights, consider an "adventure travel" pack, which is designed to weather baggage handling systems as well as wilderness. NorthFace and Lowe-Alpine make durable models. **External-frame packs** are more comfortable for long hikes over even terrain, since they keep the weight higher and distribute it more evenly. Whichever you choose, make sure your pack has a strong, padded hip belt, which transfers the weight from the back to the legs. Any serious backpacking requires a pack of at least 4000 cubic inches (65 liters). Allow an additional 500 cubic inches for your sleeping bag in internal-frame packs. Sturdy backpacks cost anywhere from $125-420. This is one area where it doesn't pay to economize—cheaper packs may be less comfortable, and the straps are more likely to fray or rip. Before you buy any pack, try filling it with something heavy and walking around the store to get a sense of how it distributes weight. A **waterproof backpack cover** or plastic garbage bags will prove invaluable if it rains, and it is always a good idea to store your belongings in plastic bags within your pack.

Boots: Be sure to wear hiking boots with good **ankle support** which are appropriate for the terrain you plan to hike. **Gore-Tex** fabric or part-leather boots are appropriate for day hikes or 2- or 3-day overnight trips over moderate terrain, but for longer trips or trips in mountainous terrain, stiff **leather** boots are highly preferable. Your boots should fit snugly and comfortably over 1 or 2 wool socks and a thin liner sock. Breaking in boots properly before setting out requires wearing them for several weeks; doing so will spare you from painful and debilitating blisters. Waterproof your boots with waterproofing treatment before going out in the woods.

Water Purification and Transport: When venturing out from developed campgrounds that have potable water, you will need to carry water and purify any that you might find along the trail. Because giardia can wreak havoc in one's digestive system (see p. 25), even water taken from the cleanest backcountry spring in the Southwest must be purified. Though iodine- and chlorine-containing tablets are the cheapest method of purification, they will not rid water of its muck or its characteristic taste. Portable **water filters** pump out a crystal clear product but often require careful maintenance and extra disposable filters. Do not ever pump dirty water unless you want to repeatedly clean or replace clogged filter cartridges. For transport, plastic **canteens** or water bottles keep water cooler than metal ones do, and are virtually shatter and leak proof. Large plastic **water bags** or **bladders** can hold up to several gallons and are perfect for travel in the desert. These containers weigh practically nothing when empty, though they are bulky and heavy when full.

Other Necessities: Raingear in two pieces, a top and pants, is far superior to a poncho. **Gore-Tex** is the best material if you are doing aerobic activity and need breathable raingear; **rubber** raingear will keep you completely dry but will get clammy if you sweat. For warm layers, **synthetics,** like polypropylene tops, socks, and long underwear, along with a fleece or pile jacket work well because they keep you warm even when wet, and dry quickly. **Wool** also stays warm when wet, but is much heavier. Never rely on **cotton** for warmth, unless you're after that inner warmth that comes from wearing "the fabric of our lives." In the wild, this "death cloth" will be absolutely useless should it get wet. When camping in autumn, winter, or spring, bring along a **"space blanket,"** which helps you to retain your body heat and doubles as a groundcloth ($5-15). Though many campgrounds provide campfire sites, you will probably want to bring a **camp stove**, especially for places that forbid fires or wood gathering. Propane-powered Coleman stoves start at

GREAT OUTDOORS

about $40; the more expensive **Whisperlite** stoves ($60-100), which run on cleaner-burning white gas, are lighter and more versatile. You need to purchase a **fuel bottle** and fill it with fuel to operate stoves. A **first aid kit, Swiss army knife, insect repellent, calamine lotion,** and **waterproof matches** or a **lighter** are other essential supplies.

....AND WHERE TO BUY IT

The mail-order/online companies listed below offer lower prices than many retail stores, but a visit to a local camping or outdoors store will give you a good sense of items' look and weight. Many local outdoor stores also have message boards where used equipment can be found.

Campmor, P.O. Box 700, Upper Saddle River, NJ 07458 (☎888-226-7667, outside US call 201-825-8300; www.campmor.com).

Discount Camping, 880 Main North Rd., Pooraka, SA 5095, Australia (☎08 8262 3399; fax 8260 6240; email info@discountcamping.com.au; www.discountcamping.com.au).

Eastern Mountain Sports (EMS), 327 Jaffrey Rd., Peterborough, NH 03458 (☎888-463-6367 or 603-924-7231; customerservice@emsonline.com; www.shopems.com). Call to locate the branch nearest you.

L.L. Bean, Freeport, ME 04033-0001 (US/Canada ☎800-441-5713; U.K. 0800 891 297; elsewhere, call US 207-552-3028; www.llbean.com). They refund/replace products that don't meet your expectations. The main store and 800 number are both open 24hr.

Mountain Designs, 51 Bishop St., Kelvin Grove QLD 4059, (☎07 3856 2344; fax 07 3856 0366; www.mountaindesign.com.au).

Recreational Equipment, Inc. (REI), Sumner, WA 98352-0001 (☎800-426-4840 or 253-891-2500; fax 253-891-2523; www.rei.com).

YHA Adventure Shop, 19 High St., Staines Middlesex, TW18, UK (☎020 7085 1900; londonw1@yhaadventure.com; www.yhaadventure.co.uk), is one of Britain's largest equipment suppliers.

LEAVE NO TRACE

The idea behind environmentally responsible tourism is to leave no trace of human presence behind. There are many practical ways to reduce the impact you leave on the wilderness. A portable **stove** is a safer (and more efficient) way to cook than using vegetation to build a campfire, but if you must make a fire, keep it small and use only dead branches or brush rather than cutting live vegetation. Make sure your **campsite** is at least 150 ft. (50m) from the nearest water, be it a spring, a stream, or a lake. If there are no toilet facilities, bury **human waste** (but not paper, which should be packed out if used) at least 6 in. (15cm) deep, above the water level, and 150 ft. or more from any water source or campsite. Always pack your **trash** in a plastic bag and carry it with you until you reach a trash receptacle. For more info on these issues, contact one of the following organizations:

Earthwatch, 3 Clock Tower Place #100, Box 75, Maynard, MA 01754, US (☎800-776-0188 or 978-461-0081; info@earthwatch.org; www.earthwatch.org).

Ecotourism Society, P.O. Box 668, Burlington, VT 05402, US (☎802-651-9818; ecomail@ecotourism.org; www.ecotourism.org).

Leave No Trace, 2475 Broadway, Boulder, CO 80304, US (☎303-442-8222 or 800-332-4100; www.lnt.org).

National Audobon Society, 700 Broadway, New York, NY 10003 (☎212-979-3000; www.audobon.org).

Tourism Concern, Stapleton House, 277-281 Holloway Rd., London N7 8HN, UK (☎020 7753 3330; info@tourismconcern.org.uk; www.tourismconcern.org.uk).

WILDERNESS AND DESERT SAFETY

GENERAL WISDOM

Stay warm, dry, and hydrated. The vast majority of life-threatening wilderness situations result from a breach of this simple dictum. On any hike, however brief, you should pack enough equipment to keep you alive should disaster befall you. This includes **raingear, hat** and **mittens, a first-aid kit, a reflector, a whistle, high energy food,** and **extra water.** On any trip of significant length, you should always carry a **compass** and a detailed **topographical map** of the area where you are hiking, preferably an official map from the US Geological Survey. Dress warmly and in layers (see p. 59). Weather can change suddenly anywhere in the region, and in the higher peaks it can snow any time of the year. Check **weather forecasts** and pay attention to the skies when hiking. Whenever possible, hike in groups or with a partner. Hiking alone greatly magnifies the risks of traveling in the wilderness. Always be sure to let someone know when and where you are hiking.

MY KINGDOM FOR A MAP. One of the most neglected tenets of wilderness safety is carrying maps wherever you go. When hiking, biking, climbing, or camping, you should ALWAYS carry a compass and use a set of detailed topographical maps. The **United States Geological Survey,** Box 25286, Denver, CO 80225 (☎888-275-8747; http://mapping.usgs.gov/mac/findmaps.html), sells indispensable 7½min. and 15min. topo maps. **Trails Illustrated,** affiliated with National Geographic (☎800-962-1643; www.trailsillustrated.com), sells larger topo maps of the Southwest's parks and other public lands.

THE DESERT AND YOU

The body loses at least a gallon of liquid per day in the desert (2 or more gallons during strenuous activity), so *always* keep drinking. Drinking huge quantities of water to quench your thirst after physical exertion is not as effective as taking preventative measures to stay hydrated. Whether you are driving or hiking, tote **two gallons of water per person per day.** Designate at least one container as an emergency supply, and always have water at your side. In the car, keep backup containers in a cooler. Drink the water you have. People have died in the desert with water they were "saving." When drinking sweet beverages, dilute them with water to avoid an over-reaction to high sugar content. Avoid alcohol and coffee, which cause dehydration. For long-term stays, a high-quality beverage with potassium compounds and glucose, such as **ERG** (an industrial-strength Gatorade available from camping suppliers), will help keep your strength up.

Most people need a few days to adjust to the heat, especially before difficult hikes. Sunglasses with 100% UV protection, sunscreen, and a hat are essential **sun protection,** but proper clothing is the most effective shield. Light-colored clothing helps reflect the sun's rays. Although it may be uncomfortable to wear a sweaty shirt, it prevents dehydration more effectively than going shirtless (for more on **heat exhaustion** and **heatstroke,** see **Essentials,** p. 24).

Heat is not the desert's only climatic extreme. At high elevations, temperatures during winter nights can drop well **below freezing**—a sweater is often necessary even in summer (see **Essentials,** p. 25). The desert is characterized by its lack of precipitation, but when it rains, it pours. **Flash floods,** especially in the spring and late summer into the fall, cause water to come down from rain-drenched higher elevations and wreak biblical devastation upon lands below, turning dry gulches into raging rivers. Canyons, streambeds, washes, and drainages of any sort can become death traps. When you are hiking in low-lying areas, be alert—check the weather forecast and don't assume that clear skies mean you are safe. Rain from hundreds of miles away can flood a canyon you are hiking in. Try not to walk in washes you can't scramble out of, beware of thunderstorms on the horizon, and never camp in washes or gullies.

THE DESERT AND YOUR CAR

Desert conditions are as grueling on cars as they are on bodies; only recently serviced cars in good condition can take the heat. Bring at least **five gallons of radiator water,** extra coolant, and a few quarts of oil (car manuals recommend appropriate oil weights for varying temperatures). Avoid running out of gas by keeping your tank above half full. In addition to a spare tire and necessary tools for the basic mishap on the road, a board and shovel are useful for sand-stuck cars. Beware of rural gravel roads that suddenly turn to sand.

Although towns are often sparse, major roads usually have enough traffic to ensure that breakdowns will be noticed. Even so, isolated areas of the region pose a threat, especially in summer. *Stay with your vehicle if it breaks down;* it is easier to spot than a person and provides crucial shade.

Turn off **air-conditioning** immediately if the car's temperature gauge starts to climb. Air from open windows should be sufficiently comfortable at highway speeds. Turning the heater on full blast will help cool the engine. If your car overheats, pull off the road and turn the heater on full force to cool the engine. If radiator fluid is steaming or bubbling, turn off the car for 30min. If not, run the car in neutral at about 1500 r.p.m. for a few minutes, allowing the coolant to circulate. Never pour water over the engine and never try to lift a searingly hot hood. **Desert water bags** are available at hardware or automotive stores for about $5-10. When strapped onto the front of the car and filled with water, these large canvas bags prevent overheating by speeding up evaporation. Driving in the evening, night, and early morning is preferable to overheating or being uncomfortably hot at midday.

FURTHER READING: WILDERNESS SAFETY

How to Stay Alive in the Woods, Bradford Angier. Macmillan ($9).

Everyday Wisdom: 1001 Expert Tips for Hikers, Karen Berger. Mountaineer ($17).

Making Camp, Steve Howe, et al. Mountaineer ($17).

FLORA AND FAUNA

INSECTS

One of the distinctive features of the Southwest desert is the abundance of scurrying, hairy, and occasionally venomous insects. Knowing these insects and keeping your distance will probably make your life less swollen and painful.

Though **spiders** have inspired many phobias and scary movies, the spiders present in the Southwest rarely pose a threat to human life. **Black Widows** are the most venomous, and are found throughout the Southwest. Adult females are characterized by a red hourglass shape on their abdomen. Though the venom of the Black Widow is 15 times as potent as the venom of a prairie rattlesnake, the small amount injected with each bite means that they rarely result in death. The **tarantula,** a large, hairy species of arachnid prevalent in the warm, dry desert regions of the Southwest, looks much scarier than it is. When provoked, the tarantula will bite, but for humans, the bite is usually merely an annoyance. Though the **brown recluse** spider is not widespread in the region, a few desert species of recluse spider do make their home in the deserts of California, Arizona, southern New Mexico, and western Texas. These spiders, as their name suggests, are shy and reclusive. However, their bites are capable of producing a nasty, festering wound.

Scorpions populate many different climates worldwide, but are a particularly notable resident of the Southwest. The characteristic features of the scorpion are two pincers (called "pedipalps") and a long barbed tail that curves skyward in aggressive or defensive situations. Only one of the nearly 100 species of scorpion indigenous to the Southwest poses any real threat to human life, and this singular species causes fatalities only in the elderly, infirm, or strongly allergic.

The best way to avoid contact with both spiders and scorpions is to always look where you are placing your hands and feet. Always **turn down sheets** before bed and **shake out clothing and boots** before putting them on, because these are the ways arachnids most often come into contact with humans. Both spiders and scorpions are nocturnal insects, so precautions are especially important in the early morning. Be careful of holes in the ground or shaded areas under rocks or wood, places where spiders and scorpions hide out during the heat of the day.

An increasing concern in the Southwest is the gradual arrival of **Africanized honey bees** (popularly known as **killer bees**) from south of the Mexican border. Though attacks are rare, six people in the United States have perished at the stingers of these insects. All of these fatal attacks occurred in the Southwest. Killer bees overwhelm their victims by sheer numbers, leaving hundreds of stings, especially on the head and face. If you encounter a swarm of aggressive bees, cover your head and seek sealed shelter in a house, shed, or car. DO NOT jump into water; the bees will wait for you to surface. Seek medical attention in cases of allergic reaction or numerous stings. Wear light-colored clothing and be alert to prevent attack.

SNAKES AND OTHER REPTILES

There is a multitude of snakes in the Southwest deserts. The only venomous species are the coral snake and several different types of rattlesnake. The **Coral Snake** is characterized by alternating red, black, and yellow bands and its small size relative to full-grown rattlesnakes. This snake delivers its potent venom by chewing on its victim. The innocuous **King Snake** is often mistaken for its evil twin because of similar red, black, and yellow stripes. The difference is the order of colors, captured in the adage, "red on yellow, kill a fellow; red on black, friend of Jack."

The **Western Diamondback Rattlesnake** is the most common and feared member of the pit viper family in the Southwest because of its mean temper and strong venom. It is the feistiest of desert snakes and causes more fatalities than any other reptile in the US. Its cousins, the **Sidewinder, Red Diamondback,** and **Speckled Rattlesnakes,** are also venomous and prevalent in the Southwest.

Most snakebites can be avoided by using common sense. Wear thick leather boots, watch where you place your feet, and listen for the rattlesnake's characteristic rattle. If you encounter a rattlesnake, stand still until it slithers away. If the snake is backed into a corner, stay still for a while and then back away slowly, stepping gently. If bitten, get to a medical facility as quickly as possible. **Tourniquets** and **anti-venom** are the only effective ways to combat the effects of the venom.

MOUNTAIN LIONS

These solitary animals are the feline regents of the Southwest. Inhabiting climates ranging from low desert to alpine forest, mountain lions (also called cougars) keep to themselves and thus seldom come into contact with humans. Most altercations result from lions protecting their young. If you happen to stumble upon a mountain lion, freeze, stand your ground, and then back away slowly to give the animal its space. There are several documented cases of mountain lions attacking young children who wandered off alone, so always make sure to keep any children or pets nearby when you are on the trail.

BEARS

BEARS WILL EAT YOU. If you are hiking in an area that might be frequented by bears, ask local rangers for information on bear behavior before entering any park or wilderness area, and obey posted warnings. No matter how irresistibly cute a bear appears, don't be fooled—they're powerful and unpredictable animals that are not intimidated by humans. No matter how much you may be hankering for a wild bear photo-op, it is a good thing when you avoid encountering bears entirely when in the wilderness. Fortunately, bears make this relatively easy—they are uninterested in humans, and tend to avoid groups of hikers they come across. Make it easy on the bears—don't sneak up on them. Travel in groups, make lots of noise, and stay on marked trails. Don't leave food or other scented items (trash, toiletries, the clothes that you cooked in) near your tent. Putting these objects into canisters is now mandatory in some national parks in the Southwest, including Yosemite. **Bear-bagging,** hanging edibles and other good-smelling objects from a tree out of reach of hungry paws, is the best way to keep your toothpaste from becoming a condiment. Bears are also attracted to any **perfume,** as are bugs, so cologne, scented soap, deodorant, and hairspray should stay at home.

If you do run into bears, proceed cautiously. If you surprised the bear or surprised each other, speak in low, soothing Barry White tones and back away slowly. Do not run, as tempting as it may be—the bear may identify you as prey and give chase. If you will be traveling extensively in bear-infested areas, consider taking **bear pepper spray**—only slightly less effective against bears than muggers. If the bear attacks, spray at his face and eyes. Without bear pepper spray, different strategies should be used with different bear species. Black bears (black coloration, tall ears, no shoulder hump) are carrion eaters; if you play dead, you are giving them a free meal. The best course of action is to fight back; resistance will deter a black bear. If you're standing toe to toe with a grizzly bear, a decided predator, fighting back will get you killed—play dead, dropping to the ground and shield your face and chest with your arms.

CACTI

More than almost any other feature, cacti give the desert its forbidding and stoic image. From the **Joshua Tree** in California to the **Yucca** in Texas, from the common **Barrel Cactus** to the rare **Organ Pipe Cactus,** these occasionally large succulent plants also lend the Southwest a characteristic stateliness and flair. Uncomfortable consequences dictate that you keep a distance from cacti at all times. You must also show respect to these magnificent succulents; damage to or removal of cacti on public lands is illegal and results in hefty fines.

ORGANIZED TRIPS AND OUTFITTERS

Organized adventure tours offer another way of exploring the wild. Stores and organizations specializing in camping and outdoors equipment can often provide good info on trips (see p. 60). Sales reps at REI, EMS, or Sierra often know of a range of cheap, convenient trips. They may also offer training programs for travelers.

When choosing an **outfitter** for a day or multi-day trip, check into their credentials and qualifications. Check local **Visitors Centers** for lists of established, experienced, and credentialed guide services and weigh your options before trusting life and limb to a person you have never met before.

The organizations below offer guided trips all over the Southwest and the entire US. Contact them for specific trips and prices.

AmeriCan Adventures & Roadrunner, P.O. Box 1155, Gardena, CA 90249 (☎800-873-5872; fax 310-324-344; UK 01892 512 700; www.americanadventures.com). Organizes group adventure camping and hostelling trips (with transportation and camping costs included) in the US, Canada, Mexico, and South America.

The National Outdoor Leadership School (NOLS), 284 Lincoln St., Lander, WY 82520-2848 (☎307-332-5300; fax 307-332-1220; admissions@nols.edu; www.nols.edu), offers educational wilderness trips all over the world, including many to the desert Southwest. They also offer courses in wilderness medicine training and leave no trace ethics.

The Sierra Club, 85 Second St., 2nd Fl. San Francisco, CA 94105 (☎415-977-5522; national.outings@sierraclub.org; www.sierraclub.org/outings), plans many adventure outings at all of its branches throughout the US, including the Southwest.

Specialty Travel Index, 305 San Anselmo Ave., #313, San Anselmo, CA 94960 (☎800-442-4922; info@specialtytravel.com; www.specialtytravel.com), is a directory listing tour operators worldwide.

TrekAmerica, P.O. Box 189, Rockaway, NJ 07866 (☎800-221-0596; www.trekamerica.com), operates small group active adventure tours throughout the US, including Alaska and Hawaii, and Canada. These tours are for 18- to 38-year-olds, and run from 1 to 9 weeks.

OUTDOOR TRAVEL PUBLICATIONS

A variety of publishing companies offer outdoors guidebooks to meet the educational needs of novice or expert. For **books** about camping, hiking, biking, and climbing, write or call the publishers listed below to receive a free catalog.

Falcon Guides, Globe Pequot Press, P.O. Box 480, Guilford, CT 06437 (☎888-249-7586; www.falcon.com). Over 1000 guides to many different outdoor-related activities. Many of the books are organized by activity and state, so they are best for the focused traveler.

The Mountaineers Books, 300 Third Ave W. Seattle, WA 98119 (☎206-284-8484; www.mountaineers.org). Over 400 titles on hiking (the *100 Hikes* series), biking, mountaineering, natural history, and conservation.

Sierra Club Books, 85 Second St. 2nd fl., San Francisco, CA 94105-3441 (☎415-977-5500; www.sierraclub.org/books). Books on the national parks and several series on different areas of the Southwest, all with an adventurous bent.

Wilderness Press, 1200 Fifth St., Berkeley, CA 94710 (☎800-443-7227 or 510-558-1666; www.wildernesspress.com). Over 100 hiking guides and maps for the western US, including *Backpacking Basics* ($10).

GREAT OUTDOORS

THE GRAND CANYON

The Grand Canyon extends from Lee's Ferry, AZ to Lake Mead, NV. In the north, the Glen Canyon Dam backs up the Colorado into mammoth Lake Powell. To the west, the Hoover Dam traps the remaining outflow from Glen Canyon to form Lake Mead, another haven for water enthusiasts. Grand Canyon National Park is divided into three sections: the most popular South Rim, the more serene North Rim, and the canyon gorge itself. Traveling between rims takes approximately five hours, either via a 13-mile hike or a long drive to the bridge in Lee's Ferry. Sandwiched between the national park and Lake Mead, the Hualapai and Havasupai Reservations also abut the river. The remote Havasupai tribe protects several of the canyon's most spectacular waterfalls and welcomes thousands of tourists each year who make the ten-mile trek to their village. With such diversity of activities in the area, the Grand Canyon and environs both entertain and inspire.

AT A GLANCE: GRAND CANYON NATIONAL PARK

AREA: 1,217,403 acres.

FEATURES: The Canyon, Colorado River, North Rim, South Rim, West Rim, Kaibab Plateau, Tonto Platform.

HIGHLIGHTS: Taking a mule ride to Phantom Ranch, rafting in luxury down the Canyon, backpacking from Rim to Rim on the South and North Kaibab Trails, standing in awe at the edge of either rim.

GATEWAY TOWNS: Flagstaff (p. 103), Williams (p. 103).

CAMPING: Mather Campground on the South Rim and the North Rim Campground require reservations ($15). Backcountry camping requires a permit ($5 per person, $10 per group).

FEES: Weekly pass $20 per car, $10 for other modes of transportation; covers both South and North Rim.

SOUTH RIM
☎928

During the summer, everything on two legs or four wheels converges on this side of the Grand Canyon. If you plan to visit at that time, make reservations well in advance for lodging, campsites, or mules, and prepare to battle the crowds. Still, it's much better than Disney World. A friendly Park Service staff, well-run facilities, and beautiful scenery help ease crowd anxiety. Fewer tourists brave the canyon's winter weather; many hotels and facilities close during the off season. Rte. 64 leading up to the Park entrance is surrounded by Kaibab National Forest, which continues above the North Rim.

▣ TRANSPORTATION

There are two park entrances: the main **south entrance** is 58 mi. north of I-40 while the eastern **Desert View** entrance is 27 mi. away, off of Hwy. 89. Both are accessed via Rte. 64. From Las Vegas, the fastest route to the South Rim is U.S. 93 S to I-40 E, and then Rte. 64 N at Williams. From Flagstaff, head north on U.S. 180 to Rte. 64.

GRAND CANYON

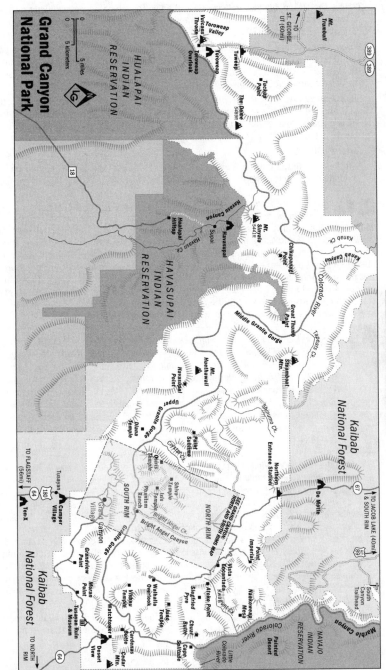

Grand Canyon
National Park

0   5 miles
0   5 kilometers

Trains: The **Grand Canyon Railway** (☎800-843-8724) runs an authentically restored train from the Williams, AZ to the Grand Canyon (2¼hr.; leaves 10am, returning 3:30pm; $68, children $27). Guided tours of the rim area run $25-35.

Buses: North Arizona Shuttle and Tours (☎866-870-8687) departs its Flagstaff depot, 1300 S. Milton St., for the Grand Canyon daily (2hr.; leaves 7:30am, 2:30pm, returns to Flagstaff 10am, 4:30pm; $20 each way). Fares don't include $6 entrance fee. Shuttles also head to Sedona twice a day ($25).

Public Transit: Free **shuttle buses** run the West Rim Loop (daily 1hr. before sunrise to sunset) and the Village Loop (daily 1hr. before sunrise to 11pm) every 10-30min. A free **hiker's shuttle** runs every 30min. between the info center and the South Kaibab Trailhead, on the East Rim near Yaki Point. (Early buses run at 4, 5, and 6am.)

Taxis: ☎638-2822.

Auto Repairs: Grand Canyon Garage (☎638-2631), east of the Visitors Center on the main road, just before the rim lodges. Open daily 8am-5pm. 24hr. emergency service.

■✳🛈 ORIENTATION AND PRACTICAL INFORMATION

Maps and signs in the park make it easy to orient yourself. Lodges and services concentrate in **Grand Canyon Village**, at the end of Park Entrance Rd. The east half of the village contains the Visitors Center and the general store, while most of the rim lodges and the challenging **Bright Angel Trail** lie in the west section. The shorter but more difficult **South Kaibab Trail** is off **East Rim Dr.**, east of the village. Free shuttle buses to eight rim overlooks run along **West Rim Dr.** (closed to private vehicles during the summer). Avoid walking on the drive; the rim trails are safer and more scenic. For most services in the park, call the **main switchboard** (☎638-2631).

 WHEN TO GO. The South Rim, open year-round, is jam-packed in the spring, summer, and fall, and only the winter offers some measure of solitude, though services are closed and temperatures are chilly (lows in the 10s and 20s, highs in the 30s and 40s). Colder and less visited than its southern counterpart, the North Rim is open for day use only from October 15 to December 1, and from December 1 to May 15, the Rim closes entirely due to snow and ice. Summer temperatures rise with visitation figures, but are highly variable from rim to rim—average summer highs are about 85°F on the South Rim, 75°F on the North Rim (due to higher elevation), and 105°F in the Inner Canyon.

Visitor Info: The first installment in the Park Service's Plan to reshape visitor flow in the crowded park, the new **Canyon View Information Plaza**, across from Mather Point just after the entrance to the park, is the one-stop center for Grand Canyon info. The Plaza houses the Visitors Center (open daily 8am-6pm), a bookstore (open daily 8am-7pm), restrooms, and helpful kiosks answering frequently-asked questions. The Visitors Center stocks copies of *The Guide* (an essential), and assorted other pamphlets. To get there, park at Mather Pt., then get out and hoof it for ½ mi. to the info plaza. For those who want to be well-prepared in advance, the Park Service, through the Grand Canyon Association, sells a variety of informational books and packets (☎800-858-2808; www.grandcanyon.com, or check out www.nps.gov/grca). The **transportation info desks** in **Bright Angel Lodge** and **Maswik Lodge** (☎638-2631) handle reservations for mule rides, bus tours, plane tours, Phantom Ranch, taxis, and more. Open daily 6am-8pm.

Bank: Bank One (☎638-2437), in Market Plaza. Full-service branch with **ATM**. Currency exchange on traveler's checks, but not cash. Open M-Th 10am-3pm, F 10am-5pm.

Luggage Storage: In Bright Angel Lodge. Open 6:30am-9pm.

Equipment Rental: In the General Store. Comfy hiking boots, socks included ($8 first day, $5 per additional day); sleeping bags ($9 first day/$5 per additional day); tents ($15 first day for a two-person, $16 first day for four-person, $9 per additional day for both); day packs ($6 for a large, $4 for a small), and other camping gear (stoves $5). Deposits required; major credit cards accepted. Open daily 7am-8:30pm.

Groceries: Canyon Village Marketplace (☎638-2262), a general store at the Yavapai Lodge complex. Open daily in summer 7am-9pm. Near the east entrance, the **Desert View General Store** serves campers. Open daily 7am-8:30pm.

Showers and Laundry: Available at concession-run **Camper Services,** adjacent to the Mather Campground in Canyon Village. Showers $1 per 5min. Laundry open 6am-9:45pm; showers 6am-11pm.

Weather and Road Conditions: ☎638-7888.

Medical Services: Grand Canyon Clinic (☎638-2551), take a left at the first stoplight after the South Rim entrance. Open M-F 7am-7pm, Sa 10am-4pm. 24hr. emergency aid.

Post Office: 100 Mather Business Ctr. (☎638-2512), in market plaza, next to the General Store. Open M-F 9am-4:30pm, Sa 10am-5pm. **ZIP code:** 86023.

ACCOMMODATIONS

Compared to the six million years it took the Colorado River to carve the Grand Canyon, the year it will take you to get indoor lodging near the South Rim is nothing. Summer rooms should be reserved *11 months in advance.* Even so, there are cancellations every day; you can check for vacancies or call the Grand Canyon operator (☎638-2631) and ask to be connected with the proper lodge. Reservations for **Bright Angel Lodge, Maswik Lodge, Trailer Village,** and **Phantom Ranch** can be made through **Xanterra Parks and Resorts,** 14001 E. Iliff, Ste. 600, Aurora, CO 80014 (☎303-297-2757). Most accommodations on the South Rim are very pricey.

Maswik Lodge (☎638-2631), in Grand Canyon Village near the rim and several restaurants. Small, clean cabins with showers but no heat are $66. Motel rooms with queen beds and ceiling fans are also available. Singles $79; doubles $121. $7-9 for each additional person. ❺

Bright Angel Lodge (☎638-2631), in Grand Canyon Village. The cheapest indoor lodging in the park, located in a historic building right on the rim. Very convenient to Bright Angel Trail and shuttle buses. "Rustic" lodge singles and doubles with shared bath $53, with private bath $71. "Historic" cabins, some of which have fireplaces, are available for 1 or 2 people $84-107. $7 per additional person in rooms and cabins. ❹

Phantom Ranch (☎638-2631), on the canyon floor, a day's hike down the Kaibab Trail or Bright Angel Trail. Male and female dorms $28; seldom-available cabins for 1 or 2 people $71.50; $10.50 per additional person. Don't show up without reservations, which can be made up to 23 months in advance. Breakfast $17; box lunch $8.50; stew dinner $20; steak dinner $29; vegetarian option $20. If you're dying to sleep on the canyon floor but don't have a reservation, show up at the Bright Angel transportation desk at 6am on the day prior to your planned stay, and take a shot on the waiting list. ❹

CAMPGROUNDS

The campsites listed here usually fill up early in the day. In the **Kaibab National Forest,** along the south border of the park, you can pull off a dirt road and camp for free. No camping is allowed within ¼ mi. of U.S. 64. Convenient **dispersed camping** can be had along the frequently traveled N. Long Jim Loop Rd.—make a right turn about 1 mi. south of the south entrance station. For quieter and more remote sites,

GRAND CANYON

follow signs for the Arizona Trail into the national forest between Mile 252 and 253 on U.S. 64. Sleeping in cars is *not* permitted within the park, but it is allowed in the Kaibab Forest. For more info, contact the **Tusayan Ranger Station**, Kaibab National Forest, P.O. Box 3088, Tusayan, AZ 86023 (☎638-2443). Reservations for some campgrounds can be made through **SPHERICS** (☎800-365-2267).

Mather Campground (call SPHERICS, ☎800-365-2267) in Grand Canyon Village, 1 mi. south of the Canyon Village Marketplace; follow signs from Yavapai Lodge. 320 shady, relatively isolated sites with no hookups. Check at the office even if the sign says the campground is full. 7-night max. stay. For Mar.-Nov., reserve up to 3 months in advance; Dec.-Feb. first come, first served. Sept.-May $12; June-Aug. $15. ❶

Ten-X Campground (☎638-2443), in Kaibab National Forest, 10 mi. south of Grand Canyon Village off Rte. 64. Removed from the highway, offers shady sites surrounded by pine trees. Toilets, water, no hookups, no showers. Open May-Sept. First come, first served; sites $10. ❶

Desert View Campground (☎638-7888), 25 mi. east of Grand Canyon Village. Short on shade and far from the hub of the South Rim, but a perfect place to avoid the crowd. 50 sites with phone and restroom access, but no hookups or campfires. Sites $10. Open mid-May to Oct. No reservations; usually full by early afternoon. ❶

Camper Village (☎638-2887), in Tusayan, 1 mi. south of the park entrance behind the general store 2-person hookups and tent sites $18-26; showers and flush toilets; $2 per additional adult. First come, first served tent sites; reservations required for RVs. ❷

Trailer Village (☎638-2631), next to Mather Campground. 84 sites designed for the RV. Showers, laundry, and groceries nearby. Office open daily 8am-noon and 1-5pm. 2-person hookups $24; $2 per additional person. Reserve 6-9 months in advance. ❷

FOOD

Fast food has yet to sink its greasy talons into the South Rim (the closest McDonald's is 7 mi. south in Tusayan), but you *can* find meals at fast-food prices, and get a slightly better return for your money.

The **Canyon Village Market Place ❶**, at the Market Plaza 1 mi. west of Mather Point on the main road, has a deli counter with the cheapest eats in the park, a wide selection of groceries, a camping supplies department, and enough Grand Canyon apparel to clothe each member of your extended family with a commemorative gift. (☎638-2262. Open daily in summer 7am-8:30pm; deli open 7am-6pm. Sandwiches $2-4.) The well-stocked **Canyon Cafe ❶**, across from the General Store, offers a wider variety of food than the deli. (Open daily 6:30am-9pm; hamburgers $3, pizza $3.50-5, dinners $5-7.) **Maswik Cafeteria ❶**, in Maswik Lodge, serves a variety of grilled food, country favorites, Mexican specialties, and healthy alternatives in a wood-paneled cafeteria atmosphere. (Open daily 6am-10pm. Hot entrees $6-7, sandwiches $3-5.) **Bright Angel Dining Room ❷**, in Bright Angel Lodge, serves hot sandwiches for $7-9. Breakfasts run $6-7 and pricey dinner entrees range $10-15. (☎638-2631. Open daily 6:30am-10pm.) Just out the door of the dining room, the **Soda Fountain ❶** at Bright Angel Lodge chills eight flavors of ice cream and stocks a variety of snack-bar sandwiches. (Open daily 8am-8pm. 1 scoop $2.)

HIKING AND BACKPACKING

Although the Grand Canyon experience for the majority of park visitors involves stepping out of the air-conditioned tour bus, walking eagerly to the rim with camera in hand, enjoying the views, snapping a few keepsake shots, and then retreating to the bus before beads of sweat begin to form, there are many more invigorating and exciting ways to enjoy the Canyon's grandeur. Outdoor recreation in the park focuses mainly on hiking and backpacking, though commercial outfits provide services like mule rides, rafting, and flightseeing.

From your first glimpse of the canyon, you may feel a compelling desire to see it from the inside, an enterprise harder than it looks. Even the young at heart and body should remember that an easy downhill hike can become a nightmarish 50° incline on the return journey: plan on taking twice as long to ascend than you took descending. Also keep in mind that the lower you go, the hotter it gets; when it's 85°F on the rim, it's around 100°F at Indian Gardens and around 110°F at Phantom Ranch. Heat stroke, the greatest threat to any hiker, is marked by a monstrous headache and red, sweatless skin. *For a day hike, you must take at least a gallon of water per person; drink at least a liter per hr. hiking upwards under the hot sun.* Apply sunscreen regularly. Hiking boots or sneakers with excellent tread are also necessary—the trails are steep, and every year several careless hikers take what locals morbidly call "the 12-second tour." Poor preparation and over-exertion greatly magnify the risks of Canyon hiking. A list of safety tips can be found in *The Guide*. Speak with a ranger before embarking on a hike—they may have important info about the trail. Hiking down to the river and back to the rim in the same day is discouraged by rangers. Resting at a campground is recommended (see **backcountry permits**). Parents should think twice about bringing children more than 1 mi. down any trail both for the child's safety and to dwarf any motivation for later revenge.

In determining what is an appropriate day hike, remember that the Canyon does not have any loops. Be prepared to retrace every single footstep uphill on the way back. For longer day hikes, it is strongly recommended that you begin before 7am. Because walking and climbing in the summer heat requires exceptional effort, the Park Service recommends not hiking between the hours of 10am and 3pm to escape the worst of the heat. Rangers present a variety of free, informative **talks** and **guided hikes;** details are listed in *The Guide.* Said rangers will also gladly offer advice regarding trail guides and maps; the *Official Guide to Hiking the Grand Canyon* published by the Grand Canyon Association is the preferred choice. The **Rim, Bright Angel, South Kaibab,** and **River Trails** are the only South Rim trails regularly maintained and patrolled by the Park Service.

Stifling heat, scarce water, and drastic elevation changes, all under the weight of a heavy pack, make **backpacking** around the Grand Canyon a grueling experience. Still, applications for **backcountry permits** far outnumber availability, especially during the summer. If you get there late in the day, you can forget about getting a permit, and plan to start earlier the next day. The most popular backpacking routes connect the rim-to-river trails listed below and demand little in the way of navigational skills. Camping along such popular corridor routes is limited to **designated areas.** The Park Service divides the park into use areas, each with restrictions on camping and recreation. Much of the park remains inaccessible to trekkers because of cliffs and other impassable terrain. The footbridge spanning the Colorado near Phantom Ranch is the only **river crossing,** making the ranch a necessary stop when traveling rim to rim. **Through-hiking** from the South to the North Rim generally connects either the Bright Angel or South Kaibab Trail with the North Kaibab Trail, covering 21-23 mi. and 10,000 ft. of elevation change. All overnight trips require a **backcountry permit** ($10 per group, $5 per person), obtainable at the Backcountry Information Center next to the Maswik Lodge (P.O. Box 129, Grand Canyon, AZ 86023; fax ☎928-638-2125; www.nps.gov/grca). Permits are available on the 1st of the month, four months before the proposed hike (e.g. July permits available March 1). Requests should include the proposed route, campsites, license plate numbers, group size, and contact info.

Rim Trail (11 mi. one-way, 4-6hr.). With only a mild elevation change (about 200 ft.) and the constant security of the nearby shuttle, the Rim Trail is excellent for hikers seeking a tame way to see the Canyon. The trail follows the shuttle bus routes along Hermit Rd. past the Grand Canyon Village to Mather Point. The Rim Trail covers both paved and unpaved ground, with 8 viewpoints along Hermit Rd. and 3 east of it. Near the Grand Canyon Village, the Rim Trail resembles a crowded city street that runs behind the lodges, but toward the eastern and western ends, hikers have a bit more elbow room. Hopi Point is a great place to watch the sun set with its panoramic canyon views—*The Guide* list times for sunsets and sunrises, and the "Choose your view" kiosk at the Visitors Center allows photographers to preview typical scenery at different locations and times of day. Bring plenty of water, as little is available along the trail.

Bright Angel Trail (up to 18 mi. round-trip, 1-2 days). Bright Angel's frequent switchbacks and refreshing water stations make it the into-the-canyon choice of moderate hikers. Depending on distance, the trail can be either a day or overnight hike. The trail departs from the Rim Trail near the western edge of the Grand Canyon Village, and the first 1-2 mi. of the trail generally attract droves of day hikers eager to try just a taste of canyon descent. Rest houses are strategically stationed 1½ and 3 mi. from the rim, each with water between May and Sept. Indian Gardens, 4½ mi. down, offers restrooms, picnic tables, 15 backcountry campsites open year-round, and blessed shade. From rim to river, the trail drops 4420 ft. Although spread over 9 mi., the round-trip is too strenuous for a day hike. With the compulsory permit, overnighters can camp at Indian Gardens or on the canyon floor at Bright Angel Campground, while day hikers are advised to go no farther than Plateau Point (12.2 mi. round-trip) or Indian Gardens (9.2 mi. round-trip). Be prepared to stand parched and exhausted as you yield and wave bitterly to tourists descending by mule train. The **River Trail** (1.7 mi.) runs along the river, connecting the Bright Angel Trail with the South Kaibab Trail.

South Kaibab Trail (7 mi. one-way to Phantom Ranch, 4-5 hr. descent). Those seeking a more challenging hike down might consider this route. Beginning at Yaki Pt. (7260 ft.), Kaibab is trickier, steeper, and lacks shade or water, but it rewards the intrepid with a better view of the canyon. Unlike most canyon-descending trails, the South Kaibab avoids the safety and obstructed views of a side-canyon route and instead winds directly down the ridge, offering panoramic views across the expanse of the canyon. Day hikes to Cedar Ridge (3 mi. round-trip; toilet facilities available) and Skeleton Point (6 mi. round-trip) are reasonable only for experienced, well-conditioned hikers, due to the trail's steep grade. For overnight hikes, Kaibab meets up with Bright Angel at the Colorado River. Fewer switchbacks and a more rapid descent make the South Kaibab Trail 1.7 mi. shorter than the Bright Angel to this point. Guests staying at the Phantom Ranch or Bright Angel Campground (the only permitted camping area on the trail) use either the Bright Angel or South Kaibab to reach the ranch. Many hikers believe that the best route is to descend the South Kaibab Trail (4-5hr.) and come back up the Bright Angel (7-8hr.) the following day. The elevation change from trailhead to river is 4880 ft.

Grandview Trail (6.4 mi. round-trip to the Mesa). The costs of hauling ore up to Grandview Point (7400 ft.) from Horseshoe Mesa (4800 ft.) along the Hopi Indian-built Grandview Trail proved too great for turn-of-the-century miners. Eventually, they gave up on mining and starting leading tourists down this harrowing descent. After hiking halfway down this wilderness trail today, however, you won't have the option of giving up as there's no water available without either descending past Horseshoe Mesa or returning to the Rim. The steep and strenuous hike requires route-finding and delicate footing on loose rocks, so hiking boots are a must. Backpackers can continue a steep 1.8 mi. to

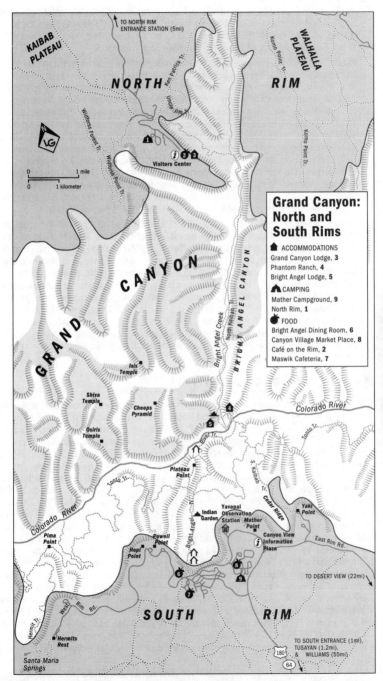

TO NORTH RIM
ENTRANCE STATION (5mi)

KAIBAB
PLATEAU

WALHALLA
PLATEAU

NORTH

RIM

Komo Point Tr.

Ken Patrick Tr.

Uncle Jim Tr.

VG

Widforss Forest Tr.

Widforss Point Tr.

Komo Point Tr.

Visitors Center

0   1 mile
0   1 kilometer

Bright Angel Creek

North Kaibab Tr.

BRIGHT ANGEL CANYON

GRAND   CANYON

Isis
Temple

Shiva
Temple

Cheops
Pyramid

Colorado River

Osiris
Temple

River Tr.

Tonto Tr.

Plateau
Point

Colorado River

Yavapai
Observation
Station

Tonto Tr.

Indian
Garden

S. Kaibab Tr.

Cedar Ridge

Yaki
Point

Pima
Point

Hopi
Point

Powell
Point

Bright Angel Tr.

Mather
Point

Canyon View
Information
Plaza

East Rim Rd.

TO DESERT VIEW (22mi)

SOUTH   RIM

Hermit Tr.

West Rim Rd.

Hermits
Rest

Santa Maria
Springs

TO SOUTH ENTRANCE (1mi),
TUSAYAN (1.2mi),
& WILLIAMS (55mi)

180

64

Grand Canyon:
North and
South Rims

🏠 ACCOMMODATIONS
Grand Canyon Lodge, **3**
Phantom Ranch, **4**
Bright Angel Lodge, **5**

⛺ CAMPING
Mather Campground, **9**
North Rim, **1**

🍎 FOOD
Bright Angel Dining Room, **6**
Canyon Village Market Place, **8**
Café on the Rim, **2**
Maswik Cafeteria, **7**

GRAND CANYON

GRAND CANYON

the Tonto Trail junction and follow the Tonto to typical canyon-floor destinations like Bright Angel Campground or Phantom Ranch. There is a reliable water source, Miners Spring, at the base of the Red Wall, 400 ft. below the eastern rim of the Horseshoe Mesa. Expect a full day of hiking to Horseshoe Mesa and back.

Hermit Trail (9.3 mi. one-way to the river). Embarking from the Hermit Trailhead at Hermit's Rest (6640 ft.), this strenuous route descends the Supai cliffs, switching back and forth frequently on loose rocks. The Hermit Trail offers panoramic views of the West Rim, less frequently seen than the rim surrounding the Grand Canyon Village because during the summer, the West Rim is accessible only by the red shuttle line. The trail ends at the base, near the Hermit Creek rapids, and water must be treated before drinking. Hikers planning to begin a multi-day trip from Hermit's Rest and in possession of the required backcountry permit may drive their vehicles to the trailhead for parking. Following the trail all the way to the Colorado covers 9.3 mi. and hikers are advised to allow at least 7hr. to reach the first overnight camping area, Hermit Creek (7.8 mi.), because of the slow pace mandated by a rocky and steep trail. Occasional rock slides and floods may obscure the trail and route-finding skills become necessary. Day hikers should not hike beyond the Santa Maria Springs, 2.5 mi. down the trail (5-6hr. each way).

Tonto Trail (up to 95 mi.). Threading its way along the entire length of the Tonto Platform, the solid sandstone Tonto Trail travels a total of 95 mi. and connects all of the other routes traveling from rim to river. The Tonto Platform, a jutting esplanade that appears table-flat from the rim actually contains many washes and gullies. The trail itself is a rugged, wilderness path and requires route-finding skills. Near Red Canyon the platform lies at 3600 ft.; by Garnet Canyon it drops to 2800 ft. Most hikers use the trail to connect other popular routes. There are 4.5 mi. of the trail between the Bright Angel and South Kaibab Trails, 21.3 mi between S. Kaibab and Grandview Trails, and 12 mi. between the Hermit Trail and Indian Gardens on the Bright Angel Trail. Traveling west past the Hermit Trail, Tonto gradually becomes less and less trafficked and route-finding grows increasingly important. Several creeks cutting through the Tonto Platform provide year-round water.

⚠ OTHER OUTDOOR ACTIVITIES

Beyond using your feet, there are other ways to conquer the canyon. **Mule trips** from the South Rim are expensive and booked up to one year in advance, although cancellations do occur. (☎303-297-2757. Day trip to Plateau Point 6 mi. down the Bright Angel Trail $127, overnight including lodging at Phantom Ranch and all meals: $343 per person.) Mule trips from the North Rim (☎435-679-8665) are cheaper and more readily available, such as the 8hr. day trip to Roaring Springs waterfall ($95). Looking up at the Grand Canyon from the wet, rubber bladder of a **whitewater raft** is also both popular, yet pricey. Trips into the Grand Canyon proper vary in length from a week to 18 days and book far in advance. The *Trip Planner* (available by request at the info center) lists several commercial guides licensed to offer trips in the canyon; check the park web site for info in advance of your visit. The only company permitted to guide one-day trips on the Colorado, **Wilderness River Adventures** (see p. 85), operates out of Page, AZ. If the views from the rim fail to dazzle and astound you, see a doctor or try the higher vantages provided by one of the park's many **flightseeing** companies, all located at the Grand Canyon Airport outside of Tuyasan. **Grand Canyon Airlines** flies 45min. canyon tours hourly during the summer. (☎866-235-9422. $75, children $45. Reservations recommended, but walk-ins generally available. Discount for lunchtime tours, 11am-2pm.) Flying smaller planes on a wider range of trips, **Air Grand Canyon** offers 30-90min. flights. (☎800-247-4726. $74-174.) Both airlines team up with Wilderness River Adventures to offer one-day combination flightseeing/rafting tours. For a rapid vertical thrill, check out the popular helicopter flights from **Papillon Grand Canyon Helicopters.** Tours of the Canyon depart as frequently as every 30min. between 8am and 5pm. (☎800-528-2418. Tours 30min.; $105, children $95. $175 per 50 min.; kids $155 per 50 min.) Both **Scenic Airlines** (☎800-634-6801) and **Air Vegas Airlines** (☎800-255-7474) offer flight/hotel/canyon tour packages out of Las Vegas's northern airport. For a list of flight companies in the park, write the Grand Canyon Chamber of Commerce, Box 3007, Grand Canyon, AZ 86023.

HAVASUPAI RESERVATION ☎928

West of the of the South Rim lies the tranquility of the Havasupai Reservation. Meaning "people of the blue-green water," the Havasupai live on the canyon floor and seasonally on the rim in a protected enclave, bordered by the national park. And what an enclave it is. Ringed by dramatic sandstone faces, their village, Supai, rests on the verdant shores of the Havasu River amidst the walls of Havasu Canyon. Just beyond town, this rushing wonder of crystal-clear water cascades over a series of spectacular falls. The grandest of them, Havasu Falls, plummets more than 100 feet into a mist-enshrouded blue-green lagoon. Beneath the falls, ecstatic visitors frolic in the waters, gleefully soaking in idyllic surroundings. Such beauty attracts thousands of visitors yearly, but luckily, a gruelling ten-mile hike separates the falls from any paved, vehicle-accessible surface and prevents the Disney-fication of the reservation. For most, blistered feet or a saddle-sore rump make bathing in the cool waters beneath the falls even sweeter.

TRANSPORTATION. Supai and the campground can only be reached by a trail that originates on the rim at the Hualapai Hilltop. To reach the trailhead, take I-40 E from Flagstaff or Williams until Rte. 66 at Seligman (40 mi. from Williams). Follow Rte. 66 for 30 mi. until it meets with Indian Rd. 18, which ends at the Hilltop after 60 mi. No roads lead to Supai, although mules and helicopters can be hired to carry bags or people. For mule reservations, contact the **Havasupai Tourist Enterprise** at 448-2141 ($75 one-way, half of which is required as a deposit; includes 4 pieces of luggage not to exceed 130 lb. total; groups leave at 10am). **Skydance Helicopter** flies between the hilltop and village four days per week. (☎800-882-1651. Flights fly every 15-20 min. on M, Th, F, and Su 9am-3pm. $70 one-way; first come, first served.) The hike down to Supai and on to the campground is not to be underestimated. The well-marked trail is a grueling, exposed 8 mi. to Supai and then an additional 2 mi. to the campground. Bring at least a gallon of water per hiker. It is also best to start hiking at dawn whether entering or leaving the Canyon. Hiking during midday is dangerous. Even day visitors have to pay the $20 entrance fee. If you anticipate staying, *do not hike down without a reservation*—you may have to turn right around and walk back to the trailhead.

PRACTICAL INFORMATION. Reservations for the campground, lodge, and mules can be made by contacting **Havasupai Tourist Enterprise.** (☎448-2141; www.havasupaitribe.com. Credit cards accepted and deposit required.) No **gas** or **water** is available past Rte. 66; stock up beforehand. Visitors must first check in at the **Tourist Office** in Supai before heading onto the campground (M-F 7am-7pm; Sa-Su 8am-5pm). If the office is closed, proceed to the campground and pay the ranger in the morning. In the village, there's a post office, general store, and cafe. The village **cafe** serves American breakfasts ($4-5) and fast-food items ranging from the $3 plate of fries to the $5 burger. (Open daily in summer 6am-7pm; Sept.-Feb. 8am-5pm.) Across the sand street, the **General Store** stocks a surprising variety of camp foods, in addition to produce and fresh dairy. Prices are expensive, but not exorbitant. (Open daily 6:30am-7pm; in winter 8am-5pm.) All **trash** must be packed out of the Reservation.

🏞️ 📷 **CAMPING AND HIKING.** The Havasupai graciously share their natural paradise with the outside world. The tribe operates the two accommodations: the 🏕️**Havasupai Campground ❷** and the **Havasupai Lodge,** both on the canyon floor. The friendly campground, 2 mi. beyond Supai, lies between Havasu and Mooney Falls. Campers will be hard-pressed to find fault with the grounds, because they border the blue-green water of the Havasu River and are near to the swimmer-friendly lagoons. The tribe charges a one-time entry fee ($20 per visitor and $10 per night) at the campground. Facilities are sparse: non-flush toilets that tend to smell up the campground, and no showers (though the falls are just a quick jaunt away). No fires are allowed, so tote your own stove or munch on dry and canned food for a few days. A spring provides fresh water. The **Havasupai Lodge ❺,** in Supai, offers basic accommodations ($75-96 for up to four people, plus the entrance fee).

The trail from Supai to the campground extends to **Mooney Falls** (1 mi. from campground), where visitors can maneuver a slippery 200 ft. descent to splash around. Next, **Navajo Falls** (1½ mi. from campground) and **Havasu Falls** (2 mi. from campground) surge over cliffs and into warm, frothy pools. Swimming and frolicking are encouraged in the falls' lagoons.

NORTH RIM   ☎928

If you're coming from Utah or Nevada, or want to avoid the crowds at the South Rim, the park's North Rim is a bit wilder, a bit colder, and much more serene—all with a view *almost* as groovy as that from the South Rim. The real difference in view has to do with the position of the sun; gazing into the canyon from the north, the sun's southerly rays are not conducive to photography. Any visit to the North Rim centers on the North Rim Lodge, an elegant structure in stone and exposed timber complete with a spacious lounge and dining room that look out into the canyon. The "other" rim entertains only a fraction of the number of visitors the South Rim sees, as over 400,000 people per year flood its observation decks. Sandwiched between canyons to the east and west, the park is most accessible along the lush Kaibab Plateau. Because of this remoteness, the North Rim tends to attract a slightly more upscale clientele, willing to shell out a few extra dollars to avoid the tiring tourist droves; expect to pay more for everything from lodging to groceries to showers. The North Rim's removed location also makes it hard to reach by public transportation, and by car, it's a long drive.

❇️ 🛈 **ORIENTATION AND PRACTICAL INFORMATION**

To reach the North Rim from the South Rim, take Rte. 64 E to U.S. 89 N, which runs into Alt. 89; from Alt. 89, follow Rte. 67 S to the edge. Altogether, the beautiful drive is over 200 mi. From Utah, take Alt. 89 S from Fredonia. From Page, take U.S. 89 S to Alt. 89 to Rte. 67 S. Snow closes Rte. 67 from early December to mid-May and park facilities (including the lodge) close between mid-October and mid-May. The visitor **parking** lot lies near the end of Rte. 67, strategically close to both the Visitors Center and lodge, about 13 mi. south of the park entrance. Trailhead parking is also available at North Kaibab and Widforss Trails and at scenic points along the road to Cape Royal.

Buses: Transcanyon, P.O. Box 348, Grand Canyon 86023 (☎638-2820). Buses run to the South Rim (5hr.; late May to Oct. leaving 7am from the North Rim Lodge; from the Bright Angel Lodge at the South Rim 1:30pm; $65, round-trip $110). Reservations required.

Public Transit: A **hikers' shuttle** runs from the Lodge to the North Kaibab Trailhead (late May to Oct. 5:20am, 7:20am; $5, $2 per additional person). Tickets must be purchased in advance at the Lodge.

Gas and Car Repairs: Chevron, on the campground road just off Rte. 67. The station does not service cars, but can arrange a tow to Kanab for repairs. 7am-7pm daily.

Visitor Information: North Rim Visitors Center (☎638-7864), on Rte. 67 just before the Lodge. Open daily 8am-6pm. **Kaibab Plateau Visitors Center** (☎643-7298), at Jacob Lake, next to the Inn. Interpretive displays provide details on the creation of the canyon and its ecosystem, and backcountry permits are issued here. Open daily 8am-5pm.

Equipment and Groceries: The **General Store,** next to North Rim Campground. Open daily 8am-8pm.

Showers and Laundromat: on the road leading to the Campground. Showers $1.25 per 5min. 7am-9pm daily.

Weather Conditions: (☎638-7888). Updated at 7am daily.

Post Office: Grand Canyon Lodge (☎638-2611). Open M-F 8am-11am and 11:30am-4pm, Sa 8am-1pm. **ZIP code:** 86052.

🏕 ACCOMMODATIONS AND CAMPING

The North Rim has only one campground, creatively named **"North Rim Campground,"** and it generally fills entirely by reservation during the summer. Cars line up at 8:30am to vie for the few spots remaining daily, but calling ahead is the safest bet. **SPHERICS** (☎800-365-2267) handles reservations. If you can't get in-park lodgings, head for the **Kaibab National Forest,** which runs from north of Jacob Lake to the park entrance. You can camp for free, as long as you're ¼ mi. from the road, water, or official campgrounds, and 1 mi. from any commercial facility. Popular undeveloped sites can be found off of Forest Route 611, at the base off Saddle Mountain. As always with dispersed camping, facilities are absent and "Leave No Trace" ethics (see **Great Outdoors,** p. 60) are a must. Less expensive accommodations may be found in Kanab, UT, 80 mi. north, where motels hover around $40.

Grand Canyon Lodge (reservations ☎303-297-2757; front desk 638-2611), on the edge of the rim. Swank rustic lodge is the only indoor rim lodging in the park. Reception 24hr. Reserve as early as six months in advance. Check out the overlook near the reception area, providing comfy seats and a truly stunning look at the chasm. Open mid-May to Oct. Singles or doubles in frontier cabins, hotel rooms $88, 4-person pioneer cabins $100, no TV's in any of the rooms. ❺

Jacob Lake Inn (☎643-7232), 32 mi. north of the North Rim entrance at Jacob Lake. Reception daily 6:30am-9:30pm. Charming lodge a gift shop, cafe, and bakery. Cabins for 2 $72-83, triples $86-88, quads $90-92; motel units $91-106. ❺

Kaibab Lodge (☎638-2389), 6 mi. north of the entrance gate, is rustic yet sophisticated. 2-person basic cabin $80, modern spaces with satellite TV $110-130. ❺

North Rim Campground (call SPHERICS, ☎800-365-2267), on Rte. 67 near the rim, the only park campground on this side of the chasm. Well-spaced pine- and aspen-shaded sites. Groceries, laundry, and showers nearby. 83 sites; no hookups. Open mid-May to mid-Oct. 7-night max. stay. Sites $15, 4 "premier sites" with canyon views $20. ❶

DeMotte Park Campground, about 16 mi. north of North Rim in Kaibab National Forest. Be an early bird to avoid disappointment; 23 woodsy sites are first come, first served and generally fill by noon. $10 per vehicle per night. No hookups. ❶

Kaibab Camper Village (☎643-7804), 1 mi. south of Jacob Lake Inn on Rte. 67. Open May to mid-Oct. 50 tent sites $12; 2-person hookups $22; $2 per additional person. ❶

Tuweep/Toroweap Campground, the national park's most remote and least crowded campground, accessible only by 60 mi. of wash-boarded dirt road (passable by sedans when dry, but be sure to have an extra tire). To find Toroweap, turn left onto BLM Rd. 109, 7 mi. west of Fredonia, AZ and follow it south 61 mi. Peering over the frightening 3000 ft. drop from Toroweap Point to the Colorado and imagining what John Welsey Powell called the "conflict of water and fire" that took place between lava flows and the roaring river makes the 2hr. drive worthwhile. Arrive early to snag 1 of the 2 amazing spots on the point. 11 primitive sites available first come, first served. Sites free. ❶

◪ FOOD

The **Grand Canyon Lodge** ❸ monopolizes in-park eating options, which tend toward the pricey side. The solution: buy groceries at the General Store and prepare your own canyon-side picnic. The lodge's dining room, treating guests to sweeping canyon views and haute cuisine, serves breakfast for $5-8, lunch for $6.50-8.50, and dinner for $13 and up. (☎638-2612, ext. 160; Open daily 6:30-10am, 11:30am-2:30pm, and 5-9:30pm. Reservations required for dinner.) Standard salads at the **Cafe on the Rim** ❷ range from $4-6, and cheese pizza by the slice goes for $2.50. (Open daily 7am-9pm. Breakfasts range $3-5.) The lodge also houses the **Rough Rider Saloon** ❷, which serves delicate baked goods and coffee in the morning and more conventional bar offerings in the afternoon. (Open daily 5:30am-9:30am and 11am-10pm. Domestic drafts $3.50, premium bottles $4.) A superb alternative to the North Rim establishments is **Jacob Lake Inn** ❸. The intimate diner counter, a fine-dining restaurant, and amiably staffed bakery combine to offer a pleasing variety of options. Pick up a gravity-defying milkshake to make the remaining miles to the rim a bit more enjoyable. (Sandwiches $6, amazing milkshakes $3, breakfasts $5-6, dinners $12-15.) **The Kaibab Lodge** ❸ presents the last dining option before North Rim eateries corner the market. (Breakfast 6am-9pm; dinner, featuring $6-8 burgers and $15-17 fish or steak, 6pm-8pm.)

◪ HIKING AND BACKPACKING

Hiking in the leafy North Rim seems like a trip to an alpine mountains. This mountain, however, is upside-down—the hike back up comes after the legs are already a little weary from hiking down. All precautions for hiking at the South Rim are even more important at the North Rim, where the elevations are higher and the air is thinner. In-depth info on trails can be found in the North Rim's version of *The Guide.* Several day hikes of variable lengths beckon the active North Rim visitor. Trails offer views rivaling those of the South Rim without the hassle of elbowing through the crowd. For an indispensable resource on North Rim Trails, pick up a copy of the *Official Guide to Hiking the Grand Canyon,* published by the Grand Canyon Association and available in all Visitors Centers and gift shops.

Bright Angel Point Trail (½ mi. round-trip, 30min.-1hr.). Trail access begins both near the Visitors Center and from the Lodge veranda. This short, paved, and relatively flat trail travels along a narrow ridge to a viewpoint offering a panorama that includes Roaring Spring Canyon, the Transept, and the South Rim. A perfect choice for visitors looking for a quick glimpse of the Canyon's grandeur.

Cape Royal Trail (½ mi. round-trip, 30min.-1hr.). A short, paved jaunt to a point acclaimed by many to be the North Rim's best scenic vantage, and is accessible to handicapped visitors. The trail departs from the parking lot at the end of the Cape Royal Rd. and travels to the edge of the Walhalla plateau (7865 ft.) for wondrous views of the Canyon. Also near the Cape Royal Rd. parking lot, the **Cliff Springs Trail** (1 mi. round-trip, 1-1½hr.) descends a narrow canyon, passing the Wahalla Glade ruins (the structural remains left by a culture inhabiting the area 3-4 thousand years ago) en route to a bubbling spring protected by towering cliffs. Resist the strong urge to sip from the natural spring; it may not be safe.

Uncle Jim Trail (5 mi. round-trip, 2-3hr.). This loop trail begins at North Kaibab Trailhead parking lot and follows the **Ken Patrick Trail** along the northernmost reaches of Roaring Spring Canyon. Just past the canyon, the trail diverges from Ken Patrick and completes a circle on a plateau that juts out in between the Roaring Springs and Bright Angel Canyons, offering superior views of both. The trail and the lookout that it approaches bear the name of early 20th-century guide and hunter, Jim Owens, who led big shots like Teddy Roosevelt and Zane Grey on mountain lion hunts. Owens claimed to have killed more than 500 of these secretive beasts himself.

Widforss Trail (9.8mi. round-trip, 6hr.). Named for landscape painter Gunnar M. Widforss who chose these vistas as subjects. Combining Canyon views with alpine forest greenery, this less traveled trail is perfect for a casual, if long, day's saunter. The trail begins at the Widforss Trailhead, clearly marked on Rte. 67 (8100 ft.) After tracing the edge of The Transept, a wide branch canyon of Bright Angel Canyon, the trail winds through the spruce fir forest characteristic of the Kaibab Plateau before arriving at splendid canyon views from Widforss Point (7900 ft.). There is no water available on the trail, so be sure to carry plenty.

North Kaibab Trail (14.2 mi. one-way to the Colorado River, 3-4 days). The North Rim's half of the Kaibab Trail, this popular and well-maintained trail descends the Roaring Spring Canyon to the Bright Angel Canyon and eventually to the Colorado, furnishing scenes that will not disappoint. Trailhead parking is in a designated lot off Rte. 67. The trail begins with a steep, 3000 ft. drop over 4.7 mi. to Roaring Spring. Day hikers are advised not to proceed beyond the spring because of the effort required in climbing back up to the rim. Moving past the Spring, the trail travels another 2.1 mi. to the Cottonwood Campground and then another 7.4 mi. to the river. Just before reaching the Colorado, the trail meets the Bright Angel and South Kaibab Trails, allowing several options for a cross-canyon hike. Hikers must yield to the mule trains that travel the upper portions of the trail.

Thunder River/Deer Creek Trails (15 mi. one-way to the Colorado). Perhaps some of the most scenic and least-traveled backpacking in the park, this trail combination promises dramatic waterfalls and sculpted narrows. The trail begins on Forest Rd. 232, accessible by turning off Rte. 67 onto Forest Service Rd. 422 W, then following 422 W to Forest Service Rd. 245, and finally turning onto Forest Service Rd. 232. The trail begins at 6400 ft. and, after descending steep cliffs, follows the Esplanade to Surprise Valley. The main trail then picks up the Thunder River, following it past a spectacular 100 ft. waterfall and eventually to the Colorado. The alternative, Deer Creek Route, leaves the Thunder River Trail in Surprise Valley, traveling west to the beautiful narrows of Deer Creek Valley and the falls where Deer Creek pours into the Colorado.

▨ OTHER OUTDOOR ACTIVITIES

Park Rangers also run nature walks, lectures, and evening programs at the North Rim Campground and Grand Canyon Lodge. Check the info desk or campground bulletin boards for schedules. If the long drive has left you sapped for a day hike, let someone else do the work. Rim-side **mule trips** go for $20, while half day options ($45) and all-day jaunts to Roaring Springs ($96) are also available through **Canyon Trail Rides** circle the rim or descend into the canyon from the Lodge. (☎435-679-8665. Open daily 7am-5pm. No credit cards.) Reservations are recommended, but because of smaller crowds, walk-ins can be accommodated more frequently than on the South Rim. To tour the Canyon along the culprit that created it, pick up a Grand Canyon River Trip Operators brochure and select from among the 20 companies offering trips down the Colorado.

GRAND CANYON

LAKE POWELL AND PAGE   ☎ 428

The decision to curb the Colorado River's steady procession to the Pacific was made in 1956, and ten years and ten million tons of concrete later, Glen Canyon Dam, the second-largest dam in the country, was completed. Stopped in its tracks in northern Arizona, the mighty river backed-up into the once remote Glen Canyon. The monolith contains hydroelectric machinery that creates energy for much of the region, and spawned a vacation destination that draws visitors to the crown jewel of a national recreation area. Lake Powell, the pelagic expanse formed by the dam, has 1960 ft. of shoreline, exceeding the amount of beach lining continental America's Pacific coast. Darting around the lake on a personal watercraft or swimming in a narrow canyon, it's hard to imagine what the area looked like when John Welsey Powell, the lake's namesake, led his crew down the Colorado in 1869.

Page (pop. 6,800) lies just southeast of the dam and features numerous businesses, all competing fiercely for the summertime dollar. The town originally housed dam workers during the dam's construction, which lasted into the mid-60's. As a launchpad from which visitors can explore the "Grand Circle" of lakes, cliffs, and canyons, Page has a healthy tourist infrastructure of motels and cheap eats, but little else. Besides the brilliant blue spread of Lake Powell, other natural wonders surround the area. Just east of Page, narrow Antelope Canyon wows visitors with sculpted sandstone and spectacular lighting. Farther east lies the Rainbow Bridge National Monument, the world's tallest natural bridge, and across the lake stretch the wild reaches of Grand Staircase-Escalante National Monument.

■✳🔀 ORIENTATION AND PRACTICAL INFORMATION

All tourist services available inside the recreation area operate under **ARAMARK,** the concessionaire contracted by the Park's Service. The company operates four major marinas: **Wahweap** on U.S. 89 in the south near the dam, **Bullfrog** and **Halls Crossing,** across the reservoir from each other, both on Rte. 276 and connected by daily ferry service, and **Hite,** hidden in Lake Powell's northernmost reaches on Rte. 95. A single info line (☎800-528-6154) handles all questions and reservations for ARAMARK facilities. Although Park Service monitoring keeps the monopoly mostly in check, services inside the recreation area are pricier than those outside.

Page continues to serve a transient crowd and has much better bargains than inside the recreation area. Motels, unspectacular restaurants, and a litany of churches line Lake Powell Blvd., a wide, U-shaped road connecting with **U.S. 89** both north and south of town. Page's economy relies almost entirely on the tourist industry, and, as such, is highly seasonal. Expect price mark-downs at those few businesses that do remain open through the winter.

Visitor Information: Carl Hayden Visitors Center (☎608-6404), just across the bridge from Page on U.S. 89 N. Open May-Sept. daily 8am-7pm; Oct.-Apr. 8am-6pm. At the **Bullfrog Marina,** 45 mi. northeast of the dam, a Visitors Center welcomes tourists entering the recreation area from Rte. 276 in Utah. Open Apr.-Oct. daily 8am-5pm. In Page, the **Chamber of Commerce,** 644 N. Navajo Dr. (☎888-261-7243), in the Dam Plaza. Carries info on local services and rentals for watersports. Open daily 9am-6pm; in winter M-F 9am-5pm. In a pinch, info kiosks at several corners of Lake Powell Blvd. have helpful info to get you through the night.

Bike Rentals: Lakeside Bicycles, 118 6th Ave. (☎645-2266). Hard trail bikes with helmet $25 per day. Open M-F 9am-6pm, Sa 8am-noon.

Showers: At Wahweap RV Park. Guests free, campers and walk-ins $2. Free outdoor beach-type showers at Lone Rock Campground.

Laundromat: Sunshine Laundry and Dry Cleaners, 131 S. Lake Powell Blvd. (☎ 645-9703). Open daily 7am-9pm. Wahweap and Bullfrog Marinas also offer machines. At Wahweap, atop the hill at the RV park.

Medical Care: Page Hospital, 501 N. Navajo Dr. (☎ 645-2424). 24hr. emergency care.

Internet Access: At the stylish **Page Public Library,** 479 S. Lake Powell Blvd. (☎ 645-4270). Open M-Th 10am-8pm, F-Sa 10am-5pm. Free Internet.

Post Office: 44 6th Ave. (☎ 645-2571). **ZIP code:** 86040. Open 8:30am-5pm M-F.

🏠 🏕 ACCOMMODATIONS AND CAMPING

Although the main drag through Page grows increasingly populated with high-end chain hotels, a few gems of an earlier, more affordable era remain. A cluster of quality budget accommodations resides on 8th Ave. between S. Navajo and Elm St. (from either direction on Lake Powell Blvd., head north on S. Navajo and make a left onto 8th Ave.). Pegged as "Page's Old Quarter," this "Avenue of Little Motels" shelters an idiosyncratic cluster of converted dam worker apartments. For the price of one night in the **Wahweap Lodge,** you could buy yourself a decent tent, and camping on the lake is beautiful and inexpensive. Visitors with boats can camp nearly anywhere along the endless lakeshore, so long as they have a **portable toilet.** The lake's marinas rent them. Don't get caught without one—the rangers are vigilant, and besides, no one wants to swim in your sewage. Away from the dam area, tent sites and hookups are available at the **Bullfrog ❶, Halls Crossing ❶,** and **Hite Marinas ❶.** Call ARAMARK (☎ 800-528-6154) for camping info. Sites $6.

Lake Powell International Hostel & Pension, 141 8th Ave. (☎ 645-3898; www.lake-powellinthostel.com). After a hiatus, this comfortable hostel with a European clientele has re-opened. Friendly owners oversee dozens of bunks ($12-15), private bedrooms with shared bathrooms ($30), and full apartments with kitchens, cable TV, VCR's, and a living room ($40 and up). Sand volleyball in the yard, basketball hoop, free shuttles to the lake and airport. Free bedding. ❷

K.C.'s Motel, 126 8th Ave. (☎ 645-2947; www.kcmotel.com). Named for the owner's affectionate Yorkie, K.C.'s offers spacious, recently renovated suites with cable TV and multiple bedrooms for discount prices. Rooms start at $39, but rates drop in winter. Online reservations accepted. ❸

Bashful Bob's Motel, 750 S. Navajo Dr. (☎ 645-3919). Bob's not embarrassed about his huge, vintage decorated rooms with kitchens, living rooms, cable TV, and free Internet access. The backyard's trees shade grillers as they eagerly cook up their next meal, perhaps even a fresh catch. Singles go from $32 and doubles start at $39, $5 per additional person; reduced winter rates. ❷

Red Rocks Inn, 114 8th Ave. (☎ 645-0062). Immense rooms at bargain prices, with kitchens and cable TV. Singles and doubles $39-54; winter rates lower. Rooms fill up quickly, so call ahead. ❸

Wahweap Campground/RV Park (☎ 800-528-6154), at Wahweap Marina. Near lake swimming areas, boat rentals, and ramps. Shuttles to the lodge, showers, laundry, general store, and Page. Tent sites $15, hookups $27. ❷

Lone Rock Campground, on Lone Rock Rd. just on the Utah side of the border. Camp anywhere on the beach to enjoy the water, the sunsets, the constant purring of RV generators, and the drone of ATVs operated by campers too lazy to walk 200 yards to the pit toilets. Water, showers, and boat ramp available. Sites $6. ❶

WATER GAUCHOS' LAMENT
Damming Motorized Recreation in the Southwest

Some take their nature with paddle, camera, and silence; others prefer fiberglass, gasoline, and the noise of churning pistons. America's National Parks have, in recent years, become a battleground for competing visions of the outdoor recreationalist's place in nature. The conflict generally pits kayakers, hikers, bikers, and climbers against dirt-bikers, ATVers, snowmobilers, and 4x4-drivers. The former outdoors ethic insists that man most enjoys nature when feeling small within it. The latter claims that man's love of the wild grows from his dominion over it. Neither side shows much appreciation for the other's chosen creed, raising a series of seemingly intractable concerns: Do parks and recreational areas demand a particular kind of use? And, more importantly, who has the right to tell me what I can and cannot do on public lands?

As the result of a lawsuit brought against the National Parks Service (NPS) by a San Francisco environmental activist group, the Bluewater Network, jet skis and all other personal watercraft (PWC) will soon disappear from Utah's Glen Canyon National Recreation area. Bluewater Network alleges that the presence of PWC in National Parks compromises the Parks Service's chartered responsibility to protect park resources for future generations. PWC manufacturers have responded to charges that a single day's ride on a PWC produces as much smog-forming air pollution as 100,000 miles of passenger car driving. However, there's little they can do to combat Bluewater Network's second complaint, namely, that "the aggravating, high-pitched noise of jetskis destroys the experience for other recreational users."

Glen Canyon National Recreation Area is currently studying the effects of PWC use on Lake Powell recreation. During an ordinary summer season, jetskis crowd the enormous reservoir. As part of the settlement with Bluewater Network, the over-arching Parks Service policy states that PWC will be banned from all NPS areas unless that area's "enabling legislation, resources, values, other visitor uses, and overall management objectives" deem PWC use appropriate. Starting September 15, 2002, PWC were no longer allowed in National Recreation Areas until the completion of analysis regarding their use. Glen Canyon won't finish its study until 2003. If the study finds that PWC are compatible with Lake Powell recreation, the craft will be allowed back on the lake; if not, they could be banished indefinitely.

PWC enthusiasts have mobilized to counter the threatened ban. The Blue Ribbon Coalition, the national lobbying group for outdoor recreation rights, joined the fight in June 2002, promising to help ensure continued PWC access on the lake. The group's motto reads: "Preserving our natural resources *for* the public instead of *from* the public." The case for the PWC side centers on recreationalist rights and choice. Despite ample rhetoric from both sides, the question of whose ideal nature the National Parks should protect remains unresolved.

Lake Powell appears representative of the battle in which low-tech environmentalists face off with mechanized thrill-seekers. In many ways it is, but a rich irony mocks the battle over a "natural" experience on Lake Powell: there's little natural about the lake to begin with. The hordes of RVs and houseboats parading the recreation area and the fact that it is, after all, a dam seem to place it firmly in the grips of the nature-dominators. Fighting for a PWC ban on the lake seems an almost absurd position in such an unnatural setting. On the other hand, conservationists should not have to wait until gas and oil leaks contaminate the reservoir—which would threaten surrounding agriculture, as well as the populations of Las Vegas and Los Angeles—and requre draining the whole "dam" thing.

Mark Kirby attended rugged Deep Springs, one of the few colleges in the US that include mending fences on their curricula. His cowboy training gave him the skills to cover the Grand Canyon, Utah and northern Nevada for Let's Go: Southwest USA 2002, the inaugural year of the Southwest book. Although he's gone on to routes in New Zealand and the Pacific, he remains a dedicated Southwesterner.

FOOD

Despite the fact that Page transforms into a bustling, cosmopolitan center for half the year, dining options in town barely escape the hum-drum steak, potatoes, and Mexican cuisine so pervasive in the area. Most eateries lie on Lake Powell Blvd., though some gather along N. Navajo Dr. There are two important bonuses to the over-abundance of Western cooking: hearty "cowboy appetite" portions at bargain "ranch-hand" prices. If the meager choices have got you down, plan your own meal at **Safeway,** 650 Elm St. (☎ 645-8155).

Ranch House Grill, 819 N. Navajo Dr. (☎ 645-1420). Try their breakfasts. The owner picked the name to evoke generous helpings of food, and his restaurant delivers. Bulging 3-egg omelettes ($4-6) come with hash browns and toast, biscuits and gravy, or two pancakes. Open daily 6am-3pm; breakfast served all day. ❶

The Sandwich Place, 662 Elm St. (☎ 645-5267) in Page plaza. "Fast food fit for grownups," including the standard regimen of deli subs and sandwiches ($4-5). Philly natives would be proud of the cheese steak ($6). Open M-Sa 11am-9pm. ❶

Dos Amigos Restaurant and Cantina, 287 N. Lake Powell Blvd. (☎ 645-9394) in the Quality Inn. Prepares delectable Mexican fare and furnishes a stunning view and patio. Deals include a bargain list of lunch specials ($5-6) and an a la carte menu (tacos begin at $2.50) that fits even the tightest of budgets. Dinners start at $11, but include a soup/salad bar. Restaurant open 7am-11pm; cantina 10am-midnight. ❸

◎ SIGHTS

Jaded with the thrills of cigarette boats and jet skis, many visitors to Lake Powell seek out slightly more sedate, but equally enthralling ways to spend a day. Both the **Rainbow Bridge National Monument** and **Antelope Canyon** draw countless visitors, who revel in awe at the exquisite artistry of water at work on sandstone canvas.

RAINBOW BRIDGE NATIONAL MONUMENT. The damming of Lake Powell created easy access to Rainbow Bridge, originally a remote wonder of the natural world. Prior to the dam, visiting the world's tallest natural bridge (290 ft.) required a journey of at least three days. Now, tourists are whisked there and back in under 5hr. on snazzy cruise ships. Despite its current tourist-attraction status, the arch remains sacred to area native cultures, a sacredness that reaches back through centuries. Out of respect for this sacredness, visitors are asked not to approach, climb on, or pass through this breathtaking lesson in erosional art. *Nonnezoshi,* or "rainbow turned to stone" in Navajo, is said to bring trouble to those who pass under it without due prayer and reverence.

Hiking to Rainbow Bridge on Navajo land requires a **hiking permit,** obtainable by writing Navajo Nation Parks and Recreation Department. *(Box 9000, Window Rock, AZ 86515)* or calling ☎ 871-6647. Most visitors, however, come by boat. A courtesy dock floats about ½ mi. from the bridge, and is reachable after 4hr. ride from either the Wahweap, Halls Crossing, or Bullfrog Marinas. Only the park concessionaire, **ARAMARK,** has permission to offer guided tours. *(☎ 800-528-6154. 7hr. full-day tours with lunch $105, children $69; 5hr. half-day tours $79, children $55.)*

ANTELOPE CANYON. Every visit to Antelope Canyon is unique because the precise angle of the sun shining through the narrow canyon opening creates a gallery of light and shadow that changes every moment. Photographers, both professional and amateur, delight in this natural studio. The canyon was rediscovered by a 12-year old girl shepherding sheep in the area in 1931, which ushered in its era as a tourist attraction. For ages, Native Americans have approached this canyon, called *Tse bighanilini* ("the place where water runs through rocks") in Navajo, with profound respect and spiritual reverence. Although the English "Antelope Canyon" lacks the Navajo's poetic flavor, visitors to the canyon cannot help but feel the same sense of reverence.

Antelope Canyon is divided by Rte. 98 into two parts: upper and lower. **Upper Antelope,** the most frequently visited, is most accessible and arguably the easier to appreciate. Descending **lower Antelope** requires climbing ladders and slipping through extremely narrow gaps. *($5 Navajo use fee; shuttle to upper canyon or mandatory guide services in lower canyon $12.50.)* For info on Antelope Canyon, stop by the Navajo Nation's **kiosk** on Rte. 98 just west of the Navajo power plant. Private tour rates are pricier than driving up to the kiosk and making arrangements directly through Navajo Nation. Locals maintain that the best viewing time is between 11am and 2pm; if you need to kill a few hours, head to Antelope Point for a swim.

OTHER (DAM) SIGHTS. For a low-key and highly informational afternoon, visit the **John Wesley Powell Museum,** where friendly staff extend the legacy of the one-armed explorer, war-hero, professor, and bureaucrat. Visitors Center inside, long-boat outside. *(6 N. Lake Powell Blvd. ☎ 645-9496. Open in summer M-Sa 9am-5pm; $7.)* The **Carl Hayden Visitors Center** at the Glen Canyon Dam guides visitors into the guts of the concrete behemoth, though in scaled-back fashion due to security measures. *(Adjacent to the dam on U.S. 89. ☎ 608-6404. Tours in summer every 30min. 8:30am-4pm; off-season every hr. Visitors Center open May-Sept. daily 8am-6pm; Oct.-Apr. 8am-5pm. Free.)*

▟ OUTDOOR ACTIVITIES

Water cowboys's dreams have come true at Lake Powell, one of the last places where jet ski rule the scene, even though their ubiquity is threatened by proposed bans. Recreation opportunities span all budgets: the affluent put in as far as six months in advance for coveted week-long rentals of houseboats while the thrifty enjoy inflatable rafts and beaches. Anglers have plenty of nooks to explore, but must do so with an Arizona or Utah fishing license. Page sells Arizona licences, which are acknowledged in Utah after being stamped ($8). Fishing is year-round. There's also plenty of hiking in narrow slot canyons, near the dam and in areas like Escalante Canyons (see p. 308) on the lake's northwest shores. Tight budget or not, each vehicle must pay a $10 fee to enter the Glen Canyon Recreation Area.

BOATING AND WATER SPORTS

Remember, your leisure pleasure is measured in horsepower. Rentals from **ARAMARK,** although convenient, tend to be pricier than renting from vendors in Page. Boats and PWC's (personal watercrafts or jet skis) are rented at each marina, with rates varying little. For a pricier, but more intimate, option, houseboats are welcomed on the lake. A 36ft. boat, sleeping 6, can be your home for 3 days and 2 nights, if you're willing to fork up the cash.

Wahweap Marina Boat Rentals (☎ 800-528-6154, ext. 8109 or 645-1111). You name it, they have it, on the water and ready to go, albeit for a good chunk of dough. Renters must be 18+ with valid ID. Prices are comparable with the other ARAMARK marinas. 14-23 ft. power boats $26 per hr., half-day $87, full-day $130, $575 per day for the "big dog"; personal watercraft $69 per hr., half-day $170, full-day $255; kayaks $10 per hour, $20 half-day, full-day $29. Reservations recommended.

Lake Powell Marine Vacations (☎ 800-530-3406), behind the Mobil on Lake Powell Blvd. A dependable alternative to pricey Wahweap rentals. jet skis $175-200 per day, speed boats $225-250 per day. Water skis, wake-boards, knee-boards available. Open M-F 9am-5pm.

Twin Finn Dive Center, 811 Vista Ave. (☎645-3114). PADI master trainer leads dives for all levels in Lake Powell, including PADI certification courses. Snorkel packages $9 per day, scuba packages $45, kayaks $35, canoes $60. Open M-Sa 7:30am-5:30pm daily.

Wilderness River Adventures, 50 S. Lake Powell Blvd. (☎645-3279) runs the only day-long float trips on the Colorado below the dam. The trips, conducted on motorized rafts, take visitors down the Colorado between towering cliffs and past the spectacular Horse-shoe Bend. Half-day $59; child $49.

DAY HIKING

Horsebend Overlook (1 mi. round-trip, ½hr.). 5 mi. south of the dam on U.S. 89. Look for turnoff just south of Mile 545, where a dirt road ascends a small hill just west of the highway. After parking on the shoulder and following the road from the hilltop, hikers behold the magnificent Horseshoe Bend. Traveling south, the river diverged around a tall sandstone spire, creating a dramatic bend in the canyon. Sunsets set the scene for a dramatic natural light show. The conditions at Horseshoe Bend will likely mirror those that created Rainbow Bridge in a few million years.

Wiregrass Canyon (6 mi. round-trip, 3-5hr.). Natural bridges, precariously perched boulders, and colorful escarpments reward the hiker willing to hike this strenuous trail. The route begins west of Lake Powell, near Big Water, UT, and descends a wash to the shores of the lake. To reach the trailhead, follow U.S. 89 west to the sign for "Big Water City" between Miles 7 and 8. Follow signs for the Glen Canyon Recreation Area and park in the Wiregrass Canyon Backcountry Use Area parking lot. The roads are passable to all vehicles when dry and completely impassable when wet. There is no actual trail to the lake—hikers scramble and follow cairns through the wash. Hiking in the wash leads past two natural bridges and several drop-offs that become waterfalls during rainstorms. Don't make the mistake of getting caught in a flash flood in an attempt to see such a spectacle. Since the hike ends at the lake, a strategically parked car along U.S. 89 or an exhausting swim to Lone Rock is needed to avoid the out-and-back hike.

Water Holes Canyon (variable distances and times). For another variation on the slot-canyon theme, visit the accessible narrows of Water Holes Canyon. The entrance to the canyon lies at Mile 542 on U.S. 89. Off the highway and up the canyon, the walls shrink into a dazzling section of narrows. In the other direction, hikers can go all the way to the Colorado, though this route requires a rope. The narrows of the canyon lie within the boundaries of the Navajo Reservation, and hiking the canyon requires a $5 permit. The best place to obtain a permit is at the Antelope Canyon kiosk on Rte. 98.

GRAND CANYON

ARIZONA

Home to the Grand Canyon, the majority of the Navajo Reservation, seven national forests, and three major cities, Arizona constantly defies its image as a land of endless stretches of desert highway. Surely, this barren land exists. The dry scrub of the Sonoran desert makes for a starkly beautiful landscape, interrupted only by myriad species of cacti or a dusty pit stop town. Driving up into the temperate forests around Flagstaff or through the red rocks of Sedona, however, exposes you to an otherworldly Arizona whose vistas can captivate you for hours, days, or weeks.

The ecological spectrum captured in the state is matched only by its cultural diversity. The huge metropolis of Phoenix provides a somewhat overwhelming big sister to the more manageable and cosmopolitan Tucson, and while these cities have made their permanent mark on the state, their existence is barely felt by the small towns that dot the legendary Route 66 and hug the Mexican border. The Navajo Nation, occupying the northeastern corner of the state, greets travelers with a distinct culture, boundless vistas, a deep sense of history, and a poverty that serves as reminder of the experience of Native Americans in the US.

From the Red Rock spires and buttes of Sedona to the spiny Sonoran Desert and the vast expanse of the Grand Canyon, Arizona is a playground for the nature lover. Adrenalin junkies can get their fix biking Sedona's single track, hiking in the Coconino Forest, or rock climbing in the red rocks. Must-see drives expose travelers to the crayola-box wonders of the Painted Desert and Petrified Forest, the metamorphosis of terrain along the Mt. Lemmon Drive, and the cliff dwellings of the Apache Trail. While in Arizona, you can easily avoid civilization, but the world-class museums and architectural curiosities of Tucson and Phoenix are not to be missed if you have time to venture into urban bustle and air-conditioning.

◪ HIGHLIGHTS OF ARIZONA

ARIZONA DESERT. Bisbee (p. 148), a laid-back artists' colony, offers picture-perfect weather and wandering in the Southeastern desert. **Chiricahua National Monument** (p. 150) offers a refreshingly untouristed wonderland of volcanic rock.

ARCHITECTURE. Frank Lloyd Wright's **Taliesin West** (p. 100) and Paolo Soleri's **Arcosanti** (p. 120) exemplify the creative architectural theories of the masters.

ON THE RESERVATION. The red-hued cliffs of **Canyon de Chelly** (p. 123) and the rainbow-tinted sands of the **Painted Desert** (p. 119) afford some of the most alluring views in the state.

GREATER PHOENIX   ☎ 602

The name Phoenix was chosen for a small farming community in the Sonoran desert by Anglo settlers who believed that their oasis had risen from the ashes of ancient Native American settlements like the legendary phoenix of Egyptian mythology. The 20th century has seen this unlikely metropolis live up to its name; the expansion of water resources, the proliferation of railroad transportation, and the introduction of air-conditioning have fueled Phoenix's ascent to its standing among America's leading cities. Shiny high-rises now crowd the business district, while a vast web of six-lane highways and strip malls surrounds the downtown area. Phoenix's rise has not been

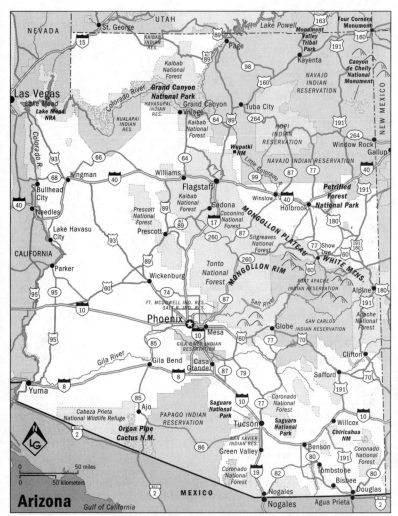

Arizona *Gulf of California*

without turmoil, though: its greatest asset, the sun, is also its greatest nemesis. The scorching heat and arid landscape may put a damper on expansion, as the wet stuff is now in short supply. For the traveler, the Phoenix sun can also be both friend and foe. During the balmy winter months, tourists, golfers, and business travelers flock to the resort-perfect temperatures. In the summer, the city crawls into its air-conditioned shell as temperatures climb to an average of 100°F and lodging prices plummet.

◪ INTERCITY TRANSPORTATION

Flights: Sky Harbor International (☎ 273-3300; www.phxskyharbor.com), just southeast of downtown. Take the Valley Metro Red Line bus into the city (5:45am-10pm, $1.25). The larg-

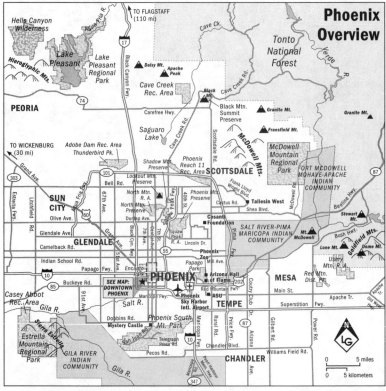

Phoenix Overview

est city in the Southwest, Phoenix is a major airline hub, and tends to be an affordable and convenient destination. **America West** (☎800-238-9292) and **Southwest** (☎800-435-9792) are the busiest airlines. To: **Los Angeles** (1 hr., 10 per day, $100); **San Francisco** (2 hr., 7-10 per day, $201); **Dallas** (1-2 hr., 5 per day, $230); **New York** (4-5 hr., 3-6 per day, $240); **Boston** (5 hr., 2-5 per day, $215).

Buses: Greyhound, 2115 E. Buckeye Rd. (☎389-4200, www.greyhound.com). To: **El Paso** (8hr., 13 per day, $35); **Los Angeles** (7hr., 12 per day, $35); **San Diego** (8hr.; 6 per day; M-Th $47.50, F-Su $49); **Tucson** (2hr., 13 per day, $14). Open 24hr. There is no direct rail service to Phoenix, but **Amtrak** (☎800-USA-RAIL, www.amtrak.com) operates connector buses to and from rail stations in Tucson and Flagstaff for those interested in train travel. The Greyhound bus station is their busiest connecting Thruway motorcoach service location.

◉ LOCAL TRANSPORTATION

Public Transportation, Downtown Phoenix: Valley Metro (☎253-5000). Most lines run to and from Central Station, at Central and Van Buren St. Routes tend to operate M-F 5am-8pm with reduced service on Sa. Fare $1.25; disabled, seniors, and children 60¢. All-day pass $3.60, 10-ride pass $12. Bus passes and system maps at the Terminal. In Tempe, the City of Tempe Transit Store, 502 S. College Ave., Ste. 101, serves as public transit headquarters. The red line runs to and from Phoenix, and last few stops of the yellow line are also in

Tempe. The red line also extends beyond Tempe to service Mesa. Bus passes and system maps at the Terminal. Loloma Station, just south of Indian School and Scottsdale Rd., is Scottsdale's main hub for local traffic. The green line runs along Thomas St. to Phoenix.

Taxis: Yellow Cab, ☎252-5252. **Discount Taxi,** ☎254-1999.

Car Rental: Enterprise Rent-a-car, 1402 N. Central St. (☎257-4177; www.enterprise.com), with other offices throughout the city. Compact cars at around $45 per day, with lower weekly and monthly rates. No surcharge for drivers over 21 (call ahead if under 21, as there are different requirements). A valid credit card and driver's license are required. N. Central St. office open M-F 7:30am-6pm, Sa 9am-noon; other offices' hours vary.

■ ORIENTATION

The intersection of **Central Ave.** and **Washington St.** marks the heart of downtown. Central Ave. runs north-south, Washington St. east-west. One of Phoenix's peculiarities is that numbered avenues and streets both run north-south; avenues are numbered sequentially west from Central, while streets are numbered east. Think of Central Ave. as the heart of town; facing north, the first road to your right is **1st St.,** the first to your left is **1st Ave.** Large north-south thoroughfares include **7th St., 16th St., 7th Ave.,** and **19th Ave. McDowell Rd., Van Buren St., Indian School Rd.,** and **Camelback Rd.** are major east-west arteries.

Greater Phoenix includes a number of smaller, independent municipalities that sometimes have different street-naming schemes. Due to the sprawl of the greater Phoenix area, you'll need a car to see many of the sights that are located outside of downtown.

NEIGHBORHOODS

Driven by dirt-cheap desert land and flat landscape, sprawl has gotten out of control in Phoenix. Once a series of independent communities, the numerous town ships of "the Valley of the Sun" (as metropolitan Phoenix is known) now bleed into one another in a continuous chain of strip malls, office parks, slums and super-resorts. The *de facto* unification of all the disparate communities has not, however, resulted in homogenization or equalization—some are magnets for tourists and money, others for illegal immigrants and crime. Since many of the most intriguing and happening locales are located outside of the downtown proper, it's useful to get acquainted with some of Phoenix' outer townships.

Just to the east of downtown Phoenix and south of the Salt River lies **Tempe,** the town that lays claim to both the third largest university in the US and the nightlife to prove it. Don't make the mistake of leaving town without experiencing at least one night as a Sun Devil (i.e. PARTY!).

East of Tempe, the suburban paradise of **Mesa** stretches out along Rte. 202. Tamer than its collegiate neighbor, Mesa is home to one of the largest Mormon colonies outside of Utah as well as a host of cheap eats and chain motels in a family-friendly environment.

Scottsdale, north of Mesa and northeast of downtown, is the playground of the (sometimes idle) rich. The very sound of the word conjures up images of expensive cars, immaculate homes, and world-renowned resorts. With its pricey accommodations but great sights, Scottsdale is a great place to visit (from Tempe).

■ PRACTICAL INFORMATION

Phoenix's explosive expansion has caused it to outgrow its original 602 area code. The city is split into three area codes, with 602 limited to Phoenix proper, 623 for

ARIZONA

IN RECENT NEWS

SHERIFF JOE

Ask anyone in Maricopa County and they're bound to have an opinion. Indeed, ask many law enforcement officials and civil rights activists country- and world-wide and they, too, are bound to have something to say about a certain Arizona sheriff. So what is it about Sheriff Joe Arpaio that reaps so much attention? One word: controversy.

In charge of the most populated county in Arizona, Sheriff Joe has instituted some divisive initiatives since his election in 1992. Among them are: the building of "tent city," in which prisoners spend blisteringly hot summer nights in the Arizona desert in old army surplus tents; the banning of smoking, coffee, pornographic magazines, and movies in prisons; and an interesting change to the prison wardrobe—mandatory pink underwear for all inmates. Yet, more than anything else, two issues have garnered the loudest reaction from challengers of Sheriff Arpaio's tactics: the establishment of the first female chain gang in the country and the installation of a webcam in a prison holding cell. Vociferous outcry over these acts from human rights groups both domestically and internationally has not deterred Sheriff Arpaio, though.

To be sure, over the past decade, Sheriff Arpaio has had little reason to back down from his aggressive policies, as he has garnered incredibly high public approval ratings (up to 85% in 1996). The reason seems to stem not so much from his charismatic appeal, but rather from the perception that Sheriff Arpaio's strict approach to punishment produces results.

(continued on next page)

western greater Phoenix, and 480 for the East Valley (including Scottsdale, Tempe and Mesa). As a consequence, even calls made within the city require an area code. *Unless otherwise noted, all listings here are within the 602 area code.*

GREATER PHOENIX

Visitor Info: Phoenix and Valley of the Sun Convention and Visitors Center (☎254-6500 or 877-225-5749, recorded info and events calendar ☎252-5588; www.phoenix-cvb.com). Downtown location: 2nd and Adams St. Open M-F 8am-5pm. Free Internet (5min. limit). Biltmore Fashion Park location: 24th St. and East Camelback. Open daily 8am-5pm. Camping and outdoors information available at the **Bureau of Land Management Office,** 222 N. Central (☎417-9200). In Tempe, try the **Tempe Convention and Business Center,** 51 W. 3rd St., #105. (☎480-894-81581; www.tempecvb.com. Open daily 8:30am-5pm.) The **Mesa Convention and Visitors Bureau,** 120 N. Center St., provides info about that neighborhood. (☎480-827-4700; www.mesacvb.com. Open daily 8am-5pm.) The **Scottsdale Convention and Visitors Bureau,** 7343 Scottsdale Mall Rd., treats visitors to a bounty of info. (☎480-945-8481; www.ci.scottsdale.az.us. Open daily 8am-6pm.)

Police: Phoenix Police Department, ☎262-6151; **Tempe Police Department,** ☎480-966-6211; **Mesa Police Department,** ☎480-644-2211; and the **Scottsdale Police Department,** ☎480-312-5000.

Hotlines: Crisis Hotline (☎254-4357). 24hr. **Gay Hotline** (☎234-2752). Daily 10am-10pm.

Hospital: Arizona State Hospital, 2500 E. Van Buren (☎244-1331). In Tempe and Mesa **Tempe St. Luke's,** 1500 S. Mill Ave. (☎480-784-5500). **Scottsdale Health Center North,** ☎480-860-3000, serves the Scottsdale area.

Internet Access: Burton Barr Central Library, 1221 N. Central Ave. (☎262-4636). Open M-Th 9am-9pm, F-Sa 9am-6pm, Su noon-9pm. In Tempe, try **Tempe Public Library,** 3500 S. Rural Rd. (☎480-350-555. Open M-Th 9am-9pm, F-Sa 9am-5:30pm, Su noon-5:30pm.) In Mesa, **Mesa City Library,** 64 E. 1st St. (☎480-644-3100. Open M-Th 9:30am-9pm, F-Sa 9:30am-6pm, Su noon-9pm.) or **@Cafe** inside **Michael Monti's Mesa Grill ❶,** 1233 S. Alma School Rd. Free and fast Internet use with purchase. Huge breakfast *burros* $3. (☎480-834-5144. Open 7am-1:30pm daily.) The **Civic Center Library,** 3839 Civic Center Rd., serves Scottsdale. (☎480-312-2476. Open M-Th 9am-9pm, F-Sa 10am-6pm, Su 1pm-5pm.)

Post Office: 522 N. Central Ave. (☎407-2028), downtown. Open M-F 8:30am-5pm. General delivery: 1441 E. Buckeye

Rd. (☎407-2051). Open M-F 7:30am-5pm. **ZIP code:** 85026. **Tempe:** 233 E. Southern Ave. (☎800-275-8777). Open M-F 8:30am-5pm. **ZIP code:** 85281. **Mesa:** 135 N. Center St. (☎800-275-8777). Open M-F 8:30am-5pm. **ZIP code:** 85201.**Scottsdale:** 7242 E. Osborne Rd. (☎480-407-2042). Open M-F 8:30am-5pm. **ZIP Code:** 85351.

⌂ ACCOMMODATIONS

Budget travelers should consider visiting Phoenix during July and August when motels slash their prices by as much as 70%. In the winter, when temperatures drop and vacancies are few, prices go up; make reservations if possible. The reservation-less should cruise the rows of motels on **Van Buren St.** east of downtown, toward the airport. Parts of this area can be unsafe; *guests should examine a motel thoroughly before checking in.* Although they are more distant, the areas around Papago Fwy. and Black Canyon Hwy. are loaded with motels and may present some safer options.

Catering to those whose money folds rather than jingles, greater Phoenix contains some of the nation's best luxury and high-end resort hotels. Although during the high season they are out of reach to most budget travelers, during the baking summer those who brave the intimidating swank will find empty rooms and ready deals. If you can stand the heat, you can live like the beautiful people, if only for a night or two. More affordable accommodations are limited, especially in Tempe/Mesa, and tend to take the form of generic, albeit respectable, chain motels.

As an alternative, **Mi Casa Su Casa/Old Pueblo Homestays Bed and Breakfast,** P.O. Box 950, Tempe 85280 (☎800-456-0682), arranges stays in B&Bs throughout Arizona, New Mexico, southern Utah, southern Nevada, and southern California. (Open M-F 9am-5pm, Sa 9am-noon. $45 and up.)

DOWNTOWN PHOENIX

Metcalf House (HI-AYH), 1026 N. 9th St. (☎254-9803), a few blocks northeast of downtown. Look for the house with lots of foliage out front. From Central Station, take bus #10 down 7th St. to Roosevelt St., walk 2 blocks east to 9th St., and turn left—the hostel is ½ block north in a shady and quiet residential area. Last bus leaves at 8:30pm. The neighborhood has seen better days, so the coin lockers available in the dorms are probably a good idea. The ebullient owner, who gushes helpful advice about the area, fosters a lively community in this decorative renovated house. Evening gab sessions common on the front porch. Dorm-style rooms with wooden bunks adjoin a kitchen and com-

(continued from previous page)

Residents voice relief in the fac that their sheriff, as they see it, vehe mently refuses to cosset criminals.

Sheriff Arpaio's critics point out however, that some crime rates have risen during Sheriff Arpaio's reign. Fo example, during the seven-year stretch from 1992 to 1999, Phoenix saw gur robbery rates rise from 115.8 to 154.2 per 100,000 people. Whether the changes instituted by the sheriff wil be vindicated by long-term effects remains to be seen.

Recently, Sheriff Arpaio was named as a possible candidate for the Repub lican Party's bid for Arizona governor After much speculation over whethe the man so popular in Maricopa County could win the statewide elec tion for Arizona's most powerful public servant, Sheriff Arpaio withdrew him self from the race. For Arizonans, his pulling out brought mixed reaction Admirers of the sheriff were upset he wouldn't be increasing his jurisdiction and overall influence, but were at the same time relieved he could focus his energies on the greater metro area Opponents of Sheriff Arpaio though the opposite—they were relieved he would not be increasing his rule, bu disconcerted that he would continue to engage his adamant *modus ope. andi* over Maricopa County.

In the near future, both opponents and proponents alike will watch with baited breath as Sheriff Arpaio imple ments a Crime of the Week campaign in which pictures of everyone arrested the day before will be posted online Only time will tell exactly what the sheriff has up his sleeve for the future of law enforcement in this pocket o the Southwest.

THE BIG SPLURGE

LIVIN' LARGE

Phoenix is a world-renowned resort destination, and it has some of the oldest and swankest hotels in the United States. During the winter high season, these plush accommodations are out of reach, but in the blazing summer months hotels are desperate enough to offer choice discounts. Live like a king and pay like a lowly duke.

■ **Arizona Biltmore,** 24th St. and Missouri (☎800-950-0086; www.arizonabiltmore.com). Designed by Frank Lloyd Wright, this lavish hotel has everything a vacationer could hope for, and the price tag to back it up. Whether you prefer golfing, hiking, biking, relaxing at the spa, or any combination thereof, it can all be found at this centrally located bastion of comfort. Prices from late May to Sept. are significantly lower than during the cooler months, though still steep for the region, starting at $175 per night. ❺

The Wyndham Buttes, 2000 Westcourt Way (☎480-225-9000; www.wyndham.com/buttesresort), in Tempe at the crossroads of Broadway and 48th St. High atop the, well, butte sits one of Tempe's most striking hotels. With two restaurants and an ever-helpful staff, the Buttes has some great deals for summer (June to mid-Aug.) travelers, with rooms starting at $89 per night. ❺

Marriot Camelback Inn, 5402 E. Lincoln Dr. (☎480-905-7997; www.camelbackinn.com), in Scottsdale. What's that smell? Oh right, that's the unmistakable scent of piles of money. This mother of the Marriot chain was built in the 1930s, and has been pampering the wealthy and their egos ever since. With amenities galore (including a renowned spa and 2 golf courses), and plummeting prices from early June to early Sept. ($159, down from $429 in the winter). ❺

mon room. Bikes for rent, and discounts to some city sights included in the price. Check-in 7-10am and 5-10pm. Chores required. $15. ❶

ExtendedStay America, 7345 W. Bell Rd. (☎623-487-0020; fax 487-0022; www.extendedstay.com), at 73rd Ave. Also in **Scottsdale** at 15501 N. Scottsdale Rd. (☎480-607-3767) and in **Mesa** at 455 W. Baseline Rd. (☎480-632-0201). Chain specializing in medium-term business travelers. Steep prices for nightly accommodation, but a bargain at the weekly rate. Immaculate rooms come with complete kitchenettes and laptop Internet hookups. Daily $55; weekly $279. ❸

YMCA Downtown Phoenix, 350 N. 1st Ave. (☎253-6181). Another option in the downtown area, the YMCA provides small, single-occupancy rooms and shared bathrooms. Various athletic facilities. A small supply of women's rooms available. Ask at the desk about storing valuables. Open everyday 9am-10pm. 18+. Daily $30; weekly $119. ❷

TEMPE

Mission Palms, 60 E. 5th St. (☎480-894-1400; www.missionpalms.com). At the base of the Tempe's Hayden Butte, this deluxe hotel is a steal in the summer for $99 per night (with prices more than doubling in the winter). Choose among the smorgasbord of amenities at your fingertips (to wit: 2 hot tubs, a pool, health club, tennis center, and standard laptop Internet hookups) to pass the time, all the while knowing that raucous Mill Ave. is merely a minute's walk away. ❺

Best Western Inn of Tempe, 670 N. Scottsdale Rd. (☎480-784-2233; www.innoftempe.com), next to U.S. 60 and Scottsdale Dr. Overall, a very well kept hotel with a friendly staff, this branch of the chain has digital cable and laptop Internet hookups in every room. Summer rooms start at $59; winter $99. ❺

Super 8 Motel, 1020 E. Apache Blvd. (☎480-967-8891; www.super8.com). Chain with digital cable standard in every room; continental breakfast, too. Consistently some of the best rates in town. Apr.-Aug. daily $39; weekly $190. Sept.-Mar. $49/$250. ❸

Days Inn Tempe, 1221 E. Apache Blvd. (☎480-968-7793; www.daysinn.com). A chain combining tidy rooms with no frills prices. Pool. Rooms in summer: $49; winter $79. ❹

SCOTTSDALE

Econolodge, Scottsdale on Fifth, 6935 5th Ave. (☎480-994-9461). Clean rooms and low prices for the location make this branch of the national chain a deal in the Scottsdale area. Singles $55. ❸

MESA

Best Western Dobson Ranch Inn & Resort, 1666 S. Dobson Rd. (☎480-831-7000 or 800-528-1356; www.dobsonranchinn.com). One block south of Highway 60 on Baseline Rd. Submitting its claim as the best resort in the area, the Ranch is a great alternative for those looking for exceptional value at a low cost. The two pools, a restaurant and massive banquet facilities are available for as little as $55 in the summer. ❹

Lost Dutchman Motel, 560 S. Country Club Dr. (☎480-969-2200). A good location by many restaurants and clean rooms are the best reasons to stay at the Dutchman. Kitchenettes available for $3. Check in 3pm; check out noon. Summer rates hover around $37 per night/$159 per week, with winter rates doubling the warmer months' prices. ❸

🗋 FOOD

While much of the Phoenix food scene seems to revolve around shopping mall food courts and expensive restaurants, rest assured that hidden jewels can be found. Downtowners feed mainly at small coffeehouses, most of which close on weekends. **McDowell** or **Camelback Rd.** offer a (small) variety of Asian restaurants. The **Arizona Center,** an open-air shopping gallery at 3rd St. and Van Buren, boasts food venues, fountains, and palm trees. Sports bars and grilles hover around the America West Arena and Bank One Ballpark. Tempe's residents fill up on bar food in the many hybrid resto-bars that cater to college kids, while both Scottsdale and Mesa have affordable and delicious options hidden in their bourgeois swanktitude or Mormon sobriety. The *New Times* (☎271-4000) makes extensive restaurant recommendations.

DOWNTOWN PHOENIX

Los Dos Molinos, 8646 S. Central Ave. (☎243-9113). From downtown, head south on Central Ave. Go very far, and once you're sure you've gone too far, go farther. Once you leave the barrio, it comes up suddenly on your right. One look and you'll know why you've made the trip; Los Dos Molinos is lively, colorful, and fun. Locals throng here on weekends, filling the indoor restaurant and the colorful courtyard, and spilling onto the street. Come early; they don't take reservations. Enchiladas $3.50, burritos $5.25-7. Open Tu-F 11am-2:30pm and 5-9pm, Sa 11am-9pm. ❶

5 & Diner, 5220 N. 16th St. (☎264-5220), with branches dotting the greater metro area. 24hr. service and all the sock-hop music that one can stand. Vinyl booths, smiley service, and innumerable juke boxes teach you what the fifties *could* have been. Burgers go for $6-7 and sandwiches are $5-7. You can get the best milkshakes in town for only $3-4. Afternoon blue plate specials change daily, but are always your money's worth (M-F 11am-4pm, $3-6). Outdoor seating with view of scenic N. 16th St. available. ❶

Gourmet House of Hong Kong, 1438 E. McDowell Rd. (☎253-4859). For those who think that quality Chinese food vanishes between the Mississippi and the West Coast, this no-frills restaurant will surely impress. They serve so many dishes that the menu comes with a table of contents. 40 kinds of soup, noodle dishes, and rare Hong Kong specialities (such as chicken feet) are unceremoniously dished out. No non-smoking section. Entrees $5-7. Lunch specials $3-5. Take-out available. Open M-Th 11am-9:30pm, F-Sa 11am-10:30pm, Su 11am-9pm. ❶

La Tolteca, 1205 E. Van Buren St. (☎253-1511). A local favorite, this unassuming cafeteria-style restaurant/Mexican grocery serves up uncommercialized Mexican fare in *grande* portions. Familiar dishes are offered alongside specialities like *cocido* soup ($5) and refreshing *horchata*, a sweet milk and rice drink ($1-2). Big burritos $3-4, dinner plates $5-6. Open daily 6:30am-9pm. ❶

Downtown Phoenix

🏠 ACCOMMODATIONS
Metcalf House, **6**
YMCA, **7**

🍎 FOOD
Gourmet House
of Hong Kong, **5**
La Tolteca, **9**

🍺 NIGHTLIFE
Ain't Nobody's Biz, **2**
Char's Has of Blues, **1**
Mr. Lucky's, **3**
Phoenix Live, **8**
Willow House, **4**

TO 🏠**1** (2mi)

E. Oak St.
E. Alvarado Rd.

W. Cypress St.
Heard Museum
E. Monte Vista Rd.
TO 🍺**2** (2mi)

Monte Vista Rd.
E. Palm Ln.

N. 3rd St.
1st St.

E. Coronado Rd.

Phoenix Art Museum
E. McDowell Rd.
TO 🍺**5** (1mi)

🍺**4**
E. Brill St.

TO 🍺**3** (2mi)
W. Willetta St.
E. Willetta St.

N. 7th Ave.
N. 5th Ave.
N. Central Ave.
Burton Barr Central Library

W. Culver St.
10 Papago Freeway
10

Portland St.
E. Portland St.
🏠**6**

1st St.
Roosevelt St.
Roosevelt St.

7th Ave.
5th Ave.
3rd Ave.
1st Ave.
Central Ave.
Garfield St.
N. 9th St.

McKinley St.
McKinley St.
3rd St.
5th St.
7th St.

Pierce St.

Fillmore St.
Fillmore St.

✉
Taylor St.
Taylor St.
🍺**8**
Arizona Center
Phoenix Union Municipal Center

Polk St.
🏠**7**
Central Bus Station
Van Buren St.
TO 🍴**9** (100yds)
& ✚ (1.5mi)

Van Buren St.
Herberger Theater Center
S. 9th St.

Monroe St.
Museum of History
HERITAGE SQUARE

Adams St.
Orpheum Theater
Renaissance Square
Phoenix Civic Plaza
Arizona Science Center

Washington St.
Visitor ℹ Information
Symphony Hall
E. Washington St.

CESAR CHAVEZ PLAZA
PATRIOT'S SQUARE

Jefferson St.
✉
Greyhound
Jefferson St.

6th Ave.
5th Ave.
4th Ave.
3rd Ave.
2nd Ave.
1st Ave.
Madison
1st St.
America West Arena
3rd St.
Jefferson St.
TO SKY HARBOR INTERNATIONAL AIRPORT (3mi)

7th Ave.
Jackson St.
Bank One Ballpark
7th St.
E. Jackson St.

Union Station Amtrak
TO 🚌 GREYHOUND (3mi)

Buchanan St.
N
LG
0   600 yards
0   600 meters

ARIZONA

TEMPE

■ **Dos Gringos Trailer Park,** 216 E. University (☎480-968-7879). The best atmosphere in Tempe, bar-none. Dos, as it's affectionately known, draws people of all walks of life with its open, laid-back feel and its inexpensive yet tasty Mexican food. Deals include a Hangover Special ($5.25) that helps one recoup from the night before, and countless meals for under $6. Open M-Sa 10am-1am, Su noon-1am. ●

■ **Long Wong's,** 701 S. Mill Ave. (☎480-966-3147). Serving up six different flavors, Wong's has the best wings in town. A hybrid bar/restaurant run by a young staff with an animated spirit. $6 for six wings, $9 for 12. Half-price wings happy hour: M-F 4-8pm. Cover $1-5, depending on the act (mostly local). 21+ in the bar. Take-out available. Open Su-Th 10:30am-11pm, F-Sa 10:30am-12:30pm. ❷

SCOTTSDALE

Greasewoods Flats, 27500 N. Alma School Rd. (☎480-585-9430). With the most eclectic mix of patrons in Scottsdale, the Flats dishes out classic American cuisine at reasonable prices, including succulent hamburgers for $6-8. Rub elbows with hippies, bikers, yuppies, bobos, and everything in between. Open M-F 10am-11pm, Sa 10am-midnight, Su 10am-10pm. ❷

Sugar Bowl Ice Cream Parlor & Restaurant, 4005 N. Scottsdale Rd. (☎480-946-0051). Get out of the heat and into this fun and flavorsome ice cream parlor for all your sweet tooth needs, where the sundaes are piled high and thick ($3-5). Open M-Sa 11am-11pm, Su 11am-10pm. ●

MESA

Ripe Tomato Cafe, 745 W. Baseline Rd. (☎480-892-4340). The biggest, fluffiest omelettes ($6) this side of the desert fill up your entire plate for breakfast or lunch. Eat inside or out, but bring your appetite. Open 6am-2:30pm daily. ●

Bill Johnson's Big Apple, 950 E. Main St. (☎480-969-6504). The sawdust on the floor will great you at this country-western style restaurant, where the food is almost as good as the Old West decor. Pick from one of the largest selections of steak around, and sample the tangy homemade BBQ sauce. Kids eat free W. Open 6:30am-10pm daily. ❷

◪ ◪ NIGHTLIFE AND ENTERTAINMENT

BARS AND CLUBS

The free *New Times Weekly*, available on local magazine racks, lists club schedules for Phoenix's after-hours scene. The *Cultural Calendar of Events* covers area entertainment in three-month intervals. *The Source*, found in bars and clubs, covers gay and lesbian nightlife. As with other aspects of Phoenix, the nightlife and entertainment prospects are better in the cooler months, but there is always something going on no matter when you visit. The scene downtown is mixed—quality clubs clustered around the sports complexes and the Arizona Center compete with topless cabarets and seedy bars. Those of college age (literally or in spirit) may find Tempe's nightlife offerings more attractive (see page p. 98).

DOWNTOWN PHOENIX

■ **Char's Has the Blues,** 4631 N. 7th Ave. (☎230-0205). Char's houses local jazz acts, and the crowds are as enthusiastic as the bands. One of Phoenix's best for foot-tapping live music. 21+. Cover Tu-Sa $3-7. Open nightly 8pm-1am, with music starting at 9pm.

ARIZONA

Rte. 88, a.k.a. **Apache Trail,** winds from **Apache Junction,** a small mining town 40 mi. east of Phoenix, through the mountains along stunning stretches of forest, desert, and lake. The trail proper is approximately 50 mi. long, starting in Apache Junction and ending at Roosevelt Lake, with a 32 mi. unpaved stretch between Tortilla Flat and Roosevelt Lake. From there, in

TIME: 2hr. driving time

DISTANCE: 50 mi.

SEASON: year-round

order to get back to Apache Junction, either retrace your steps, or follow Rte. 88 eastward toward **Globe** (32 mi.), and then take U.S. 60 west to Apache Junction. It's wise to start early in the day; even in the summer, darkness falls quickly and early and some of the sights could be closed. The route is well-traveled and safe, but be sure to fill up the gas tank before setting out—past Apache Junction, the nearest gas is 61 mi. away on U.S. 188, heading toward Globe.

Before the drive enters park property, a few touristy sites will greet you. **Goldfield Ghost Town Mine Tours,** 5 mi. north of the U.S. 60 junction on Rte. 88, offers tours of the nearby mines and gold-panning in a resurrected ghost town. (☎ 480-983-0333. Open daily 10am-5pm. Mine tours $5, ages 6-12 $3; gold-panning $4.50.) Turn right off of the trail and onto nearby Mining Camp Rd.; 1 mi. up you'll find the ever-popular **Mining Camp Restaurant ❸.** Bring your appetite; meal tickets aren't cheap, but the food is delicious and all-you-can-eat. ($16, children $9, seniors $14.35. Open Oct.-June M-Sa 4-9pm, Su noon-9pm.) Back on the trail, the **Bluebird Mine Curio Shop** is a mile farther down and is the last sight before the trail enters park property. The Bluebird is an incredible resource for area history and stories of mining lore. (Open summer daily 6am-6pm; winter 7:30am-5pm.) The first sign of crossing the invisible line into protected land is the lack of billboard advertising, which is strictly prohibited. Electricity, unfortunately, is not; powerlines will be your constant companions throughout your route.

❶ LOST DUTCHMAN STATE PARK. Steep, red, and haunting, the **Superstition Mountains** derive their name from Pima Native American legends, but they could have just as easily been named for the strange lore surrounding the legendary gold mine hidden in their hills. In the 1840s, a Mexican explorer found gold in the area but was killed before he could reveal the location of the mine. More famous is the case of Jacob Waltz, the "Dutchman" for whom the park is named (despite his being German). During the 1880s, he brought out about $250,000 worth of high-quality gold ore from somewhere in the mountains, but upon his mysterious disappearance in 1891, he left only a few clues to the whereabouts of the mine. Many who have come looking for it have died violent deaths—one prospector burned to death in his own campfire, while another was found decapitated in an arroyo. Needless to say, the mine has never been found. But if you're feeling lucky, do some "exploring" of your own—there are innumerable roads and trails in the park, as well as a campsite. Siphon Draw Trail is a demanding hike (2.5 mi. one-way), but the rewarding view is worth the difficult ascent over rocks and steep inclines. (☎ 480-982-4485. Water available; no hookups. $5 charge for day use parking, $10 for campsite.)

❷ TONTO NATIONAL FOREST. The end of Lost Dutchman State Park marks the beginning of Tonto National Forest. Your first right as you enter the camp is First Water Rd., which leads to a wealth of trailheads into the Superstition Mountains. The trailheads are well-marked, and most include maps with directions, distances, and other general info. During the summer, especially in the noontime and afternoon, the sun can be scorching and water scarce; keep this in mind before setting out on a cross-country trek.

Those who want to stick to the drive have much to look forward to. The scenery is the Trail's greatest attraction; the dramatic views of the arid landscape make it one of the most beautiful driving routes in the nation. Buttes and canyons—rust-red, desert rose, and a dozen other shades—speckle the way. Most of the rocks you see were formed in the Tertiary Period, about 29 million years ago. The majority are composed of basalt and volcanic ash; their spectacular beauty makes this region second only to the Grand Canyon as Arizona's most photographed landmark.

❸ TORTILLA FLAT. Originally a stage coach stop, Tortilla Flat now boasts a population of six and serves as a watering hole for tourists. The town keeps its spirits up and travelers nourished with a restaurant (meals $6-8), ice cream shop, and saloon. (☎ 480-984-1776. Restaurant open M-F 9am-6pm, Sa-Su 8am-7pm.)

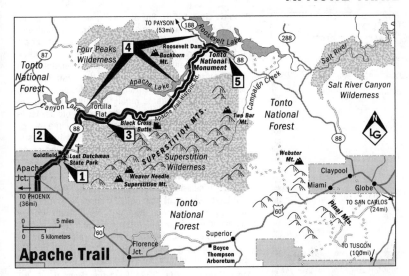

Apache Trail

◢ THE ARTIFICIAL LAKES: CANYON LAKE, APACHE LAKE, AND ROOSEVELT LAKE. The deep blue waters of these man-made lakes contrast sharply with the red- and beige-hued rock formations surrounding them. Formed early this century, partly as a result of Franklin Roosevelt's Depression-busting efforts, the dams that produced these azure jewels in the desert also supply Phoenix with power. **Canyon Lake** sees the most traffic, with enough tourist visits to justify a marina, campground, restaurant, and dinner steamship (camping sites $10-12).

The scene at **Apache Lake** is much the same; on the dirt stretch between the two it's not uncommon to see trailer-pulling trucks muscling each other for road space. **Roosevelt Lake** is more low-key and is the site of the **Theodore Roosevelt Dam,** the last dam constructed by hand in the US. On the far side of the dam you'll find the graceful Roosevelt Lake Bridge, spanning over 1000 ft. of canyon across the lake. **Inspiration Point** commands an excellent view of the area.

◢ TONTO NATIONAL MONUMENT. Five miles east of Roosevelt Dam on Rte. I-88, Tonto National Monument is the last sight on the trail proper. It preserves 750-year-old cliff dwelling ruins built by Southwestern natives. A short trail leads up to the ruins, which are set into a cliff face. The monument was constructed by the Salado. Some locals invoke the name of the Ancestral Puebloans, although "Tonto" was originally a derisive name given to the natives by the Spaniards. (Open daily 8am-4pm. $3 per person, under 17 free; free with National Parks Pass.) **Tonto National Forest** offers camping. (☎ 602-225-5200. Sites $4-11.)

Tonto National Monument marks the end of the Apache Trail proper, but the return route along Rte. 88/U.S. 60 could also prove interesting. Innumerable campgrounds flank the first stretch of Rte. 88, and gas stations and convenience stores regularly sprout to service motorists. Rte. 88 junctions into U.S. 60 five mi. west of **Miami AZ,** a tiny hamlet not to be confused with its Florida namesake.

A more promising sight is the **Boyce Thompson Arboretum** just outside the town of Superior. A desert botanical garden, the Arboretum brings together plants from every desert in the world. The grounds feature a seasonal creek, a man-made lake and a cactus garden. (☎ 520-689-2723; http://ag.arizona.edu/bta/. Admission $6, ages 5-12 $3. Open year-round daily 8am-5pm.)

THE INSIDER'S CITY

TEMPE PUB CRAWL

Tempe has more watering holes than you can swing a dead cat at. Below are Let's Go's humble suggestions for a night on the town. When you're done crawling and are ready to head home, you can grab a green line bus at any of the stops above.

1 Start the evening at **Dos Gringos Trailer Park.** Stock up on tasty Mexican food as you sip on a seemingly bottomless $4 margarita.

2 Dig into some of Arizona's finest chicken wings at **Long Wong's.** Try the suicide wings—if you dare.

3 Rack 'em up at the **Mill Cue Club,** and prepare to get schooled by the ASU kids.

4 Nurse your bruised ego back to health on sweet sweet microbrews at the **Mill Ave. Beer Co.**

5 Stagger down to the last real tavern in Tempe, the **Bandersnatch Brew Pub.** Enjoy your brew the traditionally way or, for the more adventuresome, try it topically through the "Beer in your Face Club."

6 Stumble into **Beeloe's Cafe & Underground Bar** to end the night with live music and the hip ASU crowd.

Phoenix Live, 455 N. 3rd St. (☎252-2502), at the Arizona Center. With 3 bars and a restaurant, this diverse nightclub megalopolis quakes the complex. **America's Original Sports Bar** is the largest of the 3, incorporating the restaurant in its family-friendly downstairs with loud sports fans partaking in the fun upstairs. A DJ spins Top 40. The dance floor at **Decades,** a retro club playing 60s-80s hits, is much larger and busier. For those who don't feel like sweating to the oldies, **Little Ditty's** features dueling baby grand pianos in a lounge atmosphere. $1.75 well drinks, wine, and domestic draft M-Sa 4-7pm. 21+ after 8pm. $5 weekend cover. Open Su-Th 4pm-midnight, F-Sa 4pm-1am.

The Willow House, 149 W. McDowell Rd. (☎252-0272). A self-proclaimed "artist's cove," it combines the best aspects of chic coffee house, New York deli, and quirky musicians' hangout. No alcohol. Coffee happy hour (2-for-1) M-F 4-6 pm. Open M-Th 6am-midnight, F 6am-1am, Sa 7am-1am, Su 7am-midnight. M is open mic night for musicians, Th is open mic for poetry. Nearly nightly live music starting at 8pm.

Ain't Nobody's Biz, 3031 E. Indian School Rd. #7 (☎224-9977), in the east end of the mall. This large lesbian bar is the big sister of the Tucson club of the same name. Top 40 hits play regularly, and the many pools tables mix well with the welcoming dance floor. On F and Sa, the bar attracts both men and women of vibrant lifestyles for a sure-to-be-memorable experience. 2-for-1 happy hour all Tu. 21+. Occasionally cover charge when the Biz hosts guest vocalists. Open M-F 4pm-1am, Sa-Su 2pm-1am. Credit cards not accepted, but there is an ATM.

Mr. Lucky's, 3660 NW Grand Ave. (☎246-0687), on the corner of 36th Ave. and Indian School Rd. "Real" cowboys and cowgirls giddyup to this bona fide country-western dance hall. Brush off your biggest belt buckle, don your favorite pair of Wranglers, and settle in for a night of good ol' country two-steppin'. Arrive before 9pm on F and Sa, as the place is mighty popular. Call ahead, as age restrictions vary. $5 cover. Open W-Th 7pm-1am, F 5pm-3am, Sa 7pm-3am.

Boom, 1724 E. McDowell Rd. (☎254-0231, www.boomnightclub.com). The place for young gay men in Phoenix to see and be seen, this combined bar and dance club is popular with throngs of gyrating Adonis-featured youth who like to party till the wee hours of the morning. 18+ after 10pm. Open Th-F 4pm-3am, Sa 4pm-6am.

TEMPE

■ **Beeloe's Cafe & Underground Bar,** 501 S. Mill Ave. (☎480-894-1230). Food, rock, and art are the hallmarks of the hip yet unpretentious Beeloe's. Every night of the week offers special deals to go with the live music, but get here before 9pm F and Sa ($4 cover), or you might not get in. Happy hour M-F 4pm-7pm. 21+. Open nightly 4pm-1am.

Mill Cue Club, 607 S. Mill Ave. (☎480-858-9017). For those looking to mingle in style, welcome home. The leather sofas in the corner compliment the dark-paneled walls and the rows of pool tables in the back, while the 20 oz. Long Island Iced Teas ($3.50) are sure to liven up your night. Happy hour 2pm-7pm daily, with a DJ spinning hits Tu-Sa. 21+. No cover. Open daily 2pm-1am.

Bandersnatch Brew Pub, 125 E. 5th St. (☎480-966-4438). One of the last real taverns in the greater metro area, Bandersnatch has a huge patio and a dimly lit, but amusing, inside. Food like mom used to make it and a non-embellished atmosphere are the major draws. If you're game, be sure to ask about the "Beer in Your Face Club." Happy hour M-F 3pm-7pm. 21+ after 9pm. Open M-Sa 11am-1am, Su noon-1am.

Mill Ave. Beer Co., 605 S. Mill Ave. (☎480-829-6775). The closest thing to a neighborhood bar in Tempe, the Beer Co. welcomes everyone with a smile and their pick of 160 beers. With a $5 cover, W and Th have 25¢ pitchers. Happy hour M-F 4pm-8pm. Live music F-Su. 21+ after 7pm. Open daily 11am-1am.

SPORTS

Phoenix offers many options for the sports lover. NBA basketball action rises with the **Phoenix Suns** (☎379-7867) at the **America West Arena,** while the **Arizona Cardinals** (☎379-0101) provide American football excitement. The winter sees the NHL's **Phoenix Coyotes** take to the ice, while in the summer, the women's basketball team **Phoenix Mercury** takes it to the hoop at the America West Arena. The **Arizona Diamondbacks** (☎514-8400) play at **Bank One Ballpark,** an architectural wonder complete with a retractable roof, an outfield swimming pool, and "beer gardens." (☎462-6799. Tickets start at $6. Special $1 tickets available 2hr. before games; first come, first served. Tours of the stadium offered throughout the year; proceeds benefit local charities.)

◙ SIGHTS

DOWNTOWN

Downtown Phoenix offers a few museums and mounting evidence of America's growing consumer culture. The price of most downtown attractions hovers around $7; fortunately, they are worth it.

▨THE HEARD MUSEUM. Renowned for its presentation of ancient Native American art, it also features exhibits focusing on contemporary Native Americans. There are many interactive and traveling exhibits, some of which are geared toward children. Named after notable benefactors, galleries include the Sandra Day O'Connor Gallery, which houses an exhibit on the museum's founders, and the Barry Goldwater Gallery, which displays photography of the Southwest. In addition, the museum occasionally sponsors lectures and Native American dances. (*2301 N. Central Ave., 4 blocks north of McDowell Rd. ☎252-8840, recorded info ☎252-8848. Open daily 9:30am-5pm. Free tours at noon, 1:30, and 3pm. $7, seniors $6, ages 4-12 $3, Native Americans with status cards free.*)

THE PHOENIX ART MUSEUM. The museum exhibits art of the American West, including paintings from the Taos and Santa Fe art colonies. Watch out for the "Masterworks" collection (Jan.-May), which will present pieces from masters as prolific as Van Gogh and Picasso. The permanent collection houses pieces by the *Tres Grandes* of Mexican art (Orozco, Siquiros, and Riviera) as well as works by noted American artists including Jackson Pollock and Georgia O'Keeffe. Every major European and American period has representatives on display; the Renaissance Spanish-Catholic, Latin American, and early American periods are the most complete. *(1625 N. Central Ave., at McDowell Rd. ☎257-1880. Open Tu-Su 10am-5pm, Th 10am-9pm. $7, students and seniors $5, ages 6-18 $2. Free on Th and after 4:15pm.)*

THE ARIZONA SCIENCE CENTER. The Center offers interactive science exhibits along with an IMAX theater and a planetarium. Slot the whole day if you're going with children. *(600 E. Washington St. ☎716-2000. Open W-F 10am-5pm, Sa-Tu 10am-9pm. $8, ages 4-12 and seniors $6. IMAX or planetarium ticket $3.)*

PAPAGO PARK AND ENVIRONS

The **Desert Botanical Garden,** in Papago Park, 5 mi. east of downtown, grows a colorful collection of cacti and other desert plants. The park's trails make a pleasant stroll, and many of the desert flowers are hard to find in the wild. *(1201 N. Galvin Pkwy. ☎941-1225, recorded info ☎481-8134. Open daily May-Sept. 7am-8pm; Oct.-Apr. 8am-8pm. $7.50, students with ID $4, seniors $6.50, ages 5-12 $3.50.)* Take bus #3 east to **Papago Park,** on the eastern outskirts of the city. The park has spectacular views of the desert along its hiking, biking, and driving trails. If you spot an orangutan strolling around the cacti, it's either a mirage or you're in the **Phoenix Zoo,** located within the park and boasting a formidable collection of South American, African, and Southwestern critters. *(455 N. Galvin Pkwy. ☎273-1341. Open Sept.-May daily 9am-5pm; $12, seniors $9, children $5; June-Aug. 7am-9pm; $9 seniors $7, children $5.)* The **Hall of Flame Museum of Firefighting,** just outside the southern exit of Papago Park, features antique fire engines and other firefighting equipment. *(6101 E. Van Buren St. ☎275-3473. Open M-Sa 9am-5pm, Su noon-4pm. $5, ages 6-17 $3, ages 3-5 $1.50.)* Still farther east of the city, in Mesa, flows the **Salt River,** one of the last remaining desert rivers in the US. **Salt River Recreation** arranges tubing trips, even for ice chests. *(☎984-3305. Open daily May-Sept. 9am-4pm. Tube rental $9.)*

SOUTH PHOENIX SIGHTS

For those interested in astounding Southwestern architecture, the striking **Mystery Castle** is worth the 5 mi. trip south of downtown. Built in small increments over 15 years (ca. 1930), this home is a spectacle of the creative use of space. Laugh along with the knowledgeable tour guides as they expound upon an endless supply of tidbits about the peculiarities of this masterpiece. *(800 E. Mineral Rd. ☎268-1581. Go south on Central Ave., and take a left on Mineral Rd. just before the South Mountain Park entrance. Open Oct. to mid-June Th-Su 11am-4pm. $5, seniors $4, ages 5-14 $2.)*

SCOTTSDALE

TALIESIN WEST. Taliesin West was built as the winter camp of Frank Lloyd Wright's Taliesin architectural collective; later in life he lived here full-time. Now it serves as a campus for an architectural college run by his foundation. The beautiful compound, entirely designed by the master, seems to blend naturally into the surrounding desert, and includes a studio, a Chinese cinema, and a performance hall. *(Corner of Frank Lloyd Wright Blvd. and Cactus St. ☎860-2700. Open Sept.-June daily 9am-4pm, closed July-Aug. 1hr. or 1½hr. guided tours required. See www.franklloydwright.org for specific tour info. $12.50-16, students and seniors $10-14, ages 4-12 $4.50.)* One of the last buildings he designed, the **Gammage Memorial Auditorium** stands in the Arizona State University campus in Tempe. Its pink-and-beige earth tones blend with the surrounding environment. *(Mill Ave. and Apache Blvd., ☎965-3434. Take bus #60, or 22 on weekends. 20min. tours daily in winter.)*

COSANTI. One of Wright's students liked Scottsdale so much he decided to stay. Cosanti is a working studio and bell foundry designed by the architect and sculptor Paolo Soleri. The buildings here fuse with the natural landscape even more strikingly than those at Taliesin West, and visitors are allowed to wander the grounds freely. Arriving early in the day, between 9am and noon, allows guests to watch the casting of the bronze wind bells for which Cosanti is famous. (*6433 Doubletree Rd. Traveling north on Scottsdale Rd., turn left on Doubletree Rd.; it will be on your left in about 5 blocks. Open M-Sa 9am-5pm, Su 11am-5pm. $1 donation.*)

⚠ OUTDOORS

CITY AND REGIONAL PARKS

The parks of Greater Phoenix (www.ci.phoenix.az.us/prl/index.html or www.maricopa.gov/rec_svc) offer Phoenicians and visitors alike a breathtaking (literally) escape from the urban sprawl that has come to define the greater metro area. Miles of hiking, biking, and even some equestrian trails traverse the sun-baked arid recreation areas. In all parks, be sure to use due caution and go prepared; don't forget it's the barren desert! Some sound advice for all the parks: start early, bring lots of water, keep an eye out for wildlife, and never go it alone. A quick stop by the ranger's station can help orient a newcomer to the park, and can also be an abundant source of reliable advice. There is no entrance fee to city parks, but no camping either. For regional parks, camping fees are $15 per night for sites with electricity and water and $8 for sites with no hookups. If not staying over night, park entrance fees are $3 per vehicle at all but Lake Pleasant, where there's a $5 charge per vehicle and a $2 charge per watercraft. In all regional parks, camping is limited to 14 consecutive nights.

WITHIN CITY LIMITS

SOUTH MOUNTAIN PARK. The popular trails in South Mountain Park on Central Ave. directly south of downtown offer an array of beautiful views that complement the manner in which guests reach the summit, whether it be by foot, bike, horse, or car. Picnic tables and ramadas abound. For a demanding outing, try the National Trail; for something more subdued but still difficult, Desert Classic will do. (☎ 602-495-0222. Open daily 5am-10:30pm; Summit Rd. gate closes at 9pm.)

SQUAW PEAK. Smack in the middle of the Phoenix valley and offering an extremely arduous hike for the eager trekker (with a 1200 ft. elevation gain in 1.2 mi.) stands Squaw Peak City Park and Preserve. The panorama up **Summit Trail** is worth the grueling ascent, but note that almost weekly someone—unprepared, inept, or both—is airlifted from the trail. Get to the park early, for in the winter parking spaces quickly fill up and in the summer, the weather between 11am-6pm is inhospitable to the demanding effort. (☎ 602-262-7901. Open daily 5am-11pm.)

WITHIN 45 MINUTES OF CENTRAL PHOENIX

MCDOWELL MOUNTAIN REGIONAL PARK. McDowell Mountain Regional Park is worth the 40min. drive from downtown Phoenix. With 80 campsites and a roaring fast track built specifically for trail runners, mountain bikers, and horse back riders looking to scratch gravel, McDowell eschews the myth that the desert is no place for sport. Showers are included in the camping fee. (☎ 480-471-0173. From Scottsdale Rd. take Shea Blvd. east, turn left on Palisades Blvd., which will take you into the town of Fountain Hills, and follow the signs to the park. Open 24hr.)

LAKE HAVASU CITY ☎ 928

Created by the 1938 damming of the Colorado River, Lake Havasu embodies a new West, created by tourist dollars and an urge to kick back. Entrepreneur Robert McCulloch willed the city (pop. 50,000) to life in 1963, as a place to test boat engines. He drew up a community plan, brought the London Bridge from Old England, and people arrived with boats in tow. Motorboats and jet skis endlessly churn the green waters into a roiling froth. When not thundering along, the boats float down the channel with well-oiled and bikini-clad gals reclining languidly on the bow. Spring break is prime time in this party town, as high temperatures keep the adrenaline to a minimum in the summer.

■ **ORIENTATION.** The lake is located on the California, Arizona, and Nevada borders, with the city lying in Arizona on Rte. 95, 21 mi. south of I-40. The small town of Parker lies 36 mi. to the south, and the gambling halls of Laughlin are a tempting 65 mi. north of town. **Rte. 95** runs north-south through the city, and is intersected downtown by the east-west thoroughfare **McCulloch Blvd.** Just east of Hwy. 95 is **Lake Havasu Ave.**, which shelters stucco installations of familiar fast food spots. McCulloch runs west over a channel, spanned by the actual London Bridge, and connects to The Island, a prime locale for beach resorts.

■ **PRACTICAL INFORMATION.** Greyhound (☎ 800-231-2222) has daily buses to cities in Arizona and California, including Las Vegas (3½hr., 1 per day 12:10pm, $35) and Los Angeles (5½hr., 1 per day, $55). The **Chamber of Commerce** is in English Village, a mock British square with a brewery and food stands, at the corner of Hwy. 95 and London Bridge Rd. (☎ 855-4115; open daily 9am-4pm). **City Transit Services** is on call with curb-to-curb shuttle services throughout Lake Havasu City. (☎ 453-7600. Operates M-F 6am-9pm, Sa-Su 6am-6pm. $3, under 10 $2, under 5 free.) Other services include: **laundry** at **Busy "B"**, 3201 N. Hwy. 95 (☎ 764-2440; open daily 4:30am-11pm; $1.25 wash); and the **post office,** 1750 McCulloch Blvd. (☎ 855-2361; open M-F 8:30am-5pm, Sa 10am-1pm). **ZIP code:** 86403.

■ **ACCOMMODATIONS.** There is an abundance of affordable motels along London Bridge Rd. Rates tend to be higher on summer weekends. The shiny **Windsor Inn ❸**, 451 London Bridge Rd., offers inexpensive rooms and all the desert amenities. Since you pay by the bed, two people can get single prices if they are willing to share or crash on the couch. (☎ 855-4135 or 800-245-4135. Singles Su-Th $39, F-Sa $59; doubles $45/$69.) The good-natured people at **Super 8 ❸**, 305 London Bridge Rd., offer predictable accommodations at predictable prices. (☎ 855-8844. Singles Su-Th $36, F-Sa $46; doubles $46/$56.) Campers should visit **Lake Havasu State Park ❶**, about 1 mi. up London Bridge Rd. off Rte. 95, where they will find a main campground (☎ 855-2784; 34 sites; showers, toilets, boat-launch; $14) and **Cattail Cove ❶** (60 sites; showers, toilets, RV hookups; $17, $19 for RVs).

■■ **FOOD AND NIGHTLIFE.** In addition to Lake Havasu Ave., there is also a tremendous concentration of fast food along Rte. 95, particularly where it intersects London Bridge Rd. For a less generic taste, try the Irish-inspired **Slainee's ❷**, 1519 Queens Bay Rd., which has hearty entrees ($7+, come with soup/salad), a slew of pool tables, and live tunes on weekends (☎ 505-8900; open daily 10am-1am). At the **Barley Brothers Brewery and Grill ❷**, 1425 McCulloch Blvd. on The Island, knowledgeable bartenders serve inventive brews (locally-brewed beer $4 per pint) as well as more refined cuisine. (☎ 505-7837. Open Su-Th 11am-10pm, F-Sa 11am-11pm. Sandwiches $8. Crowd is everywhere from casual to dressy.) A short, but dark, walk over London Bridge from the Brewery, the colossal **Kokomo's on the Channel** nightclub is where you can shake your sunburned booty. The open-air superclub is at the London Bridge Resort, 1477 Queens Bay Rd. Tiny mixed drinks are $4, but hold out for the DJ-announced $1 specials. (☎ 855-0888. $5 cover on weekends. Open Su-Th 11am-11pm, F-Sa 11am-1am; things pick up at 11pm.)

⬛𝄃 SIGHTS AND ACTIVITIES. The place to be in Lake Havasu is on the water. Any number of tourist publications can direct you to a reputable boat rental. Loungers should try **Windsor Beach,** 1 mi. up London Bridge Rd. off Rte. 95, in Lake Havasu State Park (day-use $8). Free beaches line the eastern shore of The Island, but swimmers can avoid boat traffic by sticking to the southern end. Take Smoketree from Rte. 95 to get to Rotary Beach, where sand, volleyball, and picnic areas await. Take London Bridge Rd. north out of the city for 3 mi., and pass the Quail Ridge residential community to get to piers that look out over the spectacular Havasu Game Preserve. Lake Havasu's other and most unusual claim to fame is the **London Bridge.** Originally built in London, England in 1824, it was painstakingly dismantled and reconstructed under the sponsorship of McCulloch. The reconstructed bridge was dedicated in October 1971. See the bridge and associated tourist "attractions" at the intersection of Rte. 95 and London Bridge Rd.

WILLIAMS
☎928

Coming from the scorching desert of southern Arizona, the climate in the higher latitudes of this Northern Arizona town will surprise—trees instead of cacti, and balmy breezes instead of blazing heat. Williams is the closest town to the Southern Rim of the Grand Canyon, accounting for the town's self-proclaimed nickname, "The Gateway to the Grand Canyon." This bit of geographical luck ensures a steady flow of tourists into Williams, and the locals are making the most of it.

The **Red Lake Hostel ❶**, about 8 mi. outside the town on the road to the Grand Canyon, offers clean, dorm-style accommodations with shared bath. (☎635-4753. Dorms $11; private rooms $33.) On the eastbound stretch of Rte. 66 at the east end of town, the **Route 66 Inn ❸** provides reliably clean and comfortable rooms at reasonable rates. Family-size suites are also available. (☎635-4791 or 888-786-6958. Singles $25 in winter, $45 in summer; doubles $32/$56; suites $55/90.) There are plenty of decent food options in Williams. **Rod's Steakhouse ❷** offers mammoth one-third-pound hamburgers for $5 during lunch hours. (☎635-2671. Open daily 11:30am-9:30pm.)

FLAGSTAFF
☎928

Born on the 4th of July, Flagstaff began as a rest stop along the transcontinental railroad; its mountain springs provided precious aqueous refreshment on the long haul to the Pacific. The past 100 years have seen the logging industry come and go, played host to a scientist in search of canal-digging Martians, and felt the unrelenting onslaught of backpackers and fannypackers alike. One thing hasn't changed, though: Flagstaff is still a major rest stop on the way to Southwestern must-sees. Travelers pass through on their way to the Grand Canyon, Sedona, and the Petrified Forest—all within day-trip distance. The energetic citizens welcome travelers to their rock formations by day and their breweries by night; many wandered into town with camera in hand and ended up settling down. Retired cowboys, earthy Volvo owners, New Agers, and rock climbers comprise much of the population.

◼ TRANSPORTATION

Flagstaff sits 138 mi. north of Phoenix (take I-17), 26 mi. north of Sedona (take U.S. 89A), and 81 mi. south of the Grand Canyon's south rim (take U.S. 180).

Trains: Amtrak, 1 E. Rte. 66 (☎774-8679). Two trains leave daily. Eastbound train leaves at 5:11am, heading to **Kansas City, MO** and **Chicago** via **Winslow** (1hr., $14-23), **Gallup, NM** (2½hr., $35-61), and **Albuquerque** (5hr., $63-110). Westbound train leaves

ARIZONA

THE HIDDEN DEAL

FLAGSTAFF TWIN HOSTELS

🔲 **Grand Canyon International Hostel,** 19 S. San Francisco St. (☎779-9421 or 888-442-2696; www.grandcanyon-hostel.com), near the train station. Sunny, clean, and classy. Despite its large size (32 beds), the hostel is blessed with friendly guests and a staff to match. Free tea and coffee, parking, and linen. Access to kitchen, TV room with cable, Internet ($2 per 30min.), free breakfast (7-10am), and laundry facilities. Showers $2. Free pick-up from Greyhound station. Offers tours to the Grand Canyon ($43) and to Sedona ($25). $5 communal dinners are occasionally organized. Reception 7am-midnight. No curfew. Occasionally will allow travelers to work for lodging—enquire with the manager. Takes reservations with credit card. 4-bed dorms Oct.-May $14, June-Aug. $16; private rooms without bath $28/$32. ❶

🔲 **Du Beau International Hostel,** 19 W. Phoenix St. (☎774-6731 or 800-398-7112; www.dubeau.net), also just behind the train station. The Du Beau lives up to its ritzy name with recently renovated dorm rooms (4-8 beds) and private bathrooms. The lively, well-equipped common room is a highlight. Reception 7am-midnight. Under the same ownership as the Grand Canyon Hostel, Du Beau offers all the same services. 8-bed dorms Oct.-May $14, June-Aug. $16. Private rooms with bath $32/38. ❶

at 9:25pm, heading to **Los Angeles** (12hr., $68-119). Occasional discount offers and specials may considerably reduce rates. Station open daily 4:45pm-7:30am.

Buses: Four separate bus lines provide service to regional destinations.

Greyhound: 399 S. Malpais Ln. (☎774-4573), across from NAU campus, 3 blocks southwest of the train station on U.S. 89A. Turn off 89A by Dairy Queen. To: **Albuquerque** (6½hr., 5 per day, $41); **Las Vegas** (5-6hr., 3 per day, $47); **Los Angeles** (10-12hr., 8 per day, $49); **Phoenix,** including airport (3hr., 5 per day, $22). Terminal open 24hr.

Sedona Shuttle Service: Coconino/Yavapai Shuttle Service (☎775-8929 or 888-440-8929) offers daily trips from Flagstaff to **Sedona.** The 1hr. trip leaves from Flagstaff M-F at 8am and 4pm, and returns from Sedona at 2:30pm. On Sa, Flagstaff-Sedona leg leaves at 10am with no return trip. No Su service. One-way $18, round-trip $36.

Grand Canyon Coaches (☎638-0821 or 866-746-8439) offers shuttle service to the **Grand Canyon.** Shuttles depart from the Flagstaff Visitors Center daily at 9am and 6:40pm and return from Maswik Lodge at the Canyon at 7am and 4:40pm. One-way $20, round-trip $40.

Northern Arizona Shuttle and Tours (☎773-4337 or 866-870-8687) provides transportation between **Phoenix** and Flagstaff. Three daily departures from the Flagstaff Visitors Center and various locations in Phoenix. One-way $30, prepaid round-trip $55. Call for departure times.

Public Transit: Mountain Line (☎779-6624). Routes cover most of town. Buses run once per hr.; route map and schedule available at Visitors Center in Amtrak station. One-way 75¢, seniors and disabled 35¢, children 60¢; book of 20 passes $13.

Taxis: Friendly Cab, ☎214-9000.

Car Rental: Enterprise Rent-A-Car (☎526-1377), Rte. 66 near the east edge of town. 21+. Rentals require a license and credit card. Open M-F 7:30am-6pm, Sa 9am-noon.

✦ 🔁 ORIENTATION AND PRACTICAL INFORMATION

The downtown area revolves around the intersection of **Beaver St.** and **Rte. 66** (formerly Santa Fe Ave.). Both bus stations, two hostels, the tourist office, and a number of inexpensive restaurants lie within ½ mi. of this spot. **S. San Francisco St.,** two blocks east of Beaver St., marks the east edge of downtown. Split by Rte. 66, the northern area is slightly more upscale while the area south of the tracks is down to earth, housing hostels and vegetarian eateries. A mountain town, Flagstaff stays temperate and receives frequent afternoon thundershowers during the summer, while the winter brings cold temperatures (averaging in the 20s) and snowfall.

Visitor Info: Flagstaff Visitors Center, 1 E. Rte. 66 (☎774-9541 or 800-842-7293), in the Amtrak station. Open M-Sa 8am-6pm, Su 8am-5pm.

Equipment Rental: Peace Surplus, 14 W. Rte. 66 (☎779-4521), 1 block from Grand Canyon Hostel. Rents tents ($7-9 per day), packs ($5-6 per day), sleeping bags ($6 per day), and stoves ($3 per day) as well as alpine, nordic, and snowshoe packages in winter. 3-day min. rental; hefty $100-200 credit card or cash deposits are required. Open M-F 8am-9pm, Sa 8am-8pm.

Laundromat: White Flag Coin-op, 16 S Beaver St. (☎774-7614), next to Macy's. Coin-operated laundry with attendant. Drop service also available. Open M-Tu 8am-9pm, W-Sa 6am-9pm, Su 6am-6:30pm.

Police: 911 Sawmill Rd. (general info ☎556-2316; non-emergencies ☎774-1414).

Pharmacy/Grocery: Fry's Food and Drug Store, 201 Switzer Canyon (☎774-2719), 1 mi. north of San Francisco St. on Rte. 66. Open daily 6am-midnight.

Medical Services: Flagstaff Medical Center, 1200 North Beaver St. (☎779-3366), provides medical services in the area, including 24hr. emergency service.

Internet Access: Free access at NAU's **Cline Library** (☎523-2171). Open M-Th 7:30am-10pm, F 7:30am-6pm, Sa 9am-6pm, Su noon-10pm. Free public access also available at the **Flagstaff Public Library,** 300 W. Aspen Ave. (☎774-4000). Open M-Th 10am-9pm, F 10am-7pm, Sa 10am-6pm, Su 11am-6pm.

Post Office: 2400 N. Postal Blvd. (☎714-9302), for general delivery. Open M-F 9am-5pm, Sa 9am-1pm. **Downtown** at 104 N. Agassiz St. (☎779-2371), 86001. Open M-F 9am-5pm, Sa 9am-1pm. **ZIP code:** 86004.

◤ ACCOMMODATIONS

When swarms of summer tourists from southern Arizona descend on Flagstaff, hotel prices shoot up. Thankfully, the town is blessed with excellent hostels. Historic **Rte. 66** is home to many cheap motels, although the private rooms at the hostels and hotels listed below rival them both in price and in quality. *The Flagstaff Accommodations Guide,* available at the Visitors Center, lists all area hotels, motels, hostels, and B&Bs. If you're here to see the Grand Canyon (who isn't?), check the notice board in your hotel or hostel; some travelers leave their still-valid passes behind, and you might find a ride to the next town as well. People staying in Flagstaff be warned: the trains operate 24hr., and their noise is inescapable.

The Weatherford Hotel, 23 N. Leroux St. (☎779-1919), on the other side of the tracks 1 block west of San

THE BIG SPLURGE

IN THE MONEY AT THE MONEY INN

Although Flagstaff is home to one of the best hostel scenes in the Southwest, it also knows how to live large. For those who want to take a break from nickel-and-diming their vacation, or for those who just can't abide without room service, Let's Go can make a few recommendations.

🖼 **Inn at 410,** 410 N. Leroux St. (☎774-0088 or 800-774-2088), the best place to stay in Flagstaff and one of the Southwest's premier B&Bs. Situated in a beautiful 1894 craftsman home, the Inn boasts 9 distinctive rooms, some with oversized jacuzzi and fireplace, decorated in classic Southwest, Victorian, or arts and crafts styles. Rooms $135-190. ❺

Birch Tree Inn, 824 W. Birch Ave. (☎744-1042 or 888-774-1042; www.birchtreeinn.com). This comfortable B&B offers 5 themed rooms in a restored 1915 Victorian home. Decor ranges from Southwestern to antique. Rooms $69-109. ❹

Inn at NAU, S. San Francisco St. in the middle of the Northern Arizona University campus, (☎523-1616; www.hrm.nau.edu/inn). The inn is operated by NAU's School of Hotel Management and staffed entirely by NAU students. Its unassuming exterior conceals 19 comfortable, spacious, and well-appointed rooms. Complimentary breakfast; all rooms have refrigerators, some have computers. With the exception of the presidential suite, all rooms $89. ❺

Francisco St. The oldest hotel in Flagstaff, dating to 1897, the Weatherford has spacious rooms with amazing balconies and bay windows. Equipped with elegant furnishings and located in the middle of downtown Flagstaff. Reservations recommended. Rooms $55. ❸

Hotel Monte Vista, 100 N. San Francisco St. (☎779-6971 or 800-545-3068; www.hotelmontevista.com), downtown. Feels like a classy hotel, with quirky decor, a bar that occasionally hosts hard-core and punk bands, with pool tables and video games downstairs. Chock-full of colorful history, the staff swears the hotel is chock-full of ghosts, too. Private rooms named after movie stars who slept there start at $70. ❹

■ CAMPING

Free backcountry camping is available around Flagstaff in specifically designated wilderness areas. Pick up a map from the **Peaks Ranger Station,** 5075 N. 89A (☎526-0866), to find out where. All backcountry campsites must be located at least 200 ft. away from trails, waterways, wet meadows, and lakes. There is a 14-night limit for stays in the Coconino National Forest. For info on campgrounds and backcountry camping, call the **Coconino Forest Service** (☎527-3600; open M-F 7:30am-4:30pm).

An alternative to backcountry camping is staying at one of the numerous maintained campsites in the forest. Many of these campsites flank the idyllic lakes to the south of Flagstaff. **Lakeview Campground ❶,** on the side of Upper Lake Mary, 11½ mi. south on Lake Mary Road (off I-17 south of Flagstaff), is surrounded by a pine forest that supports an alpine ecosystem. (Open May-Oct.; no reservations. Drinking water, pit toilets. $10 per vehicle per night.) **Pinegrove Campground ❶,** 5 mi. south of Lakeview at the other end of Upper Lake Mary, is set in a similarly charming locale. (☎877-444-6777. Open May-Oct.; reservations available. drinking water, flush toilets. $12 per vehicle.) **Ashurst/Forked Pine Campground ❶** flanks both sides of Ashurst lake, a smaller, secluded lake on Forest Rd. 82E (turn left off of Lake Mary Rd., across from Pine Grove Campground). Water and flush toilets are on-site, and the fishing is stupendous. 64 sites are available on a first come, first served basis ($10 per vehicle).

■ FOOD

All the deep-fat-frying chains are readily available outside of downtown, but near the heart of Flagstaff, the creative and off-beat rule. The downtown core brims with pubs, restaurants, and cafes with a variety of cuisines to suit all tastes.

Macy's, 14 S. Beaver St. (☎774-2243), behind Motel Du Beau, is a cheery student hangout serving only vegetarian food (and excellent vegan selections) in an earthy atmosphere. $4-7 specials change daily. Get there early and start the day with a bowl of granola ($4) and one of their fresh roasted coffees ($1-3.50). Open Su-W 6am-8pm, Th-Sa 6am-midnight. Food served until 1hr. before closing. Cash only. ❶

Pasto, 19 E. Aspen (☎779-1937), serves up delicious Italian cuisine in a high-class atmosphere. Entrees span the spectrum from seafood, chicken, and veal to more traditional pasta dishes and cost $10-18. Open Su-Th 5pm-9pm, F-Sa 5pm-9:30pm. Reservations recommended. ❸

The Black Bean, 12 E. Rte. 66 (☎779-9905), is a great place for on-the-go burritos ($3-5). They come with your choice of fixin's, and are large enough to make a hefty meal. Creative specialty wraps $5. Open M-Sa 11am-9pm, Su noon-8pm. ❶

Mountain Harvest Deli, 2 S. Beaver St. (☎779-9456), across from the Du Beau Hostel, crafts organic ingredients into tasty sandwiches, some vegetarian ($5-6). Open M-Sa 8am-8pm, Su 9am-7pm. ❶

Flagstaff

♠ ACCOMMODATIONS
Birch Tree Inn, **2**
Du Beau Hostel, **8**
Grand Canyon
   International Hostel, **10**
Hotel Monte Vista, **4**
Inn at 410, **1**
The Weatherford Hotel, **3**

🍴 FOOD
The Black Bean, **6**
Cottage Place
   Restaurant, **7**
Macy's, **11**
Mountain Harvest
   Deli, **9**
Pasto, **5**

TO MUSEUM OF N. ARIZONA (3mi) & TO GRAND CANYON (81mi)

TO ✚ (.25mi)

Columbus Ave.
Sullivan Ave.
Hunt Ave.
Fine Ave.
Elm Ave.
Dale Ave.
Cherry Ave.
Birch Ave.
Aspen Ave.
Rte. 66
Phoenix Ave.
Benton Ave.
Butler Ave.
Dupont Ave.
Brannen Ave.

Rio De Flag
Thorpe Park
Mars Hill Rd.
Thorpe Rd.
Toltec St.
Aztec St.
Mogollon St.
Bonito St.
Park St.
Sitgreaves St.
Kendrick St.
Humphreys St.
Beaver St.
Leroux St.
San Francisco St.
Agassiz St.
Elden St.
Spring St.
Summitt Ave.
Sycamore St.
Walnut St.
Grand Canyon Ave.
Coconino Ave.
Kingman St.
Florence St.
Globe St.
Tombstone Ave.
Clay Ave.
Malpais Ln.
Mikes Pike
Blackbird Roost St.

TO 🔭 LOWELL OBSERVATORY (.25mi)

Amtrak

Greyhound

TO 40 (1.5mi); PHOENIX (143mi); SEDONA (34mi)

89

Northern Arizona University

TO INN AT NAU (400yds.)

66

0   200 yards
0   200 meters

Cottage Place Restaurant, 126 W. Cottage Ave. (☎ 774-8431), Flagstaff's premier fine dining establishment, located, as the name would suggest, in a quaint cottage. Start with an order of goat cheese and chives wrapped in phyllo before splurging on their "tenderloin medallions napped with port wine demi-glace and garnished with grilled black tiger shrimp laced with Hollandaise sauce." The wine list has received the Wine Spectator Award of Excellence for the past 6 years. Appetizers $6-12, entrees $20-28. Reservations recommended. ❺

🎬 NIGHTLIFE

The students of the University of Northern Arizona provide a sizeable clientele for Flagstaff's numerous pubs, bars, and nightspots. The student body is as diverse as it is energetic, catering to a number of social and musical scenes.

Mogollon Brewing Company, 15 Agassiz St. (☎ 773-8950; mogollonbrewing.com), the perfect place to relax and savor the fine art of beer-drinking. Sample from a wide selection of delicious handcrafted ales, all brewed on site, in their rustic tap room. Live music 6 nights a week ranges from bluegrass to funk. Happy hour 4-7pm, pints $2.50. Tu night $1 beers. Open M-F 3pm-1am, Sa-Su 1pm-1am.

Charly's, 23 N. Leroux St. (☎ 779-1919), plays live jazz and blues in one of the classiest buildings in town. Live music is on the menu 6 nights a week, including patio bands on

ARIZONA

Th. Pub fare entrees $9-10. The upstairs Zane Grey Ballroom picks up the overflow, and serves nightly drink specials for $2.50. Happy hour 5-7pm. Open daily 11am-10pm. Bar open daily 11am-1am.

Joe's Place (☎ 774-6281), on the corner of Rte. 66 and Agassiz, hosts indie bands of all descriptions weekend nights. Lively everyday, M features open mic blues, Tu pool tournaments, and Su open mic, free pool, and free pizza. Happy hour from 4-7pm with $2.25 mixed drinks and $1.75 domestic bottles. Open 11am-1am.

The Alley (☎ 774-7929), on Rte. 66 near the intersection with San Francisco St. The ultimate college dive. Weekends see live music, with many out-of-towners. Happy hour M-Sa 4-7pm, and all day Su with free nacho bar. Open 3pm-1am.

The Museum Club, 3404 E. Rte. 66 (☎526-9434), a.k.a. the **Zoo,** is the premier spot for honky-tonk action. This place is the real deal—it was built during the Great Depression as a roadhouse to liven spirits. Cowboy gusto is revived daily with liquor and first-class country music. Open daily 11am-3am. Cover $3-5.

👁 SIGHTS

LOWELL OBSERVATORY. In 1894, Percival Lowell chose Flagstaff as the site for an astronomical observatory, and then spent the rest of his life here, devoting himself to the study of heavenly bodies and culling data to support his theory that life exists on Mars. The Lowell Observatory, where he discovered the planet Pluto, doubles as both a general tribute to his genius and a high-powered research center sporting five super-duper telescopes. During the daytime, admission includes tours of the telescopes, as well as a museum with hands-on astronomy exhibits. If you have stars in your eyes, come back at night for an excellent program about the night's sky and the constellations. *(1400 W. Mars Hill Rd., 1 mi. west of downtown off Rte. 66. ☎ 774-3358; www.lowell.edu. Open daily winter noon-5pm, summer 9am-5pm. Evening programs W, F, Sa 7:30pm; in summer M-Sa 8:00pm. $4, ages 5-17 $2.)*

MUSEUM OF NORTHERN ARIZONA. The more down-to-earth Museum of Northern Arizona features exhibits on the native peoples of the area. Galleries house expansive collections of Native American art, contemporary and ancient, some of which is on sale. A small natural history section also houses an intimidating dinosaur skeleton. *(Off U.S. 180, 3 mi. north of town. ☎774-5213. Open winter W-Sa 9am-5pm, summer daily 9am-5pm. $5, students $3, seniors $4, ages 7-17 $2, Native Americans with ID $2.)*

OTHER SIGHTS AND EVENTS. North of town near the museum, the **Coconino Center for the Arts** houses exhibits, festivals, performers, and even a children's museum *(☎ 779-7258 or 774-6272).* In the second weekend of June, the annual **Flagstaff Rodeo** comes to town with competitions, barn dances, a carnival, and a cocktail waitress race. Competitions and events go on from Friday to Sunday at the Coconino County Fair Grounds. *(On Hwy 89A just south of town. ☎800-638-4253.)* On the **4th of July,** the town celebrates its birthday with street fairs, live music, outdoor barbecues, a parade, and, of course, fireworks. At the tail-end of the summer (Labor Day), the **Coconino Country Fair** digs its heals into Flagstaff with rides, animal competitions, and carnival games. **Theatrikos,** a local theater group, stages plays year-round. *(11 W. Cherry Ave. ☎774-1662; www.theatrikos.com.)*

🔼 OUTDOOR ACTIVITIES

With the northern **San Francisco Peaks** and the surrounding **Coconino National Forest,** Flagstaff offers numerous options for the rugged outdoorsman or those simply

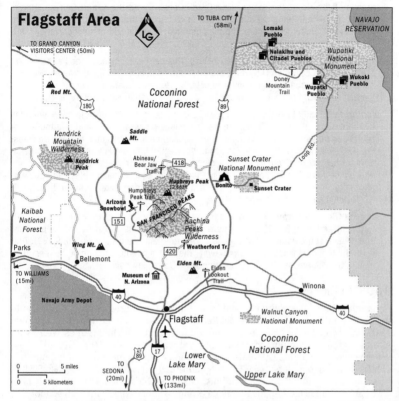

Flagstaff Area

N

TO TUBA CITY
(58mi)

NAVAJO
RESERVATION

Lomaki
Pueblo

TO GRAND CANYON
VISITORS CENTER (50mi)

Nalakihu and
Citadel Pueblos

Wupatki
National
Monument

Doney
Mountain
Trail

Wukoki
Pueblo

Red Mt.

Coconino
National Forest

180

89

Wupatki
Pueblo

Kendrick
Mountain
Wilderness

Saddle
Mt.

Kendrick
Peak

Abineau/
Bear Jaw
Trail

418

Sunset Crater
National Monument

Humphreys Peak
12,643ft

Bonito

Sunset Crater

Loop Rd.

Humphreys
Peak Trail

Arizona
Snowbowl

SAN FRANCISCO PEAKS

Kaibab
National
Forest

151

Kachina
Peaks
Wilderness

Wing Mt.

420

Weatherford Tr.

Parks

Bellemont

Elden Mt.

Elden
Lookout
Trail

TO WILLIAMS
(15mi)

Museum of
N. Arizona

Winona

Navajo Army Depot

40

Flagstaff

Walnut Canyon
National Monument

40

0   5 miles

0   5 kilometers

89   17

Lower
Lake Mary

Coconino
National Forest

TO
SEDONA
(20mi)

TO PHOENIX
(133mi)

Upper Lake Mary

interested in walking off last night's fun. Nature's playground provides skiing, hiking, biking, and general awe-struckedness. Due to the 7000 ft. altitudes, bring plenty of water, regardless of the season or activity. In late spring and summer, National and State Park Rangers may close trails if the fire danger gets too high; winter snowfalls can likewise shut down routes.

HIKING

It's important to note that many trails are multipurpose; the hiking trails of the Mary's Lakes regions also make killer single tracks for mountain bikers. The trails in the San Francisco Peaks, however, are located in the Kachina Peaks Wilderness area, and are off limits to mechanized vehicles. The Coconino National Forest has many trails for hikers of all abilities. Consult the **Peaks Ranger Station**, 5075 N. 89A (☎ 526-0866), for trail descriptions and possible closures. Be sure to carry plenty of water when you hike—most hikes do not have reliable water sources.

Humphrey's Peak (9 mi. round-trip, 6-7hr.). The single most popular trail in the area, this strenuous hike ascends Arizona's highest mountain. The trailhead can be found at the Snow Bowl Ski Area, in the first parking lot to the left. From the parking lot, the trail winds through and out of alpine forest, and eventually above tree line. The summit of Humphrey's Peak affords a 360° panoramic view of Northern Arizona, including the mesas of the Hopi reservation, Oak Creek Canyon, and the Grand Canyon. Hikers should be careful during the summer; sudden afternoon thunderstorms are not uncommon, and it's better to abandon the hike than risk being caught at such elevations in a lightning storm. 3400 ft. elevation gain. Closed in winter and early spring.

Elden Lookout Trail (6 mi. round-trip, 7-9hr.). This hard trail begins at the Peaks Ranger Station, north of town on U.S. 89. Leading to the peak of Mt. Elden, it crosses over petrified lava flows and through conifer forests, as well as an aspen grove that represents the first regrowth from a 1977 forest fire. 2400 ft. elevation gain. Open Apr.-Nov.

Weatherford Trail (17½ mi. round-trip, 9-12hr.). Originally a car track for pleasure rides by the owners of Model-T Fords, the trail has since been narrowed and repurposed for hikers and horsemen. Drive 2 mi. north of Flagstaff on Rte. 180, then turn left on Forest Rd. 420 (Schultz Pass Rd.). The road forks soon after; take the left fork and continue on 5 mi. to Schultz Tank; the trailhead is next to the tank. Winding through high elevations and alpine forests, this moderate-to-strenuous trail is an excellent place to spot bird and animal life. Great views of the countryside are afforded throughout the trail. 3200 ft. elevation gain. Open May-Nov.

Abineau/Bear Jaw Trail (6 mi. round-trip, 4-5hr.). Head north of town along U.S. 180; turn right on Forest Rd. 151 and follow it until it intersects Forest Rd. 418. Turn right and drive past the Potato Tank; 2 mi. later, the road will intersect Forest Rd. 9123J. Turn right; the trailhead is less than 1 mi. away. The trail is remote and one of the least traveled in the wilderness. 1900 ft. elevation gain. Open May-Nov.

ROCK CLIMBING

The mountainous lay of the Flagstaff area makes for a variety of mountain climbing opportunities in the area. **Vertical Relief,** 205 S. San Francisco St., in downtown Flagstaff, offers info, equipment, and guided climbs in the area, as well as an extensive indoor climbing gym with several walls. (☎556-9909 or 877-265-5984; www.verticalrelief.com. Open M-F 10am-11pm, Sa-Su noon-8pm. Guided outdoor climbs: half-day one person $160, each additional person $85; half-day $225/$125; all equipment included. Indoor climbing: day pass $14, students $12, monthly pass $59; F after 7pm is teen night, $9 day pass and $3 shoe rental with high school ID.)

There are numerous sites on the south side of Mt. Elden, around Sycamore Canyon to the southwest of Flagstaff, and on Lake Mary Rd. Few are obvious, so a guide or specialized guide book is necessary.

SKIING

The **Arizona Snow Bowl,** open from mid-December to April, operates four chairlifts (and a tow rope) and maintains 32 trails. The majestic **Humphrey's Peak,** standing a whopping 12,670 ft., is the backdrop for the Snowbowl, as well as the home of the Hopi's sacred Kachina spirits. The skiing, however, takes place on **Agassiz Peak,** the second highest peak in the San Francisco Mountains, with the main lift reaching an altitude of 11,500 ft. With an average snowfall of 260 in. and 2300 ft. of vertical drop, the Snow Bowl rivals the big-boy ski resorts of the Rockies and easily outclasses all of its Arizona competition. To reach the Snow Bowl, take U.S. 180 about 7 mi. north to the Fairfield Snow Bowl turnoff.

The Snow Bowl caters to a wide range of skiers and is evenly divided between beginner, intermediate, and advanced runs. Snowboarders are welcome. (☎779-1951; www.arizonasnowbowl.com. Open daily 9am-4pm. Lift tickets adult weekend full-day $40, half-day $32; midweek $40/$25; ages 8-12 $22/$17.) **Equipment rental** is available on the mountain. (Half-day ski package $15, full-day $20; extreme performance package $30/$20; snowboards $27/$20.)

ARIZONA

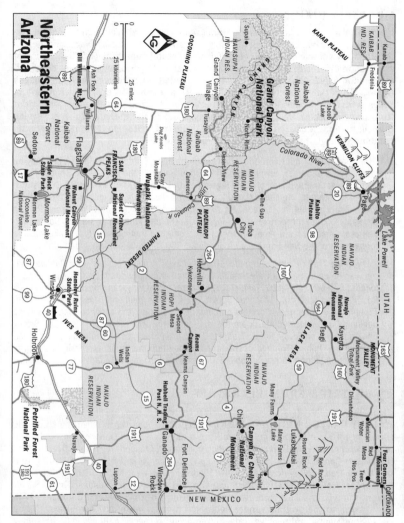

Northeastern Arizona

The Snow Bowl is open during the summer months. Visitors can ride the chairlift or hike to the top of Mt. Agassiz to experience its stunning vistas. When the air is clear, the North Rim of the Grand Canyon, the Painted Desert, and countless square miles of Arizona and Utah can be seen from the peak. (Chairlift runs late May to early Sept. daily 10am-4pm; early Sept. to mid-Oct. F-Su 10am-4pm. $9, seniors $6.50, ages 6-12 $5.)

Cross-country skiing is available at the **Flagstaff Nordic Center,** 8 mi. north of Snow Bowl Rd. on U.S. 180. There are beginner and expert routes, but the bulk of the trails are intermediate. In addition to cross-country skiing, many routes are devoted to snowshoeing. (☎779-1951. Trail pass $10, snowshoe pass $5. Basic cross-country ski package $14. Performance package $20, snowshoes $9.)

MOUNTAIN BIKING

Flagstaff also offers excellent mountain biking and attracts enough mountain bikers to keep a thriving outfitting industry going. **Absolute Bikes,** 18 N. San Francisco St., fixes any vehicle on two wheels and runs a rental operation. (☎779-5969. Front suspension $25 for first day, $15 for second, and $10 for all subsequent days; full suspension $45/25/20.) They also lead free guided rides Tuesday at 6am. **Sinagua Cycles,** 113 S. San Francisco St. (☎779-9969), a few blocks down from Absolute Bikes, leads free bike rides Monday to Friday at 4:30am, as well as an "epic ride" for advanced bikers every second Sunday. Most of the individual forest service trails in the Flagstaff area make for short cycle tracks; the do-it-yourselfer should combine several of these to make for a day of biking.

Little Bear Trail (7 mi. round-trip). There is no trailhead for the Little Bear; it can only be reached by a short (1½ mi.) ride up Little Elden Trail from the Little Elden Springs Horse Camp. To get there, drive north of Flagstaff on U.S. 89 to Elden Springs Rd. (Forest Rd. 556) and turn left. The Horse Camp is 3.5 mi. up this road. This moderate trail is great for wildlife watching, as it meanders through stands of Juniper and Ponderosa Pine. It distributes out to a trailhead at Schultz Tank and a trail junction in the heart of the wilderness; as such, it's a great means of accessing the trail network that makes up the forest north of the San Francisco mountains. 1080 ft. elevation gain. Open May-Nov.

Rocky Ridge Trail (4½ mi. round-trip). This challenging, highly technical yet relatively flat trail can be combined with the Schultz Creek Trail and the Oldham Trail. The trailhead is located on Forest Rd. 420. Take U.S. 180 north out of Flagstaff, turn right onto Forest Rd. 557, and then quickly left on Forest Rd. 420. The trailhead is very near this turn. Though the elevation gain on this particular trail is slight, the rocky surface may force beginning and intermediate riders to dismount frequently. The trail ends at the Brookbank trailhead on Forest Rd. 557 after 2.2 mi., from which it's possible to return to Flagstaff via the Oldham Trail, go deeper into the forest up the Brookbank Trail, or return to the beginning along Forest Rd. 557. Elevation gain 100 ft. Open early spring-late fall.

⚡ DAYTRIPS FROM FLAGSTAFF

WALNUT CANYON NATIONAL MONUMENT. The remnants of more than 300 rooms in 13th-century Sinaguan dwellings make up Walnut Canyon National Monument, constructed within a 400 ft. deep canyon. A glassed-in observation deck in the **Visitors Center** overlooks the whole canyon. The steep, self-guided 1 mi. round trip **Island Trail** snakes down from the Visitors Center past 25 cliff dwellings. The 0.8 mi. **Rim Trail** offers views of the canyon and passes rim-top sites. Every Saturday morning from 10am-1pm, rangers lead groups of five on 2 mi. hikes into Walnut Canyon to the original ranger cabin and more remote cliff dwellings. Hiking boots, long pants, and reservations are required for these challenging 2½hr. hikes. There's also a trailhead for the Mexico-to-Utah Arizona trail 1.7 mi. west of the entrance road. *(10 mi. east of Flagstaff, off I-40, at Exit 204. ☎526-3367. Open daily 8am-6pm; off-season 9am-5pm. $3, under 17 free. Call ahead; hours change frequently.)*

SUNSET CRATER VOLCANO NATIONAL MONUMENT. The crater encompassed by Sunset Crater Volcano National Monument appeared in AD 1065. Over the next 200 years, a 1000 ft. high cinder cone took shape as a result of periodic eruptions. The self-guided **Lava Flow Nature Trail** wanders 1 mi. through the surreal landscape surrounding the cone, 1½ mi. east of the **Visitors Center,** where gnarled trees lie uprooted amid the rocky black terrain. Lava tube tours have been permanently discontinued due to falling lava, and hiking up Sunset Crater itself is not permitted. Those intent on peering into a volcano can hike the 1 mi. round-trip trail into Lenox Crater (250 ft. elevation gain), departing the road 1 mi. east of the Visitors Center. *(12 mi. north of Flagstaff on U.S. 89.* ☎ *526-0502. Open daily 8am-6pm; off-season 8am-5pm. $3, under 16 free; includes admission to Wupatki.)* The **Bonito Campground ❶,** in the Coconino National Forest at the entrance to Sunset Crater, provides tent sites ($12; drinking water, flush toilets).

WUPATKI NATIONAL MONUMENT. Wupatki possesses some of the Southwest's most scenic Pueblo sites, situated 18 mi. northeast of Sunset Crater, along a stunning road with views of the Painted Desert. The Sinagua moved here in the 11th century, after the Sunset Crater eruption forced them to evacuate the land to the south. Archaeologists speculate that in less than 200 years, droughts, disease, and over-farming led the Sinagua to abandon these stone houses perched on the sides of *arroyos* in view of the San Francisco Peaks. Five empty pueblos face the 14 mi. road from the Visitors Center to where it reconnects with U.S. 89. The largest and most accessible, **Wupatki,** located on a ½ mi. round-trip loop trail from the Visitors Center, rises three stories. Roughly 4 mi. northwest of the Visitors Center, the spectacular **Doney Mountain Trail** climbs ½ mi. from the picnic area to the summit. Get info and trail guide brochures at the **Visitors Center.** Backcountry hiking is not permitted. *(☎ 679-2365. Open daily 8am-5pm. Monument open daily 8am-5pm.)*

NEAR FLAGSTAFF

Within two hour's drive of Flagstaff, a stunning range of Southwestern scenery and activities presents itself. To the south, a drive through beautiful red-rock country will lead you to new-agey Sedona or the refreshingly less-touristed towns of Jerome and Prescott. East of the city, Rte. 66 leads to the Petrified Forest and Painted Desert, and to the northeast, the Navajo Nation spans the rest of the state. With this in mind, don't let the Grand Canyon be your only day-trip from Flagstaff.

SEDONA ☎ 928

Since Sedona is a UFO sighting hotspot, one wonders if the Martians are simply mistaking its deep red-rock towers for home. The scores of tourists who descend upon the town year-round (Sedona and nearby Oak Creek Canyon rival the Grand Canyon for tourist mass) certainly aren't; they come for sights that

IN
RECENT
NEWS

A BURNING ISSUE

In an unprecedented move in the history of US forest management, on June 28th, 2002, the Coconino National Forest closed all land under its jurisdiction to guard against human-caused fire starts. In light of the devastation wrought by the Rodeo Fire, officials have chosen to prohibit all access to the Coconino in the hopes of preserving forest resources. The closures will be lifted as soon as sufficient rain falls to mitigate the fire danger, but with the drought now in its eighth year many fear that forest closures will become a routine feature of life in northern Arizona.

In the wake of the driest year on record, rangers report that throughout the Coconino trees currently hold less water than lumber in a lumberyard. Furthermore, as such extreme drought conditions cause trees to emit flammable substances called turpines, touching an unlit match to a tree's bark will result in spontaneous combustion.

The dry spell leading to the current crisis began in 1995 and has resulted in abbreviated ski seasons as well as devastating forest fires. While some officials note that extreme climate fluctuations have long been a feature of Southwest history, others speculate that current regional trends may be linked to global warming.

would make Newton question gravity. Dramatic copper-toned behemoths dotted with pines tower over Sedona, rising from the earth with such flair and dazzle that they feel like a perfectly manufactured tourist attraction. Some of the more creative folks in town will tell you that they were man-made, perhaps by the Egyptians. Sedona is also the New Age capital of the US, with enough spiritual healers and vortexes to alleviate any crisis, mid-life or otherwise. Though the downtown is overrun with overpriced boutiques and cafes, the rocks are simply spectacular.

ORIENTATION AND PRACTICAL INFORMATION

Sedona lies 120 mi. north of Phoenix (take I-17 north to Rte. 179) and 30 mi. south of Flagstaff (take I-17 south to Rte. 179). The airport is tiny, with no regular flights, and neither Greyhound nor Amtrak provides service to Sedona. For the car-less, the **Sedona-Phoenix Shuttle** (☎282-2066) is one of the few options, running six trips daily between the two cities ($40). The **Sedona Chamber of Commerce,** at Forest Rd. and U.S. 89A, provides info on accommodations, camping, and local attractions. (☎282-7722. Open M-Sa 8:30am-5pm, Su 9am-3pm.) The **police** department is on the main drag, U.S. 89A (non-emergency ☎282-3100). The **Sedona Medical Center,** 3700 W. U.S. 89A (☎204-3000), at the western edge of town, provides medical services in the area. The **Sedona Public Library,** 3250 White Bear Rd., has free **Internet access.** (☎282-7714. Open M noon-8pm, Tu and Th 10am-6pm, W 10am-8pm, F-Su 10am-5pm. One block north of Hwy. 89A at the west end of town.) **Post office:** 190 W. U.S. 89A (☎282-3511; open M-F 9am-5pm). **ZIP code:** 86336. **Temporary employment:** Sedona's tourist businesses furnish a wealth of opportunities for short-term work. Look for help wanted signs in shops and restaurants, or ask directly inside.

ACCOMMODATIONS

Lodging in town is a bit pricey, but a few deals can be had; however, it's not a bad idea to make Sedona a daytrip from Flagstaff or Cottonwood. Check the local papers or bulletin boards at New Age shops for opportunities (a good place to look is the string of stores on Rte. 179 near the junction with 89A, notably the purple Visitors Center). In addition, cheaper options, such as the Willow Tree Inn (see **Jerome,** p. 119), can be found in Cottonwood, 15 mi. away, where a number of budget motels line U.S. 89.

Los Abrigodos Resort & Spa, 160 Portal Ln. (☎282-1777), caters to Sedona's more affluent crowd, but offers a whole heck of a lot for the dollar. With its sprawling 22-acre compound, the resort has three restaurants, an incredible location, and its famous full-service spa. Guests are within walking distance of Talaquepaque—a beautiful, Spanish-style walking community of artsy shops and kitschy restaurants. Suites start at $165. Reservations highly recommended. ❺

Los Abrigodos Lodge, 270 N. Hwy. 89A. (☎282-7125 or 800-521-3131), boasts an incredible view of the surrounding carmine monoliths and has a pool and a spa. Within walking distance of some of Sedona's best shopping and food. Rooms from $119. ❺

White House Inn, 2986 W. U.S. 89A (☎282-6680), is one of the cheapest options, with singles and doubles, some with kitchenettes, some with gorgeous views, for $48-64. ❸

CAMPING

Most of the campsites in the area are clustered around U.S. 89A as it heads north along Oak Creek Canyon on its way to Flagstaff. There are private campgrounds aplenty, but most cater to the RV crowd rather than to backpackers. The **US Forest Service campsites** ❶ along 89A provide the best, cheapest option for tent-toters.

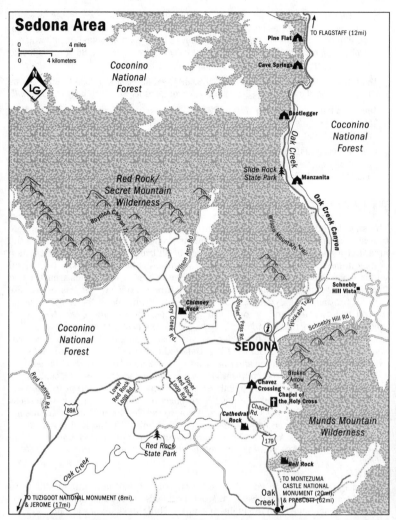

Sedona Area

Coconino National Forest

TO FLAGSTAFF (12mi)

Pine Flat

Cave Springs

Bootlegger

Coconino National Forest

Red Rock/ Secret Mountain Wilderness

Boynton Canyon Tr.

Wilson Arch Rd.

Slide Rock State Park

Manzanita

Oak Creek

Oak Creek Canyon

Wilson Mountain Trail

Chimney Rock

Dry Creek Rd.

Soldier's Pass Rd.

SEDONA

Schnebly Hill Vista

Huckaby Trail

Schnebly Hill Rd.

Coconino National Forest

Red Canyon Rd.

89A

Lower Red Rock Loop Rd.

Upper Red Rock Loop Rd.

Chavez Crossing

Broken Arrow Tr.

Chapel of the Holy Cross

Munds Mountain Wilderness

Chapel Rd.

Cathedral Rock

179

Red Rock State Park

Oak Creek

Bell Rock

TO MONTEZUMA CASTLE NATIONAL MONUMENT (20mi), & PRESCOTT (62mi)

TO TUZIGOOT NATIONAL MONUMENT (8mi), & JEROME (17mi)

Oak Creek

North of Sedona, between nine and 20 mi. from the town, four separate camp-grounds—**Manzanita, Bootlegger, Cave Springs, and Pine Flat (east and west)**—main-tain over 150 campsites. They all have similar facilities, with picnic tables, toilets, drinking water (except at Bootlegger), and trash containers located at every camp-ground. (☎527-3600 for local info; ☎877-444-6777 national reservation service number. 7-night max. stay. Tent sites $12.)

🍴 FOOD

Like many things in Sedona, restaurants can be expensive. However, there are a few good deals to be had.

Casa Rincon, 2620 U.S. 89A (☎282-4849), seemingly stares down passersby with a coyly inviting, margarita-induced smile. Boasting some of the best dining in town, Rincon attracts patrons with a daily happy hour (3-6pm; $3 margaritas), mouth-watering combination platters ($10-13), and almost daily live entertainment. Bring your appetite and check your troubles at the door. Open daily 11:30am-9pm. ❷

The Coffee Pot Restaurant, 2050 W. U.S. 89A (☎282-6626), a local favorite, serves 101 varieties of omelettes ($5-8) and 3 kinds of tacos for $4. Open daily 6am-9pm. ❶

The Red Planet Diner, 1665 W. U.S. 89A (☎282-6070), beams patrons in with a flying saucer and extraterrestrial allure. Martian milkshakes ($4) and Universal noodle bowls ($6-9) are "out-of-this-world." Open daily 11am-11pm. ❷

India Palace, 1910 W. U.S. 89A, in the Basha's shopping center, has a $6 lunch buffet with curry, vegetable stew, and tandoori chicken. The menu has vegetarian options and entrees under $10. (☎204-2300. Open daily 11am-2:30pm and 5-10pm.) ❷

▟ OUTDOOR ACTIVITIES

The singular beauty of the rock formations around Sedona make it a formidable tourist magnet. The influx of tourists means prosperity and development for the area, but it also has resulted in intense use of all trails, roads, and facilities. As a consequence, the area directly around Sedona has been especially organized within Coconino National Forest as the **Red Rock Country.** Within this area, the **Red Rock Pass** is required for parking on any of the forest service roads. Passes cost $5/$15/$20 for daily/weekly/annual coverage and are available at the ranger station, the tourist info office, and various local businesses. Rangers ticket vehicles parked on the forest roads that fail to display passes. For the best info about the area, visit the **Sedona Ranger District office,** 250 Brewer Road. Going eastbound on U.S. 89A, it's your first right before Burger King. Detailed topographical and trail maps are available, as well as camping and hiking advice. (☎282-4119. Open M-F 8am-4pm.)

Much of Sedona' environs falls into the areas of the **Red Rock Secret Mountain Wilderness** and the **Munds Mountain Wilderness.** Be sure to pay attention to the well-marked borders between the undeveloped parts of Sedona and these wilderness areas; inside the wilderness areas, in addition to the Red Rock Pass requirements, strict rules are enforced to protect the natural habitat. In the Red Rock Secret Mountain Wilderness Area, no backcountry camping is permitted, and mountain bikes and motorized vehicles are prohibited in both wilderness areas.

HIKING

It's nearly impossible to go wrong with any of the well-maintained and well-marked trails in and around Sedona. Most trailheads are located on the forest service roads that snake from the highways into the hills and canyons around Sedona. Few trails have water on them; be sure to carry plenty, especially in the summer.

Wilson Mountain Loop (4½ mi. round-trip, 5-7hr.). Not really a loop, this strenuous combination trail uses North Wilson Trail (FS #123) to ascend Wilson Mountain, and Wilson Mountain Trail (FS #10) as the descent, ending 1 mi. south of the trailhead. From the trailhead at the Encinoso picnic area, the path snakes up through a canyon to reach the bench of Wilson Mountain. At the top of this rise is an alpine meadow, offering gorgeous views of Oak Creek Canyon, the Sedona rock formations, the San Francisco Peaks, and even the Mogollon Rim. The trail then reaches the junction with the Wilson Mountain Trail, and steeply descends along a fault canyon and through sparse juniper foliage. It arrives at U.S. 89A at the picnic site under Midgley Bridge, 250 ft. lower than it began. Total elevation gain 1750 ft.

ARIZONA

IS THE FORCE WITH YOU?

Could a powerful force be lurking near the Sedona airport or parks? Psychic **Page Bryant** thought so in 1980, when she divined several vortices, or areas of great psychic and spiritual energy, around town. People who enter the vortices have claimed to have experienced episodes of extreme psychic and emotional alertness, and sometimes **spiritual healing** in the long term. Vortices have become a sensation among the New Age crowd since Bryant's discovery, and much conjecturing and scientific study on the subject has been conducted. **Extra-terrestrial meddling,** spiritual presences, high magnetism from Sedona's metal-rich rocks, and **parallel universe cross-over** have all been cited as causes. Perhaps you can unlock their mystery: the main vortices are at the airport, Bell Rock, Cathedral Rock, and Boyton Canyon.

FS #161—Huckaby Trail (5.2 mi. round-trip, 6-7hr.). This moderate trail, constructed in 1998, traverses the area between Midgley Bridge and Schnebly Rd., crossing Oak Creek. An eighth of a mile after the Schnebly Rd. trailhead, the Margs Draw trail forks to the left; keep right. 2 mi. into the trail, it crosses Oak Creek; no bridge currently exists over the water, but in normal conditions the level is low enough to permit an easy fording. The trail climbs up the canyon under Midgley Bridge via switchbacks, and ends at the same parking lot as the Wilson Mountain Loop. Total elevation gain 700 ft.

FS #47—Boynton Canyon Trail (5 mi. round-trip, 3hr.). This incredibly popular (and, as a result, often crowded) route can be accessed from the western prong of Dry Creek Rd. off of U.S. 89A in the center of Sedona. The path can be rocky at times, but the elevation gain is spread out the length of the trail, making for an easy, pleasant jaunt. Since this is a canyon trail, views are limited, and occasionally obscured by trees in the conifer forest. Total elevation gain 450 ft.

MOUNTAIN BIKING

In the words of one Sedona biker, Sedona single track unfurls like a ribbon beneath you. **Mountain Bike Heaven,** 1695 W. U.S. 89A, is the outfitter of choice for bikers in the know. Rentals are available starting at $25 per day, and they lead occasional free bike trips. (☎282-1312. Open M-F 9am-6pm, Sa 8am-5pm, Su 8am-4pm.) A guide book or map with detailed directions is a must for those interested in serious biking in the area, but a few "must do" Sedona routes are listed here. One is the Huckaby trail (see above) which, because of its rolling elevations, makes for an exciting, fast ride. Others include:

Broken Arrow (7 mi. round-trip, 3hr.). Head south on Rte. 179 for 1.3 mi., where a broken arrow sign clearly marks the turnoff to Morgan Rd. (left from the Y-intersection). The trailhead is just down the road, past a cattleguard. Barrels full of rocks serve as posts along the trail. A twisty single track leads uphill for about 1 mi. At this point, several trails branch to the left, leading to a deep sinkhole and Submarine rock along a variety of paths. Stick to the right if you want to continue along the trail, which continues for another several miles. At about the 3rd mile of the route, the trail intersects with a Jeep road at a cul-de-sac. Two bike routes radiate from the Jeep loop; the one on the right leads up to Chicken Point. The one on the left is the continuation of the trail (dubbed Little Horse), which meanders for a while, a wash, and through a gate. Past the gate, the trail twists around again, crossing a broader wash and sharply turning every which way. The trail will split off several times; generally, stay to the left. The Little Horse trailhead comes up soon, and you've rejoined Rte. 179.

Soldier's Pass (2.3 mi. round-trip, 1hr.). An entire area rather than a single ride, the maze of tracks around the Soldier's Pass trail can be very confusing, so hit the trails with one of the local bike clubs until you're familiar with the myriad tracks that criss-

ARIZONA

cross the area. The loop, however, is straight forward enough, if a bit on the short side. From Central Sedona, take Soldier's Pass north until the intersection with Rim Shadow Drive. Turn right, follow the main road to the parking lot (open 6am-8pm). From the parking lot, head up north on a Jeep road that dead-ends. A single track picks up where the road leaves off; follow this as it winds past a scattering of pools, eventually reaching the Devil's Kitchen sinkhole. From here, a single track bears left, back to the parking lot.

ROCK CLIMBING

The rock formations that punctuate the Sedona landscape provide ample, quality opportunities for aspiring spider-men. Finding some of the more out-of-the-way places (and making the most of the obvious ones) may require some expert advice. **Canyon Outfitters,** on the west side of town on U.S. 89A, can provide just that. (☎ 282-5294. Open M-F 9am-6pm, Sa 9am-5pm, Su 11am-4pm.) David, the climbing expert there, self-publishes the *Red Lizard Guide Book,* giving exact details and directions to the climbing areas around Sedona.

Some of the best sites are located just meters from uptown Sedona, at the **Uptown Crags** directly behind the shops and restaurants that front the eastern fringe of Sedona's U.S. 89A. A playground for the climber, these faces and rocky gullies provide a smorgasbord of bouldering and sport climbing opportunities. The **Coffeepot Crags,** on the north side of town by the road of the same name, provide another great spot for climbers, with a variety of routes in close proximity. The most famous single climbing spot, and the most photographed rock formation in the area, is **Cathedral Rock,** located off the east side of Rte. 179. The finest climb off of this formation is the **Mace,** a must-do for serious traditional climbers.

DRIVING

Scenic driving is nearly as plentiful as the red rocks. The Chamber of Commerce is very helpful in suggesting routes. The **Red Rock Loop** (20 mi., 1hr.) provides views of mind-blowing rock formations and a little dirt road adventure. Dry Creek and Airport Rd. are also good drives. For those hoping to see Sedona's wild off-road side, jeep tours are available from a number of companies. Generally, trips are $35-75 and 2-4hr. in length. **Sedona Adventures,** 276 N. U.S. 89A (☎ 282-3500 or 800-888-9494), offers some of the least expensive trips in the area.

👁 🗻 SIGHTS AND OTHER ACTIVITIES

RED ROCK STATE PARK. Located on the well-marked Red Rock Loop Rd. on U.S. 89A, 15 mi. west of Sedona, Red Rock State Park serves as a nature preserve and recreation area along a woody, secluded area of Oak Creek. Numerous trails criss-cross the park, and are great for wildlife watching. None of the trails are particularly challenging or steep, and no single trail is longer than 2 mi. round-trip. A brochure with detailed trail listings can be picked up at the Visitors Center. In addition to the plethora of self-guided trails, rangers lead occasional interpretive hikes—bird hikes take place on Wednesday and Saturday at 7am, hikes up Eagle's Nest Loop to the House of Apache Fire (a palatial ruined chalet) on Saturday at 8am, and full moon hikes (2 per cycle) start at 6:30pm. No swimming or wading allowed in the park. (☎ 282-6907. *Visitors Center open daily 9am-5pm. Park open Apr.-Nov. daily 8am-6pm; Oct.-Mar. 8am-5pm. $5 per car, $1 per pedestrian or cyclist.*)

CHAPEL OF THE HOLY CROSS. Lying just outside a 1000 ft. rock wall, the Chapel of the Holy Cross rests in the middle of red sandstone rock formations just outside of Sedona, and represents a feat of inspired architecture on the part of the Catholic community that funded its construction. A long winding path leads to the Chapel, inside of which candles burn around a modern icon of Jesus. While the view from the parking lot is a religious experience itself, the view from the chapel is divine. *(On Chapel Rd. ☎282-4069. Open daily 9am-5pm.)*

MONTEZUMA CASTLE NATIONAL MONUMENT. Built by the Sinagua tribe in the 12th century, this 20-room cliff dwelling was originally assumed to be an Aztec construction, with local myth claiming the Castle as Montezuma's last refuge. While it's now known that the Sinagua were unrelated to the Columbian-era Aztecs, let not the misnomer keep you from this fascinating historical site. Unfortunately, you can't get very close to the castle, but the view from the paved path below is excellent and wheelchair accessible. *(10 mi. south of Sedona on I-17. ☎567-3322. Open daily 8am-7pm, off-season 8am-5pm. $2, under 17 free.)*

MONTEZUMA WELL. A beautiful lake formed by the collapse of an underground cavern, Montezuma Well once served as the earliest irrigation system in the Southwest, built by the Sinagua who lived here. A trail winds its way around the lip of the well, highly elevated above the surface of the water, affording good views of the Verde Valley. *(Off I-17 11 mi. north of the castle. Open daily 8am-7pm. Free.)*

TUZIGOOT NATIONAL MONUMENT. Built between 1125 and 1400, this dramatic Sinaguan building stands on a ridge and overlooks the Verde Valley. The intricate structure leaves a lasting appreciation for Sinaguan architectural innovation. *(Take U.S. 89A to Rte. 279, and continue through Cottonwood to the monument, 20 mi. southwest of Sedona. ☎634-5564. Open daily 8am-7pm; in winter 8am-5pm. $2, under 17 free.)*

JEROME   ☎928

Precariously perched on the side of Mingus Mountain, Jerome once attracted miners, speculators, saloon owners, and madams who came to the city following the copper boom of the late 1800s. By 1920, the city ranked as Arizona's third largest. However, the 1929 stock market crash threw Jerome's economy into a downward spiral, and by mid-century Jerome was a ghost town. More recently, bikers, hippies, ex-cowboys, and artists have arrived, drawn by the charm and spectacular scenery of the town. Jerome's current incarnation is, in one respect, drastically different from its start—tourist mining has replaced copper mining as the main industry. Yet the strange, lively flavor of this singular town continues to thrive. The **Jerome State Historic Park**, ½ mi. off U.S. 89A just as you enter town, provides a worthwhile panoramic view of the town and a small museum. (☎634-5381. Open daily 8am-5pm. $2.50, ages 7-13 $1.) There's a small **post office** on Jerome St. 120 Main St. (☎634-8241. Open M-F 9am-5pm.) **ZIP code:** 86331.

Budget travelers should make Jerome a daytrip from Flagstaff or Phoenix, as lodging tends to be expensive. Staying over in Cottonwood, 15 mi. from both Jerome and Sedona, is a good alternative. The **Willow Tree Inn ❸**, off I-17 in Cottonwood, offers classy, comfortable rooms. (☎634-3678. Singles Nov.-Apr. $40-42, Mar.-Oct. $44-48; doubles $44-48/$50-59.) In addition, a number of budget motels are situated along U.S. 89 in Cottonwood. In town, **The Inn at Jerome ❸**, 309 Main St., is one of the lower-priced joints. The rooms are all given quaint, cute names (such as Dance Romance) that match the potpourri and wicker-work decor. (☎634-5094 or 800-634-5094. Rooms $50-90 including full breakfast.)

PETRIFIED FOREST NATIONAL PARK   ☎928

Sixty thousand acres of technicolor formations, chiseled stone ramparts, and countless stands of glistening petrified trees draw countless visitors annually, and for good reason—this geological wonderland is a unique, funtabulous experience. Some 225 million years ago, when Arizona's desert was a swampland, volcanic ash covered the logs, slowing their decay. When silica-rich water seeped through the

ARIZONA

PROTOTYPE OF A CITY The planned city of **Arcosanti**, off I-17 at Exit 262, is designed to embody Italian architect Paolo Soleri's concept of "arcology," or "architecture and ecology working together as one integral process." Arcology's main tenet is treating human habitation as an ecological problem as well as a structural one; the goal is to create a living environment that optimally fuses with the surrounding natural environment. Every facet of Arcosanti is engineered for a specific reason, melding together inhabitants' needs with the surrounding desert's resources. The result is a spectacularly efficient and utilizable use of the barren land's natural assets.

The architecture of Arcosanti is revolutionary. The building materials are modern materials—concrete, steel and insulation—but are used in a way to make it more artful than many of the expensive modern showcase buildings in L.A. and New York. Arches form working and community spaces; geometric modules stack together to form the Visitors Centers and cafeteria. Every bit of space is maximized and used ingeniously; the heating vents harness the excess heat generated by the bronze foundry, and a waterfall-on-demand flows through the community theater. When complete, the city will be extremely efficient supplying in food, power, and all other resources. Arcosanti has been under construction since 1970 and is now expected to be finished by 2010.

A great alternative to merely viewing the innovative factory town of Arcosanti is to partake in its construction. Anyone with an interest in "arcology" may participate in either the one-week ($450) or five-week ($950) programs available (prices include room and board). The first week of both workshops is a seminar led by Soleri himself, while the last four weeks of the longer program is more engaging, with time spent either building the town's structures, gardening the surprisingly fertile desert land, or both. The five-week program is particularly rewarding, as participants learn a respect for finding a reasonable median between human's needs and wants and what the earth can provide—something that only such intensive involvement can provide. (☎632-7135; www.arcosanti.org. Visitors Center open daily 9am-5pm. Tours daily every hr. 10am-4pm. $8 donation requested.)

wood, the silica crystallized into quartz, producing rainbow hues. Layers of colorful sediment were also laid down in this floodplain, creating the stunning colors that stripe its rock formations.

When a route for the transcontinental railroad was being scouted in the mid-1800s, surveyors stumbled across this incredible region. Within a few years of the building of the railroad, the "forest" became a prime attraction for sightseers and collectors and, in the decades that followed, thousands of tons of rock were removed. Local residents recognized that the supply of petrified wood was not limitless. In 1906, the area was designated a national monument, and in 1962, it was made a national park. One of the most unique attractions in the Southwest, the park welcomes over one million visitors a year. Still, much of the solitude of this magical world is preserved just out of sight of the park drive and waits to be explored by those willing to get off the beaten track.

■ ▮ **ORIENTATION AND PRACTICAL INFORMATION.** Roughly speaking, the park can be divided into two parts: the northern **Painted Desert** and the southern **Petrified Forest.** An entrance station and Visitors Center welcomes guests at each end and a 28 mi. road connects the two sections. With lookout points and trails at intervals along the road, driving from one end of the park to the other is a good way to take in the full spectrum of colors and landscapes.

You can enter the park either from the north or the south. (Open June-Aug. daily 7am-7pm; Sept.-May 8am-5pm. Entrance fee $10 per vehicle, $5 per pedestrian; $5 motorcycle.) **Amtrak** and **Greyhound** both run through **Winslow** and **Gallup, NM;** buses also stop at the Circle K in **Holbrook.** There is no public transportation to either part of the park. To access the southern section of the park, take U.S. 180 from St. Johns 36 mi. west or from Holbrook 19 mi. east. Holbrook is a major stopover town on I-40 and provides travelers with a full range of services. The **Rainbow Forest Museum** provides a look at petrified logs up close and serves as a **Visitors Center.** (☎524-6822. Open June-Aug. daily 7am-7pm; Sept.-May 8am-5pm. Free.) To reach the northern section of the park, take I-40 to Exit 311, 107 mi. east of Flagstaff and 65 mi. west of Gallup, NM. The **Painted Desert Visitors Center** is less than 1 mi. from the exit. It shows a video overview of the park every 30 min. (☎524-6228. Open June-Aug. daily 7am-7pm; Sept.-May 8am-5pm.) **Water** is available at both the Visitors Centers and the Painted Desert Inn. There's **gas** at the Painted Desert Visitors Center. In case of **emergency,** call the ranger dispatch (☎524-9726).

⛺ 🍴 ACCOMMODATIONS AND FOOD. There are no established campgrounds in the park, but **backcountry camping** is allowed in the fantastical Painted Desert Wilderness with a free permit. Backpackers must park their cars at Kachina Point and enter the wilderness via the 1 mi. access trail. No fires are allowed. For the less mobile, **free camping** is also allowed at the **Crystal Forest Museum and Gifts,** a private trading post at the junction of U.S. 180 and the park road, just outside park boundaries. (☎524-3500. Bathrooms and water.)

From Gallup to the park, Rte. 66 "ambiance" and services pretty much disappear beneath the ever-encroaching desert, but the route rises again at full strength in Holbrook, 26 mi. west of the park. Budget accommodations and roadside diners abound. To get a real taste of Rte. 66, stay at the **Wigwam Motel ❷,** 811 W. Hopi Dr., where 19 concrete tepees have awaited travelers for half a century. (☎524-3048. clewis97@apartrails.com. Reception 4-9pm. Check-out 11am. Singles $35; doubles $41. Reservations recommended Mar.-Oct.) You can experience another Rte. 66 fixture by hitchin' your horse (or, for that matter, your fuel-efficient hatchback) at **Joe and Aggie's Cafe ❶,** 120 W. Hopi Dr., where the Mexican specialties ($4-9) are hard to beat. (☎524-6540. Open M-Sa 7am-8pm.) **Gallup, NM** (see p. 398), and **Flagstaff, AZ** (see p. 103), offer more plentiful lodging and eating options.

📷 🥾 SIGHTS AND OUTDOORS. Most travelers opt to drive the 27 mi. park road from north to south, but the trip in either direction is magnificent. From the north, the first stop after the Visitors Center and the entrance station is **Tiponi Point,** one of eight Painted Desert overlooks. While it isn't necessary to park and get out at every one, visiting a couple gives a good impression of the colorful expanse to the north. From the next stop at **Tawa Point,** the **Painted Desert Rim Trail** (½ mi. one-way) skirts the mesa edge above the Lithodendron Wash and the Black Forest before ending at the showpiece lookout **Kachina Point.** The **Painted Desert Inn** (open daily 8am-4pm) at the point is a National Historic Landmark and houses a small, interesting museum. The panoramas from Kachina Point are among the best in the park, and the point provides access for travel into the **Painted Desert Wilderness,** the park's designated region for backcountry hiking and camping. There are **no trails** in the wilderness, and no permits are required for day hikes. For camping and multi-day excursions, free permits are available at the Visitors Centers.

As the road crosses I-40, it enters the Petrified Forest portion of the park. The next stop is the 100-room **Puerco Pueblo,** which was built by ancient pueblo peoples sometime before AD 1400. A short trail through the pueblo offers viewpoints of nearby petroglyphs. Many more petroglyphs may be seen at **Newspaper Rock,** but from more of a distance. Be sure to notice the incredible petrified tree cross-section encased in rock above and to the left of the glyphs.

ARIZONA

THE FIGHT OVER NAVAJO COAL

There is a very standard narrative of Anglo expansion into the wild Indian lands of the Southwest—settlers arrive to cultivate the virgin land and natives, through warfare, disease and social marginalization, disappear from the scene. The Indian, for most Americans, has turned into a nostalgic symbol of a bygone era.

Yet, Indians themselves refuse to be ignored in the land they once ruled. The Navajo Nation has taken an all-American approach in trying to defend its interests: it has filed a lawsuit. At issue is whether then Attorney General David Hodel, as the Navajo Nation alleges, socially conspired with Peabody Coal Co. to undermine contract negotiations with the tribe in the 1980s. Over half a billion dollars has been awarded already to the Navajo Nation in the matter for illegal actions made by the company and the government; payment is pending a Supreme Court appeal.

Unfortunately, the lawsuit is just the least of the nation's worries. To wit, the Navajos are beset by a host of problems, including: a lack of infrastructure, poorly paved roads, a shortage of electricity and water, high unemployment, chronic alcoholism, and limited police and fire protection. With the recent exposure given to the Navajo Nation through the aforementioned lawsuit, as well as the recent release of *Windtalkers* chronicling the Navajo's successful contribution to the American military effort in WWII, perhaps the public will realize that the Native American is not yet vanished.

The road then wanders through the eerie moonscape of **The Tepees,** before arriving at the 3 mi. **Blue Mesa** vehicle loop. This area exhibits some of the park's wildest geology. Brilliant blue clay hills are mixed with tree fragments in a sort of impressionist's daydream. The moderate **Blue Mesa Trail** (1 mi.) loops through the belly of the badlands and offers a respite from the cars and crowds. The overlook at **Jasper Forest** provides views of an area that was heavily looted by souvenir seekers around the turn of the 19th century. Farther along, **Giant Logs Trail,** near the southern Visitors Center, is peppered with fragments of the petrified wood. Both trails are less than 1 mi. and involve little elevation change but travel through the densest concentration of petrified wood in the world. Giant Logs features **Old Faithful,** which at over 9 ft. in diameter is the largest tree in the park. Picking up fragments of the wood is illegal and traditionally unlucky; if the district attorney doesn't get you, then the demons will. Those who *must* have a piece should buy one at any of the myriad kitschy stores along I-40.

NAVAJO RESERVATION

Although anthropologists believe the Navajo are descended from groups of Athabascan people who migrated to the Southwest from Northern Canada in the 14th and 15th centuries, the Navajo themselves view their existence as the culmination of a journey through three other worlds to this life, the "Glittering World." Four sacred mountains bound Navajoland— Mt. Blanca to the east, Mt. Taylor to the south, San Francisco Peak to the west, and Mt. Hesperus to the north. The land is holy to the Navajo and this is apparent in the reverence for it.

During the second half of the 19th century, Indian reservations evolved out of the US government's *ad hoc* attempts to prevent fighting between Native Americans and Anglos while facilitating white settlement on native lands. Initially, the reservation system imposed a kind of wardship over the Native Americans, which lasted for over a century, until a series of Supreme Court decisions beginning in the 1960s reasserted the tribes' legal standing as semi-sovereign nations. Today, the **Navajo Nation** is the largest reservation in America and covers more than 27,000 square miles of northeastern Arizona, southeastern Utah, and northwestern New Mexico. Home to over 180,000 Navajo, or Dineh ("the People") as they call themselves, the reservation comprises one-tenth of

For visitors to the reservation, cultural sensitivity takes on a new importance; despite the many state and interstate roads that traverse the reservation, the land is legally and culturally distinct. Superficially, much of the Navajo Nation and other reservations resemble the rest of the US. In reality, deep rifts exist between Native American and "Anglo" culture—the term used to refer to the non-reservation US society. The reservation has its own police force and laws. Driving or hiking off designated trails and established routes is considered trespassing unless accompanied by a guide. Possession and consumption of alcohol are prohibited on the reservation. General photography is allowed unless otherwise stated, but photographing the Navajo people requires their permission (a gratuity is usually expected). Tourist photography is not permitted among the Hopi. As always, the best remedy for cultural friction is simple respect.

the US Native American population. Within the Navajo borders, the smaller **Hopi Reservation** is home to around 10,000 Hopi ("Peaceable People")..

Lively reservation politics are written up in the local *Navajo-Hopi Observer* and *Navajo Times*. For a taste of the Navajo language and Native American ritual songs, tune your **radio** to 660AM, "The Voice of the Navajo." Remember to advance your watch 1hr. during the summer; the Navajo Nation runs on **Mountain Daylight Time,** while the rest of Arizona, including the Hopi Reservation, does not observe daylight savings and thus operates on Pacific Time during the warmer months and Mountain Standard Time during the cooler months. The **area code** for the reservation is 928 in Arizona, 505 in New Mexico, 435 in Utah.

Monument Valley, Canyon de Chelly, Navajo National Monument, Rainbow Bridge, Antelope Canyon, and the roads and trails that access these sights all lie on Navajo land. Those planning to hike through Navajo territory should head to one of the many **parks and recreation departments** for a backcountry permit, or mail a request along with a money order or certified check to P.O. Box 9000, Window Rock, AZ 86515 ($5 per person). The "border towns" of **Gallup, NM** (see p. 398), and **Flagstaff, AZ** (see p. 103) are good gateways to the reservations, with car rental agencies, inexpensive accommodations, and frequent Greyhound service on I-40. Budget travelers can camp at the National Monuments or Navajo campgrounds, or stay in one of the student-run motels in high schools around the reservation.

CANYON DE CHELLY   ☎928

The red-hued cliffs of Canyon de Chelly ("*d' Shay*") and the adjoining canyons in the national monument have a remarkable history, having served as a home to native peoples for almost five millennia. The Basketmaker, Ancestral Puebloan, Hopi, and, finally, the Navajo have all utilized the protection offered by the cliffs and the rich soil of the canyon floor. However, like much of the region, de Chelly's history has been colored by repeated conflicts between Native Americans and Anglos. In 1805, in what is now called Massacre Cave, 115 women and children were shot by Spanish soldiers. Later in the 1860s, the famed Kit Carson starved the Navajo out of the canyon, in order to displace them to central New Mexico.

■ ⌨ **ORIENTATION AND PRACTICAL INFORMATION.** The most common route to the park is from **Chambers,** 75 mi. south, at the intersection of I-40 and U.S. 191; you can also come from the north via U.S. 191. The monument sits 3 mi. east of **Chinle** on Navajo Rte. 7. One of the larger towns on the reservation, Chinle, at the intersection of Navajo Rte. 7 and U.S. 191, has ATMs, gas stations, grocery stores, laundromats, restaurants, a hospital, and a post office. A number of **Navajo**

ARIZONA

> **WHAT LANGUAGE IS THIS?** With the release of the Nicholas Cage vehicle Windtalkers, an odd sort of fame has emerged for the **Navajo Code Talkers** of the US Marine Corps. With the bombing of Pearl Harbor in December 1941 and subsequent hostilities, the skill and implications of Japanese code-breaking were readily apparent. In looking for a code that would stymie Japanese efforts, the US military turned to a number of young men from the Navajo Reservation. Initially, 29 Navajos were enlisted into the elite ranks of the code talkers, and by the end of the war over 400 men had entered the US Marines to make up this vital communications web in the Pacific. The code was critical to the success of a number of US engagements, including the victory at Iwo Jima, and was never broken by the Japanese. You can visit an exhibit commemorating the actions of these courageous men at the **Burger King,** of all places, along Rte. 160 in **Kayenta.**

Transit System (☎ 729-4002) buses run daily from there. The monument is also accessible via Navajo Rte. 64 out of **Tsaile,** 28 mi. northeast of the Visitors Center. The monument's **Visitors Center** is a good resource and provides sign-up sheets for the guided tours; it's also the place to fill up on water. (☎ 674-5500. Open daily 8am-5pm.) In an **emergency,** contact the park ranger (☎ 674-5500, after hours 674-5524).

■ ■ **ACCOMMODATIONS AND CAMPING.** Camp for free in the monument's **Cottonwood Campground,** 1½ mi. from the Visitors Center. This giant campground is in a lovely cottonwood grove and enjoys gentle breezes. (☎ 674-5500. 96 sites. Restrooms, picnic tables, water except in winter, and dump station. 5-night max. stay. First come, first served.) If Cottonwood is full, **Spider Rock Campground,** 8 mi. southeast of the Visitors Center near the Spider Rock turnoff, offers 40 primitive sites near the canyon rim. (☎ 674-8261. Sites $10.) The **Many Farms Inn,** 16 mi. north of Chinle and ¼ mi. north of the intersection of Navajo Rte. 59 and U.S. 191, serves as a stopover from Canyon de Chelly to Monument Valley or Navajo National Monument. Housed in the local high school, the rooms are a bit institutional with shared bathrooms, but a better deal can't be had in Navajo Nation. (☎ 781-6362. Open June-Aug. daily; Sept.-May weekdays only. Reception 7am-10pm. Check-out noon. Doubles $28.) **Gallup, NM** (see p. 398), **Farmington, NM** (see p. 395), and **Cortez, CO** (see p. 347) are the closest cities with cheap lodging options.

■ **THE RIM DRIVES.** The easiest way to see the canyon is via one of the paved Rim Drives, which skirt the edges of the canyon's precipitous cliffs. Although the drives are a little less intense than plunging into the canyon on foot or in a four-wheel-drive vehicle, they still capture the jaw-dropping sublimity of the monument. The **North Rim** (34 mi. round-trip) and the **South Rim** (37 mi. round-trip) both take a few hours to appreciate fully. Booklets on the drives (50¢) are available at the Visitors Center. Make sure to lock your car and take valuables with you.

The first stop on the North Rim Drive is **Ledge Ruin Overlook,** and while the ruins are not as spectacular as some of the others in the canyon, the spot provides excellent views of the fields that continue to be cultivated by the Navajo after hundreds of years. The next turnoff leads to the **Antelope House Overlook** and its two viewpoints. To the west, the impressive Antelope House Ruin is tucked underneath an overhang on the canyon floor, and to the east at the junction between Canyon del Muerto and Black Rock Canyon stands the **Navajo Fortress,** a buttress where Navajo warriors held off Kit Carson and his troops for several months in the 1860s. The last turnoff on the North Rim Drive heads out to the **Mummy Cave** and **Massacre Cave Overlooks.** The large dwellings in Mummy Cave Ruin are a testament to the

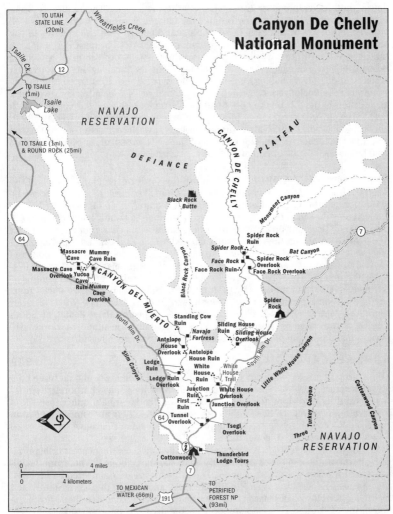

Canyon De Chelly National Monument

TO UTAH STATE LINE (20mi)

Wheatfields Creek

Tsaile Ck.

12

TO TSAILE (1mi)

Tsaile Lake

NAVAJO RESERVATION

TO TSAILE (1mi), & ROUND ROCK (25mi)

DEFIANCE

64

Black Rock Butte

CANYON DE CHELLY

PLATEAU

Monument Canyon

7

Spider Rock Ruin

Spider Rock

Bat Canyon

Massacre Cave

Mummy Cave Ruin

Massacre Cave Overlook

Yucca Cave Ruin

CANYON DEL MUERTO

Mummy Cave Overlook

Black Rock Canyon

Face Rock

Spider Rock Overlook

Face Rock Ruin

Face Rock Overlook

Spider Rock

North Rim Dr.

Standing Cow Ruin

Navajo Fortress

Sliding House Ruin

Sliding House Overlook

Antelope House Overlook

Antelope House Ruin

South Rim Dr.

Little White House Canyon

Slim Canyon

Ledge Ruin

White House Ruin

White House Trail

Cottonwood Canyon

Ledge Ruin Overlook

Junction Ruin

First Ruin

White House Overlook

Junction Overlook

Three Turkey Canyon

64

Tunnel Overlook

Tsegi Overlook

NAVAJO RESERVATION

i

Cottonwood

Thunderbird Lodge Tours

7

0   4 miles

0   4 kilometers

TO MEXICAN WATER (66mi)

191

TO PETRIFIED FOREST NP (93mi)

ARIZONA

architectural know-how of the Ancestral Puebloans. It is easy to see the indefensible predicament of the Navajo trapped in Massacre Cave. Fifteen miles north of this last overlook turnoff is the small town of Tsaile.

The **South Rim Drive** first passes the **Tunnel Overlook,** which is the starting point of many guided hikes into the canyon but does not offer much of a view. The next turn-out is the **Tsegi Overlook,** which gives an impression of the immense space inside the canyon. The views of the confluence of Canyon del Muerto and Canyon de Chelly from **Junction Overlook** are among the most spectacular in the entire monument; here you can feel the awe that each new band of travelers must have felt upon seeing the Canyon for the first time. The next stop is the **White House Overlook,** which serves as trailhead for the fantastic **White**

House Trail, as well as a great viewpoint in its own right. The moderate 3 mi. round-trip trail is the only way to enter the canyon without a guide and is well worth the couple of hours it takes to descend 600 ft. into the canyon to the ancient dwellings and grunt your way back up. Be sure to bring water, and save the overlook until afterwards to preserve the suspense of the hike. At **Sliding House Overlook,** you can see a cliff dwelling losing its battle against gravity as it actually slides off its ledge. A bit farther along the South Rim Drive, the inconspicuous **Face Rock Overlook** actually provides views of four different dwellings, all at different heights on the cliff. **Spider Rock Overlook,** the last stop on the South Rim Drive, affords great views of a narrow sandstone monolith towering 800 ft. above the canyon floor. Native American lore says the whitish rock at the top contains the bleached bones of victims of the *kachina* spirit, or Spider Woman, who has a taste for disobedient children.

🏞 **HIKING AND EXPLORING.** To explore the floor of the canyon beyond the White House Trail (see above), a **private guide** must be hired. Reservations can be made through the Visitors Center, but are not required. Two hikes led by Navajo guides enter the canyon. (4 mi. round-trip. 4hr. June-Aug. daily 9am and 1pm. $10 per person.) Traveling on the canyon floor is an incredible experience and offers a perspective on terrain that cannot be matched on the rim. Guided tours also provide access to dwellings not visible from the canyon rim. Guides for hikes and vehicle tours of the canyon can be hired through **Tsegi Guide Association.** (☎ 674-5500. 3hr. min., $15 per hr. You provide the four-wheel-drive vehicle. Required permit free at Visitors Center.) If you don't have four-wheel drive, **De Chelly Tours** (☎ 674-3772) and **Thunderbird Lodge Canyon Tours** (☎ 674-5841 or 800-679-2473) offer tours for a bit more. Horseback tours can be had at **Justin's Horse Rental,** on South Rim Dr. at the canyon's mouth. (☎ 674-5678. Open daily 9am-sundown. Horses $10 per hr., mandatory guide $15 per hr. 2hr. min. Reservations advised.)

HOPI RESERVATION   ☎ 928

Like a drop of crude oil on a Navajo nation ocean, Black Mesa and its three constitutive spurs, First Mesa, Second Mesa, and Third Mesa, have harbored the Hopi people and its traditions for over a millennium. Today inhabitants of the Hopi Reservation continue to live in the mesa top villages their ancestors founded in the AD 900s and practice the techniques of dry farming that have been passed down from generation to generation.

Exploring the reservation requires a car, especially since the nearest transportation are the trains and buses that run through **Flagstaff,** about 100 mi. from the villages, and **Winslow,** about 60 mi. away. The three mesas are connected by Rte. 264, which runs east-west between Rte. 160 and 191, and rely on the services provided by the modern towns of **Polacca** and **Kykotsmovi,** which lie beneath them. From the south, Rte. 2, 87, and 77 are all stunning scenic drives to the reservation. On Second Mesa, the **Hopi Cultural Center,** 5 mi. west of the intersection of Rte. 264 and 87, serves as a Visitors Center and contains the reservation's only museum, displaying Hopi baskets, jewelry, pottery, and info about the tribe's history. (☎ 734-6650. Open M-F 8am-5pm, Sa-Su 9am-3pm. $3, under 14 $1.) **Free camping** is allowed at ten primitive sites next to the Cultural Center. The Hopi Reservation, like the rest of Arizona, stays on **Mountain Standard Time** throughout the year. **No cameras** or other recording devices are allowed on the reservation.

The villages on **First Mesa** are the only places in the reservation really geared toward visitors. To reach the mesa top, take Rte. 264 into Polacca and follow the signs. The **Ponsi Hall Community Center** serves as a general info center and a starting point for **guided tours.** The 30-60min. tours depart throughout the day and venture to the precarious **Walpi,** perched on the southern tip of the mesa. (☎737-2262. Open June-Aug. daily 9am-6pm; Sept.-May 9:30am-5pm. Tours $5.) The villages on the **Second** and **Third Mesas** are even less developed for tourism. They each feature an array of shops and stalls hawking beautiful Hopi art including the elaborately detailed kachina dolls, which sell for hundreds of dollars. On the Third Mesa, **Old Oraibi** has been home to the Hopi since the early 1100s and challenges a few New Mexican pueblos for the title of oldest continuously inhabited village in the US.

Visitors are welcome to attend a few Hopi **village dances** throughout the year. Often announced only a few days in advance, these religious ceremonies usually occur on weekends and last from sunrise to sundown. The dances are formal occasions; do not wear shorts, tank tops, or other casual wear. Photos, recordings, and sketches are strictly forbidden. Often several villages will hold dances on the same day, giving tourists the opportunity to village-hop. The **Social** and **Butterfly Dances,** held in the fall, are a good bet for tourists. The **Harvest Dance,** in mid-September at the Second Mesa Village, is a spectacular ceremony bringing together tribes from all over the US; admission is free. Inquire at the cultural center.

NAVAJO NATIONAL MONUMENT ☎928

This small portion of the vast Tsegi Canyon system packs a big punch with two of the best-preserved Ancestral Puebloan cliff dwellings, Betatakin and Keet Seel, in the Southwest. In the second half of the 13th century, a small population of the ancestors of the modern Hopi inhabited these intricate dwellings and farmed the fertile canyon floors. Despite all the hard work put into their construction, hard times left the villages vacant by 1300. In the hundreds of years that followed, these architectural wonders were left undisturbed. Then around the turn of the 19th century, the dwellings were "discovered" by white fortune hunters and looted to fulfill the growing demand for prehistoric Southwestern artifacts. In the face of this threat, President Harding designated the area a national monument in 1909, effectively sealing the sites from further destruction. The remoteness of these dwellings, which had preserved their integrity for hundreds of years, today has a similar effect, making the Navajo National Monument a fantastic place to escape the crowds while viewing the full extent of Ancestral Puebloan architecture.

🔏 **PRACTICAL INFORMATION.** From U.S. 160, 20 mi. southwest of **Kayenta** and 50 mi. northeast of **Tuba City,** Rte. 564 travels 9 mi. north to the park entrance and Visitors Center. The Visitors Center provides helpful info and houses a number of exhibits. (☎672-2700. Open daily 8am-5pm.) The **general store,** at the junction of Rte. 564 and 160, has groceries and an **ATM.** The Visitors Center and the campground have **water.** The monument broadcasts **weather** and **road conditions** on 1610AM. No ground fires are allowed. In case of **emergency,** call 697-3211.

The free **Navajo Campground ❶,** next to the Visitors Center, is a wonderful, forested treat and a welcome relief in the summer from the heat of the flatlands. It has only 31 sites, but there's an additional overflow campground nearby with no running water. (First come, first served. 7-day max. stay. No hookups.) A quick 50 mi. east in Tuba City, the **Grey Hills Inn ❸,** less than 1 mi. east on Rte. 160 from the Rte. 264 and 160 intersection, offers motel rooms with shared bathrooms. (☎283-4450. Reception 24hr. Singles $49; doubles $54. Somewhat negotiable.)

◩ **SIGHTS.** The monument contains three cliff dwellings: **Inscription House** has been closed since the 1960s due to its fragile condition, but may reopen in the next few years; the other two sites, **Betatakin** and **Keet Seel,** admit a limited number of visitors. The stunning Keet Seel (open late May to early Sept.) can be reached only via a challenging 17 mi. round-trip **hike.** The trail drops 1200 ft. from the canyon rim to the floor and then follows the streambed to the site. Hikers can make this trip in a long day or stay overnight in a **free campground** nearby. Total access is limited to 20 people per day, so to ensure a permit on a specific date, contact the Visitors Center. For those winging it, all of the allotted permits are generally not used.

Ranger-led tours to Betatakin, a 135-room complex, are limited to 25 people and generally take 5hr. The 5 mi. hike descends 700 ft. and follows a heavily forested canyon to the site. (Late May to early Sept. 1 per day at 8:15am. First come, first served the morning of the tour.) If you're not up for a long hike, the wheelchair-accessible, 1 mi. round-trip **Sandal Trail** lets you gaze down on Betatakin from the canyon rim and includes plaques detailing the native use of local flora. The **Aspen Forest Overlook Trail,** another 1 mi. hike, winds through a canyon of aspens and firs (rarities in these parts) to a great view, albeit with no ruins. Write to **Navajo National Monument,** HC 71 Box 3, Tonalea 86044, for more info.

MONUMENT VALLEY
☎ 435

The red sandstone towers of Monument Valley are one of the Southwest's most otherworldly sights. Paradoxically, they're also one of the most familiar, since countless Westerns have used the butte-laden plain as a backdrop. For hundreds of millions of years, sediment from the Rocky Mountains was deposited in the lowland basin where these 400 to 1000 ft. monoliths now tower. Deep internal pressures then uplifted these newly formed layers of rock some 3 mi. above sea level to create an enormous plateau. Over the last 50 million years the forces of erosion have worked their magic by wearing down the layers of rock and creating the geological wonders we see today. Some years before John Wayne, Ancestral Puebloans managed to sustain small communities here, despite the hot, arid climate. Today the valley is the crown jewel of Navajo Nation Parks and Recreation.

The park entrance lies off U.S. 163, just across the Utah border, 24 mi. north of **Kayenta** and 25 mi. south of Mexican Hat. The **Visitors Center** has info on the park drive and road conditions; they can also arrange vehicle, horse, and hiking tours. (☎801-727-3353. Park and Visitors Center open May-Sept. daily 7am-7pm; Oct.-Apr. 8am-5pm. The drive closes at 6:30pm in summer and 4:30pm in winter. $3, under 7 free.) In winter, snow laces the rocky towers, and the majority of tourists flee.

Mitten View Campground ❶, ¼ mi. southwest of the Visitors Center, offers 99 sites, showers, restrooms, and panoramic views, but no hookups. (Sites $10; in winter $5. 14-day max. stat Register at the Visitors Center. No reservations.) **Goulding's Monument Valley Campground ❶,** 3 mi. west of Rte. 163 on the road opposite the tribal park, offers more protected camping but without the scenery. (☎727-3231. Laundry, showers, pool. Reception 7am-10pm. Sites $15.)

THE MOGOLLON RIM

The Mogollon Rim marks the divide between two climatic and ecological zones, producing a stretch of the state that spans from sweltering desert to more elevated woodlands. Unsurprisingly, the chunk of the state east of Phoenix, between Navajo Nation and Tucson, goes relatively untrodden. Mogollon Rim Country is largely remote and undeveloped, but it offers beautiful wilderness land for travelers yearning for a little less civilization.

PAYSON
☎ 928

Payson is the chief city of the Mogollon Rim country, located just south of the rim itself and west of the pristine Tonto National Forest. The town has seen a recent

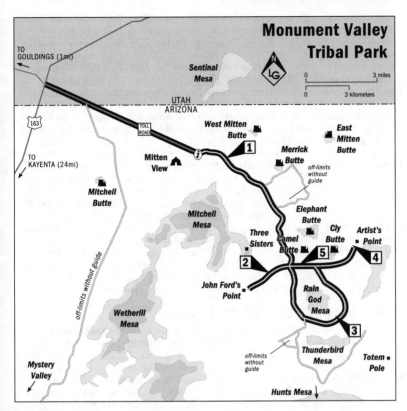

Monument Valley Tribal Park

TO GOULDINGS (1mi)

Sentinal Mesa

N

UTAH
ARIZONA

163

TOLL ROAD

West Mitten Butte **1**

East Mitten Butte

TO KAYENTA (24mi)

Mitten View

Merrick Butte

off-limits without guide

Mitchell Butte

Mitchell Mesa

Elephant Butte

Three Sisters

Camel Butte

Cly Butte

Artist's Point **4**

2

5

off-limits without guide

John Ford's Point

Rain God Mesa

Wetherill Mesa

3

Mystery Valley

off-limits without guide

Thunderbird Mesa

Totem Pole

Hunts Mesa

0   3 miles
0   3 kilometers

---

1 THE MITTENS. These matching buttes rise from the valley floor like the hands of a child buried in a snowbank. Nearby are the **Merrick Butte** and **Mitchell Mesa,** named after two prospectors killed by Utes after they claimed to have found hidden treasures of silver in the sacred valley. Let that be a lesson for tourists and developers alike.

> **TIME:** 1½ driving time
> **DISTANCE:** 17 mi.
> **SEASON:** year-round

2 THREE SISTERS AND JOHN FORD'S POINT. A few miles farther, these three pinnacles tower over the most photographed point in the park. Here John Ford captured stunning shots for *Stagecoach*, as well as other great Westerns. Today the panorama is immortalized in home video after home video.

3 TOTEM POLE. The power of erosion is on display here in this seemingly gravity-defying formation at the southeast corner of the drive.

4 ARTIST'S POINT. The power of erosion is on display here in this seemingly gravity-defying formation at the southeast corner of the drive.

5 NORTH WINDOW AND ◼ THE THUMB. This awe-inspiring gap between two large buttes down the road from the "world's largest thumb" is also the only spot in the park where you can hike without a guide. A narrow trail leaves the parking area along the base of the butte on the left and makes its way underneath its northern face to offer a escape from the cars and other visitors.

boom in growth and tourism since the completion of Rte. 87 linked it with Phoenix; the result is a pleasant and optimistic town not yet demoralized by development and gentrification. In August, Payson hosts its rodeo, the longest continually running in the world. While this may pique your curiosity, be warned: lodging prices skyrocket, and rooms as far away as Strawberry and Pine get booked up.

Located at the junction of Rte. 260 and 87, Payson finds its life's blood in the these main arteries. Rte. 87 is rechristened Beeline Hwy. for its course through the town, and Rte. 260 provides the other main thoroughfare. Tourist info can be found at the **Rim Country Regional Chamber of Commerce,** 100 W. Main St., just off of Beeline Hwy. (☎474-4515 or 800-672-9766. Open M-F 8am-5pm, Sa-Su 10am-2pm.) The **Ranger Station** is at 1009 E. Rte. 260 (☎474-7900; open M-F 8am-5pm). For non-emergencies, contact the **police,** 303 S. Beeline (☎474-5177), in City Hall. Payson houses the **Payson Regional Medical Center,** 807 S. Ponderosa St. (☎474-3222). The **post office** is at 100 W. Frontier St., a little off Beeline a block before the Chamber of Commerce. (☎474-2972. Open M-F 8:30am-4pm, Sa 9am-noon.) **ZIP code:** 85541.

A number of inexpensive motels line the major highways. **Budget Inn Suites ❸,** 302 S. Beeline Hwy., runs a comfortable and clean operation. (☎474-2201. Rooms in winter $35-69, summer $44-89.) Right next to the Best Value Inn, the **Bee Line Cafe ❷** offers up hearty portions of home-cooked meals at inexpensive prices. (☎474-9960. Daily fish specials $7. Open daily 5am-9pm.) The **Mogollon Grille ❸,** 202 W. Main St., serves up the best (albeit more expensive) food in town, and booms with live blues and folk music after 7pm Friday and Saturday. (☎474-5501. Open M-Th 11am-9pm, F-Sa 11am-10pm, Su 11am-7pm. Meals $12-15.)

TONTO NATURAL BRIDGE STATE PARK   ☎928

Located 10 mi. north of Payson on Rte. 87, the fantastic **Tonto Natural Bridge** is the longest and widest natural water crossing in North America. It is large and strong enough to support the road leading to its parking area; tourists often pass over without even realizing it. At parking level, four viewpoints give the observer an eyeful of the cavernous, cathedral-like passage. For further exploring, a path leads down to water level, and scrambling is permitted in order to pass beneath the bridge. Water dripping down from the cathedral-like natural domes that support the crossing have smoothed out the rocks inside; even the dry ones can be slippery, so bring trusty shoes and healthy common sense.

In addition to the bridge itself, the park also is home to a colony of bats, a herd of javelinas (porcine herbivores native to the Southwest), and a pride of feral cats. Be careful around the feral cats; although they make for cute pictures and physically resemble their domesticated cousins, these kitties are wild and unaccustomed to humans. (☎476-4202. Visitors Center open daily 10am-5pm. Park open Memorial Day to Labor Day daily 8am-7pm; Sept.-Oct. 8am-6pm; Nov.-Mar. 9am-5pm; Apr. 8am-6pm. $6 per vehicle.)

MOGOLLON RIM

The single most important geographic and ecological divide in Arizona, the Mogollon Rim marks the southern edge of the central woodlands climatic and ecological zones, and the northern frontier of what turns into the Saguaro desert farther south. At parts, the Rim itself looms 2000 ft. over the countryside to its south. The area is a favorite haunt of local campers and outdoors types, and has seen a certain amount of recreational development. There are a number of maintained **campsites** along the rim, and innumerable trails have been cut through the forest. Most of the area around the rim falls in the **Sitgreaves National Forest,** and the ranger station in Payson has maps of the region.

The best way to experience the Rim is to travel down **Forest Rd. 300,** which follows the Rim for most of its course between Rte. 87 and 260. This road also serves as a distributor to many of the campsites, lakes, and trailheads north of the Rim. It is just under 50 mi. in length, has no gas for its entire length, and is paved for less than 2 mi. at either end. The road can be choppy and rocky, and is exceptionally dusty in dry weather. It can be accessed from either end—the western side of Forest Rd. 300 junctions with Rte. 87 near Strawberry, some 25 mi. north of Payson. The eastern part of the road junctions with Rte. 260 some 36 mi. to the east of Payson, in the middle of nowhere. Due to the relative proximity of gas to the western end in Strawberry, it may be wiser to travel the road west to east. Less than 4 mi. into the drive, other forest roads will begin branching to the north; these lead to Rte. 87, and after 10 mi. constitute the quickest means of returning to a major paved highway. Note that not all northbound roads necessarily lead to highway; some lead to lakes and recreation sites. All roads are well marked with mileages.

The appeal of the drive lies mainly in the gorgeous views it affords of Southern Arizona, but there are other perks as well. The area near Rte. 280 features a number of **dispersed campgrounds ❶,** without facilities but also without cost. Around these campgrounds is the turn off to **Wood's Canyon Lake,** the largest of the Rim lakes and well-frequent by fishermen. **Potato Lake,** on a spur road 4 mi. in from Rte. 87 is another popular fishing hole. If fishing isn't your cup of tea, the road passes a number of historical markers, some cabin ruins, a number of trailheads all while granting its famous, mile-high view.

TUCSON   ☎ 520

A little bit country, a little bit rock 'n' roll, Tucson (TOO-sahn) is a city that carries its own tune and a bundle of contradictions. Mexican property until the Gadsden Purchase, the city retains many of its south-of-the-border influences and shares its Mexican heritage with such disparate elements as the University of Arizona, the Davis-Monthan Airforce Base, McDonald's, and Southern Baptism. Boasting mountainous flora beside desert cacti and art museums next to the war machines of the Pima Air and Space museum, the city nearly defies categorization. In the last several years, a reenergized downtown core has attracted artists and hipsters, while families and retirees populate the sprawling suburbs. Tucson offers the conveniences of a metropolis without the nasty aftertaste, and arguably better tourist attractions than almost any other Southwestern city.

ARIZONA

▌ TRANSPORTATION

Flights: Tucson International Airport (☎ 573-8000; www.tucsonairport.org), on Valencia Rd., south of downtown. Bus #25 runs every hr. to the Laos Transit Center; from there, bus #16 goes downtown. Round-trip to: **Dallas** (2hr., 4 per day, $230); **LA** (1 hr., 7 per day, $99); **Phoenix** (25min., 4 per day, $165). **Arizona Stagecoach** (☎ 889-1000) goes downtown for around $14 for one person, $3 for each additional person. 24hr. Reservations recommended.

Trains: Amtrak, 400 E. Toole Ave. (☎ 623-4442), at 5th Ave., 1 block north of the Greyhound station. To: **Albuquerque** via El Paso (4 per week, $99); **Las Vegas** via LA (3 per week, $124); **Los Angeles** (3 per week, $72); **San Francisco** via LA (3 per week, $130). Book 2 weeks ahead or rates are substantially higher. Open Sa-M 6:15am-1:45pm and 4:15-11:30pm, Tu-W 6:15am-1:45pm, Th-F 4:15-11:30pm.

Buses: Greyhound, 2 S. 4th Ave. (☎792-3475), between Congress St. and Broadway. To: **Albuquerque** (12-14hr., 5 per day, $88); **El Paso** (6hr., 12 per day, $35); **Los Angeles** (9-10hr., 4 per day, $40); and **Phoenix** (2hr., 16 per day, $15). Open 24hr.

Public Transit: Sun-Tran (☎792-9222). Buses run from the Ronstadt terminal downtown at Congress and 6th St. Fares 85¢, under 19 60¢, seniors and disabled 35¢, day pass $2. Service roughly M-F 5:30am-10pm, Sa-Su 8am-7pm; times vary by route.

Taxis: Yellow Cab, ☎624-6611.

Car Rental: AAA Tucson Auto Rental, 3150 E. Grant Rd. (☎320-1495). Rates start at $20 per day. Under 21 surcharge $10 per day. Credit card deposit required on most cars, cash deposit accepted for pre-owned rentals ($25 per day). Open M-F 8am-6pm, Sa 8am-4pm, and Su 11am-4pm.

Bike Rental: Fairwheels Bicycles, 1110 E. 6th St. (☎884-9018), at Fremont. $20 first day, $10 each additional day. Credit card deposit required. Open M-F 9am-6pm, Sa 9am-5:30pm, Su noon-4pm.

◼✳◼ 🛈 ORIENTATION AND PRACTICAL INFORMATION

Just east of I-10, Tucson's downtown area surrounds the intersection of **Broadway Blvd.** and **Stone Ave.,** two blocks from the train and bus terminals. The **University of Arizona** lies 1 mi. northeast of downtown at the intersection of **Park** and **Speedway Blvd.** "Avenues" run north-south, "streets" east-west; because some of each are numbered, intersections such as "6th and 6th" are possible. Speedway, Broadway, and **Grant Rd.** are the quickest east-west routes through town. To go north-south, follow **Oracle Rd.** through the heart of the city, **Campbell Ave.** east of downtown, or **Swan Rd.** farther east. The hip, young crowd swings on **4th Ave.** and on **Congress St.,** both with small shops, quirky restaurants, and a slew of bars.

Visitor Information: Tucson Convention and Visitors Bureau, 100 S. Church Ave. (☎624-1817 or 800-638-8350; www.visittucson.org), in the shopping plaza. Open M-F 8am-5pm, Sa-Su 9am-4pm.

Bi-Gay-Lesbian Organization: Gay, Lesbian, Bisexual and Transgendered Community Center, 300 E. 6th St. (☎624-1779). Open M-Sa 11am-7pm.

Police: non-emergency ☎791-4444.

Hotlines: Rape Crisis, ☎624-7273. **Suicide Prevention,** ☎323-9373. Both 24hr.

Medical Services: University Medical Center, 1501 N. Campbell Ave (☎694-0111).

Internet Access: Free at the **University of Arizona main library,** 1510 E. University Blvd. Open Sept.-May M-Th 7:30am-1am, F 7:30am-9pm, Sa 10am-9pm, Su 11am-1am; June-Aug. M-Th 7:30am-11pm, F 7:30am-6pm, Sa 9am-6pm, Su 11am-11pm.

Post Office: 1501 S. Cherry Bell (☎388-5129). Open M-F 8:30am-8pm, Sa 9am-1pm. **ZIP code:** 85726.

🏠 ACCOMMODATIONS

There's a direct correlation between the temperature in Tucson and the warmth of its lodging industry to budget travelers: expect the best deals in summer, when rain-cooled evenings and summer bargains are consolation for the midday scorch. **The Tucson Gem and Mineral Show,** the largest of its kind in North America, is an added hazard for budget travelers. Falling at the end of January and beginning of February, the mammoth show fills up most of the city's accommodations for its two-week run, and drives prices up considerably. Unless you've made arrangements in advance, this is a bad time to drop in on Tucson.

ARIZONA

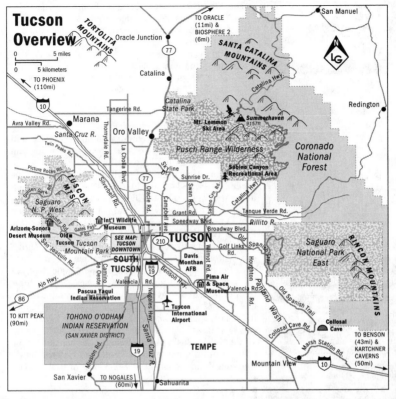

Tucson Overview

TORTOLITA MOUNTAINS

0 — 5 miles
0 — 5 kilometers

TO PHOENIX (110mi)

TO ORACLE (11mi) & BIOSPHERE 2 (6mi)

Oracle Junction

San Manuel

Catalina

SANTA CATALINA MOUNTAINS

Catalina Hwy

Redington

Tangerine Rd.

Avra Valley Rd.

Marana

Catalina State Park

Mt. Lemmon Ski Area

Summerhaven 9157ft

Santa Cruz R.

Oro Valley

Pusch Range Wilderness

Coronado National Forest

Twin Peaks Rd.

Thornydale Rd.

La Cholla Blvd.

Silverbell Rd.

Skyline

Sunrise Dr.

Sabino Canyon Recreational Area

Picture Rocks Rd.

TUCSON MTS

Golden Gate Rd.

Gates Pass Rd.

Saguaro N. P. West

Int'l Wildlife Museum

Campbell Ave

Swan Rd.

Sabino Cyn Rd.

Catalina Hwy

Tanque Verde Rd.

Kinney Rd.

Arizona-Sonora Desert Museum

Old Tucson

Tucson Mountain Park

SEE MAP: TUCSON DOWNTOWN

Grant Rd.

Speedway Blvd.

Broadway Blvd.

Rillito R.

Saguaro National Park East

RINCON MOUNTAINS

San Joaquin Rd.

Camino de Oeste

SOUTH TUCSON

210

TUCSON

Wilmot Rd.

Golf Links Rd.

Davis Monthan AFB

Old Spanish Trail

Houghton Rd.

Ajo Hwy.

Valencia Rd.

Pima Air & Space Museum

Valencia Rd.

Pantano Wash

Pascua Yaqui Indian Reservation

Nogales Hwy

Benson Hwy

Tucson International Airport

TO KITT PEAK (90mi)

TOHONO O'ODHAM INDIAN RESERVATION (SAN XAVIER DISTRICT)

Santa Cruz R.

TEMPE

Colossal Cave Rd.

Colossal Cave

TO BENSON (43mi) & KARTCHNER CAVERNS (50mi)

San Xavier

TO NOGALES (60mi)

Sahuarita

Mountain View

Marsh Station Rd.

10

Mission Rd.

⊠ **Roadrunner Hostel,** 346 E. 12th St. (☎628-4709). Wows guests with unparalleled amenities such as a giant 52 in. TV, a formidable movie collection, free high-speed Internet access, purified water, free coffee and tea, and swamp cooling. Located in a pleasant house a few blocks from downtown, the hostel is exceptionally clean and friendly. There is no curfew and no chores are required; they'll even pick you up at the Greyhound or Amtrak terminal. Apr.-Sept. international guests get 2 free additional nights when they pay for the first 2. Free linen, towels, lockers, and laundry soap. Kitchen and laundry. Dorms $18; private doubles $35. ❶

⊠ **Loews Ventana Canyon Resort,** 7000 N. Resort Dr. (☎299-2020). A quintessential 5-star hotel 5 mi. north of downtown off Oracle Rd. At the base of an 80 ft. waterfall, the incredible Ventana delivers on every level—from its relaxing spa to its championship golf course to the beautiful surrounding Catalina Mountain foothills. Singles start at $95. ❺

Hotel Congress and Hostel, 311 E. Congress (☎622-8848). Conveniently located across from the bus and train stations, and offers superb lodging to night-owl hostelers. Downstairs, Club Congress booms until 1am on weekends, making it rough on early birds. Private rooms come with bath, phone, vintage radio, and ceiling fans. The cafe downstairs serves great salads and omelettes. Dorms $17. Singles June-Aug. $29, Sept.-Nov. and May $49, Dec.-Apr. $68; doubles June-Aug. $38, Sept.-Nov. and May $53, Jan.-Apr. $82. 10% discount for students, military, and local artists. ❶

ARIZONA

THE INSIDER'S CITY

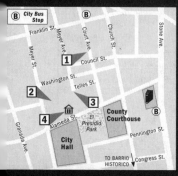

HISTORIC DOWNTOWN TUCSON

A great sample of this history can be had in a tour of historic Tucson, where the past comes alive. When touring the various sites listed here, be sure to start early in the day, as the locales below operate between 9am-5pm.

1 Start off with an early lunch at **El Charro,** Tucson's oldest Mexican restaurant, housed in a 1900s-era family home.

2 Head next to the **Edward Nye Fish House.** Built in 1867 on the site of the Presidio Barracks, it now houses the renowned Campbell Collection of Western American Art.

3 One block east, **La Casa Cordova** stands as Tucson's oldest home. It houses a Presidio exhibit on the entire area.

4 Next door, the **Tucson Museum of Art** exhibits one of the finest collections of art in Arizona.

Further down Church Ave., past the Tucson Convention Center along Chsuing St., the Barrio Historico beckons with Sonoran buildings in brightly colored adobe. Inside the Barrio is "El Tiradito," a Catholic shrine to a youth killed in a love triangle. Go there to light a candle and make a wish.

The Flamingo Hotel, 1300 N. Stone Ave. (☎ 770-1901). Houses not only guests, but also Arizona's largest collection of Western movie posters. There are dozens of rooms available, from the Kevin Costner room to the Burt Lancaster suite (both with A/C, cable TV, telephones, and pool access). Laundry facilities on-site. Singles May-Aug. $24, doubles $29; Sept.-Nov. all rooms $49; Dec.-Apr. $75. ❹

🏕 CAMPING

In addition to the backcountry camping available in the **Saguaro Park** and **Coronado Forest** (both inside and outside the Pusch Ridge Wilderness), there are a variety of other camping options. **Gilbert Ray Campground** ❶ (☎ 883-4200), just outside Saguaro West along the McCain Loop Rd., offers $7 campsites with toilets and drinking water, and is in easy reach of the city as well as all the Speedway sights. **Catalina State Park** ❶ (☎ 628-5798), north of Tucson on Oracle Rd., features $10 tent sites fully equipped with hot showers, water, and toilets. Picnic sites available. A variety of camping areas flank **Sky Island Scenic Byway** at Mt. Lemmon; an added perk of these sights is their temperate climate, even in summer. All campgrounds charge a $5 road access fee in addition to the camping costs. **Spencer Canyon** ❶ (sites $12) and **Rose Canyon** ❶ (sites $15) have potable water and toilets, while **Molino Basin** ❶ and **General Hitchcock** ❶ have toilets but no potable water (both $5). Call the Santa Catalina Ranger District (☎ 749-8700) for more info.

🍴 FOOD

As any good college town should, Tucson brims with inexpensive yet tasty eateries. Although every style of cooking is represented, south-of-the-border fare is king. Good, cheap Mexican restaurants are everywhere.

☒ elle, 3048 E. Broadway Blvd. (☎ 327-0500), brings out the gastronome in all who are fortunate enough to sample its succulent menu. Cool classical jazz resonates through this stylish eatery, as mouth-watering chicken penne ($12) is enjoyed in elle's *über*-elegant, yet welcoming, surroundings. Open M-F 11:30am-10pm, Sa 4:30pm-10pm. ❸

Time Market, 444 E. University Blvd., offers $1.75 pizza slices, enhanced by toppings like piñon nuts and smoked gouda. Calzones $6. Open daily 7:30am-10pm. ❶

La Indita, 622 N. 4th Ave. (☎ 792-0523), delights customers with traditional Mexican cuisine ($3-9) served on tasty tortillas. The food is still prepared by *la indita*

ARIZONA

Downtown Tucson

ACCOMMODATIONS
Flamingo Motel, 1
Hotel Congress and Hostel, 9
Roadrunner Hostel, 13

FOOD
Coffee Etc., 4
Elle, 11
India Oven, 3
La Indita, 6
Maya Quetzal, 7
Time Market, 2

NIGHTLIFE
Ain't Nobody's Biz, 12
Club Congress, 10
IBTs, 8
O'Malley's, 5

N

0 _____ 200 yards
0 _____ 200 meters

Granada Ave.

Franklin St.

Meyer Ave.

Council St.

Court Ave.

Washington St.

Alameda St.

Tucson Museum of Art

City Hall

Presidio Park

Pennington St.

El Paso County Courthouse

Granada Ave.

Braniff Pl.

Tucson Convention Center

Church Ave.

Ochoa

Jackson St.

Stone Ave.

Congress St.

Broadway Blvd.

12th St.

Armory Park

Stone Ave.

Scott Ave.

8th St.

7th St.

6th Ave.

Sun-Tran

Amtrak

Toole Ave.

Greyhound

Stevens Ave.

Broadway Blvd.

10th St.

9th St.

8th St.

7th St.

6th St.

5th St.

4th St.

2nd St.

11th Ave.

Queen Ave.

3rd St.

4th St.

Perry Ave.

9th Ave.

Ash Ave.

Stone Ave.

Echols Ave.

7th Ave.

Ferro Ave.

6th Ave.

Arizona Ave.

5th Ave.

Herbert Ave.

4th Ave.

Huff Ave.

3rd Ave.

Bean Ave.

2nd Ave.

1st Ave.

Euclid Ave.

University Blvd.

Tyndall Ave.

Park Ave.

Catalina Park

University of Arizona

TO (1mi)

TO (1mi)

TO UNIVERSITY OF ARIZONA LIBRARY (300yds)

TO UNIVERSITY OF ARIZONA (300yds)

Fairwheels Bicycles

TO (1.5mi)

herself, and as a result, the food has a bit of added kick. Open M-Th 11am-9pm, F 11am-6pm, Sa 6-9pm, Su 9am-9pm. ❶

India Oven, 2727 N. Campbell Ave. (☎326-8635), between Grant and Glenn, offers relief when you've had enough Mexican food. The garlic *naan* ($2.35) is exquisite. Daily $6 lunch buffet. Open daily 11am-2:45pm and 5-10pm. Vegetarian dishes $6-7, tandoori meats and curries $6-9. ❶

Coffee Etc., 2830 N. Campbell Ave. (☎881-8070); has unbeatable hours (open daily 24hr.). A Tex-Mex coffee shop. Offers sandwiches and light meals from $5-10. ❷

🎵 🎶 NIGHTLIFE AND ENTERTAINMENT

The free *Tucson Weekly* is the local authority on nightlife, while the weekend sections of the *Star* or the *Citizen* also provide good coverage. Throughout the year, the city of the sun presents **Music Under the Stars,** a series of sunset concerts performed by the **Tucson Symphony Orchestra** (☎792-9155). For **Downtown Saturday Nights,** on the first and third Saturday of each month, Congress St. is blockaded for a celebration of the arts with outdoor singers, crafts, and galleries. Every Thursday, the **Thursday Night Art Walk** lets you mosey through downtown galleries and studios. For more info, call **Tucson Arts District** (☎624-9977). UA students rock 'n' roll on **Speedway Blvd.,** while others do the two-step in clubs on **N. Oracle.** Young locals hang out on **4th Ave.,** where most bars have live music and low cover charges.

Club Congress, 311 E. Congress St. (☎622-8848), has DJs during the week and live bands on weekends. The friendly hotel staff and a cast of regulars make it an especially good time. M is 80s night with 80¢ drinks. Congress is the venue for most of the indie music coming through town. Cover $3-5. Open daily 9pm-1am.

O'Malley's, 247 N. 4th Ave. (☎623-8600), is a good spot with decent bar food, pool tables, and pinball. As its name implies, this is a better place to nurse your pint of Guinness than it is to get your groove on. Cover Th-Sa varies. Open daily 11am-1am.

IBT's, on 4th Ave. at 6th St. (☎882-3053), the single most popular gay venue in Tucson, can be hard to spot—there is no sign and the is door unmarked. Once you've spotted the stucco building halfway down the block, however, there's no mistaking it; you've found IBT's. It pumps dance music in its classic club environment to a weekend capacity crowd. W and Su drag shows wow audiences. Open daily 9am-1am.

Ain't Nobody's Biz, 2900 E. Broadway Blvd. (☎318-4838), in a shopping plaza, is the little sister of its Phoenix namesake, and is the big mama of the Tucson lesbian scene. A large bar, 'Biz' attracts crowds of all backgrounds and has some of the best dancing in Tucson. Open daily 11am-1am.

👁 SIGHTS

UNIVERSITY OF ARIZONA. Lined with cafes, restaurants, galleries, and vintage clothing shops, **4th Ave.** is an alternative magnet and a great place to take a stroll. Between Speedway and Broadway Blvd., the street becomes a historical shopping district with increasingly touristy shops. Lovely for its varied and elaborately irrigated vegetation, the **University of Arizona's** mall sits where E. 3rd St. should be, just east of 4th Ave. The **Center for Creative Photography,** on campus, houses various changing exhibits, including the archives of Ansel Adams and Richard Avedon. (☎621-7968. Open M-F 9am-5pm, Sa-Su noon-5pm. Archives available to the public, but only through print-viewing appointments. Free.) The **Flandrau Science Center,** on Cherry Ave. at the campus mall, dazzles visitors with a public observatory and a laser light show.

climbing to 9157 ft. above sea level, the Mt. Lemmon Drive is a virtual trans-national trip from the deserts of Mexico to the conifer forests of Canada. Along the ascent, drivers are witness to breathtaking metamorphosis of terrain. *Road construction will plague the Mt. Lemmon Drive until at least the fall of 2002. Road closures and delays are frequent. Call 751-9405 for current info.*

Mt. Lemmon Scenic Drive

The 50 mi. round-trip drive begins northwest of downtown Tucson along the **Catalina Hwy.,** off Tanque Verde Rd. Venturing into the **Coronado National Forest,** the road passes rolling hills of Sonoran desert scrub, Saguaro cacti, and mesquite trees. Past the Molino Canyon vista point, a Forest Service entrance station collects fees. There is no charge to drive, but if you plan on hiking any of the numerous trails or picnic grounds that line the road, a $5 day-use permit must be purchased. Beyond the entrance station, the road continues to climb on its way through five different life zones. Desert lowland gives way to semi-desert grassland and oak forests which change into mixed pine and oak woodlands at about 6000 ft. **Windy Point Vista,** true to its name, provides views of Tucson, the **Patagonia Mountains,** and on clear days, the **Sierra de San Antonio** of Mexico. Just before Mile 20, the **Palisades Visitors Center** offers restrooms, brochures, and ranger advice. From here, the vegetation continues to morph into a ponderosa pine forest, as the road climbs to over 8000 ft. The final life zone is the mixed conifer forest with temperatures that are on average 20°F cooler than Tucson.

At Mile 25, the drive meets the access road for the **Mt. Lemmon Ski Valley**. The season runs from mid-December to April, with balmy temperatures making for comfortable, convenient skiing. Although the Valley may be pint-sized, with only one ski lift and 18 trails (20% beginner, 38% intermediate, 42% advanced), it punches over its weight with its proximity to downtown Tucson, inexpensive tickets and gloriously sunny weather. (☎520-576-1321. 950 ft. vertical drop. Adult weekend full day $32, half day $28; adult weekday $28/$23; over 65 and active military $27/$27; under 12 $13/$11.)

The climax of the drive is the village of **Summerhaven,** whose surroundings look more like the northern Rockies than southern Arizona. Pine trees dominate, clustering around steep, craggy mountainsides. **Alpine Lodge** houses skiers in the winter and those fleeing the oppressive heat in the summer. (☎576-1744. Doubles $69 M-Th, $89 F-Su. $10 per extra person.)

If you're travelling by 4x4, Summerhaven need not be the end of your road trip. A roughly 30 mi. travel road links Summerhaven with **Oracle, AZ,** connecting to Rte. 77 via W. American Ave.

TIME: 1½ hr. driving time

DISTANCE: 50 mi.

SEASON: year-round

(☎621-7827. Open M-Tu 9am-5pm, W-Sa 9am-5pm and 7-9pm, Su noon-5pm. $3, under 14 $2. Shows $5/$4, seniors and students $4.50.) The **University of Arizona Museum of Art** offers visitors a free glimpse of modern American and 18th-century Latin American art, as well as the singularly muscular sculpture of Jacques Lipchitz. The very best student art is exhibited here too. *(1031 N. Olive. ☎621-7567. Open M-F 10am-3pm, Su noon-4pm.)*

TUCSON MUSEUM OF ART. This major attraction presents impressive traveling exhibits in all media, in addition to its permanent collection of varied American, Mexican, and European art. Historic houses in the surrounding and affiliated Presidio Historic Block boast an impressive collection of Pre-Columbian and Mexican folk art, as well as art of the American West. *(140 N. Main Ave. ☎624-2333. Open M-Sa 10am-4pm, Su noon-4pm. Closed M between Memorial Day and Labor Day. $5, seniors $4, students $3, under 13 free. Everyone free on Su.)*

SIGHTS ON WEST SPEEDWAY. As Speedway Blvd. winds its way west from Tucson's city center, it passes by a variety of sights. Closest to the city, the **International Wildlife Museum** is wild but lifeless—the creatures were stuffed long ago. *(4800 W. Gates Pass Rd. ☎617-1439. Open M-F 9am-5pm, Sa-Su 9am-6pm, last entrance at 4:15pm. $7, seniors and students $5.50, ages 6-12 $2.50.)* Farther west, Speedway's name changes to Gates Pass Rd. and later junctions into Kinney Rd. **Gates Pass,** west of the International Wildlife Museum on the way to Kinney Rd., is an excellent spot for watching the rising and setting sun. The left fork leads to **Old Tucson Studios,** an elaborate Old West-style town constructed for the 1938 movie *Arizona* and used as a backdrop for Westerns ever since, including many John Wayne films and the 1999 Will Smith vehicle *Wild Wild West.* It's open year-round to tourists, who can stroll around in the Old West mock up, view gun-fight re-enactments and other tourist shows and, if fortunate, watch the filming of a current Western. *(☎883-0100. Open daily 10am-6pm, sometimes closed on M in winter. Call ahead as occasionally Old Tucson is closed for group functions. $15, seniors $13.45, ages 4-11 $9.45.)* Those opting to take the right fork will eschew the Wild Wild West for the merely wild West; less than 2 mi. from the fork lies the **Arizona-Sonora Desert Museum,** a first-rate zoo and nature preserve. The living museum recreates a range of desert habitats and features over 300 kinds of animals. A visit requires at least 2hr., preferably in the morning before the animals take their afternoon siestas. *(2021 N. Kinney Rd. ☎883-2702. Follow Speedway Blvd. west of the city as it becomes Gates Pass Rd., then Kinney Rd. Open Mar.-Sept. daily 7:30am-5pm; Oct.-Feb. 8:30am-5pm, June-Sept. Sa 7:30am-10pm. $9, Nov.-Apr. $10, ages 6-12 $1.75.)*

PIMA AIR AND SPACE MUSEUM. This impressive museum follows aviation history from the days of the Wright brothers to its modern military incarnations. Exhibits on female and African-American aviators are interesting, but the main draw is acres of decommissioned warplanes. *(☎574-0462. Open M-F 7am-3pm, Sa-Su 7am-5pm; in summer daily 9am-5pm. $7.50, seniors $6.50.)* Tours of the **Davis-Monthan Air Force Base** are offered at the museum. *(5 tours per day M-F. $5, ages 6-12 $3.)*

CAVES. Caves are all the rage in Tucson. The recently opened **Kartchner Caverns** State Park is enormously popular, filled with magnificent rock formations and home to over 1000 bats. This is a "living" cave, which contains water and is still experiencing the growth of its formations, so while conditions may be damp, the formations shine and glisten in the light. Taking a tour is the only way to enter the cave. *(Located 8 mi. off I-10 at Exit 302. ☎586-4100. Open daily 7:30am-6pm. 1hr. tours run every 30min. 8:30am-4:30pm. Entrance fee $10 per vehicle, tour $14, ages 7-13 $6. Reservations strongly recommended.)* Near **Saguaro National Park East** (see p. 139), **Colossal Cave** is one of the only dormant (no water or new formations) caves in the US. A variety of tours are offered; in addition to 1hr. walking tours that occur throughout

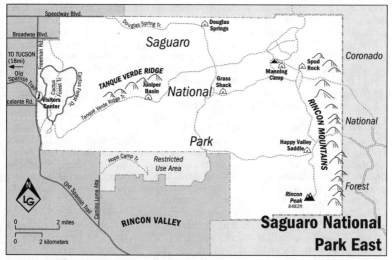

Saguaro National Park East

the day, a special ladder tour through otherwise sealed-off tunnels, crawlspaces, and corridors can be arranged. (☎647-7275. Open mid-Mar. to mid-Sept. M-Sa 8am-6pm, Su 8am-7pm; mid-Sept. to mid-Mar. M-Sa 9am-5pm, Su 9am-6pm. $7, ages 6-12 $4. Ladder tour: Sa 5:30-8pm; $35, includes meal and equipment rental, reservations required.)

OUTDOOR ACTIVITIES

SAGUARO NATIONAL PARK WEST

North of the desert museum, the western half of Saguaro National Park (Tucson Mountain District) has limited hiking trails and an auto loop. The **Bajada Loop Drive** runs less than 9 mi. but passes through some of the most striking desert scenery the park has to offer. The paved nature walk near the **Visitors Center** passes some of the best specimens of Saguaro cactus in the Tucson area. The towering cacti take decades to reach maturity and don't start sprouting their trademark raised arms until around age 75. There is no camping available in the park, and mountain biking is allowed only on vehicle roads and not on the hiking trails. (☎733-5158. Park open 24hr.; Visitors Center daily 8:30am-5pm; auto loop 7am-sunset. Free.)

There are a variety of hiking trails through Saguaro West; **Sendero Esperanza Trail,** beginning at the Ez-kim-in-zin picnic area, is the mildest approach to the summit of **Wasson Peak,** the highest in the Tucson Mountain Range (4687 ft.). This moderate trail winds 4 mi. one-way to reach the peak. No reliable water is available along the trail—be sure to carry plenty. The **Hugh Norris Trail** is a slightly longer, slightly more strenuous climb to the top of Wasson Peak, and it offers gorgeous desert views the whole way. Five miles one-way, the round-trip hike will take most of the day. The trailhead is clearly marked, off the Bajada Loop Drive.

SAGUARO NATIONAL PARK EAST

Also known as the Rincon Mountain District, the eastern portion of the park lies east of the city on **Old Spanish Trail;** take I-10 E to Exit 279 and follow Vail Rd. to Old Spanish Trail. **Backcountry camping** is allowed; free mandatory permits may be picked up at the **Visitors Center** any time until noon on the day of camping. Mountain biking is permitted inside the park, but only around the **Cactus Forest Loop Drive** and **Cactus Forest Trail,** at the western end of the park near the Visitors Center. (☎733-5153. Visitors Center open daily 8:30am-5pm. $6 per vehicle, $3 per pedestrian.)

The trails in Saguaro East are longer than those in the western part of the park. With over 128 mi. of trails, many hikes must be done over the course of two days (trailside camp sites are available). One of the only trails that can easily be completed in a single day is the **Cactus Forest.** Smaller trails and trail systems branch off of Cactus Forest. In the Rincon Valley area, the **Hope Camp Trail** is less than 3 mi. one-way, but must be shared with horses.

TUCSON MOUNTAIN COUNTY PARK

Located west of Tucson along Speedway/Gates Pass/Kinney, Tucson Mountain County Park includes Gates Pass itself as well as many of the Tucson mountains. A variety of trailheads, picnic areas, and a campsite radiate from Kinney Road. For drivers, the **McCain Loop Rd.** loops around the Arizona-Sonora Desert Museum and passes through some of the most rugged and wild stretches of desert. Entrance to the park is free, and mountain biking is permitted.

The **Golden Gate Loop** is one of the longer trails in the park. An easy 8 mi. loop with little elevation change, the trail circles Golden Gate Mountain. The trailhead for the Golden Gate Trail is not available directly from the road; instead, park on one of the lots on eastern Gates Pass Rd. and follow David Yetman Trail 0.5 mi. to the trailhead. The loop crosses several washes that can present hazards during sudden thunderstorms that sometimes strike in the summertime.

From the same trailhead, the **David Yetman Trail** presents a more difficult, 11.6 mi. round-trip loop, though it may be shortened by exiting via trailheads on Gates Pass Rd. and Camino de Oeste. In addition to its desert splendor, the Yetman trail passes a ruined stone building formerly owned by an *Arizona Daily Star* editor.

SABINO CANYON

Northeast of downtown Tucson, the cliffs and desert pools of **Sabino Canyon** provide an ideal backdrop for picnics and day hikes. To get there, take Speedway Blvd. to Swan Rd. to Sunrise Dr. The entrance is at the cross of Sunrise Dr. and Sabino Canyon Rd. Locals beat the Tucson heat by frolicking in the water holes during the summer. No cars are permitted in the canyon, but a shuttlebus makes trips through it. (☎749-2861. Runs July-Nov. every hr. 9am-4pm, Dec.-June every 30min. dawn to dusk; $6, ages 3-12 $2.) The National Forest's **Visitors Center** lies at the canyon's entrance. (☎749-8700. Open M-F 8am-4:30pm, Sa-Su 8:30am-4:30pm.)

The forest area outside the canyon is the **Pusch Ridge Wilderness,** which is located within the **Coronado National Forest.** The northern and eastern border of the wilderness is the Mt. Lemmon Hwy., and the wilderness stretches to the south and west sides of the Coronado National Forest. Hiking trails cross through the Forest, Wilderness and Sabino Canyon in furious multitude. **Biking** within the park is only permitted 5am-9pm, and not on Wednesday or Saturday. In the Pusch Wilderness Area, biking is forbidden, while in the rest of the Coronado forest it is permitted.

■ DAYTRIPS FROM TUCSON

BIOSPHERE 2. Ninety-one feet high, with an area of more than three acres, Biosphere 2 is sealed off from Earth—"Biosphere 1"—by 500 tons of stainless steel. In 1991, eight research scientists locked themselves inside this giant greenhouse to cultivate their own food and knit their own socks as they monitored the behavior of five man-made ecosystems: savanna, rainforest, marsh, ocean, and desert. After two years, they began having oxygen problems and difficulty with food production. No one lives in Biosphere 2 now, but it's still used as a research facility. The Biosphere is 30min. north of Tucson; take I-10 west to the "Miracle Mile" exit, follow the miracles to Oracle Rd., then travel north until it becomes Rte. 77 N. From Phoenix, take I-10 to Exit 185, follow Rte. 387 to Rte. 79 (Florence Hwy.), and proceed to Oracle Junction and Rte. 77. Guided 2hr. tours include two short films, a walk through the laboratory's research and development models for the Biosphere 2 ecosystems, and a stroll around Biosphere 2 itself, including the crew's living quarters. Walking around unchaperoned is also permitted. (☎896-6200 or 800-838-2462. Tours daily 9am-4:30pm, grounds open 8:30am-5:30pm, last admission at 5pm. $13, seniors and students $11.50, ages 13-17 $9, ages 6-12 $6.)

MISSION SAN XAVIER DE BAC. Built by the Franciscan brothers in the late 1700s, this is the northernmost Spanish Baroque church in the Americas, and the only such church in the US. Located on the Tohono O'odham Indian Reservation, there were few opportunities and fewer funds to restore it until the late 20th century. In the early 90s, a local group gathered money in order to preserve and protect this singular church; since then, the mortar has been restored, the frescoes have been retouched and preserved, and the statuary cleaned of centuries of soot and desert sand. The result is a dazzling house of God, well-earning its nickname "white dove of the desert." (South of Tucson off of I-19 to Nogales, take the San Xavier exit and follow the signs. ☎294-2624. Open for viewing 8am-6pm; masses held daily. Admission is free both to the church and to small adjoining museum, although donations are accepted.)

SOUTHERN ARIZONA

South of Tucson, Arizona boasts some of the most fascinating and idiosyncratic geology, wildlife, and small towns that the state has to offer. From the border town of Nogales to the Disneyland-esque Tombstone and the artist colony of Bisbee, life in southern Arizona cannot be simply categorized. The inimitable volcanic rock of Chiricahua National Monument provides a spectacle for the senses, and if you're willing to make a trek, the extremely remote and untouristed Organ Pipe Cactus National Monument will not disappoint.

ORGAN PIPE CACTUS NATIONAL MONUMENT ☎520

Cozying up to the Mexican border, the lonely dirt roads of Organ Pipe Cactus National Monument encircle an extraordinary collection of the flora and fauna of the Sonoran Desert. Foremost among them is the Organ Pipe Cactus itself, which is common in Mexico but found only in this region of the US. Its texture and color are similar to those of a Saguaro, but while the Saguaro is commonly shaped like a body with two or more arms, the Organ Pipe Cactus consists only of arms, which sprout tentacle-like from the soil.

▓ ⁊ ORIENTATION AND PRACTICAL INFORMATION. Located on U.S. 85, 22 mi. south of the tiny hamlet of **Why,** Organ Pipe Cactus Monument is one of the most isolated national parks in the US. It's nearly empty during the summer, but in the cooler winter months the campground usually fills up on weekends. The **Visitors Center,** on Rte. 85, 5 mi. north of the Mexican border, distributes maps and provides hiking recommendations (☎387-6849; open daily 8am-5pm). The adjacent **Twin Peaks Campground ❶** offers water, restrooms, and grills, but no hookups (tent sites $10). **Back-country camping ❶** requires a $5 permit from the Visitors Center, which is good for 14 days of camping. For further info, write to the Superintendent, Organ Pipe Cactus National Monument, Rte. 1 Box 100, Ajo AZ 85321-9626. The closest indoor accommodation is in **Lukeville,** a border town with a gas station, hotel, and border crossing. The **Gringo Pass Campground and Motel ❸** has several

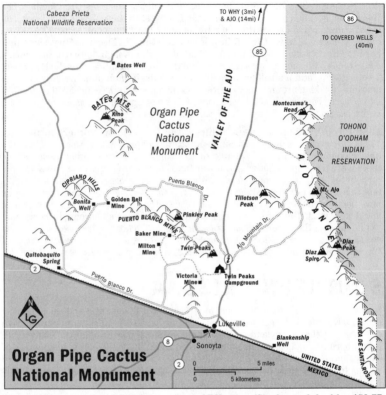

Cabeza Prieta
National Wildlife Reservation

TO WHY (3mi)
& AJO (14mi)

86

TO COVERED WELLS
(40mi)

85

Bates Well

BATES MTS.
Kino
Peak

Organ Pipe
Cactus
National
Monument

VALLEY OF THE AJO

Montezuma's
Head

TOHONO
O'ODHAM
INDIAN
RESERVATION

CIPRIANO HILLS

Puerto Blanco Dr.

Bonita
Well

Golden Bell
Mine

Pinkley Peak

PUERTO BLANCO MTNS.

Baker Mine

Milton
Mine

Twin Peaks

Tillotson
Peak

Ajo Mountain Dr.

AJO RANGE

Mt. Ajo

Diaz
Peak

Quitobaquito
Spring

2

Puerto Blanco Dr.

Victoria
Mine

Twin Peaks
Campground

Diaz
Spire

N
LG

Lukeville

8

Sonoyta

**Organ Pipe Cactus
National Monument**

2

Blankenship
Well

UNITED STATES
MEXICO

SIERRA DE SANTA ROSA

0   5 miles
0   5 kilometers

motel-style rooms in addition to a mass of RV sites. (Singles and doubles $52-77; triples $87; quads $95. Hookups and tent sites $11. RV lots closed in summer.) **Ajo,** 14 mi. north of the park boundary, has a greater array of lodging and services.

◤ **OUTDOOR ACTIVITIES.** Two scenic loop-drives penetrate the park's desert landscape and lead to a few trailheads. Both are winding and unpaved, but should pose no problems for an ordinary car. *Be sure to keep your speed low.* No water is available along either drive. The **Ajo Mountain Drive** (21 mi. round-trip; 2hr.) circles along the foothills of the steep, rocky Ajo Mountains, the highest range in the area. On the other side of the park, the **Puerto Blanco Drive** (53 mi. round-trip; 4-5hr.) winds through the colorful Puerto Blanco Mountains, passing oases, cacti, and abandoned mines along the way. An exceptional feature along the drive is **Quitobaquito,** a spring, creek, and marshland in the area where the drive meets the Mexican border. In stark contrast to the baking heat and relative silence of the desert, the oasis is at least 10°F cooler and hums with insects, song birds, and other animals. The road leads to the pond and marsh, and a short ¾ mi. spur heads toward the spring. In the midst of your cool respite, however, be aware that the busy Mexican Rte. 2 zips by merely 100 yards away from the spring, and with large breaks in the fencing. As of late June 2002, thefts from cars have been reported from the parking lot. Don't leave your CD player, video camera, digital camera, laptop, silverware, Mondrian, or Ming vase in plain sight.

KITT PEAK Harboring 22 telescopes about 90 min. west of Tucson off Rte. 86, **Kitt Peak Observatory** is home to the world's second largest collection of optical telescopes (the largest collection is in Chile). To gain permission to erect the first telescope on this Tohono O'odham sacred mountain, the original builders wowed the elders into agreeing to its construction by treating them to a night of star-gazing in Phoenix. Since then, most of the wowing has been done by tourists, who drive up the steep and windy access road to see the stars or just the telescopes. Daytrippers can wander around the compound or take one of the free daily tours. The more committed are encouraged to sign up for an evening program—an amateur astronomer's fantasy, it includes binocular- and telescope-based stargazing in some of the best conditions on earth. It can get cold at night, so dress appropriately. (☎520-318-8726. Open daily 9am-3:45pm. Daytime tours at 10, 11:30am, 1:30pm. Suggested donation $2. Evening program runs 3½hr. $36, seniors $26, students with ID $25; by reservation only. Fee includes a light dinner.)

Several hikes offer an excellent means of experiencing the park. Be sure to carry plenty of water whenever venturing out in the park. About halfway around the loop of the Ajo Mountain Drive lies the beginning of the **Estes Canyon-Bull Pasture Trail.** This strenuous 4.1 mi. round-trip hike climbs through the mountains to a plateau that affords an astounding view from all sides. An easier trek leads to **Victoria Mine,** the oldest gold-and-silver mine in the area (4.5 mi. round-trip). For those who prefer two wheels, most roads in the park double as biking trails, but be sure to exercise caution on the busy thoroughfares through the park.

I-19: TUCSON TO NOGALES

A modern interstate super-highway, I-19 is rarely without a coterie of gas stations and fast-food stands. The 63 mi. between Tucson and Nogales are no exception. The road surface is immaculate, and varies between four and six lanes for the duration. Between Tucson and Nogales, a couple of sights warrant mention. About 15 mi. north of Nogales, **Tubac** is the first European settlement in Arizona. First settled in 1752 by Spanish soldiers, Tubac bears remains from earlier Native American habitation. Today, the town flourishes as a touristy arts-and-crafts center with dozens of shops selling Latin American goods. The original *presidio* built by those Spanish soldiers of yore has been preserved as a state historical park. (☎398-2252. Open daily 8am-5pm. $3, ages 7-13 $1.) A few miles farther south, **Tumacacori National Historic Park** preserves the remains of a Franciscan mission dating back to 1795. Frequently ravaged by Apache, the church was rebuilt in 1822, but the cemetery is the original. (☎398-2341. Open 8am-5pm. $3.)

NOGALES   ☎520

Nogales is as American as apple pie—if instead of apple, you used jalapeño peppers and instead of pie crust a flour tortilla. The Mexican side of the city boasts over 200,000 people, while the American district measures in at only 20,000. Store signs are bilingual or Spanish-only, half of the TV stations are Mexican, and even the highway mileage signs are done Mexican-style; between here and Tucson, all distances are given in kilometers. Welcome to Mexico's northern-most city.

Nogales lies at the southern terminus of I-19, which continues into Mexico as Hwy. 15, and splits with its commercial doppelganger, "Business I-19", a.k.a. Grand Ave., for the length of the town. The two merge north of town, and are linked by shopping-mall-lined Mariposa Rd. Rte. 82 connects Nogales to the smaller communities in Arizona's southeastern pocket, branching off of Grand

ARIZONA

CROSSING THE BORDER There are border checkpoints on Grand Ave. in the middle of Nogales and on I-19 west of the city. The Grand Ave. crossing sees heavy local traffic while the I-19 crossing is where larger commercial vehicles and long-distance travelers cross. Crossing into Mexico in Nogales is easy; no visas are required for entry if you stay for less than 72 hours and travel less than 21km. Although only proof of citizenship is necessary for these daytrips (a valid or expired passport, birth certificate, or naturalization forms), in most cases these documents aren't even checked. Longer excursions into Mexico are more complicated. Citizens of the United States, Australia, Japan, and most larger European countries do not have to get a visa so long as they do not engage in profitable activities or intend to study. For more information, visit the Mexican consulate on Grand Ave. or www.consulmexico.org. I you plan on driving your car in Mexico, you must purchase Mexican car insurance before you cross the border, as American insurance does not always transfer. Consult your individual agency. A host of stores along Grand Ave. sell Mexican insurance.

Getting back into the United States is not quite so simple; American customs and immigration officials keep a close eye on the traffic that passes this border. Hour-long delays at the Nogales crossing are not uncommon, and wave-throughs unheard of. American citizens have to worry most about customs rather than immigration; the inspectors will ask about contraband. They may also inspect obvious hiding places for illegal immigrants. Tourists to the US crossing the border should be aware of their visa status to ensure that there will be no problem with readmittance; visitors from nations qualifying them for visa exemption needn't worry—you will be asked to fill out a form, but that's all. Students, legal immigrants, and aliens on work visas should be more wary; there are usually restrictions on readmittance in those circumstances. *(INS port of entry ☎ 287-3609, Border Patrol ☎ 377-6000. Border open daily 6am-10pm.)*

Ave. near northern downtown and leading to Patagonia, Tombstone, and Bisbee. A railroad follows Business I-19 through the city, directly west of Morley Rd.

The **Greyhound** bus terminal, 35 N. Terrace Ave., is close to the border, west of Grand Ave. From there, tickets may be purchased to Phoenix (3½-5hr., 11 per day, $20-31) and Tucson (1½hr., 2 per day, $8). **Visitor info** is available at the **Tourist Center**, at the north end of town. Follow the signs. (☎ 287-3685. Open M-F 8am-5pm.) Other services include: **police,** 777 N. Grand Ave. (☎ 287-9111); **Carondelet Holy Cross Hospital,** 1171 W. Target Range Rd. (☎ 285-3000), off of I-19 at the last exit before the border; and the **post office,** 300 N. Morley Ave., one block east of Grand Ave. (☎ 287-9246. Open M-F 9am-5pm, Sa 9am-1pm.) **ZIP code:** 85621.

Unfortunately, budget accommodations in Nogales are a bit dodgy. The chain motels along Mariposa and Grand are inexpensive and reliable, though fairly colorless. An independent option, **Time Motel ❷** on Grand Ave., provides guests with TV, A/C, phone, and a pool at budget prices. (☎ 287-0702. In summer singles $32, doubles $36; in winter $36/$40.) Cheap Mexican food can be had south of the border, but if you're craving a sojourn from the tyranny of the burrito, check out **Sweets 'n' Subs ❶,** 1855 N. Grand Ave., a combination bakery and sub shop. Try an enormous $3 ham-and-cheese sub. (☎ 281-4299. Open M-F 6am-6pm, Sa 6am-5pm.)

ROUTE 82/80: NOGALES TO TOMBSTONE

The stretch of state highway linking Nogales and Tombstone passes through stretches of wilderness punctuated only by small, picturesque townships that

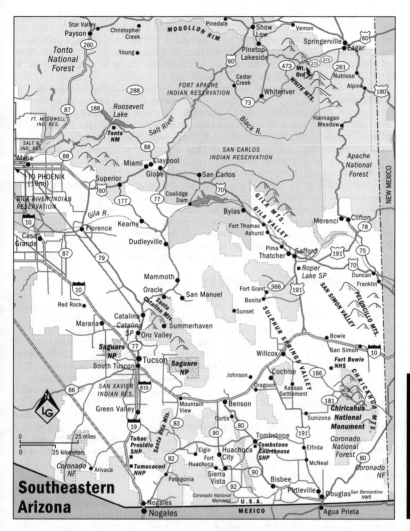

Southeastern Arizona

cater to tourists. The 71 mi. between the two towns are some of the most pleasant you'll ever drive. With towns such as Patagonia and Sonoita along the way, there is no shortage of gas stations, but prices and hours tend to be best in Nogales and drivers are advised to fill up there.

The landscape around the road is composed mainly of desert scrub. Immediately outside Nogales, the road crosses the **Santa Cruz River.** Past the river, the highway is flanked on either side by the **Coronado National Forest,** a woodsy backdrop to the rugged landscape, and then reaches **Patagonia Lake State Park.** Formed when Sonoita creek was dammed in the late 60s, the lake is used by locals for all water sports, and the park offers a **campground ❶,** a beach, and excellent fishing

(☎520-287-6965. 110 sites, showers. $10 per night, $15 for hookups, $5 day use. Entrance closed 10pm-5am.) Past the park, buttes and rock formations rise on either side of the road leading up to **Patagonia.** A picturesque town, it prospered from both the railroad and ranching, and managed to survive the fall of both. **Internet access** is available at the **Town Library,** 346 Duquesne St. (☎394-2010. Open M, W and F 10am-5pm; Tu 10am-6:30pm; Sa 10am-2pm.)

The highway continues past Patagonia along the Sonoita Creek before entering **Sonoita** itself. The small town boasts some of Arizona's prized vineyards and excellent eateries. **Grasslands Restaurant & Bakery ❶,** 3119 Rte. 83, is among the best eateries, with organic food made on the spot daily. (☎455-4770. Baked goods $1-5. Open for lunch Th-Su 8am-3pm, dinner Th-Sa 5-8pm.) Sonoita's surrounding vineyards are worth the stop, both with a myriad of homegrown wines to sample and, of course, buy. Nine miles south of town in the village of Elgin sits the large **Elgin Complex Winery,** with its house pride, "Tombstone Red," being the state's best-selling wine. (☎455-9309. Tours daily 10am-5pm.) Further south, **Sonoita Vineyards** offers visitors breathtaking views of the valley, as well as of the sprawling vineyards. (☎455-5893. Open M-F 10am-4pm.) The next 38 mi. pass through nearly barren wilderness; only buttes and distant mountains serve to break the lull of the desert. **Fairbank,** the sole town on this stretch, is so small that it is barely noticeable. Approaching Tombstone, the scenery morphs into a Hollywood Western—buzzards circling and heat blasting. The only thing missing are the cattle skulls.

CORONADO NATIONAL FOREST

Split by I-19 coming into Nogales from Tucson, two giant chunks of the Coronado National Forest fill up most of Santa Cruz County. The alpine climate around Nogales is a cooler, wetter contrast to the desert that surrounds Tucson. The **ranger station,** just north of Nogales on I-19 at the Ruby Rd. Exit, provides maps of the area, including detailed trail descriptions on request. (☎520-281-2296. Open daily 8am-4:30pm.) The Tucson-based **Southern Arizona Hiking Club** (☎520-751-4513; www.sahcinfo.org) leads guided hikes in the area—call or pick up their bulletin at the ranger station for more info. No mountain bikes are permitted in designated wilderness areas; check with rangers for details about restrictions.

There are surprisingly few maintained campgrounds in the area. The **Bog Springs Campground ❶,** with 13 sites, toilets, and water, provides convenient access to several hikes (sites $10). Another campground sits to the west of Nogales along Ruby Rd., accessible from the Ruby Rd. Exit off of I-19. **White Rock Campground ❶,** on Pena Blanca Lake, offers fishing, a boat launch, and drinking water (sites $5). **Backcountry camping ❶** is free, but requires a permit.

◪ OUTDOOR ACTIVITIES. There are plenty of **hiking** opportunities in the forest. All of the hikes listed here are off-limits to mountain bikes and are closed in the winter. The strenuous **Old Baldy Trail** (#372) is the most direct way of reaching the summit of Mt. Wrightson, the highest peak in the Santa Rita range (elevation gain 4050 ft.). To access the trailhead, take I-19 N from Nogales to the Continental Rd. Exit. From there, take Madera Canyon Rd. (Forest Rd. 62) until the Roundup Picnic area. Turn left, and there is a parking lot for the trailhead. This 4.5 mi. round-trip trail ascends through a variety of mountain habitats, and the gorgeous views from the top of the mountain showcase the entire Southern Arizona Mountain ranges. The **Super Trail** (#134) is the easier and longer (8.1 mi.) ascent up Mt. Wrightson, with a milder elevation gain. It shares a trailhead with Old Baldy, and features the same mountain views. The two trails trace a figure-8, so it's possible to switch between them midway. The **Bog Springs/Kent Springs Loop** (#156/157) meanders through stands of sycamore, juniper, and walnut, in addition to the Arizona bamboo that flourishes in this surprisingly green and moist area. To access the 4.5 mi. loop trail, use the directions to Madera Canyon Rd., but instead of driving to Roundup picnic area, drive to Bog Springs Campground, park in the parking area, and follow the old roadbed past campground #13. (1800 ft. elevation gain.)

Although the above trails are all off-limits to bikes, there are some opportunities for mountain bikers in the area. The rigorous 13 mi. **Elephant Head Mountain Bike Route** (#930/930A) follows a variety of single-track trails and forest roads between its northern end on Proctor Rd. (Forest Rd. 70) and the **Whipple Observatory Visitors Center,** its southern terminus (1000 ft. elevation gain). To reach the northern end, take I-19 to Madera Canyon Rd. After 11 mi., turn onto Prescott Rd. (Forest Rd. 70), and follow it for 2 mi., until the route begins at the road's junction with Forest Rd. 4074. To access the south end, take I-19 to the Canoa Rd. Exit, and drive along the east frontage road parallel to the freeway southbound until you reach Elephant Head Rd. on your right. Turn down the road and take the next left onto Mt. Hopkins Rd., which leads all the way to the Visitors Center, where the route begins.

BENSON   ☎ 520

A quaint hub between Tucson and Tombstone, Benson offers transportation services as well as some good food and lodging. **Amtrak** stops by on its way in and out of Tucson, but there is no ticket office. At the **Benson Flower Shop, Greyhound,** 600 E. 4th St. ,(☎ 800-231-2222) stops on its way to **Los Angeles** ($38; M-F 8am, 12:40pm, 9pm) and **El Paso** ($33; M-F 8:55am, 7:35pm). The ▓Benson Motel ❷, 185 E. 4th St., has masterfully restored rooms, each with its own car garage. The attention to detail at this Western-themed motel is second to none. (☎ 520-586-3340. Singles $30, doubles $33.) Down the road, the **Horse Shoe Cafe ❶,** 154 E. 4th St., dishes out great buffalo burgers ($6.50) and other American classics in a no-frills atmosphere. (☎ 586-3303. Open daily 6am-9pm.)

TOMBSTONE   ☎ 520

Long past its glory days when Tombstone was the largest city between the Pacific and the Mississippi, the town has sanitized itself from an authentic, debauched and dangerous Western town into a Cowboy Disneyland. In Tombstone you can get anything you want—as long as it's a shot of rot-gut or a gunfight re-enactment.

By inviting visitors to view the barnyard where Wyatt Earp and his brothers kicked some serious butt, Tombstone has turned the **shootout at the O.K. Corral,** on Allen St. next to City Park, into a year-round tourist industry. (☎ 457-3456. Open daily 9am-5pm. $2.50.) The voice of Vincent Price narrates the town's history next door to the O.K. Corral in the **Tombstone Historama,** while a plastic mountain revolves onstage and a dramatization of the gunfight is shown on a movie screen. (☎ 457-3456. Shows daily every hr. 9am-4pm. $2.50.) Site of the longest poker game in Western history (8 years, 5 months, and 3 days), the **Bird Cage Theater,** at 6th and Allen, was named for the suspended cages once housed prostitutes. (☎ 457-3421. Open daily 8am-6pm.) John Slaughter battled outlaws at the **Tombstone Courthouse,** at 3rd and Toughnut St. The courthouse is now a museum. (☎ 457-3311. Open daily 8am-5pm. $2.50, ages 7-13 $1.) The **tombstones** of Tombstone, largely the result of all that gunplay, stand in Boothill Cemetery on Rte. 80 just north of town. (☎ 457-3421 or 800-457-3423. Open daily 7:30am-6pm. Free.) For something different, the **Rose Tree Museum,** at 4th and Toughnut St., shelters the largest rose tree in the world. (☎ 457-3326. Open daily 9am-5pm. $2, under 14 free.)

ARIZONA

A good idea is to stay in Benson and commute out for a day in Tombstone. If you want to stay in town, the **Larian Motel ❷**, on the corner of Fremont and 5th, is clean, nicely furnished, and roomy, and within easy walking distance of all sights. (☎ 457-2272. Singles $40-45, doubles $45-59.)

Nellie Cashman's Restaurant ❶, named after the "angel of the mining camps" who devoted her life to clean living and public service, is a little less Old West and a bit more down-home. Delicious ½ lb. hamburgers start at $5.50. (☎ 457-2212. Open daily 7:30am-9pm.) For a bit of moonshine and country music, smell your way to **Big Nose Kate's Saloon,** on Allen St., named for "the girl who loved Doc Holliday and everyone else too." Bartenders serve drinks like "Sex in the Desert." (☎ 457-3107. Open daily 10am-midnight.)

To get to Tombstone, head to the Benson Exit off I-10, then go south on Rte. 80. The nearest **Greyhound** station is in **Benson** (see above). The **Douglas Shuttle** (☎ 364-9442) has service to Tucson ($10), Bisbee ($5), and Benson ($5). The **Tombstone Visitors Center** provides info and maps, although Tombstone is so small that nothing is hard to find. (☎ 457-3929. Open M-F 9am-4pm, Sa-Su 10am-4pm.) The Tombstone **Marshal's office** (☎ 457-2244) is just behind City Hall. **Internet access** is available at **Desert Gold Web Services** on Freemont. (☎ 457-3250. Open 7am-6pm. 15¢ per min.) The **post office** is at 516 E. Allen St. **ZIP code:** 85638

BISBEE   ☎ 520

One hundred miles southeast of Tucson and 20 miles south of Tombstone, mellow Bisbee, a former mining town, is known throughout the Southwest as a laid-back artists' colony. Once renowned for its mines and labor troubles (in 1918, at the end of World War I, 1200 striking miners were deported at gunpoint to the desert in New Mexico), now Bisbee's citizens are probably further left then the union agitators they once deported. Visitors revel in the town's proximity to Mexico, picture-perfect weather, and excellent, relatively inexpensive accommodations. The few sights in town are mine-related, but Bisbee is a terrific place to stroll, window-shop, and drink coffee in an artsy cafe.

🔁 **PRACTICAL INFORMATION.** Bisbee is not served by Greyhound. **Douglas Shuttle** (☎ 364-9442), a local line, links Bisbee with surrounding cities including Tombstone ($5) and Tucson ($15). Maps, brochures, and advice on the area can be had at the **Chamber of Commerce,** 31 Subway St. (☎ 432-5421. Open M-F 9am-5pm, Sa-Su 10am-4pm.) Pick up one of their maps: the streets of Bisbee are labyrinthine, and without a map you will be lost. With a map you'll still be lost, but you'll feel better. **Cranberry Mercantile,** on Brewer's Gulch Ave. north of downtown, is one of the few grocers in old Bisbee. (☎ 432-3488. Open M-Sa 7am-9pm, Su 10am-9pm.) **Canyon Wash Laundromat,** on Tombstone Canyon Rd., is near the south of town (open 8am-8pm). The **post office,** on Main St., is one block south of the highway exit. (☎ 432-2052. Open M-F 8:30am-4:30pm.) **ZIP code:** 85603

🔁🖸 **ACCOMMODATIONS AND FOOD.** About a 10min. walk from downtown, the **Jonquil Inn ❷**, 317 Tombstone Canyon, offers clean and smoke-free rooms. (☎ 432-7371. Singles $40-45, doubles $50-60; in winter about $10 more.) On Tombstone Canyon Rd., at the south end of town, the **School House Inn ❸** houses guests in a remodeled 1918 school house. Rooms are all themed and vary in size; the Principal's Office is palatial indeed, while the numbered classrooms have a cozier sort of charm. (☎ 432-2966 or 800-537-4333. All rooms have private bath, full breakfast included, TV in common room. No children under 14. Single bed $55; double/queen/king $60-80; 2-bed suite $90.)

ARIZONA

DELUGE The concept of a monsoon is more evocative of Indochina than Arizona, but the seasonal storms that batter the southern part of the state are aptly named. June in Arizona delivers stereotypical desert weather: heat, sun, more heat, and more sun. Perhaps only a lonely cloud mars the perfect blue sky in Tucson in late June, but come the 4th of July, it's joined by a regular posse of precipitation. After the intense dry heat of June, the monsoonal flow arrives in July and August. Though the temperature remains fairly high, daily thunderstorms pop up and pour down on the desert. These storms have a few peculiarities. Due to the lack of moisture in the desert, vast quantities of dust are taken up into the clouds, producing intense static electricity and some of the most spectacular lightning in the world. The storms are also extremely localized; it is possible to cross the street in Tucson and go from sunny weather into the teeth of driving rain. Apart from being a meteorological curiosity, these storms also pose dangers to travelers. Hiking at high altitudes during stormy weather increases the risk of lightning strikes and exposure. The faint of heart, and those who faint in the heat, should consider visiting southern Arizona in the winter months, when the only extreme weather will be on the Weather Channel in your overpriced hotel room.

A number of cheap eateries line the main drags of downtown. Most have classic American fixins' for around $4-8. A meat-a-tarian can get a fix at **Old Tymers ❷**, with steak ($11) and hamburger ($5) any way they like, from bleeding to burnt. (☎432-7364. Open Su-Th 11am-9pm, F-Sa 11am-10pm.)

◙ SIGHTS. Queen Mines, on the Rte. 80 interchange entering Old Bisbee, ceased mining in 1943 but continues to give educational 1¼hr. tours. (☎432-2071. Tours at 9, 10:30am, noon, 2, and 3:30pm. $10, ages 7-15 $3.50, ages 3-6 $2.) The Smithsonian-affiliated **Mining and Historical Museum,** 5 Copper Queen, highlights the discovery of Bisbee's copper surplus and the lives of the fortune-seekers who extracted it. (☎432-7071. Open daily 10am-4pm. $4, seniors $3.50, under 16 free.)

For a less earthly and more heavenly experience, visit the **Chihuahua Hill Shrines.** A 25min. hike over rocky ground leads to a Buddhist, and then a Mexican Catholic shrine. The Catholic shrine is older and has the prime real estate on the peak, but both have been lovingly constructed and cared for. The Catholic shrine is exceptional in its complexity, including numerous statues of the Madonna as well as dioramas of the Saint's lives and a towering cross. The Buddhist shrine is lower key, but includes several works of rock art as well as innumerable prayer flags and pictures of the last two Dalai Lamas. To reach these shrines, head to Cranberry Mercantile. To the left of the store, two staircases head up the hill; take the leftmost (the one marked by a hemp leaf, not the one stamped USA). After the climb up the stairway, turn right and follow a concrete driveway for a very short time. Right before the private property sign, turn right off of the paved road and start hiking through the rock. At the cross, bear up and follow the markers.

↰ OUTDOOR ACTIVITIES. About 18 mi. west of Bisbee along Rte. 92, along the Mexican border, **Coronado National Memorial** marks the place where Francisco Coronado and his expedition first entered American territory. A small Visitors Center houses exhibits about the expedition and a video documenting the famous voyage. The park contains a few hiking trails, including the southernmost section of the **Arizona Trail,** and offers the chance to do some independent spelunking. **Coronado Cave,** a small, relatively dry cave, is 0.8 mi from the Visitors Center along a short, steep path. A free permit is required to explore the cave, and can be picked up at the Visitors Center as long as each spelunker has a flashlight. The cavern

ARIZONA

isn't vast, but it's large enough to make for an interesting 1½hr., despite juvenile graffiti scrawled across a couple of overhangs. (☎ 366-5515. Park open daily dawn to dusk. Visitors Center open daily 8am-5pm.) **Ramsey Canyon Preserve,** 5 mi. farther down the road, attracts nearly as many bird-watchers as birds. In the middle of migratory routes for many North American birds, thousands of hummingbirds throng here in the late summer. Other species, including the golden eagle and a number of bats, pass through en masse. A short 0.8 mi. trail meanders through the manicured grounds, passing by a hummingbird garden, a frog pond, and a butterfly park. (Open daily 8am-5pm. $5, under 16 free; first Sa of every month free.)

CHIRICAHUA NATIONAL MONUMENT ☎520

Over 25 million years ago, Chiricahua was a thick heap of volcanic ash extruded from the nearby Turkey Creek Caldera. Fortunately, since then the never-to-be-underestimated powers of erosion have sculpted the hardened rock into spectacular formations with forbidding mountains in the background. Pillars of stacked stones cluster in groups, and tons of rock are perched precariously, appearing as though they'll fall immediately—they've been like that for hundreds of years. A cross between Zion and Bryce Canyon, Chiricahua was aptly called the "Land of the Standing-Up Rocks" by Apaches and the "Wonderland of Rocks" by pioneers. And while Chiricahua nearly equals the natural splendor of Bryce and Zion Canyons, it happily falls short of their popularity, indulging in peace and tranquility.

█!█ ORIENTATION AND PRACTICAL INFORMATION. Chiricahua is 40 mi. from I-10 and 70 mi. from Bisbee (see p. 148); from Bisbee, go east on Rte. 80 to Rte. 191 N, then to 181 N. The **Visitors Center** is just beyond the entrance station. (☎ 824-3560, ext. 104. Open daily 8am-5:30pm. Entrance fee for vehicles $6, pedestrians $3.) All of the park, except for a strip around the main road, is federally designated wilderness. No backcountry camping, bicycles, or climbing allowed.

█ █ ACCOMMODATIONS AND CAMPING. Although no backcountry camping is permitted along the trails, there is an established **campground ❶** inside the park. It features toilets, picnic grounds, water, and easy access to the park trails, but unfortunately, no showers. (24 sites. 14-day max. stay. $8.) The only nearby roofed accommodations are offered by the plush, ranch-style **Chiricahua Foothills Bed and Breakfast ❹**, with well-decorated rooms facing a green courtyard. Lunch and dinner are available on request at extra cost. (☎ 824-3632. Doubles $70.)

█ HIKING. There is a bountiful selection of **day hikes** in the monument. Many of the trails depart from the Echo Canyon parking lot, near the end of the main road. The longest loop possible from this trailhead rewards hikers with extraordinary views of and passage through the monument's incredible rock formations. From the parking lot, the **Echo Canyon Trail** leads 1.6 mi. through an impressive cluster of formations before junctioning with the **Hailstone** and **Upper Rhyolite Trails.** Take Hailstone and the **Ed Riggs Trail** for a fairly strenuous, 3.4 mi. loop and a quick return to the parking lot. For a longer loop, continue down the Upper Rhyolite Trail 1.1 mi. farther as the path wanders through pine forest. The trail junctions with the **Sarah Deming Trail,** which steeply ascends the opposite face of the canyon. After 1.6 mi., the high point of the hike is reached, and you may either hike the **Heart of Rocks Scenic Loop** to get a panoramic view of the entire vista, or continue immediately along **Big Balanced Rock Trail,** which winds across ridge tops for 1 mi. The Big Balanced Rock Trail eventually bleeds into **Mushroom Rock Trail.** Here, there is also a 0.5 mi. spur leading to the aptly named **Inspiration Point,** which affords a commanding view of the formations and canyons below. The return trip follows the level Mushroom Rock and Ed Riggs Trails, with more forest and fewer views than the Echo Canyon beginning. Together, they are approximately 2 mi. in length. The whole loop clocks in at 7.4 mi. and takes 4-5hr.; add 1.1 mi. and 45min. for the Heart of Rocks Loop and for the Inspiration Point Trail. The trail is fairly strenuous, and no reliable water is to be had along its length. The trails are clearly marked both at the trailheads and junctions and on the free monument map provided, but for added peace of mind and safety, 25¢ can buy you a more detailed **trail map.** The central loops are the bread and butter of Chiricahua, leading through the most spectacular country and racking up the brunt of the monument's mileage, but a couple of side treks also merit attention. The 5 mi. round-trip **Natural Bridge Trail,** off the main road on a clearly marked trailhead 1½ mi. past the Visitors Center, gains and loses 500 ft. over 2.5 mi., ending at a point where the rocks have formed a small natural bridge. The trail takes 3hr. to complete. Another trail leads from a parking lot at the extreme end of the main road up to the top of **Sugarloaf Mountain,** affording gorgeous views of the mountain crags and valleys. Approximately 500 ft. are gained over the steep, 0.8 mi. trail. Allow 2hr. for the hike.

CALIFORNIA

California's desert divides roughly into the Low and High Deserts, names which indicate differences in both altitude and latitude. The Sonoran, or Low Desert (see p. 185) occupies southeastern California from the Mexican border north to Needles and west to the Borrego Desert. The Mojave, or High Desert, averages elevations of 2000 ft., spanning the southern central part of the state, bounded by the Sonoran Desert to the south, San Bernardino and the San Joaquin Valley to the west, the Sierra Nevadas to the north, and Death Valley to the east. Four major east-west highways cross the desert. In the Low Desert, Interstate 8 hugs the California-Mexico border, while Interstate 10 passes Joshua Tree and Palm Springs. Interstate 15 cuts through the heart of the Mojave from Barstow, the Mojave's main pit stop, on to Las Vegas, while Interstate 40 cuts southeast through Needles and on to the Nevada desert. West of the desert, Los Angeles provides a major hub for travel throughout the Southwest, and Route 395 provides a major route up the east side of the Sierras to Reno.

■ HIGHLIGHTS OF CALIFORNIA

DEATH VALLEY. Visit the lowest point in the US at **Badwater** (p. 172), or hike to **Telescope Peak** (p. 173).

JOSHUA TREE. Take on the world-class boulders at the **Wonderland of Rocks** and **Hidden Valley** (p. 184).

GHOST TOWNS. Explore the ghost towns of the California Desert, including **Bodie** (p. 165) and **Skidoo** (p. 174).

LOS ANGELES

With a desert basin center, two mountain ranges cross the region, and 81 miles of dazzling coastline, Los Angeles County juggles multiple personalities. Here, myth and anti-myth stand comfortably side by side. Some see in its sweeping beaches and dazzling sun a demi-paradise, a land of opportunity where the most opulent dreams can be realized. Others point to its congestion, smog, and crime, and declare Los Angeles a sham—a converted wasteland where TV-numbed masses go to wither in the sun.

While not a Southwestern city itself, L.A. provides a convenient place into which to fly, and after a night on the town, rent a car and head east into the great outdoors. For more detailed info on the sights and activities that L.A. has to offer for a more extended stay, see ▨*Let's Go: California 2003.*

▣ TRANSPORTATION

INTERCITY TRANSPORTATION

Flights: Los Angeles International Airport (LAX) (☎310-646-5252), is in Westchester, about 15 mi. southwest of downtown, 10 mi. south of Santa Monica. LAX can be a con-

fusing airport, but there are plenty of electronic kiosks both inside and out providing info in myriad languages. Airport police (☎310-646-7911) available 24hr.

Trains: Amtrak, 800 N. Alameda St. (☎213-683-6729 or 800-872-7245), rolls into Union Station, at the northwestern edge of downtown Los Angeles.

Buses: Greyhound, 1409 N. Vine St. (☎800-231-2222), 1 block south of Sunset in Hollywood. A downtown station, in a rough neighborhood, is at 1716 E. 7th at Alameda St.

LOCAL TRANSPORTATION

Subway: With new sections on the Red Line branch created especially to cart tourists around, the **MTA subway** (☎800-266-6883; www.mta.net) is now one of the easiest ways to travel. Fare $1.35, with transfers $1.60; seniors and handicapped 45¢/55¢. All lines run daily 5am-11pm.

Buses: Nary an Angeleno will suggest moving about L.A. in anything but a car, but L.A.'s **MTA buses** (☎800-266-6883 for schedules; www.mta.net) are not altogether useless. Fares $1.35, with transfer $1.60; seniors and handicapped 45¢/55¢; exact change required. Weekly passes $11. The local **DASH shuttle** (☎213-808-2273; www.ladot-transit.com) serves major tourist destinations in many communities, including Downtown, Hollywood, Fairfax, Midtown, Crenshaw, and Van Nuys/Studio City, and Venice in the summer. Open M-F 6:30am-6:30pm, Sa 10am-5pm. Fare 25¢. Around Santa Mon-

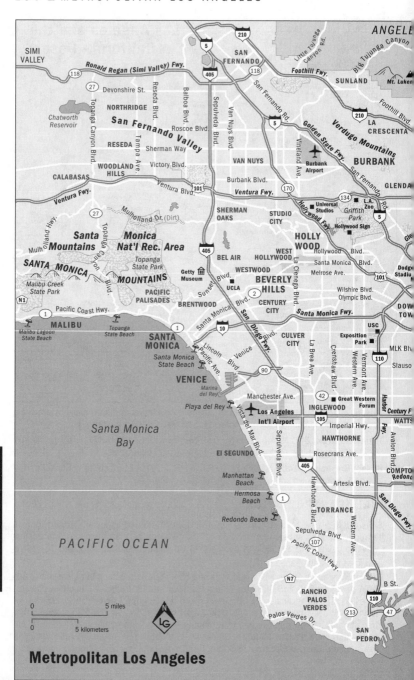

Metropolitan Los Angeles

CALIFORNIA

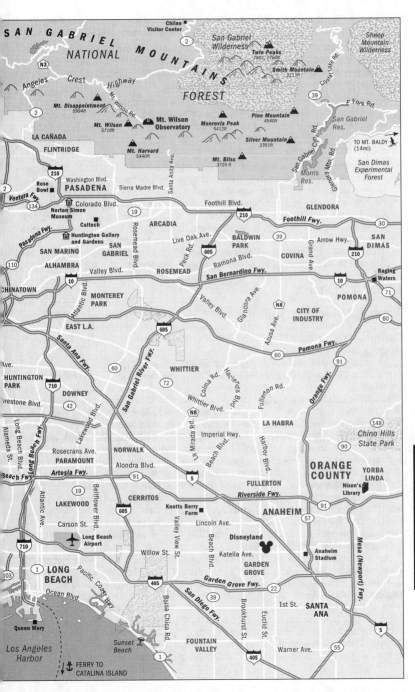

SAN GABRIEL
NATIONAL
MOUNTAINS
FOREST

Chilao
Visitor Center

San Gabriel
Wilderness

Sheep
Mountain
Wilderness

Twin Peaks
7601, 7760ft
Smith Mountain
5111ft

Coyote Lake Rd.

E Fork Rd.

San Gabriel
Res.

TO MT. BALDY
(14mi)

San Dimas
Experimental
Forest

N3

Angeles   Crest   Highway

Mt. Disappointment
5994ft

Mt. Wilson
5710ft

Mt. Wilson
Observatory

Monrovia Peak
5412ft

Pine Mountain
4540ft

Silver Mountain
3391ft

Mt. Harvard
5440ft

Mt. Bliss
3725 ft

San Gabriel Cyn. Rd.

Glendora Mtn. Rd.

Morris
Res.

San Gabriel Res.

LA CAÑADA
FLINTRIDGE

PASADENA

Washington Blvd.

Rose
Bowl

Ventura Fwy.

Norton Simon
Museum

Colorado Blvd.

Sierra Madre Blvd.

Santa Anita Ave.

Foothill Blvd.

GLENDORA

Foothill Fwy.

SAN
DIMAS

Arrow Hwy.

Caltech

Huntington Gallery
and Gardens

SAN MARINO

ALHAMBRA

Pasadena Fwy.

ARCADIA

Rosemead Blvd.

Live Oak Ave.

Peck Rd.

BALDWIN
PARK

COVINA

Grand Ave.

Raging
Waters

SAN GABRIEL

Valley Blvd.

ROSEMEAD

Ramona Blvd.

San Bernardino Fwy.

CHINATOWN

Atlantic Blvd.

MONTEREY
PARK

Valley Blvd.

Glendora Ave.

Azusa Ave.

CITY OF
INDUSTRY

POMONA

EAST L.A.

Santa Ana Fwy.

Pomona Fwy.

HUNTINGTON
PARK

WHITTIER

Colima Rd.

Hacienda Blvd.

Fullerton Rd.

Orange Fwy.

DOWNEY

Whittier Blvd.

LA HABRA

Chino Hills
State Park

irestone Blvd.

Lakewood Blvd.

Imperial Hwy.

Beach Blvd.

Harbor Blvd.

Rosecrans Ave.
PARAMOUNT

NORWALK

La Mirada Rd.

ORANGE
COUNTY

YORBA
LINDA

Artesia Fwy.

Alondra Blvd.

FULLERTON

Nixon's
Library

Beach Fwy.

Alameda St.

LAKEWOOD

Bellflower Blvd.

CERRITOS

Riverside Fwy.

Carson St.

Knotts Berry
Farm

Lincoln Ave.

ANAHEIM

Atlantic Ave.

Long Beach
Airport

Valley View St.

Beach Blvd.

Disneyland

Anaheim
Stadium

Mesa (Newport) Fwy.

LONG
BEACH

Pacific Coast Hwy.

Willow St.

Katella Ave.

GARDEN
GROVE

Ocean Blvd.

Bolsa Chica Rd.

Garden Grove Fwy.

San Diego Fwy.

Queen Mary

Los Angeles
Harbor

FERRY TO
CATALINA ISLAND

Sunset
Beach

Brookhurst St.

Euclid St.

1st St.   SANTA
ANA

Warner Ave.

FOUNTAIN
VALLEY

CALIFORNIA

ica, the **"Big Blue Bus" (BBBus)** provides service to local destinations. Fare 50¢, transfers to MTA buses 25¢. **Unless otherwise noted, all route numbers are MTA.**

Taxis: Cabs are costly, but if you need one, it's best to call **Independent** (☎213-385-8294 or 800-521-8294), **L.A. Taxi/Yellow Cab Co.** (☎310-715-1968 or 800-200-1085), or **Bell Cab** (☎888-235-5222). Fare is about $2 per mi. anywhere in the city and approximately $30-38 from airport to downtown.

Car Rental: Although traffic is a nightmare, L.A. may be the most difficult city in the U.S. to get around without a car. It may also be a difficult place for younger travelers to **rent** a car. Most places will not rent to people under 21, and the ones that do are likely to impose a surcharge that only movie stars can afford to pay (nearly double the standard rate). Drivers between 21 and 25 will incur a lesser surcharge.

Bicycles: Unless you have legs and lungs of steel, a bicycle in L.A. is useful only for recreational purposes. Air quality is poor, distances are long, and drivers aren't used to looking out for cyclists. The people at **L.A. Bike Tours,** 6729¼ Hollywood Blvd., might be able to convince you that there are some areas that are *best* explored by bike—at the very least it means one less tour bus. If you are not in a group, it's best to stick to designated bike paths, of which there are many. The most popular routes are the **South Bay Bicycle Path** (19 mi.), running from Santa Monica to Torrance, **San Gabriel River Trail** (37 mi.), the traffic-free **Upper Río Hondo** (9 mi.) and **Lario Trails** (22 mi.), and **Kenneth Newell Bikeway** (10 mi.), through residential Pasadena. *Avoid night biking.*

✴ ORIENTATION

A mere 419 mi. south of San Francisco and 127 mi. north of San Diego, the City of Angels spreads its wings across the flatland basin between the coast of Southern California and the inland San Gabriel Mountains. You can still be "in" L.A. even if you're 50 mi. from downtown.

A legitimate **downtown** Los Angeles exists, but it won't help orient you to the rest of the city. The heart of downtown, full of towering skyscrapers, is relatively safe on weekdays, but *avoid walking there after dark and on weekends*. The predominantly Latino section of the city is **East L.A.,** which begins east of downtown's Western Ave. with **Boyle Heights, Montebello,** and **El Monte.** North of East L.A., **Monterey Park** is one of the few cities in the US with a predominantly Asian-American population. The **University of Southern California (USC), Exposition Park,** and the mostly African-American districts of **Inglewood, Watts, Huntington Park,** and **Compton** stretch south of downtown. **South Central,** the name by which this area is known, has built a reputation for its crime rate and offers little to attract tourists.

Glittering **Hollywood** lies northwest of downtown. **Sunset Blvd.,** which runs from the ocean to downtown, presents a cross-section of virtually everything L.A. has to offer: beach communities, lavish displays of wealth, famous nightclubs, and sleazy motels. The **Sunset Strip,** hot seat of L.A.'s best nightlife, is the West Hollywood section of Sunset Blvd. closest to Beverly Hills. Hollywood Blvd. runs just beneath the celebrity-ridden **Hollywood Hills.**

The region known as the **Westside** encompasses prestigious **West Hollywood,** Westwood and Westwood Village, Century City, Culver City, Bel Air, Brentwood, and **Beverly Hills.** Westside's attractions include the **University of California at Los Angeles (UCLA),** in Westwood, and fashionable Melrose Ave. hangouts in West Hollywood. The name **West L.A.** is a municipal distinction that refers to Westwood and the no-man's land inland of Santa Monica that includes Culver City and Century City. The area west of downtown and south of West Hollywood is known as the **Wilshire District. Hancock Park,** an affluent residential area, covers the northeast portion of the district and contains the Los Angeles County Museum of Art.

AREA CODES. L.A. is big. Really big. There are many area codes. Here's a handy guide to them all:
213 covers downtown L.A., Huntington Park, Vernon, and Montebello.
213 and **323** cover Hollywood. (Mostly 323, but some are still 213.)
310 and **424** cover Malibu, Pacific Coast Highway, Westside, parts of West Hollywood, Santa Monica, south and east L.A. County, and Catalina Island.
626 covers the San Gabriel Valley and Pasadena.
818 covers Burbank, Glendale, San Fernando Valley, Van Nuys, and La Cañada.
909 covers the eastern border of L.A. County.

The **Valley Region** sprawls north of the Hollywood Hills and the Santa Monica Mountains. For most people, the valley is, *like*, the **San Fernando Valley,** where almost 2 million people wander among malls and TV studios. The valley is also home to **Burbank** and **Studio City.** The basin is bounded to the north and west by the Santa Susanna Mountains and the Ronald Reagan Fwy. (Rte. 118), to the south by the Ventura Fwy. (Rte. 134), and to the east by the Golden State Fwy. (I-5). The **San Bernardino Valley,** home to about 2 million residents, stretches eastward from Los Angeles south of the San Gabriel Mountains, and includes the city of **Pasadena**.

Eighty miles of beaches line L.A.'s **coastal region. Zuma** is northernmost, followed by **Malibu,** which lies 15 mi. up the coast from **Santa Monica.** A bit farther south is the distended beach-side freak show known as **Venice.** The beach towns south of Santa Monica include **Manhattan, Hermosa,** and **Redondo Beaches**. South across the Palos Verdes Peninsula is **Long Beach.** Furthest south are the **Orange County** beach cities: Seal Beach, Sunset Beach, Huntington Beach, Newport Beach, and Laguna Beach. Confused yet? Everyone is. Invest in maps.

🔃 PRACTICAL INFORMATION

Visitor Information: Los Angeles Convention and Visitors Bureau, 685 S. Figueroa St. (☎213-689-8822), between Wilshire Blvd. and 7th St. in the Financial District. Distributes *Destination: Los Angeles,* a free booklet with tourist and lodging info. Open M-F 8am-5pm, Sa 8:30am-5pm.

Weather Conditions: ☎213-554-1212, **Highway Conditions:** ☎800-427-7623.

Police: 1358 N. Wilcox Ave. (☎213-485-4302), in Hollywood.

Rape Crisis: ☎310-392-8381.

24hr. Pharmacy: Sav-On, 3010 S. Sepulveda Blvd. (☎310-478-9821), in West L.A. For other 24hr. locations, call 800-627-2866.

Hospitals: Cedars-Sinai Medical Center, 8700 Beverly Blvd. (☎310-855-5000, emergency 423-6517). **Good Samaritan Hospital,** 616 S. Witmer St. (☎213-977-2121, emergency 977-2420). **UCLA Medical Center,** 10833 Le Conte Ave. (☎310-825-9111, emergency 825-2111).

Post Office: Central branch at 71301 S. Central Ave. (☎800-275-8777). Open M-F 7am-7pm, Sa 7am-3pm. **ZIP Code:** 90001. Hollywood branch at 1615 Wilcox Ave. (☎800-275-8777). Open M-F 8:30am-5:30pm, Sa 8:30am-3pm. **ZIP code:** 90028.

🏠 ACCOMMODATIONS

As in any large city, cheap accommodations in Los Angeles are often unsafe. It can be difficult to gauge quality from the exterior, so ask to see a room before you spend any money. Be suspicious of rates below $35; they're probably not the kind of hotels in which most travelers would feel secure. For those willing to share a room and a bathroom, hostels are a saving grace, although Americans should be aware that many only accept international travelers. These hostels require an international passport, but well-traveled Americans with proof of travel (passports, out-of-state identification, or plane tickets often do the trick) may be permitted to stay. It never hurts to ask for off-season or student discounts, and occasionally managers will lower prices to snare a hesitant customer.

In choosing where to stay, the first consideration should be location. If you don't have wheels, you would be wise to decide which element of L.A. appeals to you the most. Those visiting for beach culture would do well to choose lodgings in Venice or Santa Monica. Avid sightseers will probably be better off in Hollywood or the more expensive (but cleaner and nicer) Westside. Downtown has numerous public transportation connections, but is unsafe after dark. Even those with cars should choose accommodations proximate to their interests to keep car-bound time to a minimum. *Listed prices do not include L.A.'s 14% hotel tax.*

HOLLYWOOD

Hollywood Bungalows International Youth Hostel, 2775 W. Cahuenga Blvd. (☎888-259-9990; www.hollywoodbungalows.com), just north of the Hollywood Bowl. Located deep in the hills of Hollywood, this newly renovated mini-compound cultivates a wacky summer-camp atmosphere complete with spacious rooms and nightly jam sessions. Bean-shaped pool, weight room, theater with big screen TV, and mini-diner. Cable and VCR in all rooms. Internet access available. 3 meals served per day (breakfast $3.50; dinner $10). Lockers 25¢. Linen and parking included. Laundry ($1.25 wash; 75¢ dry). Check-in 24hr. $14 airport shuttle. Stay 3 nights for free one-way transportation to airport. **Passport and international airline ticket or college ID required.** Co-ed dorms (6-10 beds) with bathroom $15-19; private doubles house up to 4 people for $59. ❶

USA Hostels Hollywood, 1624 Schrader Blvd. (☎323-462-3777 or 800-524-6783; www.usahostels.com), south off Hollywood Blvd., west of Cahuenga Blvd. Stay for more than a day at the hostel and get free pickup from airport, bus, and train stations. This lime-green and blue-dotted chain hostel is packed with young people looking to have some fun. Special events are offered seven nights a week, highlighted by free comedy W and Su. Purchase a raffle ticket in exchange for a beer or a shot. Beach shuttles run T, Th, and Su free of charge. To use lockers, bring your own lock or buy one for $3. All-you-can-eat pancakes, linen, and parking included. Dinner $5. **Passport or proof of travel required.** Dorms (6-8 beds) with private bath $17; private rooms for 2-4 people $38-46. Prices discounted $1-2 during winter off-season. ❶

Orange Drive Manor, 1764 N. Orange Dr. (☎323-850-0350). This pleasant, converted mini-mansion located in a quiet residential neighborhood is the perfect retreat for tranquility. Don't be confused by the lack of a sign—this house is your hostel. Small cable TV lounge and limited kitchen with microwave and fridge. Spacious, clean rooms with antique furniture. Internet access available. Lockers 75¢. Bring your own towel. Parking $5 per night. Reservations recommended. **US citizens and non-students permitted.** Dorms (4-6 beds), some with private baths, $19-23; private rooms $37-47. Minimal discount with ISIC card. No credit cards. ❷

SANTA MONICA AND VENICE

🏨 **Los Angeles/Santa Monica (HI-AYH),** 1436 2nd St. (☎310-393-9913; www.hilosangeles.org), Santa Monica. Take MTA #33 from Union Station to 2nd St. and Broadway, BBBus #3 from LAX to 4th St. and Broadway, or BBBus #10 from Union Station. Located only one block from the promenade, this hostel can afford to be choosy. It enforces a no-alcohol policy and 10pm-8am quiet hour. Rooms are small but common spaces well kept and well attended. Newly renovated kitchen, 2 nightly movies, library,

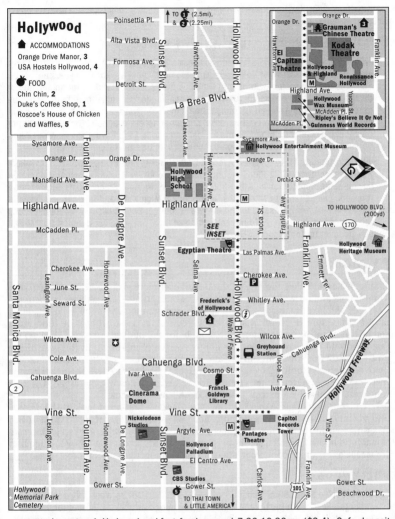

Hollywood

🏠 ACCOMMODATIONS
Orange Drive Manor, **3**
USA Hostels Hollywood, **4**

🍎 FOOD
Chin Chin, **2**
Duke's Coffee Shop, **1**
Roscoe's House of Chicken
and Waffles, **5**

central courtyard. Various breakfast foods served 7:30-10:30am ($2-4). Safe deposit boxes and lockers. Laundry wash $1, dry 75¢. Pay garages nearby. 24hr. security and check-in. 10 consecutive day max. stay. In summer, reserve well in advance by phone or at www.hiayh.org. 4-10 bed dorms $25-27, non-members $28-30; private doubles $67-73. Group packages available for 8+ people. ❷

Cadillac Hotel, 8 Dudley Ave., Venice (☎310-399-8876; www.thecadillachotel.com), directly off the Ocean Front Walk, in Venice. $11 airport shuttle. Discounted car rental with free pickup. Free parking. Sauna, rooftop sundeck with spectacular view, and well-equipped gym. All rooms have TVs and private baths. Internet access $1 per 10min. Laundry 75¢ wash, 50¢ dry. No kitchen. Reservations recommended. Four persons dorms $25. Work in exchange for night stay. "Family room" with queen and bunk $99.

Standard room $89. Requires 2 out of 3 of the following: valid driver's license, credit card, or passport. ❷

WESTSIDE: BEVERLY HILLS AND WESTWOOD

Orbit Hotel and Hostel, 7950 Melrose Ave. (☎323-655-1510; www.orbithotel.com), west of Fairfax Ave. in West Hollywood. Opened by 2 young L.A. locals 3 years ago, Orbit deserves top honors for location and livability. It sets a high standard for hostel interior design from fashion-conscious furniture to air circulation via large room fans. Spacious retro kitchen and big-screen TV lounge area, small courtyard, and a party room for late night. Free breakfast. Free TV show tickets. Internet access available. Car rental $20 per day. Parking available. 6-bed dorms $17; 4-bed dorms $20. Private rooms with TV and bath $45. Dorms accept international students with **passport** proof only. ❶

Hotel Claremont, 1044 Tiverton Ave. (☎310-208-5957 or 800-266-5957), in Westwood Village near UCLA. Pleasant and inexpensive for its locale. Owned and operated by the same family that built the hotel over 60 years ago. Clean rooms with antique dressers, ceiling fans, private baths, and phones. Microwave and free coffee offered in the lobby next to a pleasant, Victorian-style TV lounge. Daily maid service. Reservations recommended, especially in June graduation season. Singles $45; doubles $51; 2 full-size beds for up to 4 people $60. ❷

FOOD

Eating in Los Angeles, the city of the health-conscious, is more than just *eating*. Thin figures and fat wallets are a powerful combination—L.A. lavishes in the most heavenly and healthy recipes. There are also restaurants where the main objective is to be seen and the food is secondary, as well as those where the food itself seems too beautiful to be eaten. Fortunately for the budget traveler, L.A. elevates fast-food and chain restaurants to heights virtually unknown in the rest of the country. For the supreme burger-and-fries experience, try **In 'n' Out Burger,** a beloved chain symbolized by a '57 Chevy. **Johnny Rocket's** revives the never-really-lost era of the American diner; their milkshakes are a heady experience. The current craze is "healthy Mexican"—**Baja Fresh** leads the pack.

L.A.'s enormous public markets give the visitor a first-hand look at the variety and volume of foodstuffs available here. **Farmer's Market,** 6333 W. 3rd St., Wilshire District, at Fairfax Ave., has over 160 produce stalls, as well as international food booths, handicraft shops, souvenir stores, and a phenomenal juice bar. **Trader Joe's** is a super-cool chain specializing in budget gourmet food.

HOLLYWOOD

Duke's Coffee Shop, 8909 Sunset Blvd. (☎310-652-3100), in West Hollywood. The legendary Duke's is the best place in L.A. to see hung-over rockers looking for an all-day breakfast. If the seats don't testify to it, the walls will—they are plastered with autographed album covers. Communal, canteen-style tables are a regular meeting place. Try "Sandy's Favorite" (with green peppers, cubed potatoes, and scrambled eggs) for $7.25. Entrees $5-11. Attendant parking in rear $1. Open M-F 7:30am-8:30pm, Sa-Su 8am-3:30pm. ❷

Roscoe's House of Chicken and Waffles, 1514 Gower St. (☎323-466-7453). The downhome feel and all-day menu makes this dive a popular spot for regular folk and celebs alike. Try "1 succulent chicken breast and 1 delicious waffle" ($7). Be prepared to wait on weekends. Open Su-Th 8:30am-12am, F-Sa 8:30am-4am. ❷

Chin Chin, 8618 Sunset Blvd. (☎310-652-1818; www.chinchin.com), in West Hollywood. Other locations in Brentwood, Beverly Hills, Studio City, Marina del Rey, and

Encino. Grab a pair of sunglasses and sit on the patio—you'll feel just like the celebrities who surround you. This chic Chinese place is extremely popular with lunchtime crowds for its handmade "dim sum and then sum" ($10.75). Chinese Chicken Salad ($8) is the sort of Californian Chinese cuisine befitting a restaurant whose name means "to your health." Take-out available. Open Su-Th 11am-11pm, F-Sa 11am-1am. ❷

SANTA MONICA

⊠ **Fritto Misto,** 601 Colorado Ave. (☎310-458-2829), at 6th St. This "Neighborhood Italian Cafe" allows patrons to create their own pasta ($6+). The flexible made-to-order menu ($10-14), and cheery, helpful waitstaff make your meal an enjoyable one. Numerous vegetarian entrees $8-11. Daily hot pasta specials $8. Weekend lunch special (11:30am-4pm) features all-you-can-eat calamari and salad for $10. Monster omelettes served Su 11:30am-4pm ($7-8). Open M-Th 11:30am-10pm, F-Sa 11:30am-10:30pm, Su 11:30am-9:30pm. ❷

Big Dean's "Muscle-In" Cafe, 1615 Ocean Front Walk (☎310-393-2666), just a few steps from the Santa Monica Pier. No pretense here: it's sun, sand, sauerkraut, and *cervezas!* Home of the management-proclaimed "burger that made Santa Monica famous" ($5.75). Bratwurst $2.50 (with kraut $3), veggie burgers $4.75. Toast Happy Hour with $2 domestic beers (M-F 4-8pm). Open weekdays 10am and weekends 10:30am until dark, or until the everybody-knows-your-name regulars empty out. ❶

VENICE AND MARINA DEL REY

⊠ **Rose Cafe and Market,** 220 Rose Ave. (☎310-399-0711), at Main St. Gigantic rose-painted walls, local art, industrial architecture, and a gift shop might make you think this is a museum. But the colorful cuisine is the main display. Healthy deli specials, including sandwiches ($6-8) and salads ($4-7) available starting 11:30am. Limited menu after 3pm. Open M-F 7am-7pm, Sa 8am-7pm, Su 8am-5pm. ❷

Aunt Kizzy's Back Porch, 4325 Glencoe Ave. (☎310-578-1005), in Marina Del Rey. Hidden in a vast strip mall at the intersection of Glencoe Ave. and Mindanao Way. Actually done up to look like a back porch, Aunt Kizzy's is a little slice of Southern heaven, serving up heaping portions of down-home cooking. Specialties like Cousin Willie Mae's smothered pork chops and Aunt Johnnie's fried chicken crowd the plate with cornbread muffins and a selection of two vegetables from fresh collard greens to creamy red beans. Save room for Aunt Kizzy's $3 sweet potato pie. Dinner $12-13; buffet brunch $8. All-you-can-eat brunch buffet is a steal at $13 (Su 11am-3pm). Open M-Th 11am-9pm, F-Sa 11am-11pm, Su 11am-10pm. ❸

Big Daddy's, 1425 Ocean Front Walk (☎310-396-4146), cross Market Ave. With surfboard tables and the Beach Boys blaring, this is the ultimate burger and beach food shack. Let these grillmasters serve up anything the heart desires but can't quite handle. $1 menu includes hot dogs, pizza, fries, vanilla ice cream, and more. Burgers $4+. Fried everything (zucchini $4; calamari $6). Smoothies $2-5. Churros from an authentic Mexican machine with chocolate, strawberry, or caramel sauce center $2. Open M-F 11am-9pm, Sa-Su 8am-10pm. ❶

BEVERLY HILLS

⊠ **Al Gelato,** 806 S. Robertson Blvd. (☎310-659-8069), between Wilshire and Olympic St. Popular among the theater crowd for its proximity to the Beverly Hills Theater, this homemade gelato spot also does large portions of pasta with a delicious sweet basil tomato sauce. Giant meatball ($4.75) and rigatoni ($11). Skip the tiramisu ($5.50) and just stick to the gelato ($3.75-5.75). Made-to-order cannoli ($4.50). Open Tu, Th, Su 10am-midnight; F-Sa 10am-1am. No credit cards. ❷

NIGHTLIFE

Before setting off to the real heart of the Southwest, be sure to hit some L.A. night-life at least once. It's the best you'll come by for the duration of your travels.

LATE-NIGHT RESTAURANTS

Fred 62, 1850 N. Vermont Ave. (☎323-667-0062), in **Los Feliz.** "Eat now, dine later." Headrests and toasters at every booth. Hip, edgy East L.A. crowd's jukebox selections rock the house. The waffles ($4.62—all prices end in .62) are divine. Open 24hr.

The Rainbow Grill, 9015 Sunset Blvd. (☎310-278-4232; http://rainbowbarand-grill.com), in **West Hollywood,** next to the Roxy. Dark red vinyl booths, dim lighting, and loud music set the scene. An insane rainbow of guests play their parts. Marilyn Monroe met Joe DiMaggio on a blind date here. Brooklyn-quality pizza $6; calamari $8; grandma's chicken soup $3.50. Open M-F 11am-2am, Sa-Su 5pm-2am. Free parking.

COMEDY CLUBS

L.A. Improv, 8162 Melrose Ave. (☎213-651-2583), in **West Hollywood.** L.A.'s best tal-ent, like Robin Williams and Jerry Seinfeld, have shown their faces here; Drew Carey and Ryan Stiles often join the show. Dinner at the restaurant (entrees $6-14) includes priority seating for the show. 18+. Cover $10-15. 2-drink min. Shows Su-Th 8pm, F-Sa 8:30 and 10:30pm. Bar open daily until 1:30am. Reservations recommended.

Groundling Theater, 7307 Melrose Ave. (☎323-934-9700; www.groundlings.com), in **Hollywood.** The best improv and comedy "forum" in town. The Groundling's alums include Pee Wee Herman and many current and former *Saturday Night Live* regulars like Will Farrell, Julia Sweeney, and Chris Kattan. Don't be surprised to see *SNL* producer Lorne Michaels sitting in the back. Lisa Kudrow of *Friends* got her start here, too. Mostly polished skits. Cover $7-18.50. Shows Tu and Th 8pm, F-Sa 8 and 10pm, Su 7:30pm.

BARS

Beauty Bar, 1638 Cahuenga Blvd. (☎323-464-7676), in **Hollywood.** A combination bar and beauty parlor. It's like getting ready for the prom all over again, except that the drinking starts before rather than after. Drinks like "Shampoo" are $5-7. Smoking room with hair-setting seats. Manicures, "up 'dos," and henna tattoos Th-Sa nights with a spe-cialty drink ($10). DJ nightly at 10pm. Open Su-W 9pm-2am, Th-F 6pm-2am, Sa 8pm-2am.

Miyagi's, 8225 Sunset Blvd. (☎323-656-0100), on **Sunset Strip.** With 3 levels, 5 sushi bars, and 7 liquor bars, this Japanese-themed restaurant, bar, and lounge is the latest Strip hotspot. "*Sake* bomb, *sake* bomb, *sake* bomb" $4.50. Open daily 5:30pm-2am.

The 3 of Clubs, 1123 N. Vine St. (☎323-462-6441), in **Hollywood.** In a small strip mall beneath a "Bargain Clown Mart" sign, this simple, classy, spacious, hardwood bar is famous for appearing in 1996's *Swingers.* DJ F-Sa, live bands Th. Open daily 7pm-2am.

The Room, 1626 Cahuenga St. (☎323-462-7196), in **Hollywood.** A speakeasy that emp-ties into an alley, the very popular Room almost trumps The 3 of Clubs. No advertising, no sign on the door. 2nd location in **Santa Monica** at 14th St. and Santa Monica Blvd. Open daily 8pm-2am.

CLUBS

Largo, 432 N. Fairfax Ave. (☎323-852-1073), in **West Hollywood.** Elegant and intimate sit-down (or, if you get there late, lean-back) club. Original rock, pop, and folk sounds along with comedy acts. Cover $2-12. Open M-Sa 8:30pm-2am.

Derby, 4500 Los Feliz Blvd. (☎323-663-8979), in **Hollywood.** The concept of the Derby was conceived by Cecil B. DeMille in the 1920s. Today this joint is still jumpin' with the kings of swing. Ladies, grab your snoods, because many dress the 40s part. Choice Italian fare from Louise's Trattoria next door. Full bar. Free Lindy Hop and East Coast swing lessons Sa 7:30pm. Cover $5-10. Open daily 7pm-2am.

Key Club, 9039 Sunset Blvd. (☎310-274-5800), on **Sunset Strip.** A colossal, crowded multimedia experience complete with black lights, neon, and a frenetic dance floor. Live acts and DJ productions, depending on the night. 4 full bars. Cover $10-55. Open on club nights 10pm-2am, live music nights 7pm-2am.

GAY AND LESBIAN NIGHTLIFE

Abbey Cafe, 692 N. Robertson Blvd. (☎310-289-8410), in **West Hollywood,** at Santa Monica Blvd. This cafe becomes a lounge, bar, and dance club as the moon rises. Impeccable service, tasteful decor. Open daily noon-2am.

U.S. 395: L.A. TO RENO

The well-traveled corridor between Los Angeles and Reno, U.S. 395 passes just to the east of the mountains surrounding Death Valley. Several towns along the way, including Lone Pine, Bishop, and Lee Vining, provide excellent stop-overs from which to explore the unlimited activities in the nearby White Mountains, Yosemite National Park, and Death Valley.

LONE PINE   ☎760

This little bump in the road may be the best kept secret in wild America. Featured in hundreds of movies, TV programs, and commercials, Lone Pine may also be the biggest star in America. The rugged, boulder-strewn hills, with the towering Sierras in the distance, provide a gorgeous backdrop for story-telling; you've probably seen some gunslinger trotting through this wide, dusty frontier.

■ ☑ **ORIENTATION AND PRACTICAL INFORMATION.** Straddling U.S. 395, Lone Pine is the first Sierra town northeast on Rte. 136 from Death Valley. Since Greyhound has canceled service to the Eastern Sierra, getting to Lone Pine by bus is rather difficult. You can take Greyhound or Amtrak to Carson City, where **CREST** (☎800-922-1930) departs on Rte. 395 Tuesday, Thursday and Friday at 2pm, and arrives in Bishop, 60 mi. to the north, at 6:30pm. A non-connecting bus passes through Bishop on its way to Lone Pine on Monday, Wednesday and Friday. Contact CREST to figure out the best way to match up buses. **Visitor Info** is available at the **Interagency Visitors Center,** at U.S. 395 and Rte. 136, about 1 mi. south of town (☎876-6222 or 877-253-8981; open July-Sept. daily 8am-5:50pm; Oct.-June 8am-4:50pm), the **Chamber of Commerce,** 126 S. Main St. (☎876-4444; open M-Sa 9am-5pm), and the **Mount Whitney/Inyo National Forest Ranger Station,** 640 S. Main St., where travelers can find outdoors info and pick up **wilderness permits.** (☎876-6200. Open daily 7am-noon and 1-4:30pm.) Other services include: **Inyo County Sheriff,** Lone Pine Substation, S. Washington St. (☎876-5606); **Southern Inyo Hospital,** 501 E. Locust St. (☎876-5501); **Internet access: Lone Pine Public Library,** on S. Washington St. (☎876-5031; open M-Tu and Th-F 9am-noon and 1-5pm, W 6-9pm, Sa 10am-1pm); and the **post office,** 121 Bush St., between Jackson and Main St. (☎876-5681; open M-F 9am-5pm). **ZIP code:** 93545.

CALIFORNIA

⌐⌐ ACCOMMODATIONS AND FOOD. Many clean but high-priced motels are available here. Weekdays are cheapest, but rates fluctuate widely depending on demand; make reservations or arrive early. The ⬛**Historical Dow Hotel ❷**, 310 S. Main St., welcomes visitors with couches, a TV, fireplace, pool, and jacuzzi. (☎876-5521; reservations 800-824-9317. Doubles from $38, with private bathroom from $52.) Camping is cheap, scenic, and conveniently located. As with motels in the area, make reservations or arrive early. The **Whitney Portal Campground ❶**, on Whitney Portal Rd., 13 mi. west of town, sits amid evergreens, a rushing stream, and phenomenal views. (Ranger ☎876-6200; reservations 800-280-2267. 7-night max. stay. Open June-Oct. Sites $14; group sites $30.)

Lone Pine has its share of coffee shops and 24hr. mini-marts, but not much else. Grab groceries in town at **Joseph's Bi-Rite Market,** 119 S. Main St. (☎876-4378. Open daily 8am-8pm.) Most restaurants are plain, but cheap, decent fare is available.

◪ SIGHTS. Along Whitney Portal Rd., **Movie Road** leads to the scenic **Alabama Hills,** where many a Hollywood Western was filmed. The **Eastern California Museum,** 155 N. Grant St., off Market St. in Independence, has a specialized collection featuring local Paiute and Shoshone handicrafts, exhibits on miners and ranchers, and a display on the Manzanar relocation camp. (☎878-0258. Open Su-M and W-Sa 10am-4pm. Donation $1.) On U.S. 395, between Lone Pine to the south and Independence to the north, lies the **Manzanar National Historic Site,** symbolic of one of the most shameful chapters in American history. Previously known as a "relocation" camp, it was the first of 10 internment centers that the US established after Pearl Harbor to contain Japanese Americans.

◪ HIKING. The most significant trek in the area is the hike to the top of **Mt. Whitney,** an 11 mi. one-way journey that will take two-three days. While the strenuous hike does not require technical mountain climbing skills, hikers should beware of the dangers of high altitudes and bears. Visit the **Whitney Trailhead Ranger Station** (☎876-6200), on Whitney Portal Rd., 13 mi. west of Lone Pine, before setting out. Hiking permits for day and overnight use are required. Write to the Mount Whitney Ranger Station at 640 S. Main St., Lone Pine, CA 93545. Include desired dates and number of people. For climbers, Mt. Whitney's **East Face** is a year-round challenge.

Many moderate **day hikes** explore the Eastern Sierra out of the Whitney Portal. The **Cottonwood Lakes Trail** (10,000 ft. at the trailhead) squeezes between the forests that abut the John Muir Wilderness and Sequoia National Park. Follow Whitney Portal Rd. for 4 mi. from Lone Pine and take Horseshoe Meadow Rd. 20 mi. to the trailhead. The hour-long hike along **Horseshoe Meadow Trail** to **Golden Trout Wilderness** passes several dozen high mountain lakes that mirror the Inyo Mountains. **Horseshoe Meadow ❶** has camping (sites $6) and equestrian facilities ($12 per horse, in case you brought one). The **Whitney Portal Trail** offers a more challenging, 6hr. hike from the Lone Pine campground to Whitney Portal campground.

If you've got bulletproof muscles and high-octane willpower, you may want to enter one of the toughest races in the world. Each spring, Lone Pine hosts the **Death Valley to Mt. Whitney Race** for both runners and cyclists. The arduous trek departs Stovepipe Wells (elevation 5 ft.) in Death Valley and struggles over an undulating 100 mi. course to the 8300 ft. Whitney Portal. Day one is 78 mi.; day two climbs the last 22. This brutal exercise makes a marathon look like an April stroll.

LEE VINING AND MONO LAKE   ☎760

One million years old, Mono Lake is the Western Hemisphere's oldest enclosed body of water. Today, Mono supports not only its own delicate and unique ecosystem but also the water needs of greater metropolitan L.A. Seventy miles north of Bishop on 395, Lee Vining provides stunning access to Yosemite via Inyo National Forest, as well as the best access to Mono Lake and the ghost town of Bodie.

■✦ **ORIENTATION AND PRACTICAL INFORMATION.** The **Mono Lake Committee and Lee Vining Chamber of Commerce,** at Main and 3rd St., provides info on activities in the area as well as lake preservation info. (☎647-6595; www.monolake.org or www.leevining.com. Open late June to Labor Day daily 9am-10pm; Labor Day to late June 9am-5pm.) **Mono Basin National Forest Scenic Area Visitors Center,** off U.S. 395, ½ mi. north of Lee Vining, offers info on Mono County's wilderness areas. (☎873-2408. Open M-F 9am-5:30pm; in winter M-F 9am-4pm.) Rent kayaks at **Caldera Kayaks,** at Crowly Lake Marina, Mammoth Lakes. (☎935-4942. Half-day $20, full-day $30, tour $60.) The **post office** is in a big brown building on 4th St. (☎647-6371. Open M-F 9am-2pm and 3-5pm.) **ZIP Code:** 93541.

▐█ **ACCOMMODATIONS AND FOOD.** Accommodations can be pretty pricey, but the cheapest options are to be found on **Main St.,** or 10 mi. south of town on the 14 mi. **June Lake Loop.** The best options include **El Mono Motel ❸,** at Main and 3rd St. (☎647-6310; singles $49); **Inn at Lee Vining ❸,** at Main and 2nd St. (☎647-6300; rooms from $45); and **Gateway Motel ❺,** in the center of town (☎647-6467; in summer from $89, in winter from $49). Most area campsites are clustered west of Lee Vining along Rte. 120. **Lundy** and **Lee Vining Canyons ❶** are the best locations for travelers headed for Mono Lake. (No water. Open May-Oct. Sites $7.)

Lee Vining Market, on U.S. 395 at the southern end of town, is the closest thing to a grocery store. (☎647-1010. Open Su-Th 7am-9:30pm, F-Sa 7am-10pm.) **Nicely's ❶,** on U.S. 395, just north of the Visitors Center, is a local favorite with the ambience of a diner. (☎647-6477. Open daily 6am-10pm; in winter closed W. Entrees $5-9.) **Mono Cone ❶,** on U.S. 395 at the northern end of town, is a local institution whose opening signals the beginning of summer. (☎647-6606. Open daily 11am-7pm.)

▣▲ **SIGHTS AND OUTDOORS.** One of the area's best-preserved ghost towns, **Bodie** was "the most lawless, wildest, and toughest mining camp the West has ever known," although it doesn't look that way now. Lying off U.S. 395 32 mi. north of Lee Vining and 13 mi. east of Rte. 270, the town is strewn with abandoned automobiles, machinery, and other historic trash, which is well preserved by the dry climate and the state government.

In 1984, Congress set aside 57,000 acres of land surrounding Mono Lake and named it the **Mono Basin National Forest Scenic Area** (☎873-2408). To get there, take U.S. 395 S to Rte. 120, then go 4 mi. east and take the Mono Lake South Tufa turnoff 1 mi. south to Tufa Grove. For a $3 fee (national parks passes accepted), travelers may investigate the **South Tufa Grove,** which harbors an awe-inspiring hoard of calcium carbonate formations. The Mono Lake Committee offers **canoe tours** of the lake that include a crash course in conservation and Mono's natural history. (☎647-6595. 1hr. tours depart from South Tufa at Mono Lake mid-June to early Sept. Sa-Su at 8, 9:30, and 11am; bird-watching is better on earlier tours. Tours $17, ages 4-12 $7. Reservations required.)

The unique terrain of this geological playground makes it a great place for hikers of all abilities. Easy trails include the quarter-mile **Old Marina Area Trail,** east of U.S. 395, 1 mi. north of Lee Vining, the **Lee Vining Creek Trail,** which begins behind the Mono Basin Visitors Center, and the **Panum Crater Trail,** 5 mi. south on U.S. 395 near the South Tufa turnoff. Those undaunted by the prospect of a punishing trek should head 10 mi. east of U.S. 395 on Rte. 120, where an exceptionally steep trail leads to the glistening **Gardisky Lake.** Another peaceful but tough hike starts at

Lundy Lake, off U.S. 395 north of Lee Vining, and leads to **Crystal Lake** and the remains of an old mining town. The hike gains 2000 ft. in its 3 mi. ascent, and the well-maintained trail offers little shade. The Visitors Center offers tours of sights, including June Lake and **Panum Crater,** an expansive site of recent volcanic activity (640 years ago) that will boil your blood.

DEATH VALLEY NATIONAL PARK ☎760

The devil owns a lot of real estate in Death Valley. Not only does he grow crops (at the Devil's Cornfield) and hit the links (at the Devil's Golf Course), but the park is also home to Hell's Gate itself. It's not surprising, then, that the area's astonishing variety of topographical and climatic extremes can support just about anyone's idea of the Inferno. Visitors can stare into the abyss from the appropriately named Dante's View, one of several panoramic points approaching 6000 ft. in elevation, or gaze wistfully into the heavens from Badwater, which (at 282 ft. below sea level) is the lowest point in the Western Hemisphere. Winter temperatures dip well below freezing in the mountains, and summer readings in the valley rival even the hottest Hades. In fact, the second-highest temperature ever recorded in the world (134°F in the shade) was measured at the Valley's Furnace Creek Ranch on July 10, 1913. On that day, ranch caretaker Oscar Denton said, "I thought the world was going to come to an end. Swallows in full flight fell to the ground dead... when I went out to read the thermometer with a wet towel on my head, it was dry before I returned." Fortunately, the fatal threshold of 130°F is rarely crossed, and the region can sustain an intricate web of life. Many threatened species, including the desert tortoise and the desert bighorn sheep, inhabit Death Valley.

In 1849, a group of immigrants looking for a shortcut to California's Gold Country led ox-drawn wagons over the ridges of the Great Basin and down into the valley's salt beds. After weeks of searching for a western pass through the Panamint Range (losing one of their party in the process), the group found a way out. Looking back at the scene of misery, someone exclaimed, "Goodbye, death valley!" thus naming the area for posterity. After this tragedy, few were anxious to return. In 1883, however, miners discovered borax (a type of salt), and gold claims followed about two decades later. Soon mining provided fortunes for a few and a livelihood for many in towns like **Rhyolite** and **Skidoo.** Eventually, rapid depletion of resources transformed boom towns into ghost towns. With no promise of new industry, most have forsaken the valley, leaving it largely undisturbed. A tourist influx began in 1933, when the government set aside over three million acres of this desert wilderness, making it the largest US national park outside Alaska.

CALIFORNIA

AT A GLANCE: DEATH VALLEY NATIONAL PARK	
AREA: 3,367,626 acres.	**GATEWAY TOWNS:** Beatty (p. 175), Shoshone (p. 175), Lone Pine (p. 163).
FEATURES: The Valley, Furnace Creek, Badwater, Panamint Range, Telescope Peak, Amargosa Range, Scotty's Castle, Devil's Golf Course.	**CAMPING:** 30 day max. stay, 14 days at Furnace Creek. Backcountry camping free, must be 2 mi. from all roads and ¼ mi. from all backcountry water sources.
HIGHLIGHTS: Hiking to Telescope Peak, visiting the lowest point in the US at Badwater, hike up the trail-less alluvial fan and narrows at Red Wall Canyon, drive to Dante's view for the panorama and a break from the heat.	**FEES:** Weekly pass $10 per vehicle, $5 per pedestrian or bike; collected at Furnace Creek Visitors Center, Grapevine, Stovepipe Wells, and Beatty.

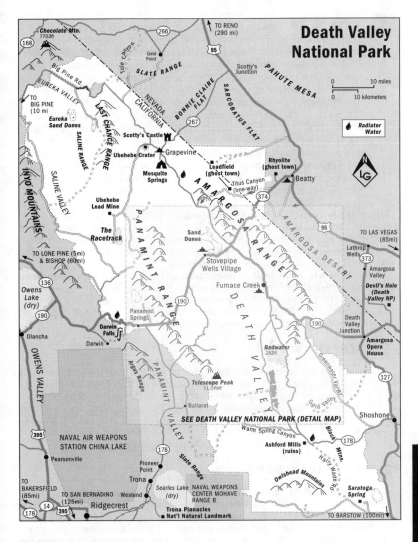

Death Valley
National Park

TO RENO
(290 mi)

Radiator
Water

SEE DEATH VALLEY NATIONAL PARK (DETAIL MAP)

⌐ TRANSPORTATION

Cars are the best way to get to and around Death Valley (3½hr. from Las Vegas; 5hr. from L.A.; 7hr. from Tahoe City; 10½hr. from San Francisco), and renting a car is more flexible than any bus tour. The nearest agencies are in Las Vegas (see p. 193), Barstow (see p. 176), and Bishop (see p. 164).

Conditions in Death Valley are notoriously hard on cars. Radiator water (*not* for drinking) is available at critical points on Rte. 178 and 190 and Nevada Rte. 374. There aren't many **gas stations** in the park, so keep the tank near full at all times. Check ahead for road closings; do not drive on wet backcountry roads.

WHEN TO GO. Although the average high temperature in July is 116°F and the nighttime low 89°F, even summer visits can be enjoyable with conservative planning. To this end, the Furnace Creek Visitors Center distributes the free pamphlet, *Hot Weather Hints.* To enjoy the many hiking and camping options, however, visit in winter, *not* summer. Winter is the coolest time (40-70°F in the valley, freezing temperatures and snow in the mountains) and also the wettest, with infrequent but violent rainstorms that flood canyons and obliterate roads. Call ahead for road and trail closings. In March and April, desert wildflowers bloom everywhere, but the floral season is accompanied by tempestuous winds that whip sand into a blinding frenzy for hours or even days. From late October to mid-November, over 50,000 people pack Death Valley's facilities during the **49ers Encampment Festival.** Traffic jams, congested trails and campsites, long lines for gas, and 4hr. waits at Scotty's Castle plague the area during the winter holidays, Easter, Thanksgiving, and many winter weekends.

Although **four-wheel-drive** vehicles and **high-clearance** trucks can be driven on narrow roads that lead to some of Death Valley's most spectacular scenery, these roads are intended for drivers with backcountry experience and are dangerous no matter what you're driving. In case of a breakdown, stay with your vehicle or find nearby shade. (For more tips, see **Great Outdoors** p. 62.)

No regularly scheduled **public transportation** services Death Valley. **Guaranteed Tours,** with a depot at the World Trade Center on Desert Inn Rd. between Swensen and Maryland Pkwy. in Las Vegas, runs bus tours from Las Vegas to Death Valley. (☎ 702-369-1000. Open for reservations daily 6am-10:45pm. 9½hr. tours depart Tu, Th, and Sa 8am. $120, includes continental breakfast and lunch.)

▓ ORIENTATION

Of the seven park entrances, most visitors choose **Rte. 190** from the east. The road is well maintained, the pass is not too steep, and the Visitors Center is relatively close. But since most of the major sights adjoin the north-south road, the daytripper with a trusty vehicle can see more of the park by entering from the southeast (**Rte. 178 W** from **Rte. 127** at Shoshone) or the north (direct to Scotty's Castle via Nevada **Rte. 267**). Unskilled mountain drivers in passenger cars should not attempt to enter on the smaller Titus Canyon or Emigrant Canyon Dr.

▓ PRACTICAL INFORMATION

Furnace Creek Visitors Center (☎ 786-3200; www.nps.gov/deva), on Rte. 190 in the Valley's east-central section. For info write: Superintendent, Death Valley National Park, Death Valley, CA 92328. Guides and topographical hiking maps ($4-8), schedules of activities and guided hikes, and weather forecasts. A 12min. slide show, a short movie (every hr.), and nightly lectures in winter provide further orientation. Park entrance fee can be paid here. Open daily 8am-6pm.

Ranger Stations: Weather report, weekly naturalist program, and park info at each station. Emergency help provided. **Grapevine** (☎ 786-2313), at Rte. 190 and 267 near Scotty's Castle; **Stovepipe Wells** (☎ 786-2342), on Rte. 190; and **Shoshone** (☎ 832-4308), at Rte. 127 and 178 outside the valley's southeast border. Also in **Beatty, NV** (☎ 702-553-7200), on Nevada Rte. 374. All are technically open daily 8am-5pm, but rangers are often out of the office and in the park.

Death Valley Hikers' Association: For info write c/o Darrell Tomer, P.O. Box 123, Arcata, CA 95521. The *Dustdevil* is their stellar publication.

CALIFORNIA

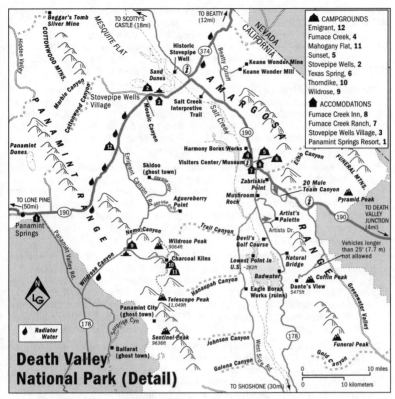

Death Valley National Park (Detail)

CAMPGROUNDS
Emigrant, **12**
Furnace Creek, **4**
Mahogany Flat, **11**
Sunset, **5**
Stovepipe Wells, **2**
Texas Spring, **6**
Thorndike, **10**
Wildrose, **9**

ACCOMODATIONS
Furnace Creek Inn, **8**
Furnace Creek Ranch, **7**
Stovepipe Wells Village, **3**
Panamint Springs Resort, **1**

Gas Stations: Get gas outside Death Valley at Lone Pine, Olancha, Shoshone, or Beatty, NV, or pay 50¢ more per gallon in Death Valley. For gas in the Valley: Furnace Creek Visitors Center (open 7am-7pm), Stovepipe Wells Village (open 7am-9pm), Panamint Springs (open 7am-5pm), or Scotty's Castle (open 9am-5:30pm). Don't play macho with the fuel gauge; fill up often. **AAA towing service, propane gas,** and **diesel fuel** available at the Furnace Creek Chevron.

Laundromat: (☎ 786-2345), on Roadrunner Ave. at Furnace Creek Ranch. $1 each for wash and dry. Open 24hr.

Showers: Stovepipe Wells Village (☎ 786-2387). Non-guests $2. Open daily 9am-9pm. Also, **Furnace Creek Ranch** (☎ 786-2345) $2. Open daily 9am-11pm.

24hr. Ranger Dispatch and Police: ☎ 786-2330.

Post Office: Furnace Creek Ranch (☎ 786-2223). Open M, W and F 8:30am-3pm; Tu and Th 8:30am-5pm. **Postal Code:** 92328.

▮ ▮ ACCOMMODATIONS AND FOOD

Affordable beds and inexpensive meals can be as elusive as the bighorn sheep. Motel rooms in the surrounding towns are much cheaper than those in Death Valley itself, but are over an hour away from all the top sights. Never assume that rooms will be available in the Valley. In the winter, camping with a stock of grocer-

CALIFORNIA

ies saves money and driving time but can be uncomfortable in the summer, especially at lower elevations. (For more affordable accommodations outside the Valley, see **Life After Death Valley,** p. 175.) For those who wish to make their own meals, **Furnace Creek Ranch Store** is well stocked but expensive. (☎786-2381. Open daily 7am-9pm.) **Stovepipe Wells Village Store** is smaller and also expensive. (☎786-2578. Open daily 7am-9pm.) Both stores sell charcoal, firewood, and ice.

Stovepipe Wells Village (☎786-2387), 30 mi. northwest of Furnace Creek Visitors Center on Rte. 190, is a great in-park option when camping becomes too hot to handle. The village offers comfortable rooms, a mineral water swimming pool, and all the amenities one could ever need. The dining room offers plenty of food at stiff prices (breakfast buffet 7-10am, $8; dinner buffet 6-9pm, $17). Rooms for up to 2 people $50-92; each additional person $11. RV sites available. Full hookups $20. ❸

Panamint Springs Resort (☎775-482-7680; www.deathvalley.com), 23 mi. east of the park's western border on Rte. 190, is remote but comfortable. The complex includes a restaurant and bar, 18 rooms, RV hookups, campsites, and gas. None of the rooms include TV or phones, but a pay phone is available for public use. The only other tie to civilization is the thunderous roar of naval fighters as they loop and corkscrew overhead on maneuvers from China Lake Naval Weapons Station. Doubles from $65. RV sites $10-25, campsites $10. ❶

Furnace Creek Ranch Complex (☎786-2345, reservations 800-236-7916; www.furnacecreekresort.com), once housed and fed Death Valley's borax miners. Today, it is flooded with tour bus refugees who challenge the adjacent 18-hole golf course (the country's lowest at 214 ft. below sea level) and relax in the 85°F spring-fed swimming pool. Complex has a cafeteria (open daily 6-10am, 11am-2pm, and 6-9:30pm) and a few pricier restaurants. Older cabins with A/C and 2 double beds $102; remodeled motel-style accommodations $133-154. Prices $15 more on holiday weekends. ❺

Amargosa Hotel (☎852-4441), at Death Valley Junction, Rte. 127 and 190, 29 mi. east of Furnace Creek. In a Spanish-style plaza developed by ballet dancer Marta Becket. 4 rooms feature Becket's murals; the other 10 are clean but mural-free. Though the hotel is a welcome retreat in the desert, visitors might be left feeling bored. Other than the opera (see **Southeast of Death Valley,** p. 175), the hotel is the *only* thing in Death Valley Junction. Reception open daily 10am-8pm. Singles from $49; doubles from $66. ❷

Furnace Creek Inn (☎786-2345, reservations 800-236-7916; www.furnacecreekresort.com), 3 mi. west of the Visitors Center on Rte. 190, is a virtual oasis in the middle of the desert. This luxurious inn offers beautiful rooms, gardens with babbling brooks, a pool and tennis courts, and an upscale bar and restaurant. All the grandeur does not come without a price; rooms start at $155 during the summer. Over the winter holidays they can go for as much as $365. ❺

CAMPING

The National Park Service maintains nine campgrounds in Death Valley; all provide an inexpensive and comfortable way of seeing the park as long as time of year is taken into consideration. Some of the hottest are closed during the summer (Sunset, Texas Spring, and Stovepipe Wells), and Thorndike and Mahogany Flat are closed due to snow and ice in the winter. Pay attention to elevation; the higher up you are, the more comfortable your visit will be when the temperature climbs into the triple digits. The Visitors Center (see **Practical Information,** p. 168) keeps records about site availability; be prepared to battle for a space if you come during peak periods (see **When to Visit,** p. 167). All campsites have toilets, but none have showers. Campers can't always count on available water, so always pack your own. The Visitors Center has unlimited free water, though it's as warm as bath water. Collecting wood is forbidden everywhere in the park, so pack your own firewood and bring a stove and fuel to use where open fires are prohibited. Roadside camping is not permitted, but **backcountry camping ❶** is free and legal, provided you check in at the Visitors Center and pitch tents at least 2 mi. from your car and any road, and ¼ mi. from any backcountry water source. All sites limit stays to 30 days except Furnace Creek, which has a 14-day limit.

Furnace Creek (☎800-365-2267), 196 ft. below sea level, north of the Visitors Center. Furnace Creek is particularly uncomfortable in summer, even though many of the 136 sites are shaded. Usually fills up first in winter, especially with RVs. Near Furnace Creek Ranch facilities ($2 shower access; laundry). 14-day limit. Reservations Oct.-Apr. Sites $16 in winter, $10 in summer. ❶

Sunset, 196 ft. below sea level, and **Texas Springs,** sea level, in the hills above the Furnace Creek Ranch Complex. These two sites are the best place for tents near Furnace Creek activities. Over 1000 sites available, some with shade. For wind protection, stick close to the base of the hills. Generators prohibited. Water, some tables. Open fires permitted. Flush toilets and dump station. Open Oct.-Apr. Sites $10-12. ❶

Stovepipe Wells, at sea level. Near airstrip, 4WD trails, and sand dunes. Reminiscent of a drive-in movie lot. Tents compete with RVs for 190 gravel sites. Spots near the trees afford more protection from sandstorms. Close to hotel and general store. A few tables and fireplaces. (Don't confuse it with the trailer park.) Open Oct.-Apr. Sites $10. ❶

Mesquite Springs, 1800 ft., near Scotty's Castle, 2 mi. south of Grapevine Ranger Station. Located in a small valley, some of the 30 sites offer shade and protection from the wind. Listen for coyote and owls. Picnic tables, water, and flush toilets. Open fires permitted. Sites $10. ❶

Emigrant, 2100 ft., off Rte. 190, 9 mi. west of Stovepipe Wells Village across from the ranger station, on the way down from Towne Pass through Panamint Range. Tents only. Gorgeous view of Stovepipe Wells and the Valley, though sites are located directly next to Rte. 190. 10 sites can be comfortable even in the summer. Flush toilets and water. No fires. Free. ❶

Wildrose, 4100 ft., on the road to the Charcoal Kilns in Wildrose Canyon, at the end of Emigrant Canyon Rd. An old summer residence of the Shoshone Indians, this shady mountainside has the most comfortable temperatures in the park. Convenient base for trips to Skidoo, Aguereberry Point, and Telescope Peak. Water and pit toilets. Open fires permitted. 30 sites. Free. ❶

Thorndike, 7500 ft., and **Mahogany Flat,** 8200 ft., 10 mi. east of Wildrose beyond the Charcoal Kilns in Wildrose Canyon. Depending on conditions, a sturdy car with an able driver may make it to either site, although 4WD is preferable. Hiking in may be a better option. 16 sites. No trailers. Gets cold and dark early; the sun sets quickly in the canyon. Can be snowy even in Apr. and Oct. Pit toilets. No water. Open Mar.-Nov. Free. ❶

🔍 SIGHTS

Plan your approach to Death Valley carefully. The park is large, and unplanned visits tend to be scattered and unrewarding. If exploring the valley in a day, adopt a north-south or south-north route, rather than heading directly to the Furnace Creek Visitors Center on Rte. 190, which connects east with west. Camera-toters should keep in mind that the best photo opportunities are at sunrise and sunset.

SCOTTY'S CASTLE. Remarkably out of place in the desert, this castle's imaginative exterior rises from the sands, complete with minaret and Arabian-style colored tile. The saga of the Castle's construction began with the friendship between Chicago insurance millionaire Albert Johnson and the infamous flim-flam man Walter Scott (a.k.a. "Death Valley Scotty"). When Johnson fell ill, his doctor suggested that he move to a warm, dry locale, and Scotty convinced him to build this palatial hacienda in Death Valley. Scotty became Johnson's caretaker for the rest of their lives, enjoying fame as the world's most famous "permanent guest/leech" since Rasputin. The well-furbished interior provides welcome relief from the heat (Humbert Humbert sought shelter here in Vladimir Nabokov's *Lolita*); though the waterfall in the living room has been switched off, the player piano and organ remain. *(From Rte. 190, look for sign near mile marker 93 and take road junction to Park Rte. 5; follow Rte. 5 for 33 mi. to castle. ☎ 786-2392. Open daily 9am-5pm. Tours $8, seniors and ages 6-11 $4; every hr. May-Sept., more frequently Oct.-Apr. You can purchase tickets until 1hr. before closing, but there are often lines.)*

DEVIL'S GOLF COURSE. Cyclical flooding and evaporation nurtures the ongoing formation of gnarled salt pillars. In the burning heat of summer, one can hear faint metallic tinklings as the salt crystals expand and shatter. Refrain from walking far into the salt pan to avoid hurting yourself on the jagged formations, and be careful not to damage the fragile crystals. *(15 mi. south of the Visitors Center.)*

BADWATER. A briny pool four times saltier than the ocean, this body of water is huge in the winter, but withers into nothing more than a large puddle in summer. The surrounding salt flat dips to the lowest point in the Western Hemisphere—282 ft. below sea level. Note the sign bolted high on the canyon wall opposite the pool that indicates sea level. The pools shelter the extremely threatened Badwater snails, many of which are crushed by thoughtless waders. Stay out of the water to avoid injuring its fragile ecology. *(18 mi. south of the Visitors Center.)*

◪ HIKING AND BACKPACKING

It is not an exaggeration to say that tourists die every year while foolishly hiking with too little water in the brutal heat. There are summer days too hot to hike even with abundant water. Severe heat exhaustion strikes even the fittest people, so do not overestimate your tolerance. Another danger is **flash flooding.** Especially when hiking in canyons, be aware of the weather forecast and always have an escape route out of the canyon should torrents of water come pouring down the canyon.

During the summer, most hikers escape to the high elevations of the Panamint and Amargosa Ranges. During winter, hiking in the valleys and badlands is tolerable, even pleasant. Rangers and the handouts they dispense give the distances and times of recommended hikes. Always bring a map with you—a few steps off the trail and you are in real wilderness.

AROUND FURNACE CREEK AND BADWATER

This is the hottest region of the park. If you *must* hike here in the summer, carry a liter of water per hour and make sure that you are off the trail by 10-11am.

Natural Bridge Canyon (1 mi. round-trip, 1hr.). The trailhead is located at Natural Bridge parking area; take Badwater Rd. 13¼ mi. south of Rte. 190, take a left, and follow the unmarked, graded road 1½ mi. to the parking area. A large, conglomerate natural bridge stands 0.3 mi. up the trail and a bit farther, the trail ends at a series of dry falls.

Desolation Canyon (2 mi. round-trip, 2hr.). To access this trail, go 3¾ mi. south of Rte. 190 on Badwater Rd.; go left on Desolation Canyon Rd., and take the left fork to the end. The trail leads up a narrow slot canyon. Make a right at all forks in the canyon.

Dante's Ridge (1-8 mi. round-trip). The trailhead is at Dante's View parking area; to access, go east on Rte. 190 and just before leaving the park, make a right on the road that leads 13 mi. to Dante's View. From the viewpoint, the trail leads 0.5 mi. north along a ridge to a first summit. Though the trail ends, the ridge continues 3.5 mi. to the summit of Mt. Perry.

NEAR STOVEPIPE WELLS

Sand Dunes (2 mi. one-way). Trailhead 22 mi. north of the Visitors Center. The most accessible dunes for day hikers lie 2¼ mi. east of Stovepipe Wells Village; use the parking area and follow the 2 mi. trail. Although barefoot climbing on the dunes can be sensuous, be wary of tumbleweeds and mesquite spines while clambering over these 150 ft. hills. In the late afternoon, the dunes (favorites of photographer Ansel Adams) glow with a golden sheen. If you try to emulate the master, know that sand will fool your light meter; increase exposure one F-stop to catch such details as footprints and ripples.

Mosaic Canyon (4 mi. round-trip, 2-3hr.). To access, take the turnoff from Rte. 190, 1 mi. west of Stovepipe Wells, to the 2½ mi. gravel road up the alluvial fan, accessible on foot, horseback, or car. A ½ mi. corridor of painted and eroded marble walls, this site stands as a true natural wonder. A simple trail leads from the parking lot around the canyon to some awesome vistas. Occasional bighorn sheep sightings are a bonus.

IN THE PANAMINTS

Telescope Peak Trail (14 mi. round-trip, 7-10hr.). A steep trail leads up to the 11,049 ft. summit of this peak, the highest in the park. The strenuous hike begins at Mahogany Flat Campground and gains 3000 ft. of elevation, passing charcoal kilns and bristlecone pines and providing unique views of both Badwater and Mt. Whitney. You should buy maps of the area at the Visitors Center or a ranger station. The trek becomes a technical mountain climb in winter, requiring ice axes and crampons. The snow usually melts by June. If your car is low-clearance, you might have to start the hike at Charcoal Kilns. If this is the case, add 3.5 mi. to your round-trip distance.

Wildrose Peak Trail (8.4 mi round-trip, 4-6hr.). From the Charcoal Kilns parking area, this trail gains 2000 ft. as it winds north to Wildrose Peak. Less crowded than Telescope, it's a good alternative in winter when snow does not usually affect this summit.

NORTHERN DEATH VALLEY

Ubehebe Crater and Peak. Only 8 mi. west of Scotty's Castle, this blackened volcanic blast site is nearly 1 mi. wide and 462 ft. deep, with a spectacular view. The 0.5 mi. gravel trail leading to the floor of the crater increases one's appreciation for the hole's dimensions, but not nearly as much as the grueling climb back out. An unpaved, four-wheel-drive road continues 23 mi. south of the crater to the vast Racetrack Playa, a dried-up lake basin providing access to Hidden Valley and White Top Mountain. See the trails left by mysterious moving rocks on this lake basin. For an outstanding view of the Racetrack, follow the **Ubehebe Peak Trail** (6 mi. round-trip) from the Grandstand parking area along a steep (2600 ft. elevation gain), rocky trail. Some scrambling is required at the end of the climb.

Fall and Red Wall Canyons. Both canyons are accessible from the Titus Canyon Mouth parking area, 3 mi. east of Scotty's Canyon Rd. between the Visitors Center and Scotty's Canyon. There are no trails up either canyon, so the routes necessitate some route-finding and plenty of arduous hiking. Fall Canyon is the next canyon north of Titus Canyon, and the mouth of the canyon lies only 0.5 mi. north of the parking area. Red Canyon's mouth is 1.5 mi. farther north of Fall Canyon and requires hiking up an alluvial fan for access to the canyon proper. While Red Wall is less frequented, both canyons are spectacular and offer some of the most spectacular narrows in the park.

CALIFORNIA

⚠ OTHER OUTDOOR ACTIVITIES

Ranger-led programs are generally unavailable in summer, but many popular programs, such as the **car caravan tours** and **interpretive talks,** are available in winter and spring. Astronomy buffs should speak to one of the rangers—they often set up telescopes at Zabriskie Point and offer freelance stargazing shows. During **wildflower season,** rangers offer tours of the blooming sites. Wildflower-watching is best after a heavy rainfall.

Driving is a popular activity in the park, and is especially nice in the summer, when a car affords a tenuous climate control. (For more on park driving and its special hazards and necessary precautions, see **Transportation,** p. 167.) Here are some of the park's most beloved drives.

Zabriskie Point. This route is 3 mi. south of Furnace Creek. Immortalized by Michelangelo Antonioni's 1970 film of the same name, Zabriskie Point is a marvelous place from which to view Death Valley's corrugated badlands at sunrise. For an intimate view of them, take the short detour along 20-Mule-Team Rd. The well-maintained dirt road is named for the gigantic mule trains that used to haul borax 130 mi. south to the rail depot at Mojave. The view of the choppy orange rock formations is particularly stunning late in the day, when the dried lakebeds fill with auburn light. Before the sunset ends, scamper 2 mi. (and 900 ft.) down Gower Gulch to colorful **Golden Canyon,** where the setting sun makes the cliffs glitter like fool's gold.

Artist's Drive. Off Rte. 178, 10 mi. south of the Visitors Center, this one-way loop twists its way through brightly colored rock formations. The loop's early ochres and burnt siennas give way at Artist's Palette to sea green, lemon yellow, periwinkle blue, and salmon pink mineral deposits in the hillside. The effect is most intense in the late afternoon as the colors change rapidly with the setting sun. The dizzying 9 mi. drive turns back on itself again and again, ending up on Rte. 178 only 4 mi. north of the drive's entrance.

Emigrant Canyon Rd. This winding road leads from the Emigrant Campground to Wildrose Canyon Dr. Along the way, there is a turnoff for the four-wheel-drive skedaddle to the ruins of Skidoo, a ghost town at 5700 ft. in the Panamint Range. Skidoo was the backdrop for the only full-length movie ever shot in Death Valley (Erich von Stroheim's *Greed,* 1923). A few miles down Emigrant Canyon Rd. is the turnoff for the dirt road to **Aguereberry Point** (which may require four-wheel drive), known for its fine sunset views. A left turn at Wildrose Canyon Dr. and a 10 mi. drive up this road will bring you to the ten conical furnaces known as the **Charcoal Kilns,** huge ovens that once fired 45 cords of wood at a time to make charcoal for mines.

BUY A BURRO Animal life persists in Death Valley, despite its desolate environment. Fragile pupfish inhabit tiny pools, and rare desert bighorn sheep traipse through rocks at higher elevations. The infamous **Death Valley burros**—beasts of burden transported from their native Middle East in the 1850s and freed when the automobile made them obsolete—unwittingly decimated the park's bighorn sheep population by wolfing down edible shrubs and fouling the water. Several years ago, the park service authorized a three-year burro banishment plan to get their asses out of there: they were sold as pets. Over 6000 have been removed, and though the ban no longer stands and burros are no longer a threat to the park, they may still be adopted for $75. Contact the California Federal Building, 2800 Cottage Way #E2841, Sacramento 95825 (☎916-978-4725).

LIFE AFTER DEATH VALLEY

BEATTY   ☎775

When approaching Death Valley from the north, consider kicking back briefly in the town of **Beatty, NV.** Situated 90 mi. northwest of Las Vegas on Rte. 95, Beatty offers weary travelers A/C and gambling facilities in an effort to make up for the desolation of the Valley. Compared to those in Reno and Las Vegas, Beatty's casinos are very relaxed. Wager as little as $1 at blackjack and jaw with the dealers, folks who play slow and seem genuinely sorry to take your money. All casinos are theoretically open 24hr., but by 2am the dealers start eyeing the clock.

Info can be found at **Beatty Visitor Information Center,** 119 E. Main St. (☎553-2424. Open M-F 10am-3pm.) There is public Internet access for a nominal fee at the **Beatty Public Library.** (☎553-2257. Open M, W, and Th 9am-3pm; Tu noon-7pm; Sa 9am-noon.) The **Beatty Ranger Station** is well stocked with books, maps, and safety info for desert-bound drivers. (☎553-2200. Open Tu-Sa 8am-4pm.) Sleep in peace at the **Stagecoach Hotel ❸,** on Rte. 95 ½ mi. north of town. Amenities include a pool, jacuzzi, casino, and bar. The hotel's restaurant serves up diner favorites 24hr. a day; dinners range from $6-10. (☎533-2419. Singles and doubles from $35.) Cheaper rooms can be found at the **El Portal Motel ❷,** on Rte. 374, one block from the junction with Rte. 95. (☎553-2912. Singles $30; doubles $33.) The **Happy Burro Inn ❸,** at Rte. 95 and 3rd St., has clean rooms and $15 RV hookups. The kitchen also serves up standard lunch counter fare. (☎553-2225, casino 553-2445. Kitchen open 24hr. Singles $35; doubles $40; prices $5 higher when they start to fill up.) Don't miss gas and water at the service station before leaving town.

Just outside of Beatty, heading toward Death Valley on Rte. 374, the ghost town of **Rhyolite** decays in the sweltering heat. **Rhyolite** exploded after prospector Shorty Harris's 1904 discovery of gold in the area. For several madcap years, the town pitched ahead in a frenetic rush of prospecting, building, and saloon hopping. At its height, it was home to an opera house and a stock exchange, but townsfolk fled when a 1911 financial panic struck. The jail and train depot still stand, but the most infamous relic of Rhyolite's crazy heyday is the **Bottle House,** constructed from 51,000 liquor bottles by miner Tom "Iron Liver" Kelly. Newer works of art by area intelligentsia fill a free public sculpture garden on the city's south side, which includes a gigantic cinder-block nude.

WEST OF DEATH VALLEY

Ghost towns and a few slightly more populated communities are the only developments that remain on Rte. 190 west of the park. In **Olancha,** the **Ranch Motel ❸,** on U.S. 395, provides clean, homey rooms in cottage-type buildings. (☎764-2387. Singles $49; doubles $59; cabins which sleep 4-8 $130. Rates may vary with the Lone Pine Film Festival or on other holiday weekends.)

Further north along U.S. 395 at the junction with Rte. 136 is the town of **Lone Pine.** Sitting at the base of Mt. Whitney, the shade of the high Sierra Nevadas can be a welcome refuge from the heat of the desert (see **Lone Pine,** p. 163).

SOUTHEAST OF DEATH VALLEY

In **Death Valley Junction,** at Rte. 127 and 190, 29 mi. from Furnace Creek, lives mime and ballet dancer Marta Becket, whose **Amargosa Opera House,** is the sole outpost of high culture in the desert. Becket incorporates parts of classical ballet, modern dance, and pantomime into a one-woman show with 47 different characters, drawing packed houses. (☎852-4441. Performances Oct., Dec.-Jan., and May Sa; Nov. and Feb.-Apr. M and Sa. Shows begin at 8:15pm. $15.)

CALIFORNIA

The town of **Shoshone,** at Rte. 127 and 178, 56 mi. southeast of Furnace Creek, serves as a gateway to Death Valley and a base for outdoor adventures. The **Charles Brown General Store and Service Station** is a good place to stock up and fill up. (☎852-4242. Open daily 8am-9pm.) Next door is the brown **Shoshone Inn ❹,** which offers clean but run-down rooms, a swimming pool, and cable TV. (☎852-4335. Singles $53; doubles $63.) The nearby **Shoshone Trailer Park ❶** has RV hookups, showers, a pool, and even some shade. (☎852-4569. Sites $10, full hookup $15.) Or stop by **Cafe Si Bon ❷,** an outpost of French cuisine in the middle of the desert. Crepes, coffee, and Internet access come at fair prices. (☎852-4224. Crepes $5-7, Internet $1 for 10min. Open M, Th, F 10am-4pm, Sa-Su 10am-6pm.)

South of Shoshone is the small town of **Tecopa,** which offers hot springs and a hostel for outdoor adventurers. Follow the signs to the **Desertaire Hostel HI-AYH ❶,** 2000 Old Spanish Trail Hwy., for knowledgeable owners and cheap sheets. (☎852-4580. Check-in 5-9pm. Closed in June Dorm beds $12).

ROUTE 66 AND INTERSTATE 40

Route 66 was designated as such in November of 1926, replacing the National Trails Highway as the principal road for commerce and immigration between the Mississippi Valley and Southern California. Running from Chicago to Los Angeles and spanning seven states, the road was taken by Okies fleeing the Dust Bowl, by wide-eyed Easterners seeking to partake in the post-war boom around L.A., and later by tourists looking for the Grand Canyon and Disneyland.

If the Smithsonian Museum is America's attic, Rte. 66 is its junk drawer, featuring the remnants of an earlier tourist culture. Greasy-spoons, gaudy motels, and odd little towns—all without their former luster—testify to the American urge to bring fun and self-transformation to even the harshest places. The shift over the last generation toward the super-interstate, with its generic restaurants and chain motels, suggests a fundamental transformation in the lifestyle of Middle America.

Much of Rte. 66 has been swallowed up by the interstate or left to languish in the form of gravel or forlorn dirt. In other places, it trucks on as a patchwork of state and county roads (businesses along it sell $4 maps tracing its modern-day route). A good portion is not worth traveling, particularly the stretches through the vast emptiness of deserts and plains, where the only difference between Rte. 66 and I-40 is that the interstate is invariably faster and more convenient.

BARSTOW   ☎760

Sitting midway between L.A. and Vegas on I-15, Barstow (pop. 23,056) is replete with cheap eats and rooms, not to mention the beauty of the California desert for those willing to explore the hot, desolate area.

🛈 **PRACTICAL INFORMATION.** The **Amtrak train** station, 685 N. 1st St. (☎800-USA-RAIL/872-7245), lacks ticket counters, so buy your tickets over the phone. One northbound and one southbound train leave the station per day. One train departs for L.A. (4am, $27). **Greyhound buses,** 681 N. 1st St. (☎256-8757 or 800-231-2222; open M-F 9am-2pm, Sa 3:30pm-6pm), go to L.A. (8 per day, $24) and Las Vegas (7 per day, $25). The **Barstow Chamber of Commerce,** 409 E. Fredrick, off Barstow Rd., has info on hotels, restaurants, and sights. (☎256-8617. Open M-F 10am-4pm.) Other services include: **police,** 220 E. Mountain View Rd. (☎256-2211); **Barstow Community Hospital,** 555 S. 7th St. (☎256-1761); and the **Post Office,** 425 S. 2nd Ave. (☎800-275-8777. Open M-F 9am-5pm, Sa 10am-1pm.) **Postal Code:** 92312.

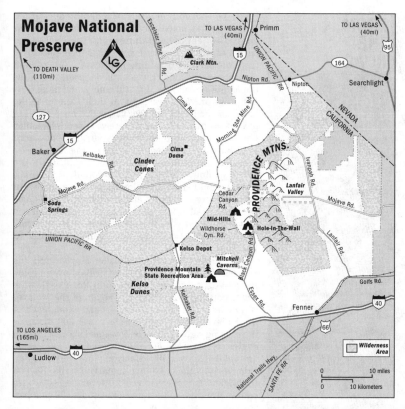

Mojave National Preserve

TO DEATH VALLEY
(110mi)

Excelsior Mine Rd.

TO LAS VEGAS
(40mi) Primm

TO LAS VEGAS
(40mi)

Clark Mtn.

UNION PACIFIC RR

Nipton Rd. Nipton

Searchlight

NEVADA
CALIFORNIA

127

15

Cima Rd.

Morning Star Mine Rd.

Baker

Kelbaker Rd.

Cinder Cones

Cima Dome

PROVIDENCE MTNS.

Ivanpah Rd.

Lanfair Valley

Mojave Rd.

Mojave Rd.

Soda Springs

Cedar Canyon Rd.

Mid-Hills

Hole-In-The-Wall

UNION PACIFIC RR

Wildhorse Cyn. Rd.

Black Canyon Rd.

Lanfair Rd.

Kelso Depot

Providence Mountain State Recreation Area

Mitchell Caverns

Kelso Dunes

Kelbaker Rd.

Essex Rd.

Golfs Rd.

Fenner

TO LOS ANGELES
(165mi)

40

Ludlow

National Trails Hwy.

SANTA FE RR

66

40

Wilderness Area

0   10 miles
0   10 kilometers

ACCOMMODATIONS AND FOOD. East Main St. offers all the usual chains, but the best value is the **Best Motel ❷**, 1281 E. Main St., which is fairly clean, quite friendly, and has all the usual motel amenities. (☎ 256-6836. Singles $34; doubles $38. Weekly rates available.)

Every restaurant chain this side of the Pecos has a branch on Main St. You'll find a more inviting variety in Barstow's local offerings. **Rosita's Mexican American Food ❷**, 540 W. Main St., has a festive dining room filled with the aromas of its tasty offerings. (☎ 256-9218. Lunch specials Tu-F under $5. Dinners $6-11. Open Tu-Sa 11am-9pm, Su 10am-9pm.) For some good, basic, hearty italian food, head to **DiNapoli's Firehouse Italian Eatery ❸**, 1358 E. Main St. (☎ 256-1094. Dinner entrees $8-15. Open Su-Th 11am-9pm, F-Sa 11am-10pm.)

EASTERN MOJAVE DESERT   ☎ 760

The land between I-15 and I-40 is among the most isolated in California. There are few towns, and you can never assume that services will be available between Barstow and Baker along I-15 or Barstow and Needles along I-40. Travelers who only use these towns as pit stops miss out on the Mojave's stunning natural attractions. Many of the region's attractions exist within the confines of the Mojave National

CALIFORNIA

FROM THE ROAD

BRIGHT LIGHTS CAST A BIG SHADOW

Las Vegas dominates the landscape in southern Nevada, so it only seems fitting that the city's materialistic, over-the-top spirit sends ripples that extend far into the more desolate reaches of the surrounding desert. The tiny cities of Jean and Primm, which are both miles south of Vegas, showcase thrill rides, cheap food, and plenty of gambling. Traveling farther into the Mojave Desert, however, visitors can detect more subtle Sin City influences. The pit-stop town of Baker, hawking fast food and desert adventures, is an unlikely suspect, but still shows some of the big city panache of the region's glittery flagship destination. Baker's California zip code renders it unable to use gambling to attract visitors, so it has made a name for itself by trumping up, electrifying, and shamelessly promoting the location's most palpable feature: the heat. Its 134ft. thermometer, built in 1991, records temperatures on a scale larger than any other such instrument in the world. The mercury-filled obelisk can be seen from miles away, and bright neon lights make it a lighthouse in the desert night. While speeding past the city, my easily amused mind found it difficult to resist the urge to guess which three-digit number the temperature had risen to, before comparing my estimate to the actual one broadcast boldly several stories in the air. Plucky, sweltering Baker proved it belongs on the same block as Las Vegas, excessively flaunting its desert climate to attract consumers that keep local cash registers jingling.

—Robert Cacace

Preserve. 1.6 million acres of federally stewarded desert scenery boasts dry lake beds, volcanic cinder cones, sweeping sand dunes, and the occasional splash of water. Dramatic geological formations rise from the seemingly infinite landscape, and resilient creatures crawl along the scorched terrain. Serene as the emptiness may be, it is still empty, and most drivers press onward, praying that their cars up to the task (see **The Desert and Your Car,** p. 62). Stop in Baker to visit the **Mojave National Preserve Desert Information Center,** which supplies friendly suggestions about popular recreation spots, maps of the area, more detailed directions, and a modest exhibit on the area's geology. (☎ 733-4040. Open daily 9am-5pm.) Hunting and fishing are allowed in the preserve, but finding water may be an angler's toughest challenge. Deer and quail are popular targets in season, but can only be hunted with the possession of a California State Fish and Game hunting license, available at Wal-Mart.

Afton Canyon Natural Area (Baker Mojave info line ☎ 733-4040) lies 36 mi. northeast of Barstow en route to Las Vegas. Follow I-15 to Afton Rd. The flowing water you see in this "Grand Canyon of the Mojave" is no mirage, but a rare above-ground appearance of the Mojave River. Canyon walls tower 300 ft. above the rushing water and its willow-lined shores. Golden eagles, bighorn sheep, and desert tortoises reside around the canyon. **Hikers** may explore the caves and side canyons tucked along unmarked trails. Bring a flashlight. Visitors can stay in 22 developed sites with water, fire pits, tables, and restrooms ($6 per person).

The **Kelso Dunes** in the Mojave National Preserve blanket a spectacular, barren landscape. Stretching lengths of 4 mi. and reaching heights of 700 ft., the dunes are off-limits to off-road vehicles. It takes 2-3hr. one-way to hike from the trailhead to the dune summit, and bear in mind that the formation acts as a giant oven in the summer—don't get baked. From the top you can hear the dunes sing on a windy day—the cascading sand groans like bending metal. The preserve plans to open a multi-million dollar Visitors Center at Kelso Depot in the middle of 2003. The dunes are about 30 mi. southeast of Baker via Kelbaker Rd. from Barstow; either take I-40 to the Kelbaker Rd. Exit (80 mi. to the east) or I-15 to Baker. Kelbaker Rd. itself is a phenomenal vantage point from which to see every conceivable desert formation from the Kelso Dunes and crusty lava flows to glacier-hewn granite heaps. Wildlife abounds, and the abandoned railstop of Kelso has an eerie ghost-town ambience. If you're coming from the east, take the clay-red, two-lane Cima Rd. south to Kelso, and look for the dunes to the west.

Providence Mountains State Recreation Area, P.O. Box 1, Essex 92332, is a popular, high-altitude (4000-5000 ft.) region with six primitive campsites (☎928-2586; sites $8) and a **Visitors Center,** on Essex Rd., 17 mi. north of I-40. View the spectacular **Mitchell Caverns** on an informative 1½ mi. tour through the stalactite-cluttered limestone chambers. (1½hr. June-Aug. Sa-Su 1:30pm; Sept.-May M-F 1:30pm; Sa-Su 10am, 1:30, and 3pm. $3, 16 and under free; tour reservations may be made with a $1 surcharge by calling 928-2586.)

There are 61 primitive but beautiful sites in the Providence Mountains at the **Mid Hill** (surrounded by pinyon and juniper trees, and unseasonably cool due to 5600 ft. elevation) and **Hole-in-Wall campgrounds ❶** (4200 ft.) in the East Mojave National Scenic Area. Both are $12 and provide limited water and pit toilets but no hookups. The road into Mid Hill isn't paved and is not recommended for RVs. From Essex Rd., follow Black Canyon Rd. to Mid Hill or Wild Horse Canyon Rd. to Hole-in-Wall. Consult a park service newsletter for the location of other roadside and backcountry campsites.

Dune buggies and **jeeps** are still permitted at the **Dumont Dunes,** just off Rte. 127 about 33 mi. north of Baker. Look for the 3.5 mi. road turning off of 127 just after Harry Wade Rd. There is no sign; keep your eyes peeled. The dunes are strewn with man-made striations—those from WWII training exercises are still visible in parts of the Mojave. Tracks persist in the sands for decades, so consider what legacy you want to leave behind.

The **Baker Bun Boy ❷** is a good place to stop for coffee and conversation in the pit stop town of Baker. The bacon cheeseburger ($8) is a safe bet. (☎733-4660. Open daily 6am-midnight.) For a slightly less conventional meal, try **The Mad Greek ❷**, just across Baker Blvd. The $7.50 Kefte-k-Bob brings shades of Athens to the Mojave Desert. (☎733-4354. Open daily 6am-midnight.) Even if you tried, you couldn't miss Baker's claim to fame: the **world's tallest thermometer.**

THE HIGH DESERT

The High Desert is the picture of desolation. The Mojave, however, conceals unlikely treasures for those patient and brave enough to explore it. Genuine summer attractions are rare, but temperate winters allow one to trudge across drifting dunes and creep through spooky ghost towns.

JOSHUA TREE NATIONAL PARK ☎760

When devout Mormon pioneers crossed this faith-testing desert in the 19th century, they named the enigmatic tree they encountered after the Biblical prophet Joshua. The tree's crooked limbs resembled the Hebrew general, who, with his arms upraised, seemed to beckon them to the Promised Land. Even today, Joshua Tree National Park inspires reverent awe in those who happen upon it. Piles of wind-sculpted boulders, flanked by seemingly jubilant Joshua trees, hearken to the magnificent devastation of Jericho.

In recent years, climbers, campers, and daytrippers from Southern California have added to the mosaic. The boulder formations strewn across the desert badlands have nearly limitless potential for first ascents. "Josh," as outdoor enthusiasts call it, has become a world-renowned mecca for both casual and elite climbers. History buffs will appreciate the vestiges of human occupation—the ancient rock petroglyphs, 19th-century dams built to catch the meager rainfall for livestock, and gold mine ruins that dot the landscape. But the most attractive

CALIFORNIA

AT A GLANCE: JOSHUA TREE NATIONAL PARK	
AREA: 1,017,748 acres.	**GATEWAY TOWNS:** Twentynine Palms, Yucca Valley, Joshua Tree.
FEATURES: Pinto Mountains, Hexie Mountains, Eagle Mountains, and Little Bernadino Mountains, High/Low Desert Transition Zone, Lost Palms Oasis.	**CAMPING:** Park campgrounds free to $35. Registration is required for back-country camping.
HIGHLIGHTS: Climbing virtually any-place in the park, hiking to the top of Ryan Mountain, camping at the more remote Belle Campground, driving the four-wheel-drive Park Geology Rd.	**FEES:** Weekly pass $10 per vehicle, $5 per pedestrian or bike.

aspect of Joshua Tree is its remoteness and its freedom from the commercial mayhem that has infested many national parks, for its natural beauty is interrupted only by a few paved roads and signs.

At the north entrance to the park lies **Twentynine Palms,** settled after World War I by veterans-turned-homesteaders looking for a hot, dry climate to soothe their gas-seared lungs. Today, the town also hosts the world's largest U.S. Marine Corps base, as well as lavish murals depicting people and events from the town's past.

▐ TRANSPORTATION

The park is ringed by three highways: **Interstate 10** to the south, **Route 62 (Twentynine Palms Highway)** to the west and north, and **Route 177** to the east. The northern entrances to the park are off Rte. 62 at the towns of **Joshua Tree** and **Twentynine Palms.** The south entrance is at **Cottonwood Spring,** off I-10 at **Route 195,** south of Palm Springs near the town of Indio. The **park entrance fee,** valid for seven days, is $5 per person or $10 per car.

▐ PRACTICAL INFORMATION

WHEN TO GO. The desert is very arid and dry. It is best to avoid visiting Joshua Tree from June to September. The park's most temperate weather is in late fall (Oct.-Dec.) and early spring (Mar.-Apr.); temperatures in other months often span uncomfortable extremes (summer highs 95-115°F, winter lows 30°-40°). For more advice on beating the heat, see **The Desert and You,** p. 61

Visitor Information:

Headquarters and Oasis Visitors Center, 74485 National Park Dr. (☎367-5500; www.joshua-tree.org), ¼ mi. off Rte. 62 in Twentynine Palms, is the best place to familiarize yourself with the park. Friendly rangers, plus displays, guidebooks, maps, and water. Open daily 8am-5pm.

Cottonwood Visitors Center, at the southern gateway of the park, 7 mi. north of I-10 and 25 mi. east of Indio. Information, water, and picnic areas are available here. Open daily 8am-4pm.

Indian Cove Ranger Station, 7295 Indian Cove Rd. (☎362-4367). Open Oct.-May daily 8am-4pm; summer hours vary.

Twentynine Palms Chamber of Commerce, 6455 Mesquite Ave., Ste. A (☎367-3445), provides info on murals, transportation, town accommodations, and food. Open M-F 9am-5pm; may close for lunch.

Joshua Tree National Park

CALIFORNIA

Mojave Desert

Colorado Desert

CAMPGROUNDS
Belle, **6**
Black Rock Canyon, **1**
Cottonwood, **8**
Hidden Valley, **3**
Indian Cove, **2**
Jumbo Rocks, **5**
Ryan, **4**
White Tank, **7**

Palm Springs

Morongo Valley
Yucca Valley
Twentynine Palms

LITTLE SAN BERNARDINO MOUNTAINS

SAN ANDREAS FAULT

COLORADO DESERT

MOJAVE DESERT

Transition Zone

PLEASANT VALLEY

HEXIE MOUNTAINS

PINTO MOUNTAINS

PINTO BASIN

COTTONWOOD MOUNTAINS

EAGLE MOUNTAINS

COXCOMB MOUNTAINS

SHEEP HOLE MOUNTAINS

Eureka Peak 5518ft
Quail Mtn. 5814ft
Ryan Mtn. 5457ft
Queen Mtn. 5677ft
Monument Mtn. 4834ft
Pinto Mountain 3983ft
Aqua Peak 4416ft

Hi-Desert Nature Museum

TO LOS ANGELES (98mi)

TO MARINE CORPS AIR GROUND COMBAT CENTER (3mi)

TO AMBOY & 40 (48mi)

TO PARKER (60mi)

TO BLYTHE (35mi)

TO MECCA & SALTON SEA (13mi)

TO MECCA & SALTON SEA (8mi)

Desert Hot Springs
Cathedral City
Rancho Mirage
Indio
Coachella
Chiriaco Summit

West Entrance Station
Entrance Station
North Entrance Station
Oasis Visitors Center
Oasis of Mara
Fortynine Palms Oasis
Barker Dam
Lost Horse Mine
Keys View
Geology Tour Road
Cholla Cactus Garden
Ocotillo Patch
Cottonwood Visitor Center
Lost Palms Oasis
Cottonwood

California Riding and Hiking Trail

Pinto Basin Rd.
Old Dale Rd.
Black Eagle Mine Rd.
Gold Crown Rd.
Pinkham Canyon Rd.
Berdoo Canyon Rd.
Thermal Cyn. Rd.
Kaiser Rd.
Adobe Rd.
Amboy Rd.
Canyon Rd.
Indian Cove Rd.
Park Blvd.
Joshua Tree
Indian Ave.
Twentynine Palms Hwy.
Joshua Lane
Yucca Trail Dr.
La Contenta Rd.
Alta Loma
Dillon Rd.
INDIO HILLS
Sheep Pass

0 5 miles
0 5 kilometers

Rock Climbing Gear and Guiding: Nomad Ventures, 61795 Twentynine Palms Hwy. (☎366-4684), in the town of Joshua Tree, has a ton of gear, information and advice, especially for more experienced climbers. **Joshua Tree Climbing School** (☎800-890-4745; www.rockclimbing.com) will set you up with gear, guiding, and instruction, no matter what level of experience you have.

Emergency: 24hr. Dispatch (☎909-383-5651). Call collect.

Medical Services: Hi-Desert Medical Center, 6601 White Feather Rd. (☎366-3711), in Joshua Tree. Emergency care 24hr.

Internet Access: Tommy Paul's Beatnik Cafe (see Food, p. 183).

Post Office: 73839 Gorgonio Dr. (☎800-275-8777), in Twentynine Palms. Open M-F 8:30am-5pm. **Postal Code:** 92277.

ACCOMMODATIONS

Those who cannot stomach the thought of desert campgrounds but want to spend more than a day at the park can find inexpensive motels in **Twentynine Palms,** the self-proclaimed "Oasis of Murals." The **29 Palms Inn ❹,** 73950 Inn Dr., is an attraction in itself. Its 19 distinctly different rooms face the Mara Oasis, which has supported life for over 20,000 years. More recently, the life here has been of the celebrity genus, with guests like Michelle Pfeiffer and Nicholas Cage. Robert Plant gets the most attention; he composed his post-Zeppelin hit "29 Palms" here. (☎367-3505. Reservations required Feb.-Apr. Doubles June-Sept. Su-Th $50-80, F-Sa $65-105; Oct.-May $10-20 extra. Cottages for 4-8 people and air-stream trailers also available for rent.) Clean, reliable **Motel 6 ❸,** 72562 Twentynine Palms Hwy., has a pool. (☎367-2833. Singles $40-44; doubles $46-50; each additional adult $3.) While creating the album *Joshua Tree* in 1987, U2 stayed in one of the 10 units at the **Harmony Motel ❹,** 71161 Twentynine Palms Hwy. (☎367-3351. All rooms recently refurbished; have A/C. One-bed singles and doubles $50-60, more for kitchen.)

CAMPING

Camping is an enjoyable and inexpensive way to experience the beauty of the park, except in the scorching heat of summer. Even then, when the sun goes down the temperatures drop to comfortable levels. Pre-noon arrivals are the best way to guarantee a site, since most campgrounds in the park operate on a first come, first camp basis and accept no reservations (campgrounds that require separate fees do take reservations). Spring weekends and holidays are the busiest times. Reservations can be made for group sites only at Cottonwood, Sheep Pass, Indian Cove, and Black Rock Canyon through **DESTINET** (☎800-436-7275). Well-prepared and experienced campers can register at the Visitors Center for a backcountry permit. All campsites have tables, firepits, and pit toilets. There are no hookups for RVs, and only those campgrounds that take reservations offer water or flush toilets—those who plan a longer stay should pack their own supplies. (14-day max. stay Oct.-May; 30-day camping limit each year.)

Indian Cove, 3200 ft., on the north edge of Wonderland of Rocks. Enter at the north entrance on Indian Cove Rd. off of Twentynine Palms Hwy. Rains create dramatic waterfalls. Popular spot for rock climbers. 107 sites. Sites $10; 13 group sites $20-35.

Jumbo Rocks, 4400 ft., near Skull Rock Trail on the eastern edge of Queen Valley. Take Quail Springs Rd. 15 mi. south of the Visitors Center. The highest and coolest campground in the park, featuring many sites surrounded by—who would imagine—jumbo rocks. Front spots have shade and protection. Wheelchair accessible. 125 sites. Free.

White Tank, 3800 ft. Few people, but watch for coyotes that may try to keep you company. Cowboys built up White Tank as a reliable cattle watering hole. 15 sites amid huge boulder towers. Free.

Hidden Valley, 4200 ft., in the center of the park off Quail Springs Rd. Secluded alcoves are perfect for pitching tents, and enormous shade-providing boulders serve as perches for viewing the sun at dawn and dusk. Its proximity to Wonderland of Rocks and the Barker Dam Trail makes this a rock climber's heaven. The 39 sites fill up quickly. Free.

Sheep Pass, 4500 ft., in center of the park near the trail to Ryan Mountain. Huge boulders and lots of Joshua trees make this site fairly cool and secluded. 6 group spots only, which can be reserved up to 3 months in advance. $20-35.

Belle, 3800 ft., within view of the Pinto Mountains, is an ideal place to stare at the starry heavens. 18 sites tucked away in the crevices of large boulders. Free.

Ryan, 4300 ft., has fewer rocks, but also less privacy and less shade, than nearby Hidden Valley. The 3 mi. round-trip trail ascends to Ryan Mountain, which served as the headquarters and water storage for the Lost Horse gold mine. The sunrise is spectacular from nearby Key's View (see p. 185). 31 sites. Free.

Black Rock Canyon, 4000 ft., at the end of Joshua Ln. off Rte. 62 near Yucca Valley. Good for those who haven't camped before, due to the proximity of Yucca Valley, water, and a ranger station. A great place to spot animals, and there are various hiking trails nearby. Wheelchair accessible. 100 sites. Reservations accepted. Sites $10.

Cottonwood, 3000 ft., offers no shade from the open Colorado Desert portion of the park, but it's the first place where wildflowers appear after sufficient rain. (To find out when, see **Wildflower Hotline,** p. 184.) Flush toilets and running water. Wheelchair accessible. 62 sites, 30 in summer. Sites $8; 3 group sites for 10-70 people $25.

FOOD

Although there are no food facilities within the park, Twentynine Palms offers both groceries and grub. While the food is not exactly of the gourmet variety, it's certainly possible to eat well. If you are willing to cook, the **Stater Brothers** supermarket, 71727 Twentynine Palms Hwy., saves you a bundle and offers a good selection. (☎367-6535. Open daily 6am-11pm.) The other option is fast food or its local equivalent. **The Finicky Coyote ❶,** 73511 Twentynine Palms Hwy., is a cafe with sandwiches, coffee drinks, smoothies, and ice cream that will make you howl. (☎367-2429. Open M-Th 6am-6pm, F 6am-7pm, Sa-Su 7am-3pm.) **Rocky's New York Style Pizza ❸,** 73737 Twentynine Palms Hwy. is where all the locals go to satisfy their cravings. (☎367-9525. Open daily 11am-10pm. Pizzas and subs $7-15.) The friendly folks at **Tommy Paul's Beatnik Cafe ❶,** 61597 Twentynine Palms Hwy., in the town of Joshua Tree, serve hot coffee, but you may prefer to douse your heat-addled brain in frosty beer or ice cream while you search the Internet for heat stroke treatments. (☎366-9799. Open W 11am-midnight, Th and Su 11am-9pm, F-Sa 11am-11pm. Internet access 15¢ per min.)

OUTDOOR ACTIVITIES

Over 80% of Joshua Tree is designated wilderness, safeguarded against development, and lacking paved roads, toilets, and campfires. The park offers truly remote territory for backcountry desert hiking and camping. Hikers who seize the oppor-

CALIFORNIA

tunity should pack plenty of water and keep alert for flash floods and changing weather conditions. Be sensitive to the extreme fragility of the desert and refrain from venturing off established trails. Do not enter abandoned mine shafts, as they are unstable and often filled with poisonous gases.

The tenacious wildflowers that struggle into colorful bloom each spring (mid-Mar. to mid-May) attract thousands of visitors. More robust plants like Joshua trees, cholla, and the spidery ocotillo have adapted to the severe climate in fascinating ways. To avoid the social stigma accompanying floral ignorance, get updates on the blooming status of yucca, verbena, cottonwood, mesquite, and dozens of other wildflowers by calling the **Wildflower Hotline** (☎818-768-3533). The beds of wildflowers provide a habitat for Joshua Tree's many animal species, and the trees and reeds of the park's oases play host to ladybugs, bees, golden eagles, and bighorn sheep. Kangaroo rats, lizards, and stinkbugs scamper about at all times of the day, while wily coyotes, bobcats, and the occasional rattlesnake stalk their prey (including, if you're not careful, you or your unleashed pet) after dusk.

ROCK CLIMBING

The crack-split granite of Joshua provides some of the best rock climbing and bouldering on the planet, for experts and novices alike. The world-renowned boulders at **Wonderland of Rocks** and **Hidden Valley** are always swarming with hard-bodied climbers, making Josh the most climbed area in America. Because of the area's limitless potential, enumerating climbs is impossible; check with **Joshua Tree Climbing School** (see p. 182). Adventurous novices will find thrills at the **Skull Rock Interpretive Walk,** which runs between Jumbo Rocks and Skull Rock. The walk offers not only info on local plants and animals, but also exciting yet non-technical scrambles on monstrous boulders. Before placing or replacing any bolts or other permanent protection, check with a ranger to see if your route is in designated wilderness. *Bolts are no longer allowed* within wilderness portions of the park.

HIKING

Despite the plethora of driving routes, hiking is perhaps the best way to experience Joshua Tree. The desert often appears monotonous through a car window, and it is only when walking slowly that one begins to appreciate the subtler beauties of the park. On foot, visitors can tread through sand, scramble over boulders, and walk among the park's hardy namesakes.

The Visitors Center has info on the park's many hikes, which range from a 15min. stroll to the **Oasis of Mara** to a three-day trek along the **California Riding and Hiking Trail** (35 mi.). The ranger-led **Desert Queen Ranch Walking Tour** covers the restored ranch of resourceful homesteader Bill Keys ($5; call for reservations). Anticipate slow progress even on short walks; the oppressive heat and the scarcity of shade can force even the hardiest of hikers to feel the strain.

Barker Dam Trail (1.1 mi. round-trip, 1hr.). Next to Hidden Valley and beginning in the Barker Dam parking lot, this route is often packed with tourists, but its painted petroglyphs and eerie tranquility make it a worthwhile stroll.

Lost Horse Mine/Mountain (4.1-8.2 mi. round-trip). The trailhead is located near the end of the road to Key's View. The mine rests in peace at the end of 2 mi., commemorating the region's gold prospecting days with rusted machinery and abandoned mineshafts. If you don't want to return yet, keep following the trail up to the saddle of Lost Horse Mountain and beyond; the trail loops around to return to the trailhead.

Ryan Mountain (3 mi. round-trip, 2hr.). From the top, the boulders in the encircling valley bear an uncanny resemblance to enormous beasts of burden toiling toward a distant destination. Bring lots of water for the strenuous, unshaded climb to the summit.

DRIVING, FOUR-WHEELING, AND BIKING

The craggy mountains and boulders of Joshua Tree acquire a fresh poignancy at sunrise and sunset, when an earthy crimson washes across the desert. Daytrippers forgo these moments of quiet serenity for which the High Desert is justly renowned. A self-paced **driving tour** is an easy way to explore the park and linger until a later hour. All park roads are well marked, and signs labeled "Exhibit Ahead" point the way to unique floral and geologic formations. One of these tours, a 34 mi. stretch across the park from Twentynine Palms to the town of Joshua Tree, provides access to the park's most outstanding sights and hikes. An especially spectacular leg of the road is **Keys View** (5185 ft.), 6 mi. off the park road just west of Ryan Campground. On a clear day, you can see forever—or at least to Palm Springs and the Salton Sea. It's also a great spot to watch the sunrise and take short hikes. The longer drive through the park from Twentynine Palms to I-10 traverses both High and Low Desert landscapes. The **Cholla Cactus Garden,** a grove of spiny succulents, lies in the Pinto Basin just off the road.

Those with **four-wheel-drive** vehicles have even more options, including the 18 mi. **Geology Tour Rd.,** which climbs through striking rock formations and ends in the Little San Bernardino Mountains. In the spring and fall, **bikers** can enjoy these roads, especially the unpaved and relatively unpopulated four-wheel-drive-only roads through **Pinkham Canyon** and past the **Black Eagle Mines.** Both begin at the Cottonwood Visitors Center. Bikers should check the park guide for more info.

YUCCA VALLEY ☎760

Yucca Valley, northwest of the park, is graced with a few unusual attractions and a genuinely helpful **California Welcome Center,** 55569 Twentynine Palms Hwy. (☎365-6323. Open M-F 9am-5pm, Sa-Su 10am-2pm.) The **Hi-Desert Nature Museum,** in Yucca Valley's Community Complex, accessible by Damosa Rd., has several precious gemstones, as well as captive scorpions and snakes. (☎369-7212. Open Tu-Su 10am-5pm. Free.) Or drive out to the infamous "energy machine" known as the **Integratron.** The drive is a bit twisty, so pay attention. To get to the Integratron from Yucca Valley, take Hwy. 62 to Old Woman Springs Rd. Turn left and go 10 mi. to Landers. Turn right at Reche Rd. and go 2 mi. to Belfield Rd. Turn left and go about 1 mi. The Integratron is at the end of the paved road. Created by the eccentric George Van Tassel in the 1950s, the metallic-and-wood structure was supposed to create a "powerful vortex for physical and spiritual healing," but Van Tassel died mysteriously before finishing it. Visitors are now lead on tours throughout the strange structure. (☎362-3126; www.integratron.com. Tours F-Su noon-4pm. $5.)

THE LOW DESERT

Only a few resilient species have learned to flourish amidst the dust and broken rocks of the Low Desert. Most of them live around Palm Springs.

PALM SPRINGS ☎760

From its first known inhabitants, the Cahuilla Indians, to today's geriatric fun-lovers, the restorative oasis of Palm Springs (pop. 43,520) has attracted many. The medicinal waters of the city's natural hot springs ensure not only the vitality of its wealthy residents, but also its longevity as a resort town. While Palm Springs is home to gaggles of retirees, it is also a winter retreat for fat-cat golfers and a prime destination for gay and lesbian travelers. With warm winter temperatures, celebrity residents, and more pink than a Miami Vice episode, this desert city provides a sunny break from everyday life.

CALIFORNIA

▐ TRANSPORTATION

Airport: Palm Springs Regional, 3400 E. Tahquitz-Canyon Rd. (☎318-3800). State and limited national service.

Buses: Greyhound, 311 N. Indian Canyon Dr. (☎325-2053 or 800-231-2222), near downtown. Open daily 8am-6pm. To: **L.A.** (9 per day; $17-19, round-trip $32-34); **San Diego** (9 per day, $25); and **Las Vegas** (6 per day, $52.50). No advance purchase necessary.

Public Transportation: SunBus (☎343-3451). Local bus service connecting all Coachella Valley cities (info office open daily 5am-10pm). Lines #23, 24, and 111 cover downtown and surrounding locales. The *SunBus Book,* available at info centers and in most hotel lobbies, includes schedules and a system map. Fare $1, transfers 50¢.

Taxis: Yellow Cab (☎345-8398) and **A Valley Cabousine** (☎340-5845) operate 24hr.

Trains: Amtrak, the corner of N. Indian Canyon Rd. and Amado Rd. (☎800-872-7245).

Car Rental: Starting at about $35 per day (excluding insurance); higher in winter. **Rent-A-Wreck,** 67555 Palm Canyon Dr. #A105, Cathedral City (☎324-1766 or 800-535-1391; www.rentawreck.com). Usually only rents to those 21 and older, but may rent to 18-20 yr. olds who meet certain qualifications. $10 surcharge for those under 25. **Budget** (☎327-1404 or 800-221-1203), at Palm Springs Regional Airport. Must be 21 with major credit card; under 25 surcharge $20 per day.

Bike Rental: Bighorn Bicycles, 302 N. Palm Canyon Dr. (☎325-3367). Mountain bikes $8 per hr., $22 for 4hr., $29 per day. Bike tours available. Open Sept.-June Th-Tu 8am-4pm; closed July-Aug. **Tri-A-Bike,** 44841 San Pablo (☎340-2840), in Palm Desert. Mountain bikes $7 per hr., $19 per day, or $65 per wk. Open M-Sa 10am-6pm, Su noon-5pm.

▐ ORIENTATION

Depending on traffic, Palm Springs is a two- to three-hour drive from L.A. along **Interstate 10.** Approaching from the north on I-15, take I-215 East to Rte. 60 East to I-10 East. From I-10 East, exit at Indian Ave., which becomes **Indian Canyon Drive,** the major north-south thoroughfare. To orient yourself, find Indian Canyon Dr. and the North-South stretch of **Palm Canyon Drive,** the city's two main drags, which connect to I-10. East Palm Canyon Dr. borders the southern edge of the city. There are two major east-west boulevards: **Tahquitz-Canyon Road** runs east to the airport, while **Ramon Road,** four blocks to the south, provides access to I-10.

▐ PRACTICAL INFORMATION

Visitor Information: Visitors Center, 2781 N. Palm Canyon Dr. (☎778-8415 or 800-347-7746; www.palm-springs.org), 1 block beyond Tramway Rd. on the right. Free hotel reservations and friendly advice. Pick up *The Desert Guide* or *Play Palm Springs* for attractions and entertainment. Open daily 9am-5pm. **Chamber of Commerce,** 190 W. Amado Rd. (☎325-1577; www.pschamber.org). Grab the seasonal *Palm Springs Visitors Guide,* buy a map ($1), or make hotel reservations. Open M-F 8:30am-4:30pm.

Laundromat: Arenas Coin-Op, 220 E. Arenas Rd. (☎322-7717), ½ block east of Indian Canyon Dr. Wash $1.75, dry 25¢ per 10min. Open daily 6:30am-9pm.

Road Conditions: ☎800-427-7623. **Weather Conditions:** ☎345-3711.

CALIFORNIA

Police: 200 S. Civic Dr. (☎323-8116).

Rape Crisis Hotline: ☎568-9071.

Medical Services: Desert Regional Medical Center, 1150 N. Indian Canyon Dr. (☎323-6511).

Internet Access: Palm Springs Public Library, 300 S. Sunrise Way (☎322-7323). Free access available in 30min. slots. Open M-Tu 9am-8pm, W-Th and Sa 9am-5:30pm, F 10am-5:30pm.

Post Office: 333 E. Amado Rd. (☎800-275-8777). Open M-F 9am-5pm, Sa 9am-1pm.

Postal Code: 92262; General Delivery 92263.

▚ ACCOMMODATIONS

Like most famous resort communities, Palm Springs caters mainly to those seeking a tax shelter, not a night's shelter. Nonetheless, affordable lodgings are surprisingly abundant. Motels slash their prices 20-40% in the summer, and comparison shopping will get you far. Many hotels offer discounts through the Visitors Center, and promotional publications often have terrific coupon deals, offering rooms for as little as $25. There is a concentration of inexpensive motels at the bend where East Palm Canyon Dr. becomes South Palm Canyon Dr. Motels in nearby communities such as Cathedral City and Desert Hot Springs are even more affordable. Reservations may be necessary in the winter. Prices listed don't include the county's 10% accommodation tax.

Orchid Tree Inn, 251 S. Belardo Rd. (☎325-2791 or 800-733-3435). Large rooms with tasteful Spanish ambiance overlook a courtyard with lush gardens and pool. Tucked away off the main downtown strip, this hotel is quiet but provides easy access to restaurants, shopping, and clubs. 1- or 2-person rooms start at $65 mid-week in July and Aug., but increase to $110-130 during the winter. Weekend rates $15-20 more. Studios, suites, and bungalows also available. ❺

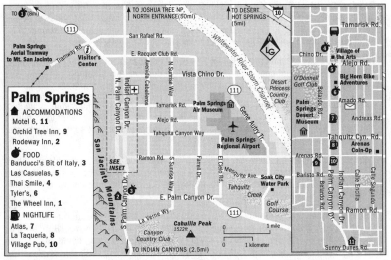

Miracle Springs Resort and Spa, 10625 Palm Dr. (☎251-6000 or 800-400-4414; www.miraclesprings.com), in Desert Hot Springs. The newer and more luxurious of two hotels perched atop the famed hot springs of Palm Springs. 110 spacious units with bedrooms and living areas, some of which overlook the 8 pools of "miracle" water. Spa, casino, restaurants, and banquet facilities available within the complex. Standard rooms start at $99 in the off-season, but increase to $139 during the winter. Pool-side rooms and deluxe suites $599. ❺

Desert Hot Springs Spa Hotel, 10805 Palm Drive. (☎329-6000 or 800-808-7727; www.dhsspa.com) has slightly cheaper and much less swanky rooms than its next door neighbor. It still looks down on the famed hot springs, however. Rooms from $89. ❺

Rodeway Inn, 1277 S. Palm Canyon Dr. (☎325-5574 or 800-829-8099). Large, clean rooms with refrigerators and phones. Laundry, continental breakfast, and a shaded courtyard surrounding a pool and jacuzzi. Singles July-Aug. Su-Th from $44, F-Sa $60; Sept.-June $69-$125. ❹

Motel 6, 660 S. Palm Canyon Dr. (☎327-4200 or 800-466-8356), conveniently located south of the city center. Other locations at 595 E. Palm Canyon Dr. (☎325-6129) and 63950 20th Ave. (☎251-1425), near the I-10 off-ramp. Each has a pool and A/C. Singles $38; doubles $44, $4 higher on weekends. ❸

Palm Court Inn, 1983 N. Palm Canyon Dr. (☎416-2333 or 800-667-7918), between I-10 and downtown. Inside the melon-colored walls are 107 rooms as well as a pool and jacuzzi. June-Sept. singles $59; doubles $69. Oct.-May singles $69; doubles $79. All prices slightly higher on weekends. Look for discount coupons in visitors' guides. ❹

🍴 FOOD

Palm Springs offers a kaleidoscope of sumptuous food, from the classic greasy spoon to ultra-trendy fusions of multiple cuisines. However, high prices limit the scope of viable options for budget travelers. To cook for yourself, head to **Ralph's,** 451 S. Sunrise Way, for groceries. (☎323-9799. Open daily 6am-1am.)

🍽 **Banducci's Bit of Italy,** 1260 S. Palm Canyon Dr. (☎325-2537). The promise of delicious Italian food draws crowds to this Palm Springs staple every night of the week. For a rich treat, try their fettucine alfredo, which comes with antipasto, minestrone soup, and buttery garlic bread ($13). Entrees from $8-15. Open daily 5-10pm. ❸

🍽 **Thai Smile,** 651 N. Palm Canyon Dr. (☎320-5503). Just as friendly as the name implies, Thai Smile serves authentic and inexpensive Thai cuisine. Vegetarian options (Tofu pad thai $7). Don't miss the $5 lunch specials. Open daily 11:30am-10pm. ❷

Las Casuelas—The Original, 368 N. Palm Canyon Dr. (☎325-3213). Its immediate success made chainhood inevitable, but locals insist that The Original lives up to its name. Authentic Mexican dishes (from $6) and colorful decor give it that south-of-the-border feel. Open Su-Th 10am-10pm, F-Sa 10am-11pm. ❷

Tyler's, 149 S. Indian Canyon Dr. (☎325-2990). The patio at this small cafe tucked in the middle of La Plaza is perfect for people-watching. Enjoy classic American fare, or treat yourself to a malt or root-beer float. Burgers $3-6. Soda-fountain drinks $2.50-4. Open M-F 11am-4pm, Sa 11am-5pm; in summer Tu-Sa 11am-4pm. ❶

The Wheel Inn, 50900 Seminole Dr. (☎909-849-7012), in Cabazon, directly off the stretch of I-10 west of Palm Springs. Legendary joint where Pee-Wee Herman met Simone after his encounter with Large Marge. Those unfamiliar with haute cinema still come for the daily specials ($6-7) or tasty pie ($2.50-3.75). The inn displays the friendly dinosaurs seen in *Pee-Wee's Big Adventure*. Open 24hr. ❷ The **gift shop,** 50800 Seminole Dr. (☎909-849-8309), in the brachiosaurus's belly, sells tons of stuff you won't need, but may be unable to resist. Open daily 6am-10pm.

👁 🏃 SIGHTS AND ACTIVITIES

Most people come to Palm Springs to drink, party, and schmooze with celebs, but the city also has its share of sights. Mt. San Jacinto State Park, Palm Springs's primary landmark, offers a variety of outdoor recreation. Hiking trails in the park are accessible year-round via the tram, and cross-country skiing is available in winter at higher elevations, though access is certainly easier and cheaper from nearby Idyllwild. Despite its benign appearance, remember that **Palm Springs is just a damp patch of otherwise ferocious desert, and precautions should be taken.** Summertime highs can reach well into the triple digits.

DESERT HOT SPRINGS SPA. A trip to Palm Springs would not be complete without a visit to the town's namesake. This spa features eight naturally heated mineral pools of different temperatures, as well as saunas, professional massages, and body wraps. *(10805 Palm Dr. in Desert Hot Springs. ☎800-808-7727. Open daily 8am-10pm. M and W $5; Tu $3; Th men $3, women $5; F men $5, women $3; Sa-Su $6. After 3pm weekdays $3, weekends $4. Holidays $7. Rates include admission to pools, dry sauna, and locker rooms.)*

PALM SPRINGS DESERT MUSEUM. This remarkable museum features frequently changing exhibits centered on art, history, and culture. The museum sponsors performances in the 450-seat **Annenberg Theatre** (☎325-4490) as well as curator-led field trips into the canyons in winter. *(101 Museum Dr. Take SunBus #111. ☎322-4839. Open Tu-Sa 10am-5pm, Su noon-5pm. $8; seniors $6.50; students, ages 6-17, and military $3.50. Free first F of each month. Field trips $3.)*

UPRISING ROCKCLIMBING CENTER. Prep for nearby Joshua Tree at this gigantic outdoor climbing structure (the only one of its kind in the US). Whether you're a beginner or a seasoned climber, you'll find a fun challenge cranking on plastic rock beneath a canopy that wards off the sun. Expert instruction and supervision available; excursions on real rock by arrangement. *(1500 Gene Autry Trail. ☎888-254-6266; www.uprising.com. Open July-Aug. Tu-F 4-8pm, Sa-Su. 10am-6pm; Sept.-June M-F 10am-8pm, Sa-Su 10am-6pm. Day pass $15, equipment rental $7. Lessons from $45 per day.)*

PALM SPRINGS AIR MUSEUM. Featuring an extensive collection of WWII aircraft and memorabilia, the museum is enjoyable for aviation buffs and novices alike. *(745 N. Gene Autry Trail, near the airport. ☎778-6262. Open Sept.-May daily 10am-5pm; June-Aug. daily 8am-3pm. $8, seniors $6.50, children $3.50.)*

PALM SPRINGS AERIAL TRAMWAY. If Mt. San Jacinto's 10,804 ft. escarpment is too much for your legs to take, this world-famous tram can whisk you to the top on a 15min. ride. At 8516 ft. above the desert, the observation deck has excellent views of the Coachella Valley and provides access to several trails. *(On Tramway Rd. off North Palm Canyon Drive. ☎325-1449 or 325-1391; www.pstramway.com. Trams run at least every 30min.; M-F 10am-8pm, Sa-Su 8am-8pm. Last tram down at 9:45pm. Round-trip $21, seniors $19, ages 3-12 $14, ages 2 and under free.)*

INDIAN CANYONS. These four canyons offer the city's only naturally cool water, as well as remnants of the Cahuilla Indian communities. Ranger-led tours demonstrate how the Cahuilla people once utilized the area's flora and fauna, which includes the world's densest patch of naturally occurring palm trees. In the cooler months, these canyons are beautiful places to hike, picnic, or horseback ride.

CALIFORNIA

(Three of the canyons are located 5 mi. south of town at the end of S. Palm Canyon Dr. ☎325-3400 or 800-790-3398. Open daily 8am-5pm. Tours M-Th 10am-1pm, F-Su 9am-3pm. $6; students, seniors, and military $4.50; ages 6-12 $2; 5 and under free. Tours $6; children $2. Tahquitz Canyon is located at the west end of Mesquite Rd. ☎416-7044. It has a separate Visitors Center, as well as a spectacular 60 ft. waterfall during the winter. Tours $12.50, children $6.)

TENNIS AND GOLF. Palm Springs has several public tennis and golf facilities. There are eight courts at **Ruth Hardy Park.** *(700 Tamarisk Dr., at Avenida Caballeros. Open dawn-dusk.)* **Tahquitz Creek Golf Resort,** managed by Arnold Palmer, claims to be one of the nation's top municipal golf courses. *(1885 Golf Club Dr. ☎328-1005. 18 holes M-F $28, Sa-Su $35; in winter M-F $60-90, Sa-Su $70-95. Discounts after 10pm. Fees include carts.)* The city's **Recreation Division** has more info on Palm Springs's many lawns and links. If you stay at any of the nicer hotels and resorts in the area, many have deals with private clubs and extend privileges to their guests. *(☎323-8273.)*

KNOTT'S SOAK CITY WATER PARK. Immersed in the life-source of desert existence, fun-lovers of all ages surf, slide, and soak in the wave pool, inner tube river, and on 18 different waterslides and attractions. *(Off I-10 South on Gene Autry Trail between Ramon and E. Palm Canyon Dr. ☎327-0499. Open Mar. to Labor Day daily 11am-6pm; Labor Day to Oct. Sa-Su 11am-6pm. $22, children under 5 ft. and seniors $13, under 3 free. $13 after 3pm. Parking $6.)*

CELEBRITY TOURS. Find further evidence that celebrities are wealthier and more glamorous than you—just don't expect to see an actual celebrity. Your closest brush with fame might be seeing Bob Hope's gardener weeding outside of Bob's high adobe wall. The 1hr. tour drives past 30-40 celebrity homes and includes guided narration. *(4751 E. Palm Canyon Dr., Ste. D. ☎770-2700. Open in winter daily 8am-5pm; summer Tu-Sa 7:30am-2:30pm. Guided tours from $17, seniors $15, under 17 $8.)*

WIND FARM TOURS. The unusual topography and outrageous temperatures of the Palm Springs region generate some of the world's strongest sustained winds. On the wind farm, about 3500 high-tech windmills harness this energy. Even if you forgo the tours, given by **Windmill Tours, Inc.,** drive down I-10 to see the oddly spectacular forest of whirling blades. *(Located 1¼ mi. west of Indian Canyon Drive on 20th Ave., just across I-10. ☎251-1997. Open M-Sa; 4 tours per day: 9, 11am, 1, and 3pm. Reservations required. $23, seniors $20, students $15, ages 6-13 $10, under 6 free.)*

◐ NIGHTLIFE

The glitz of Palm Springs doesn't disappear with the setting sun—the city's nightlife is almost as heralded as its golf courses. Although a night of total indulgence here might cost a small fortune, several bars provide nightly drink specials and lively people-watching. **La Taquería,** 125 E. Tahquitz Way (☎778-5391), specializes in ultra-fresh and healthy Mexican cuisine; the mist-enshrouded tile patio is great for sipping Moonlight Margaritas ($6). Locals hang at the **Village Pub,** 266 S. Palm Canyon Dr., for easygoing beer-swilling and folksy live rock. The crowd is usually over 25, but it gets younger on the weekends. (☎323-3265. 21+. Open daily 11am-2am.) Those willing to open the wallet a little wider for a night on the town can head to **Atlas,** 210 S. Palm Canyon Dr. The hip, ultra-modern restaurant and dance club is in the heart of downtown. It's fusion specialties are just as modern. (☎325-8839. Entrees $15-25. Local DJs nightly. 21+ for dancing. Open daily 11am-2pm.)

Palm Springs is a major destination for gay and lesbian travelers. The gay scene sparkles with bars, spas, and clothing-optional resorts. The comprehensive *Gay Guide to Palm Springs,* available at the Visitors Center, helps you get started.

● SEASONAL EVENTS

Village Fest (☎320-3781) takes over Palm Canyon Dr. downtown every Thursday night from 6 to 10pm (in summer 7-10pm). Vendors from surrounding communities market food, jewelry, and local crafts in a bargain bonanza, while townsfolk enjoy live music and entertainment.

Attempting to fulfill his campaign promise to heighten Palm Springs's glamour quotient, former mayor Sonny Bono instituted the annual **Nortel Networks Palm Springs International Film Festival** (☎778-8979; Jan. 9-20 in 2003). The **57th Annual National Date Festival,** Rte. 111 in Indio (☎863-8247. Feb. 14-23 in 2003), is not a hook-up scene but a bash for dried-fruit lovers. Palm Springs is also famous for its tennis and professional golf tournaments, like the **44th Annual Bob Hope Chrysler Classic** (☎346-8184; Jan. 27-Feb. 2 in 2003) and the LPGA's **32nd Annual Kraft Nabisco Championship** (☎324-4546).

NEAR PALM SPRINGS

Living Desert Wildlife and Botanical Park, 47900 Portola Ave., Palm Desert, 1½ mi. south of Rte. 111, has oryx, camels, and meerkats alongside indigenous flora. Wear sunscreen and bring water because there isn't much shade, though misters are provided. (☎346-5694; www.livingdesert.org. Open Sept.-June daily 9am-5pm, last admission at 4pm; July-Aug. daily 8am-1:30pm, last admission at 1pm. Sept.-June $8.50, seniors and military $7.50, ages 3-12 $4.50; July-Aug. $6.50, ages 3-12 $3.50.)

Since the **Coachella Valley** is the self-proclaimed "Date Capital of the World," comb your hair, suck down a breath mint, and head to the **Shields Date Gardens,** 80225 Rte. 111, in nearby Indio. This palm grove sets itself apart from the rest by presenting an amusing and free informational film titled *The Romance and Sex Life of the Date* in addition to the usual date shakes and gift boxes. (☎347-0996 or 800-414-2555. Open Sept.-May daily 8am-6pm; June-Aug. daily 9am-5pm.) If Palm Springs isn't enough of a zoo, you can observe wildlife at the **Big Morongo Canyon Preserve,** off Rte. 62, a sanctuary for birds and other animals. (☎363-7190. Open daily 7:30am-dusk. Free.) Northeast of Palm Springs in Thousand Palms, the **Coachella Valley Preserve** has a Visitors Center that can help you plan a hike through mesas, bluffs, or the **Thousand Palms Oasis,** which are homes to the protected fringe-toed lizard. (☎343-2733 or 343-4031. Open Sept.-June sunrise-sunset.)

CALIFORNIA

NEVADA

The mountains and deserts of Nevada's Basin and Range region stretch for hundreds of miles. Legalized prostitution and gambling mark the state as a purveyor of loose Wild West morality. The Nevada Test Site, north of Las Vegas, represents one of mankind's most ignominious projects: the embattled land surrounding the site is so absent of life that it's the proposed repository for the nation's nuclear waste. Beyond some patches of bright lights, sin, and showtunes, Nevada is empty, dusty, and unkind to flesh and bone.

Despite this widespread sense of natural, environmental, and moral desolation, Nevada shelters pockets of prosperity and fecundity within the borders of the fastest growing state in the land. Booming population growth in Las Vegas makes this concrete oasis one of the West's most popular residential communities, and it can be a hellishly good time. Similar growth surrounds Nevada's northern metropolitan center, Reno. The high peaks of the Snake, Ruby, and Jarbidge areas are aberrations in the desert, supporting a rich and fertile variety of unique ecosystems. Uncrowded and pristine, these Nevada lands afford the opportunity for real wilderness solitude. Three massive bodies of water—the mammoth, man-made Lake Mead, the crystalline blue Pyramid Lake, and the mountain-ringed Lake Tahoe—provide refreshing retreats from brutal desert heat.

Nevada also harbors a rich variety of cultures. The industrious Basque people continue to work the land in northern Nevada, infusing the area with their vibrant culture and unique cuisine. The modern boomtown of Elko has become a preserver of cowboy culture through its Western Folklife Center and its annual Cowboy Poetry and Music Gatherings. Burning Man, the annual performance art spectacle, rises up out of the Black Rock desert, sandwiched between tiny Winnemucca and blue-collar Gerlach.

▩ HIGHLIGHTS OF NEVADA

GREAT BASIN. This addition to the national park system boasts several worthwhile sights and activities—hike up Wheeler Peak (p. 213), explore the dazzling Lehman Cave (p. 211), and see bristlecone pine groves, the earth's oldest organisms (p. 212).

LEAVING LAS VEGAS. Tear yourself away from the slots and tables (p. 200) so that you can scale some gnarly walls at **Red Rocks** (p. 206), check out the enormity of **Hoover Dam** (p. 206), rent a boat on **Lake Mead** (p. 207), or hike at **Valley of Fire.**

ELKO. Go for a morning hike in the **Ruby Mountains** (p. 235), and spend the afternoon brushing up on cowboy culture (p. 235).

LAS VEGAS   ☎ 702

Rising out of the barren Nevada desert, Las Vegas is a shimmering tribute to excess and materialism. Gambling, whoring, and mob-muscle built this city, and continue to add to its dark mystique. Mafia influence in Vegas has notably diminished in the last thirty years, however, having been replaced by the even more notorious and powerful, if family-friendly, corporate mob. In the new Las Vegas, boutique shops, theme park casinos, and a nonstop carnival atmosphere provide a

Nevada

way into the wallets of all ages and degrees of risk aversion. The recent residential boom attests to the changing face of one of America's fastest growing cities, as blocks upon blocks of pastel cookie-cutter homes stretch toward the mountains. Rather than calming the Vegas scene, metropolitan growth has heightened tourism and taken excess to new levels. Nowhere else in America do so many shed their inhibitions and indulge otherwise dormant appetites. Vegas is still about money and sex (but mostly money). The opulent mega-casinos that dominate Vegas are unbelievably successful at maximizing profits, be it with over-the-top entertainment, fine dining, or by squeezing out billions from its 0.5% advantage in blackjack. Yet, for every winner, we all know, there's always a loser. There's a broken heart and a busted wallet for every twinkling light in the Vegas.

⌐ TRANSPORTATION

Flights: McCarran International (☎261-5211), at the southwestern end of the Strip. Main terminal on Paradise Rd. Vans to the Strip and downtown $4-5; taxi $10-15.

Buses: Greyhound, 200 S. Main St. (☎384-9561 or 800-231-2222), downtown at Carson Ave. To: **Flagstaff** (5-7hr., 3 per day, $46.50) and **L.A.** (5-7hr., 10 per day, $34).

Public Transportation: Citizens Area Transit or **CAT** (☎228-7433). Buses #117, 301, and 302 serve downtown and the Strip. Buses #108 and 109 serve the airport. All are wheelchair accessible. Buses run daily 5:30am-1:30am (24hr. on the Strip). Routes on the Strip $2, residential routes $1.25, seniors and ages 6-17 60¢. **Las Vegas Strip Trolleys** (☎382-1404) cruise the Strip every 15min. daily 9:30am-1:30am. $1.65; use exact change.

Taxis: Yellow, Checker, Star (☎873-2000). Initial charge $2.30, each additional mi. $1.80. For pickup, call 30min. beforehand. Wheelchair accessible cabs available.

Car Rental: Sav-Mor Rent-A-Car, 5101 Rent-A-Car Rd. (☎736-1234 or 800-634-6779), at the airport. From $35 per day, $149 per week; 150 mi. per day included, each additional mi. 20¢. Must be 21+, under-25 surcharge $8 per day. Discounts can be found in tourist publications. Open daily 5:30am-1am; airport window opens at 7am.

◢ ORIENTATION

Driving to Vegas from L.A. is a straight, 300 mi. shot on I-15 N (4½hr.). From Arizona, take I-40 W to Kingman and then U.S. 93 N. Las Vegas has two major casino areas. The **downtown** area, around 2nd and Fremont St., has been converted into a pedestrian promenade. Casinos cluster together beneath a shimmering space-frame structure covering over five city blocks. The other main area is the **Strip,** a collection of mammoth hotel-casinos along **Las Vegas Blvd.** Parallel to the east side of the Strip and in its shadow is **Paradise Rd.,** also strewn with casinos. As in any city with a constant influx of money, some areas of Las Vegas are unsafe, so remain on well-lit pathways and don't wander too far from major casinos and hotels. Valeting your car at a major casino and sticking to Fremont St. are a safe bet. *The neighborhoods just north of Stewart St. and west of Main St. in the downtown vicinity are especially demanding of caution.*

Despite, or perhaps as a result of, its reputation for debauchery, Las Vegas has a **curfew.** Those under 18 are not allowed unaccompanied in most public places Sunday through Thursday from 10pm to 5am and Friday through Saturday from midnight to 5am. Laws are even harsher on the Strip, where no one under 18 is allowed unless accompanied by an adult from 9pm to 5am Monday through Friday and 6pm to 5am on the weekends. *The drinking and gambling age is 21.*

◪ PRACTICAL INFORMATION

Visitor Information: Las Vegas Convention and Visitors Authority, 3150 Paradise Rd. (☎892-0711; fax 226-9011), 4 blocks from the Strip in the big pink convention center by the Hilton. Up-to-date info on headliners, conventions, shows, hotel bargains, and buffets. Open daily 8am-5pm.

Tours: Gambler's Special bus tours leave L.A., San Francisco, and San Diego for Las Vegas early in the morning and return at night or the next day. Ask at tourist offices in the departure cities or call casinos for info. **Coach USA,** 4020 E. Lone Mountain Rd. (☎384-1234 or 800-634-6579). Guided "neon and lights" night tour (3½hr., 1 per day, $39). Bus tours from Las Vegas to **Hoover Dam/Lake Mead** (4 hr., 2 per day,

NEVADA

$39) and the **Grand Canyon's South Rim** (full-day, includes continental breakfast, box lunch, and tours; $149). Discounts with coupons in tourist publications and for ages 3-11. Reserve at least 24hr. in advance.

Bank: Bank of America, 1140 E. Desert Inn Rd. (☎654-1000), at the corner of Maryland Pkwy. Open M-Th 9am-5pm, F 9am-6pm. Phone assistance 24hr.

ATMs: In all major casinos, but there is at least a $2 charge for each transaction.

Bi-Gay-Lesbian Organization: Gay and Lesbian Community Center, 953 E. Sahara Ave. (☎733-9800). Open M-F 11am-7pm, Sa 10am-3pm.

Laundry: Cora's Coin Laundry, 1099 E. Tropicana Rd. (☎736-6181). Open 8am-8pm. Wash $1-3.

Road Conditions: ☎877-687-6237. **Weather Conditions:** ☎263-9744.

Marriage: Over 115,000 couples a year trek to Las Vegas to tie the knot because of its lenient regulations and ubiquitous chapels. **Marriage License Bureau,** 200 S. 3rd St. (☎455-4415), in the courthouse. 18+ or 16 with parental consent. Licenses $35; cash only. No waiting period or blood test required. Open M-Th 8am-midnight, F-Su 24hr.

Divorce: Must be a Nevada resident for at least 6 weeks; process often takes 3 weeks. $152 filing fee. Permits available at the courthouse M-F 8am-5pm. Visit the Family Court at 601 N. Pecos Rd. for more information (☎455-4415).

Police: ☎795-3111.

24-Hour Crisis Lines: Compulsive Gamblers Hotline, ☎800-567-8238/LOST-BET. **Gamblers Anonymous,** ☎385-7732. **Rape Crisis Center Hotline,** ☎366-1640. **Suicide Prevention,** ☎731-2990.

Internet Access: Clark County Library, 1401 E. Flamingo Rd. (☎507-3400), one block east of Maryland Pkwy. Open M-Th 9am-9pm, F-Sa 9am-5pm, Su 1-5pm.

Post Office: 301 E. Stewart Ave. (☎800-275-8777), downtown. Open M-F 8:30am-5pm. General Delivery pickup M-F 9am-2pm. **ZIP code:** 89101.

▞ ▞ ACCOMMODATIONS AND CAMPING

Even though Vegas has over 100,000 rooms, most hotels fill up on weekend nights. If you get stuck, call the **Room Reservations Hotline** (☎800-332-5333), or go to one of the tourist offices. The earlier you reserve, the better chance you have of snagging a special rate. Room rates in Vegas fluctuate, and many hotels have different rate ranges for weeknights and weekend nights. The prices below are only a general guide; you can often get better deals during slow periods, but could be unpleasantly surprised if you try to reserve for a convention weekend. A room that costs $30 during a promotion can cost hundreds during conventions (two major conventions are in Jan. and Nov.). Check free, readily available publications such as *What's On In Las Vegas, Today in Las Vegas, 24/7, Vegas Visitor, Casino Player, Tour Guide Magazine, Best Read Guide,* and *Insider Viewpoint of Las Vegas* for discounts, coupons, general info, and schedules of events.

Strip hotels are at the center of the action and within walking distance of each other, but their inexpensive rooms sell out quickly. Many have reasonable rates Sunday through Thursday, but prices can triple on the weekends or when a convention is in town. There is a cluster of inexpensive motels north of the Strip (1200-1400 S. Las Vegas Blvd.), but these are far from the action and located in a sketchy part of town. Another cluster is located around Sahara Rd. and S. Las Vegas Blvd. Motels also line **Fremont Street,** though this area is a little rougher; it is

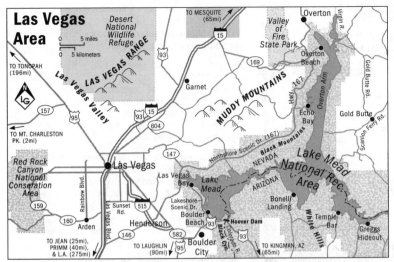

Las Vegas Area

TO MESQUITE (65mi)
TO TONOPAH (196mi)
TO MT. CHARLESTON PK. (2mi)
Desert National Wildlife Refuge
LAS VEGAS RANGE
Las Vegas Valley
Garnet
Valley of Fire State Park
Overton
Virgin R.
Overton Beach
Overton Arm
Gold Butte Rd.
MUDDY MOUNTAINS
Echo Bay
Gold Butte
Scanlon Ferry Rd.
Red Rock Canyon National Conservation Area
Las Vegas
Las Vegas Bay
Lake Mead
Northshore Scenic Dr. (167)
Black Mountains
NEVADA
ARIZONA
Bonelli Landing
Lake Mead National Rec. Area
White Hills
Temple Bar
Greggs Hideout
Rainbow Blvd.
Las Vegas Blvd.
Sunset Rd.
Arden
Henderson
Lakeshore Scenic Dr.
Boulder Beach
Boulder City
Hoover Dam
Colorado R.
Black Canyon
TO JEAN (25mi), PRIMM (40mi), & L.A. (275mi)
TO LAUGHLIN (90mi)
TO KINGMAN, AZ (65mi)

best to stay in one of the casinos in the **Fremont Street Experience** (see **Casinos,** p. 200) itself. There is another concentration of inexpensive motels along the southern stretch of the Strip, across from the ritzy **Mandalay Bay.** Another option, if you have a car, is to stay at one of the hotel-casinos in either Jean, NV (approximately 30 mi. south on I-15, near the California border) or Primm Valley (approximately 45 mi. south on I-15). These tend to be less crowded and much cheaper than in-town hotels, and you get the full resort casino experience.

Those under 21 may run into difficulty getting a room in Las Vegas. State law makes it illegal for any hotel/casino to rent a room to anyone under this age. However, most hotels are lenient, especially during slower periods. If you run into trouble, head to one of the smaller motels or hostels without casinos attached. **The 9% state hotel tax is not included in room rates listed below.**

🏨 **Silverton,** 3333 Blue Diamond Rd. (☎800-588-7711; www.silvertoncasino.com). Cheaper because it's off the Strip, this spooky ghost town-themed gambling den has a re-creation every Su night of a great Wild West tradition—the luau. Free Las Vegas Blvd. shuttle for guests until 10pm. Singles start at $29 Su-Th, F-Sa $49; doubles $39/$69. RV park is also available (hookups $27). ❸

🏨 **San Remo,** 115 E. Tropicana Ave. (☎800-522-7366). Just off the Strip, this is a smaller, friendlier version of the major player casinos, without the gimmicks, crowds, and high prices. Live entertainment every night. Rooms may go as low as $29 during slow periods, but are usually Su-Th $42, F-Sa $70. ❸

🏨 **Whiskey Pete's** (☎800-248-8453), in Primm Valley, NV, 45 mi. south of Vegas on I-15, just before the California border. Whiskey Pete's is the cheapest of 3 Western-themed casinos right in the middle of the desert. Cheap as fool's gold and home to the wildest roller coaster in Nevada ($6). Su-Th $19, F-Sa $50; prices vary with availability. ❸

🏨 **USAHostels Las Vegas,** 1322 Fremont St. (☎385-1150 or 800-550-8958; www.usa-hostels.com). A funky, fun place to stay, though it is far from the Strip and in an unattractive neighborhood. Rooms are clean, the international staff is friendly, and the atmosphere caters to students and international travelers. Private and dorm rooms are available, along with a pool, jacuzzi, laundry, kitchen and billiard room. Shared bath-

THE INSIDER'S CITY

BUDGET CASINO CRAWL

Sin City doesn't have to be expensive. Try this route for a dazzling night in Vegas for under $30.

1 Get started at the **Paradise Buffet at the Flamingo** (733-3111) at 2:30pm. Gorge on two endless buffet lines for only $10.

2 Walk off your meal by touring through the opulent **Grand Canal Shops at the Venetian.** Gondoliers sing along the indoor canal.

3 At the **Forum Shops at Caesar's Palace,** watch as day changes into night on the skylike ceiling. An animatronics show welcomes guests to Caesar's world every hour.

4 At dusk, cross the strip to the **Eiffel Tower at the Paris**. For $9, trek up to the top of this 50 story structure for an unbeatable view of the city.

5 After sunset, the free **Water Show at the Bellagio** takes place every 15min. on an outdoor lake and is tough to beat. Grab your camera for this spectacular water ballet.

6 Starting at 8pm, you can watch roaring, foaming **Volcano at the Mirage** erupt every 15min.

7 For a true pyrotechnics treat, watch the **Pirate Battle at Treasure Island.** Swashbuckling happens

rooms. Offers free pickup from Greyhound station. Su-Th dorms $14-19, F-Sa $17-23; suites $40-42/$49-51. **Must have international passport, proof of international travel, or student ID. ❷**

Goldstrike, 1 Main St. (☎472-5000 or 800-634-1359), in Jean, NV, 30 mi. south of Vegas on I-15 (Exit 12). Vegas-style casino has various inexpensive restaurants (prime rib $7, dinner buffet $7.50). A genuine Vegas experience at cut-rate prices. Loose slots and low-limit tables. Rooms Su-Th $20-30, F $40, Sa $50; additional person $3. ❸

Somerset House Motel, 294 Convention Center Dr. (☎888-336-4280; www.somersethouse.com). A no-frills establishment within short walking distance of the major Strip casinos. Many rooms feature kitchens; all 104 units are large and impeccably clean. Dishes and cooking utensils provided upon request. Singles Su-Th $35, F-Sa $44; doubles $44/$55. Additional person $5; rates lower for seniors. ❸

Las Vegas International Hostel (AAIH/Rucksackers), 1208 S. Las Vegas Blvd. (☎385-9955). Though the rooms are clean, the neighborhood surrounding this European-flavored joint is not. Numerous strip clubs and "adult" motels that rent rooms by the hour line this part of the Strip. However, the staff is friendly and the hostel itself is safe. Shared bathrooms. Key deposit $5. Reception 7am-11pm. Check-out 10am. 6-person dorms Apr.-Nov. $12 with IHA membership or student ID; singles $26-28. ❶

Palace Station, 2411 W. Sahara Ave. (☎800-634-3101). Free shuttles to Las Vegas Blvd. run from 8:45am-12:15am. Has all the features of a Strip hotel. Home of the largest slot win in history—$25,000,000. Rooms Su-Th $40-80, F-Sa $100-130; additional person $10. ❺

Glass Pool Inn, 4611 S. Las Vegas Blvd. (☎439-6800 or 800-527-7118). Offers old but clean rooms south of the Strip. Its claim to fame: an above-ground pool with windows that peer underwater. Singles and doubles Su-Th $29-39, F-Sa $59. ❸

Circus Circus, 2880 S. Las Vegas Blvd. (☎800-444-2472). Check out the awesome Adventuredome Theme Park and the clown shop. Su-Th $39-79, F-Sa and holidays $79-159; rollaway bed $12. Fills 3-4 months in advance. ❺

CAMPGROUNDS

Lake Mead National Recreation Area (☎293-8906), 25 mi. south of town on Rte. 93/95. Numerous campsites available throughout. Showers only at Calville and Overton Beach. Sites with flush toilets $10. ❶

Valley of Fire State Park (☎ 397-2088), 60 mi. north of Vegas, along Rte. 169. A splendid campground near the ancient petroglyph site of Atlas Rock. No electricity or hookups. Sites $13. ❶

Circusland RV Park, 500 Circus Circus Dr. (☎ 734-0410). Pool, jacuzzi, convenience store, showers. Open 6am-midnight. Hookups Su-Th $19, F-Sa $21. ❷

🍴 FOOD

Sloshed and insatiable gamblers gorge themselves day and night at Vegas's gigantic buffets. For the bottomless gullet, there is no better value than the caloric intensity of these eateries. Beyond the buffets, Vegas has some of the best restaurants in the world, though there's little for the true budget adventurer.

▨ Carnival World Buffet at the Río, 3700 W. Flamingo Rd. (☎ 252-7777). Hands down the greatest buffet in Vegas. Enjoy truly delicious food from any of the 11 stations, each reflecting a different theme. Breakfast $8 (8-10:30am), lunch $11 (11am-3:30pm), dinner $15 (3:30-11pm). ❸

Benihana Village at the Las Vegas Hilton, 3000 Paradise Rd. (☎ 732-5755). Indoor village theme created with fish-filled pond, rain, and multi-level dining area. Sit down and watch your five-course meal flashingly prepared by charismatic hibachi chefs. A slight splurge, filling entrees are worth every penny of the $16-30 price tag. Open nightly 5:30-10:30pm. ❺

The Plaza Diner, 1 Main St. (☎ 386-2110), near the entrance to Jackie Gaughan's Plaza Hotel/Casino. Cheap prime rib dinner $6 (noon-midnight). Open 24hr. $1 beers. ❷

Rincon Criollo, 1145 S. Las Vegas Blvd. (☎ 388-1906), across from Las Vegas International Hostel. Dine on filling Cuban food beneath a wall-sized photograph of palm trees. Daily special including rice and black beans $6.50. Hot sandwiches $3.50-4.50. Open Tu-Su 11am-9:30pm. ❶

Battista's Hole in the Wall, 4041 Audrie Ave. (☎ 732-1424), right behind the Flamingo. Adorning the walls are 28 years' worth of celebrity photos and novelties from area brothels, as well as the head of "Moosolini," the fascist moose. Dinner, with the house wine ($18), is pricey but worth it. Open Su-Th 4:30-10:30pm, F-Sa 4:30-11pm. ❺

Mediterranean Cafe, 4147 S. Maryland Pkwy. (☎ 731-6030), serves up fresh, delicious Greek and Mediterra-

THE LOCAL STORY

CHEAP RENT, BIG TIPS

Ralph Griffo, a resident of Las Vegas, is a former blackjack dealer at the renowned Horseshoe Casino.

Q: Where do you come from?
A: New York City.
Q: So you're not a native Las Vegan. What made you make the move out West?
A: Well, basically it was because of housing; real estate was kind of high in New York, and real estate was cheap in Las Vegas. So, we came here on vacation—about 17 of us—and we decided we liked some houses here, and we left the deposits to move out here.
Q: Do you enjoy gambling in the casinos out here?
A: I like to gamble once in a while.
Q: Do you have any experience working at the casinos? I understand they employ a lot of people around here.
A: Yes, I dealt blackjack at Binion's Horseshoe, that's in downtown Las Vegas.
Q: Did you ever meet any famous people while dealing?
A: I remember once dealing to Dennis Rodman.
Q: What's the biggest payoff you ever had to deal out as a blackjack dealer down there?
A: Actually, I had a guy at the blackjack table playing two hands, $25,000 each hand. He'd win a few, and once he actually hit blackjack. On one of those hands, I had to pay him $37,500.
Q: Did he leave a big tip?
A: Yeah, he tipped about $5,000 altogether.

nean specialties. Try the yummy combo plate with couscous and tabouli ($9) or a big falafel and hummus pita bread sandwich ($5). Open M 11am-9pm, Tu-Th 11am-1am, F-Su 11am-3am. ❷

Saizan, 115 E. Tropicana Ave. (☎739-9000), in San Remo. The best sushi bar near the Strip offers only the freshest sushi and sashimi. The Yumyum roll ($8) lives up to its name. Open daily 5:30pm-midnight. ❸

◉ SIGHTS

Before casinos inject you full of glitz and suck you dry of greenbacks, explore some of the simpler oddities of the city. Fans of classical music and kitsch will be delighted by the renovated **Liberace Museum,** 1775 E. Tropicana Ave., and its exhibits of the showman's velvet, rhinestone, fur, and suede stage costumes. (☎798-5595. Open M-Sa 10am-5pm, Su 1-5pm. $12, students and seniors $8, under 12 free.) Silly exhibits at the **Guinness World Records Museum,** 2780 S. Las Vegas Blvd., showcase repulsive and intriguing human oddities, display record-setting events captured on video, and allow visitors to compare their dimensions to those of some giants. (☎792-3766. Open daily 9am-8pm. $6.50, students and seniors $5.50, ages 5-12 $4.50.) It's been said that God made men, and Sam Colt made 'em equal. Experience coltish justice at the **Gun Store,** 2990 E. Tropicana Ave. Ten dollars plus ammo lets you try out an impressive array of pistols, including the enormous Magnum 44. For $30, let loose by firing 50 rounds of a machine gun at the on-site range. (☎454-1110. Open daily 9am-6:30pm.)

Way out in Primm Valley along I-15 near the Cali border, the **Desperado Roller Coaster** is the tallest and fastest bad-boy in the Vegas area, and one of the best coasters on the West Coast. (☎800-248-8453. Open Su-Th 11am-8pm, F-Sa 11am-midnight. $7.) Offering services from 3min. drive-through whirlwinds to elaborate fantasy-themed extravaganzas, the **Little White Wedding Chapel,** 1301 Las Vegas Blvd., is a mainstay of the city's matrimonial traditions. Luminaries like Michael Jordan and Sally Jessy Raphael have been hitched here. A life-changing drive through the wedding tunnel begins at a romantic $40 (plus a donation to the minister) and possibilities expand with the imagination. (☎382-5943. No reservations required for the drive-through services. Have your marriage license ready. Open 24hr.)

🏛 CA$INOS

Attracting tourist dollars with food, liquor, and fun has been taken to another level by casinos spend millions of dollars to fool guests into thinking they are somewhere else. Spittin' images of Venice, New York, Río, Paris (complete with Eiffel Tower), Cairo (complete with the Egyptian Pyramids), and Monte Carlo already thrive on the Strip. Efforts to bring families to Sin City are evident with the surplus of shopping malls, arcades, amusement parks, and themed hotels.

Gambling is illegal for those under 21. If you are of age, look for casino "funbooks" that allow gamblers to buy $50 in chips for only $15. Cash goes in a blink when you're gambling, so it pays to have a budget. Be aware of your surroundings and guard your winnings.

Casinos, nightclubs, and some wedding chapels are open 24hr. There are far more casinos and far more attractions within them than can be listed here; use the following as a compendium of the best, but explore the Strip for yourself. Check with the Visitors Center for more casino listings (see p. 195).

TO TEXAS (1.5mi)
& FIESTA (1.5mi)

95

515

Binion's
Horseshoe

Main St.
Station

"The Fremont St.
Experience"

The Fitzgerald

Golden
Nugget

PLAZA

0   1000 yards

0   1 kilometer

N

LG

Tonopah Dr.

Shadow Ln.

Fremont St.

Carson St.

Bridger St.

Main St.

Casino Ctr Blvd.

3rd St.

4th St.

Las Vegas Blvd.

Lewis St.

582

3rd St.

Maryland Pkwy.

Clark St.

Bonneville Ave.

14th St.

15th St.

16th St.

TO SUNCOAST
(3mi)

159

Valley Medical Center

University Medical
Center

Gass St.

Hoover St.

Coolidge St.

7th St.

8th St.

159

Charleston Blvd.

Grand Central Parkway

604

Colorado Ave.

Commerce St.

Utah St.

Franklin St.

Sweeney St.

13th St.

15th St.

7th St.

Hassett St.

Little White
Wedding Chapel

8th St.

New York St.

Oakey Blvd.

Rexford St.

Canosa Ave.

10th St.

11th St.

Oakey Blvd.

Valley View Blvd.

Rancho Dr.

Oakey Blvd.

Philadelphia St.

Tam Dr.

Fairfield

6th St.

St. Louis Ave.

I-15

Western St.

Stratosphere

Talbot St.

Chapman St.

Sahara Ave.

589

Las Vegas Blvd.

Sahara Ave.

589

Guinness World
Records Museum

Sahara

Karen Ave.

Circus
Circus Dr.

Wet 'n' Wild

Las Vegas
Hilton

Kendale

Vegas Valley St.

La Canada St.

Riviera Blvd.

Riviera

Las Vegas
Country
Club

Palora St.

Golden Arrow St.

Stardust

Joe W. Brown Dr.

Las Vegas
Hilton

The Strip

Rancho Dr.

Westwood Ave.

Highland Ave.

Industrial Rd.

Convention Center Dr.

Las Vegas
Convention
Center

Bel Air Dr.

Sombrero St.

Channel
8 Dr.

Debbie
Reynolds Dr.

Desert Inn Rd.

Pinehurst Dr.

Fashion
Show Mall

Spring Mountain Rd.

604

Sands Ave.

Burbank Ave.

Sierra Vista St.

Swenson St.

Dumont St.

Cambridge St.

Commanche St.

Cherokee St.

Treasure
Island

Country Club St.

Elm Dr.

Katie St.

The Venetian

Imperial
Palace

Audrie St.

Twain Ave.

Palo Verdes St.

Northrup
St.

Maryland Pkwy.

Cambridge St.

Spencer St.

The Mirage

Rio
Suite
Hotel

Caesar's
Palace

Flamingo
Hilton

10

Barbary Coast

Howard Hughes Pkwy.

Flamingo Rd.

The
Palms

9

Bellagio

Bally's

Jockey
Club

Paris

Salton St.

Paradise Rd.

University
of Nevada
Las Vegas

Eym Dr.

Brussels St.

Las Vegas Blvd.

Aladdin

I-15

Monte
Carlo

New York
New York

MGM Grand

Audrie St.

Koval Ln.

Hard Rock
Casino

Lana St.

Harmon Ave.

Las Vegas
International
Golf Center

Thomas
& Mack
Center

Thom &
Mack

TO LIBERACE
MUSEUM (.6mi)

Wilbur St.

Excalibur

604

Reno Ave.

Tropicana

Giles St.

Tropicana Ave.

Swenson St.

Hacienda Ave.

Industrial Rd.

Luxor

Hacienda Ave.

Mandalay Bay

Diablo Dr.

McCarran
International
Airport

Richard St.

Kelly St.

The Four
Seasons

Dewey Dr.

12

Russell Rd.

TO JEAN & 13 (30mi);
PRIMM VALLEY & 14(45mi)
Ogendo Rd.

Tourist
Bureau

Kitty
Hawk St.

TO BLUE DIAMOND
RD. (3 mi) & 15

Wynn Rd.

Hewemon St.

Las Vegas

■ ACCOMMODATIONS

Circus Circus, **6**
Glass Pool Inn, **12**
Goldstrike, **13**
Las Vegas Int'l Hostel
  (AAIH/Rucksackers), **3**
Palace Station, **5**
San Remo, **11**
Silverton, **15**
Somerset House
  Motel, **7**
Whiskey Pete's, **14**

🍖 FOOD

Batista's Hole
  In The Wall, **10**
Plaza Diner, **1**
Rio's Carnival World
  Buffet, **9**
Rincon Criollo, **2**

🍸 NIGHTLIFE

The Beach, **8**
Goodtimes, **4**

NEVADA

202 ■ LAS VEGAS

THE STRIP

The undisputed locus of Vegas's surging regeneration, the Strip is a seeming fantasy land of neon, teeming with people, casinos, and restaurants. The nation's 10 largest hotels line the legendary 3½ mi. stretch of Las Vegas Blvd. named an "All-American Road" and "National Scenic Byway." Despite the corporate facade, porn is still peddled in the shadow of family fun centers, and night denizens sporting open alcohol containers wander the street in search of elusive jackpots.

Aladdin, 3667 S. Las Vegas Blvd. (☎785-5555). More of a sight than a casino, the decor of this spectacle outshines its facilities. The Desert Passage shopping area is a mile-wide desert town complete with "weather patterns" and ambient noise.

Circus Circus, 2880 S. Las Vegas Blvd. (☎734-0410). While parents run to card tables and slot machines downstairs, children spend *their* quarters upstairs on the souped-up carnival midway and in the titanic video game arcade. Within the hotel complex, Grand Slam Canyon is a Grand Canyon theme park with a roller coaster and other rides, all contained inside the bright pink "adventuredome." Open daily 24hr. Free daily shows, every half-hour 11am-midnight.

Rio Suite Hotel and Casino, 3700 W. Flamingo Rd. (☎252-7777). Just across I-15 on Flamingo Rd., the all-suite Rio hotel boasts clubs, restaurants and a casino floor with a Brazilian carnival. The ceiling of the Masquerade Village is the site of a a bead-tossing, beverage-sipping, music-pumping good time.

Mirage, 3400 S. Las Vegas Blvd. (☎791-7111). Arguably the casino that began Vegas's reincarnation from decay in the early 90s. Among its attractions are a dolphin habitat, Siegfried and Roy's white tigers, and an equally flaming volcano that erupts in fountains and jets of fire every 15min.

MGM Grand, 3799 S. Las Vegas Blvd. (☎891-7979). A huge bronze lion guards this casino, and a couple of live felines can be seen inside at the lion habitat. In addition to more than 5000 rooms, the MGM hosts world-class sporting events and concerts.

Caesar's Palace, 3570 S. Las Vegas Blvd. (☎731-7110). At Caesar's, busts abound: some are plaster, while others are barely concealed by the low-cut costumes worn by the cocktail waitresses. Neither is real. The pricey Forum Shops began the high-end shopping craze at Strip casinos, and continue to lure consumers with fine eateries and two animatronic shows. (Shops open M-F 10am-11pm; Sa-Su 10am-midnight.)

Excalibur Hotel and Casino, 3850 S. Las Vegas Blvd. (☎800-937-7777). Medieval mock-up hurls visitors centuries into the past. A life sized castle with drawbridge and moat, two enormous towers of rooms, and a kiddie carnival area. Acts as one terminal of the monorail connecting to the Luxor and Mandalay Bay.

New York, New York, 3790 S. Las Vegas Blvd. (☎740-6969). Towers mimic the Manhattan skyline, re-creating the glory of the Big Apple at this tacky casino. Traverse the sidewalk under a replica of the Brooklyn Bridge. Roller coaster open daily 11am-11pm; $10, 2nd ride half-price.

Flamingo Las Vegas, 3555 S. Las Vegas Blvd. (☎800-732-2111). Mobster Bugsy Siegel bucked the cowboy casino trend with this resort-style Strip casino in 1946, thereby setting Vegas's trajectory for decades to come. Sprawling pool area plays home to penguins, flamingos, and fish.

Luxor, 3900 S. Las Vegas Blvd. (☎262-4000). This non-generic casino and architectural marvel recreates the majestic pyramids of ancient Egypt in opaque glass and steel. Wander into the depths of the desert at the **King Tut Tomb and Museum.** Museum open daily Su-Th 9am-11pm; $5.

NEVADA

Treasure Island, 3300 S. Las Vegas Blvd. (☎894-7111). At Treasure Island, throngs of pushy people struggle to see a campy send-up of pirate lore. In the Pirate Show, a British navy vessel engages a galleon of roguish sea criminals, resulting in one of the best free shows in Vegas. Shows every 1½hr. Inside, the Kahunaville bartenders spin, toss, flip, and launch drinks against a flashy Hawaiian backdrop.

Stratosphere Casino Hotel and Tower, 2000 S. Las Vegas Blvd. (☎380-7777). The tallest structure west of the Mississippi River, the 1149 ft. free-standing tower can be seen from anywhere in the city, and affords postcard-like photo opportunities. The world's two highest thrill rides rumble atop its observation deck, and another is slated to open. $7 to head up to the tower. Rides open 10am-1am; $5-8.

Bellagio, 3600 S. Las Vegas Blvd. (☎888-987-6667). Boasts the distinction of being the world's largest five-star hotel. The classy Bellagio has a magnificent collection of art and carefully maintained botanical gardens that change with the seasons. Muscle your way up for a view of the spectacular Water Show on its outdoor lake, where water jets elegantly propel streams of water several stories into the air during a musical aquatic ballet. Daily water shows every quarter hour, noon-11pm; free.

Paris, 3655 S. Las Vegas Blvd. (☎946-7000). This is the smallest of the "theme" casinos, with all of the attractions of the real Paris, including mimes and tasty crepes. Almost to scale Eiffel Tower houses a restaurant and a beautiful view at its summit.

Venetian, 3355 S. Las Vegas Blvd. (☎ 733-5000). This huge casino features the upscale **Grand Canal Shoppes,** through which runs a 3 ft. deep chlorinated "canal." Singing gondoliers push tourists along in small boats while everyone else takes pictures. Architectural replicas of Venetian plazas, bridges, and towers adorn the Strip-side exterior.

DOWNTOWN AND OFF-STRIP

The tourist frenzy that grips the Strip is slightly less noticeable in old Downtown Vegas. The Glitter Gulch offers smaller hotels, cheaper alcohol and food, and some serious gambling. The family atmosphere of the Strip is entirely lacking, however. Years of decline were reversed with the 1995 opening of the Fremont Street Experience. The open desert sky above that thoroughfare is but a memory, and in its place, a canopy of neon, playing laser light shows throughout the night has arisen. The transformation of the neighborhood was furthered with the construction of a pedestrian promenade that now represents Fremont St. Despite the renewal, avoid Stewart and Main St. at night.

Northwest of the downtown area, tiny casinos cater to Vegas residents tired of crowds and lines. These "locals" often offer generous "comps" (free food, alcohol, and rooms), and hidden culinary gems. On Lake Mead Blvd., the **Texas Station** (at N. Rancho, Lake Mead Blvd. ☎631-1000) runs one of the busiest casinos in town. Across the street, the **Fiesta Casino Hotel** (2400 N. Rancho Dr. ☎800-731-7333) boasts a humongous sports book. The **JW Marriot Las Vegas Casino and Spa,** 221 Rampart Blvd. (☎869-7777) pampers guest with luxury Mediterranean style accommodations and a world-class spa.

Las Vegas Hilton, 3000 Paradise Rd. (☎697-8700). This casino is a "can't miss" stop thanks to its enormous "Las Vegas Hilton" sign. Inside, the $70 million Star Trek Experience immerses you in the Trekkie universe. Entrance to the "experience" also includes admission to the Star Trek Museum, which sets forth this cultural phenomenon with astonishing intricacy. Open daily 11am-11pm; $25.

Binion's Horseshoe Hotel and Casino, 128 E. Fremont St. (☎382-1600). The Binion family brought their love of high-stakes gaming from Texas. Site of the World Series of Poker, this is a serious gambler's paradise. High craps odds, single-deck blackjack, and a willingness to honor almost any bet are Horseshoe hallmarks.

NEVADA

BLACKJACK Blackjack is the most popular table game in Vegas. You can buy a little card in most gift shops that lists the most statistically sensible strategy for various hands. You can use the card at the tables, but you must not set it on the table. Blackjack dealers will also tell you what your best move is. There are various counting systems for blackjack that allow exceptionally astute gamblers to tilt the advantage slightly in their favor. Such strategies are only for the gifted, and Vegas casinos offset this edge by dealing from multiple decks within a shoe. The house makes billions off arrogant novices who are certain that they're the savant who can outsmart the house. All of the major casinos offer free daily instruction in most table games, and you should take advantage of these sessions if you want to have any hope of holding onto your cash. Also be sure to ask about local house rules that may make one particular table or casino a better bet.

The Plaza Casino, 1 Main St. (☎386-2110). Majestically stands guard over the touristy Fremont St. Experience. Center Stage Restaurant furnishes a great view of the nightly light shows.

Golden Nugget, 129 E. Fremont St. (☎386-8121). Injecting a touch of Strip-like class into the downtown area, this perennial four-star hotel charms with marble floors, elegant chandeliers, and high-end gambling.

ENTERTAINMENT

Vegas entertainment revolves around the casino axis. Extra bucks will buy you a seat at a made-in-the-USA phenomenon: the Vegas spectacular. These stunning, casino-sponsored productions feature marvels such as waterfalls, explosions, fireworks, and casts of thousands (including animals). You can also see Broadway plays and musicals, ice revues, and individual entertainers in concert. All hotels have city-wide ticket booths in their lobbies. Check out some of the ubiquitous free show guides (*Las Vegas Today, Best Read Guide, Today in Las Vegas, What's On*) for summaries of shows, as well as times and prices. Some "production shows" are topless; most are tasteless. One exception: the ▧**Cirque de Soleil**'s creative shows—*O* and *Mystere*—are bank-busting yet awe-inspiring displays of human agility and physical strength. "Limited view" tickets are discounted, and the view isn't that limited.

For a show by one of the musical stars who haunt the city, such as **Celine Dion** or **Wayne Newton**, you may have to fork over $50 or more. "Magicians of the Century," **Siegfried and Roy,** go for a fabulous $105.50 at the Mirage. Incredible impersonator/singer/dancer Danny Gans also entertains at the Mirage, and tickets run $80-100. "Revues," featuring imitations of (generally deceased) performers are far more reasonable. The **La Cage** drag show at the Riviera features dressed-to-the-nines "female impersonators" imitating all of your favorite divas for $30.

NIGHTLIFE

Nightlife in Vegas gets rolling around midnight and runs until everyone drops—or runs out of money. Cabs languish in line, waiting to take inebriated clubhoppers to the next happening joint. To save cash on covers and still see the hot spots, try heading to some places before the midnight rush, or on off-nights.

The Bars at the Hard Rock Casino, 4455 Paradise Rd. (☎693-5000). Youthful crowd and electric atmosphere at this circular bar in the middle of the casino floor. Go late and gawk at

NEVADA

whatever sweaty rock legend has wandered offstage at "The Joint" (a hot and intimate rock venue). Drinks $3-7. No cover. Open 24hr.

C2K Mega Club at the Venetian, 2800 S. Las Vegas Blvd. (☎933-4255). The casino's palatial showroom is transformed nightly into a mind-shattering *über*-club. Techno, techno, techno. Cover: men $10, women $5; Su women free. Open W-Su 11pm-dawn.

Ra, 3900 S. Las Vegas Blvd. (☎262-4000). Egyptian-themed nightclub at the Luxor, contains a sushi bar and state-of-the art sound system. Arguably Vegas's hottest club with famous DJs, it's the place to see and be seen. Cover $20, depending on the event and who you know. Open W-Sa 10pm-6am.

Club Río, 3700 W. Flamingo Rd. (☎247-7977). Another "in" place at which to gyrate all night long to grinding techno. Video walls radiate sultry and energizing images of the dance floor. If you don't look "in," you'll stand "out." Cover: men $10, women $5. Open W-Sa 10:30pm-dawn.

Club Paradise, 4416 Paradise Rd. (☎734-7990), across from Hard Rock Casino. Repeatedly voted best gentleman's cabaret (read: strip joint) in America. It's safe, and the g-strings stay on. Beer $6, cocktails $6-8. Cover $10. Open M-F 4pm-6am, Sa 6pm-6am.

Goodtimes, 1775 E. Tropicana Ave. (☎736-9494), is a gay bar/dance club in the renovated Liberace plaza with a $10 all-you-can-drink special on Mondays and bumping tunes that help it live up to its name. Open 24hr.

Hookah Lounge, 4147 S. Maryland Pkwy. (☎731-6030), features more than 20 flavored tobaccos (no opium, though) and a funky, intimate vibe that attracts pre-club crowds. Full bar and flavored teas. Open M-Th 5pm-1am; F-Sa 5pm-3am.

The Beach, 365 Convention Center Dr. (☎731-1925*).* At this tropical-themed club, there are 2 levels and dance floors where DJs spin Top 40 and hip hop. Tough on ID's; dress code strictly enforced. Ladies drink free Su-M, W before midnight. No cover. Open Su-Th 10pm-4am, F-Sa 10pm-6am; sports bar open 24hr., lunch served after 11am.

Bar at Times Square, 3790 S. Las Vegas Blvd. (☎740-6969), attempts to duplicate the laid-back atmosphere of an NYC bar, with dueling pianos playing requests just across from the "New York Slot Exchange." Cover $10 on weekends. Open Su-Th 8pm-3am, F-Sa 8pm-4am.

LEAVING LAS VEGAS

Away from Vegas, the mountains and lakes offer wonderful opportunities for outdoor recreation. Roadtrippers stop to gawk at the monumental engi-

IN RECENT NEWS

VEGAS FACES A LIQUID ASSETS SHORTAGE

Asked to support Venetian canals, ubiquitous gushing fountains, elaborate water ballets, and more than 1.5 million residents, all amid southern Nevada's dry desert surroundings, it comes as no surprise that water shortages plague the region. Despite the underground springs in the area, Las Vegas (Spanish for "the meadows") has not been heavily irrigated since prehistoric times. Explosive urban sprawl, coupled with a borderline abusive use of water at big-name casinos, is rapidly beginning to outstrip the supply of water allotted to Nevada by the states sharing the rushing Colorado River. Las Vegas's apportionment, which is the lowest of the states sharing the river, is a meager 300,000 acre-feet of water. With more than 5000 people moving to the area each month, the only conceivable solution may be to cut the ceaseless influx of residents. Southern Nevada is rapidly exhausting its stores of conserved water, forcing it to dip into reserves that neighboring Arizona does not yet need to rely on. Expanding Arizona urban areas make that solution less viable with each passing year. Experts are fearful that water restrictions may not solve the growing problem, and it is far from clear that a population accustomed to gluttonous water use is willing to change its ways.

neering of the Hoover Dam, boaters enjoy the strikingly blue waters of Lake Mead, and hikers and climbers test the pristine stone at Red Rocks and Mt. Charleston. Near Lake Mead, the Valley of Fire's arid Southwestern landscapes sizzle. While Las Vegas swelters, the higher elevations around it are cool, and the skiing is good in the winter. North of Vegas, 11,918 ft. Mt. Charleston offers temperate alpine climates even when Vegas swelters in 110°F heat. Should the urge to strap on some hiking shoes strike you, Mt. Charleston and Kyle Canyon can accommodate your desires. In early spring, the Mary Jane and Big Falls trail reveals awesome vistas of sublime Kyle Canyon and cascading waterfalls. The trailhead can be reached via Kyle Canyon Rd. (Rte. 157), and welcomes hikers to the 1.5 mi. trek that climbs 1000ft. For more experienced hikers, try the 11 mi. north loop that ascends to the peak of the mountain. At Mummy Mountain, visitors are treated to a panoramic view of the Vegas Valley, with Lake Mead in the distance. (Take U.S. 95 N out of Las Vegas and watch for the left turn into the park about 18 mi. out of town.)

RED ROCK CANYON

Just 20 mi. west of the Strip, the Red Rock Canyon National Conservation Area escarpment is a stupendous network of crimson sandstone bluffs and washes. From Vegas, take Charleston Blvd. (Rte. 159) west and continue for about 10min. until you reach the signs indicating the turn for the 197,000-acre park. You can either stick to the 13 mi. **scenic auto route** (open 6am-8pm; $5), or hike into the desert itself. Red Rocks is also one of America's premier **rock climbing** destinations, and hikers can watch the rock-jocks hang from the bluffs. An excellent **Visitors Center** introduces visitors to the myriad wonders of this flourishing desert ecosystem with interactive exhibits and guided walking tours. (☎363-1921. Open daily 8am-4:30pm during off-season; 8am-5pm during the summer.) The **campground ❶** is located off Rte. 159 near the Visitors Center, with picnic tables, grills, water, and toilets, but no hookups, for $10. For group site reservations call the Visitors Center. Backcountry camping and overnight climbing require permits. (☎647-5050. Free.) The most popular hikes are those through the washes of the first and second pullouts along the scenic road. **Pine Creek Canyon** also has short easy hikes.) At the base of Wilson Cliffs, **Spring Mountain Ranch State Park** houses a 520-acre historic ranch and scenic picnic sites. Each vehicle that enters the park is charged $5, and is granted access to the ranch (1pm-4pm daily) and the opportunity to follow guided tours (several per day, call 875-4141 for more details.)

HOOVER DAM

Built to subdue the flood-prone Colorado River after state leaders were given control over their stretch of the snaking waterway, this looming ivory monolith took 5000 men five years of seven-day weeks to construct. By the time of the dam's completion in 1935, 96 men had died. Their labor rendered over a 726 ft. colossus that now shelters precious agricultural land, pumps big voltage to Vegas and L.A., and furnishes a watery playground amid the sagebrush and mountains. Though the dam has altered the local environment, it is a spectacular engineering feat, especially given the comparatively primitive state of heavy excavation equipment at the time of its construction. The scaled-down tours and interpretive center explore the dam's history. (☎294-3510. Take U.S 93/95 south 18mi. from Las Vegas. Head east 4mi. on U.S. 93 until you get to the winding dam road. Open daily 9am-5pm; exhibits close at 5pm. Self-guided tours with short presentations $10, seniors $8, ages 7-16 $4. Parking on the Nevada side costs $5; free on the Arizona side.)

LAKE MEAD

When the Colorado River met the Hoover Dam Lake Mead was formed. This 100 mi. oasis became the unlikely location for the country's first national recreation area. Take Lake Mead Blvd. (Rte. 147) east 14 mi. There is a $5 fee to enter the recreation area. Follow Rte. 147 to Rte. 167, which frames the western shore of the lake, shuttling visitors from Boulder Beach in the south to Overton in the north.

First-time visitors to the lake will benefit from a trip to the **Alan Bible Visitors Center**, 4 mi. east of Boulder City, and its informative brochures and maps. (☎293-8990. Open daily 8:30am-4:30pm.) For maps and abundant information about area services, pick up the *Desert Lake View* at one of the several ranger stations dotting Lake Mead's shores. Backcountry hiking and camping is permitted in most areas. Hunters can target deer and bighorn sheep in season, and should contact the **Nevada Division of Wildlife** (NDOW; ☎486-5121) for information on obtaining licences and information on firearm restrictions. Those interested in casting their line can expect bites from large striped bass, and the area around Boulder Beach is promising. Despite these other diversions, Lake Mead is sustained by the multitude of weekend adventurers driving white pickup trucks with jet skis in tow. For those who come unprepared, boats and other watercraft can be rented at the various concessionaires along the shores. **Boulder Beach** is accessible by Lakeshore Dr., off U.S. 93. (☎800-752-9669. Jet skis $50 per hr., $270 per day; fishing boats $55 per 4hr., $100 per day.)

Alongside the Park Service **campsites ❶** ($10), concessionaires usually operate RV parks (most of which have become mobile home villages), marinas, restaurants, and occasionally motels. More remote concessionaires, including **Echo Bay Resort ❺**, offer motel and camping options. (☎800-752-9669. Singles overlooking lake $85; doubles $100; hookups $18.) Its restaurant, **Tale of the Whale ❶**, is decorated in nautical motifs, furnishes glimpses of Lake Mead, and cooks up $6 burgers and numerous daily specials. The resort rents jet skis ($50 per hr., $270 per day) and fishing boats ($30 for 2hr., $75 per day).

Northwest of Lake Mead, brilliantly colored rocks come alive in striking formations at the **Valley of Fire.** The robust crimson sandstone evokes landscapes usually associated with southwestern Utah. Rte. 169 bisects the park and leads to the extensive exhibits and short films on display at the **Visitors Center.** (☎397-2088. Open daily 8:30am-4:30pm.) Hiking areas are prevalent, and there are many sites with ancient petroglyphs. Campgrounds at the western end of the park near **Atlas Rock ❶** offer 51 sites. ($13, with showers, water, and toilets; no hookups.) The most direct route to the park from Las Vegas carries you north along I-15 for 45mi. Head east on Rte. 169 for 10mi. and enter the park for a $5 fee.

EAST CENTRAL NEVADA

Nearly 200 mi. south of Interstate 80 and 250 mi. north of Las Vegas, amid desert vegetation, the Snake Range, containing the highest peaks of the Basin and Range province, rises from the scrub. Due to the area's continued obscurity, the mining town of Ely and the backcountry of Great Basin National Park remain relatively undisturbed by the West's droves of summer tourists.

ELY   ☎775

With nearly 70 lonely mi. of U.S. 6 separating Ely and the entrance to Great Basin National Park, this mining and gaming town hardly fits the profile of a typical "gateway" city. However, its barren surroundings make Ely the locus of west-cen-

NEVADA

tral Utah and east-central Nevada traffic. Development of the area's copper resources brought the county seat, an influx of residents, and a railroad system. Ely is still a mining town, however, though it has recently adapted to its new role as a crossroads for visitors in search of the West's many treasures.

■■ **ORIENTATION AND PRACTICAL INFORMATION. U.S. 6, 50,** and **93** meet in Ely and radiate towards Reno, Vegas, Utah, Idaho, and California. Most **gas stations** lie along these arteries. Restaurants, shops, banks, historic casinos, and countless budget motels line Ely's Autland St., the downtown extension of U.S. 93 S. **Nevada Express,** 426 Campton St., across from Sacred Heart Catholic Church (☎775-289-2877, M-F 7:30am-5:30pm), runs round-trip buses to Vegas (every Tu and F; one-way $47, round-trip $84.) You'll need a car to travel from Ely to **Great Basin National Park** (p. 208) or surrounding areas. For tourist info, visit the **White Pine County Chamber of Commerce,** at 636 Autland St. (☎289-8877. Open M-F 9am-5pm; for info on weekends, visit the Hotel Nevada.) **Ely Ranger District,** 350 E. 8th St., provides info on the Humboldt National Forests near Ely and Great Basin National Park. Other services include: **William Bee Ririe Hospital,** 1500 Ave. H (☎289-3001); **free Internet access** at White Pine County Library, 900 Campton St. (☎289-3737; open M-Th 9am-6pm, F 9am-5pm, every other Sa 10am-2pm); and the **post office,** 415 5th St., at Clark (☎289-4537; window open M-F 10am-3pm). **ZIP code:** 89301.

■■ **ACCOMMODATIONS AND FOOD.** many of Ely's 21 hotels are located on Aultman St. The **Hotel Nevada ❶,** 501 Aultman St., a downtown hot spot, has 13 dirt-cheap rooms available (singles $20, doubles $25). These rooms go extremely fast and normal rates approach $40 for a single. (☎888-406-3055. Reserve ahead to ensure the cheap rate.) Down Aultman, the **Rustic Inn ❶,** 1555 Aultman St., has gleaming white towels and clean, wood-paneled rooms looked over by friendly owners. (☎289-6797. Singles $25-30, doubles $37+.) **La Fiesta ❶** prepares a succulent selection lunch specials ($5.75-6.25), all served with rice and beans. (☎289-4112. Open daily 11am-10pm, lunch specials 11am-3pm.) Aultman St. has several steak-and-potatoes chow-houses, including downtown casinos. Gigantic **Gorman's Market,** 1689 E. 7th St., fulfills supermarket needs. (☎289-3444. Open daily 7am-10pm.)

GREAT BASIN NATIONAL PARK   ☎775

Established in 1986, Great Basin National Park preserves ancient glaciers, prehistoric pine trees, a diverse fauna, and miles of unrefined trails. As the only national park fully within Nevada's borders, Great Basin borrows its name from one of the state's most salient features. The basin area extends through much of Nevada, and is so named because no precipitation falling in the region reaches the ocean. Eastern Nevada's Snake Range forms the spine of the park, with various creeks, lakes, and forest spreading out from its peaks. Despite the apparent desolation of the area's vast desert stretches, high alpine areas created by the towering ranges support a surprising variety of diverse biological communities. Great Basin National Park shelters rare species from the ancient bristlecone pine to the mountain lion. Located far from any major metropolitan area, Great Basin allows visitors to explore its natural richness in peace.

■■ **ORIENTATION AND PRACTICAL INFORMATION**

Tucked away quietly in eastern Nevada, Great Basin National Park lies 243 mi. from **Salt Lake City** (see p. 238) and 74 mi. from **Ely** (see p. 207), its nearest Nevada

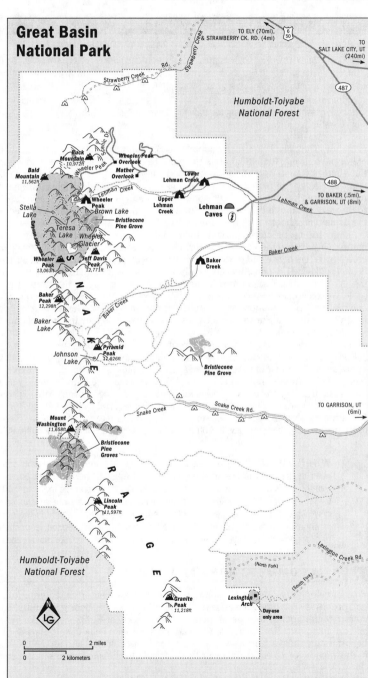

Great Basin
National Park

TO ELY (70mi),
& STRAWBERRY CK. RD. (4mi)

6
50

TO
SALT LAKE CITY, UT
(240mi)

Strawberry Creek

Rd.

Strawberry Creek

487

Humboldt-Toiyabe
National Forest

Wheeler Peak
Scenic Dr.

Buck
Mountain
10,972ft

Wheeler Peak
Overlook

Mather
Overlook

Lower
Lehman Creek

488

Bald
Mountain
11,562ft

Wheeler Peak

Lehman Creek

Upper
Lehman
Creek

Lehman
Caves

TO BAKER (.5mi),
& GARRISON, UT (8mi)

Lehman Creek

Wheeler
Peak

Brown Lake

Stella
Lake

Bristlecone
Pine Grove

Teresa
Lake

Wheeler
Glacier

Baker Creek

Davis Creek

Wheeler
Peak
13,063ft

Jeff Davis
Peak
12,771ft

Baker
Creek

S

Baker
Peak
12,298ft

N

Baker Creek

Baker
Lake

A

Johnson
Lake

Pyramid
Peak
11,926ft

K

Bristlecone
Pine Grove

E

Snake Creek

Snake Creek Rd.

TO GARRISON, UT
(6mi)

Mount
Washington
11,658ft

Bristlecone
Pine
Groves

R

A

Lincoln
Peak
11,597ft

N

Humboldt-Toiyabe
National Forest

G

E

Lexington Creek Rd.

(North Fork)

(South Fork)

Granite
Peak
11,218ft

Lexington
Arch

Day-use
only area

N
LG

0   2 miles

0   2 kilometers

NEVADA

AT A GLANCE: GREAT BASIN NATIONAL PARK	
AREA: 77,100 acres.	**GATEWAY TOWNS:** Ely (p. 207), Baker.
FEATURES: Wheeler Peak, Lehman Caves, Bristlecone Pine Groves.	**CAMPING:** Park campgrounds $10; backcountry camping free, no permit required.
HIGHLIGHTS: Touring the Grand Palace Room in Lehman Caves, hiking to the summit of Wheeler Peak, hiking the Baker Lake Trail.	**FEES:** No entrance fee, admission to Lehman Caves $2-8.

neighbor. The park lies directly south of U.S. 6/50 off Rte. 487 and 488. Only one major paved road, **Rte. 488,** enters the park, in the northeast corner, and leads to the Visitors Center and all four developed campgrounds. Improved gravel roads grant access to the park's northern and eastern edges, and a high-clearance dirt road ventures into the park's wild southern mountains. Ely bills itself as a gateway to the park, although the small town of **Baker** (5 mi. from the Visitors Center) and the **Border Inn** (about 11 mi. from the park on U.S. 6/50) also provide basic services.

As any trip to a national park should, a visit to Great Basin begins with a informational foray into the Visitors Center. The **Great Basin National Park Visitors Center** greets travelers at the end of Rte. 488 with a bookstore, cafe, theater, and park info desk. (☎234-7331. Open June-Aug. daily 7am-6pm; Sept.-May 8:30am-5pm.) Hunting, ATV use, or possession of firearms and fireworks are not permitted in the park. **Backcountry camping** does not require a permit, but the park recommends completing a backcountry registration form at the Visitors Center before beginning your trek. The Forest Service prohibits pets on trails or in the backcountry, and dogs must be leashed while in campgrounds. Mountain bikers can pedal any of the park's developed roads but are excluded from the trail system.

Because the park is still relatively new, on-grounds facilities remain in a developmental stage; most of the nearest available services are in Baker. The **Border Inn** (see p. 210) offers non-guest showers ($3), a convenience store, a greasy-spoon diner, and the only gas between Ely and Delta, UT (10¢ per gallon more expensive than standard prices). The nearest comprehensive **medical facility** is 70 mi. away in Ely, although the Park Service is prepared to conduct emergency rescues. The **post office** is also in Baker (open M-F 8:30am-4:30pm, Sa 8:30-11:30am). **ZIP code:** 89311.

WHEN TO GO. Because of its elevation, Great Basin remains tolerably cool, even in the thick of the summer; in July and August, the two most popular months to visit, highs hover in the mid-80s. Winter highs average in the low 40s with lows in the 10s and 20s. Due to low visitor turnout and weather restrictions, only Lower Lehman Campground remains open year-round. Although the park rarely experiences significant crowding, visitors in the off season, especially backcountry skiers, have the entire park as their personal outdoor playground.

 ## ACCOMMODATIONS AND CAMPING

Four developed campsites accommodate Great Basin visitors in addition to several primitive sites along Snake and Strawberry Creeks and nearly unlimited backcountry camping. All four developed campgrounds cost $10 per night per vehicle and are filled on a first-come, first-served basis. **Wheeler Peak Campground ❶** (9890 ft.) offers the most scenic sites, nestled among aspen groves and alpine meadows in the shadow of 13,000 ft. Wheeler Peak. Access to the sites comes at the end of the serpentine Wheeler Peak Scenic Drive, a road not recommended for vehicles over 24 ft. (37 sites, 1 wheelchair accessible. Open June-Sept. Pit toilets and potable water.) Following the graded gravel road south from Rte. 488 leads to **Baker Creek Campground ❶** (7530 ft.), a serene spot perched on the banks of Baker Creek. (32 sites, 2 with wheelchair access. Open May-Oct. Pit toilets and potable water.) **Upper** (24 sites, 1 site with wheelchair access; open May-Oct., try sites 17-24 for a more removed and spacious stay) and **Lower** (11 sites; open year-round) **Lehman Creek Campgrounds ❶,** close to the Visitors Center and Lehman Caves, guard the banks of Lehman Creek along the first 3 mi. of the Wheeler Mountain Scenic Drive. Both campgrounds tend to crowd quickly, so plan on arriving early. Both sites have pit toilets and potable water. Both Upper Lehman and **Wheeler Creek** Campgrounds host informational evening ranger talks during summer months. Scenic **primitive camping ❶,** which offers pre-dug fire pits, rewards the visitor willing to travel gravel roads off the beaten path. **Snake Creek Rd.,** 5 mi. south of Baker along Rte. 487, follows the fertile watershed Snake Creek area and allows easy access to six primitive sites. **Strawberry Creek Rd.,** 3.2 mi. from the U.S. 50/6 and Rte. 487 junction, leads to four primitive sites along Strawberry Creek.

Motels are rare, but the **Border Inn ❷,** straddling the UT/NV border along U.S. 50/6, proffers sizeable rooms with miniature TVs and VCRs. (☎ 234-7300. Singles $31-33.) For four walls and a mattress somewhat closer to the mountains, try the **Silver Jack Motel ❸,** at 14 Main St. in Baker. (☎ 234-7323. Singles $37-42.)

⬛ FOOD

Catering to those unwilling to trek to Baker or beyond, the **Lehman Caves Cafe ❶,** at the Visitors Center, serves breakfast items ($3), deli sandwiches ($5), and ice cream, while also peddling all variety of national park memorabilia. (Open Apr.-Oct. same hours as Visitors Center.) For a more substantial menu, check out **T&D's ❶** restaurant, bar, and convenience store in Baker. (☎ 234-7264. Restaurant open F-M 7am-8:30pm, Tu-Th 11am-8:30pm; bar 11am until everyone leaves; store daily 8am-6:30pm.) The store stocks grocery and camping essentials, and the restaurant serves deli sandwiches ($4.50), burgers ($3.75-6), pizza, breakfasts ($3-4; Th-Su), and country favorites like chicken fried steak ($7-9).

⬛ SIGHTS

Because much of it remains undeveloped, exploring the far reaches of the park requires a good pair of hiking boots, plenty of water, several days of food, and strong legs. Luckily for those not enthusiastic about hauling a 60 lb. pack through the backcountry, the park's most notable features, **Wheeler Peak, Bristlecone Groves, Lexington Arch,** and **Lehman Cave,** are accessible by car or a combination of car and short hike. For the experienced spelunker, the park contains extensive limestone caves. Exploring these caves requires a permit from the Park Service, acquired two weeks in advance and with proof of significant prior caving experience. Mountain bikers, in addition to riding park roads, will relish excellent riding at the BLM's **Sacramento Pass Recreation Site,** east of the park along U.S. 50/6.

LEHMAN CAVE

Absalom Lehman discovered these splendid caves in 1885, and by the turn of the century he was charging visitors for the pleasure of exploring them by candlelight. They continue to delight travelers. The Park Service prohibits self-guided tours, offering three varieties of **guided tours:** entrance into the first room only (30min.; $2, under 12 free), a tour of three of the four rooms (1hr.; $6; under 12 $3), and a tour of the spectacular **Grand Palace Room** (1½hr.; $8, under 12 $4). The cave

OH $#&%!!! The dendrochronologist's worst nightmare: meticulously counting the rings on a tree you've just cut down only to discover that you've killed the world's oldest living organism. Such a disaster occurred in 1964 when a researcher cut and sectioned a Great Basin bristlecone pine that had been growing on the side of Mt. Wheeler for 4900 years. These gnarled trees grow far apart from one another and often look dead or dying. Their sporadic spacing protects them from lightning-induced fires, as trees remain far enough from each other to prevent a blaze from spreading. Their lifeless appearance stems from their irregular growing cycles. During wet years, the bristlecone develops as any other tree would, thickening its girth and sending out new shoots. Unlike other trees, however, the bristlecone stops growing entirely during dry years, an ability that allows the tree to conserve resources. This ability to slip into stasis gives the ancient trees their battered, dying look. Understanding this growth/stasis cycle and measuring the width of bristlecone rings has provided vital climatological data about the past 4500 years. Scientists continue to study the trees to learn about ancient climates, but, learning from their colleague's folly, they now use core-sampling as an alternative to cutting and sectioning.

remains a cool 50°F, refreshing on the shorter tours, but chilly for the Grand Palace tour. (☎234-7331, advanced tickets ext. 242. Tours frequent during June-Aug. 8am-4:30pm; 4 per day Sept.-May 9am-3:30pm. Reservations recommended during summer. No children under 5 permitted on the Grand Palace tour.)

LEXINGTON ARCH
A mammoth, six-story limestone arch protected by the park's southeast corner, Lexington Arch provides evidence of nature's powerful craftsmanship. To experience this sublime sculpture, travel south 10.7 mi. from Baker, through Garrison, UT, to the sign for Lexington Arch. Follow the rough, high-clearance dirt road 12 mi. to the parking area and then grab water, some food for the road, and sunscreen for a 1.7 mi. one-way hike, rising 820 ft. to the base of the Arch.

BRISTLECONE PINE GROVE
The Great Basin Bristlecones, gnarled but beautiful trees, are the world's oldest living organisms (see **Oh $#&%!!!**, p. 212). Bristlecones demonstrate the extremes of biological adaptation to harsh environments; the trees regularly grow high on mountain slopes where no other trees can survive by deadening themselves until more hospitable times allow it to flourish. Although there are several Bristlecone groves throughout the park, the grove below Wheeler Peak offers the easiest access. Follow the Wheeler Peak Scenic Drive to the end and take the trail (2.8 mi. round-trip) from **Bristlecone Trailhead** to the famous trees. Ranger-guided tours of the grove depart from the trailhead at 10am daily during the summer.

◢ OUTDOOR ACTIVITIES

WHEELER PEAK SCENIC DRIVE
Beginning just down the hill from the Visitors Center, the Wheeler Peak Scenic Drive winds 12 mi. through changing biological communities and climates to 10,000 ft. to Laden with sharp curves and switchbacks, the road demands careful driving and takes 20-30min. one-way. As the road climbs, it passes first through greasebrush and sagebrush, then piñon pines and junipers, then ponderosa pines, white fir, and mountain mahogany, and finally through spruce, limber pine, and

high alpine aspen groves. As late as June, snowbanks line the summit area, and make the warm desert weather at the base a pleasant memory. **Mather Overlook** and **Wheeler Peak Overlook** furnish awe-inspiring views of jagged Wheeler Peak and Wheeler Glacier. The scenic drive also serves various campgrounds, trailheads, and interpretive hikes, but is closed during the winter months.

DAY HIKING

Several trails along the Wheeler Peak Scenic Drive grant ample opportunities to peel off the car seat and stretch weary legs. For a less crowded jaunt, try the longer trails departing from the Baker Creek Trailhead.

Mountain View Nature Trail (0.3 mi. round-trip; 30min.). Beginning behind the Visitors Center, this trail provides a brief glimpse into park biology and geology for those pressed for time. Stop in the Visitors Center for the informative trail guide.

Alpine Lakes Loop Trail (2.7 mi. round-trip; 1½-2½hr.). This gradual climb (600 ft. elevation gain) on a heavily used trail allows quick approach to 2 scenic lakes, Stella and Teresa. Trailhead located at the end of Wheeler Peak Scenic Drive.

Wheeler Peak Trail (8.6 mi. round-trip; 5-8hr.). From the trailhead parking lot near the top of the scenic drive, this strenuous trek (elevation gain 3000 ft.) follows the precipitous ridgeline, affording endless views east and west. Because of the afternoon thunderstorm threat, hikers should start early and bring warm clothing and raingear. Expert hikers ought to be careful of altitude sickness and rapidly changing weather conditions.

Baker Lake Trail (12 mi. round-trip; 6-9hr.). This saunter to pristine Baker Lake is for the ambitious day-hiker. The trail begins at the Baker Lake Trailhead at 8000 ft. and climbs gradually to 10,620 ft. Few attempt the long haul, creating backcountry solitude along a well-marked trail. The hike can also be done as a 2-day up-and-back overnight trip.

Lehman Creek Trail (7 mi. round-trip; 4-6 hr.). The only day hike set aside for year-round use, this uphill jaunt hugs a babbling creek for much of its course. Trail can be accessed at either Wheeler Peak or one of the Lehman campgrounds.

BACKPACKING

Southern stretches of the park offer countless possible wilderness routes for the experienced hiker. There are no trails south of Snake Creek, and proficient map and compass skills should accompany any expedition into this area. Since much of the backcountry ventures above 9000 ft., snow cover prevents passage for most of the year. North of Snake Creek and in the Mt. Moriah Wilderness across U.S. 50/6 from the park, several well-trodden routes offer options for the less experienced.

Baker Lake/Johnson Lake Loop (13.1 mi. round-trip; 2-3 days). Beginning at the Baker Lake trailhead (8000 ft.), this hike travels to Baker Lake and over a high ridge (11,290 ft.) to Johnson Lake. Both lakes offer solitude and scenic camping. Signs and indications of frequent travel mark the way, with the exception of the steep climb between Baker and Johnson Lakes, where it's everyone for themselves over the ridge. A variant of this loop travels from Baker Lake up the south gorge of Baker Peak (12,298 ft.) and along the knife-like ridgeline to Wheeler Peak.

Hendry's Creek Trail (11 mi. round-trip; 2-3 days). Located in the expansive Mt. Moriah Wilderness, this popular trail climbs from 7000 ft. to the summit of Mt. Moriah (12,050 ft.). A major draw of this trek is the possibility for some truly scenic alpine camping on the **Table** (11,000 ft.), an immense, flat meadow offering spectacular views of the Snake Range and a small grove of bristlecones. For access, follow "Forest Access" signs off U.S. 50/6, past the Rte. 487/U.S. 50 junction.

NEVADA

I-80: THE NORTHERN CORRIDOR

Spanning 400 miles from Reno to Wendover, Interstate 80 is the lifeblood of northern Nevada, funneling commercial traffic and the occasional tourist from California to Utah and back again. Amtrak runs one train per day along this route, making scheduled stops in Winnemucca, Elko and Reno. Northern Nevada might not be the most hospitable and welcoming region of the Southwest, but the wild Ruby Mountains, the mind-blowing Black Rock Desert, and the cowboy culture of Elko are a few points of interest in the region.

RENO   ☎ 775

Reno, with its decadent casinos cradled by snowcapped mountains, captures both the natural splendor and capitalist frenzy of the West. Acting as the hub of northern Nevada's tourist cluster that includes nearby Lake Tahoe and Pyramid Lake, the self-proclaimed "biggest little city in the world" does a decent job of compressing the gambling, entertainment, and dining experience of Las Vegas into a few city blocks. Built as much around the allure of a quick buck as a quick break-up, the city rose to prominence as a celebrity destination where getting a divorce was easier than making a hard eight on the craps table. Whatever your reason for visiting, Reno continues to be the Sierra's alternative to Vegas, attracting gamblers who crave the rush of hitting it big without the theme-park distractions.

▐▀ TRANSPORTATION

Flights: Reno-Tahoe International Airport, 2001 E. Plumb Ln. (☎328-6400), on U.S. 395 at Terminal Way, 3 mi. southeast of downtown. Most major hotels have free shuttles for guests; otherwise, take bus #13. Taxis from downtown to the airport $9-11.

Trains: Amtrak, 135 E. Commercial Row (☎329-8638 or 800-872-7245). Ticket office open daily 8:30am-4:45pm. Arrive 30min. in advance to purchase tickets. One train per day travels to **Sacramento**, continuing on to **San Francisco** via bus.

Buses: Greyhound, 155 Stevenson St. (☎322-2970 or 800-231-2222), half a block from W. 2nd St. Open 24hr. Higher prices F-Su. To: **Las Vegas** (1 per day, $72, one-way express); **San Francisco** (17 per day, $30-33, one way).

Public Transportation: Reno Citifare (☎348-7433) serves the Reno-Sparks area. Main terminal at 4th and Center St. Runs daily 5am-7pm, although city center buses operate 24hr. Buses stop every 2 blocks, and service runs to the airport. $1.25, ages 6-18 90¢, seniors and disabled 60¢. Carson City, $3 one way.

Taxis: Yellow Cab, ☎355-5555. **Reno-Sparks Taxi Cab,** ☎333-3333.

Car Rental: Savers Rent-a-Car, 1201 Kietzke (☎786-6444 or 888-432-3455). 23+ with own liability insurance; can purchase collision insurance. Prices begin at $23 per day for 150 mi. of driving. Credit card or $300 cash deposit required. Open 8-7 daily.

✱ ℹ ORIENTATION AND PRACTICAL INFORMATION

Only 14 mi. from the California border and a 443 mi. desert sprint north of Las Vegas, Reno sits at the intersection of **I-80** and **U.S. 395,** which runs along the eastern slope of the Sierra Mountains and the scenic Truckee River. Scan West Coast papers or Internet travel sites for "gamblers' specials" on bus and plane fare—some even include casino credits.

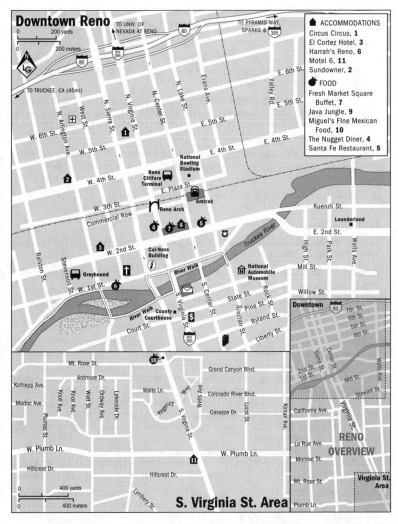

Downtown Reno

ACCOMMODATIONS
Circus Circus, 1
El Cortez Hotel, 3
Harrah's Reno, 6
Motel 6, 11
Sundowner, 2

FOOD
Fresh Market Square
Buffet, 7
Java Jungle, 9
Miguel's Fine Mexican
Food, 10
The Nugget Diner, 4
Santa Fe Restaurant, 5

S. Virginia St. Area

Most major casinos are "downtown" on Sierra and Virginia St., between 2nd and 4th St. The neon-lit streets of downtown Reno are heavily patrolled in summer, but **avoid walking alone** near the northeastern corner at night. Virginia St. south of the Truckee River has cheaper accommodations and good food, and is serviced by the #1 bus running from downtown Reno to the Meadowood Mall. In Sparks, which lies just to the northeast, several casinos line I-80. The *Reno/Tahoe Travel Planner*, available at the Visitors Center, contains a local map and is an excellent city guide. *The official drinking and gambling age is 21*, but enforcement varies.

Visitor Information: Reno-Sparks Convention and Visitors Center Cal-Neva Building, 100 N. Virginia St. (☎800-367-7366; www.playreno.com or www.renolaketahoe.com),

NEVADA

on the 2nd fl. of the Cal-Neva Building. Pamphlets, a Reno Historical Society exhibit, and the Reno-Sparks Chamber of Commerce on the 16th fl. Open daily 9am-5pm.

Quick Cash: ATMs in most casinos. Most charge $1.50 for out-of-state withdrawals.

Library: Downtown Reno Library, 301 S. Center St. (☎327-8300). Free public Internet access against the soothing backdrop of an indoor fountain. M-W 10am-8pm; Th-F 10am-6pm; Sa 10am-5pm; Su noon-5pm.

Marriage: Men and women over 18 (and those 16-17 with a parental OK) can pick up a marriage license at the **Courthouse,** 75 Court St. (☎328-3274), for $50 (cash)—all you need is a partner and an ID. Open daily 8am-midnight, including holidays. Numerous chapels in Reno are eager to help you tie the knot.

Divorce: To obtain a divorce permit, you must be a resident of NV for at least 6 weeks and pay a $150 fee. Permits are available at the courthouse divorce office M-F 8am-5pm; an uncontested divorce may take up to 4 months. Call 328-3535 for info.

Laundromat: Launderland & Coin-op Laundry, 680 E. 2nd St. (☎329-3733). Wash $1.75-$4.50, drying is free. Open daily 7am-10:00 pm; last load 9:00pm.

Road Conditions: ☎877-687-6237.

24hr. Crisis Lines: General Counseling and Rape Crisis, ☎800-992-5757. **Compulsive Gamblers Hotline,** ☎800-522-4700.

Medical Services: St. Mary's Hospital, 235 W. 6th St. (☎770-3000; emergency ☎770-3188), near Arlington Ave. 24hr.

Post Office: 50 S. Virginia St. (☎786-5936). Open M-F 8:30am-5pm, Sa 10am-2pm, to pick up packages only. **ZIP code:** 89501.

▛ ACCOMMODATIONS

While weekend prices at casinos are usually on the high side, gambler's specials, weekday rates, and off-season discounts provide some great, cheap rooms. Prices fluctuate, so call ahead. **Silver Legacy ❸,** 407 N. Virginia St. (☎800-687-7733), **Circus Circus ❹,** 500 N. Sierra St. (☎329-0711), and **Sundowner ❸,** 340 N. Arlington Ave. (☎786-7050), have been known to offer good deals to go along with their central locations and massive facilities. (Rates can get as low as $32, but they generally hover around $50 for a single.)

Be advised—heterosexual prostitution is legal in most of Nevada (though not in Reno itself), which may be reflected by certain motels being cheap but lacking a particularly wholesome feel. The prices below don't include Reno's **12% hotel tax.**

Harrah's Reno, 219 N. Center St. (☎800-427-7247). A Reno staple, Harrah's provides big, clean rooms in a central downtown location. Two towers of rooms, six restaurants, an arcade, and a health club leave little to be desired. The casino attracts large crowds and houses Planet Hollywood's Reno branch, a great place to grab a mixed drink. Call ahead for rates/availability. Singles, doubles M-Th start at $49; F-Su $89. ❺

Fitzgerald's Casino/Hotel, 255 N. Virginia St. (☎1-800-535-5825). Resting at the base of the Reno arch, this 351-room hotel/casino offers cheap, clean rooms right at the heart of the city. Airport shuttle service ($2.65) and free valet parking for guests. S-Th $30; F-Sa $50. ❸

Circus Circus, 500 N. Sierra St. (☎329-0711 or 800-648-5010). Entertainment for all ages can be found in this 1500 room family hotel and casino. Acres of casinos, restaurants, a new workout room, carnival activities, and a real live big top. Rooms are large, posh, and quiet. Call for discounts. Su-Th from $34, F-Sa from $60. ❹

Motel 6 1901 S. Virginia St. (☎827-0255), 1½ mi. down Virginia St. at Plumb Ln. Though a short hike from downtown Reno, this chain offers neat, comfortable rooms and HBO, pool access, and laundry facilities. Smoking and non-smoking quarters available. Singles June-Sept. Su-Th $40; F-Sa $50; Oct.-May $36/$45. ❸

El Cortez Hotel, 239 W. 2nd St. (☎322-9161). 116-room downtown hotel. A/C, cable TV, exposed pipes, and thin walls. Singles Su-Th $29, F-Sa $38; doubles $43/$49. ❷

El Dorado Motel, 1607 S. Virginia St. (☎323-6055). Not to be confused with the downtown hotel giant, this no-frills option has tiny, sparsely decorated rooms which are clean enough. HBO, no A/C. Singles Su-Th $30; F-Sa $40; more expensive on holidays. ❷

CAMPGROUNDS

Campers can make the drive to the woodland campsites of **Davis Creek Park ❶**, 17 mi. south on U.S. 395, then follow the signs ½ mi. west. (☎849-0684. Open daily 8am-9pm, but campers can self-pay at the gates at any time of day. Free picnic area open daily 8am-9pm, complete with volleyball courts and a trout-packed Ophir Creek Lake. Sites $13, each additional car $5; pets $1; showers and toilets on site.) After camping at the base of Slide Mountain, visitors can hike its Ophir trail, which ascends over 4,000 ft. to meet the Tahoe Rim Trail. The difficult climb is 6.1 mi. each way. You can also camp along the shore at **Pyramid Lake** (see p. 229). To stay closer to Reno, park and plug in your RV overnight at **KOA ❶**, 2500 E. 2nd St. (☎1-888-562-5698. Hookups $29), right near the Reno Hilton. Campers receive access to the Hilton's pool. Call ahead for availability.

FOOD

Food prices in Reno are low, but the quality doesn't have to be. Casinos offer a wide range of all-you-can-eat buffets and 99-cent breakfasts. Buffet fare can be greasy and overcooked, but you can find a good combination of quality and cost. Escaping the ubiquitous buffets is worthwhile, as inexpensive eateries provide Mexican and Basque food.

Miguel's Fine Mexican Food, 1415 S. Virginia St. (☎322-2722). Miguel's Mexican fare is praised by locals and critics alike. A substantial lunch menu ($6-9) offers delicious food in handsome servings. The taquitos ($3) and sopapillas (3 for $1) are scrumptious. Entrees $5-10. Open Su noon-8pm; Tu-Th 11am-9pm; F-Sa 11am-10pm. ❷

Fresh Market Square Buffet (☎786-3232), 2nd fl. in Harrah's. Prime rib, crab legs, and shrimp run along the numerous buffet tables. In addition to the cooked-to-order prime cut of beef, diners can sample Asian cuisine, pizza, traditional American fare, and desserts. Breakfast buffet $7, lunch $7, dinner $11. Champagne brunch Sa-Su 8am-2pm $11. Open M-F 7am-2pm and 4-9pm, Sa-Su 8am-2pm and 4-9pm. ❸

Santa Fe Restaurant, 235 Lake St. (☎323-1891), in the Santa Fe Hotel, in the heart of downtown. When the Basques migrated from the Pyrenees, they brought their cuisine with them. Hearty, Americanized portions are served up family-style. Oxtail, beef tongue, and pigs feet alternate as side dishes, while top sirloin steak, chicken, and pork chops are mainstays. Lunch $11. 7-course dinner $15. Open daily 11am-2pm and 6-9pm. ❸

Java Jungle, 246 West 1st St. (☎329-4484), just past West St., along the river. The fun jungle theme exudes from its pores with numerous plants and giraffe prints. Enjoy your coffee ($1.25), espresso or sandwich ($5) on the outdoor patio in view of Wingfield Park. For $1.75, the Italian sodas are a great way to cool off in the summer: choose from over 30 flavors. Open Su-Th 6am-11pm; F-Sa 7am-midnight; extended summer hours. ❶

The Nugget Diner, 233 N. Virginia St. (☎ 323-0716), Treat yourself at this crowded greasy spoon in the back of the tiny Nugget Casino. The "Awful Awful" burger comes with all the trimmings and heaps of fries for only $3.50. Breakfast, served all day, is cheap and fast. Open M-Tu 7am-11pm, W-Su 7am-4am. ❶

🎵 ENTERTAINMENT

Reno is a big adult amusement park. Many casinos offer free gaming lessons; minimum bets vary between establishments. Drinks are usually free if you're gambling, but alcohol's inhibition-dropping effects can make betting a bad experience. You cannot collect big winnings if you are under 21, so consider your jackpot a donation to the casino's coffers.

Almost all casinos offer live nighttime entertainment, but most shows are not worth the steep admission prices. **Harrah's,** however, is an exception, carrying on a dying tradition with it's **dinner shows** in Sammy's Showroom. Starting at $32.50, Harrah's offers dinner at one of its restaurants and a performance by headlining impersonator Gordie Browne, named "Entertainer of the Year" by the *Sacramento Bee.* At **Circus Circus,** 500 N. Sierra (☎ 329-0711), a small circus above the casino performs "big top" shows every ½ hr. These shows and others are listed in the weekly *Showtime. Best Bets* and *Fun & Gaming* provides listings of discounted local events and shows. The *Nevada Events & Shows* section of the Nevada visitors' guide lists sights, museums, and seasonal events. More info is in the *Reno Gazette-Journal* and *News & Review.*

There's far more to Reno than its casinos. In late November, Reno's **River Holiday and Festival of Trees** (☎ 334-2262 or 334-2414) uses the Truckee River Walk and the island setting of Wingfield Park to celebrate the holiday spirit. The park is decorated with lights and trees as artists sell their wares, performers entertain crowds, and children are treated to a visit from Santa.

Cultural events heat up in the summer, such as the popular five-year-old **Artown** festival (☎ 322-1538; www.artown.org), held every July for the entire month. The event features dance, jazz, painting, and basketry, and everything is free. In August, local Basque traditions, dancing, food, and music break through the seams of the blanketing casino culture at Reno's annual **Basque Festival** (☎ 787-3039).

The first week in August roars into chrome-covered, hot-rod splendor with **Hot August Nights** (☎ 356-1956), a celebration of classic cars and rock 'n' roll. The annual **Reno Rodeo** (☎ 329-3877), one of the biggest in the West, gallops over eight days in late June. In September, the **Great Reno Balloon Race** (☎ 826-1181), in Rancho San Rafael, and the **National Championship Air Races** (☎ 972-6663; www.airrace.org), at the Stead Airport, draw an international group of contestants who take to the sky as spectators look on. Also in September, nearby Virginia City hosts **Camel Races** (☎ 847-0311) during the weekend after Labor Day, in which camels and ostriches race through town.

LAKE TAHOE   ☎ 530/775

Tahoe's natural beauty attracts outdoor fanatics from across the globe, and its burgeoning entertainment and hotel industry eagerly supports their efforts. In a town without an off-season, visitors can revel in an array of activities from keno to kayaking. After roads were cut into the forested mountain terrain, new money arrived with casinos, summer homes, and motels. Now, everyone can enjoy Tahoe's pure blue waters, tall pines, and high-rises silhouetted by the deep auburn glow of the setting sun. An outdoor adventures's dream in any season, Tahoe has miles of biking, hiking, and skiing trails, long stretches of golden beaches, lakes stocked with fish, and many hair-raising whitewater activities.

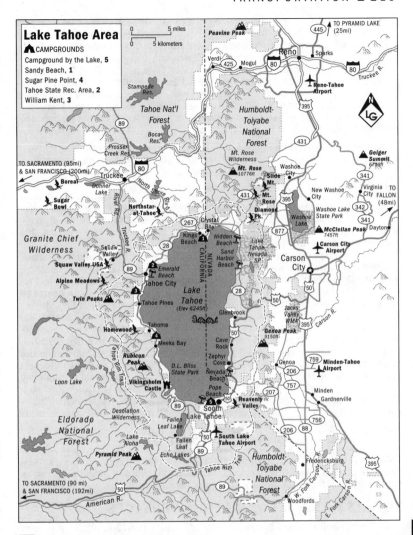

Lake Tahoe Area

▲ CAMPGROUNDS

Campground by the Lake, **5**
Sandy Beach, **1**
Sugar Pine Point, **4**
Tahoe State Rec. Area, **2**
William Kent, **3**

0 _____ 5 miles
0 _____ 5 kilometers

⊏ TRANSPORTATION

Buses: Greyhound, 3794 Montreal Rd. (☎530-543-1050 or 800-231-2222), in the Tahoe Colony Inn at the Raley's Shopping Center. To **San Francisco** (3 per day, $27-29) and **Sacramento** (3 per day, $21-23). Station open daily 8am-7pm.

Trains: Amtrak (☎800-USA-RAIL/872-7245) runs a bus from its San Joaquin and Capitol train routes to Pre-Madonna Casino off I-15 and Whiskey Pete's Casino in **Stateline, NV.** These trips are long and costly. Call for rates, which fluctuate greatly.

Public Transit: Tahoe Casino Express (☎800-446-6128) provides shuttle service between the Reno airport and South Shore Tahoe casinos (daily 6:15am-12:30am;

$19, round-trip $34, up to 2 children under 12 free). **Tahoe Area Regional Transport** or **TART** (☎550-1212 or 800-736-6365; www.laketahoetransit.com) connects the western and northern shores from Incline Village to Tahoe City to Tahoma (Meeks Bay in summer). Stops daily every hr. or half-hr. 6:30am-6pm, depending on the route. Buses also run out to Truckee and Squaw Valley several times per day. Exact fare required. $1.25, day pass $3. **South Tahoe Area Ground Express** or **STAGE** (☎541-6328) operates around South Tahoe and hourly to the beach. It connects Stateline and Emerald Bay Rd. $1.25, day pass $2, 10-ride pass $10. Most casinos operate free shuttle services along U.S. 50 to California ski resorts and motels. A summer bus program connects STAGE and TART at Meeks Bay 6am-midnight.

Car Rental: Enterprise (☎775-586-1077), in the Horizon lobby in Stateline, NV. Must be 21+ with credit card. From $41 per day, $199 per week with unlimited mileage.

◪ ORIENTATION

In the northern Sierra on the California-Nevada border, Lake Tahoe is a 4hr. drive from San Francisco. Lake Tahoe rests 118 mi. northeast of Sacramento and 35 mi. southwest of Reno on I-80. From the Carson City and Owens Valley area, **U.S. 395** runs north-south 20 mi. from Tahoe's eastern shore.

The lake is divided into two main regions, known as **North Shore** and **South Shore.** The **North Shore** includes Kings Beach, Tahoe City, Tahoe Vista, and Incline Village, while the **South Shore** has Emerald Bay, South Lake Tahoe City, and Stateline. Proclaimed "The Most Beautiful Drive in America," **U.S. 50** combines with **Routes 28 and 89** to form a 75 mi. asphalt ring around the lake; the complete winding, sloping loop takes nearly 3hr. Rte. 89 is also known as **West Lake Boulevard** and **Emerald Bay Road,** while Rte. 29 becomes **North Lake Boulevard** and **Lakeshore Drive** in Tahoe City and on the western shore, and **South Lake Tahoe Boulevard** turns into **Highway 50.**

Road conditions in Tahoe can be treacherous from September-May, when tire chains may be required and a 4WD vehicle is highly recommended. As Tahoe is a popular weekend destination, traffic is fierce on Friday afternoons and Sunday evenings. During winter, cars on the way to or from Tahoe City ski resorts pack the roads around 9am and 5pm. If there is road work near the small town of Tahoe City, forget trying to get there on either Rte. 28 or 89 from the South Shore.

◪ PRACTICAL INFORMATION

Tahoe is littered with tourist information and Visitors Centers, often with more than one in each town. Brochures offer valuable lodging and dining coupons, as well as information about Tahoe's thriving wilderness activities.

TOURIST AND INFORMATION SERVICES

US Forest Service Visitors Center, 870 Emerald Bay Rd. (☎573-2600), 2 blocks north of S. Lake Tahoe on Rte. 89. Supervises campgrounds and recreation trails. Mandatory wilderness permits for backcountry hiking available. Open M-F 8am-4:30pm.

Lake Tahoe Visitors Center (☎573-2674), 3 mi. north of South Lake Tahoe on Rte. 89. Hiking trailheads and detailed maps of the area. Sells permits for entering Desolation Wilderness. Camping fee $5 per person per night, $10 per person for 2 or more nights, $20 for 1-year pass. Under 12 free. Reservations ($5) are available for overnight permits June-Sept. Open daily 8am-5pm, with extended summer hours.

Visitor information: (☎573-2674). **Lake Tahoe/Douglas Chamber of Commerce,** 195 U.S. 50 (☎775-588-4591; www.tahoechamber.org), in Stateline, NV. Open daily 9am-5pm. **Tahoe North Visitor Resort Association,** 950 N. Lake Blvd. (☎583-3494). Staff helps with reservations. Open M-F 7am-9pm, Sa-Su 9am-3pm. **Incline Village and Crystal Bay Visitors Bureau,** 969 Tahoe Blvd. (☎800-GO-TAHOE/468-2463; www.gotahoe.com). Open M-F 8am-5pm, Sa-Su 10am-4pm.

LOCAL SERVICES

Banks: US Bank, 705 N. Lake Blvd. (☎583-2346), in Tahoe City. Open M-Th 9am-5pm, F 9am-6pm. **24hr. ATM. Bank of the West,** 2161 Lake Tahoe Blvd. (☎531-3390), in S. Lake Tahoe. Open M-Th 9am-5pm, F 9am-6pm, Sa 9am-1pm. 24hr. ATM.

Library and Internet Access: South Lake Tahoe Library, 1000 Rufus Allen Blvd. (☎573-3185). Open Tu-W 10am-8pm, Th-Sa 10am-5pm. **Tahoe City Library,** 740 N. Lake Blvd. (☎583-3382) Tu and Th-F 10am-5pm; W noon-7pm; Sa noon-4pm. Free.

Laundromat: The Big Tree Cleaners, 531 N. Lake Blvd. (☎583-2802), in Tahoe City. Wash $1.50, dry 25¢ for 10min. Open M-F 9am-6pm. **Uncle Bob's Laundromat,** 2180 Lake Tahoe Blvd. (☎542-1910), in S. Lake Tahoe. Wash $1.25-1.50, dry 25¢ for 8min. Open daily 7am-10pm.

EMERGENCY AND COMMUNICATIONS

Road Conditions: California ☎800-427-7623; Nevada ☎702-793-1313.

Police: Sheriff's offices are located at 1352 Johnson Blvd. (☎542-6100), in S. Lake Tahoe; 2501 N. Lake Tahoe Blvd. (☎581-6310), in Tahoe City.

Crisis Hotlines: General ☎800-992-5757. **Gamblers Anonymous** ☎583-8941. **Tahoe Women's Services** ☎546-3241.

Medical Services: Barton Memorial Hospital at 3rd St. and South Ave (☎541-3420), in S. Lake Tahoe. **Incline Village Community Hospital,** 880 Alder Ave. (☎775-833-4100, in Incline Village. **Tahoe Forest Hospital,** at Donner Pass Rd. and Pine Ave. (☎587-6011), in Truckee.

Post Office: Tahoe City, 950 N. Lake Blvd. #12 (☎800-275-8777), in the Lighthouse Shopping Center. Open M-F 8:30am-5pm, Sa noon-2pm. **Postal Code:** 96145. **South Lake Tahoe,** 212 Elk Point Rd. (☎588-5419). Open M-F 8:30am-5pm, Sa 10am-2pm. **Postal Code:** 96151.

 The area code for Lake Tahoe is **530** unless otherwise specified. The Nevada side is **775.**

▐ ACCOMMODATIONS

The strip off U.S. 50 on the California side of the border supports the bulk of the South Shore's motels. Particularly glitzy and cheap in South Lake Tahoe, motels also line the quieter area along Park Ave. and Pioneer Trail. The North Shore offers more woodsy accommodations along Rte. 28, but rates are especially high in Tahoe City, where lodgings are booked solid and well in advance for weekends and holidays at sky-high prices. Fall and spring are the most economical times of the year to visit Tahoe because of the off-season bargains. Look for discount coupons in newspapers. Nearby campgrounds are a good option in warmer months.

Tahoe City Inn, 790 N. Lake Blvd. (☎581-3333 or 800-800-8246; www.tahoecity-inn.com), next to Safeway in Tahoe City. Deluxe rooms sporting glass block walls, jacuzzis, and mini-fridges. Comfy queen beds, coffeemakers, and cable TV complete the package. Rooms with VCRs are more costly, but visitors get free access to extensive video library. Late Apr. to mid-June and late Sept.-late Nov. Su-Th $49, F-Sa $66; extra bed $10. Prices rise during peak season. ❹

Tamarack Lodge, 2311 N. Lake Tahoe Blvd. (☎583-3350 or 888-824-6323), 3 mi. north of Tahoe City, across from Star Harbor. Clean lodge in the woods. Outdoor BBQ and fireplace, phones, cable TV, and friendly management. Rooms from $44. ❸

Cedar Glen Lodge, 6589 N. Lake Blvd. (☎546-4281 or 800-500-8246; www.cedarglen-lodge.com), in Tahoe Vista. Modest rooms complimented by numerous amenities. Private beach access, heated pool, and indoor and outdoor hot tub and sauna. Grounds include BBQ pits, playground, hammock, lots of flowers, and a tiny rabbit hutch. Morning newspaper and continental breakfast included. Cottages with kitchens also available. Open 8am-8:30pm. Singles from $65. ❹

Firelite Lodge, 7035 N. Lake Tahoe Blvd. (☎800-934-7222), in Tahoe Vista. Sleek, modern quarters complete with kitchenette, patio overlooking pool, and spa. Call ahead to reserve one of the 26 rooms. Open daily 8am-10pm. Singles in summer and winter from $59; off-season singles begin at $49. ❹

Doug's Mellow Mountain Retreat, 3787 Forest Ave. (☎544-8065), in S. Lake Tahoe. From the north turn left onto Wildwood Rd., and after 3 blocks take a left on Forest Ave.; it's the 6th house on the left. Easygoing Doug supplies a modern kitchen, BBQ, fireplace. Internet access $5 per. hr. Bedding included. No curfew, flexible checkout times. Dorms $15 per person; private rooms available. Discounts for stays over a week. ❶

Royal Inn, 3520 Lake Tahoe Blvd. (☎800-556-2500), in S. Lake Tahoe. Queen beds and desk space, along with a ton of cable TV channels. Continental breakfast, laundry facilities on premises. Singles Su-Th $35; doubles $59. Weekends and holidays see greatly inflated rates, but don't be bashful about mentioning that *Let's Go* brought you here—you may be handsomely rewarded. ❺

⛺ CAMPING

At its Visitors Center, the **US Forest Service** provides up-to-date information on camping (see **Tourist and Information Services,** p. 220). *North Tahoe Truckee This Week*, a free publication, prints info about grounds. **Route 89** is scattered with state campgrounds from Tahoe City to South Lake Tahoe. Campgrounds are often booked in July and August, so reserve well in advance; call the **National Recreation Reservation System** or **NRRS** (☎877-444-6777; www.reserveusa.com) for US Forest Service campgrounds, the **California Campground Reservation System** or **CCRS** (☎800-444-7275, outside California 619-452-1950) for California State Parks, or the **National Park Reservation System** (☎800-365-2267). The NRRS and CCRS charge a non-refundable reservation fee and ask for a credit card number. Backcountry camping is allowed in designated wilderness areas with a permit from the Forest Service (see **Tourist and Information Services,** p. 220). The only campground open year-round is **General Creek** ❶ in Sugar Pines State Park; all others are generally open from Memorial Day to Labor Day.

The 63,960 acres of **Desolation Wilderness** on the western side of Lake Tahoe are free of substantial human presence. Camping here is only for the experienced. The heavily protected area boasts glacial lakes and valleys, granite peaks, and sub-alpine forests that comprise some of the region's most breathtaking vistas. To maintain the grounds, Congress has introduced new permit costs and zoning regulations as part of the "Recreation Fee Demonstration Program." The **Granite Chief Wilderness** is a less traveled area. Next to the Alpine Meadows and Squaw Valley ski resorts, the wilderness overlooks the Lake Tahoe Basin. Visitors are free to day hike without a wilderness permit. Free campfire permits are required and issued by the US Forest Service (see **Tourist and Information Services**, p. 220). The **Mount Rose Wilderness,** one of the nation's newest, is located in the northeast area of the Lake Tahoe Basin (accessible via Rte. 431) and can be traversed without a permit.

> **Tahoe State Recreation Area** (☎ 583-3074), at the northeast end of Tahoe City on Rte. 28. 1 acre of land along the lake and road, with a long pier. Water, flush toilets, showers ($5). Open May-Nov. 38 sites $15-16; $1 per dog per day. ❶

> **Sandy Beach** (☎ 546-7682), off Rte. 28 in Tahoe Vista. Rocky soil beneath pine trees and adjacent to a sandy beach. Hookups, water, flush toilets, and showers. 44 very visible sites $15-20; pets $1.50 per day. ❷

> **Campground by the Lake** (☎ 542-6096), 1150 Rufus Allen Blvd., in S. Lake Tahoe. City-run campground operates over 160 sites on 35 acres, just across from beach and picnic areas. Free casino shuttle, showers and flush toilets included. Open April 1-Oct. 31. Sites $18; RV hookups $25; pets an additional $1. ❷

> **Sugar Pine Point State Park** (☎ 525-7982), on the west shore, 1 mi. south of Tahoma, and across Rte. 89, just a few mi. north of Meeks Bay. Popular grounds include tennis courts, cross-country ski trails, bike trails, nature center, the historic Ehrman mansion, and lakeside dock. Water, BBQ pits, and flush toilets. Hot showers 50¢. Open year-round. 175 sites $16; day use $2, seniors $1. ❷

> **William Kent** (☎ 583-3642), on Rte. 89, 2 mi. south of Tahoe City, is one of the most popular campgrounds on the west shore. Beach access across Rte. 89. Clean flush toilets and water. Open June-Labor Day. 92 sites $16. ❷

◪ FOOD

In the south, the casinos offer perpetually low-priced buffets, but bar and grilles and burger joints dot the lakeshore, promising reasonable prices, similarly large portions, and much better food. Groceries are cheaper on the California side. Try **Safeway,** in S. Lake Tahoe, at Lake Tahoe Blvd. and Johnson St. (open 24hr.), or in Tahoe City at 850 N. Lake Blvd. (open daily 7am-10pm). Alternatively, you could go *au naturel* at **New Moon Natural Foods** 505 W. Lake Blvd., just south of Tahoe City. (☎ 583-7426. Open M-F 10am-7pm, Sa-Su 10am-6pm.)

> **Lakehouse Pizza,** 120 Grove St. (☎ 583-2222), in Tahoe City. The kitchen turns out small but tasty pizzas from $9. Standard breakfast specials $3-7. California salad and sandwiches $7. Open M-Th 8am-10pm, F-Sa 8am-11pm. ❷

> **The Fire Sign Cafe,** 1785 W. Lake Blvd. (☎ 583-0871) 2 mi. south of Tahoe City, 100 yards south of TART stop. Big breakfasts served at this woodsy location. Large omelettes, complete with homefries and a muffin, for only $6. Look out for daily lunch deals. Open daily 7am-3pm. ❷

> **Fast Eddie's Texas-Style BBQ,** 690 N. Lake Blvd. (☎ 583-0950), in Tahoe City. The beef brisket ($15) takes 10hr. to cook, but you get it in 10min. Everything is slow-cooked with oak firewood, and you can taste the difference. Dinner entree prices run high, so try the juicy burgers ($7). Open daily 11am-10pm. ❸

> **Red Hut Waffles,** 2749 Lake Tahoe Blvd. (☎ 541-9024), and 227 Kingsbury Rd. (☎ 588-7488). Homestyle cooking. Waffle piled with fruit and whipped cream $5.75. Bottomless coffee $1.25. Open daily 6am-2pm. No credit cards. ❷

> **Sprouts Natural Foods Cafe,** 3123 Harrison Ave. (☎ 541-6969), at the intersection of Hwy. 50 and Alameda Ave. All-natural food in unnaturally large portions, this place keeps everyone satisfied. Try the breakfast burrito with avocados ($5), or the tasty smoothies ($3-3.75). Open daily 8am-10pm. ❶

NEVADA

🏔 OUTDOOR ACTIVITIES

SUMMER ACTIVITIES

BEACHES

Many beaches ring Lake Tahoe, providing the perfect setting for a day of sunning and people-watching. Parking generally costs $5; bargain hunters should leave cars in turnouts on the main road and walk to the beaches.

NORTH SHORE. Sand Harbor Beach, south of Incline Village, has gorgeous granite boulders and clear waters that attract swimmers, sunners, scuba divers, and boats to its marina. The parking lot ($5) is usually full by 11:30am. **Commons Beach Park,** in the heart of Tahoe City just off N. Lake Tahoe Blvd., contains a playgound for kids, an acre of beach for sunbathing, and access to lake waters for swimming. City planners intend to add a bike trail, more beach, and picnic areas. **Kings Beach** has volleyball nets, picnic tables with grills, a basketball court, and a playground. Jet-skis, sailboards, and kayaks can be rented at both beaches. Parasailing and waterskiing are also available.

SOUTH SHORE. Pope Beach, at the southernmost point of the lake off Rte. 89, is a shaded expanse of shoreline that becomes less trafficked on its east side. **Nevada Beach,** 3 mi. north of South Lake Tahoe, is close to the casinos off U.S. 50, offering a sagebrush sanctuary with a picturesque view of sun-kissed mountains. **Zephyr Cove Beach,** about 15 mi. north of South Lake Tahoe, has completely renovated its impressive facility, hosting a youthful crowd keen on beer, beaches, and bikinis. It is also the launch site for the famous M.S. Dixie II, which cruises the lake.

WEST SHORE. Meeks Bay, 10 mi. south of Tahoe City, is family-oriented, social, and equipped with picnic tables, volleyball, motorboat and kayak rental, camping areas, and a store. In summer, the Tahoe City and South Tahoe buses connect here. Five miles south of Meeks Bay, the **D.L. Bliss State Park**, 17 mi. south of Tahoe City on Rte. 89, has a large beach on the small Rubicon Bay. Stand atop Rubicon Point and peer into the crystalline lake. The trailhead of the Rubicon Trail leads to the peaceful Vikingsholm mansion. Parking here ($5) is very limited, so check at the Visitors Center at the entrance or look to park on the road and walk in. **Chambers Beach,** between Homewood and Tahoma, draws an energetic crowd of families and young hipsters who occupy the public volleyball courts. Visitors to **Emerald Bay** often marvel at the the scene. Circled by neat rows of green pines, the bay boasts the distinction of being named National Natural Landmark, and affords access to Vikingsholm and the "Tea House" on Fannette Island.

HIKING

Hiking is a great way to explore the Tahoe Basin. The Visitors Center and ranger stations provide detailed info and maps for all types of hikes. Backcountry users must obtain a wilderness permit from the US Forest Service (see **Tourist and Information Services,** p. 220) for any hike into the Desolation Wilderness; only 700 hikers are allowed in this area on any given day. Due to erratic weather conditions in the Sierra, hikers should always bring a jacket and drinking water. Buy a topographical map before you go and ask where the snow has (or has not) melted—it's not usually gone until July and finding a trail under a foot of hard snow is next to impossible. **Alpenglow Sport Shop,** 415 N. Lake Blvd., in Tahoe City, carries an array of equipment and sells great trail maps, but any found at the numerous outdoorsy stores are adequate. (☎ 583-6917. Open M-F 10am-6pm, Sa-Su 9am-6pm.)

After decades of work, the 165 mi. **Tahoe Rim Trail** has been completed, but upkeep and maintenance continues daily. The hiking trail encircles the lake, following the ridge tops of the Lake Tahoe Basin. Hiking is moderate to difficult, with an average grade of 10%. On the western shore, it is part of the Pacific Crest Trail. Trailheads abound throughout the region, so consult Visitors Centers for those nearest you. Frequently trafficked trailheads include Spooner Summit at the U.S. 50/Rte. 28 junction and Tahoe City off Rte. 89 on Fairway Dr.

NORTH SHORE. The **Granite Chief Wilderness,** behind Squaw Valley, is a great option; its rugged hiking trails and mountain streams wind through secluded forests and fields of wildflowers. The **Stateline Lookout,** running 0.5 mi., provides a knowledgeable staff and telescope views of the lake. From Rte. 28, go north on Reservoir Dr., make a right on Lakeshore, and a left on Forest Service Rd. 1601. Watch trout breed at Martis Creek Lake on the 3 mi. **Wildlife Creek Wildlife Area Loop,** just south of Truckee. Take Hwy. 267 9 mi. north from Kings Beach. The **Marlette Lake Trail** begins at Spooner State Park, NV, at the junction of U.S. 50 and Rte. 28. It leads 5 mi. through the moderately difficult terrain of the Tahoe Rim Trail from Spooner Lake to Marlette Lake. At 10,778 ft., **Mount Rose,** in the Toiyabe National Forest, is one of the tallest mountains in the region as well as one of the best climbs. (Info ☎ 775-882-2766. Open M-F 8am-4:30pm.) The 6 mi. trek starts out as an easy dirt road hike but becomes a rocky scramble after mile three. Take Rte. 431 from Incline Village to the trailhead, which is 1 mi. south of the summit.

SOUTH SHORE. The southern region of the basin offers many moderate to strenuous hiking trails. Many visitors find the picturesque **Emerald Bay** to be an essential stop and photo opportunity. This crystal-clear pocket of the lake embraces Tahoe's only island and most photographed sight—tiny, rocky Fannette. The alpine lakes and dramatic waterfalls make this a mini-paradise. **Emerald Bay State Park,** which connects to the Desolation Wilderness, offers hiking and biking trails of varying difficulty, camping, and terrain for rock climbing. The parking lot collects a $3 day use fee. One of the best hikes in Tahoe is the **Rubicon Point Trail,** which wraps 5 mi. around the beach and granite cliffs of Emerald Bay. The trailheads are at D.L. Bliss Park and Vikingsholm. The **Eagle Falls Trail** is accessible from Vikingsholm's parking lot by hiking to Eagle Lake (1 mi.) and into the Desolation Wilderness. (Permits required for this hike, and there is a fee for overnight camping; for details on these regulations, see **Desolation Wilderness,** p. 222.)

Those looking for a more leisurely excursion will enjoy the nature trails around the Taylor Creek Visitors Center, north of South Lake Tahoe on Hwy. 89. The **Lake of the Sky Trail** (0.5 mi. round-trip) is dotted with informative signs about the origins of the lake, its early inhabitants, and its current animal populations.

Lower and **Upper Echo Lakes,** off U.S. 50 south of Tahoe, are a smaller, wilder version of Tahoe; granite tablets and pine trees tower around the lakes, producing an unmatched feeling of seclusion. **Echo Chalet,** 2 mi. west of U.S. 50 near the top of Echo Summit, operates **boat** service across the lake. (☎ 659-7207. Runs daily 8am-6pm. No reservations. One-way $7 with at least 2 people; pets $3.) This is the most affordable way to satiate motorboat-related desires. From the drop-off point, a well-maintained trail (part of the Pacific Crest Trail) skirts the north side of the lakes to the Upper Lake boat landing and into the Desolation Wilderness. Day hiking wilderness permits are available at the chalet; mandatory overnight permits are issued at the forest service (see **Wilderness Permits,** p. 220). Another 2 mi. along U.S. 50, just before Twin Bridges, is the **Horsetail Falls** trailhead. The waterfalls

> # FROM CREST TO CREST: THE TRAIL OF
> # THE WEST
> As the longest hiking path in America, the **Pacific Crest Trail (PCT)** snakes, swerves, and scales up 2638 mountainous miles from Mexico to Canada, passing through all sorts of climates from deserts to sub-Arctic regions along the way. True to its name, the PCT always keeps to the crests—the trail maintains an average elevation of over 5000 ft. It dishes out quality as well as quantity; there's an amazing view from the summit of **Mount Whitney** (14,494 ft.), the highest peak in the contiguous United States. Although the PCT was begun in 1968, the trailblazing task was so immense that it was not officially completed until 1993.
>
> No matter how much of the trail you choose to take on, proper supplies, conditioning, and acclimatization are vital. The **Pacific Crest Trail Association** (☎916-349-2109 or 888-728-7245; www.pcta.org) gives tips on how to prepare for the journey. Contact them at 5325 Elkhorn Blvd., Box 256, Sacramento 95842.

here make those at Eagle Lake look like leaky faucets. To access them, you'll have to make the short (1.3 mi.) but tough hike through the slippery canyon. Inexperienced hikers should beware—each year, several people have to be rescued by US Forest Service helicopters.

ROCK CLIMBING

The **Alpenglow Sport Shop,** 415 N. Lake Blvd., in Tahoe City, provides free rock and ice climbing literature, and rents climbing shoes for $8 a day. (☎583-6917. Open M-F 10am-6pm, Sa-Su 9am-6pm.) **Headwall Climbing Wall,** at Squaw Valley, offers several challenging routes in the Cable Car Building. (☎583-7673. Open daily 10am-5pm. $12 per day, indoor shoe rental $4 per day.)

There are many popular climbs in Lake Tahoe, but climbing should never be undertaken without knowing the ropes—proper safety precautions and equipment are a must. Those unprepared for dangerous climbs can try bouldering at **D.L. Bliss State Park** and at **Split Rock** in Donner Memorial State Park. The climbing at **Donner Summit** is world-renowned. Along Old Hwy. 40 by Donner Pass, climbers ascend **School Rock** (beginner) or the precarious **Snow Shed** (advanced). A host of popular climbing spots are scattered through South Shore and the Donner Summit area. The super-popular **Ninety-Foot Wall** at Emerald Bay, **Twin Crags** at Tahoe City, and **Big Chief** near Squaw Valley, are some of the more famous area climbs. **Lover's Leap,** in South Lake Tahoe, is an incredible (and an incredibly crowded) climb of two giant cliffs. East of South Lake Tahoe off U.S. 50, **Phantom Spires** has amazing ridge views, while **Pie Shop** has great exposure.

SEEING THE SIGHTS

Heavenly Mountain (see **Winter Activities,** below) whisks visitors along at 13 ft. per sec. to Heavenly's summit. At the observation deck, recreational opportunities compliment the view. (☎775-586-7000. Runs daily 10am-sunset. $20, ages 6-12 $12.)

Squaw Valley (see below) also offers a scenic tram ride that climbs to the mountaintop High Camp, with a year-round ice-skating rink, tennis club, pool, spa, mountain bike and hiking trails, and the world's highest bungee jumping tower. Restaurants and shops at the top are pricey. (Runs daily June-Aug. 10am-9pm; in Sept. 10am-4pm. $17, under 12 $5; after 5pm $8.)

For a closer view of the waters, the **M.S. Dixie II Paddlewheeler** cruises Lake Tahoe in style from its Zephyr Cove dock, at 760 Hwy. 50. With up to five tours per day, the ride includes a video of the ecosystem that thrives under the lake's calm surface. (☎775-589-4906. Tours $24. Dinner/dancing $49. Breakfast $27. Champagne brunch $29.) On the North Shore, the **Tahoe Gal,** 850 N. Lake Tahoe Blvd., in the Lighthouse Shopping Center, makes a floating foray into Lake Tahoe with five daily cruises. The Happy Hour Cruise offers discounted drinks and two adult tickets for the price of one. (☎800-218-2464. Happy Hour Cruise 4:30pm. Tickets $20.)

WINTER ACTIVITIES

DOWNHILL SKIING

With its world-class alpine slopes, knee-deep powder, and notorious California sun, Tahoe is a skier's mecca. There are approximately 20 ski resorts in the Tahoe area. The Visitors Center provides info, maps, publications like *Ski Tahoe* (free) and *Sunny Day* (free, with excellent area maps), and coupons (see **Tourist and Information Services,** p. 220). For daily ski info updates, use www.tahoesbest.com/skitahoe. All the major resorts offer lessons and rent equipment. Look for multi-day packages that offer significant discounts over single-day rates. Lifts at most resorts operate daily 9am-4pm; arrive early for the best skiing and shortest lines. Prices do not include ski rental, which generally costs $15-20 for a full day. Skiers on a tight budget should consider night skiing or half-day passes. Numerous smaller ski resorts offer cheaper tickets and shorter lines. **Diamond Peak Ski Resort** (☎775-832-1177), off Country Club Dr. in Incline Village, has a snowboard park and is right on the beach, while **Sugar Bowl** (☎426-9000), 3 mi. east on Old Hwy. 40 off I-80 at Soda Springs Exit, recently doubled in size and has decent terrain. Skiing conditions range from bikini days to frost-bitten finger days, and snow (artificial or otherwise) might cover the slopes into early summer. Off-season skiing may not compete with winter skiing for snow quality, but it's generally much cheaper. **Rates listed below are for winter.**

Squaw Valley (☎583-5585 or 888-SNOW-321/766-9321; www.squaw.com), off Rte. 89, north of Alpine Meadows. The site of the 1960 Olympic Winter Games, and with good reason—the groomed bowls make for some of the West's best skiing. Squaw boasts 4200 acres of terrain across 6 Sierra peaks. The 32 ski lifts—including the 110-passenger cable car and high speed gondola—access high-elevation runs for all levels. Open late Nov.-June 1. Full-day lift ticket $56, half-day $39, seniors and 13-15 $28, over 76 and under 12 free. Night skiing (until mid-Apr. daily 4-9pm) $20. Non-skiing cable car ride $16, after 4pm $65.

Alpine Meadows (☎583-4232 or 800-441-4423), on Rte. 89, 6 mi. northwest of Tahoe City. An excellent, accessible family vacation spot and local hangout with more than 2000 skiable acres. Not as commercial as Squaw, it has long expert bowls with good powder skiing, but few beginner runs. Full-day lift ticket $54, ages 7-12 $10, ages 65-69 $30, over 70 $8, under 6 $6. Basic ski rental $27, under 13 $18.

Heavenly (☎775-586-7000), on Ski Run Blvd. off U.S. 50 (South Lake Tahoe Blvd.), is the largest and most popular resort in the area, with over 4800 skiable acres, 29 lifts, and 84 trails. Over 10,000 ft. high, it is Tahoe's highest ski resort. Few shoots or ridges. Its lifts and slopes straddle the California-Nevada border and offer dizzying views of both. Full-day lift ticket $57, ages 13-18 $47, seniors and ages 6-12 $29.

Rose (☎800-SKI-ROSE/754-7673), 11 mi. from Incline Village on Rte. 431, is a local favorite because of its long season, short lines, and intermediate focus. Full-day lift ticket $45, seniors $25, ages 13-17 $35, ages 6-12 $12, over 70 (mid-week) and under 6 free; half-day $35, ages 13-17 $30. Tu 2 for 1 tickets, W student discounts.

Boreal (☎426-3663), on I-80, 10 mi. west of Truckee, opens earlier than most resorts and saves skiers the drive to Tahoe. Voted "Best Place to Snowboard" by locals. Mostly

NEVADA

beginner and intermediate slopes are good for snowboarding. 9 lifts and 41 trails. Open Nov.-Apr. Ski 9am-9pm. Full-day lift ticket $34, ages 5-12 $10, over 60 $18, over 70 and under 5 free. Call about midweek discounts and night skiing.

Northstar (☎ 562-1010; www.skinorthstar.com), on Rte. 267 13 mi. north of Tahoe City, is a family-oriented ski area with an emphasis on beginning and intermediate trails. 200 new acres on Lookout Mountain cater to advanced skiers. Family dining is available at any of the 6 restaurants on or near the mountain. Full-day lift ticket $54, ages 13-22 $44, under 13 $17.

CROSS-COUNTRY SKIING AND SNOWSHOEING

One of the best ways to enjoy the solitude of Tahoe's pristine snow-covered forests is to cross-country ski at a resort. For more detachment, rent skis at an independent outlet and venture onto the thick braid of trails around the lake. **Porters** (☎ 587-1500), at the Lucky-Longs Center, in Truckee, and 501 N. Lake Blvd., in Tahoe City (☎ 583-2314; open daily 8am-6pm), rents skis for $9-12.

Royal Gorge (☎ 426-3871), on Old Hwy. 40 below Donner Summit, is the nation's largest cross-country ski resort, with 90 trails covering 170 mi. of beginner and expert terrain. Warming huts provide a respite during your trek. **Spooner Lake,** at the junction of U.S. 50 and Rte. 28, offers 57 mi. of machine-groomed trails and incredible views. (☎ 775-749-5349. $15, children $3; mid-week special $11.

Snowshoeing is easier than cross-country skiing, and allows you to traverse more varied terrain. Follow hiking or cross-country trails, or trudge off into the woods (make sure to bring a map). Equipment rentals are available at many sporting goods stores for about $15 per day. Check local ranger stations for ranger-guided winter snowshoe hikes.

🔊 NIGHTLIFE

There are varying degrees of nightlife in Lake Tahoe. In Tahoe City, most of the nightlife is centered around the pub scene. On the South Shore, however, it's a little more glitzy—that's where you find the late-night gambling and dancing. To get in, you'll need a state ID or license; international residents need passports.

Caesar's Palace, 55 U.S. 50 (☎ 888-829-7630). Roman theme extends through large casino, intimate sportsbook, restaurants, and clubs. Within Caesar's, popular **Club Nero** (☎ 775-586-2000) is a hotspot for dancing and drinking, with $2 drinks on M. Cover $5-25. Open daily 9pm-early morning.

The Brewery, 3542 S. Lake Tahoe Blvd. (☎ 544-2739). Stop in and try one of the 6 microbrews on tap. Sassy Bad Ass Ale packs a fruity punch, and pizzas (starting at $9) come crammed with as many toppings as you want. Laid-back atmosphere makes this spot a favorite for locals. Open daily 11am-10pm; later hours during peak seasons.

NEAR LAKE TAHOE

The area surrounding Lake Tahoe is a rare find in the High Sierra: a pristine mountain setting with nearby outposts of urbanization, offering the best of both worlds. Lake Tahoe and Donner Lake glitter in both sun and snow. Innumerable outdoor recreation opportunities reel in visitors by the score; after the sun goes down, they all head to beachside barbecues, the dimly lit yuppie bars of Tahoe City, or the glitzy gambling of South Lake Tahoe and Reno, just across the Nevada border.

NEVADA

BLACK ROCK SAFETY. As already indicated, safety concerns are serious business in the Black Rock Desert. The playa is composed of silt and clay, so mucky conditions may arise without warning. *Extreme caution should be exercised when driving off-road.* Many people who become stuck in the winter and spring must wait until the dry season to retrieve their cars. If you become stuck, wait with the vehicle rather than braving the desert environment. Check playa conditions at the **BLM** offices at **Gerlach** (see p. 231) or **Winnemucca** (see p. 231) before heading out. When in the desert, always carry abundant water, food, and sunscreen. Be sure to tell someone where you plan to go and when you plan to be back. Finally, several accidents have occurred when visitors have attempted to cross the train tracks at the playa's eastern edge. Despite its remoteness, the playa sees heavy train traffic from the Union-Pacific line; be cautious near the tracks.

PYRAMID LAKE   ☎ 775

When John Fremont "discovered" Pyramid Lake in 1844, he saw a rock structure near its shore that looked enough like a pyramid to give the lake its name. Pyramid Lake represents different things to different people: a playground to local boating enthusiasts, a scenic wonder to tourists, and a financial and cultural lifeblood to the Paiute people. Drawing its water from Lake Tahoe through the modest flow of the Truckee River, Pyramid, like most other Great Basin lakes, is pluvial: it has no outlet. The lake, just 33 mi. north of Reno, is a contained vacation destination for the fishers, campers, and boaters who pack its shores every summer.

Dirt roads depart from Rte. 445 and lead to the shoreline along the west side of the lake, but many are soft and sandy and require four-wheel drive. Caution is therefore advised, as sand conditions can change rapidly from compact to treacherous without warning. After **Warrior Point,** the road becomes gravel, and it's slow going from there. Be prepared to share the road with thrill-seeking dirt-bikers and dune buggy riders. Route 447 shoots up the east side of the lake, but a view of the water is blocked by surrounding mountains and miles of sandstone desert.

Whether boating, fishing, or camping, a permit is required. The **Ranger Station** (☎ 476-1155) and **Pyramid Lake Marina** (☎ 476-1156) in Sutcliffe, along the western side of the lake, sell permits for different activities. (Day use $5, camping $5, boating or fishing $6.) The marina hosts a comprehensive mini-museum that provides an excellent introduction to the natural history of the lake and the cultural history of the Paiute people. It also sells fishing tackle, camping gear, gas, food, and beverages and rents boats. (Boats $12-45 per hr., depending on size and horsepower. Discounts for 6hr. rentals.) Its **RV park** offers full hookup sites with shower and laundry facilities ($15). For those without an RV, **Crosby Lodge** (☎ 476-0400; make a right before heading to the Marina off the Sutcliffe exit) has cabins and converted RVs that sleep up to seven. Cabins start at $40, and Crosby's has a bar, restaurant, convenience store, and grille to meet most immediate needs.

Eight and a half miles north of Sutcliffe lies **Warrior's Point Park,** one of the most popular, developed sites in the park for camping. Take the gravel road 3½ mi. to the Willows, a verdant vein of trees and grass that winds from the mountains to the lake. From here, there is a great view of the **Needles,** the elegant tufa formations along the northern tip of the lake.

The **Pyramid Lake Museum and Visitors Center,** along the southern tip of the lake, ¼ mi. west of the junction of Rte. 446 and 447 and adjacent to the high school, is distinguished by its unconventional architecture; the building is crafted to evoke a sense of pride accessible to all Native American nations. Rotating exhibits showcase historic and contemporary Paiute culture. (☎ 574-1088. M-F 8am-4:30pm.

NEVADA

FISH OR FAMINE During the first half of the 20th century, Pyramid Lake attracted celebrity anglers ranging from Herbert Hoover to Clark Gable, all striving to snag a big Lahontan Cutthroat trout. In 1925, an angler pulled a world-record 41 lb. trout out of the lake. By the mid-1940s, however, the Cutthroat was extinct in Pyramid Lake. Anglers had found such good luck with enormous fish because, thanks to the 1902 Newlands Reclamation Act, farmers near Fallon, NV diverted much of the Truckee's flow for agriculture. Decreased water in the Truckee destroyed the Cutthroat's spawning grounds, leaving only the oldest, biggest fish in the lake. By 1968, the lake's level had dropped over 80 ft. Recent litigation by tribal authorities has resulted in a settlement agreement with all parties claiming water rights in the Truckee Basin. Since 1997, thanks to this agreement and above-average rainfall, the lake level has risen nearly 20 ft. Aggressive fishery work by the Pauite tribe has enabled the re-introduction of the Cutthroat, making the Lake once again an angler's paradise.

Free.) Following Rte. 447 5 mi. north past the town of Nixon, County Rd. 5, a well-compacted dirt road, veers off to the left. This route provides excellent views of the **Stone Mother,** the **Fremont Pyramid,** and **Anaho Island,** which reveal local wildlife and meaningful cultural symbols.

BLACK ROCK DESERT WILDERNESS

In December 2000, the federal government designated much of this desert as a National Conservation Area and marked ten distinct areas within the desert as National Wilderness Areas, making it 2000 square miles of the wildest areas in the US. However, this undisturbed and primitive central Nevada wilderness does not welcome exploration. The Black Rock Desert is inhospitable, virtually devoid of water, often impassable in any type of vehicle, and full of hot springs scalding enough to boil flesh. Despite these dangers—or because of them—the Black Rock has recently become a playground for a variety of limit-challenging recreationalists. Activities conducted recently in the area include land sailing, arts festivals, no-limits golf, amateur rocketry, mountain biking, and pick-up truck croquet with a seven-foot ball. With new federal protection, the evocative, otherworldly expanse of desert and mountains will continue to inspire and entice artists, outdoorsmen, and thrill-seekers for years to come.

■ **ORIENTATION.** The Black Rock Desert lies in northwest Nevada, the barren remnant of ancient Lake Lahontan. Extensive block-faulting is responsible for the several mountain ranges jutting out of the desert floor, the high water table, and the presence of hot springs. The Black Rock extends north from Gerlach, NV, beginning in an immense playa (a dry lake bed once submerged under 500 ft. of water) that changes only 5 ft. in elevation over a 25 mi. stretch. The desert then splits into two wings, with one wing jutting northwest towards Cedarville, CA and bound on the west by the **High Rock Canyon Area.** The second wing extends towards the **Jackson Mountains** in the northeast and includes the Quinn River Valley. As a general rule, exploring the desert requires a four-wheel-drive vehicle with high clearance and durable tires. From Gerlach, Rte. 34 ventures north to Black Rock, providing travelers with a paved road and numerous gravel offshoots into the playa. Driving past High Rock Lake requires high clearance and four-wheel drive.

■ **OUTDOOR ACTIVITIES.** Off-roading is the area's primary form of recreation, but the inexperienced should heed the words on a Gerlach restaurant's wall: "Black Rock, where the pavement ends and the West begins." **Rte. 34,** headed north along the Granite Range, is a reliable county road passable to most vehicles. Sheer and spectacular cliffs in High Rock Canyon dazzle hikers and drivers alike, although reaching the canyon by road past High Rock Lake requires high-clearance and four-wheel drive. High Rock Canyon also offers the Black Rock's only **rock climbing**. Rte. 49, the Jungo Rd., travels between Gerlach and Winnemucca and, although the road is flat and well-compacted, jagged rocks near Gerlach make heavy-duty tires a necessity.

Most visitors to the Black Rock Desert venture no farther than the playa northeast of Gerlach. The spacious and undisturbed playa welcomes all varieties of eccentric pursuits, but come prepared with your own equipment: no outfitters supply gear for playa adventures like land sailing or turbine-engine racing. The historic **Applegate-Lassen Pioneer Trail** runs through the desert, darting between the Black Rock's many hot springs. The BLM discourages hot spring use because even those springs not ordinarily hot enough cause serious burns can occasionally produce plumes of heat hot enough to kill. Both the Trego hot springs in the northeast of Gerlach near the railroad and several springs west of the Soldier's Meadow Ranch are cool enough to permit soaking.

GERLACH   ☎ 775

Although the Black Rock is administered from Winnemucca's Bureau of Land Management, Gerlach, nearest the playa, acts as a staging ground for Black Rock enthusiasts. The tiny town 60 mi. north of Pyramid Lake is a mixture of traditional, blue-collar mining folks with a small, avant-garde population of artists. The railroad is the biggest presence in Gerlach; the Burning Man offices is the second biggest. Several **restaurant/saloons** line Main St., but the nearest store lies south on Rte. 447 in Empire, NV. Gerlach has its own **gas station** at the southern entrance to town that also distributes BLM pamphlets and provides reports of playa conditions. **Bruno's ❷**, on Main St., offers Gerlach's only accommodations, and its diner-esque restaurant serves up deliciously and famously hearty homemade ravioli and thick milk shakes. (☎ 557-2220. Restaurant open daily 5am-9pm. Small singles with a black-and-white TV start at $32.) When passing through Gerlach, take a detour down **Doobie Ln.** to see the "world's only drive-through folk art experience." Named for local DeWayne Williams and his conspicuous substance habit, this 2 mi. drive showcases a delightfully postmodern collection of aphorisms, affirmations, memorials, marriage commemorations, Christian revelations, and local advertising. Each item appears painted in white on rock—contemporary petroglyphics. To find Doobie Ln., bear right at the 447/34 Junction and travel 2 mi. to Guru St. Gerlach also serves as staging ground for the annual **Burning Man Festival** (see p. 232). Burning Man organizers maintain a small field office and museum, or, more appropriately, a collection of artifacts from previous festivals, next to the Burning Man offices on 390 Main St.

WINNEMUCCA   ☎ 775

Before Winnemucca assemblyman Phil Tobin's 1931 gambling bill was approved in Nevada, his town existed as a sleepy wagon crossing and mining site. After gaming's meteoric ascent, Tobin's prophecy seems to have come true: "Nevada would be a place today where people hurry through if the [gambling] bill had not been passed." The growing town of Winnemucca boasts large casinos, varied recreational activities, and a distinctive Old West charm that fueled it most recent wave of reinvention. Today, the buckaroo crowd is older: Winnemucca tourism is all about the AARP, the retirement lifestyle, and the nickel slots, dawn to dusk and dusk to dawn.

NEVADA

BURNING MAN FESTIVAL Every year on Labor Day, volunteers transform the Black Rock Playa near Gerlach, NV into Black Rock City, a city-as-art-installation that hosts the Burning Man Festival. Burning Man is a communal celebration of self-expression. Organizers tout its non-commercial virtue: there's no money in Black Rock City and barter reigns. More importantly, Burning Man admits no spectators; everyone must contribute their own creativity. Participants express themselves by doing everything from donning alien suits to offering free shaves to performing daring pyrotechnic displays. The weekend's celebration culminates when an enormous wooden human sculpture bursts into flames. To find out more about this ephemeral event, peruse the web site (www.burningman.com) or call 415-863-5263. If you happen to be in Gerlach in the weeks preceding or following Labor Day, stop by the Burning Man offices, 390 Main St., to get a taste of the event's culture.

🔣🔢 ORIENTATION AND PRACTICAL INFORMATION. Originally a simple crossing of the Humboldt River, Winnemucca today stands at the crossroads of I-80 and U.S. 95, a location ideal for snagging dollars from travelers and tourists headed in all directions. Winnemucca Blvd. is the main strip in town, lined with motels and casinos. To the east, the Sonoma Mountains provide outdoor excitement, especially at popular Water Canyon. The **Humboldt County Chamber of Commerce and Visitors Center** is located in a vacated casino at 30 W. Winnemucca Blvd. (☎ 623-2225). Pick up one of their useful brochures comparing lodging and dining options. (Open M-F 9am-5pm; Sa 9am-4pm; Su 11am-4pm.) **Greyhound,** 665 Anderson St. (☎ 623-4464), runs six buses daily east and west along I-80. Open irregularly; call ahead. **Amtrak** stops on Railroad St. between Melarkey and Lay. To: **Reno** (1 per day, $32, locals warn that it often runs behind schedule) and **Salt Lake City** (1 per day, $58). For medical needs, try the **Humboldt General Hospital,** (☎ 623-5222) 118 E. Haskill St. **Free Internet access** is available at the **Humboldt County Library,** 85 E. Fifth St. (☎ 623-6388), with extended hours Tu-W. **Post Office** can be found at 850 Hanson St. (☎ 623-2456). Local **ZIP code:** 89445.

🏠🍴 ACCOMMODATIONS AND FOOD. Winnemucca Blvd. acts as the arena for a fierce Darwinian struggle among an overpopulation of motels, hotels, and casinos. Often, singles can be had for as low as $30. Far enough outside of town for a glimpse of desert solitude, **Hi-Desert RV Park ❶,** 5575 E. Winnemucca Blvd. (☎ 623-4513), touts grassy, full hookups for $22.50 and tents for $16. **Model T Hotel and Casino ❷,** 1130 W. Winnemucca Blvd. (☎ 623-2588), offers a peaceful atmosphere, and comes at the right price. For $29 year-round, the snazzy rooms are a real steal, complete with A/C and HBO. RV park furnishes hookups for $22. For campers, the BLM's **Water Creek Recreation Area ❶,** up Water Canyon Rd., contains many aspen-shaded and free campsites.

At **Las Margaritas ❷,** 47 E. Winnemucca Blvd. (☎ 625-2262) fruity margaritas compliment mountainous Mexican delights. The super burrito ($8) requires a super appetite. Diners are welcomed with a towering basket of tortilla chips, salsa, and pico de gallo. Open daily 11am-10pm. Basque food has been served up family-style since 1863 at the **Winnemucca Hotel and Bar ❸,** 95 Bridge St. Winnemmucca's oldest building houses a family kitchen that serves up epic, traditional meals. Six-course lunch special is a steal at $7 while dinner is $14. (☎ 623-2908. Open daily; lunch 12-1pm; dinner 6:15-9pm.) **The Griddle ❶,** 460 W. Winnemucca Blvd., offers no surprises, just tasty breakfast favorites. A stack of three hotcakes runs $4.25. (☎ 623-2977. Open M-F 5am-8pm, Sa-Su 5am-12pm.

NEVADA

🔼 **OUTDOOR ACTIVITIES.** Although Winnemucca is not a traditional outdoors destination, the surrounding desert mountains cater to a wide range of activities. **Water Canyon** provides ample opportunity for a not-too-strenuous day hike; the Santa Rosa Mountains offer several hikes featuring beautiful wildflowers and wildlife. About ½ mi. after the BLM sign on Water Canyon Rd. begins the **Bloody Shins Trail**, a single-track mountain-bike trail established by local bikers from **Bikes and More,** 423 Bridge St. (☎ 625-2453). Visit the shop for info about biking on old mining roads, dune skiing, and, in winter, the backcountry snow recreation. The **Bureau of Land Management Office,** 5100 E. Winnemucca (☎ 623-1500), provides info about local recreational activities, including four-wheeling on the sand dunes north of town along U.S. 95. Also inquire about the drive through scenic **Pleasant Valley** to a variety of trails in the Humboldt National Forest and Santa Rosa Wilderness Area. The Winnemucca BLM office also administers the **Black Rock Desert**. For those in search of a different type of "gaming," Winnemucca acts as the epicenter of chukar hunting. A native of Southeast Asian ranges, the chukar—along with other birds—are common near Winnemucca. For more info, contact the Winnemucca office of the Nevada Division of Wildlife (NDOW; ☎ 623-6565).

ELKO AND THE RUBY MOUNTAINS ☎ 775

While countless other Nevadan towns have decayed, Elko (pop. 34,047) has charted a different course. The West's three most prosperous industries—mining, ranching, and gaming—have nurtured Elko's sharp ascent. Now, 1993's "Best Small Town in America" proudly serves as the commercial and governmental heart of northern Nevada, welcoming visitors from across the country thanks to its new airport. It will continue to thrive, at least until the costs of extracting microscopic gold particles from the Carlin Trend begin to exceed the profits, which have flooded Elko with cash since the mid-1960s. Prosperity has set the stage for modernity's clash with tradition, which becomes apparent as boot repair shops brush up against yoga centers and cellular phone suppliers.

🏳 TRANSPORTATION

Flights: Elko Regional Airport (☎ 738-5138), off Mountain City Hwy. New airport terminal. gives roaring evidence of its presence as flights soar over Idaho St. **Skywest** routes flights through nearby major airports, while **Casino Express** flies to many West Coast destinations for $109.

Trains: Station at 12th and Sharp St.; follow signs from 12th St. **Amtrak** (☎ 800-872-7245) runs trains east and west near I-80. To: **Reno** (6hr., 1 per day, $52) and **Salt Lake City** (6hr., 1 per day, $40).

Buses: Greyhound, 193 W. Commercial St. (☎ 738-3210), a block and a half west of the post office, runs 6 buses daily along I-80. To: **Reno** (5hr., 3 per day, $45.50-48.50) and **Salt Lake City** (4½hr., 4 per day, $47.50-50.50).

Public Transit: Northeastern Area Transit (☎ 777-1428) operates city buses up and down Idaho St. ($1) and to Spring Creek ($2).

Taxi: Elko Taxi, ☎ 738-1400.

✳🏳 ORIENTATION AND PRACTICAL INFORMATION

Located on I-80 near the Idaho and Utah borders, Elko spreads out along Idaho St., with the center of downtown at the intersection of 5th St. and Idaho. Fast food and motels cluster near the I-80 interchanges. Northwest of town, Mountain City Hwy.

NEVADA

gives way to a shopping plaza, a Wal-mart, and cookie-cutter housing developments. Heading southeast, the suburban community of Spring Creek is sandwiched between Elko and the verdant Ruby Mountains. To reach the Rubies, take either 12th St. or 5th St. to the Lamoille Highway. Set against the Rubies, Lamoille itself is a charming ranch town with two excellent family-owned restaurants.

Visitor Information: Elko Chamber of Commerce, 1405 Idaho St. (☎738-7135), at Sherman Station. Contains pamphlets upon pamphlets of Elko info. Ask about Elko's **brothels** sprinkled along 3rd St.; the town has more than any other city in the nation. The Visitors Center itself is an exhibit of transplanted log cabins from the Old West. The **Elko Convention Center and Visitors Authority** 700 Moren Way, (☎800-248-3556) off of College Ave. on Idaho, hosts Elko's major events and hold valuable info for travellers.

Police: 1401 College Ave. (☎777-7103).

Hospital: Northeastern Nevada Regional Hospital, 2001 Errecart Blvd (☎738-5151).

Internet access: The **Elko Public Library,** 720 Court St. (☎738-3066), offers free access. Open M-Th 9am-8pm and F-Sa 9am-5pm.

Post office: 275 3rd St. (☎777-9803). **ZIP code:** 89801.

■ ■ ACCOMMODATIONS AND CAMPING

Inexpensive rooms abound in Elko, nearly all of them along Idaho St. The National Forest offers several scenic campsites throughout Lamoille Canyon.

▨ **Pine Lodge and Lamoille Inn** (☎753-6542), on Rte. 227 in Lamoille, 18 mi. south of Elko. Small, cozy, and family-owned. The Inn offers 3 rooms for $65 each, double/triple occupancy w/ living room area, A/C, and satellite TV; kids stay free. Call in advance to reserve a room. ❹

Economy Inn, 411 10th St. (☎800-565-3286), at the intersection of Idaho St. and 10th. King-size bed with large pillows ensures a great night's sleep. HBO, A/C, microwave, fridge, coffeemaker, and charming pastel decor. Singles rarely go above $25 throughout the year; doubles $29. ❷

Towne House Motel, 500 W. Oak St. (☎738-7269), off W. Idaho St. Clean, inexpensive rooms with microwave, refrigerator, A/C. Singles $25-30, doubles $32-36. ❷

During summer months, excellent camping attracts many to Lamoille Canyon, about 20 mi. south of town. To reach the canyon, take the Forest Rd. 660, which runs miles into the Rubies' scenic recess. There are developed campsites, potable water, and vault toilets at **Thomas Creek Campground ❶.** (Tent sites $12.) For free, dispersed camping, take the dirt road leading to **Lamoille Campground ❶** and camp at one of the already-used sites along the road (not at the campground itself).

■ FOOD

Elko has a surprisingly eclectic collection of eateries. Most restaurants lie along Idaho St., although the strip malls surrounding town also shelter a few jewels. For Basque eating and a tasty steak, check out the three restaurants on Silver St. between 3rd and 5th St. **Roy's Grocery,** 560 Idaho St. (☎738-3173), carries an extensive selection of Mexican items in addition to the standard line up.

Elko Dinner Station, 1430 Idaho St. (☎738-8528). Far East meets Old West with cuisine drawn from disparate sources. Heaping plates of fried rice start at $6, while the perfectly-cooked NY steak, served with fries and soup/salad, is worth the $13 price tag. Open daily 11am-9:30pm. ❷

9 Beans and a Burrito (☎ 738-7898), in Elko Junction Shopping Plaza, off Mountain City Highway. Burritos at this popular Mexican joint start as low as $1.85. A meal-sized chicken soft taco is only $3. Open M-Sa 7:30am-9:30pm, Su 8am-8:30pm. ❶

The Grill at O'Carroll's Bar (☎ 753-6451), on Rte. 227 in Lamoille. Delicious breakfasts are perfect after a night in Lamoille Canyon. Similarly excellent lunch/dinner menu. Succulent and juicy ribeye steak on a slice of sourdough runs only $7. Tu-W 8am-4pm; Th-M 8am-8pm. ❷

🔵 📍 SIGHTS AND FESTIVALS

Elko celebrates cowboy culture with museums, exhibits, and annual events. The **Western Folklife Center,** 501 Railroad St. (☎ 738-7508; Open Tu-Sa 10am-5pm), is perhaps the premier national institution devoted to the subject. Its annual **National Cowboy Poetry and Music Festival,** held in late January (☎ 738-7508), draws sagebrush bards and crowds of thousands from throughout the West to its downtown facility. Other important Elko events include the **National Basque Festival** (☎ 738-6215), held in early July, and the enormous **Elko Mining Expo** (☎ 738-4091), held in mid-June. The most popular is the **Silver State Stampede** (☎ 738-3085), which draws large crowds at the city fairgrounds in July. Elko also boasts the highly informative **Northeastern Nevada Museum,** 1515 Idaho St. (☎ 738-3418). With exhibitions including archives of local history, contemporary art, mining, Nevada's largest gun collection, and a host of hunting-trophy taxidermies with animals from all seven continents, the museum could hardly fail to please.

Just a short drive from Elko, visitors can tour the working ranches and beautiful vistas of cowboy country. Rte. 228, reached via Rte. 227 south of Elko, furnishes glimpses into the West's past. A slew of ranches package this experience into commercial opportunities, granting outsiders a chance to live the cowboy life, if they have credit cards in tow. Contact the Visitors Center for more info.

🏔 OUTDOOR ACTIVITIES

Elko is tucked between two glaciated ranges, the Jarbidge and the Rubies. For info on outdoor activities, contact the **Forest Service,** 2035 Last Chance Rd. (☎ 738-5171; Open M-F 7:30am-4pm), and be sure to grab a copy of their guide to the Rubies. The recreational use officer at the Elko **BLM Office,** 3900 E. Idaho St. (☎ 753-0200; Open M-F 7:30am-4:15pm), will fit wilderness itineraries to visitors' needs, as well as give advice about popular, yet untrammeled, outdoors sites. Camping essentials, advice on hiking in the Rubies, and cross-country ski rental are available at the **Cedar Creek Clothing Company,** 453 Idaho St. (☎ 738-3950). The store also offers local Larry Hyslop's compendium of info on hikes in the Rubies. Visit **T-Rix Bicycles,** (717 W. Idaho St., ☎ 777-8804, just west of Mountain City Hwy.), to discuss the area's hottest single-track rides, or rent a bike for $25 per day.

The **Ruby Mountains** are the primary playground for Elko's wilderness fanatics. The most easily accessible area in the Rubies is Lamoille Canyon, dubbed "Nevada's Yosemite" by enthusiasts. Much of the land surrounding the National Forest is private, making access difficult. Difficult access, however, means that by going off-trail from Lamoille, experienced backpackers can spend days in trailless, infrequently-traveled wilderness. Hiking season in the Rubies begins in mid-June and lasts into the fall, but prepare for snow in the higher reaches into July. Relatively new to the recreation scene, **South Fork State Recreation Area** is perched just 10 mi. south of Elko, off Rte. 228. Nevada's most recent addition to its wealth of state parks boasts a large reservoir, campgrounds, and hiking. South Fork plays host to watersport enthusiasts from May through October.

BACKPACKING

The **Ruby Crest National Recreation Trail** begins at the end of the Forest Rd. 660 and winds 40 mi. through the Ruby Wilderness to Harrison Pass. This remote route begins at 8800 ft., averages 9500 ft., and finishes at Harrison around 7500 ft. Expect to see few other hikers and limited water during the middle section of the hike, and budget four to five days for completion of the trip.

DAY HIKES

Lamoille Lake/Liberty Pass (4-7 mi. round-trip, 3-6hr.). Following the first 3.5 mi. of the Ruby Crest trail, this day hike begins at 8800 ft. and climbs to Liberty Pass at 10,500 ft., passing several small lakes and the larger Lamoille Lake. Keep your eyes peeled for mountain goats and bighorn sheep. Many day hikers turn around after 2 mi. at Lake Lamoille. Snow lingers at higher elevations well into summer.

Island Lake (4 mi. round-trip, 2-3hr.). The trailhead lies just before the parking lot at the end of Lamoille Canyon Rd. This hike switches back and forth along the canyon's northern edge and climbs to beautiful Island Lake.

Thomas Canyon Trail (4 mi. round-trip, 2-3hr.). From the trailhead at the rear of the Thomas Canyon Campground, the trail climbs gradually straight through the canyon following the creek and culminates at a glacial cirque with two cascading waterfalls.

OTHER OUTDOOR ACTIVITIES

The Rubies offer excellent backcountry skiing in winter. Alpine skiing, 5 mi. north of Idaho St. at **Elko's Sno-Bowl,** gains more fans each season. **Cedar Creek Clothing Co.** (see p. 235) is a good resource for backcountry skiing info. Rock climbers have installed a few anchors on western faces near the entrance to the canyon. Bird enthusiasts camp at alpine sites to see exotic Himalayan Snowcocks as they fly at dawn from their high glacial-cirque perches. This rare species took to the area after being introduced in the 1960s and 70s. Southeast of the mountains, the **Ruby Lake Wildlife Refuge** is a motor lodge for migrating waterfowl in spring and fall. Reach the refuge and its campground by following Rte. 228 out of Spring Creek over the recently paved Harrison Pass. Some fowl hunting is allowed in the refuge, but more extensive access to big game can be found in the Ruby Valley. Bighorn sheep as well as antelope, deer, and mountain goat gather in the area around Elko. Contact the **Nevada Division of Wildlife** (**NDOW;** 1375 Mountain City Hwy; ☎ 738-6006) for more info. Anglers, after obtaining the required license, can try their luck in many of the areas lakes, reservoirs, and rivers. Contact NDOW for specifics.

WENDOVER AND BONNEVILLE SALT FLATS   ☎ 775

Straddling the Utah-Nevada border, Wendover presents a much-needed respite from miles of destitute desert expanses. The respite does not promise much, being merely a sterile strip of casinos, banks, motels, and fast food. The town has two notable features. Just east of Wendover, the **Bonneville Speedway** has hosted land speed records racing since 1914. Southeast of town on the flats surrounding the airport, Enola Gay pilots used dummy bombs to drill the procedures involved in atomic deployment in the months leading up to August 11, 1945. Visit the **Nevada Welcome Center,** 735 Wendover Blvd. (☎ 664-3138. Open daily 9am-5pm, sometimes earlier), for info on Wendover's historic and current sites and attractions. If stranded in Wendover and desperate for relief, try the **Greyhound** station, 215 E. Wendover (☎ 465-2595). The **Wendover Library,** 490 Camper Dr. (☎ 664-2572), provides Internet access during its limited afternoon hours.

Wendover is a weekend getaway town for gambling folk, so rates for accommodations fluctuate wildly depending on the day of the week and season of the year. Call ahead a couple of days before your visit to get a better idea of prices. On the Nevada side of Wendover Blvd., five casinos nearly monopolize the lodging market. Weekday rates as low as $22 per night welcome the savvy bargain hunter, but on busy weekends, prices soar and rooms book rapidly. At the far Nevadan end of Wendover Blvd., **The Red Garter Casino** (☎982-2111) seduces guests with arrestingly low promotional rates. The **Rainbow** (☎800-217-0049) and the **Peppermill** (☎800-648-9660) employ the familiar mirrors-and-flashing-lights strategy to entice passersby. Motel prices on the Utah side tend to follow the casino rate trends, making for a tough sell against the casinos' newer furnishings. Try the **Motel 6,** 561 E. Wendover Blvd. (☎665-2267) for immense rooms. Wendover also hosts a **KOA Campground ❶,** 651 N. Camper Dr., that accommodates RVs and tent-campers alike. (☎664-3221. Tent sites $19, hookups $21.) The casinos, along with the usual fast-food suspects, also on Wendover Blvd., control the Wendover dining sce+

NEVADA

UTAH

From the majestic peaks of the Wasatch Mountains to the sculpted slickrock of its southern deserts, Utah is a and of contrasts, surprises, and profound beauty. Whether hiking deep within the cathedral of a slot canyon, floating weightlessly atop the Great Salt Lake or traversing a knifeblade ridge in Zion, a visitor can not help but wonder at the power of nature and the enormity of geologic time.

Anglo settlement of this ancient land began in 1847, when Brigham Young arrived in the Salt Lake Valley with his band of Mormon pioneers. Today over 60% of the state's population belongs to the Church of Jesus Christ of Latter Day Saints, and Mormon heritage defines Utah's modern culture. Still, the state is not nearly as homogeneous as stereotypes might suggest. Bolstered by the 2002 Olympic Games, Salt Lake City plays host to an array of diverse communities. In the south, vivacious Cedar City draws thousands to its annual Shakespeare Festival.

Most Utahns live in the 100 mi. Salt Lake metropolitan corridor between Ogden and Provo, leaving the rest of the land sparsely populated. Five spectacular national parks (Zion, Bryce, Capitol Reef, Canyonlands and Arches) stretch across the southern desert, offering technicolor canyons, bizarre rock formations and unlimited hiking. Throughout the state, remote alpine forests and rugged wilderness areas provide for solitude, adventure and infinite awe. In the winter, the Wasatch Mountains, rising as a backdrop to Salt Lake City, draw hundreds of thousands of skiers with the world's best powder and top-notch resort facilities.

Visitors to Utah should know something of the peculiarities of Mormon culture. While polygamy is a thing of the past, members of the Church of Jesus Christ of Latter Day Saints are prohibited from smoking and drinking caffeine or alcohol. Although coffee and cigarettes are fairly easy to obtain in larger communities, alcohol is harder to come by, especially anything stronger that Utah's watered down (3.2% alcohol) beer.

SALT LAKE CITY   ☎ 801

Tired from five gruelling months of travel, Brigham Young looked out across the Great Salt Lake and proclaimed: "This is the place." In this desolate valley he knew that his band of Mormon pioneers had finally found a haven where they could practice their religion freely, away from the persecution they had faced in the East. To this day, Salt Lake City is still dominated by Mormon influence. The Church of Jesus Christ of Latter-Day Saints (LDS) owns the tallest office building downtown and welcomes visitors to Temple Square, the spiritual epicenter of the

---

◪ HIGHLIGHTS OF UTAH

MOAB. Though the area has quickly become a mecca for outdoors enthusiasts, hiking in the **Needles** (p. 284), exploring the remote **La Sal Mountains** (p. 276), and climbing the **Fisher Towers** (p. 275) will get you away from the crowd.

HIGHWAYS. Rte. 95 (p. 307) and **Rte. 12** (p. 312) offer unmatched roadside vistas.

WILDERNESS. The high peaks of the **Uintas** (p. 266), and the narrows of **Escalante** (p. 308) encompass boundless acres of pristine wildlands.

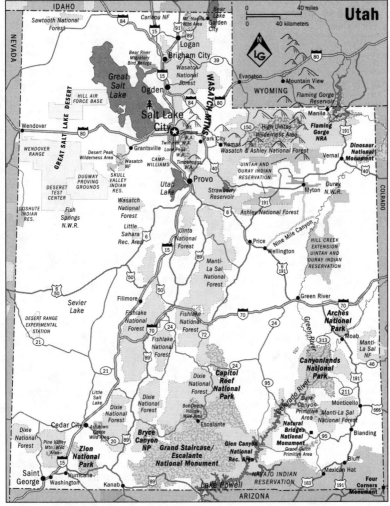

Mormon religion. Despite its commitment to preserving tradition, Salt Lake is rapidly attracting high-tech firms, as well as droves of outdoor enthusiasts drawn by world-class ski resorts, rock climbing, and mountain trails. The city, for all its homogeneity, supports a surprising variety of culturally diverse communities.

◼ INTERCITY TRANSPORTATION

Flights: Salt Lake City International, 776 N. Terminal Dr. (☎575-2400), 6 mi. west of Temple Sq. UTA buses #50 and 150 run between the terminal and downtown for $1.25, but service ends at 6pm on Su and buses leave only hourly M-Sa 7-11pm. Taxi to Temple Sq. costs about $15. **Southwest Airlines** (☎800-435-9792) flies to: **Oak-**

Salt Lake City

🏠 ACCOMMODATIONS
Armstrong Mansion B&B, **5**
Avenue's Hostel, **4**
Hotel Monaco, **8**
City Creek, **3**
Ute Hostel, **11**

🍴 FOOD AND DRINK
Metropolitan, **10**
Orbit, **7**
Park Cafe, **12**
The Pie, **6**
Red Iguana, **1**
Sage's Cafe, **9**
Tibet Cafe, **2**

land ($135), **Las Vegas** ($110), **Los Angeles** ($135), **Baltimore** ($323), and **Phoenix** ($142).

Trains: Amtrak, 340 S. 600 W (☎322-3510). *Be aware: the station is in an unsafe area of town.* To **Denver** (15hr., 1 per day, $75-112) and **San Francisco** (19hr., 1 per day, $77-115). Station open daily 10:30pm-6am.

Buses: Greyhound, 160 W. South Temple (☎355-9579), near Temple Sq. To: **Denver** (7-10hr., 5 per day, $54); **Las Vegas** (12-13hr., 2 per day, $49); and **Los Angeles** (15-18hr., 2 per day, $93). Open daily 6:30am-11:30pm, summer 6:30am-2:30am, ticket window until 10:30pm.

▣ LOCAL TRANSPORTATION

Public Transit: Utah Transit Authority (UTA) (☎743-3882). Frequent service to University of Utah campus; buses to Ogden (#70/72/73 express), suburbs, airport, mountain canyons, and the #11 express runs to Provo ($2.25). New trax light rail follows Main St. from downtown to Sandy and to the University of Utah. Buses every 20min.-1hr. M-Sa 6am-11pm. Fare $1-2, senior discounts, under 5 free. Maps available at libraries and the Visitors Center. Buses and trains traveling downtown near the major sites are free.

Taxis: Ute Cab, ☎359-7788. **Yellow Cab,** ☎521-2100. **City Cab,** ☎363-5550.

Car Rental: Enterprise, 1148 S. Main St. (☎534-1622). 21+ rentals require a license and credit card. Cars start at $40 per day. Open M-F 7:30am-6pm, Sa 9am-noon.

ORIENTATION

Salt Lake City's grid system may seem confusing at first but makes navigation easy once you get the hang of it. Brigham Young designated **Temple Sq.** as the heart of downtown. Street names increase in increments of 100 and indicate how many blocks east, west, north, or south they lie from Temple Sq.; the "0" points are **Main St.** (north-south) and **South Temple** (east-west). State St., West Temple, and North Temple are 100 level streets. Occasionally, streets are referred to as 13th S or 17th N, which are the same as 1300 S or 1700 N. Local address listings often include two numerical cross streets, acting as a type of coordinate system (no maps needed!). A building on 13th S (1300 S) might be listed as 825 E. 1300 S, meaning the cross street is 800 E (8th E). Smaller streets and those that do not fit the grid pattern sometimes have non-numeric names.

PRACTICAL INFORMATION

Visitor info: Salt Palace Convention Center and Salt Lake City Visitors Bureau, 90 S. West Temple (☎534-4902). Located in Salt Palace Convention Center, 1 block south of Temple Sq. Open daily 9am-5pm.

Hotlines: Rape Crisis, ☎467-7273. **Suicide Prevention,** ☎483-5444. Both 24hr.

Gay/Lesbian Information: The Little Lavender Book (☎323-0727), distributed twice yearly, presents a directory of gay-friendly Salt Lake City services.

Laundry: McFarlands Cleaning Centers, 154 S. 400 E. (☎531-6684). Open daily 7am-9:30pm. Self service machines and professional dry cleaning available.

Police: 315 E. 200 S (non-emergency ☎799-3000).

Medical services: University Hospital, 50 N. Medical Dr. (emergency ☎581-2291).

Internet access: Salt Lake Public Library, 209 E. 500 S (☎524-8200). Free Internet access. M-Th 9am-9pm; F-Sa 9am-6pm; Su 1-5pm. Free Internet access is also available at the **Family Search Center** on Temple Sq. M-Sa 9am-9pm.

Post office: 230 W. 200 S, 1 block south and 1 block west of Visitors Center. Open M-F 8am-5pm, Sa 9am-2pm. **ZIP code:** 84101.

Employment: The ski hills around Salt Lake city employ literally thousands of workers over both the ski season and the summer months. Positions include everything from lift operator to ski medic to massage therapist. Most hiring is now done through the individual resorts' web sites, although Snowbird (see p. 248) also makes use of a job hotline (☎947-8240). Work at ski hills typically entails a commitment for most of the season. However, the restaurants in the Park City resort are usually willing to pick up short-term staff during the high season. There the procedure is more informal; show up with resume in hand, and ask if they need anyone.

BE PREPARED A few blocks away from Temple Square stand 15 silos containing roughly 19 million lbs. of grain. Owned by the Mormon Church, the contents of these particular silos are not for sale. They are a reserve. For when things break down. For the Second Coming.

THE LOCAL STORY

THE MORMON PHENOMENON

In 1827, in an obscure town in upstate New York, the angel Moroni delivered to Joseph Smith a set of soft golden tablets upon which was inscribed a prophetic record in mystical language. Aided by divine guidance and stone spectacles, Smith translated the plates to English and published the Book of Mormon in 1830, the date traditionally marking the founding of the Church of Jesus Christ of Latter Day Saints.

Though the tablets vanished soon afterwards, Smith's church grew rapidly. Facing persecution, they were forced further and further west. In 1846, 30,000 Mormon pioneers were expelled from Nauvoo, IL, resulting in the Great Trek that would ultimately lead to the founding of Salt Lake City.

Mormons hold their faith to be the restoration of true Christianity. Just as the Bible tells the story of the eastern half of the world, the Book of Mormon is both a history of the ancient Americas and a record of Christ's coming to the New World. The first people described in the Book of Mormon crossed the ocean between 2200 BC and 300 BC; the second group, mostly descendents of Joseph, arrived around the time of the Roman Empire.

The 113 LDS temples throughout the world serve as venues for a number of unique and often misunderstood ceremonies. Sunday services are deemed too mundane for these sacred spaces, and only the worthy— church members certified by their bishop to have paid their dues and not cheated on their spouses—may enter. Inside, members engage in the rituals of "sealing" and perform "work for the dead."

(continued on next page)

⚐ ACCOMMODATIONS

Affordable chain motels cluster at the southern end of downtown, around 200 W and 600 S, as well as on North Temple.

Base Camp Park City, 268 Historic Main St. (☎655-7244 or 888-980-7244; www.parkcitybasecamp.com), 30 mi. east of Salt Lake City on I-80 and south on Rte. 224. This brand new, state-of-the-art, dazzling, and friendly hostel offers 70 affordable beds in an exorbitant town. Free Internet, free parking, discounts on selected Main St. restaurants, spectacular movie/DVD theater, and free transportation to Deer Valley, The Canyons, and Park City. Taxis/shuttles from Salt Lake City airport available. Winter dorms $35, summer $25; private room (sleeps up to 4) $120/$80. Make reservations as far in advance as possible during ski season as the hostel tends to fill up rapidly. Online booking possible. ❷

Ute Hostel (AAIH/Rucksackers), 21 E. Kelsey Ave. (☎595-1645 or 888-255-1192), near the intersection of 1300 S and Main. Located 2 blocks from new UTA trax line for easy downtown/ski-shuttle access. Young international crowd. Free pickup can be arranged from airport, Amtrak, Greyhound, or the Visitors Center. Kitchen, no curfew, free tea and coffee, parking, linen. Check-in 24hr. 14 dorm beds, $15 each. 2 private rooms, $25 singles; $35 doubles. Reservations only accepted in advance with pre-payment, recommended from July-Sept. and Jan.-Mar. No credit cards. ❶

The Avenues Hostel (HI-AYH), 107 F St. (☎359-3855), 15min. walk from Temple Sq. in a residential area. Free parking, 2 kitchens. Reception 7:30am-noon, 4pm-10:30pm. Dorms $17 (non-members); doubles $36 (non-members), plus $5 key deposit. Reservations recommended July-Aug. and Jan.-Mar. ❶

City Creek Inn, 230 W. North Temple (☎533-9100; citycreekinn.com), a stone's throw from Temple Sq. Offers 33 tastefully decorated, immaculate ranch-style rooms for cheaper rates than any of its downtown competitors. Singles $53; doubles $64. ❸

Armstrong Mansion Bed and Breakfast, 667 E. 100 S (☎531-1333 or 800-708-1333). This over-the-top romantic getaway features 15 sumptuously decorated Victorian rooms, many with jacuzzis only a few feet from the bed. Rates range from $119 for a basic room with king to $229 for the honeymoon suite in the tower. ❺

Hotel Monaco, 15 W. 200 S (☎990-9709; www.monaco-saltlakecity.com). Salvador Dalí at the French Riviera. Complimentary massages, tarot card readings, and nightly wine receptions. The staff of the

Monaco will furnish your room with a bowl of goldfish on request. Pet-friendly. Singles and doubles from $199. ❺

🏕 CAMPING

The mountains rising to the east of Salt Lake City offer comfortable summer camping with warm days and cool nights. Rocky **Little Cottonwood Canyon** offers tent sites at **Tanners Flat** ❶ (39 sites, water faucets and flush toilets; $12; open early May to late Oct.) and **Albion Basin** ❶ (25 sites, water faucets and pit toilets; $12; higher altitude; open early July to late Sept.). **Big Cottonwood Canyon** has camping at **Spruces** ❶ (97 sites, water faucets and flush toilets; $14; open late May to early Oct.) and **Redman** ❶ (43 sites, water faucets and pit toilets; $12; open mid-June to late Sept.). To find the campgrounds, take I-215 to Exit 7 (6200 S) and follow the signs to Big or Little Cottonwood Canyon. Brown recreation signs point the way to the campsites, which lie roughly 30 mi. from downtown Salt Lake. On weekends, get there early; for summer weekends, call in advance. The **Salt Lake Ranger District** (☎943-1794) fields calls for camping reservations and more info.

◪ MORAL FIBER

Good, cheap restaurants are sprinkled around the city and its suburbs. Despite its white bread reputation, Salt Lake hosts a number of ethnic cuisines. Cheap Mexican eateries have proliferated, as have brewpubs in the downtown area. If you're in a hurry downtown, **ZCMI Mall** and **Crossroads Mall**, both across from Temple Sq., have standard food courts. For groceries, large franchise stores serve the Salt Lake area, found mostly outside of downtown on major thoroughfares like State St. or N. Temple.

▦ **Sage's Cafe,** 473 E. 300 S (☎322-3790). This organic, vegan cafe is a nexus of culinary and political revolution. Describing themselves as "culinary astronauts," talented chefs produce a surprising variety of delectable dishes. Weekday lunch buffet $6.75. Be sure to try a refreshing soy milkshake ($4) or sample from their smoothie selection (also $4). Open W-Th 11am-10pm, F 11am-11pm, Sa 9am-11pm, Su 9am-10pm. ❶

Red Iguana, 736 W. North Temple (☎322-4834), across the bridge from downtown in the bright orange building. This immensely popular eatery serves up authentic pre-Columbian Mexican food. A la carte burritos, enchiladas, tacos ($5-7), and combo plates ($10-12). Open M-Th 11am-10pm, F 11am-11pm, Sa noon-10pm, Su noon-9pm. ❷

(continued from previous page)

"Sealing" binds spouses and family members together for all eternity, while "work for the dead" allows non-Mormon ancestors the privilege of higher degrees of Mormon salvation. Church members can "stand in" for their deceased relatives by being baptized again (twice per dead ancestor) by immersing themselves in the baptismal waters. However, spirits can choose to accept or reject Mormon blessings.

To pay for elaborate temples and maintain the church welfare network, members are required to tithe 10% of their annual income. In addition, most Mormon men, and a growing number of women, serve two-year missions in far-flung corners of the world. As a result, the Mormon church is the world's fastest growing religion.

While many still associate Mormonism with polygamy, the practice of having multiple wives was officially overturned by a prophetic revelation in 1890. Similarly, a policy barring blacks from holding church offices was overturned in 1978.

And just as its missions have attracted millions of converts, the Mormon Church has also proven highly adept at managing its worldly affairs. Church assets stand at over $30 billion, and its annual revenue stream of approximately $6 billion, $5 billion of which derives from tithing, places it midway up the Fortune 500 list between Paine Webber and Nike. Its holdings, many of them wholly-owned businesses, range from America's largest beef ranch to the Beneficial Life Insurance Corp.

For more information, visit www.mormon.org. Those curious about the purpose of life may wish to click on the "Purpose of Life" heading which will explain things in detail.

Park Cafe, 604 E. 1300 S (☎487-1670), at the south end of Liberty Park. Eclectic menu in a classy little joint. Breakfasts $6-8, lunches $7-9, light dinners (Th-Sa only) $8-10. Open Su-W 7am-2:30pm, Th-F 7am-2:30pm and 5pm-9pm, Sa 5pm-9pm. ❷

Orbit, 540 W. 200 S (☎322-3808; www.orbitslc.com), close to the dance clubs in the old industrial district. One of the city's newest and trendiest eateries, Orbit boasts sleek decor and a diverse crowd. Sandwiches ($7-10), dinner entrees ($10-16), and pizzas ($8-10). Open M-W 11am-11pm, Th-F 11am-1am, Sa 10am-1am, Su 10am-10pm. ❸

The Pie, 1320 E. 200 S (☎582-0193), next to the University of Utah. This subterranean college hangout serves up large pizzas (starting at $8) late into the night. Open M-Th 11am-1am, F-Sa 11am-3am, Su noon-11pm. No credit cards. ❶

Tibet Cafe Shambala, 382 4th Ave. (☎364-8558), in a quiet residential neighborhood northeast of Temple Sq. Enjoy the bountiful lunch buffet ($6) under the beneficent gaze of the Dalai Lama. Entrees $5-7. Open M-Sa 11am-3pm and 4-9:30pm. ❶

Metropolitan, 173 W. 300 S (☎364-3472), serves up exquisite cuisine in an elegant atmosphere. While entrees can reach up to $30, a separate bistro menu offers gourmet options for $15. Live Jazz Sa. Open Tu-Sa 5:30pm-10pm. Reservations recommended. ❺

◎ SIGHTS

LATTER-DAY SIGHTS. The majority of Salt Lake City's sights are sacred to the Church of Jesus Christ of Latter-Day Saints and are free. The seat of the highest Mormon authority and the central temple, **Temple Sq.** is the symbolic center of the Mormon religion. The square has two **Visitors Centers,** north and south. Visitors can wander around the flowery 10-acre square, but the sacred temple is off-limits to non-Mormons. An automated visitor info line (☎800-537-9703) provides up-to-date hours and tour info. Forty-five-minute tours leave from the flagpole every 15min., showing off the highlights of Temple Sq. *The Testaments,* a film detailing the coming of Jesus Christ to the Americas (as related by the Book of Mormon), is screened at the **Joseph Smith Memorial Building.** *(☎240-4383 for film show times, 240-1266 to arrange a tour. Open M-Sa 9am-9pm. Free.)*

Temple Sq. is also home to the **Mormon Tabernacle** and its famed choir. Weekly rehearsals and performances are free. *(Organ recitals M-Sa noon-12:30pm, Su 2-2:30pm; in summer also M-Sa 2-2:30pm. Choir rehearsals Th 8-9:30pm; choir broadcasts Su 9:30-10am, must be seated by 9:15am.)* In the summer, there are frequent free concerts at **Assembly Hall** next door. *(☎800-537-9703)*

The **Church of Jesus Christ of Latter Day Saints Office Building** is the tallest skyscraper in town. The elevator to the 26th floor grants a view of the Great Salt Lake in the west opposite the Wasatch Range. *(40 E. North Temple. ☎240-3789. Observation deck open M-F 9am-5pm.)* The LDS church's collection of genealogical materials is accessible and free at the **Family Search Center,** 15 E. South Temple St., in the Joseph Smith Memorial Building. The Center has computers and staff to aid in your search. The actual collection is housed in the **Family History Library.** *(35 N. West Temple. ☎240-2331. Center: Open M-Sa 9am-9pm. Library: Open M 7:30am-5pm, Tu-Sa 7:30am-10pm.)*

CAPITOL HILL. At the northernmost end of State St., Utah's **capitol building** features beautiful grounds, including a garden that changes daily. *(☎538-3000. Open M-F 8am-5pm. Tours M-F 9am-4pm.)* Down State St., the **Hansen Planetarium** has free exhibits and laser shows set to music. *(15 S. State St. ☎531-4925. Open M-Th 9am-9pm, F-Sa 9:30am-midnight, Su 1-5pm. Laser show $6, planetarium science show $4.50.)*

MUSEUMS. At the **Children's Museum,** you can build houses with enormous Legos or work in the "color factory." *(840 N. 300 W. ☎322-5268. Take bus #70. Open M-Th and Sa 10am-6pm, F 10am-8pm. $3.75, under 1 free.)* Visiting exhibits and a permanent collection of world art wows enthusiasts at the newly expanded **Utah Museum of Fine Arts,** on the University of Utah campus. (☎ 581-7332. Open M-F 10am-5pm, Sa-Su noon-5pm. Free.) Also on campus, the **Museum of Natural History** focuses its display space on the history of the Wasatch Front. (☎ 581-6927. M-Sa 9:30am-5:30pm, Su noon-5pm. $4, ages 3-12 $2.50, under 3 free.) The **Salt Lake Art Center** displays an impressive array of contemporary art and documentary films. (20 S. West Temple. ☎ 328-4201. Open Tu-Th and Sa 10am-5pm, F 10am-9pm, Su 1-5pm. Suggested donation $2.)

THE GREAT SALT LAKE. The Great Salt Lake, administered by Great Salt Lake State Marina, is a remnant of primordial Lake Bonneville and is so salty that only blue-green algae and brine shrimp can survive in it. The salt content varies 5-27%, providing unusual buoyancy. No one has ever drowned in the Great Salt Lake—a fact attributable to the Lake's chemical make-up. Decaying organic material on the lake shore gives the lake its pungent odor, a stench that locals prefer not to discuss. **Antelope Island State Park ❶,** in the middle of the lake, has beaches, hiking trails, camping, picnic spots, and buffalo. (☎ 625-1630. It is nearly impossible to get to the Lake without a car; bus #37 "Magna" will take you within 4 mi., but no closer. To get to the south shore of the lake, take I-80 17 mi. west of Salt Lake City to Exit 104. To get to the island, take Exit 335 from I-15 and follow signs to the causeway. Open daily 7am-10pm; in winter dawn to dusk. Day use: vehicles $8, bicycles and pedestrians $4. Camping $10 per vehicle for first night, $8 each additional night. Reservations recommended; call 800-322-3770.)

⚄ ⚅ ENTERTAINMENT AND NIGHTLIFE

Concerts abound in the sweltering summer months. At 7:30pm every Tuesday and Friday, the **Temple Sq. Concert Series** presents a free outdoor concert in Brigham Young Historic Park, with music ranging from string quartet to unplugged guitar (☎ 240-2534; call for a schedule). The **Utah Symphony Orchestra** performs in **Abravanel Hall,** 123 W. South Temple (☎ 533-6683; office open M-F 10am-6pm; tickets Sept. to early May $15-40; limited summer season: call 1 week in advance.) The University of Utah's **Red Butte Garden,** 300 Wakara Way (☎ 587-9939; www.redbuttegarden.org), offers an outdoor summer concert series with quality national acts.

1998 NBA Western Conference Champion **Utah Jazz** (season Oct.-Apr.; tickets $10-83) take the court at the **Delta Center,** 301 W. South Temple (☎ 325-7328).

The free *City Weekly* lists events and is available from bars, clubs, and restaurants. Famous teetotalers, the early Mormon theocrats instated laws making it illegal to serve alcohol in a public place. Hence, all liquor-dispensing institutions fall under the "private club" rubric and serve only members and their "sponsored" guests. In order to get around this cumbersome law, most bars and clubs will charge a "temporary membership fee" that's essentially the same as a cover-charge. The result of all this is a surprisingly active nightlife, centered on S. West Temple and the run-down blocks near the railroad tracks. For an alternative to the club scene, check out the classic movie screenings ($4) at **Brewvies,** 667 S. 200 W (☎ 355-5500). This movie theater-*cum*-brewpub lets you enjoy local microbrews along with your Hitchcock. Call for showtimes. 21+.

Bricks, 200 S. 600 W (☎ 238-0255), Salt Lake's oldest and largest dance club, featuring 2 floors of thumping house, multiple bars, an outdoor patio, pool tables, and the city's best sound system. Bricks also hosts national acts that span the musical spectrum. Separate 18+ and 21+ areas. Cover $5-7. Open nightly 9:30pm-2am.

Club Axis, 108 S. 500 W (☎ 519-2947; clubaxis.com), Salt Lake's version of a pretentious super-club, complete with multiple dance floors, lounges, and a jungle-themed bar. F gay/alt. lifestyle night, W and Sa dress to impress. Separate 18+ and 21+ areas. Cover $5-7. Open W-Sa 10pm-2am.

UTAH

HOW TO BRING THE OLYMPICS TO UTAH

In 1995, Salt Lake City was ecstatic to learn that it had been chosen as the venue for the 2002 Winter Olympics. Preparations immediately began for the construction of Olympic-caliber facilities. In January 1999, however, jubilation turned to shock as allegations of bribery emerged. An International Olympic Committee (IOC) report revealed that the city had, in fact, conducted shady dealings and bribed IOC members in charge of choosing the 2002 host city. The Salt Lake City organizing committee raised $400,000 in scholarship money and awarded it to 13 people, six of whom were IOC member relatives. Allegedly, the organizing committee also provided visiting IOC delegates with escorts during their visit to Salt Lake City, although these allegations rest on the testimony of purportedly "unreliable" prostitutes. On one occasion, organizers presented the visiting IOC president with a $9000 pistol and an $1800 shotgun as souvenirs of his visit to the West. As outrageous as these bribes appear, much speculation remains as to whether bribery has long been a part of the wooing that cities conduct to attract IOC votes. Either way, the Salt Lake organizing committee got caught red-handed. Two men stood trial for bribery, but the city got to keep its Games.

Xscape, 115 S. West Temple (☎539-8400; clubaxis.com), Salt Lake's newest and second-largest club features dance music on F and Sa and live acts M-Th. 2 main dance floors, lounges, bars, and pool tables sprawl over 6 stories. Live shows all ages, club nights 21+. Cover $5-7. F-Sa club nights 9pm-2am; live acts, ranging from gutter punk to space rock, usually begin at 6:30pm.

Dead Goat Saloon, 165 S. West Temple (☎328-4628), showcases local jazz and blues acts in a relaxed atmosphere that includes pool, darts, and a grill. 21+. Signature M blues night starts at 9:30pm. Open M-F 11:30am-2am, Sa-Su 6pm-2am.

Zipperz, 155 W. 200 S (☎521-8300). A diverse mix of the Salt Lake gay and lesbian crowd flocks to this classy bar/dance club. Sip your martini while relaxing in the wingchairs by the window or get your groove on in the second-story dance floor. W 80s. night, Sa dance party. F 18+, all other nights 21+. Cover $5-6. Open nightly Su-Th 2pm-2am, F-Sa 5pm-2am.

⛷ SKIING

Utah sells itself to tourists with pictures of intrepid skiers on pristine powder, hailed by many as "the greatest snow on earth." Seven major ski areas lie within 45min. of downtown Salt Lake, making Utah's capital a good, inexpensive base camp from which to explore the winter vacation paradise of the Wasatch Mountains. Nearby **Park City** is the quintessential ski town with the excellent but lonely ⛺**Base Camp Park City** (see p. 242) as its only budget option. Be sure to call or check ski area web sites for deals before purchasing lift tickets. In addition to being a good source of fun, the Utah ski hills are also an excellent source of employment. If you are interested in working while you ski, check the employment section on each hill's web site or call Snowbird's job hotline (☎947-8240).

Alta (☎359-1078; www.alta.com), 25 mi. southeast of Salt Lake City in Little Cottonwood Canyon. Cheap tickets; magnificent skiing. In business since 1938, this funky, no-frills resort continues to eschew both opulence and snowboarding. 8 lifts, 1 high-speed and 5 tows, serve 54 trails (25% beginner; 40% intermediate; 35% advanced) on 2200 skiable acres. 500 in. of champagne powder annually. Season mid-Nov. to mid-Apr. with skiing daily from 9:15am-4:30pm. Lift tickets: full day $38, half-day $29, day pass for beginner lifts only $22. Offers a joint ticket with nearby Snowbird for $68. Rentals: 4 rental shops in Alta ski village offer competitive rates.

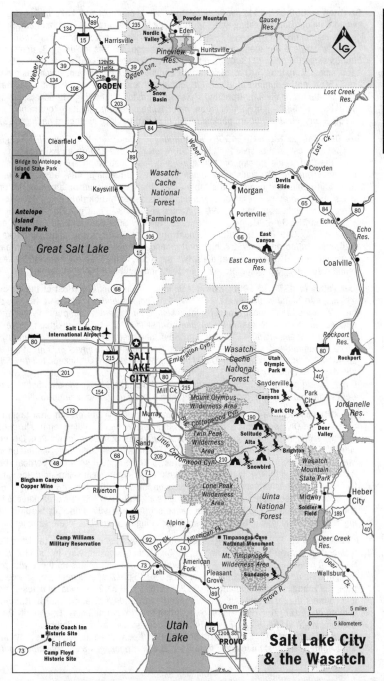

Salt Lake City
& the Wasatch

Brighton (☎800-873-5512; www.skibrighton.com), south of Salt Lake in Big Cotton-wood Canyon. Bargain skiing and snowboarding in a down-to-earth atmosphere. Brighton is especially family- and beginner-friendly, but features a snowboarding park and virtually limitless backcountry skiing for the virtuoso. 10 lifts including 3 high-speed quads serve 66 trails (21% beginner; 40% intermediate; 39% advanced) on 850 skiable acres. More than 500 in. of snow falls annually on the mountain, which has a base of 8750 ft. and a summit of 10,500 ft., creating a vertical drop of 1750 ft. Open early Nov. to late Apr. daily 9am-4pm and M-Sa until 9pm for night skiing. Lift tickets: full-day $39, half-day $34, night $24, children under 10 free. Rentals: adult ski/board package $26 per day, child ski/board package $18, high performance ski/board package $32.

The Canyons (☎435-649-5400; www.thecanyons.com), in Park City. With lodges, shops, and restaurants styled in chic Southwestern motifs and an abundance of territory, The Canyons is quickly becoming a world-class destination. 16 lifts, including 7 high-speed, serve 146 trails (14% beginner; 44% intermediate; 42% advanced) on 8 mountain peaks and over 3500 skiable acres. The recently built Dreamscape lift provides access to more intermediate terrain. Skiers and snowboarders enjoy 3190 ft. of vertical thrill, with a summit of 9990 ft. Annual snowfall 355 in. Open Nov.-Apr. daily M-F 9am-4pm, Sa-Su 8:30am-4pm. Lift tickets: full day $62, half-day $45; children and seniors $31/$24. Rentals: adult ski/board package $34 per day, child ski package $24, child board package $27, high performance ski package $40. Free season pass in exchange for 1 day of work at the resort per week. Call ahead for more info. A year-round resort, it offers hiking, horseback riding, and mountain biking in the summer.

Deer Valley (☎435-649-1000; www.deervalley.com), in Park City. Host of the slalom, moguls, and aerial events of the 2002 Winter Olympics and a genuine world-class ski area. With the area's most expensive lift tickets, Deer Valley attracts primarily the affluent, leaving the slopes sparse for pristine bowl skiing. 19 lifts, 6 high-speed, serve 88 trails (15% beginner; 50% intermediate; 35% advanced) on 1750 acres. Featuring a 9570 ft. summit and a 3000 ft. vertical drop, the mountain receives 300 in. of annual snowfall. No snowboards. Skiing Dec.-Apr. daily 9am-4:15pm. Lift tickets: full-day $67, half-day $46; children $36/$28; senior $46/$30. Rentals: adult ski package $39 per day, child ski package $28, high performance ski package $49. In the summer months, Deer Valley offers hiking, mountain biking, horseback riding, and a camp for kids.

Park City (☎435-649-8111; www.parkcitymountain.com). Its exceptional facilities earned it the Olympic snowboarding events in 2002. With mad skiing terrain, luxurious lodging, and a lift connecting the mountain to the town's posh storefronts, Park City provides. 15 lifts, 5 high-speed, whisk skiers to 100 trails (18% beginner; 44% intermediate; 38% advanced) on 3300 skiable acres. 350 in. annual snowfall. Vertical drop 3100 ft. Season mid-Nov. to mid-Apr. Open daily 9am-4pm, night skiing until 9pm after Dec. 25. Lift tickets vary by season; high season full-day $60+, half-day $42; ages 65-69 $30; 70+ free. Rentals: adult ski package $20 per day, child ski package $17, snowboard packages $32, high performance ski package $37. Park City features hiking, mountain biking, climbing, and horseback riding opportunities in the summer.

Snowbird (☎742-2222 or 800-640-2002; www.snowbird.com) sprawls up the Little Cottonwood, a canyon world-renowned for its high-quality powder. Now in its 31st year, Snowbird offers challenging skiing for all levels and resort amenities for those who prefer light days on the slopes. 13 lifts, including an 125-passenger aerial tram, service 85 trails (27% beginner; 38% intermediate; 35% advanced) on 2500 skiable acres. 2 new lifts connect the resort with Alta. Annual snowfall 500 in. Vertical drop 2900 ft. from a summit of 11,000 ft. Skiing and snowboarding mid-Nov. to mid-May. Open daily 9am-4:30pm; night skiing W and F until 8:30pm. Tickets: full-day including tram $56, lifts only $47; half-day $48/$40; 2 children under 12 free with adult. Joint ticket with Alta $68. Rentals: adult ski packages from $19, child ski packages $16, snowboard packages $29, high performance ski package $40. Also hosts backcountry skiing and mountaineering courses. Snowbird offers extensive summer hiking and biking opportunities.

Solitude (☎800-748-4754; www.skisolitude.com), in Big Cottonwood Canyon south of Salt Lake. Budget prices for luxurious runs at a beautiful resort. Uncrowded slopes and 20km of nordic trails at Silver Lake (8700 ft.) promise tranquility. 7 lifts, 1 high-speed, serve 63 trails (20% beginner; 50% intermediate; 30% advanced) on 1200 skiable acres. Vertical drop 2050 ft. from a summit of 10,035 ft. Annual snowfall 500 in. Season Nov. to late Apr. Skiing and snowboarding daily 9am-4pm. Lift tickets: full-day $44, half-day $37, seniors (60-69) $37, over 70 free, children $14. Nordic Center full-day $10, half-day $7. Rentals: adult ski package $24 per day, snowboards $28, high performance ski package $38. Summertime hiking and biking opportunities.

◪ OTHER OUTDOOR ACTIVITIES

Salt Lake area outdoor enthusiasts cherish the easy access to trailheads, fishing, skiing, and climbing of the Wasatch Front Range. Most popular points of access lie within a 30min. drive from downtown Salt Lake. **Mill Creek Canyon, Big Cottonwood Canyon,** and **Little Cottonwood Canyon** all cut into the Wasatch immediately east of town. Access to these canyons is off Wasatch Blvd. which runs parallel to the southbound stretch of I-215. **UTA** shuttles serve all three canyons regularly. The easiest place to obtain info on the canyons and other area recreational possibilities is the **Forest Service Information Station** in **REI**, 3285 E. 3300 S (☎466-6411; open Tu-Su). Dispersed camping is allowed in all three canyons but is prohibited within ½ mi. of the road. Forest service regulations prohibit dogs from the Cottonwood Canyons, as both provide drinking water to the Salt Lake metropolitan area. The **Great Western Trail,** a developing long route that will eventually connect Canada and New Mexico, winds through the area, with a trailhead at the top of Mill Creek Canyon. Most trails remain within their canyon, making for excellent day hikes.

The mountains rising west of the city also offer a range biking trails. **Wild Rose Mountain Sports,** 702 Third Ave., rents full-suspension bikes from $25 per day and gives expert trail advice. (☎533-8671. Open M-Th 9:30am-7pm, F-Sa 9:30am-6pm.)

Both Big and Little Cottonwood Canyons feature extensive **rock climbing.** Difficult bouldering problems can be found along the first five mi. of Little Cottonwood. **Ice climbers** pick their way up ice falls on the south side of the canyon. **Exum Mountain Adventures** offers private guiding services as well as courses in avalanche safety, crevasse rescue, basic mountaineering, and rock climbing for all levels. (☎550-3986. One-day group rock course $90 per person, $215 for private lesson, weekend winter ice climb $90 per person.)

◪ DAYTRIPS FROM SALT LAKE CITY

DESERET PEAK WILDERNESS

Forty-seven miles west of Salt Lake lies an imposing wilderness area providing succor from the Wasatch Front weekend crowds. The Deseret Peak Wilderness, designated in 1984, includes 25,508 acres, with elevations ranging between 5500 and 11,000 ft. Wildlife is abundant, including deer, coyotes, mountain lions, wild horses, and bald and golden eagles. Higher elevations feature jagged escarpments, tranquil basins, and all varieties of alpine flora.

To reach Deseret Peak, take I-80 west from Salt Lake about 20 mi. to Rte. 36 south. Follow signs for Rte. 138 west and Grantsville. Once in Grantsville, stock up on supplies and travel through town to the brown Forest Service sign for North and South Willow Canyon Rds. The most popular access to the area is from the Loop Campground at the end of South Willow Canyon Rd. The road lies 6 mi. south of Grantsville. North Willow Canyon Rd. is less traveled and spotted with campsites, many of them trash-littered. For summer hiking, be sure to bring plenty of water and sunscreen; temperatures can exceed 90°F and altitude amplifies the damaging effects of UV radiation. Also, check the forecast before embarking on a hike, as violent thunderstorms frequently ravage the wilderness area.

The most popular Deseret Peak Wilderness hike, and arguably the most spectacular, leads to the summit of the peak itself. On summer weekends expect to encounter a few other hikers, but otherwise, be prepared to climb in solitude. The trail begins at 7440 ft. at the end of the South Willow Canyon Rd. Follow the **Mill Fork Trail** to the **Deseret Peak-Vickory Trail.** Vibrant aspen grove foliage awaits the fall hiker along the Mill Fork. Once on the Deseret Peak Trail, the final part of the climb winds through rugged terrain, but the views are well worth the extra exertion. Trailhead to summit (11,031 ft.), the route stretches 4 mi. Coming down from the peak, follow the Deseret Peak-Vickory Trail north along the ridge to the **Dry Lake Fork Trail.** This trail intersects the Mill Fork Trail about 1.1 mi. from South Willow Canyon Rd. The Dry Lake descent route is also about 4 mi., making for a round-trip of 8 mi. Expect to spend about 8hr. on the trail: despite its popularity with the locals, the Forest Service ranks the trail as very difficult.

TIMPANOGOS CAVE NATIONAL MONUMENT

Legend has it that a set of mountain lion tracks first led Martin Hansen to the mouth of the cave that today bears his name. **Hansen's Cave** forms but one-third of the cave system of American Fork Canyon, collectively called Timpanogos Cave. Situated in a rich alpine environment, Timpanogos is a true gem for speleologists (cave nuts) and tourists alike. Though early miners shipped boxcar loads of stalactites and other mineral wonders back east to sell to universities and museums, enough remain to bedazzle guests for the 1hr. walk through the caves. Today, the cave is open to visitors only via tours led by rangers.

Timpanogos Cave National Monument is solely accessible via Rte. 92 (20 mi. south of Salt Lake City off I-15, Exit 287; Rte. 92 also connects with Rte. 189 northeast of Provo). The **Visitors Center** dispenses tour tickets and info on the caves. Summer tours tend to sell out by early afternoon; reservations for busy summer weekends should be made as early as 30 days in advance but in less busy times are accepted at the Visitors Center up to the day before the tour. Bring water and warm layers: the rigorous hike to the cave climbs 1065 ft. over 1.5 mi., but the temperature remains a constant 45°F inside. (☎ 756-5238. Open mid-May to late Oct. daily 7am-5:30pm. 3hr. hikes depart daily 7am-4:30pm every 15min. $6, ages 6-15 $5, Golden Age Passport and ages 3-5 $3, age 2 and under free.)

The National Monument is dwarfed by the surrounding **Uinta National Forest,** which encompasses the mountains of the Wasatch Range. The **Alpine Scenic Drive (Rte. 92)** leaves the Visitors Center and heads southwest through endless aspen groves, providing excellent views of Mt. Timpanogos and other snowcapped peaks. The loopy 20 mi. drive is laden with switchbacks and takes close to 1hr. in one direction. This road will take you past many trailheads. The Forest Service charges $3 for recreation along the road on national forest land (pass good for three days). The climb to the summit of sheer **Mt. Timpanogos** (11,749 ft.) starts either from the Aspen Grove Trailhead (6860 ft.) or from the Timpooneke Trailhead (7260 ft.). The **Timpooneke Trail** (16.2 mi. round-trip to the summit) lies on the cave side of the scenic drive and meets the summit trail at Emerald Lake. The **Aspen Grove Trail** (19.8 mi. round-trip to the summit) ascends from the other side of the scenic drive, climbing 6.9 mi. to Emerald Lake and the summit trail. Both hikes are very strenuous and can be treacherous in spring or early summer when precipitous rock faces and slick snowfields make for a deadly combination. Expect the ascent to require at least a full day, and though the trails are reasonably well marked, rangers recommend that you bring a map and compass and be prepared for severe weather. The **Silver Lake Trail** (3.6 mi. round-trip, moderately difficult, 4hr.) offers a pleasant afternoon's hike, climbing from 7600 ft. to 9000 ft. Find the trailhead in the North Fork of **American Fork Canyon,** on Forest Rd. 9, just before the Granite Flat Campground. Those camping in this area should take precautions to store their food out of the reach of bears. For more info, pick up an Uintas National Forest trail guide at the **Pleasant Grove Ranger District ❶** (☎ 785-3568), 390 N. 100 E, Pleasant Grove.

The ranger district also has info on the campgrounds in the area (☎ 800-280-2267 for reservations; sites $11-13). **Backcountry camping ❶** throughout the forest requires no permit or fee as long as you respect minimum-impact guidelines. While the National Park Service forbids camping within the national monument itself, **Little Mill Campground ❶**, on Rte. 92 past the monument ($11, open early May to late Sept.) provides an excellent jumping-off point from which to beat the Timpanogos Cave crowds. Once in the Wasatch Range, services are extremely limited. Rte. 89 in nearby Pleasant Grove and Orem has gas stations, supermarkets, and fast food.

SUNDANCE RESORT

Just a short drive up Rte. 189, Robert Redford's **Sundance Resort** boasts 450 acres of pristine Utah powder and surprisingly reasonable lift ticket rates. Sundance is the best lesser-known ski resort in the country, and while lodging rates there are sky high, nearby Provo makes a good base. Three lifts provide access to a wide variety of terrain over a vertical drop of 2150 ft. UTA buses provide transportation between Provo's Mt. Timpanogos Transit Center and Sundance 8am-6pm daily. Call 888-743-3882 for more info. A year-round resort, in summer Sundance offers excellent hiking, biking, and horseback riding opportunities. (☎ 255-4107; www.sundanceresort.com. Full-day lift ticket M-F $28, Sa-Su $34, children $16, seniors $10. Ski and snowboard rentals available. Open late Nov. to early Apr. 9am-4:30pm. Sundance also offers 15 mi. of groomed nordic trails and 6mi. of separate snowshoe trails. Nordic trail fee $11, nordic ski/boot rentals $18, snowshoe rentals $10.) In Provo, the **Safari Motel ❷**, 250 S. University Ave., furnishes a few of its 30 large rooms with microwaves and refrigerators. (☎ 373-9672. Singles $35 in winter, $39 in summer; doubles $39/$49.)

OGDEN   ☎ 801

A citadel of Mormonism and a "good place to raise a family," Ogden's tourist appeal lies in its proximity to excellent outdoor opportunities in its hinterland.

■ ⁊ **ORIENTATION AND PRACTICAL INFORMATION.** Breaking with Mormon tradition, Ogden's north-south streets are generally named for presidents, while east-west streets are numbered. Most banks and a number of hotels lie along Washington Blvd., as does the mall (at 24th St.). The section of 25th St. between Wall and Grant Ave. is Ogden's historic center and boasts a variety of restaurants and shops. Harrison Blvd.,which defines the eastern limit of town, runs past Weber State and a variety of restaurants, accommodations, and services. **Express Shuttle** (☎ 300-397-0773) travels the 30 mi. between Ogden and the airport. Shuttles leave every hour on the hour (24hr. $26, each additional person $10.) **Greyhound,** 2393 Wall Ave. (☎ 394-5573), next to Union Station, has five buses daily to Salt Lake City (45min., $12), two to Logan (1-2hr., $15), two to Bringham

FROM THE ROAD

ON THE EDGE

It was the one section I didn't even bother to read. My mom gave me one of those survival books for Christmas, and I dutifully memorized key sections on stopping runaway camels and what to do in case of an alien abduction. The chapter on what to do if your car is hanging off the edge of a cliff, though, struck me as rather contrived. If your car's hanging off a cliff, I thought, you're screwed. Next page.

At 8:30pm on June 18, my friend Matt was driving down the dirt road through Nine-Mile Canyon on the way from Vernal, to Price. A car appeared around a blind corner. We swerved right, going into a ditch. The front right tire hit a small boulder and the rear of the car swung right, slamming into wall of the canyon as we skid diagonally across the roadway, and I closed my eyes before we bounced off the other vehicle and came to a rest tilted backwards at a 45° angle with the right front tire about two feet in the air.

A second elapsed. I opened the door and got out, slowly, deliberately. Matt forced his door open and squeezed through. I looked down. One hundred feet.

At that moment a feeling of deep contentment bordering on joy began to grow in me that persisted long after the fact. No one in either vehicle was injured, and standing there in the middle of the dirt road, Matt and I embraced each other. Later the wrecker would come, mumbling "this'll be interesting" as he stepped down from his truck, excited by the challenge. The car would be winched back onto the road, loaded onto a truck, and taken away. Life would go on, a little more real. *—Evan North*

City (30min., $10), four to Denver (10-14hr., $56.50), two to L.A. (18hr., $99), and two to Las Vegas (8-10hr., $49). The **Ogden Convention and Visitors Bureau,** 2501 Wall St. (☎627-8288; open M-Sa 8am-6pm), in Union Station, has brochures on the area and houses a helpful **Forest Service Information Desk.** Though trains no longer stop in Ogden, **Union Station,** situated at the base of historic 25th St., houses a number of elegant and engaging museums, notably the **Utah State Railroad Museum** and the **Browning/Kimball Car Museum.** (Open summer M-Sa 10am-6pm, Su 11am-3pm; winter M-Sa 10am-5pm. $4.) Medical care is found at **McKay-Dee Hospital Center,** 4401 Harrison Blvd. (☎627-2800). **Free Internet access** is available at many terminals in the Weber County Library, 2464 Jefferson Ave. (☎337-2632; open M-Th 10am-9pm, F-Sa 10am-6pm, Su 1-5pm). **Post office:** 2730 Washington Blvd. (open M-F 8:30am-5pm, Sa 10am-noon). **Employment:** Seasonal work abounds at Snowbasin and Powder Mountain. Job listings are available online; alternatively, call Snowbasin to request an application (☎399-1135). **ZIP code:** 84401.

🏠🍴 ACCOMMODATIONS AND FOOD. The corporate chain-gang clusters around the Ogden exits from I-15. With a convenient downtown location, the **Western Colony Inn ❸,** 234 24th St., offers large, clean rooms for excellent rates. (☎627-1332. Singles start at $43 in summer, $40 in winter, $4 per additional occupant.) Just a short drive up Ogden Canyon, the Ogden Valley provides abundant camping on the shores of Pineview Reservoir. Both **Anderson Cove ❶** and **Jefferson Hunt ❶** lie along Rte. 39 roughly 15 mi. east of the city. (Mid-May to mid-Sept. Vehicles $14 at Anderson, $12 at Jefferson; water and pit toilets at both facilities.) **Bangkok Garden ❶,** 2462 Grant Ave., delivers delicious $5 Thai and Chinese lunch specials. (☎621-4049. Open M-Th 11am-9pm, F 11am-10pm, Sa 1-10pm.) Up the canyon in Huntsville, Utah's oldest bar, **The Shooting Star Saloon ❶,** on 2nd St. S, combines Polish knockwurst and two beef patties to create a burger ($5.50) noted as one of the nation's best. (☎745-2002. 21+. Open W-Sa noon-11pm, Su 2-11pm.)

⛷ SKIING. Ogden Valley boasts two premier ski resorts. **Snowbasin,** off Rte. 39 in Ogden Valley, hosted the 2002 Olympic downhill competition on a course hailed by many ski champions as the best in the world. Olympic-driven construction brought state-of-the-art lifts and new lodges to the mountain. Nine lifts, including a high-speed quad and two gondolas, service 55 trails (20% beginner; 50% intermediate; 30% advanced) on 3200 acres of diverse skiing. Skiers descend from a peak of 9340 ft. to a 6400 ft. base. (☎399-1135; www.snowbasin.com. Open late Nov. to Apr. daily 9am-4pm. Snowboards allowed. Annual snowfall 400 in. Full-day $48, half-day $31; under 12 $23/$22; over 65 $36/$25. Discount cards available. Child ski rental packages $14 per day, adult $20 per day. Child snowboard packages from $23 per day, adult $28 per day.) **Powder Mountain,** east of Eden in Ogden Valley, delivers on the powder it promises. Seven lifts serve 81 trails (10% beginner; 50% intermediate; 40% advanced) on 2800 acres of groomed runs and another 2700 acres of pristine backcountry. The mountain's summit (8900 ft.) tops a vertical drop of 2000 ft. (☎745-3772; www.powdermountain.com. Open mid-Nov. to mid-Apr. daily 9:30am-4:30pm, night skiing 4:30-10pm on selected runs. Snowboards welcome. Annual snowfall 500 in. Full-day $37, half-day $30; under 13 $20/$17; over 65 $30/$25; night skiing $16. Adult ski rental packages $15 per day, children $10 per day. Snowboard, powder skis, and high performance packages $27 per day.) **Nordic Valley,** a small, local-use resort, has fewer services and a shorter season, but offers cheaper prices (full-day Su-F $10, Sa $20). Two double chairs service 16 runs on 100 acres of varied terrain (30% beginner; 40% intermediate; 30% advanced). All runs open for night skiing. Rentals available. (☎800-745-3511. Open mid-Dec. to mid-Mar. M-Th 5-10pm, F-Sa 9am-10pm, Su 9am-4pm.)

◪ **OTHER OUTDOOR ACTIVITIES.** The bulk of Ogden's outdoor recreation takes place up in Ogden Canyon. To reach the canyon, take 12th St. east out of town until it becomes Canyon Rd. (Rte. 39). Outdoor info is available at the **Forest Service Information Center** in Union Station.

By far the most popular canyon trail, the 3½hr. **Indian Trail** leaves Rte. 39 at the Coldwater Canyon Trailhead and winds over 4.3 mi. of moderately difficult terrain to the easternmost end of 22nd St. in Ogden. A more strenuous hike, the **Ben Lomond Trail,** ascends roughly 4000 ft. to the top of Ben Lomond Peak. Starting at North Fork Park in Ogden Valley, the trail traverses 7.3 mi. of rocky terrain to the 9712 ft. summit and demands an entire day. From the top, climbers rejoice at sweeping views of the Great Salt Lake. The **Wheeler Trail** complex, accessible from just below the Pineview Reservoir dam, is a favorite of local mountain bikers. For bike rental in the Ogden Valley, stop by **Diamond Peak Sport and Ski** in Eden. (☎745-0101. Open summer M-Sa 10am-6pm; winter M-Sa 8am-10pm, Su 8am-6pm. From Rte. 39, turn left over the Pineview Dam onto Rte. 158. Bike rentals from $20 per day. Tu group trail ride and Th group road ride leave from the store at 6pm.) Ogden locals spend weekends on the water at Pineview Reservoir. To rent a wave-runner, visit **Chris's,** along Rte. 39 in Huntsville. (☎745-3542. Open 9am-7pm. $125 per day. Customer's car must have tow hitch in order to transport wave-runner to lake.) Downtown Ogden offers water-borne recreation of its own at a new kayaking park, where 24th St. meets the Weber River.

LOGAN AND BEAR LAKE   ☎435

In 1824, when Ephraim Logan descended into the beautiful Cache Valley, he encountered a hardy group of fur trappers. Solitary by nature and by trade, these rugged outdoorsmen gathered infrequently to talk, barter, and, of course, party like animals. Utah State students have taken up the mantle of their forefathers, and Logan still knows how to throw a raucous party. The bustling hamlet is a college town through and through, replete with cultural events, cheap restaurants, and, unfortunately, expensive lodging.

UTAH

⊞ ⚡ ORIENTATION AND PRACTICAL INFORMATION. The city spreads out along Rte. 89 (called Main in town), extending toward the mountains through a charming downtown stretch. 500 N leads to the Utah State Campus, whereas 1400 N accesses a growing infestation of strip malls. Following Rte. 89 through town leads to Logan Canyon, an impressive and imposing scenic byway. After winding through the canyon to the northeast, Logan Canyon Rd. terminates at Garden City on the impossibly turquoise Bear Lake, a popular resort destination and watersports haven. **Greyhound,** 754 W. 600 N (☎752-2877; open M-F 9:30am-noon and 2-7:30pm), runs two buses daily to Salt Lake City (2hr. 3:35am and 6:40pm; $16.25 one-way). For more info about Logan, the Cache Valley, Logan Canyon, and Bear Lake, stop first at the **Cache Chamber of Commerce,** 160 N. Main, for helpful literature. (☎752-2161. Open summer M-Sa 9am-5pm, winter M-F 9am-5pm.) In Garden City, the **Bear Lake Visitors Center,** on Logan Canyon Hwy., has information on activities at Bear Lake. (☎946-2760. Open summer M-Sa 10am-6pm, Su 11am-5pm.) **IHC Logan Regional Hospital** (☎716-1000) provides full medical care at 1400 N and 500 E in Logan. For medical assistance in Garden City, head to **Bear Lake Memorial Hospital's Fast Aid Medical Clinic** (☎208-847-1630), a small 24hr. clinic on Logan Canyon Hwy. **Free Internet access** is available at Logan's Cache County Library, 255 N. Main (open M-Th 10am-9pm, F-Sa 10am-6pm). **Post office:** 151 N. 100 W (☎752-7246; open M-F 8:30am-5:30pm, Sa 8:30am-12:30pm). **ZIP code:** 84321.

⚡⚡ FOOD AND ACCOMMODATIONS. Logan lodging is steep and dominated by national chains. **Days Inn ❸,** 364 S. Main, has the lowest rates in town and spotless rooms with microwaves and minifridges. (☎753-5623. Singles start at $40 in winter, $50 in summer; doubles $50/$60.) On the glamorous, resort-dominated Bear Lake, the **Bear Lake Motor Lodge ❸,** 50 S. Bear Lake Blvd., rents bright, clean rooms, some with kitchenettes. (☎946-3333 or 946-2971. Singles $49 in summer, $39 in winter; $10 per extra person. Reservations needed summer weekends.) Ten miles south of Garden City on Rte. 30, **Rendezvous Beach State Park ❶** has 186 sites along the shoreline. (☎946-3343. Running water, toilets, and showers. Tent sites $14, full hookups $20.) The Forest Service-operated **Sunrise Campground ❶,** above Garden City along Logan Canyon Hwy., perches over Bear Lake in an aspen forest. (Open mid-May to mid-Oct. Toilets and running water. Tent sites $12.)

Logan offers an uncommon variety of reasonably priced restaurants, representing many types of ethnic fare. Most restaurants lie along Main, although the shopping plazas north of downtown also house Logan eateries. Don't miss the 1920s-era soda fountain at the town classic **■Bluebird Cafe ❷,** 19 N. Main. Its tasty and inexpensive traditional American fare (lunches $4-5, dinners $8-10) is famous as far away as Ogden. (☎752-3155. Open M-Th 11am-9:30pm, F-Sa 11am-10pm.) The chic **Caffe Ibis ❶,** 52 Federal St., one block past 100 N off Main, has creative deli sandwiches, soups and salads ($3-8), and specialty coffees and is popular with the student crowd. (☎753-4777. Open M-Th 6am-9pm, F-Sa 6am-10pm, Su 8am-6pm.)

⚡ OUTDOOR ACTIVITIES. Rte. 89 between Logan and Bear Lake has "scenic byway" designation, and the helpful **Forest Service Information Center** welcomes visitors at the canyon's entrance. (☎755-3620. Open M-F 8am-4:30pm.) Stop for the useful brochure guide to the canyon and for the historical kiosk, as well as info on other scenic area routes. Mile markers along the byway correspond to descriptions in the brochure, making for a comprehensive tour of the canyon. Along the road, pull-outs allow parking for such activities as **spelunking, backcountry skiing, day hiking, fly fishing,** and **rock climbing.** For sport and traditional climbers alike, the canyon's limestone walls cater to all ability levels. Canoe, kayak, ski, and hiking gear rental, as well as books, maps, and advice, are available at **Trailhead,** 117 N.

Main. (☎783-1541. Open M-Sa 10am-6pm. Backpacks $5 per day; cross-country skis $10; snowshoes $8; canoes $20; kayaks $15.) For mountain bikes and snowboards, **Norda's Mountain Outfitters** is less than a block away at 77 N. Main. (☎752-2934. Open M-Sa 10am-7pm. Full-suspension bikes $25 per day; snowboards $20; basic skis $16, high end $25.) **Bitter Sweet,** 51 S. Main, offers three-day climbing lesson packages for $85, rents climbing shoes ($4), and sells other climbing equipment. (☎752-8152. Open summer M-Sa 9am-6pm, winter M-Sa 10am-10pm.)

NORTHEASTERN UTAH

Centered on the small town of Vernal, this portion of Utah lies in the northern reaches of the Colorado Plateau, bounded by the high peaks of the Uintas. Tracts of land composing the Uintah and Ouray Indian Reservation dot the landscape. The cooler climate of the Uintas and the waters of Flaming Gorge and the Green River provide visitors with a pleasant break from the parching summer heat.

VERNAL   ☎435

Historically an important mining and cattle center, Vernal has shifted to a Dinosaurland tourism economy. Vernal's geographic location allows speedy access to the lush, high Uintas, the ancient canyons of Dinosaur National Monument, and the blazing red walls of Flaming Gorge. Though not a destination in and of itself, Vernal prides itself on being a friendly base for regional exploration.

ORIENTATION AND PRACTICAL INFORMATION. To see virtually all there is to see in Vernal, drive down U.S. 40. A stopover town for nearly a century, Vernal has evolved to meet the needs of vacationers just passing through. Strip malls vie for highway-front real estate. **Greyhound** runs buses to **Denver** (8hr., 2 per day, $56) and **Salt Lake City** (4½hr., 2 per day, $35) from Frontier Travel, 72 S. 100 W (☎789-0404; open M-F 8:30am-5:30pm). **The Northeast Utah Visitors Center,** 235 E. Main (☎789-7894; open daily 8am-9pm), provides info on Vernal, the Dinosaur National Monument, and other regional recreational activities. Pick up maps of hiking and biking trails here. The **Ashley Valley Medical Center,** 151 W. 200 N (☎789-3342), treats rafting injuries and all other ailments. For **free Internet access** in Vernal, visit the Ashley County Public Library, 155 E. Main, down the road from the Visitors Center. (☎789-0091. Open M-Th 10am-9pm, F-Sa 10am-6pm.) Mail kitschy dinosaur postcards from the **post office,** 67 N. 600 W (open M-F 9am-5pm, Sa 10am-1pm). **ZIP code:** 84078.

ACCOMMODATIONS AND CAMPING. There's plenty of camping in and around Vernal for those who prefer the convenience of remaining close to civilization and avoiding the scorching heat of the National Monument. Just north of town on Rte. 191, **Steinnaker State Park ❶** has 29 well-developed sites with water spigots and flush toilets on a gorgeous beach and reservoir. (☎789-4432. Open Apr. to mid-Oct. Tent sites $11.) For the camping amenities that only a KOA can provide, head to **Campground Dina RV Park ❶**, 930 N. Vernal Ave., about 1 mi. north of Main on U.S. 191 in Vernal. (☎789-2148 or 800-562-7574 for reservations. Heated pool, showers, laundry, convenience store. Grassy tent sites for up to 2 people $18, full hookups $22, each additional person $2. Call ahead for summer weekends.)

Although camping is choice near Vernal, the town does support several motels. In high-demand summer months, be aware that prices may not match quality. The comfortable **Sage Motel ❸**, 54 W. Main, has standard rooms, A/C, satellite TV, and free local calls. (☎789-1442 or 800-760-1442. Singles $45 in winter, $50 in summer;

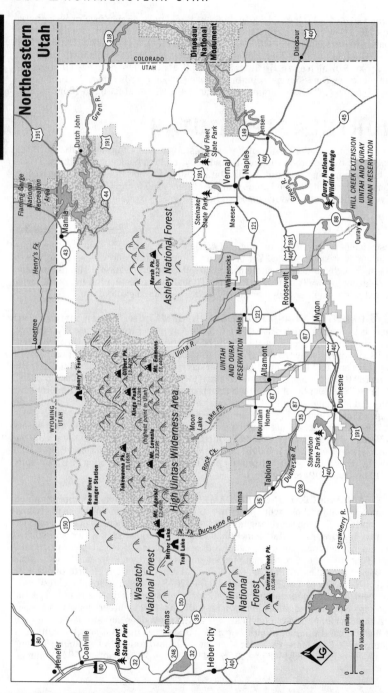

Northeastern Utah

doubles $55/$60.) On the outskirts of town toward the National Monument, **Split Mountain Motel** ❷, 1015 E. U.S. 40, has clean rooms with A/C, microwave, and minifridge. (☎789-9020. Singles $40 in winter, $45 in summer; doubles $50/$55.)

■ **FOOD.** The **7-11 Ranch Restaurant** ❶, 77 E. Main, in Vernal, packs in locals and tourists for monster breakfasts ($5) and fresh java. (☎789-1170. Open M-Sa 6am-11pm; breakfast served until noon.) Imported to the **Weston Inn** from nearby LaPointe, **Stockman's** ❶, 1684 W. U.S. 40, lures hordes of hungry Vernalites for an exciting menu of Southwest cuisine, steak, and seafood. Burgers ($5-7) and gargantuan decadent desserts ($5-6) are highlights. (☎781-3030. Open Tu-F 10am-11pm, Sa 11:30am-11pm.) Homemade salsa is the special at **LaLa's Fiesta** ❷, 550 E. Main. Lunch and dinner specialties begin with the *chile relleno* (2 for $5), and all meals are under $9. (☎789-2966. Open M-Sa 11am-9pm.) If stocking up for a camping excursion, visit **Jubilee Foods**, 575 W. Main (☎789-2001; open until midnight).

■ **SIGHTS AND OUTDOORS.** Housed in the same building as the Visitors Center, **The Field House**, built in 1958, offers a complex overview of the geology and natural history underlying the paleontological abundance of the area. A small laboratory demonstrates how bones are extracted from rock. (☎789-3799. Open in summer daily 8am-9pm; in winter 9am-5pm. $5.) For Western history buffs, the **Western Heritage Museum**, 328 E. 200 S, offers revealing info about Josie Basset and the Wild Bunch. (☎789-7399. Open M-F 9am-6pm, Sa-Su 10am-5pm. Free.) A **Western Park** (☎789-1352) at the same address hosts weekly competitions and a National Rodeo every July. For another perspective on Western culture, the **Northern Ute Indian Pow Wow**, held on the 4th of July in Ft. Duchesne, west of Vernal, draws large crowds from throughout northeast Utah.

As a gateway, Vernal is surrounded by outdoor destinations with no real attraction or park of its own. However, enterprising outfitters offer products and services to accommodate a variety of outdoor sports in the region. **Basin Sports**, 551 W. Main (☎789-2199; open M-F 9am-7:30pm, Sa 9am-7pm), sells budget outdoor gear for camping, hunting, and rafting. **Altitude Cycle**, 510 E. Main #8, rents Cannondale bikes in the off season and provides free advice on area riding year-round. (☎781-2595. Open M-F 10am-6pm, Sa 9am-5pm. Bike rentals Sept.-May. Bikes from $10 per hr., $25 per half day, $35 per full day. Coed group rides W, women's rides F evenings.) **River Runners' Transport**, 417 E. Main, is Vernal's do-it-yourself river-running contractor, a great alternative to all of the rafting outfits in town. They offer boat rentals and vehicle shuttling services for those brave enough to run the rivers on their own; they will coordinate entire rafting vacations. (☎800-930-7238. Open M-Sa 8am-5pm. Rafts from $85 per day, kayaks $25 per day, canoe package $45 per day. Call well in advance for reservations.) A dive shop? In the desert? In business for more than a decade, **Atlantis Divers**, 206 W. Main, offers beginner open-water certification ($250) in Flaming Gorge, as well as more extreme river and ice diving. (☎789-3616. Open M-F 9am-6pm, Sa 8am-1pm.)

DINOSAUR NATIONAL MONUMENT ☎435

Poised at the confluence of the Green and Yampa Rivers, the 330-square-mile Dinosaur National Monument is a natural historian's promised land. These rapidly flowing tributaries of the Colorado have sliced through the eons recorded in sedimentary stratigraphy, creating both an informative lesson in geology and a tantalizing morsel of eye candy. Of course, there are the fossils too: the world's most concentrated collection of Jurassic Era dinosaur bones. On top of these large saurian remains, the monument's sandstone cliffs served as a canvas upon which

UTAH

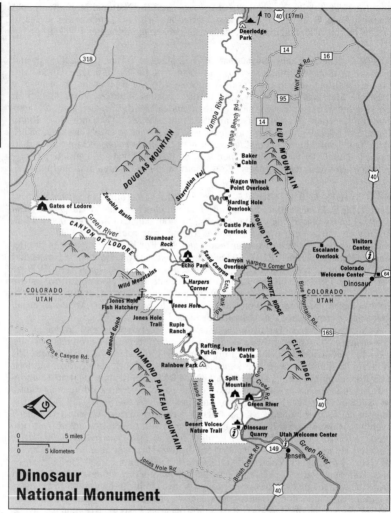

**Dinosaur
National Monument**

Archaic and Fremont Native Americans carved a dazzling iconography. Amid these natural and man-made wonders, the monument provides a superb arena for outdoor recreation, whether hiking, biking, backpacking, or river running.

✴ 🛈 ORIENTATION AND PRACTICAL INFORMATION

The national monument's western and main entrance lies 20 mi. east of Vernal, on Rte. 149, which splits from U.S. 40 southwest of the park in Jenson, UT. Several other roads access the park: Jones Hole Rd. in the northwest, Rte. 318 and a 10 mi. unpaved road in the north, Harper's Corner Rd. in the south and Deerlodge Rd. in the east from U.S. 40, east of Elk Springs, CO. Once inside the park, pay a visit to

UTAH

the **Dinosaur Quarry Visitors Center,** a remarkable Bauhaus building that houses exhibits, a bookstore, and an exposed river bank brimming with dinosaur bones. During the summer, a **shuttle** whisks passengers up the ½ mi. to the Visitors Center; between Labor Day and Memorial Day cars can drive directly to the Center. (☎781-7700. Open June-Aug. 8am-7pm, Sept.-May 8am-4:30pm.) A second Visitors Center at **Monument Headquarters,** 45 mi. along Hwy. 40 from the Rte. 149 turnoff in Dinosaur, CO, has info on scenic canyons and river running, but no fossils. (☎970-374-3000. Open June-Aug. daily 8am-6pm, Sept.-May M-F 8am-4:30pm.) There are no **services** within the national monument. **Gas** is available in Vernal and Jenson, UT, and Dinosaur, CO. Multi-day campers should stock up on food in Vernal, which also provides the closest restaurants and indoor accommodations.

Wise travelers avoid the scorching summer sun by visiting in the spring and fall, but most people come in the summer, primed to fight the heat and the crowds. To protect the monument from this heavy tourist influx, the Park Service has instated a series of **regulations.** Vehicles must stay on designated roads, campfires should be built only in firepits, pets must be leashed at all times and are not allowed on trails or in the backcountry, and hunting of any kind is illegal. *The monument's greatest hazards threaten visitors during the sweltering summer months: be sure to drink plenty of water and apply sunscreen frequently.*

CAMPING

The monument contains six designated camping areas. The most easily accessible site during summer months, **Green River ❶,** lies along Cub Creek Rd. about 5 mi. from the entrance fee station. (88 sites. Flush toilets and water. $12.) Nearby **Split Mountain ❶** hosts only groups during the summer, but is open to all during winter months. For both campgrounds, water is turned off in the winter and tent sites are free. The monument's four other designated camping areas all require more effort to reach. To access the sites at **Rainbow Park ❶,** a popular put-in for single-day rafting trips, go 3 mi. on Rte. 149 from U.S. 40 to Brush Creek Rd.; follow Brush Creek 5 mi. and turn right on Island Park Rd. (acceptable for low-clearance vehicles but impassable when wet). The campsites are at the end of the road, 16 mi. from the turnoff. (2 sites. Pit toilets, no water. Free.) **Echo Park Campground ❶,** 13 mi. along Echo Park Rd. off the Harper's Corner Drive, is perched on a high-clearance, four-wheel-drive road above the confluence of the Green and Yampa Rivers. Views of the rivers and canyons at Echo Park rank among the monument's best. (9 sites. $6. Pit toilets and water in summer only, free when water is turned off.) The northern- and easternmost corners of the monument also have campsites, at **Gates of Lodore ❶** (17 sites; $6; pit toilets and water in summer only, free when water is turned off) and **Deerlodge Park ❶** (8 sites, pit toilets, no water; free). Gates of Lodore lies 10 mi. east of Rte. 318, and Deerlodge Park is 17 mi. off U.S. 40 in Colorado.

"SCIENCE FIRST, MEN!" In early June, 1869, intrepid explorer and avid naturalist John Wesley Powell, missing an arm and lashed to his boat, led a team of eight "mountain men" into the Gates of Lodore, at the northern tip of today's Dinosaur National Monument. Powell, the self-reliant, decorated Civil War hero, professor of Natural History, and later director of the US Geological Survey, lived the rugged, independent life that makes the modern outdoorsman feel envious and downright feeble. Yet, despite the heroics involved in leading a team down the treacherous waters that had ruined earlier expeditions, Powell downplayed the adventurousness of his "scientific" mission. In the face of constant danger he insisted on taking scientific measurements, and at journey's end his main regret was not the hardship for himself and his men, but instead that they hadn't taken enough data. His crew probably thought him crazy, as demonstrated by the incident at Disaster Falls in Lodore. One of the ships had capsized and broken apart on the rocks, but the cabin had remained intact, wedged next to a large boulder downstream from the falls. Fearing the loss of all of his precious barometers (they'd all been foolishly stored in one boat), Powell sent several men out into the raging river on a recovery mission. When the men reached the boat, they began shouting ecstatically. As Powell recounts in his journal, he was surprised to see such exuberance over the recovery of the scientific instruments that his men considered utterly ridiculous. The men, it turns out, were in fact celebrating the discovery of an intact whiskey barrel, which they dragged joyously back to shore. To Powell's relief, they also remembered to retrieve a few of the barometers. No hardship too great in the name of science. Or whiskey, as the case may be.

OUTDOOR ACTIVITIES

The national monument offers a variety of informational and recreational activities, catered to suit all lengths of stay. For those passing through, a stop at the Dinosaur Quarry Visitors Center provides an overview of the monument's features, as well as the chance to see a dinosaur-bone-riddled riverbank. For travelers with time to see more, there are miles of road, trail, and river to explore.

ON THE RIVER

Perhaps the best way to see Dinosaur National Monument is as the early explorers did: by boat. A day or multi-day float down the Green or Yampa River funnels travelers through roaring rapids and magnificent canyons. Numerous rafting outfits operate in the area, but only two have permits to run daily rafting trips. Daily trips float from Rainbow Park to the take-out near Split Mountain Campground. **Don Hatch River Expeditions,** 221 N. 400 E. in Vernal, is descended from one of the nation's earliest commercial rafting enterprises. Well-respected Hatch Expeditions floats through the monument and the nearby Flaming Gorge. Be sure to request a paddle trip if you're interested in helping steer the raft. (☎789-4316 or 800-342-8243; www.hatchriver.com. Open M-F 9am-5pm. One-day trip $66, age 6-12 $56; seniors 10% off. Advance reservations recommended.) **Adrift Adventures,** at the corner of Rte. 149 and U.S. 40 in Jenson, UT, runs daily trips through Split Mountain Gorge as well as multi-day trips in Colorado and Utah. (☎800-824-0150. Open M-Sa 8am-6pm, Su 8am-5pm. Trips leave daily at 9am from the store. One-day trip $66, children $55. Advance reservations recommended.)

It is possible for experienced river runners with their own equipment to gain access to the monument's rivers, but this requires a lot of forethought, planning, and luck. Applications ($15 non-refundable fee) must be submitted by February 1 for summer trips, and in 2000, only 300 permits were randomly awarded to a pool of 4500 applicants. Applicants are notified of lottery selection by March 1 and must then submit a secondary application. Those who win must pay an extra fee for the permits (one-day $25, multi-day up to 5 days $125, each additional day $35) and follow a list of park regulations for boating. Call 970-374-2468 for more information and to request an application (office open M-F 8am-noon).

ON THE ROAD

There are two paved scenic driving tours of the park, as well as an extensive web of four-wheel-drive and high-clearance roads. Inquire at the Visitors Center for road conditions and specific driving advice.

Cub Creek Scenic Drive (22 mi. round-trip, 1-3hr.). Beginning at the Quarry Visitors Center, this drive winds past striking mountains, ambling rivers, prehistoric rock art, and ends at the Josie Morris Homestead. A guide to the drive (available at the Visitors Center; 50¢) points out notable features along the way. Examine the whimsical and mysterious lizards, goats, princesses, and hunters carved into the boulders by ancient artists. Stretch your legs at the end of the drive, either on the **Hog Canyon Trail** (1 mi.) or the **Box Canyon Trail** (¼ mi.); both hikes are easy and descend into breathtaking canyons.

Harper's Corner Rd. (62 mi. round-trip, 2-4hr.). This paved route begins at the Headquarters Visitors Center and climbs to a spectacular vantage point for viewing the canyons sculpted by the Green and Yampa rivers. At road's end, the moderate 2 mi. **Harper's Corner Trail** leads to one of the park's most magnificent views and should not be missed. The Park Service warns that open grazing occurs along the road, creating a serious driving hazard for cars traveling at high speeds.

ON THE TRAIL

Exploring the monument on foot provides a way to dodge summer crowds, as most tourists see the park from behind auto glass; it also gives a good sense of desert travel's difficulty. Be sure to pack plenty of water and sunscreen. The **Desert Voices Trail** (2 mi. round-trip) offers a moderate hike departing from the Split Mountain boat ramp and provokes reflection on the desert environment with a series of interpretive signs. A more challenging glimpse of desert environs faces hikers on the **Sound of Silence Hike** (2 mi. round-trip), along which hikers must navigate using only a series of landmarks; there is no trail. Sound of Silence departs from Cub Creek Rd. halfway between the entrance gate and Split Mountain Campground. To experience the fertile riparian ecosystems that flourish even in the desert heat, try the stream-side **Jones Hole Trail** (8 mi. round-trip). This moderate hike begins at the Jones Hole Fish Hatchery, accessible via Jones Hole Rd.

FLAMING GORGE ☎ 435

The fading light of the sunset turns the walls of Red Canyon to glowing embers, hence the moniker "Flaming Gorge." Natural beauty alone, however, didn't satisfy the electricity and water demands of the Bureau of Reclamation; a BOR dam completed in 1964 as part of the Colorado River Storage Project now generates power for 150,000 homes. Today, the reservoir and over 200,000 surrounding acres, ranging from alpine wilderness and dramatic canyons in the south to high desert in the north, are protected as the Forest Service's Flaming Gorge National Recreation Area. Outdoors enthusiasts, especially boaters and fishermen, descend into the gorge every summer to take advantage of this altered landscape.

Called "the world's longest art gallery," the sandstone cliffs of Nine-Mile Canyon have served as a canvas for Native American artists throughout the ages. Though people have inhabited the canyon for 12,000 years, the majority of the petroglyphs, held to be some of the best in the world, date roughly from AD 1000. The Scenic Backcountry Byway travels 78 miles from Myton to Wellington, though the majority of the petroglyphs appear along a 50 mi. corridor toward the southern end. The name "Nine-Mile Canyon" derives from a surveying map produced by John Wesley Powell's expedition through Utah in 1869. Powell's mapmaker found a small creek at the ninth mile marker, dubbing it "Nine-Mile Creek."

A roadtrip through the canyon can begin either from the north or south. From Rte. 40 in the north, a sign points the way to Nine-Mile Canyon 1½ mi. west of Myton. Be sure to take a left at the first fork in the road. The 32 mi. gravel road leading from Myton to the canyon is not especially scenic and without Fremont art. From the south, the main access route is 8 mi. east of Price in the town of Wellington. Turn north on 2200 E (Soldier Creek Road) at the Chevron Station. The first 12 miles of the road, up to the Soldier Creek Mine, are paved.

At least a full day should be dedicated to driving the canyon, allowing 4hr. for driving and time for walks to and from the petroglyphs. The road surface is poor and impassible in wet weather. Washboard ruts, punctuated by the occasional axle-breaking pothole, reduce speed to 20 m.p.h. Sandy patches and blind corners mandate extreme caution.

There are no services along the byway. Stock up on water, food, and gas before you go. A spare tire and emergency kit are also a good idea. Binoculars and a local canyon guide help to precisely locate petroglyphs. **Nine-Mile Canyon Ranch Bunk and Breakfast ❶**, 25 mi. north of Wellington, offers the only indoor accommodations in the canyon, complete with home-cooked meals. (☎435-637-2572; www.ninemilecanyon.com. Bunk rooms $60, cabins $40; camping with water, toilets, and picnic tables $10.) Camping is allowed even if the owners are away. Summer temperatures can soar to near 100°F, and proper viewing of much of the art requires leaving the car. Although most of the land along Nine-Mile Canyon belongs to private ranchers, some primitive camping can be found 13 mi. up **Gate Canyon.** Mountain bikers frequently ride the canyon and side loops in tributary canyons.

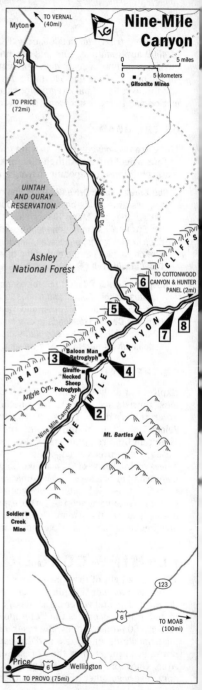

NINE-MILE CANYON

Note that the mile markers along the canyon start from Wellington but are equally useful to southbound travelers as navigational aids.

TIME: 4hr. driving time

DISTANCE: 78 mi.

SEASON: year-round

1 PREPARATION. Starting in Price, a quick stop at **Eastern Utah College's Prehistoric Museum,** 153 E. Main St., provides enriching background knowledge. (☎637-5060. Open summer daily 9am-6pm. $3 suggested donation.) In Vernal, the **Northeast Utah Visitors Center,** 235 E. Main, stocks a variety of helpful pamphlets on the canyon. (☎789-7894. Open daily 8am-9pm.) For general info and info on biking, contact the **Price BLM Office,** 125 S. 600 W. (☎636-3600; open M-F 7:45am-4:30pm).

2 MILE 26: THE FIRST PETROGLYPHS. A rocky outcropping protected by a squat wooden fence appears 26 mi. north of Wellington. The rocks just inside the fence display a number of petroglyphs. This extensive collection serves as an excellent way to train the eye what to look for when driving up the canyon; most other panels are more difficult to spot. Before leaving, glance up to spot an impressive panel carved into the rock just above a narrow ledge.

3 MILE 30: HARPER. Thirty miles past Wellington rests an assemblage of battered structures that have the look of an old homestead site. These abandoned buildings were part of the once-bustling town of Harper, which used to spread nearly 1 mi. along the canyon. Able to flourish while the road served as the principal link between Price and the Uintah Basin, Harper went bust when the railroad diverted freighters away from the canyon.

4 MILE 31.5: PIG HEAD ROCK. Rounding a corner brings into view a gigantic boulder, perched perilously close to the road. Don't worry, it won't fall—it's been there since pioneer days. Some say it looks like Porky Pig; pre-Disney pioneers called it "Giant's Chew of Gum." About 20 ft. farther up the road, a well-trodden foot path leads to a smattering of petroglyphs. After examining the main panel, follow the outcropping left and right for more viewing.

5 MILE 34: GATE CANYON. After passing several ranch buildings, Nine-Mile Canyon Rd. meets a junction with Gate Canyon and the road to Myton. Gate Canyon earned its name for a stone arch that once spanned the canyon over the road. Stagecoach employees destroyed the decaying arch at the turn of the century to protect travelers. The road was built after the Civil War by the 9th Cavalry, an African-American company.

6 MILE 38.7: THE GRANARY. A cattle-guard crosses the road just before it bends around a towering, sheer rock face. Spotting the intact granary high on the cliff requires either very careful eyes or binoculars, since it hides against a background of light-colored rock, perched on a ledge about 300 ft. above the canyon floor. For those with good memories, the Prehistoric Museum exhibit contains a photograph of the granary useful in helping to pick it out against the cliff face. The Fremont people used granaries to store and protect surpluses of corn, beans, and squash.

7 MILE 42.7: RASSMUSSEN'S CAVE. The cave, really an alcove, was used heavily by the Fremont people, as evidenced by the numerous petroglyphs and the depressions worn into the rock by corn grinding. Earlier excavations at the cave unearthed mummies and native artifacts. Today, the alcove suffers from visitor negligence—trash and graffiti soil the once-beautiful site.

8 MILE 45: THE HUNTER PANEL. One and a half miles up Cottonwood Canyon, which lies roughly 44 mi. from Wellington, is the drive's most famous petroglyph, the hunter panel. A complex scene depicting a herd of prey and a native hunter poised for the kill, this remarkable glyph culminates a visit to the canyon.

⚡ 🛈 ORIENTATION AND PRACTICAL INFORMATION

From Vernal, UT, follow scenic byway U.S. 191 north to the recreation area. Signs explain the geologic history of the area along the spectacular ascent through the foothills. The reservoir extends as far north as Green River, WY, and is also accessible from I-80. A recreation pass ($2 per day, $5 per 16 days) can be obtained at the **Flaming Gorge Visitors Center,** on U.S. 191 atop the Flaming Gorge Dam, or at most stores surrounding the Gorge. The Visitors Center also offers free tours of the dam and power plant. (☎885-3135. Open daily 8am-6pm; off-season 10am-4pm.) A few miles off U.S. 191 and 3 mi. off Rte. 44 to Manila, the **Red Canyon Visitors Center** hangs 1360 ft. above the reservoir, offering breathtaking views into the canyon. (☎889-3713. Open late May to Aug. daily 10am-5pm.) Gas and other services cluster around the dam and the towns of Manila and Dutch John, UT. **Post Office:** 4 South Blvd., in Dutch John (☎885-3351. Open M-F 7:30am-3:30pm, Sa 8:30am-11am and 1:45-3:15pm.) **ZIP code:** 84023.

🏠 🏕 ACCOMMODATIONS AND CAMPING

Camping in the area is scenic and accessible. Visitors Centers can offer sound advice on how to pick from the over 30 campgrounds spread around the lake. A number of sites can be reserved by calling 888-444-6777 at least five days in advance. The 19 secluded sites at **Dripping Springs ❶,** just past Dutch John on Rte. 191, are some of the most coveted, due to their prime fishing location. (Sites $14. Pit toilets, water available early May to mid-Oct.; open with no fee rest of year. Reservations accepted.) **Canyon Rim ❶,** on the road to the Red Canyon Visitors Center, offers a feeling of high-country camping with nearby views of the red-walled gorge and convenient access to the Canyon Rim Trail. ($14. Pit toilets, water available mid-May to mid-Sept.; open with no fee untill snow forces closure.) Several miles past Dutch John, the popular **Mustang Ridge Campground ❶** lies just above an excellent swimming hole and a boat ramp. ($16. Water, flush toilets. Open mid-May to mid-Sept.) The immense **Firefighter's Memorial Campground ❶,** on Rte. 191 south of the dam, has numerous large, shady sites, some with hillside views of the reservoir. ($14. Water, pit toilets. Open mid-May to mid-Sept.) Showers are available at **Deer Run, Cedar Springs, Firehole,** and **Mustang Ridge** ($3 for non-campers).

While camping is cheaper, indoor lodging can be found at **Red Canyon Lodge ❸,** 2 mi. before the Visitors Center on Rte. 44. While this lodge offers location, views, and year-round activities more in line with a luxury resort, budget cabins are available. (☎889-3759; www.redcanyonlodge.com. Private lake, restaurant. 2-person cabins with restrooms $55, 4-person $65; each additional adult $6, each child under 12 $2; rollaway beds $6 per night.)

Twenty-eight miles north on Rte. 44, the town of **Manila** boasts a collection of motels, though the dollar doesn't buy much in the way of quality during the summer. In town, the **Steinnaker Motel ❷,** at the intersection of Rte. 43 and 44, offers five rooms that are cramped but clean, some with kitchenette. (☎784-3104. Check-in at the Chevron station. Singles $36; doubles $44; tax included.)

🏔 OUTDOOR ACTIVITIES

FISHING AND BOATING

The Flaming Gorge Reservoir and the Green River below the dam offer some of the best fishing in the country. Fishing **permits** ($8 first day, $6 each additional day) are available at Flaming Gorge Lodge, Dutch John Recreation Services, and most stores in Manila. **Cedar Springs Marina,** 3 mi. before the dam, rents pontoon, ski, and fishing boats and offers guided fishing trips. (☎889-3795. Open daily 8am-6pm. 10-person pontoon boats from $120 for 3hr., $200 per day. 6-person ski boats $130/$220; skis $15 per day. 6-person fishing boats $50/90.) Nearby, **Flaming Gorge Lodge** rents fishing rods, as well as offering summer seasonal employment. Check the web site for details. (☎889-3773; www.fglodge.com. Open daily 6:30am-8pm. $15 per day.) At **Lucerne Valley Marina,** 7 mi. east of Manila off Rte. 43, you can procure a 14 ft. fishing boat for $75 a day. (☎784-3483. Open daily around 7am-9pm. $50 deposit required.)

RIVER RUNNING

The stretch of the **Green River** from the base of the **dam** to the **Gates of Lodore** in Dinosaur National Monument (see p. 257) does not require a permit and contains several named rapids. Below the dam, management of the river is divided into three sections: **Spillway to Little Hole, Little Hole to Indian Crossing,** and **Indian Crossing to the Gates of Lodore.** The first section, a popular, 7 mi. trip, can take 1-3hr., depending on outflow from the dam (daily outflow can range from 830 to 4500 cubic feet per second). There is no camping between the Spillway and Little Hole. The next section, 7.5 mi. from Little Hole to Indian Crossing, demands 3-4hr. of float time and is speckled with developed campsites available to rafters. Fewer rafters continue on for the remaining 30.8 mi. to the Gates of Lodore, although no permit is required until the boundary of the National Monument. For more info on floating the Green, contact the **Flaming Gorge Ranger District,** at the corner of Rte. 43 and 44 in Manila. (☎784-3445. Open M-F 8am-4:30pm.)

Several companies rent rafts to self-guided rafters and provide shuttle services up and down the waterway. **Green River Outfitters,** at the Rte. 66 gas station in Dutch John, offers guided fishing trips, in addition to raft rental and shuttle services. (☎885-3338. 2-person kayak $30 per day, 6-, 7-, 8-, 10-, and 14-person rafts $45-80. Moving a vehicle from the dam to Little Hole costs $25.) The **Flaming Gorge Recreation Service,** at the Conoco Station in Dutch John, rents the same sort of equipment. (☎885-3191. 2-person kayaks $39 per day, 7-person rafts $49 per day, 8-person rafts $59. Shuttling between the dam and Little Hole costs $47, to move a vehicle $32. Waverunners $150 per day.)

HIKING AND BIKING

Although most reservoir recreationalists stick to boats, water skis, and fishing poles, the area offers an extensive network of hiking and biking trails. One of Utah's most traveled thoroughfares, I-15 ferries red-rock-hungry tourists from the Salt Lake City Airport to their chosen destination in southern Utah. Although the towns along the highway tend toward the boring side, the amphitheater in Cedar Breaks and the Shakespeare festival in Cedar City merit stops on the way to Utah's national parks. The **Canyon Rim Trail,** a moderate 5 mi. one-way hike, has access points at the Red Canyon Visitors Center, and the Red Canyon, Canyon Rim, Green Lake, and Greendale campgrounds. From the Visitors Center to Canyon Rim Campground, the trail traces the edge of Red Canyon for about a mile before splitting into two forks. The left fork follows the rim of the canyon, while the right cuts inland to Green Lake before the trails meet up again and continue to the Greendale Overlook. Starting at Canyon Rim Campground, the trail can also be done as a 2.7 mi. loop. Another popular hike begins at **Dowd Mountain** and descends 1500 ft. into Hideout Canyon over the course of 5 mi. To access the trail, turn at signs for the mountain off Rte. 44 south of Manila. The first mile is relatively flat and boasts spectacular views of the gorge. Beginning at the base of the dam, the **Little Hole**

UTAH

A ROYAL ROMP FIT FOR A KING. Despite inconvenient access, the trailhead leading to Utah's highest peak, **Kings Peak** (13,528 ft.), is routinely packed during summer months. A shot at bagging Utah's highest begins in Lonetree, WY. First, stock up on provisions and fill up with gas. If approaching from I-80 in Wyoming, Mountain View provides the last services. From Flaming Gorge in Utah, Manila has the last gas stations and markets. The sign for Rte. 290 lies hidden off Rte. 414, the major thoroughfare. To find the turn, clock 22 mi. from Mountain View, WY and take the right onto gravel past the first cluster of buildings. On Rte. 290 S, the sign for Henry's Fork Trailhead appears immediately. Follow signs for Henry's Fork and Forest Service Rd. 077 to the trailhead, where there are four campsites and a pit toilet. The hike to the summit requires at least two days, stretching 32 mi. from trailhead (9400 ft.) to summit along the most traveled route. The 11 mi. from Henry's Fork to the basin below Gunsight Pass (11,800 ft.) is relatively easy and heavily traveled. Ford Henry's Fork via the footbridge at Elkhorn Crossing and continue toward Gunsight. At Gunsight, the main trail dips in Painter Basin before climbing back up to Anderson Pass (12,600 ft.). From here, the summit lies nearly 1 mi. to the south, along a ridge that requires trailless scrambling over boulders. The main route demands very fit lungs and legs, but no technical expertise. An **alternate route** diverges from the main trail at Gunsight Pass, skirting the shoulder of an unnamed peak to arrive at Anderson Pass more quickly and directly. This route requires extensive scrambling over talus and a difficult, non-technical climb over a small cliff. Many cairns make the first half of the route easy to follow, but once you're on the shoulder, a map is absolutely necessary. Inexperienced mountaineers should stick to the main trail, especially on the way down. Most Kings Peak hikers spend a night or two near **Henry's Lake.** Enough snow melts by July 1 to clear the summit route, and it remains open until the first autumn snowfall. Afternoon thunderstorms are a danger that make summiting in the morning an absolute necessity. Topo maps are available from local ranger stations for $7.

Trail follows the Green River for 7 mi. to Little Hole. The trail is mostly flat and offers beautiful scenery and excellent opportunities for wildlife viewing.

All hiking trails in the recreation area also allow mountain bikers. The strenuous **Elk Park Loop** (20 mi.) departs Rte. 44 at the signs for Deep Creek Campground, follows the Deep Creek Rd. to Forest Rd. 221 and Forest Rd. 105, skirts Browne Lake, and then runs single-track along the **Old Carter and South Elk Park Trails.** For more info on hiking and biking trails, grab the helpful pamphlets available at the Visitors Centers and the Flaming Gorge District Ranger Station.

For the traveler in search of yet more spectacular geology, the **Sheep Creek Geologic Loop,** an 11 mi. scenic backway off Rte. 44 just south of Manila, winds through a canyon lined with towering rock formatting, sculpted strata, and desert wildlife.

HIGH UINTA WILDERNESS   ☎ 435

The High Uinta (you-IN-tah) Wilderness Area offers a welcome respite from the crowded trails of the Wasatch Range. Within its 460,000 acres, it contains 500 lakes and several 13,000 ft. peaks, including Kings Peak, Utah's highest. Parts of the Uintas suffer from the same popularity and overuse as the Wasatch Front, but for the backpacker willing to wander off the beaten path, the Uintas reward with some of Utah's most pristine alpine environments. The mountain range itself differs from all others in the region, and most ranges in the US, with its east-west rather than north-south orientation. Powerful, high-angle faulting lifted the 600- million-year-old Uinta parent rocks and glaciers sculpted the terrain, combining to create a striking and varied topography. The resulting mountain block shelters a rich variety of wildlife, including raptors, moose, trout, elk, and black bears.

■ ⓘ ORIENTATION AND PRACTICAL INFORMATION

The High Uinta Wilderness Area covers a substantial portion of northeastern Utah and is therefore accessible from several different highways and trailheads. The most heavily used sections of the wilderness are the **Mirror Lake Scenic Byway** in the western corner and the **Henry's Fork/Kings Peak** area in the northeast. The **Wasatch-Cache** and **Ashley National Forests** jointly administer the wilderness. Depending on your planned destination, the following ranger stations oversee the area and are of help to visitors: in the west, **Kamas Ranger District,** 50 E. Center St. (☎783-4338; open M-F 8am-4:30pm); in the east, **Vernal Ranger District,** 355 N. Vernal Ave. (☎789-1181); and in the south, **Roosevelt Ranger District,** 244 W. U.S. 40 (☎722-5018).

The small, rural **Kamas** serves as a gateway to the western portion of the wilderness. The town has gas stations, restaurants, and lodging spread out along Rte. 34, although camping is the. To stock up on groceries before heading into the woods, stop by **Kamas Food Town,** a large, full-service grocer at 145 W. 200 S (☎783-4369; open M-Sa 7am-9pm, Su 9am-7pm).

⚠ OUTDOOR ACTIVITIES

WESTERN UINTA WILDERNESS

The easiest access to the western portion of the Wilderness Area is the Mirror Lake Scenic Byway. The byway, **Rte. 150,** leaves Kamas and meanders 46 mi. through high alpine-scapes and past glistening mountain lakes to the northern edge of the Wasatch-Cache National Forest. The road skirts the wilderness, with several trailheads yielding access to truly remote lands. Following Rte. 150 the full 78 mi. leads to Evanston, WY and I-80. Two ranger stations serve the byway, the **Kamas Ranger District,** on Rte. 150 in Kamas, and the **Bear River Ranger Station,** on Rte. 150 at the northern limit of the national forest. Both stations provide extensive info on recreational, camping, and scenic opportunities, including the new mile-by-mile guide to the scenic byway ($8). Travel along the byway requires a pass ($3), available at both ranger stations and many stores in Kamas.

Both developed and primitive campsites line the scenic byway at regular intervals. All developed sites have pit toilets and potable water, but there are no shower facilities. By far the most popular campground, **Mirror Lake,** at Mile 31.5, lies on the banks of the byway's namesake lake. (79 sites. $12, $5 per extra vehicle.) For the crowd-averse, both **Washington Lake** (36 sites; $12) and **Trail Lake** (60 sites; $12) campgrounds, at Mile 25, offer shady sites nestled on the shores of tranquil alpine lakes. Many primitive sites can be seen from the byway and are the safest fee-free camping bet for those lacking the high clearance needed to explore rough Forest Service roads.

Several popular **day hikes** lie along the full length of the byway. The **Ruth Lake Trail** (2 mi. round-trip, easy to moderate, 1½ hr., water available on trail) begins at Mile 35 of the drive and climbs gently only 200 ft. to the lake (10,300 ft.). The **Bald Mountain Trail** (4 mi. round-trip, strenuous, 2½ hr., no water available on trail), begins at Mile 29 and leads from the trailhead at Bald Mountain Pass (10,715 ft.) to Bald Mountain Peak (11,943 ft.). The summit provides dazzling views of the peaks comprising the westernmost spine of the High Uintas. During winter months, the Forest Service plows Rte. 150 up to the Soapstone turnoff, enabling **cross-country skiers** to enjoy a trail (7.7 mi.) between Yellow Pine and Soapstone. For other hiking and backpacking trails, the well-marked **Mirror Lake, Highline, Wolverine, Christmas Meadows,** and **East Fork Bear River** trailheads all provide ready trail access.

EASTERN UINTA WILDERNESS

Reaching trailheads that access the eastern portion of the wilderness area requires significantly more effort than from the scenic byway in the west. Trailheads surround the wilderness area, but reaching many of them demands travel on rough, washboard Forest Service roads. Access to the southern and eastern trailheads begins from Rte. 87 heading north from Duchesne or Rte. 121 north from Roosevelt. Two small Wyoming towns, **Mountain View** and **Lonetree,** serve as gateways to trailheads in the northeast.

Most people focus on Kings Peak when hiking in the eastern Uintas. For more ideas, stop by the Forest Service offices in Roosevelt or Vernal (see p. 255). Hikers tackling the wilderness from the north should stop by the **Mountain View Ranger Station,** 321 Rte. 414 in Mountain View WY, for information and trail conditions (☎307-782-6555. Open M-F 8am-4:30pm.) All camping within the eastern wilderness area is primitive, but many trailheads have toilet facilities. For a unique brand of "roughing it," spend a night or several at the primitive **Spirit Lake Lodge ❸,** just east of the wilderness area, nestled in a high basin surrounded by commanding peaks. The lodge, decorated with a delightful blend of diner kitsch and hunting trophies, serves three meals a day and offers guests access to a stable of horses and a fish-filled alpine lake. (☎880-3089. No running water and 2hr. of electricity per day. Cabins start at $34. Horse rides $10 per hr.; boat rentals $30 per day. Call ahead for directions and reservations.)

EAST CENTRAL UTAH

Extreme sports, ranching, and wilderness solitude mix in the Moab area to form a wacky Western concoction as enigmatic as Utah itself. The area's parks are its biggest draw. Remote Canyonlands provides a counterpoint to accessible Arches, with the La Sal Mountains providing a scenic backdrop to both.

MOAB   ☎435

A town without historic buildings or cultural offerings, Moab may at first seem nonsensical as a major tourist destination...until you look up to the towering sandstone of the Moab and Swiss Cheese Rims, that is. As has always been the case, the canyonlands that surround Moab are the real draw for both residents and visitors. Moab first flourished in the 1950s, when uranium miners rushed to the area and transformed the town from a quiet hamlet into a gritty desert outpost with a phosphorescent glow that hasn't left the town since. Today, the mountain bike has replaced the Geiger counter as the principal tool of outdoor recreation, and heavily laden SUVs lurch into town filled to the brim with passengers eager to bike and climb the red slickrock, raft whitewater rapids, and explore surrounding Arches and Canyonlands National Parks. The town itself has changed to accommodate the new arrivals; cafes and t-shirt shops now fill the rooms of the old uranium building on Main. The influx of outdoors-minded transplants has also had an effect on the town's politics, making Moab one of the more liberal towns in Utah.

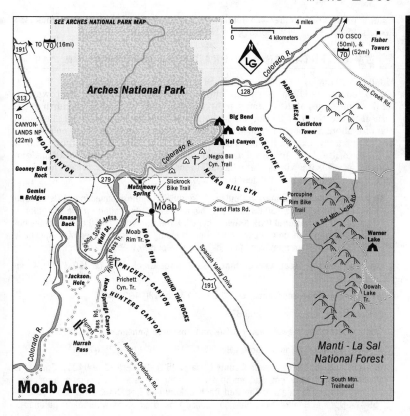

▐◄ TRANSPORTATION

Canyonlands Field (☎ 259-7421), 20 mi. north of town on U.S. 191, offers charter plane service to Western hubs, through operators like **Redtail Aviation** and **Great Lakes Airlines.** Flights to destinations including Denver, Salt Lake City, and Phoenix can run as low as $100 when arranged far enough in advance. The closest **Amtrak** and **Greyhound** stations are in Green River, 52 mi. northwest of town. Some hotels and hostels will pick guests up from the train or bus for a fee. In addition, **Bighorn Express** (☎ 888-655-7433) makes a daily trip to and from the Salt Lake City airport, with stops in Green River and Price along the way. Shuttles leave from the Ramada Inn, 182 S. Main. (Departs Salt Lake City airport at 2pm, departs Moab at 7:30am. 4½ hr. trip. $49 each way. Reservations recommended.)

A car is a handy tool for exploring Moab and its environs but unlike in much of the rest of southeastern Utah, is not a necessity. **Roadrunner Shuttle** (☎ 259-9402) and **Coyote Shuttle** (☎ 259-8656) can take you where you want to go on- or off-road in the Moab area, each specializing in bike ($10-12), river, and airport ($12) shuttles but accommodating individualized needs. **Thrifty Car Rental,** 711 S. Main (☎ 259-7317), in the Moab Valley Inn, offers both cars and 4x4s as well as one-way rentals to a number of Colorado and Utah destinations. If you're hankering for an off-roading excursion, **Farabee 4x4 Rentals,** 83 S. Main (☎259-7494), and **Slickrock Jeep Rentals,** 284 N. Main (☎259-5678), are both good choices.

✦ ⁊ ORIENTATION AND PRACTICAL INFORMATION

Moab sits 30 mi. south of I-70 on U.S. 191, just south of the junction with Rte. 128. Grand Junction is 112 mi. northeast, and Monticello is 53 mi. south. The town center lies 5 mi. south of the entrance to Arches National Park and 38 mi. north of the turnoff to the Needles section of Canyonlands National Park. U.S. 191 becomes Main for about 5 mi. through downtown. Drivers eastbound into Moab on I-70 who don't mind a few extra miles should take Exit 212, which leads past the shambles of Cicso to Rte. 128. This jewel among desert roads parallels the sparkling Colorado River, affording vistas of the La Sal Mountains and red rock towers for 45 mi. until it terminates at U.S. 191 just north of Moab.

Visitor Info: Moab Information Center, 3 Center St., at the intersection of Center and Main (☎259-8825 or 800-635-6622). This umbrella organization for the Chamber of Commerce, the **National Park Service,** the **US Forest Service,** and the **BLM,** doles out copious information on the city and the surrounding outdoors. (Open Mar.-Apr. daily 8am-7pm; May 8am-8pm; June to mid-Oct. 8am-9pm; Nov.-Feb. 9am-5pm.)

Laundry: Country Clean Laundromat, 588 S. Kane Creek Blvd. (☎259-3987). Open daily 7am-9pm.

Weather and Road Conditions: ☎801-524-5133 or 800-492-2400.

Police, 121 E. Center St. (☎259-8938).

Crisis Center: Seekhaven Family Crisis and Resource Center, ☎259-2229.

Medical Services: Allen Memorial Hospital, 719 W. 400 N (☎259-7191).

Internet Access: Free at **Grand County Library,** 25 S. 100 E (☎259-5421). Open M-W 9am-9pm, Th-F 9am-7pm, Sa 9am-5pm. Access the net as well as a wide array of sandwiches and coffee treats at **The Red Rock Bakery and Net Cafe,** 74 S. Main (☎259-5941). Open M-Sa 7am-6pm, Su 7am-5pm; $1 per 5min., 75¢ with bakery purchase.

Bookstore: Back of Beyond Books, 83 N. Main St. (☎259-5154 or 800-700-2859), sports a splendid selection of local interest books. Open Mar.-Oct. daily 9am-10pm, Nov.-Feb. 9am-6pm.

Post Office: 50 E. 100 N (☎259-7427). Open M-F 8:30am-5:30pm, Sa 9am-1pm. **ZIP code:** 84532.

⁊ ACCOMMODATIONS

Chain motels clutter Main, but Moab is generally not cheap and fills up fast in spring and summer, especially on weekends. Off-season rates can fall by half.

■ **Lazy Lizard International Hostel,** 1213 S. U.S. 191 (☎259-6057; www.gj.net/~lazylzrd). Look for the "A1 Self Storage" sign 1 mi. south of Moab on U.S. 191. The owners of this well-maintained hostel go out of their way to be helpful; they'll give you the lowdown on the Moab scene and arrange trips through local companies. The kitchen, VCR and extensive video library, laundry, and hot tub are at your disposal and draw an interesting mix of college students, international backpackers, and the odd aging hippie. 24 dorm beds, 11 private rooms, 8 cabins, and tent camping area. Showers for non-guests $2. Internet access $1 per 10min. Reception 8am-11pm, but late arrivals can be arranged. Check-out 11am. No curfew. Reservations recommended for weekends in the spring and fall. Dorms $8; private rooms for 1 or 2 from $20; cabins sleeping up to 6 $25-44; tent sites $6. ❶

Hotel Off Center, 96 E. Center St. (☎259-4244), a block off Main. This converted office building rents eclectically lavish rooms accented by antique items such as a miner's hat, fishing nets, and a Victrola. The gracious owners are continually renovating, much to the delight of the many returning guests. Shared bath and kitchen. Open approximately Mar.-Nov. 4 bed dorm $12; singles $39; doubles $49. ❶

Silver Sage Inn, 840 S. Main (☎259-4420). This motel offers the best rates in town for its simple, clean rooms in a small, somewhat institutional building. Reception 7am-10pm. Check-out 11am. Apr.-Oct. singles $40, doubles $45; Nov.-Mar. $25/$30. ❷

Apache Motel, 166 S. 400 E (☎800-228-6882 or 259-5727). Sleep where John Wayne slept. Follow the proud signs and hitch your horse outside a quiet, spotless room before heading into town to maintain a little law and order. When you're all done, you can wash off the red dust in their swimming pool. Reception 7am-11pm. Check-out 11am. Rooms $29-85, ranging with business. AAA discount. ❷

CAMPING

One thousand campsites blanket the Moab area, so finding a place to sleep out under the stars shouldn't be much of a problem, even in the busiest seasons. Most private campgrounds target RVs, but tenters can find dozens of sites along the river and some select private grounds. Refreshingly pure water is available at Matrimony Spring near the intersection of U.S. 191 and Rte. 128, a literal watering hole treasured by locals.

Goose Island, Hal Canyon, Oak Grove, and Big Bend, Rte. 128 (☎259-2100). This series of developed campgrounds inhabits the south bank of the Colorado River 3-9 mi. northeast of downtown Moab. Many of the sites are shaded, and the location couldn't be better. All sites have picnic table and fire pits, but there are no hookups or showers. Check-out noon. Sites $10. ❶

Negro Bill, Drinks Canyon, Upper Big Bend, Rte. 128 (☎259-2100). For those willing to rough it, these semi-developed camping areas are interspersed among the more developed sites on Rte. 128. They feature fire rings and pit toilets. The flat, shaded sites at the utterly un-P.C. Negro Bill are the best. Check-out noon. Sites $5. ❶

Up the Creek Campground, 210 E. 300 S (☎259-6995). This secluded, shaded campground, just a walk away from downtown, caters solely to tent camping, unlike the RV-oriented sites that rule in town. 20 sites. Showers ($5 for non-guests). Check-out 11am. Open Mar.-Oct. $10 per person. ❶

FOOD

Moab's eateries cover a more cosmopolitan range than most Utah towns of its size to accommodate discerning visitors and many budgets. **City Market** vends groceries and quick deli meals at 425 S. Main (☎259-5181; open daily 6am-midnight). Another option is **Moonflower Market (Moab Community Coop),** 39 E. 100 N, an oasis of organic and health. Check the bulletin board inside for rides all over the western US and apartment listings. (☎259-5712. Open M-Sa 9am-8pm, Su 10am-3pm.) Restaurants in Moab tend to shut down by 10pm.

The Moab Diner and Ice Cream Shoppe, 189 S. Main (☎259-4006). The retro booths might take you back to the 50s at this friendly diner, but with veggie specials and tasty green chili ($4-10), the food won't. Grab breakfast here and you'll be set until dinnertime. Open Su-Th 6am-10pm, F-Sa 6am-10:30pm. ❷

UTAH

■ **EklectiCafe**, 352 N. Main (☎259-6896). Look for the larger-than-life coffee cup mosaic out front. All weariness and worries of the road dissipate here amidst the greenery and folk art on the shady front deck. The wide array of ambrosial pastries, coffee drinks (all made with organic, fair-trade beans), breakfasts ($3-7), and lunch options ($4-8) are available to go, but you'd be passing up on unbeatable atmosphere, which includes live roots music on Su mornings and whenever local musicians feel the spirit move them. Open M-Sa 7:30am-2:30pm, Su 7:30am-1pm. ❶

Desert Bistro, 92 E. Center St. (☎259-0756). When typical roadside fare falls short of satisfying, stretch your budget at this sanctuary of fine dining. Local art bedecking the walls, a choice wine list, and fish and game specials leave little to be desired. This is still Moab though; don't feel compelled to dress up, and give your spruced-up waiter a second look to determine whether he's one of the diehards you climbed or biked alongside earlier in the afternoon. Entrees $18-25, salads $6-8. Opens at 5:30pm daily. ❺

Peace Tree Juice Cafe, 20 S. Main (☎259-8503). After a hot day in the desert, cool off here with a delicious smoothie or fresh juice ($2.50-5). More substantial fare is also served, including a wide variety of vegetarian delights, wraps and salads ($4.50-6), and breakfast munchies ($1.50-5.50). Open daily 8am-6:30pm. ❶

Eddie McStiff's Microbrewery & Family Restaurant, 57 S. Main (☎259-2337), in the self-titled plaza. This popular joint offers 13 interesting beer flavors such as raspberry and jalapeño, as well as quality pizzas ($4.50-14) and burgers ($5-7). For vegetarians, great salads are available too. Open daily 5:30-10pm; bar open until approx. 1am. ❷

Breakfast at Tiffany's, 90 E. Center St. (☎259-2553). Audrey Hepburn would be proud of this hole in the wall that adds a little Fifth Ave. flare to an otherwise Western town. The creative fare ($4-7) defies the bacon-and-eggs standard, and the sun-drenched patio encourages lingering. Open M-F 7am-3pm, Sa-Su 7am-noon. Cash only. ❶

Banditos Grill, 467 N. Main St. (☎259-3894). Popular with locals, this spot boasts Mexican authenticity and delivers massive portions for reasonable prices. The grilled salmon burrito ($7.50) is especially good. Open daily 11am-10pm. ❷

■ ENTERTAINMENT AND NIGHTLIFE

Moab's handful of bars resound with rollicking good fun on weekend nights starting at about 9pm. **The Río Colorado Restaurant and Bar,** 100 W and Center St., is the place to go for live music on Friday and Saturday nights, and one of few places in town serving hard drinks. (☎259-6666. Open daily 4-9pm, bar until 1am.) **Woody's Tavern** at Main St. and 200 S also serves the hard stuff, and fills up with folks looking for a mellow night of pool or a rough-and-tumble rager. The musically minded should showcase their talent at the **Branding Iron** on Saturday nights, south of town on U.S. 191 at the corner of Spanish Trail Rd.

Starting Labor Day weekend and continuing for the next two weeks every September, the **Moab Music Festival** brings a variety of acts to several stunning venues against the scenic backdrop of canyon country. For tickets and information, call 259-7003 or visit www.moabmusicfest.org.

■ OUTDOOR ACTIVITIES

Moab can serve as home base for almost any conceivable desert activity, and in many cases is the preeminent locale. For **mountain biking, rafting, hiking, rock climbing,** and **four-wheeling,** it doesn't get much better than Moab.

MOUNTAIN BIKING

More than any other destination in the West, Moab is synonymous with mountain biking. More people come to ride Moab's **Slickrock Trail** than any other route in the world, but it is only one of many fantastic rides in the area. Other routes provide equally challenging biking and views without the sometimes overwhelming crowds. In all cases, be sure to ride only on open roads and trails, stay clear of cryptobiotic soil, and protect water sources. The desert environment may seem harsh, but it recovers slowly from the impact of thousands of mountain bike rides.

There is no shortage of bike shops in Moab, and all charge similar rates for rentals ($32-35 per day for half suspension, $38-40 for full suspension, $50 for top-end demos). **Rim Cyclery,** 94 W. 100 N holds a strong reputation as the shop that started it all. (☎259-5333. Open Su-Th 9am-6pm, F-Sa 8am-6pm.) For those interested in hiring a bike for multiple days, **Poison Spider Bicycles,** 497 N. Main, reduces rates for additional days. (☎259-7882 or 800-635-1792; www.poisonspiderbicycles.com. Open daily 8am-6pm.) Other outfitters, including **Moab Cyclery,** 391 S. Main (☎259-7423 or 800-451-1133; www.escapeadventures.com) and **Chile Pepper Bike Shop,** 702 S. Main (☎259-4688 or 888-677-4688), offer mountain bike tours in the surrounding area as well as in Canyonlands ($50-70 without rental, $75-120 including rental). Several companies (each owing its name to the same cartoon show) provide shuttle service to bikers: **Coyote** (☎259-8656), **Roadrunner** (☎259-9402), and **Acme** (☎260-2534). Popular destinations cost $10-12 per rider, and some companies charge a minimum rate per trip. Riders should carry plenty of **water** and consult the incredibly useful set of topo maps, **Moab East** and **Moab West,** which describe numerous rides in reliable detail and show elevation profiles ($10 each).

> **Slickrock Bike Trail** (9.6 mi. round-trip, plus a 2.2 mi. practice loop). The trailhead is on Sand Flats Rd., 2.3 mi. from its intersection with Millcreek Dr., which begins on 400 East in town. This loop tackles the intense terrain of Moab's slickrock while showing off the spectacular scenery. This technically and physically difficult ride constantly changes elevation as it traverses the red sandstone above Moab and the Colorado River. No net elevation change. Rideable year-round. Sand Flats Recreation Area fee $3.

> **Porcupine Rim** (21 mi.). This challenging ride, a favorite among locals, embarks from near two metal stock tanks on the north side of Sand Flats Road, 11 mi. from Moab. After a 4 mi. climb to High Anxiety View-

THE HIDDEN DEAL

ALFONSO'S MEXICAN FOOD

A quick look at and inside Alfonso's at 812 S Main St. in Moab fails to impress; the square building and molded plastic booths fit the formula of an American fast-food joint, and its location along the strip south of town near McDonald's and Wendy's marks it for easy dismissal.

But this ain't no Taco Bell. Underneath the facade, this restaurant is the budget traveler's dream come true. Monstrous burritos are just $2.25-4, and numerous a la carte options fulfill every size craving for a pittance (tacos from $1.75). However, you don't taste the price—Alfonso's comes closer to authentic Mexican cuisine than anyplace else for hundreds of miles. According to a discerning local, "it's everything great about Mexican food without the bugs." Customers used to Americanized Mexican fare may have to ask what composes *carnitas* or balk initially at the liberal use of lard, but once Alfonso's never fails to win over even the most skeptical. No other place in town could even approach Alfonso's in fueling an action-packed itinerary of Moab area exploration. ☎259-0963. Open 8am-midnight. Take-out available. ➊

point and outstanding views of Castle Valley, the trail descends on jeep roads and technical singletrack for 10 mi. until it reaches Rte. 128, 7 mi. from Moab. A shuttle is desirable, but the ride can be done as a 32 mi. loop.

Poison Spider Mesa (12 mi. round-trip). The trailhead for this moderate route is on Potash Rd. 279 (Rte. 279) at the "Dinosaur Tracks" sign. The climb up onto Poison Spider Mesa and Little Arch is tough, but you are rewarded with a killer descent. Or, the confident can choose the challenge of the exposed and vertigo-inducing Portal Trail, which turns the ride into a loop and should not be attempted by any but the most skilled riders. 860 ft. elevation gain (all lost on the way back). Rideable year-round.

Gemini Bridges (14 mi.). This trail begins on Rte. 313, 12.6 mi. from its intersection with U.S. 191 north of Moab. Besides a brief ascent out of Little Canyon, riders enjoy mostly long downhills on this pleasant entry-level route which passes the interesting formations of Gemini Bridges and Gooney Bird Rock and provides spectacular views of Arches and Behind the Rocks. The trail emerges on U.S. 191 north of Moab. A shuttle is necessary, or the ride turns into a 50+ mi. loop. 380 ft. elevation gain, 1830 ft. drop.

Hurrah Pass Trail (19.2 mi. round-trip). This ride can be begun anywhere in downtown Moab; no shuttle is necessary (mileage is measured from the end of the pavement on Kane Creek Blvd.). This out-and-back route on a graded dirt road offers a good introduction to mountain biking as it climbs high above the Colorado River. 900 ft. elevation gain. Rideable year-round.

RIVER RUNNING (RAFTING AND KAYAKING)

Next to mountain biking, rafting on the Colorado River is Moab's biggest draw. Every day, bus loads of visitors are whisked north along Rte. 128 to the **Fisher Towers** put-in. For those in search of bouncier thrills, May and June bring big water in the Colorado's **Westwater** and **Cataract Canyons**. Westwater trips range from one ($125) to three ($435) days, while Cataract and other longer stretches of the Colorado can be explored via multi-day trips. Countless raft companies based in Moab offer trips that cater to every imaginable type of rafter, from the four-year-old looking forward to his first time in a boat to the wily veteran who knows she's ready to handle whatever Class V+ rapids are thrown at her. For basic day-long trips, reservations are rarely necessary, and all the outfitters offer essentially the same trips. **Canyon Voyages Adventure Co.**, 211 N. Main (☎259-6007 or 800-733-6007; www.canyonvoyages.com), **Tag A Long Expeditions**, 452 N. Main (☎259-8946 or 800-453-3292), and **Western River Expeditions**, 1371 N. U.S. 191 (☎259-7019 or 800-453-7450), all have good reputations and are well established. You can choose between a full-day voyage ($44-49 including lunch, children $33-37) and half-day excursions ($33-36, children $26-29). The superb guides at **OARS/North American River Expeditions**, 543 N. Main (☎259-5865 or 800-342-5938), specialize in extended expeditions ranging from overnights in Cataract Canyon to week-long journeys and beyond.

Those who prefer to tackle the turbid water in a more independent and hands-on fashion should consider cruising at their own pace in an inflatable or touring kayak, or squeezing into a whitewater kayak for a real wild ride. All three types can be rented for $35 per day at **Canyon Voyages** (see above listing), but prior experience is required for the more technical boats. One-way river shuttles can be arranged with them too, as well as one- to three-day courses in whitewater kayaking (from $210 including equipment rental). Most of the extended trips offered by Canyon Voyages and OARS allow the option of paddling a kayak through the flatwater sections of the river.

ROCK CLIMBING

Unsurprisingly, Moab and its environs are a climbing paradise that beckons wall-rats from all over the world. While many of the routes challenge top climbers and

HOLE-LY MACKEREL (OR MULE)

Using only hand-powered drills and dynamite, Albert Christensen spent 12 years creating the bizarre **Hole 'n the Rock,** 15 mi. south of Moab on U.S. 191, a tribute to the days of Jell-O molds and chrome. This 14-room house carved out of a sandstone cliff boasts 5000 sq. ft. of living space, an impressive array of amateur mule and horse taxidermy, and several likenesses of two of Christensen's heros, Jesus Christ and Franklin Delano Roosevelt. Albert's wife, Gladys, kept the dream alive after his death in 1957 and opened the house to the public. She died in 1974, but this tribute to kitsch continues on with a well-appointed gift shop, featuring Elvis memorabilia and mesh hats in addition to daily tours. (☎686-2250. Open mid-Apr. to mid.-Oct. daily 9am-6pm; late Oct. to early Apr. 9am-5pm. Tours $4, children $3.)

require a great deal of technique, beginners with a little grit and determination can scale the red rock too. **Pagan Mountaineering,** located in McStiff's Plaza on S. Main, has a good selection of gear for sale and can provide info on area climbs. (☎259-1117. Open M-Sa 10am-7pm, Su 10am-5pm.) The folks at ◪**Moab Cliffs and Canyons,** 63 E. Center St., initiate the inexperienced and hone the skills of the more practiced. From a seemingly vertical wall or the exhilarating summit of a 400 ft. tower, the price of hiring a guide's individualized instruction will feel well worth it. (☎259-3317 or 877-641-5271; www.moabcliffsandcanyons.com. Half day of climbing $100 for one person, $85 each for 2, $65 each for 3. Canyoneering from $85/65. Shoe/harness rental $5. Group class meeting every W at 5pm $15.) **Moab Desert Adventures** (☎260-2404) also runs classes and guided trips at just slightly higher prices. Eric Bjornstad's **Desert Rock** guidebook series, widely available in bookstores and gear shops, delves into the details of many of the routes in the Moab area. Countless sport climbs exist in the area, especially up in the **La Sal Mountains,** where summer climbers escape the savage desert heat. For those interested in getting on the rock in a slightly less involved way, great bouldering can be had at **Big Bend Boulders** on Rte. 128 across from the Big Bend Campground, near the entrance to Arches National Park, and quite likely in the vicinity of your campsite. The following areas are hallowed ground to climbers:

Wall Street, located along the north bank of the Colorado, rises up from Potash Rd. (Rte. 272) northwest of Moab. Conveniently close to town and shaded in the afternoon, the vertical sandstone affords over 100 one-pitch routes for crag-style climbing (some bolted, but most traditional) ranging from 5.6 to 5.12, with most around 5.10. A great place to meet other climbing enthusiasts.

Indian Creek, renowned for world class **crack climbing,** is reached by a 50 mi. drive south of Moab on Rte. 211 near the Needles district of Canyonlands. Hundreds of famed cracks from 5.10 and up captivate experienced climbers.

Fisher Towers, northeast of town along Rte. 128 on the Colorado, is a classic for technical aid climbing, but most routes require extensive gear and a great deal of faith in the crumbly-looking Cutler sandstone. Notable exceptions are **Ancient Art Tower,** a formation straight out of Dr. Seuss, whose corkscrew summit can be free-climbed and is more moderate, and the one-pitch route at the trailhead on **Lizard Rock.**

Castle Valley, also along Rte. 128, 5 mi. west of Fisher Towers, features towers of calcified Wingate Sandstone recognizable as the epitome of desert free climbing. The most classic, **Castleton Tower,** a symmetrical 400 ft. monolith, can be ascended along routes ranging from 5.9 to 5.12. A host of other superb formations include the **Rectory,** the **Priest,** the **Nuns, Sister Superior,** and **Parriott Mesa.**

ABBEY'S ROAD For many, the essays and novels of Edward Abbey most eloquently capture the untamed expanses of the American West. Born in Pennsylvania, he fell in love with the region upon his first visit and devoted the rest of his life to fiercely defending it from the US's westward march of "progress." He spent three seasons as a park ranger at Arches National Park, delighting in the solitude of the desert. Abbey later penned a celebrated series of essays on life in the desert based on his years spent wandering around Moab and Canyonlands. He captured their enigmatic beauty in his passionate and often acerbic manner—Abbey's passages vividly evoke the unforgiving, sun-parched landscape he loved. *The Monkey Wrench Gang*, Abbey's novel about an amusing, incomprehensibly radical foursome rebelling against the pillaging of the wilderness, serves as inspiration for environmentalists everywhere and provided the emotional and psychological blueprint for Earth First!, an activist environmental group. As Abbey once wrote, "For us the wilderness and human emptiness of this land is not a source of fear but the greatest of its attractions."

HIKING

Amazing hiking abounds in the Moab area, and whether you're looking for a couple peaceful hours or a full-day slog, the options are nearly endless. The **La Sal Mountains,** which lie east of Moab and rise to heights over 12,000 ft., are often forsaken for the allure of the nearby slickrock, but offer incredible wilderness. More info on hikes around Moab and in the La Sals is available at the Moab Info Center.

IN THE LA SALS. The **South Mountain Trail** is on the La Sal Pass Rd. about ¼ mi. from the **Brumley Creek-La Sal Springs Trail.** This moderate hike, passable May through October, is one of the most scenic in the La Sals, circumscribing the 11,535 ft. South Mountain. The trail passes through varied terrain as it crosses a number of basins. The route ends at the La Sal Rd., about 4 mi. east of where it begins, so the hike can be made into an approximately 9 mi. loop. The **Oowah Lake-Clarks Lake Trail** begins on Geyser Pass Rd. south of Haystack Mountain. An easy hike passable May through October, it climbs down from 10,000 ft. along the **Geyser Pass Rd.** to 8800 ft. at **Oowah Lake,** passing through aspen, fir, and beautiful meadow. The 3 mi. one-way trail may be combined with the **Boren Mesa Trail** and a portion of the Geyser Pass Rd. to make an enjoyable 9 mi. loop.

AROUND MOAB. The **Portal Overlook Trail** (980 ft. elevation gain) begins at JayCee Park Recreation site on Rte. 279, 4.2 mi. west of its junction with U.S. 191. This moderately easy 4 mi. round-trip trail, hikeable year-round, climbs above the Colorado to afford a panoramic view of the Moab Valley, the La Sal Mountains, and the Colorado River. Much of the trail follows cairned ramps of Kayenta sandstone to this breathtaking destination. The trailhead for the **Negro Bill Canyon Trail** (330 ft. elevation gain) is located on Rte. 128, 3 mi. east of its junction with U.S. 191. An easy 4 mi. round-trip jaunt hikeable year-round, it follows a perennial stream up the scenic Negro Bill Canyon. The 243 ft. Morning Glory Bridge, the sixth longest natural rock span in the US, spans a side canyon approximately 2 mi. up. For a bird's-eye view of the Behind the Rocks area sandstone fins, hike up the **Hidden Valley Trail,** accessible by driving 3 mi. south from town on U.S. 191, turning right onto Angel Rock Rd., and right again onto Rimrock Rd. This easy trail climbs 680 ft. over 2 mi. up to a broad shelf between the higher Moab rim and Spanish Valley below to the east. By continuing onto the Moab Rim jeep and mountain bike trail, the hike can be extended 3 more mi. to the Colorado River. About 4.7 mi. down Castle Valley Rd. off Rte. 128 east of Moab, the **Castleton Tower Approach Trail** affords panoramic views of Castle Valley, its numerous lovely sandstone formations, Porcupine Rim, and the La Sals close by to the south. Of course, the view from the summit of Castleton Tower 400 ft. above is even better, but you'll have to bring rock climbing gear to enjoy that 2.5 mi. round-trip, 1300 ft. elevation gain.

FOUR-WHEELING

There are thousands of miles of jeep trails in Grand County. Unless you have previous experience off-roading, most of these routes are not the sort of thing that you'll want to dive (or drive) right into. Unlike with most biking or hiking, it is very easy to end up over your head very quickly. The Visitors Center can provide info specific to your vehicle's and your own abilities. Popular easier routes include **Gemini Bridges,** beginning on U.S. 191 just south of its intersection with Rte. 131, and some routes in the **Behind the Rocks** area. A definite second-best option is to let someone else do the driving for you. Numerous companies throughout town offer tours of the backcountry on a daily basis, and are willing and able to take you on the area's most extreme trails. Of course, this option is quite expensive. **Farabee Adventures, Inc.,** 401 N. Main (☎259-7494 or 888-806-5337), and **Dan Mick's Guided Tours,** 600 Millcreek Dr. (☎259-4567), specialize in four-wheel-drive trips.

ARCHES NATIONAL PARK ☎435

"This is the most beautiful place on earth," novelist Edward Abbey wrote of Arches National Park. Although the number of visitors has increased from a few hundred in Abbey's day to a few hundred thousand today, nothing else has changed. Thousands of sandstone arches, spires, pinnacles, and fins tower above the desert with almost overwhelming grandeur. Some arches are so perfect in form that early explorers believed they were constructed by a lost civilization. The reality may be even more astounding: over the course of millions of years, bits and pieces of the porous sandstone were broken off in cycles of freezing and thawing, and what remained was then sculpted by wind and water into its current flowing forms. Deep red sandstone, green piñon trees and juniper bushes, and the occasional ominous thunderclouds against a strikingly blue sky combine to shape an unforgettable palette of color. However, this rainbow cannot be appreciated fully with a museum-like reserve from behind the tinted windows. Throw yourself into the painting and explore this magnificent land on foot.

■ ♦ 🛈 ORIENTATION AND PRACTICAL INFORMATION

Although no public transportation serves Arches, a number of shuttle bus companies, including **Roadrunner Shuttle of Moab** (☎259-9402), travel to the park. The park entrance is on U.S. 191, 5 mi. north of Moab and 25 mi. south of the junction of U.S. 191 and I-70. A 18 mi. paved road bisects the park and, along with a number of spur roads, offers access to the most popular hiking trails, formations, and viewpoints. The **Visitors Center,** to the right of the entrance station, has some interesting exhibits and a bevy of rangers on duty. (☎719-2299. Open daily 8am-4:30pm; extended hours approximately Mar.-Sept.) For **weather and road info,** call 800-492-2400

AT A GLANCE: ARCHES NATIONAL PARK	
AREA: 76,519 acres.	**GATEWAY TOWNS:** Moab (p. 268).
FEATURES: Arches, arches, arches!	**CAMPING:** Devil's Garden Campground $10 in summer.
HIGHLIGHTS: Driving to the Windows, Delicate Arch, and Devils Garden, hiking to Delicate Arch.	**FEES:** Weekly entrance pass $10 per carload, $5 per pedestrian or biker.

WHEN TO GO. While many visitors come in the summer, 100°F temperatures make hiking difficult. If you will be hiking in the summer, be sure to bring plenty of water. The best time to visit the park is in the spring and fall, when temperate days and cool nights combine to make for a comfortable stay. In the winter, white snow provides a brilliant contrast to the red arches.

(Utah) or 877-315-7623 (Colorado). Write the Superintendent, Arches National Park, P.O. Box 907, Moab, UT 84532 for more info.

CAMPING

The park's only campground, **Devil's Garden ❶,** has 52 excellent campsites nestled amid piñon pines and giant red sandstone formations. The campsite is within walking distance of the Devil's Garden and Broken Arch trailheads; however, it is a long 18 mi. from the Visitors Center. Sites are first come, first served except for large groups, and the campground tends to fill every night. There are bathrooms and running water, but no showers. (☎719-2299. No wood gathering. Open year-round. 1-week max. stay. Sites $10.)

If the heat becomes unbearable at Arches, the aspen forests of the **Manti-La Sal National Forest** offer respite. Take Rte. 128 along the Colorado River and turn right at Castle Valley, or go south from Moab on U.S. 191 and turn left at the Shell Station. There are a number of campgrounds here including **Warner Lake ❶,** where beautiful sites sit 4000 ft. above the national park and are invariably several degrees cooler (sites $10; Oowah Lake sites free). Oowah, a 3 mi. hike from the Geyser Pass Rd., is a rainbow trout haven. Fishing permits are available at stores in Moab and at the Forest Service Office, 62 E. 100 N, for $5 per day. Contact the Manti-La Sal National Forest Moab/Monticello Ranger District (☎259-7155).

SIGHTS AND OUTDOORS

DRIVING

The 18 mi. main park road serves as the virtual greatest hits of Arches for those with limited time or limited interest in braving the desert heat. The park boasts the heaviest concentration of natural arches on the planet, and many are pinpointed on the free map and guide that is passed out at the entrance station. Leaving the Visitors Center, the drive first encounters **Courthouse Towers** and **Park Avenue,** which in their thin verticality are strangely reminiscent of a mainstreet facade from a movie set. A 1 mi. trail promenades down this stretch before meeting up again with the park drive. The road then passes **Petrified Dunes, The Great Wall,** and **Rock Pinnacles** before arriving at the gravity-defying **Balanced Rock.** Immediately after the turn-out for Balanced Rock, a spur road heads out to the fantastical **Windows** section. Here it seems that everywhere you turn another arch comes out of the woodwork, and an easy 1 mi. trail allows visitors to get up close and personal with such goliaths as **North Window, South Window,** and **Turret Arch.** Visitors occasionally come across petroglyphs left on the stone walls by the Ancestral Puebloans and Utes who wandered here centuries ago. Two-and-a-half miles north of the turnoff to the Windows, another spur road sets out for the Delicate Arch. A trail climbs up to the arch, but to view the spectacular formation without the long hike, take the **Delicate Arch Viewpoint Trail** from the Delicate Arch Viewpoint parking area. This 300 ft. trail takes around 15min. Beyond the Delicate Arch turnoff is the maze of **Fiery Furnace.** Access to this labyrinth of canyon bottoms beneath cliffs

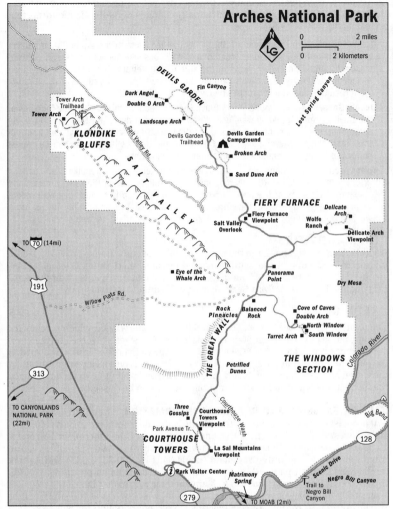

Arches National Park

N LG

0   2 miles
0   2 kilometers

DEVILS GARDEN

Fin Canyon

Lost Spring Canyon

Dark Angel
Double O Arch

Tower Arch
Trailhead

Tower Arch

Landscape Arch

KLONDIKE
BLUFFS

Devils Garden
Trailhead

Devils Garden
Campground

■ Broken Arch

S
A
L
T

V
A
L
L
E
Y

Salt Valley Rd.

■ Sand Dune Arch

FIERY FURNACE

Delicate
Arch

■ Fiery Furnace
Viewpoint

Wolfe
Ranch

Salt Valley
Overlook

Delicate Arch
Viewpoint

TO 70 (14mi)

191

■ Eye of the
Whale Arch

Panorama
Point

Dry Mesa

Willow Flats Rd.

313

Rock
Pinnacles

Balanced
Rock

Cove of Caves
Double Arch

■ North Window

TO CANYONLANDS
NATIONAL PARK
(22mi)

Turret Arch ■ ■ South Window

THE
GREAT
WALL

Petrified
Dunes

THE WINDOWS
SECTION

Colorado River

Big Bend

Three
Gossips

Courthouse
Towers
Viewpoint

Courthouse Wash

128

Park Avenue Tr.

COURTHOUSE
TOWERS

■ La Sal Mountains
Viewpoint

Scenic Drive

Negro Bill Canyon

ⓘ Park Visitor Center

Matrimony
Spring

279

Trail to
Negro Bill
Canyon

TO MOAB (2mi)

and monoliths requires an additional fee. Rangers lead groups from the Visitors Center twice daily in summer, but those who can attest to adequate hiking credentials can explore it on their own for less. (Tours often fill up 1-2 days early; reservations can be made 7 days in advance in person. $6, children $3. Permit for unguided travel $2.) At the road's end lies **Devil's Garden,** a wonderland of rock.

HIKING

While the red slickrock vistas from the road may seem unbeatable, the park's eponymous arches are best appreciated up close. To experience them more intimately, load up on water and sunscreen and seek out the formations on foot. For detailed maps and info on hiking, corner a ranger at the Visitors Center. Hiking in the park is hard to beat, especially in the cool days of spring and fall. Stay on trails; the land may look barren but the soil actually contains cryptobiotic life forms that are easily destroyed by footsteps.

Delicate Arch (3 mi. round-trip, 2-3hr.). This trail leaves from the Wolfe Ranch parking area, 1.2 mi. off the main road. Much of this strenuous hike follows cairns over exposed slickrock, offering excellent views of the surrounding terrain. The arch itself has been exquisitely eroded and can only be fully appreciated from beneath. 480 ft. elevation gain. Hikeable year-round except when wet.

Devil's Garden (7.2 mi. round-trip, 3-5hr.). The trailhead for this challenging loop lies at the Devil's Garden parking area, at the end of the main road. The hike requires some scrambling over rocks, but travelers will be rewarded by the 8 arches visible from the trail. Start early in the morning or at the end of the day, as the crowds can be almost suffocating. Not recommended in wet or snowy conditions.

Tower Arch (3.4 mi. round-trip, 2-3hr.). Find the trailhead at the Klondike Bluffs parking area via the Salt Valley Rd. This moderate hike explores one of the more remote, and less crowded, areas of the park. The trail ascends a steep but short rock wall before meandering through sandstone fins and sand dunes. The Salt Valley Rd. is often washed out, so check with the Visitors Center before departing. Hikeable year-round.

OTHER ACTIVITIES

Rock climbing is also popular in the park. A number of guide books provide specific info on routes. None of the features named by the United States Geological Services (USGS) may be climbed, but an abundance of classic ascents await the vertically inclined, including **Owl's Head. Bike** travel is limited to roads only.

GREEN RIVER   ☎ 435

The town of Green River (pop. 860) straddles the waterway on which it relies for not only name but also livelihood, an oasis in the vast desert traversed by the interstate. Long a crossroads, from the early days of the Denver-Río Grande Railroad to the construction of Interstate 70, today Green River survives as a center for rafting the Green and Colorado and, believe it or not, melon farming. If you're in town for the harvest, the watermelon and cantaloupe are not to be missed.

■ ■ **ORIENTATION AND PRACTICAL INFORMATION.** Green River lies along I-70 just east of its intersection with U.S. 191 N, 185 mi. southeast of Salt Lake City, 102 mi. west of Grand Junction, CO, and 160 mi. east of the junction of I-70 and I-15. Main St., the only thoroughfare in town, runs between two exits off I-70. The town is home to the only **Greyhound** (☎ 564-3421 or 800-231-2222) and **Amtrak** (☎ 800-872-7245) stops in all of southeast Utah, thanks to its proximity to I-70. Buses stop at the **Rodeway Inn,** 525 E. Main, on their way to Salt Lake (185 mi.), Las Vegas (400 mi.), or Denver (350 mi.). The train, which stops at the south end of Broadway, comes through once a day in each direction, bound for Salt Lake City or Denver. You may have to ask for it to stop in town.

The **Visitors Center,** located in the **John Wesley Powell Museum,** 885 E. Main, is well stocked with brochures about town services and the surrounding outdoors. (☎ 564-3526. Open June-Aug. daily 8am-8pm; Sept.-May 8am-5pm.) The adjacent museum captivates history buffs and others with river lore and a slideshow narrated by excerpts from Powell's journals. (☎ 564-3427. $2, youths $1. Same hours as Visitors Center.) There's a **laundromat** at the Shady Acres RV Park and Campground, 350 E. Main. (☎ 564-8290. Open daily 6am-11pm.) Other services include: **weather and road conditions,** ☎ 800-492-2400; **Emery County Sheriff,** 48 Farrer St. (☎ 564-3431); **Green River Medical Center,** 305 W. Main (☎ 564-3434); free **Internet access** at the **Green River City Library,** 85 S. Long St. (☎ 562-3349; open M-F 10am-

6pm); and the **post office**, 20 E. Main (☎564-3329; open M-F 8:30am-noon and 1-4:30pm, Sa 8:30-11:30am). **ZIP code:** 84525.

⚑🖸 ACCOMMODATIONS AND FOOD. Main is lined with budget motels. One of the cheapest is **Robbers Roost Motel ❷**, 225 W. Main, which offers clean, basic rooms and the added bonus of a pool. (☎564-3452. Reception 7am-2am. Check-out 10:30am. Singles $29; doubles $39. Rates drop in winter.) Another option is the similarly priced **Mancos Rose Inn ❷**, 20 W. Main. (☎564-9660. Reception 24hr. Check-out 11am.) Campers are in for a treat along the water's edge at the **Green River State Park ❶**, 145 S. Green River Blvd. Its 40 grassy sites and showers make for a relaxing spot to recuperate from or prepare for a day on the river. (☎564-3633. Check-in 3pm, check-out 2pm. Sites $14. No hookups.)

Ben's Cafe ❶, 115 W. Main, dishes out ample portions of Mexican and American food. Bargain breakfasts range $3.75-6, and a $5-8 lunch isn't far behind. (☎564-3352. Open daily 7am-10pm.) Head to **Ray's Tavern ❷**, right next door at 26 S. Broadway, with its rafting t-shirt wallpaper for some serious grillin' (½ lb. burger with fries $5.70) as well as pizzas ($9-14) served on tree-trunk tables. (☎564-3511. Open 11am-10pm.)

⚑ OUTDOOR ACTIVITIES. Predictably, the town's grandest offering is the river itself, and rafting trips depart frequently from late spring through early fall. Two reputable local outfitters are **Moki Mac River Expeditions,** 100 S. Sillman Ln. (☎564-3361 or 800-284-7280), and **Holiday Expeditions,** 1055 E. Main (☎801-266-2087 or 800-624-6323). Both offer a day trips on the Green (for about $55) as well as multi-day trips on the Green, the Colorado, and other Western rivers. Holiday also features expeditions combining rafting with mountain biking.

To see the spectacular terrain of this country from the banks rather than the river, the **Green River Scenic Drive** is an appealing option. This drive traces the river through Gray Canyon for almost 20 mi., offering plenty of diversions for those interested in biking, hiking, swimming, and camping. From the center of town head east on Hastings Rd. and turn left. Eight miles out at Swasey Beach, the pavement ends and the road stays just above the river for the remainder of the drive, to a rock formation bearing a likeness to Queen Nefertiti.

Thanks to an uplift 40-60 years ago and the subsequent forces of erosion, the spectacular topography of the **San Rafael Swell** is a wonderland for hikers, backpackers, and bikers. This kidney-shaped area, located just off I-70 19 mi. west of Green River, has been designated a Wilderness Study Area (WSA) by the BLM and is up for inclusion in the National Park system as a National Monument. For the time being, however, the San Rafael is little known to tourists in comparison to Utah's other outdoor hotspots. The Visitors Center in Green River provides information on road conditions and a free guide to the **San Rafael Desert Loop Drive,** which begins just south of town and follows the river to **Horseshoe Canyon,** an extension of Canyonlands National Park, and then links up with Rte. 24 to skirt the edge of the sawtooth ridge that marks the eastern rim of the swell, called **San Rafael Reef,** before intersecting with I-70. This 100 mi. scenic drive can be combined with the Bicentennial Highway (Rte. 95) departing from Hanksville. **Backcountry camping** is usually allowed along the route (check with the BLM in advance), and developed sites are available for a fee at **Goblin Valley State Park** south of the swell near Temple Mountain and Crack Canyon just off Rte. 24.

Crystal Geyser, about 10 mi. south of town, erupts every 14-16hr. for about 30min. at a time, shooting a jet of water 80-100 ft. high. Environmental purists may be surprised to learn that the seemingly natural scenic phenomenon owes its origin to the oil extraction industry; the geyser formed in 1936 after a petroleum test well was drilled on the riverbank. Drive east on Main over I-70 and turn left onto the frontage road. After 2.7 mi., turn right and continue 4.4 mi. to the geyser.

UTAH

CANYONLANDS NATIONAL PARK   ☎ 435

Those who make the trek to Canyonlands National Park are rewarded with a pleasant surprise: the absence of people. The sandstone spires, roughly cut canyons, and vibrantly colored rock layers of this awe-inspiring landscape are often passed up by those on a time budget, and many visitors bid them good riddance—without the onslaught of RVs and tour buses, some of the wildest land in the lower 48 is given room to breathe. When the park was established in 1964, much of the territory had yet to be mapped or fully explored, and was traveled only by Native Americans, cowboys, outlaws, and miners. In some sections of the park, not much has changed. Due to the park's sheer size and awe-inspiring panoramas, those willing to get off the beaten path will experience a vast beauty unlike that of any other park. Like the Utes, mountain men, and fortune-hunters that came before them, visitors must come well prepared—there are few amenities in the park, and those who venture out commit themselves to a real outdoor experience.

AT A GLANCE: CANYONLANDS NATIONAL PARK

AREA: 337,598 sq. mi.

FEATURES: Green and Colorado Rivers, The Needles, Island in the Sky, The Maze.

HIGHLIGHTS: Hiking in the Needles, off-roading on White Rim Road, touring Horseshoe Canyon.

GATEWAY TOWNS: Moab (p. 268), Monticello.

CAMPING: Squaw Flat Campground (The Needles) $10, Willow Flat Campground (Island in the Sky) $5; permits required for overnight backcountry travel.

ENTRANCE FEES: Weekly pass for vehicles $10, pedestrians and bikers $5.

✦ ORIENTATION

The Green and Colorado Rivers divide the park into three districts, and themselves comprise the fourth. Because each region is essentially self-contained, once you've entered one district, getting to another requires retracing your steps and reentering the park, a trip that can last from several hours to a full day. To get to the **Needles,** take Rte. 211 W from U.S. 191, about 40 mi. south of Moab or 14 mi. north of Monticello. Farther north, **Island in the Sky** is the most easily accessible district from Moab—the entrance station and Visitors Center sit about 22 mi. southwest of the Rte. 313 W turnoff from U.S. 191, 10 mi. north of Moab. To reach the **Maze** district from I-70, take Rte. 24, 15 mi. west of Green River, 29 mi. to a turnoff just south of the entrance to Goblin Valley State Park. The **Rivers** district features great stretches of flat water as well as some world-class rapids. Above the confluence, both rivers remain calm as they wind their way through the layered sandstone, cutting two deep canyons. The power of their combined flow in the southern portion of the park makes for incredibly fast and powerful whitewater raging through Cataract Canyon. For more info on rafting in Canyonlands, visit the rafting companies based in Moab (see p. 268).

WHEN TO GO Summer temperatures in Canyonlands often top 100°F. The spring and fall are the best times of the year for hiking and backpacking, with highs ranging 60-80°F. Be aware, however, that temperatures fluctuate greatly over the course of a day, and it is not unusual for an 80°F day to turn into a 40°F night. Although there is not much snowfall in Canyonlands, winter highs range 30-50°F, with lows 0-20°F, and even a little bit of snow can render many areas of the park impassable.

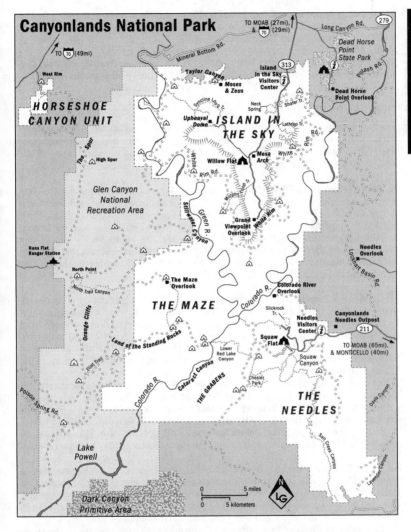

🛈 PRACTICAL INFORMATION

Coyote Shuttle (☎259-8656) and **Roadrunner Shuttle of Moab** (☎259-9402) both provide taxi service to the Needles and Island in the Sky districts. For general info
before plunging into the different districts, visit Monticello's **Multiagency Visitors
Center,** 117 S. Main (☎587-3235 or 800-574-4386; open M-F 8am-5pm, Sa-Su 10am-
5pm), or the **Moab Information Center,** 3 Center St. (☎259-8825 or 800-635-6622.
Open July-Aug. daily 8am-9pm, Sept.-Oct. and Apr.-May 8am-7pm, Nov. 9am-7pm,
Dec.-Mar. 9am-5pm, May-June 8am-8pm.) The **Bureau of Land Management** presides
over the Green and Colorado upstream from the park. For more info, contact the

Grand County Travel Council (☎800-635-6622) or the **Moab Area BLM Office** (☎259-6111). For recorded river flow info, call 801-539-1311. **Rim Cyclery**, 94 W. 100 N (☎259-5333), and **Pagan Mountaineering**, 88 E. Center St. (☎259-1117), both in Moab, offer a full range of outdoor gear. There is no **gas** or food available in the park, and no **water** available in Island in the Sky or the Maze. **Weather and Road Conditions:** ☎800-492-2400 or 964-6000. Write to Canyonlands National Park, 2282 S.W. Resource Blvd., Moab, UT 84532, or call 259-7164 for more info.

THE NEEDLES

The Needles region, named for its Cedar Mesa sandstone spires, offers unparalleled hiking amid arches, canyons, and Native American ruins. Hiking and four-wheel-drive trails offer excellent views of both rivers and make for some of the best day trips and overnight treks in the park.

🚩 **PRACTICAL INFORMATION.** The **Needles Visitors Center**, 35 mi. west of U.S. 191, is a good place to fill up on water and to pick the brains of rangers before setting out. (☎259-4711. Open Mar.-Oct. daily 8am-5pm; Nov.-Feb. 8am-4:30pm.) Just outside the park boundary and 1 mi. from the Visitors Center, the **Needles Outpost** houses a limited and expensive grocery store and gas pump. (☎979-4007. Open daily 9am-6pm.) Services including an **ATM, grocery store, hospital,** and **post office** are available in **Monticello**, 50 mi. southeast of the park. **Water** is available at the Visitors Center and at Squaw Flat Campground.

🏕 **CAMPING. Squaw Flat Campground,** 4 mi. west of the Visitors Center on a well-marked spur of the main park drive, offers 26 sites that occupy a sandy plain surrounded by giant sandstone pinnacles, many of which provide glorious shade from the blazing sun. (☎259-4711. Flush toilets and running water. No wood gathering. 14-night max. stay. Check-out 10am. Sites $10; Dec.-Jan. free.) To stay at the great **backcountry** campsites to be found throughout the district, obtain a permit from the Visitors Center (backpacking permit $15, overnight 4x4 permit $30).

For some great overlooks at elevations above 8000 ft., camp in the **Monticello District** of the **Manti-La Sal National Forest,** south of Needles. The campsites in the forest here are almost always cooler than those within the park. Two campgrounds are easily accessible from Rte. 211: **Buckboard**, 11½ mi. south of Rte. 211 (16 sites, 10 with full hookup; $9), and **Dalton Springs**, 13 mi. south of Rte. 211 (18 sites, 16 with full hookup; $9). Both campgrounds are open from late May to September.

🥾 **HIKING.** Hiking options from the Needles area are more developed than in any other district, and numerous itineraries are possible along the interconnecting trails. The majority of trails traverse a mixture of slickrock and sandy washes surrounded by the surreal landscapes of the Needles themselves. Almost any hike in this region is bound to be a good one, but some favorites stand out.

The moderate **Chessler Park Loop** travels through slickrock country to the spectacular Chessler Park, 960 acres of grassy meadows surrounded by magnificently rainbowed hoodoos. Starting at the base of Elephant Hill, the 11 mi. round-trip hike encircles the meadow, winding through a series of deep, narrow fractures along the way, and experiences little elevation change. The **Druid Arch** hike follows the Chessler Park Loop for a few miles before branching off into Elephant Canyon and the arch. The moderately difficult 11 mi. round-trip route provides some of the most spectacular views in the Needles as it makes its way up a steep climb that requires both a ladder climb and some scrambling to the arch.

A moderate 7.5 mi. trail leads between **Big Spring** and **Squaw Canyon**. The trailhead is located along Squaw Flat Loop "A." Rambling through varied terrain in two canyons, this trail serves as great introduction to the Needles. The section between the canyons climbs steep grades along exposed slickrock benches and is dangerous when wet. The **Slickrock Trail** departs from a well-marked turn-out near the end of the park drive. A short route that provides a good taste of slickrock country, this easy 2.4 mi. round-trip hike offers several viewpoints of the river canyons and the surrounding terrain. You may even see bighorn sheep.

◪ BACKPACKING, ROCK CLIMBING, AND FOUR-WHEELING. Backpacking opportunities abound in the Needles. Make sure you get a permit at the Visitors Center before setting out ($15; reservations recommended for spring and fall), and bring plenty of water; reliable water sources can be few and far between (or nonexistent). The challenging 22.5 mi. one-way **Salt Creek Canyon Trail** begins at Peekaboo Camp and plunges into some of the wildest terrain in the district. It follows the canyon's main drainage through dense brush and cottonwood groves before picking up an old four-wheel-drive trail. Those without high-clearance four-wheel-drive vehicles can begin the hike 3.5 mi. north of Peekaboo at Cave Spring or at the southern end of the canyon at Cathedral Butte. Allow two days to complete the one-way trip, camping at semi-developed sites along the way. The 18.9 mi. **Lower Red Lake Canyon** hike begins at the Elephant Hill Trailhead. This strenuous route climbs through the Grabens before descending the steep talus slope of Lower Red Lake Canyon to the banks of the Colorado, affording great views of the river and the Maze on the opposite bank. Allow two days; the only camping is at-large.

A multitude of **rock climbing** routes are easily accessible throughout the park, but none of the routes are bolted and most are difficult to top rope, so they are not for beginning climbers. Talk to a park ranger for more info. Myriad rock outcroppings please amateur and hard-core boulderers almost everywhere in the park.

More than 50 mi. of backcountry roads blanket the Needles, providing access to campsites, trailheads, and natural wonders and some great rides for high-clearance, **four-wheel-drive** vehicles. Permits are required for four-wheel-drive day use and can be obtained at the Visitors Center (14-day pass $5). The **Elephant Hill** route is one of the most difficult four-wheel-drive roads in Utah and should not be attempted by inexperienced drivers. Those willing to risk life, limb, and vehicle are rewarded with spectacular views and access to some of the more remote parts of the park and the surrounding area. The road also offers some challenging riding for mountain bikers. The more moderate **Colorado Overlook** route presents a four-wheeling experience better suited for less seasoned drivers, as well as some excellent biking. The last 1½ mi. of the road presents large rocks and stair-step drops.

ISLAND IN THE SKY

A towering mesa which sits within the "Y" formed by the two rivers, Island in the Sky affords fantastic views of the surrounding canyons and mountains and offers the most readily accessible drive-through experience of the park for travelers short on time, in addition to plenty of hiking and backcountry jeep roads for a more in-depth visit. The mesa is not an island but more of a peninsula, connected to a plateau by an isthmus or "neck" that stretches between two canyons and is just wide enough to allow the road to pass over.

◪ PRACTICAL INFORMATION. The **Island in the Sky Visitors Center,** 22 mi. southwest from the intersection of U.S. 191 and Rte. 313, provides orientation and sells the only **water** in this area of the park to travelers. (☎ 259-4712. Open Apr.-Oct. daily 8am-6pm, Nov.-Mar. 8am-4:30pm.) Moab (p. 268), 32 mi. from the park, provides many services including **banks, grocery stores,** a **hospital,** and a **post office.**

UTAH

⚸ CAMPING. Willow Flat Campground sits high atop the mesa, approximately 8 mi. south of the Visitors Center on a well-marked 1 mi. turnoff from the park drive. At 6000 ft., the campground provides a respite from the heat of much of the surrounding countryside. (12 sites. Pit toilets, no water. 14-night max. stay. Check-out 10am. Sites $5.) **Dead Horse Point State Park,** on Rte. 313, 22 mi. south of the junction with U.S. 191, offers more luxurious camping as well as its fair share of astounding sights, including a view of the Colorado that many say surpasses any in the Island of the Sky section of the national park. (21 sites. Water, hookups, and covered picnic tables. Sites $14, including admission to park. **Visitors Center** open daily 8am-5pm. Entrance fee $7.) For more info, write the Park Superintendent, Dead Horse Point State Park, Box 609, Moab, UT 84532, or call 259-2614 or 800-322-3770 (open daily 6am-10pm). **Free camping** is allowed in designated primitive campsites on **BLM** land along Rte. 313 east of the park. Be warned that the BLM's liberal hospitality extends to mining companies, which make an occasional ruckus in the area.

▨ HIKING. Trails on the Island in the Sky offer spectacular views; a short hike makes a fruitful diversion. Routes that drop below the mesa top tend to be primitive and rough. Hikes are marked with cairns and signs at junctions and trailheads and may be tackled without a permit. The **Neck Spring Trail** begins across from the overlook just south of the Neck. This moderate 5 mi. round-trip hike stays on the mesa top as it loops above the Taylor Canyon, which makes the northern "moat" of Island in the Sky. The trail passes a spring that was used by ranchers, as well as relics of these operations. (300 ft. elevation change. Hikeable year-round.) The moderate 8 mi. round-trip **Syncline Loop** begins at the end of the park road at the Upheaval Dome Trailhead and encircles the breathtakingly surreal **Upheaval Dome,** as well as providing access to both the Green River and the crater. A 3.5 mi. spur leaves the trail about halfway through and heads west to the White Rim Rd. and the Green River. Near this point, a 1.5 mi. spur strikes out into the middle of the crater's moonscape. (1300 ft. elevation change.)

Starting at the well-marked trailhead along the Grand View Point Spur, the **Murphy Loop** crosses the mesa top before dropping down Island in the Sky and heading out onto Murphy Hogback, which features excellent views of the White Rim and surrounding canyons. The moderately strenuous 10.5 mi. route then follows the White Rim Rd. for a little over 1 mi. before climbing back up to the mesa top. (1500 ft. elevation change. Hikeable year-round.) The strenuous **Lathrop Canyon** hike drops pretty much straight off Island in the Sky and descends to the banks of the Colorado River. The 17 mi. round-trip route passes through varied terrain from the grasslands of the mesa top, across the slick sandstone of its red rock sides, and to the sandy washes and groves of cottonwoods that lead to the mighty river. Find the well-marked trailhead on the main park road in the large meadow south of the Neck. Bring plenty of water for this long trip, which is equally enjoyable when done in two days, although it can reasonably be completed in one long day. (2000 ft. elevation change. Hikeable year-round.)

⚒ BACKPACKING, BIKING, AND FOUR-WHEELING. Backpacking routes in Island in the Sky aren't as developed or varied as the routes in the Needles, but some good treks can still be found. **Taylor Canyon,** which drops from the Island in the Sky to the Green River, offers a good overnight hike, combining the Alcove Spring Trail and the four-wheel-drive road that heads from the White Rim up to Taylor Camp. A loop route including **Upheaval Canyon** is also a good option. Backpacking permits are required and can be obtained at the Visitors Center.

As is true with the other districts in Canyonlands, four-wheel-drive vehicles and mountain bikes share the same routes because mountain bikes are not allowed on hiking trails. The 100 mi. White Rim Rd. offers premier off-roading in Canyonlands for both drivers and bikers. Spectacular views of the Colorado and Green Rivers, the surrounding canyons and mountains, and Island in the Sky are ubiquitous along the route. The full loop usually takes two to three days for vehicles and three to four days for mountain bikes. The trail is moderately difficult for both bikes and cars, and some sections, including the Lathrop Canyon Rd., Murphy's Hogback, Hardscrabble Hill, and the Mineral Bottom switchbacks, are challenging. Reservations are required for four-wheel-drive trips, and permits are required for overnight trips ($30). Drivers and bicyclists must stay in designated campsites.

THE MAZE

The most remote district of the park, the rugged Maze is a veritable hurly-burly of twisted canyons made for *über*-pioneers with four-wheel-drive vehicles or a yen for demanding backcountry walkabouts. The Maze also provides closest access to the outlying Horseshoe Canyon, which boasts what is considered the most significant rock art in North America.

🛈 PRACTICAL INFORMATION. The **Hans Flat Ranger Station,** 75 mi. from I-70 and 60 mi. from the junction of Rte. 24 and 95 in Hanksville, is an invaluably informative resource for Maze exploration. The station has **no services** or **water.** (☎ 259-2652. Open daily 8am-4:30pm.) Green River, approximately 90 mi. north on I-70, offers most services including an **ATM, grocery store,** and **post office.** Hanksville, 60 mi. south, provides more limited services. No permanent water sources are available. None of the hiking trails in the region are wheelchair accessible. There are no entrance fees in the Maze district.

🛈 CAMPING. There is no developed campground comparable to campgrounds in the Needles and Island in the Sky districts, but numerous **primitive campgrounds** dot the terrain. Some of the most popular campgrounds for visitors embarking on (relatively) brief excursions into the Maze include North Point, High Spur, and Maze Overlook. All campgrounds operate on a first come, first served basis.

🛈 HORSESHOE CANYON. This detached unit of Canyonlands boasts some of the best works of rock art in North America. The **Great Gallery** includes well-preserved, life-sized figures featuring detailed designs. The canyon sits approximately 30 mi. east of Rte. 24 on a spur off the road to Hans Flat Ranger Station. Visitors may stay at the **campsite** on BLM land at the West Rim trailhead (pit toilet, no water). A 6hr., 6.5 mi. guided **hike** into Horseshoe Canyon leaves the West Rim trailhead at 9am on Saturday and Sunday from April through October. This trail, which drops 750 ft. into the canyon, can also be hiked without the ranger escort. *Be sure to bring plenty of water.*

🛈 OUTDOOR ACTIVITIES. Like everything else in the Maze, **hiking** trails are primitive. A number of trails lead into canyons and to viewpoints, but tend to be marked only with cairns or not marked at all, and are only accessible via four-wheel-drive roads. Many of the canyons look alike and require basic **rock climbing** maneuvers in order to gain access. A topographic map is essential. One multi-day route readily accessible for standard vehicles is **North Trail Canyon.** The hike begins for those with two-wheel drive at the **North Road Junction,** 2½ mi. southeast of the Hans Flat Ranger Station. This moderately strenuous 30 mi. round-trip route drops through steep, rocky terrain from the Orange Cliffs mesatop into Elaterite Basin before heading out to water the stupendous views of the Maze Overlook. (1000 ft. elevation change. Hikeable year-round.)

Four-wheel-drive roads in the Maze district are extremely difficult and should not be attempted by inexperienced drivers. Visitors should be aware that all routes present considerable risk of vehicle damage, and should come prepared to make basic vehicle repairs. In addition, drivers must provide their own toilet systems. For those seasoned veterans who are not deterred by all the obstacles that the Maze has to throw at drivers, the region offers a considerable network of roads that lead to myriad canyons and vistas. The **Flint Trail** is the most popular trail in the district, but is closed in the winter due to its extremely slippery clay surface.

INTERSTATE 15 SOUTH

One of Utah's most-traveled thoroughfares, Interstate 15 is an express trip south of Salt Lake City, ferrying red-rock-hungry tourists from the Salt Lake City Airport to their chosen destination in southern Utah. Although towns along the highway tend toward the boring side, the amphitheater in Cedar Breaks and the Bard's work on stage in Cedar City merit stops on the way to Utah's national parks.

CEDAR CITY   ☎ 435

Southern Utah's college town, Cedar City exudes energy, especially when summer crowds pour in for the annual Shakespeare Festival. East of town, the Dixie National Forest and Brian Head Resort lure visitors with endless views and world-class hiking and biking, while the fantastical red sandstone sculpture garden of Cedar Breaks National Monument will inspire the imagination.

■■ 🔁 **ORIENTATION AND PRACTICAL INFORMATION. Skywest Airlines** (☎800-453-9417) flies between Cedar City and **Salt Lake City** ($150 one-way) out of **Cedar City Regional Airport,** west of town. **Greyhound,** 1744 W. Royal Hunte Dr. (☎867-5828), stops in Cedar City on its routes up and down the I-15 corridor. **To: Salt Lake City** 4hr., 2 per day, $41; **Las Vegas** 3hr., 5 per day, $32.; **Denver** 8-10hr., 3 per day, $87.) For **Festival Taxi Cab Co.,** call 586-7186.

The **Iron County Visitors Center,** 581 N. Main, houses a friendly staff and a copious collection of brochures and maps. (☎586-5124. Open M-F 8am-5pm.) For **outdoor info,** visit the **Cedar City BLM,** 176 E. D.L. Sargent Dr. (☎586-2401; open M-F 8am-4:30pm), or the **Cedar City Ranger District,** 1789 N. Wedgewood Ln. (☎865-3200; open M-F 8am-5pm). Services include: **Valley View Medical Center,** 595 S. 75 E (☎586-6587); **Internet access** at the **Cedar City Memorial Library,** 136 W. Center St. (☎586-6661; open M-Th 9am-9pm, F-Sa 9am-6pm); and **post office,** 333 N. Main (☎586-6708; open M-F 8:30am-5:30pm, Sa 8:30am-12:30pm). **ZIP code:** 84720.

🔁🗒 **ACCOMMODATIONS AND FOOD.** Economy motels flourish on Main St., sustained by the Utah Shakespearean Festival, during which room prices soar. For high-quality rooms and friendly service, try **Cedar Rest Motel ❷,** 479 S. Main St. (☎586-9471. Singles $30 in winter, $50 in summer; doubles $36/$60.) **Cedar City KOA ❷,** 1121 N. Main St., boasts a heated pool, laundromat, and private video and DVD theater. (☎586-9872. Tent sites $25 for 2 people, each additional person $3; super-sites with large pull-throughs and Internet access $35.) Abundant camping fills the mountains west of Cedar City. The convenient **Cedar Canyon Campground ❶,** on Rte. 14, 12 mi. from Cedar City, offers 19 tent sites with water and vault toilets ($8). Camping is also available in the national monument (see p. 290).

While fast-food joints populate the areas of town near I-15 interchanges, downtown Cedar City offers a number of high-quality, budget-priced dining options. For lunch, a light dinner, a late-night snack, or cappuccino, the **Pastry Pub ❶,** 86 W.

Center St., is a Cedar City fixture. The Pub decor makes for pleasing contrast with the array of healthy sandwich ($3.50-5) and salad ($5) options. (☎867-1400. Open M-Sa 7:30am-10pm, during the festival M-Sa 7:30am-midnight.) Head to **Hunan Chinese Restaurant ❶**, 501 S. Main, for delectable $4-6 lunch specials and $6-8 dinner entrees. (☎586-8952. Open M-F 11am-9pm, Sa noon-9pm.)

🟦 **SIGHTS.** Every summer, thousands of theater connoisseurs from across the country descend on Cedar City for the annual 🔲**Utah Shakespearean Festival.** Held in a traditional Elizabethan theater on the Southern Utah University campus between mid-June and mid-October, the Tony Award-winning festival presents several Shakespearean selections and a repertoire of modern works. Between two and five shows are performed daily, at four venues. (☎800-752-9849 for tickets and info. Tickets $12-42. Student rush tickets 30min. before show 50% off.)

🔲 **HIKING.** The **Ashdown Gorge Wilderness Area,** administered by the Dixie National Forest, abuts the western edge of Cedar Breaks National Monument, east of Cedar City, and offers an excellent arena for experienced backcountry hikers and backpackers to explore dramatic canyons and hike into the monument from the bottom. Trailheads leading into the wilderness depart from both Rte. 14 and Rte. 143. Maps and info on the wilderness area are available at the Cedar City Ranger District office. A popular and challenging trail in the wilderness area, the **Rattlesnake Trail** departs from Rte. 143 at 10,460 ft., just beyond the park's northern boundary, descending 3,607 ft. into the canyon. Traveling 5 mi. one-way, it parallels the rim of the monument, offering endless views of both the monument and **Ashdown Gorge.** The trail's end joins the 2.5 mi. **Potato Hollow Trail,** which connects with Forest Rd. 301 for those interested in through-hiking and shuttling cars. The hike can be done in one very long day or an easier two; hikers should be aware that Ashdown Gorge is prone to flash flooding.

East of Cedar City, the **Virgin River Rim Trail** makes for an excellent introduction to any trip to Zion National Park with its breathtaking views of the Virgin River headwaters and the distant Zion Canyon monuments. The entire trail is 32 mi., beginning at **Woods Ranch** just before the Cedar Canyon Campground on Rte. 14 and ending at **Strawberry Point** along Forest Service Rd. 058. For hikers interested in shorter excursions, several trails climbing south from **Navajo Lake** make shorter treks. To reach Navajo Lake, drive 25 mi. on Rte. 14 east of Cedar City and turn right on the Navajo Lake Rd.

🔲 **SKIING.** Beyond Cedar Breaks National Monument on Rte. 143 lies **Brian Head Resort,** a quiet ski hamlet and premier mountain biking resort. The slopes envelop two mountains surrounding town, providing a variety of terrain for skiers and snowboarders of all ability levels. Brian Head may be smaller than other Utah resorts, but its size brings a small-town feel lacking in decadent resort towns like Park City. Six lifts serve 500 skiable acres and a 1707 ft. vertical drop. The base elevation is Utah's highest resort elevation at 9600 ft., and 425 in. of snow fall annually on the mountain. Fifty-three runs (30% beginner; 40% intermediate; 30% advanced) descend the mountain, and 42 mi. of **cross-country trails** (50% beginner; 30% intermediate; 20% advanced) serve the nordic enthusiast. (☎677-2035. Ski season Nov. to early Apr. Slopes open daily 9:30am-4:30pm; night skiing F-Sa and holidays 3:30-10pm. Full-day pass $38, half-day $33; seniors and ages 6-12 $25/$17. Adult ski packages $23, child ski packages $15; adult snowboard packages $30.) During summer months, Brian Head offers mountain bikers over 160 mi. of some of the nation's finest singletrack. The resort provides shuttle service to area trailheads, as well as chairlift rides for bicyclists. A free brochure entitled **Bike Brian Head,** available at the resort offices on Rte. 143 and the Cedar City Visitors Center,

FROM THE ROAD

VERTICAL DAY

I heard a woman on the Zion shuttle say that she once hiked both Observation Point and Angel's Landing in one day. By then it was already past noon—I knew I had my work cut out for me. But it was mid-summer and eight hours of daylight beckoned.

I loaded up on trail mix and started the first one. Booking up the trail full-hrottle, whizzing by German and Korean tourists, I suddenly hit a dead end. The trail ended at a little spring. Damn, wrong trail. No time to appreciate nature here. I charged down and started on the other one.

As sweat poured off me, I began to see that doing this in the 100° degree mid-day heat might not have been the best idea. After the first 1000 ft. or so the trail entered a narrow canyon, providing momentary shade.

Countless switchbacks later, up and down, I made it back, made myself some dinner, and started up Angel's Landing. I knew I really had to hurry this time, as getting stuck up here in the dark would be a problem. Plus, I had the sense that the two kids behind me, visibly quite in love, might want some privacy up there.

The steep switchbacks lead to a rather horrible thing called the "water-wiggles"—a near-vertical squiggle of rail leading straight up the mountain. From there the trail skates atop a ridge to the summit. Looking down the 500 ft. sheer drop-offs on either side, I thought about how lucky it was that I wasn't afraid of heights.

At the top, I experienced one of the finest views in America. Sated, I made my way down slowly, carefully, reaching the bottom just as darkness enveloped the canyon, exhilarated that I had conquered the day. *—Evan North*

has listings of area routes. **Georg's**, in Brian Head, rents full suspension bikes from $30 per day. (☎677-2013. Open June to late Sept. 8am-5pm.)

CEDAR BREAKS NATIONAL MONUMENT

Shaped like a gigantic ampitheater, the semicircle of canyons that makes up Cedar Breaks National Monument measures more than 3 mi. in diameter and 2,000 ft. in depth. A gallery of sandstone spires decorate the alternately red, orange, and yellow surface of the bowl. To reach this marvel of geology, take Rte. 14 east from Cedar City and turn north on Rte. 148. A 28-site **campground** ❶ perched at 10,200 ft. (open June to mid-Sept.; water, flush toilets; sites $12) and the **Visitors Center** (☎586-0787; open May-Sept. daily 8am-6pm) await at **Point Supreme.** There are no services inside the monument; the nearest gas, food, and lodging are found either in Cedar City or Brian Head. (☎586-9451. Entrance $3; under 17 free.)

Tourists travel to the Monument nearly exclusively for the view, most easily reached by parking at the Visitors Center and walking to Point Supreme, or by stopping at one of several vistas along the 5 mi. stretch of scenic Rte. 143. The Monument has two established trails that provide for a more extended visit. Originating at the **Chessman Ridge Overlook** (10,467 ft., roughly 2 mi. north of the Visitors Center), the popular 2 mi. round-trip **Alpine Pond Trail** follows the rim to a spring-fed alpine lake whose waters trickle into the breaks, winding toward slow evaporation in the Great Basin. The hike takes 1-2hr. and is accompanied by an instructive trail guide available at the Visitors Center or trailhead ($1). The 4 mi. round-trip **Ramparts Trail** departs from the Visitors Center at 10,300 ft. and traces the edge of the amphitheater through a Bristlecone grove to a 9950 ft. point, providing spectacular views of the terrain below. Though reaching the monument during the winter proves difficult on snowy roads, cross-country skiers cherish the rolling meadows and serene winter scenery.

HURRICANE AND LA VERKIN   ☎435

Hurricane ("Hurakin") and La Verkin don't offer much as sister gateway towns, but they do have location on their side, acting as a crossroads between Zion, Bryce, Lake Powell, and the Grand Canyon. Visitor info can be found at the **Hurricane Chamber of Commerce**, 95 S. Main. (☎635-3402. Open M-F 9:30am-1pm.) In La Verkin, **Farmers Market,** 495 N. State St., is the largest "big-city" grocer close to Zion National Park and should satisfy even the pickiest of grocery shoppers. (☎635-0774. Open 5:30am-midnight.) The

Hurricane **post office** is at 1075 W. 100 N., off Rte. 9 between Lin's Market and US Bank. (☎635-4781. Open M-F 8:30am-5:30pm, Sa 9am-1pm.) **ZIP code:** 84737.

The crown jewel of the towns is the ⊠**Dixie Hostel (HI-AYH) ❶**, 73 S. Main, 20 mi. west of Zion in Hurricane. This bright, airy, and immaculate hostel is a comfortable stay and only 2hr. from Las Vegas, Lake Powell, the North Rim, and Bryce Canyon. (☎635-8202. Linen, laundry, kitchen, and continental breakfast. Internet access $1 per hr. Dorms $15; singles $35.) Just down the street from the hostel, the **New Garden Cafe ❶**, 138 S. Main, dishes out light vegetarian and health-conscious fare ($5-7) in a new-age atmosphere. Lounge on the porch with the locals and discuss the medicinal properties of Mormon Tea. (Open daily 9am-2pm.)

PARKS OF SOUTHWESTERN UTAH

Bryce Canyon, Zion, and Capitol Reef National Parks lie in a northeast-to-southwest-oriented line running through the southwest portion of the state, connected by Rte. 9, U.S. 89, and Rte. 12. These popular parks are dwarfed by Grand Staircase-Escalante National Monument, the new kid on the block, sprawling south and east of Bryce Canyon and west of Capitol Reef. To the north of Rte. 12 between Bryce and Capitol Reef, the Dixie National Forest encompasses much of the Aquarius Plateau.

ZION NATIONAL PARK   ☎435

Russet sandstone mountains loom over the puny cars and hikers that flock to Zion National Park in search of the promised land, and rarely does Zion disappoint. Some 13 million years ago, the ocean flowed over the cliffs and canyons of Zion. When the sea subsided, it left behind only the raging Virgin River, whose watery fingers continue to sculpt the smooth white and pink rock monuments. In the northwest corner of the park, the walls of Kolob Terrace tower thousands of feet above the river. Elsewhere, branching canyons and rock formations showcase erosion's unique artistry. In the 1860s, Mormon settlers came to the area and enthusiastically proclaimed that they had found Zion, the promised land. Brigham Young disagreed, however, and declared that the place was awfully nice, but "not Zion." The name "not Zion" stuck for years until a new wave of entranced explorers dropped the "not," giving the park its present name. The park might very well be the fulfillment of biblical prophecy for outdoor recreationalists. With hiking trails nonpareil and challenging and mysterious slot canyons set against a tableau of sublime sandstone, visiting Zion is a spiritual event.

✦ ORIENTATION

The main entrance to Zion is in **Springdale**, on Rte. 9, which borders the park to the south along the **Virgin River**. From I-15, take either the **Hurricane** or **La Verkin** exits.

AT A GLANCE: ZION NATIONAL PARK

AREA: 146,592 acres.

FEATURES: Great White Throne, Kolob Canyons, Virgin River.

HIGHLIGHTS: The Riverside Walk, Angel's Landing, trekking the Narrows, backcountry hikes.

GATEWAY TOWNS: Springdale (borders park), Hurricane/La Verkin (p. 290).

CAMPING: South and Watchman Campgrounds $14, Lava Point free, $5 permit required for overnight backcountry travel.

ENTRANCE FEES: Vehicles $20; pedestrians $10.

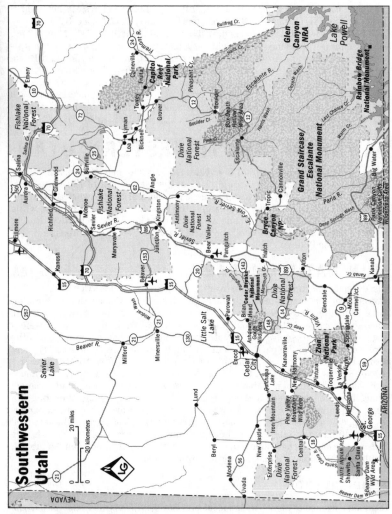

Rte. 9 continues through the park and connects with Zion's eastern boarder via a long tunnel. Approaching from the east, pick up Rte. 9 from U.S. 89 at Mt. Carmel Junction. To reach the less visited **Kolob Canyons,** take Exit 40 off I-15. This entrance connects with Zion Canyon only by the rubber soles of hiking boots.

Zion divides neatly into three distinct regions. In **Zion Canyon** proper, the heart of the park, visitors stand awestruck in the shadows of towering crags like **The Great White Throne, Angels Landing, The Temple of the Virgin,** and the **Temple of Sinawava.** This is Zion at its postcard-picture best. In the westernmost corner of the park, separated from Zion Canyon by the high Kolob Terrace, lie **Kolob Canyons** and the immense **Kolob Arch.** On the park's eastern limit, the **Zion-Mt. Carmel Hwy.** winds past painted slickrock and colorful mesas. All three areas offer their own unique

UTAH

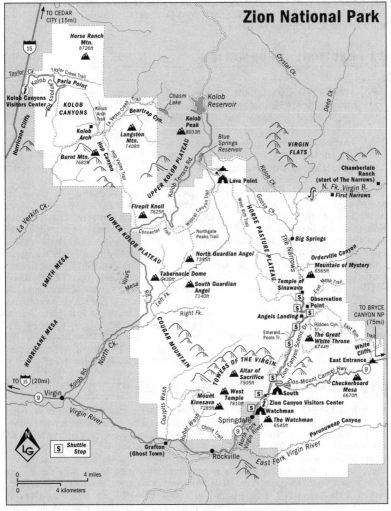

Zion National Park

insight into the haphazardly creative power of geologic processes, torrential rainfall, and raging rivers.

TRANSPORTATION

No unauthorized traffic may travel the Zion Canyon Scenic Drive during summer months. **Free shuttles** run between Springdale and the Temple of Sinawava (the northmost stop in the canyon) beginning at 5:30am. Shuttles run every 30min. early in the day, with increased frequency in the late morning and afternoon. The last shuttle leaves the Temple of Sinawava at 11pm. **Parking** is available at the Visitors Center, but the Park Service advises leaving cars in Springdale and taking the

UTAH

shuttle into the park. The Visitors Center lot generally fills entirely between 11am and 3pm during summer months. Overpriced **gasoline** is available just outside both the east and south park entrances.

⁊ PRACTICAL INFORMATION

WHEN TO GO. Crowds of hikers, backpackers, and scenic-view-seeking tourists flock to Zion between Memorial Day and Labor Day, overcrowding campgrounds and parking facilities. For the visitor with a more flexible travel schedule, the cool Zion spring and fall offer a less crowded park and a more comfortable climate. Between May and October, daily high temperatures range 70-105°F with lows 45-75°F. During winter months, highs range 45-80°F, dipping below freezing some nights.

The brand new, ecologically harmonious **Zion Canyon Visitors Center,** just inside the south entrance, houses an info center, bookstore, and backcountry permit station. At the west entrance to the park, the **Kolob Canyons Visitors Center** offers info on the Kolob Canyon Scenic Drive and the surrounding trail system, books, maps, and displays on the formation of the Kolob Arch. (Park info ☎ 772-3256. Both centers open in summer daily 8am-7pm; reduced winter hours.) Just outside the main entrance in Springdale, the **Happy Camper** grocer, 95 Zion Park Blvd., stocks camp food, fresh produce, and meat. (☎ 772-3402. Open daily 7:30am-10pm.) **Zion's Bank,** 921 Zion Park Blvd., and **ATMs** serve tourists in Springdale. In case of an **emergency,** call 772-3322. **Internet access** is available for $3 for 15min. at Sol Foods, across the footbridge from the Visitors Center, but is only $1 per hr. at the **Springdale Branch Public Library,** 898 Zion Park Blvd. (☎ 772-3676; open M, W, F 10am-6pm; Tu, Th 10am-9pm; Sa 10am-5pm). **Post offices** are found in the Zion Park Lodge (☎ 772-3213; open M-F 8am-5pm, Sa 9am-noon) or at 624 Zion Park Blvd. in Springdale (☎ 772-3950; open M-F 8am-1pm and 2-5pm, Sa 9am-noon). **ZIP code:** 84767.

⌂⌂ CAMPING AND ACCOMMODATIONS

More than 300 sites are available at the **South** and **Watchman Campgrounds ❶,** near the brand-new Visitors Center. Campgrounds fill quickly in summer; arrive before noon to ensure a spot. **Watchman Campground** takes reservations, but **South** is first come, first served. (☎ 800-365-2267 for Watchman reservations. Water, toilets, and sanitary disposal station. Both $14. Open year-round.) Avoid the crowds at the six free primitive sites at **Lava Point,** a nearly 1hr. drive from the Visitors Center, in close proximity to the panoramic Lava Point overlook and the Western Rim Trailhead. (Open June-Nov.) To find Lava Point, turn right off Rte. 9 at the sign for the Kolob Reservoir in Virgin and follow signs for the campground. **Zion Canyon Campground ❶,** 479 Zion Park Blvd., refreshes the weary, hungry, and filthy with a convenience store, pizzeria, grocery store, showers ($3 for non-guests), and coin-op laundry. (☎ 772-3237. Office open daily 8am-9pm. Store open daily 8am-9pm; off-season 8am-5pm. Sites for 2 $18, full hookups $22; $3.50 per additional adult, $2 per additional child under 15.) **Zion Frontier Campground ❶,** ¼ mi. outside the east entrance, sits 1000 ft. higher and about 10°F cooler than the sites inside the park, and offers a laundromat, showers, restaurant, and gas station. (☎ 648-2154. Office open 24hr. 60 tent sites $12, 19 hookups $20, tepees and a hogon $20, cabins $25.)

For those inclined toward indoor accommodations, Springdale's least expensive lodging, the family-owned **El Río Lodge ❸,** 995 Zion Park Blvd., welcomes guests with clean rooms, friendly service, and dazzling views of the Watchman Face.

THE CABLE GUYS Imagine how the sandstone monuments of Zion Canyon would look as you glance back over your shoulder and descend rapidly over 2000 ft., attached to a thin cable and at the mercy of whoever is controlling the brakes. Such were the rides on the **Cable Mountain Draw Works** during the first two decades of the 20th century. Spanning a 2000 ft. vertical drop from the summit of Cable Mountain to what is today the Weeping Rock shuttle stop, the cable first carried lumber from the high mesa of the east rim to the valley floor in 1901. From their arrival, settlers in Springdale, an area forested only by poor-quality cottonwoods, had faced the tedious task of hauling lumber from the mountaintops, a job that could require as long as two weeks per load. When Brigham Young visited the area in 1863, he prophesied that one day, lumber would descend from the cliffs "like a hawk flies." Such colorful imagery inspired young David Flanigan to begin construction on the cable works around 1898. By 1901, lumber traveled from peak to valley in less than 3 min., a remarkable increase in efficiency. According to David Flanigan's diary, the cable work's first passenger, a family dog, was "real scairt" after its first ride on the cableworks. Falling 2000 ft. in 3 min. was quite a thrill, and lumber workers regularly used the works to travel to and from the mesa. In 1930, the National Parks Service removed the cable, fearing injury to visitors. Now, watching the escarpments' heights receding rapidly into the blue sky above is an experience that promises to be a Zion visitor's last.

(☎ 772-3205 or 888-772-3205. Singles $47; doubles $52; winter rates dip to around $35.) Across the street, the **Terrace Brook Lodge ❸**, 990 Zion Park Blvd., offers clean and reasonably inexpensive rooms. (☎ 800-342-6779. Singles $55, with 2 beds $71; $10 less in winter. Inquire about AAA discounts.)

◪ FOOD

The **Zion Canyon Lodge,** located in Zion Canyon halfway to the Temple of Sinawava, houses the only in-park concessions. Inside, the cafeteria-style **Castle Dome Cafe ❶** serves the standard fare of hamburgers, personal pizzas, and deli sandwiches. (Open daily 11am-7pm. Entrees $3-6.) Upstairs, the **Zion Lodge Dining Room ❷** offers a $7 all-you-can-eat breakfast buffet, $5-8 affordable lunches, and $13-20 pricey dinners (☎ 772-3213. Open daily 6:30-10:30am, 11:30am-3pm and 5:30-9pm). Good deals on high-quality food in Springdale can easily be found. ◪**Sol Foods ❶**, 95 Zion Park Blvd., connected with the Visitors Center by footbridge, is locally owned and exceptionally friendly. In addition to sandwiches, burgers ($5-6), and baked goods, Sol Foods boasts an extensive vegetarian menu. Hearty breakfasts ($4-6) are served during summer. (☎ 772-0277. Open daily 8am-9pm; shorter hours in winter.) A local favorite, **Oscar's Cafe ❷**, 948 Zion Park Blvd., specializes in innovative Mexican entrees ($8-11), juicy garlic burgers ($5-7), and delicious breakfasts ($4-8) served in a decked-out venue. (☎ 772-3232. Open daily 8am-10pm.) Carbo-craving backpackers and local devotees flock nightly to the **Zion Pizza and Noodle Co. ❷**, 686 Zion Park Blvd., to devour unique pizzas ($9-14) and pasta platters ($10). (☎ 772-3815. Open daily for dinner at 4pm.)

◪ HIKING AND BACKPACKING

Zion offers a wide variety of trails suitable for a broad spectrum of ability levels. Within Zion Canyon, some trails meander peacefully near the path of the Virgin River; others ascend the walls and will have you praying for a stray mule to show up. The park's famous slot canyons challenge the adventuresome, and a number of backcountry treks traverse spectacular and varied terrain. As always, be vigilant in preparing yourself for your time on the trails. Zion is situated in a desert, and heat exhaustion and dehydration are constant threats. Drink copious amounts of water, apply sunscreen liberally, and avoid hiking in the middle of the day. Any hiking itineraries that include portions in slot canyons or other terrain prone to flash flooding should begin with a check of the day's forecast at a Visitors Center.

DAY HIKING

Riverside Walk (2 mi. round-trip, 2-3hr.). Zion's most used trail, the Riverside walk can resemble a city sidewalk on busy summer afternoons. This easy trail begins at the last shuttle stop, the Temple of Sinawava, and follows the Virgin River between towering sandstone cliffs. A concrete surface makes the trail accessible to anyone. Many visitors hiking through the mid-day heat cool off at trail's end with a quick dip in the Virgin. From the end of Riverside walk, day-hikers can venture up into the **Narrows** (see p. 298).

Watchman Trail (2 mi. round-trip, 2-3hr.). Embarking from the Watchman Campground (¾ mi. south of the Visitors Center) and less crowded than other short Zion hikes, this moderate hike climbs to a plateau adjacent to the mammoth Watchman. From the plateau, visitors have excellent views of West Temple and the Temple of the Virgin across the canyon, the Watchman above, and Springdale below. Hiking in the late afternoon or early evening avoids the blistering mid-day heat. 350 ft. elevation gain.

Emerald Pools (interlocking network of trails; round-trip distances vary 1.2-3.1 mi.; 1-3hr.). With sparkling pools and cascading waterfalls, this trail can be completed with several variations of length and difficulty. Access to the pools begins at both the Zion Lodge and Grotto shuttle stops. The easy 0.6 mi. one-way leg between Zion Lodge and Lower Emerald pool grants paved access all the way to the pool. Although the trails themselves are heavily used and easily followed, the surrounding terrain is dangerous. Several reckless hikers have died taking "the fast way down" the sheer faces between the pools. Proper footwear (closed-toed shoes with good treads) is recommended for the hike to the upper pools. Elevation gain 70-350 ft. depending upon route.

Hidden Canyon (2 mi. round-trip, 3hr.). Originating at the Weeping Rock shuttle stop, this moderately difficult paved trail, inscribed into the solid sandstone face, winds rapidly to the end of Hidden Canyon. Sheer drop-offs make the trail a nightmare for the acrophobic. The canyon itself, carved by a seasonal drainage, affords magnificent examples of the artistic talent of rapidly moving water. At trail's end, hikers yearning for more can scramble trail-less farther up the mountain. 850 ft. elevation gain.

Observation Point (8 mi. round-trip, 5hr.). Ascending from the Weeping Rock shuttle stop, the highly strenuous yet mostly paved trail to Observation Point climbs steep sandstone faces and shoots through narrow canyons en route to a staggeringly beautiful vantage point. From amid a grove of ponderosa pine, Gambel Oak, and Manzanita, the summit rewards determined climbers with sweeping views of Zion Canyon. This trail may be inadvisable for those afraid of heights. 2150 ft. elevation gain.

Angels Landing (5 mi. round-trip, 4hr.). This trail packs a lot of climbing into a short distance, making it one of the park's most strenuous hikes. The rewarding views at the end makes achy legs and wheezy lungs seem inconsequential. In fact, there's little that doesn't seem inconsequential from Angels Landing, a magnificent crag that rises nearly 1500 ft. from the valley floor. The trail begins at the Grotto shuttle stop and picks its way up sandstone faces, traveling through the famous "Walters Wiggles," a series of tight switchbacks carved out of the rock in the 1920s, before reaching Scout Point after 1.8 mi. From Scout Point, the route to the summit traverses a knifeblade ridge that drops off to the valley floor on both sides. Chains, carved steps, and footstep-worn sandstone provide ample assistance in making it to the top. 1500 ft. elevation gain. Not advised for those afraid of heights.

BACKCOUNTRY HIKING

The park requires permits ($5), obtainable at either Visitors Center, for day travel on routes outside the canyon and for backcountry camping. Popular hikes like the West Rim have limits on the number of people permitted to use the trails per day, and reservations are accepted up to three days in advance. For extensive info on backcountry routes and procedures, pick up a copy of the *Zion Backcountry Planner* at either Visitors Center. **Water** may or may not be available along the trails depending upon the season. Check the water source board at the **Backcountry Desk** in Zion Canyon Visitors Center before departing.

Most backcountry hikes in Zion are one-way, requiring either a two-vehicle shuttle or the services of a shuttle company. The friendly young locals at **Zion Canyon Transportation** (☎877-635-5993) provide service to remote locations throughout the park, dependent on demand.

West Rim Trail (14 mi. one-way, 2 days). Starting on the high Kolob Plateau in the park's north central area, this moderately strenuous trek follows the West Rim of Zion Canyon to the Grotto picnic area. From high above, the trail offers awe-inspiring views of narrow slot canyons and Zion Canyon's monoliths. Because of these vantages, the trail receives more use than any other backcountry trail in Zion, and the backcountry office issues a limited number of permits each day. Most hikers complete the trek in 2 days, camping overnight at one of many established backcountry sites along the trail. To find the trailhead, travel north from Virgin along the Kolob Rd. and turn right at the signs for Lava Point Campground. Bear left past the ranger station and follow the steep dirt road to the trailhead. The hike begins by tracing the precipitous edge of the Horse Pasture Plateau. Traveling south, the first 8 mi. remain relatively constant in elevation, but the last 5 mi. drop dramatically. A series of 3 springs usually provides water along the route, but check the water source board at the Backcountry Desk to be sure.

East Rim Trail (10.5 mi. or more). This strenuous through-hike connects the park's east entrance (approximately 5850 ft.) with the Weeping Rock shuttle stop (4360 ft.). From either starting point, the trail climbs to Stave Spring Junction. The trail offers views of Angels Landing and Cathedral Mountain in Zion Canyon, and perspectives of several of the park's seldom-seen features like Checkerboard Mesa and the White Cliffs. In late spring and early summer, fields of wildflowers consume the east rim, painting the hillsides a motley collection of brilliant hues. An energetic visitor could hike over Stave Spring, and arrive 7hr. later in Zion Canyon. Alternately, a series of short diversions to spectacular vantages from Cable Mountain, Deertrap Mountain, and the east boundary barricade make the East Rim a popular 2-3 day backpacking destination. Check with the Backcountry Desk for water availability.

Wildcat Canyon Trail (5.8 mi. one-way, 4hr. or more depending on the route chosen). A moderate hike traveling from the Kolob Rd. to the Western Rim trailhead, this 500 ft. climb traverses part of the Kolob Plateau. Views of dark basaltic lava flows along the trail contrast with the white sandstone characteristic of Zion. The hike can be extended into an overnight with the addition of the 1.2 mi. Northgate Peaks Spur Trail. Camping along the spur ranks among the park's most scenic. To find the trail, follow the Kolob Rd. north from Virgin. During winter months, the trail acts as a popular cross-country ski destination. In combination with the Hop Valley, Connector, and Western Rim trails, Wildcat Canyon can serve as a leg on a multi-day backcountry trip. Check with the Backcountry Desk for water availability.

Hop Valley Trail (6.7 mi. one-way, 4-6hr.). Beginning from the Kolob Rd., this excursion accesses La Verkin Creek and the Kolob Arch from the east. Backcountry restrictions assure a relatively uncrowded hike, with only 3 groups permitted per day. The trail winds through a park en route to a steep descent to La Verkin Creek. Watch for cattle in the park during summer months and use their well-worn trails to help route-finding along the stream. During summer months, the stream occasionally disappears into the sand, so plan to carry plenty of water. Several established campsites line the hillside just before the descent to La Verkin Creek.

⚠ OTHER OUTDOOR ACTIVITIES

CANYON HIKES AND CANYONEERING

For those adept at rock climbing and rappeling, Zion offers countless opportunities for canyoneering. Descending thousands of feet through narrow slot canyons provides an exhilarating and exhausting glimpse of the powerful natural forces that continue to shape Zion Canyon. The National Park Service prohibits commercial guiding inside the park, so visitors planning to canyoneer must come equipped with their own ropes, hardware, and skill. For detailed info on canyoneering, consult the Backcountry Desk at the Zion Canyon Visitors Center.

A limited number of people are allowed to tackle the park's most popular canyon hikes each day. Permits for hiking the Narrows from north to south are available at the backcountry desk at 8am the day before the proposed hike. For the Subway, hikers must apply to a lottery three months in advance to obtain reservations, though a limited number of walk-in permits are available a day in advance.

The Narrows (16 mi. one-way, 1-2 days). This Zion classic trek follows the Virgin River from the park's northern border to the Temple of Sinawava. More than 60% of the hike is actually in the river, with depths ranging from ankle-deep to mid-chest. During winter months, the hike requires a wetsuit and other protective clothing. The narrow passages, despite their scenic beauty, present a lethal flash-flood threat, and all hikers planning to attempt the Narrows should check on the anticipated weather in advance. Even with a promising weather report, sudden summer thunderstorms anywhere in the Virgin River basin can catch hikers unaware with downriver flash flooding. Walking sticks and sturdy hiking shoes protect trekkers from ankle sprains on terrain described as "hiking on slippery bowling balls." The **Zion Adventure Company,** 36 Lion Blvd., rents Narrows hiking packages that include Neoprene socks, canyoneering shoes, and walking sticks. (☎772-1001; www.zionadventures.com. Open summer daily 7:30am-8pm; reduced winter hours. $16 per day.) There are 3 ways to hike the Narrows. The first, most popular, and easiest, begins by hiking up the Virgin River past the end of the Riverside Walk. Other hikers shuttle to the northern end of the trail, at the Chamberlain Ranch, and complete the hike in either one gruelling 12hr. day or as an overnight hike. 12 coveted campsites serve backpackers about halfway between the Chamberlain Ranch and the Riverside Walk. As the hike is one-way, starting at Chamberlain Ranch requires either a 2-car shuttle or a commercial shuttle. To reach the trailhead, turn north off Rte. 9 two mi. east of the park's east entrance at the sign for "Zion Ponderosa Resort and Ranch." Though the first half of the roughly 20 mi. road to Chamberlain Ranch is paved, the dirt portion is impassible by all vehicles when wet. Two companies run daily shuttles to the trailhead, both for $25 per hiker. **Zion Canyon Transport** (☎877-635-5993) departs from the Zion Canyon Visitors Center at 6am daily, and occasionally also runs shuttles at 9am ($30 per person) if enough people sign up. **Springdale Cycles** (☎800-776-2099) offers shuttle service departing from their shop at 932 Zion Park Blvd. at 6:45am daily. Both companies require reservations. Only 80 hikers per day can receive permits to hike south from Chamberlain Ranch. No reservations are accepted; hikers must obtain permits from the Backcountry Desk the day before departing.

La Verkin Creek to Kolob Arch (7.2 mi. one-way, 4-6hr.). This trek follows La Verkin Creek between towering sandstone faces and past cascades, pools, and numerous springs to the Kolob Arch. The mammoth arch is one of the world's tallest and is a popular destination for Zion hikers. Because of heavy use, the trail is limited to 15 groups per day. Although the relatively flat hike can be travelled as a long 1-day round-trip, inviting side canyons and the scenic Beartrap Canyon Falls make a strong case for camping overnight to allow time to explore. Established campsites line the trail along the creek. To find the trailhead, enter the park at the Kolob Canyons entrance and follow the Kolob Canyons Scenic Drive 3.5 mi. to Lee Pass and the trailhead. To extend the hike into a multi-day trek, consider following the Hop Valley Trail to the Connector, Wildcat Canyon, and Western Rim Trails.

The Subway (4.5-9.5 mi. one-way). Traveling the Left Fork of North Creek, The Subway involves scrambling over boulders, rappeling down rock faces, and swimming in frigid pools sandwiched in gaps between sandstone walls too narrow for the sun to reach. Two routes can be taken: from the top down or from the bottom up. The bottom route begins at the Left Fork Trailhead off Kolob Canyon Rd., travels 4.5 mi. up the canyons before returning the same way, and requires route-finding skills, stream crossings, and boulder scrambles. The more intense top route embarks from the Wildcat Canyon Trailhead (also off Kolob Canyon Rd.), travels 9.5 mi. to the Left Fork Trailhead, and demands at least 60 ft. of rope or webbing for rappeling. The thrills of traversing such inhospitable terrain attract droves of hikers, and the Park Service limits use to 50 people per day. Applications to the Subway lottery must be submitted three months in advance and hikers are notified one month before their departure date. Visit www.nps.gov/zion or call 772-0170 for more information and an application. The Park Service also saves 10 permits each day to accommodate walk-ins (non-refundable permit fee $5), but be sure to get in line bright and early, as one person can take all 10.

MOUNTAIN BIKING

Inside the national park, bicycles can travel only on park roads; no trail riding is permitted. The Zion Canyon Scenic Drive, closed to car traffic, makes for an excellent ride, allowing visitors to avoid the pseudo-urban experience of crowds and obstructed views characteristic of shuttle rides into the canyon. Trail riding is available just outside of the park along the extensive trail system at **Gooseberry Mesa.** The advanced terrain challenges enthusiasts, and the impressive views of Zion inspire all. Ask for directions and trail info at one of the two Springdale bicycle shops. A local bike guru offers abundant advice on mountain biking and all other conceivable forms of Zion Canyon recreation at **Bike Zion,** 1458 Zion Park Blvd. (☎ 772-2453. Open daily 8am-6pm. Rigid bike full-day $23, half-day $17; front suspension $29/$22; full suspension $35/$27.) **Springdale Cycle,** 932 Zion Park Blvd., offers high-quality bikes at competitive prices and offers single and multi-day tours. (☎ 800-776-2099; www.springdalecycles.com. Open M-Sa 9am-7pm. Front suspension full-day $30, half-day $20; full suspension $40/$30; kids $15/$10.)

DRIVING

Although Zion cannot be truly experienced from behind the windows of a car or shuttle bus, these drives may provide an excellent counterpart to the more active experiences that will define your time here.

Zion-Mt. Carmel Highway. After passing through the remarkable Zion Canyon Tunnel, Rte. 9 winds through dazzling slickrock domes and mesas. A panoply of soft reds and whites treats the eyes as the road turns in never-ending switchbacks. Scenic pull-outs at points including Checkerboard Mesa, a formation decorated with symmetrical square panels of pink and white, allow for quick photo opportunities.

Zion Canyon Scenic Drive. Shuttle buses departing frequently from the Visitors Center travel up and down Zion Canyon, offering a glimpse of the park's tremendous and majestic sandstone monoliths. A round-trip ride on the shuttle requires about 90min.

Although the Park Service uses shuttles with large picture windows, the staggering size of the faces makes it hard to appreciate the immensity of the formations.

OTHER ZION ACTIVITIES

On scorching summer days, many visitors to Zion enjoy the cooling waters of the lower Virgin River. **Zion Tubing,** 180 Zion Park Blvd., rents tubes for floating a 2½ mi. segment of the lower Virgin and provides shuttle service. (☎772-8823. Open late Feb. to Nov. daily 7:45am-9pm. $11; shuttles $2 per person.) For a more intense afternoon at the park, visit the **Zion Adventure Company** (see p. 298). They offer introductory canyoneering course in narrow slot canyons just outside the park (4-5hr.; $99). Fearless **rock climbers** occasionally scale the enormous walls of Zion Canyon, but the climbing is at a level intended only for near-professionals and should not be attempted by any but the best.

BRYCE CANYON NATIONAL PARK ☎435

One of the West's most vivid landscapes, Bryce Canyon brims with slender rock spires (hoodoos). What it lacks in Grand Canyon-esque magnitude, Bryce makes up for in intricate beauty. Early in the morning or late in the evening, the sun's rays bring the hoodoos to life, transforming them into color-changing stone chameleons. The first sight of the canyon can be breathtaking: as Ebenezer Bryze, a Mormon carpenter with a gift for understatement, put it, the canyon is "one hell of a place to lose a cow."

■ ？ ORIENTATION AND PRACTICAL INFORMATION

From the west, Bryce Canyon lies 1½hr. east of **Cedar City** (see p. 288); take either Rte. 14 or Rte. 20 to U.S. 89. From the east, take I-70 to U.S. 89, turn east on Rte. 12

AT A GLANCE: BRYCE CANYON NATIONAL PARK	
AREA: 35,835 acres.	**GATEWAY TOWNS:** Tropic, Panguitch.
FEATURES: The main amphitheater of Bryce Canyon, Paunsaugunt Plateau, Pink Cliffs, countless hoodoos.	**CAMPING:** Park campgrounds $10, backcountry camping permit $5.
HIGHLIGHTS: View the Bryce sunset from Sunset Point, hike the Peekaboo Loop, cross-country ski the Under-the-Rim trail in complete solitude.	**FEES:** Weekly pass $20 per car, $15 if parking outside the park; $10 per bike or pedestrian.

in Panguitch. Most visitors travel from the south, taking U.S. 89 to Rte. 12 after visiting Lake Powell, the Grand Canyon, or Flagstaff, AZ.

Public Transportation and Parking: During the summer, **parking** inside the park varies from crowded to non-existent. To assuage the traffic problem, the Park Service has implemented a shuttle system, serving the viewpoints around Bryce Ampitheater, the Visitors Center, and Ruby's Inn. Private vehicles can travel park roads, but the Park Service offers a $5 admission discount to those who park at Ruby's Inn and ride the shuttle into the park. Busses run roughly every 10-15min.

Visitor Information: The **Visitors Center** (☎834-5322), lies just inside the park. A helpful backcountry desk provides info on recreation opportunities in the area. Open June-Aug. daily 8am-8pm; Apr.-May and Sept.-Oct. 8am-6pm, Nov.-Mar. 8am-4:30pm.

UTAH

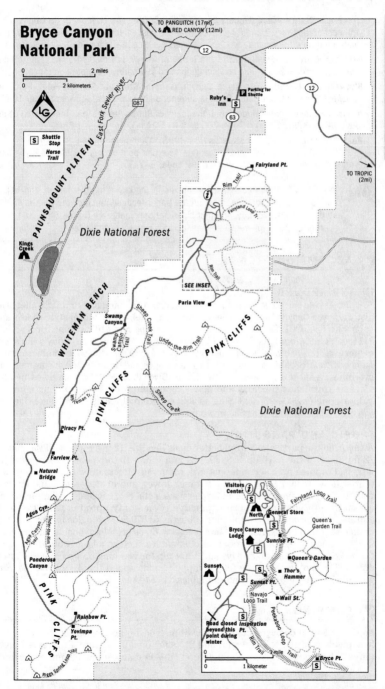

Bryce Canyon National Park

0 ___ 2 miles
0 ___ 2 kilometers

S Shuttle Stop
- - - - Horse Trail

TO PANGUITCH (17mi),
& ▲ RED CANYON (12mi)

12

Parking for Shuttle
Ruby's Inn
P
S
63

PAUNSAUGUNT PLATEAU

East Fork Sevier River

087

12

■ Fairyland Pt.

TO TROPIC
(2mi)

Rim Trail

Fairyland Loop Tr.

Dixie National Forest

Kings Creek

SEE INSET

Rim Trail

Paria View ■

WHITEMAN BENCH

Swamp Canyon

Swamp Canyon Trail

Sheep Creek Trail

Under-the-Rim Trail

PINK CLIFFS

PINK CLIFFS

Dixie National Forest

Sheep Creek

Whiteman Tr.

■ Piracy Pt.

■ Farview Pt.

■ Natural Bridge

Agua Cyn.

Agua Canyon Trail

Under-the-Rim Trail

Ponderosa Canyon

PINK CLIFFS

■ Rainbow Pt.
Yovimpa Pt.

Riggs Spring Loop Trail

Visitors Center **(i)**
S
North
General Store
Bryce Canyon Lodge
S
Sunrise Pt.

Fairyland Loop Trail

Queen's Garden Trail

■ Queen's Garden

Sunset ▲
S
Sunset Pt.
■ Thor's Hammer

Navajo Loop Trail

■ Wall St.

Peekaboo Loop Trail

X
Road closed beyond this point during winter
Rim Trail
Inspiration Pt.

½ mile

■ Bryce Pt.
S

0 ___ 1 kilometer

Groceries: Doug's Place Grocery Store (☎679-8600), 141 N. Main St. in Tropic, UT, 7 mi. east of the Rte. 12 and 63 junction. Has the best selection of any area grocery store with affordable prices and favorites like Nutella. Open in summer daily 7am-9:30pm.

ATM and Currency Exchange: In the lobby of Ruby's Inn (☎834-5341), the official "beaten track" of Bryce Canyon visiting, located just north of the park entrance.

Showers and Laundry: The **Bryce Canyon General Store,** at Sunrise Point. Purchase shower tokens at the register. Open in summer daily 8am-8pm. Showers $2 per 10min.

Internet Access: Terminal located in the lobby of Ruby's Inn ($1 per 4min.). Free at the **Panguitch Public Library,** 25 S. 200 E (☎676-2431). Open M-F 1-6pm.

Post Office: In Ruby's Inn Store (☎834-8088). Window open M-F 8:30am-noon and 12:30-4:30pm. No credit cards accepted. A second post office is inside the Bryce Canyon Lodge and only open in summer. **ZIP code:** 84717.

WHEN TO GO. Peak visitation occurs in the late spring, summer, and fall, until snow descends in earnest on the park. Because much of the park is situated in the high country, summer highs are only moderate (in the 80s), and an average of 95 in. of snow blankets the high country each winter.

ACCOMMODATIONS

IN AND AROUND THE PARK

Sleeping inside the park requires either a tent and sleeping bag or a fat wallet. The historic **Bryce Canyon Lodge ❺,** the only in-park hotel, offers motel-style rooms and cabins. (☎834-5361. Open Apr.-Oct. Rooms for 2 people $100; cabins for 2 people $111; each additional person $5.) Just outside the park entrance, Ruby's Inn's less expensive little-brother motel, the **Bryce View Lodge ❸,** on Rte. 63, combines convenience with affordable prices. (☎834-5180. Singles and doubles $60 in summer, $44 in winter.) A short drive west on Rte. 12, the **Bryce Pines Motel ❸,** family-owned for 45 years, furnishes spacious and newly renovated rooms surrounding a heated indoor pool. (☎800-892-7923. Singles $50; economy doubles $64; deluxe doubles $75. Rates drop as much as $20 in winter.)

TROPIC AND PANGUITCH

Away from the park, rates drop; better deals line Rte. 12 in Tropic, and Panguitch, 23 mi. west of the park on U.S. 89, has more than 15 inexpensive, independent motels. For most area accommodations, room rates fluctuate with the season and tourist flow. Winter rates are much, much lower, and in slow summers, bargain walk-in rates abound. ⬛**Bybee's Steppingstone Motel ❷,** 21 S. Main in Tropic, offers clean, bright, spacious and inexpensive rooms only minutes from the park entrance but far away from the tourist bustle. (☎679-8998. Singles in summer $40; doubles $45.) In Panguitch, the ⬛**Marianna Inn ❷,** 699 N. Main, boasts immaculate, spacious, newly remodeled rooms and amenities such as a large outdoor pergola for relaxing on hot summer days and a hot tub for warming up on chilly fall afternoons. The Inn also has one fully equipped handicapped room. (☎676-8844. Singles $35 in summer, $30 in winter; doubles $45/$40.)

CAMPING

North and **Sunset Campgrounds ❶,** both within 3 mi. of the Visitors Center, offer toilets, picnic tables, potable water, and 216 sites on a first come, first served basis (sites $10). Arrive early to claim a good site, as many spots are uncomfortably close to neighbors or situated on sloping ground. No RV hookups are available inside the park, but the North Campground has a $2 dump station. Two popular campgrounds lie just west of Bryce on Rte. 12 in the Dixie National Forest. The **Kings Creek Campground ❶**, 11 mi. from Bryce on Forest Service Rd. 087 off Rte. 12 (look for signs to Tropic Reservoir), features spacious sites. Refresh yourself with a quick dip in Tropic Reservoir, just a stone's throw from the campground. Group sites are available with reservations. (☎800-280-2267. Sites $10. Drinking water, flush toilets. Open May 21 through Labor Day.) West of the park on Rte. 12, the **Red Canyon Campground ❶** has 36 well-developed sites on a first come, first served basis amid the glory of the red rocks. The campground lies rather close to the road, but the shade and scenery make it a prime location. (Sites $11. Drinking water, flush toilets. Showers $2 per 8min.) For an affordable RV hookup near the park, try the **Bryce Canyon Pines Campground and RV Park ❶**, on Rte. 12 several miles west of the Rte. 63 junction. (☎800-892-7923. Tent sites $17, hookups $23.)

▐ FOOD

Inside and immediately surrounding the national park, feeding options are scarce. A hot dog ($2) or a packaged sandwich ($3) awaits famished tourists at the **Bryce Canyon General Store** at the Sunset Point overlook (open 8am-8pm). For a sit-down lunch inside the park, try the reasonably priced burgers ($5-6) and sandwiches ($5.50-6.50) at the **Bryce Canyon Lodge Dining Room ❶**. (☎834-5361. Open daily 6:30-10:30am, 11am-3:30pm, 5:30-9:30pm.) With a little driving time, more affordable and varied alternatives multiply. Unlimited thick, golden brown pancakes ($2) await starving passersby at the **Hungry Coyote ❷**, on N. Main in Tropic. Bring an enormous appetite if you hope to finish more than two or three of these monsters. Dinner, with all-you-can-eat soup and salad bar, is just $8. (☎679-8811. Open Apr.-Oct. daily 6:30-10:30am and 5-10pm.) Several miles west of the park on Rte. 12, the **Bryce Pines Restaurant ❸** earns its distinction as a local favorite by serving delicious home-cooked meals complemented by fresh soups and an endless selection of homemade pies. (☎834-5441. Open in summer daily 6:30am-9:30pm. Sandwiches $5-8; dinner entrees $13-19.) Twenty-three miles west of the park in Panguitch, **Grandma Tina's Spaghetti House ❷**, 525 N. Main, specializes in hearty Italian eating with a vegetarian emphasis. (☎676-2376. Open in summer daily 7am-11pm. Lunch pastas $5-6; dinners $10-12.)

▚ OUTDOOR ACTIVITIES

The 18 mi. park road travels south from the Visitors Center, offering a variety of vantage points from which to gaze out upon the land beyond the Paunsaugunt Plateau. Some viewpoints like **Sunset, Sunrise,** and **Natural Bridge** offer close-up views of notable formations like **Thor's Hammer.** Other places like **Bryce** and **Inspiration Points** deliver panoramic views of the entire Bryce amphitheater. For some fabulous photographs of the amphitheater, catch the light of the rising sun from Inspiration Point as it illuminates the hoodoos. The final two viewpoints along the drive, **Rainbow** and **Yovimpa Points,** impart views extending nearly 100 mi. to the North Rim of the Grand Canyon.

As awe-inspiring as the vast forest of **hoodoos** may appear from the rim of the alcove, the individual hoodoos themselves, seen up-close, demonstrate peculiar quirks and foibles. The best way to appreciate these towering spires is by descending into the ampitheater, either by foot or on horseback. Several companies offer trail rides in and around Bryce Canyon, although only **Canyon Trail Rides,** inside the Bryce Canyon Lodge, offers trips that travel to the canyon floor. (☎679-8665. 2hr.

HOW DO YOU HOODOO Sweating under the scorching summer sun during a walk through Bryce Canyon, it's hard to visualize the wintry ice responsible for the amphitheater's striking hoodoo formations. How could water create such a dramatic, almost cave-like topography in dry desert plateau that receives less than 18 in. of annual precipitation? The answer begins 10-15 million years ago, when powerful collisions of the earth's crust caused the extensive series of faults and uplifts known today as the Colorado Plateau. At Bryce, the Paunsaugunt Plateau rose along fault lines from the surrounding sediments to heights approaching 10,000 ft. At such an elevation, nighttime winter temperatures average well below freezing, but during the day, year-round sunlight lifts temperatures high enough to melt the snow and ice. When the snow, having melted and seeped into cracks in the rock during the day, refreezes at night to ice, it expands by up to 9% and exerts intense pressure on the rock. This process of melting and refreezing, known as frost wedging, occurs as many as 200 times per year. The linear organization of the hoodoos results from this process because most of the cracks in the rocks are straight fault-created lines. During the spring thaw, melting snow and ice also help to sculpt the hoodoos. Run-off travels down the plateau toward the Paria River, eroding the surface by both the mechanical process of lifting rock particles and the chemical process of dissolving calcium carbonate particles in the limestone. The more calcium carbonate present in the rock, the more rapidly it erodes. Some areas of limestone contain less calcium carbonate than others and remain intact while gullies form around them. These less-concentrated limestone rocks eventually become the tops of hoodoos, called capstones, as the ground surrounding them erodes away. When marveling at these spectacular spires in the dry summer heat, remember with equal wonder the frosty forces at work in forming them.

rides $30, half-day $45.) For yet another perspective on the famous hoodoos, try a helicopter flight from **Helivision,** located at Ruby's Inn. (☎ 834-5341. 15-20min. flyovers from $55 per person; 2-person min. Longer flights over all of Bryce Canyon and into Grand Staircase-Escalante also available.) During winter months, a thick blanket of snow covers the Bryce landscape, painting the amphitheater's bizarre spires a resplendent white. Park visitation shoots up in October as guests flock to see the display created by the season's first snow. **Cross-country skiers** enjoy these snowy views all winter long while traversing several established trails along the Canyon Rim. Skiers should remember to beware of cornices, fragile cusps of snow forming along the canyon edge that can collapse without warning. Although **biking** inside the park is limited to paved surfaces, the Red Canyon region of the Dixie National Forest that surrounds the park offers some well-respected rides. Stop by the **Visitors Center,** on Rte. 12 west of the park, for details. (☎ 676-2676. Open in summer daily 8am-6pm.)

DAY HIKING

Hikers weaving between hoodoos follow in the footsteps of famous outlaws like Butch Cassidy, who found the area's maze-like geography perfect for hiding out. Hiking in Bryce is fantastic, but visitors traveling from sea level should remember that at park elevation (8000-9000 ft.), the air is thinner, and climbing several hundred feet back up to the rim is likely to be at least twice as hard as descending. The park's guide, called the *Hoodoo,* offers short descriptions of Bryce hikes. For more detailed info, ask a ranger in the Visitors Center or pick up a copy of *Bryce Canyon National Park: Day Hikes and Backpacking Trails,* published by the Park Service and Bryce Canyon Natural History Association.

Rim Trail (5.2 mi. one-way, 2-3hr.). Tracing the edge of the spectacular Bryce amphitheater, this moderately strenuous trail travels from Bryce Point (8280 ft.) to Fairyland Point (7804 ft.). Between Sunrise and Sunset Points (0.5 mi. one-way), the flat and paved trail is wheelchair-accessible. As no shuttle service is available at Fairyland Point, hikers in search of an easy stroll may wish to take the shuttle back to their cars from Sunrise Point (a 2.7 mi. one-way trip) rather than continue on. However, the segment between Sunrise and Fairyland Points (5 mi. round-trip) is less crowded. Along the entire route, looking east affords breathtaking views of the hoodoos and the distant Aquarius Plateau. Light shines most beautifully on the hoodoos and less severely on you early in the morning and late in the afternoon.

Navajo Loop (1.3 mi. round-trip, 1-2hr.). This steep, moderately strenuous hike is made famous by postcards depicting majestic Douglas Fir trees growing between the towering limestone walls of "Wall Street," a narrow slot canyon. The route begins at Sunset Point (8000 ft.) and descends 521 ft. over a series of tight switchbacks to a junction with Queen's Garden Trail before climbing back via a different trail. En route, hikers get close-up views of the precarious Thor's Hammer hoodoo and relief from the blistering heat inside Wall Street. An alternate route picks up the Queen's Garden Trail at the bottom, following it up to Sunrise Point and then following the Rim Trail (0.5 mi.) back to Sunset. Trail guide available in the Visitors Center.

Queen's Garden Trail (1.8 mi. round-trip, 1-2hr.). One of Bryce's easier trails, the hike begins at Sunrise Point (8017 ft.) and descends slowly 320 ft. to the Queen Victoria Pinnacle, a rocky spire resembling a queen on her throne. To hike back, follow the same path you descended or pick up the Navajo Loop Trail at the base for more variety.

Peekaboo Loop Trail (4.1 mi. round-trip, 3-4hr.). Descending roughly 1000 ft. from Bryce Point, this highly strenuous, breathtaking hike weaves through a forest of hoodoos and firs, providing some of the best views in the park. The 1.1 mi. trail from Bryce Point to the Peekaboo Loop winds down an exposed face and offers a remarkable panorama of the amphitheater and the town of Tropic below. Hikers can continue up the same path back to Bryce Point after completing the 3 mi. loop, but a better option is to connect the trail with the Navajo Loop and return via Sunset Point. For the most spectacular hoodoo-viewing, take a left on the Peekaboo Loop after descending from Bryce Point. At the junction in 1.7 mi., follow the signs to the Navajo Loop and turn left at the intersection with that trail. This route ascends to Sunset Point and the canyon rim via the famous "Wall St." slot canyon. From there, hikers can return to their cars at Bryce Point via the shuttle or the Rim Trail.

BACKPACKING

Nearly all visitors to Bryce Canyon remain high above the amphitheater, perhaps venturing on a few day hikes amongst the hoodoos but leaving the national park's backcountry untrammeled. Backpacking offers much different scenery than day-hiking. Multi-day treks escape the amphitheater's hoodoos and sand hills for high alpine forests and meadows. The Park Service regulates backcountry use and camping with a permit system. **Backcountry permits** ($5) are available at the Visitors Center and are issued beginning at 8am the day before the proposed trip. Before making plans, stop by the Visitors Center to discuss your route with a ranger and pick up a copy of the free *Backcountry Hiking and Camping Guide*. Bryce has two main backcountry trails:

Riggs Spring Loop (9 mi., 1-2 days). The loop explores the remote southern portion of the park, beginning at the Rainbow Point parking area and descending 1700 ft. to the Pink Cliffs heading toward Riggs Spring (7443 ft.). After 5.7 mi., the trail joins the Under-the-Rim Trail to return to Rainbow Point. 3 designated campsites lie widely separated along the trail. The short distance involved makes the Riggs Spring Loop an excel-

This 122-mile stretch of Rte. 95 between Blanding and Hanksville, known as the **Bicentennial Highway** because it was built in 1976, is one of the most scenic in the lower 48, as well as a pleasure to cruise with little danger of tailgating traffic. From the cliff dwellings of the architecturally adept Ancestral Puebloans to the modern-day engineering feats of Lake Powell, from the heights of the Henry Mountains to the canyon bottoms of Natural Bridges, Route 95 offers a diverse cross-section of southern Utah. The highway also mirrors part of the routes taken by Mormon settlers as they pushed into this uncharted part of the state. Traveling beside and through such natural and cultural highlights, this drive makes a good anthropology, geology, and history lesson rolled into one.

Unlike many of the other scenic routes of the Southwest, Rte. 95 is not some dusty, twisting desert road but instead a properly maintained, state-funded highway. As such, the typical hazards—washboard ridges, rocks and potholes—aren't a significant concern. A more significant concern is fuel - the only town along the drive is tiny Fry Canyon, about 40 mi. from Blanding. Outside Fry Canyon, gas sources are unreliable, and even those in the hamlet are not open 24hr. Do yourself a favor, and fill up in Blanding.

1 BEAR'S EAR PASS. Seven miles west of Blanding on Rte. 95, a sign for **South Cottonwood National Forest Access** indicates a road which leaves the highway, climbing north up the southern slopes of the Abajo Mountains. The pavement ends after several miles, and the terrain changes dramatically as the road rises. Before long, the slopes are blanketed with lush grass, shaded by massive birches. After miles of travel in the surrounding semi-arid terrain, this oasis is a welcome surprise. After 26 mi., the road passes between twin buttes dubbed the **Bear's Ears** before descending 6 mi. to Rte. 275, the access road to Natural Bridges. All told, the 32 mi. route should take about 1-2hr. and is easily passable in good conditions.

2 BUTLER WASH INDIAN RUINS. The turn-off for these well-preserved **Ancestral Puebloan cliff dwellings** is about 10 mi. west of Blanding on the right-hand side of the road. A 0.5 mi. hike leads to an overlook of the ruins, which are tucked underneath an overhang at the head of **Butler Wash.** These ruins bear many similarities to the sites at Mesa Verde but also share similarities with Kayenta culture sites like those found at Navajo National Monument.

Route 95
Bicentennial
Highway

ROUTE 95 — THE BICENTENNIAL HIGHWAY

3 COMB RIDGE. The slope beyond the Butler Wash site is part of this impressive ridge, which ran unbroken on a north-south axis through much of southeastern Utah. A bit farther south, the highway blasts through this wall of sandstone, catering to modern travelers. The Hole-in-the-Rock pioneers were not so lucky and had to make their way down to Bluff, UT to find a way

TIME: 3hr. driving time
DISTANCE: 112 mi.
SEASON: Year-round

through. The ridge is even more impressive when viewed from the west, so make sure to take a look behind you once you've passed through the road-cut.

4 MULE CANYON INDIAN RUINS. These Ancestral Puebloan ruins, which lie alongside the highway about 20 mi. west of Blanding, have been carefully reconstructed by the University of Utah and give a good sense of a small mesa-top village. An interesting exhibit explains many aspects of Basketmaker and Ancestral Puebloan culture. You can set up **camp** for free at this spot.

5 NATURAL BRIDGES NATIONAL MONUMENT. 35 mi. west of Blanding, Rte. 275 diverges to the geological wonders of Natural Bridges (see p. 321).

6 DARK CANYON. Fifty miles west of Blanding is the **Fry Canyon Lodge,** which provides expensive gas to go along with expensive "backcountry" dining and accommodations. About 10 mi. farther, the highway crosses over a small wash, just before **San Juan County Rd. 2061,** which climbs into and out of White Canyon, heading north to Dark Canyon and some of the most remote canyoneering and hiking in the country. This road should not be attempted without a high-clearance vehicle. Contact the San Juan Resource Center in Monticello (☎ 587-1500) for more info.

7 GLEN CANYON NATIONAL RECREATION AREA. Rte. 95 crosses into the recreation area where a well-marked access road to the lake and White Canyon immediately turns off to the left. The road then crosses White Canyon before coming to the Farley Canyon turnoff about 70 mi. from Blanding and then crossing the Dirty Devil River near the town of **Hite** (water, gas, groceries, marina, and campground). If Hite's crowds and noise don't suit you, seek solitude along the lake at the end of one of three unpaved roads which leave Rte. 95 in succession southeast of Hite. Just west of the turnoff for Dark Canyon, **Blue Notch Canyon Rd.** winds up numerous switchbacks to the incredibly blue mesa top. The road, marked C.R. 2061, can be tough on cars and may force a turnaround after 11 mi., but eventually peters out at the lakeshore. **White Canyon** and **Farley Canyon** provide easier, if somewhat less scenic, access to Lake Powell a few miles closer to Hite. The campgrounds here, like the ones at Hite and the end of Blue Notch Canyon Rd., are primitive and charge a $6 fee.

8 HENRY MOUNTAINS. After crossing the once-mighty Colorado where it stops pooling behind the reservoir, Rte. 95 climbs out of canyon country and parallels the majestic Henry Mountains, the last mountain range in the contiguous US to be named and explored. About 100 mi. northwest of Blanding and 20 mi. south of Hanksville, the **Bull Creek Pass National Backcountry Byway** leaves Rte. 95 to the west and climbs into the mountains. There are a number of campsites on this drive and some spectacular scenery—you could see a wild herd of bison! Parts of the road are okay for cars, but don't attempt the entire 56 mi. loop without a high-clearance, four-wheel-drive vehicle. Contact the BLM in Hanksville (☎ 542-3461) for more info.

lent choice for the time-crunched backpacker—a cool, late afternoon hike provides access to remote campgrounds, and an early morning return allows for quick turn-around to the next destination. As a day hike, however, the trail proves much more strenuous, with a total of 3400 ft. of elevation change. As the summer heat often bakes all moisture out of the surrounding landscape, check with the Visitors Center before departing to find out if there is water at Riggs Spring.

Under-the-Rim Trail (23 mi. one-way, 3-4 days). Bryce's backcountry thoroughfare, this route travels south-north, paralleling the park road. Because so few visitors travel the Bryce backcountry, the trail remains uncrowded even in summer and affords a real taste of solitude as it winds through forests and meadows. From Rainbow Point at the south-ernmost end of the park to Bryce Point, the trail descends a total of 2000 ft. over the course of 19 mi., occasionally traveling up moderate inclines, before regaining roughly 1500 ft. in the last 4 mi. Several connector trails descending from the rim provide options for hikes of variable lengths. Water sources are intermittent and unreliable; check with the Visitors Center for water availability and to reserve a campsite before departing. Though shuttles no longer serve the southern portion of the park, hikers can often get rides back to their cars at Rainbow Point from other visitors. Hitch-hiking within the park is prohibited, but the rangers at the Visitors Center can arrange pick-up.

GRAND STAIRCASE-ESCALANTE NATIONAL MONUMENT ☎ 435

The last virgin corner of US wilderness to be captured by cartographer's pen, Grand Staircase-Escalante National Monument remains remote, rugged, pristine, and beautiful. This 1.9 million-acre expanse of painted sandstone, high alpine plateaus, treacherous canyons, and raging rivers shelters diverse areas of geological, biological, and historical interest. The name "Grand Staircase" refers to the exposed layers of stratigraphy, rising in a colorful and continuous series of cliffs from Lake Powell to Bryce Canyon. Diverse and unique biological communities flourish in isolation, ranging from fragile cryptobiotic crusts to hardy, 1400-year-old pines. Human occupation and use of the area likewise has a varied history, from the Ancestral Puebloan and Fremont cultures, who left petroglyphs, grana-ries, and pottery, to the Mormon pioneers, who fought the desert mile-by-mile in establishing Hole-in-the-Rock Trail. The western portion of the monument guards the impressive and inspiring Vermillion Cliffs, the labyrinthine Paria Canyon, and the geologically spectacular East Kaibab Monocline. On the high Kaiparowits Plateau, located in the central area of the monument, invaluable fossils provide scientists' only current insight into certain Cretaceous mammals. In the east, the Escalante River offers countless challenging and scenic hiking opportunities through narrow slot canyons and fertile riparian areas. All of these outstanding features, hidden away in wild expanses of sandstone, make the monument one of the most intriguing and mysterious areas of the west.

✈ ? ORIENTATION AND PRACTICAL INFORMATION

An entire lifetime could be spent wandering the 1.9 million acres of the Grand Staircase. As such, several communities serve as gateways to different portions of the monument. In the north, scenic **Rte. 12** travels between **Bryce** (see p. 300) and **Capital Reef National Park** (see p. 313), passing through the towns of **Escalante** and **Boulder,** UT and offering prime access to the Escalante River and its canyons. In the south, **Rte. 89** cuts into the monument above **Lake Powell** (see p. 80) and provides access to **Cottonwood Canyon Rd.**

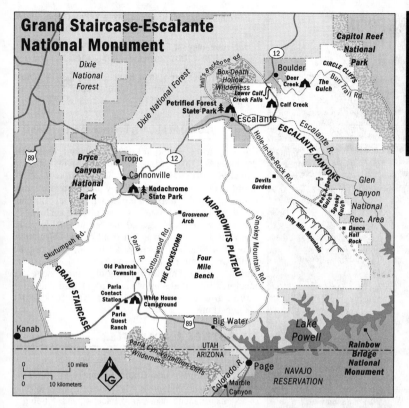

Grand Staircase-Escalante National Monument

Visitor Information: Escalante Interagency Visitors Center, 755 W. Main (☎826-5499; open mid-Mar. to Oct. daily 7:30am-5:30pm, Nov. to mid-Mar. M-F 8am-4:30pm), in Escalante. Within the hub for Grand Staircase-Escalante info, helpful and friendly staff steer eager hikers to appropriate routes and dissuade the over-ambitious from attempting Box-Death Hollow in the middle of monsoon season. Two info centers are located strategically on either end of the Cottonwood Canyon Rd. In the South: **Paria Contact Station,** 30min. west of Lake Powell on U.S. 89. Open Mar.-Nov. daily 8:30am-4:15pm. In the north: **Cannondale Visitors Center,** 10 Center St. (☎679-8981; open Mar.-Nov. daily 8am-4:30pm), near Rte. 12 in Cannondale. The BLM web site is also quite helpful: www.ut.blm.gov/monument.

Groceries: Bestway Groceries, 9 W. Main (☎826-4226). Stocks Escalante's only selection of grocery items. Open M-Sa 8am-8pm.

Bank/ATM: Wells Fargo, on W. Main in Escalante. Exchanges foreign currency; 24hr. ATM. Open M-F 9am-3pm.

Laundry and Showers: Broken Bow RV Park, on W. Main in Escalante. Showers $4; coin-op laundry.

Medical Services: Kazan Memorial Clinic, 65 N. Center St. (☎826-4374), in Escalante. Visiting physicians from Panguitch treat locals and visitors M, W, and F. Doctors

FROM THE ROAD

BENEATH THE DESERT

For all the years that he'd led trips in Escalante, Rick hadn't found a way to upclimb that slot. The canyon, only a foot or two wide and at least three hundred deep, dead-ended in a dry waterfall that appeared to extend all the way to the surface.

He'd been planning to go exploring on Friday, and when I came by the day before he offered to take me along. As we set out the next morning, into the slickrock desert on the east end of the Monument, Rick hid the keys to the Jeep in a secret compartment and had me memorize a number of key landmarks. In case he fell down a cliff, a rock outcropping and fault line on the side a distant mesa would guide me back to the car.

Hiking across the slickrock, we would stop every few minutes to pick up pieces of rock. Fragments of arrowheads and ancient stone tools, their edges worn dull, littered the landscape, remnants of a native civilization that lived atop these petrified sand dunes some 2000 years ago.

Fifteen minutes into the wilderness Rick drew a map on the sandstone with an arrowhead. There were two side canyons in this area that he'd never explored; one of them, he thought, should lead to the top of the waterfall. We descended into one canyon and climbed out to the edge of another. Rick tossed a pebble to check the depth. Clink. It sounded shallow, and we were about to start climbing down when we heard another clink, then another, more distant.

We turned back to the first canyon and followed it as it cut downward through the slickrock.

(continued on next page)

---

available Tu and Th at the **Bryce Valley Clinic,** 10 W. Center St. (☎679-8545), in Cannonville.

Internet Access: Escalante Public Library, 90 N. 100 W (☎826-4200). Open M-F 2:30-6:30pm.

Post Office: Escalante Post Office, 230 W. Main (☎826-4314). Open M-F 8:30am-4pm, Sa 8:30am-noon. **ZIP code:** 84726.

🏠 🍴 ACCOMMODATIONS AND FOOD

Catering to the backpacker/hiker crowd, **Escalante Outfitters ❷,** 310 W. Main, welcomes the desert-dirty and wilderness-weary back to civilization with seven simple yet elegant cabins. They also house a small camping supply shop and a cafe with an all-you-can-eat salad bar and the area's best pizza. (☎826-4266. Cabins $25, tents $10; salad bar $6, subs $4-5, pizza from $10.) On the terrace in front of the 🔲**Trailhead Cafe ❶,** 100 E and Main, relax to soothing reggae beats or classic rock anthems as you sip an herbal smoothie ($3). This local hangout serves espresso, masterfully grilled sandwiches ($5-7), and delicious baked goods. (☎826-4714. Open Apr.-Nov. daily 7:30am-10pm.)

🥾 OUTDOOR ACTIVITIES

 Venturing into Grand Staircase-Escalante National Monument intimidates even the most experienced hikers and backpackers. Finding water is always difficult, and deadly flash floods can strike without warning during summer. Don't come to the monument expecting to find a network of developed trails; every hike requires detailed topo maps and route-finding and often scrambling across rugged, rattlesnake-infested terrain. Because summer temperatures get dangerously high, most hikers visit in spring and fall. For the well-prepared and informed hiker, the Grand Staircase-Escalante Monument represents a remote swath of the wild American West, ripe for exploration; for the careless and unprepared, the monument can mean death or serious injury.

Owing to the rugged nature of the monument, a guided trip is perhaps the best way to make the most of a visit to Escalante. 🔲**Excursions of Escalante,** with offices in the Trailhead Cafe at 125 E. Main St. (☎800-839-7567; www.excursions-escalante.com), provides professional yet relaxed guide services, tailored to meet the client's needs. Even a short, inexpensive half-day hiking trip ($45) offers an up-close, physically challenging look at some breathtaking slot and box canyons. Extreme slot-canyon adventures and overnight treks are also offered. Mention *Let's Go* for a 15% discount. **Escalante Outback Adventures** (☎877-777-7988), in the Utah Canyons Shop at 325 W. Main, handles local hiker shuttle services ($1 per mi.). The service is pricey for individual hikers, but it's a good bargain for a group. This outfitter also conducts various guided tours: a sunset tour ($38), an archaeological tour ($32), and a slot-canyon tour ($65).

Any trek or drive into the monument, whether for an afternoon or a month, should begin at the Escalante Interagency Office. The extensive map collections and route knowledge offered by the staff help ensure both safety and fun.

HIKING AND BACKPACKING

A **free backcountry permit** is required for all multi-day trips into the monument. The most popular destination for backpacking trips is the **Canyons of Escalante,** in the eastern portion of the monument. Cutting through the slickrock toward Lake Powell, the Escalante and its feeder drainages create a practically endless series of canyons ripe for exploration. Many routes require technical canyoneering skills. Primary access to the canyons of Escalante comes via the **Hole-in-the-Rock Rd.,** heading south from Rte. 12 east of Escalante. The southern stretches of the road require four-wheel drive, but access to the popular **Peek-A-Boo** and **Spooky** slot canyons is available to two-wheel-drive vehicles. For one of the most challenging routes in the area, inquire about the **Box-Death Hollow** at the interagency office in Escalante. This 30 mi. trek through **Death Hollow Wilderness** travels through narrow slot canyons north of town and earns its name because of frequently lethal flash floods. The hike should not be underestimated, as it involves technical climbing skills and long stretches of swimming with a heavy pack through stagnant pools.

Travelers with enough time for an afternoon's constitutional can hike the 3 mi. one-way trail to the cascading, 126 ft. **Lower Calf Creek Falls,** the only developed route in the monument. The trail originates at the Calf Creek Campground, on Rte. 12 halfway between Boulder and Escalante, and generally takes 3-4hr. round-trip.

CAMPING

Dispersed, backcountry camping is permitted in most sections of the monument, but some restricted

(continued from previous page)

To the right lay an impossibly narrow fissure, perhaps only a foot or two wide, extending 100 ft. between the sky and darkness. We had found the top of Rick's waterfall. Debris carried by flash floods—logs, sticks, and rocks—cluttered the edge, and we set to work removing it.

I put on my harness while Rick anchored the rope. We were unable to remove some of the larger debris so I had to squeeze between fallen logs to enter the crevice. Gradually the canyon opened up and I could climb down by pressing my back against one wall and feet against another. The floor, a thin ribbon of dark sand, came into view far below as the air grew cooler. Wedged into the rock I spotted a splintered femur bone, hopefully human.

Rick climbed down after me, hauled the rope through and we began working our way out. High above, the sky appeared sometimes as a thin blue ribbon, sometimes only as an orange glow as the rock closed overhead. The floor was either too wet or too narrow to walk upon, forcing us to span the walls with hands on one side and feet on another.

Gradually the fissure widened and we sat down in the sand to have lunch. I asked Rick about the flash floods that form these canyons. He said he loved to see one, from the top, of course. Imagine, he said, 60 ft. of water screaming through here scouring the walls smooth as it hurls an avalanche of debris at the Escalante River.

But it was a clear day, and no sudden rush of water came pouring in on us. Instead, we emerged blinking out of the canyon, tired but happy.

If you want to try the canyon yourself, call Rick at **Excursions of Escalante** (see p. 310). *—Evan North*

areas do exist. Check at the Interagency Office for more info.

A number of campgrounds serve the Escalante area. Within the monument, the 13 shaded sites at the **Calf Creek Campground ❶**, 15 mi. east of Escalante on Rte. 12, offer access to the Calf Creek Falls Trail. ($7. Flush toilets, drinking water.) Six miles east of Boulder, the seven primitive sites at **Deer Creek ❶** lie off the scenic Burr Trail Rd. ($4; pit toilets, no water).

Two state parks adjoining the monument provide more developed, and expensive, sites. West of Escalante in Cannonville, the stunning **Kodachrome Basin State Park ❶** boasts 27 sites ($14; showers, drinking water, flush toilets). Camping at **Escalante Petrified Forest State Park ❶**, located just west of Escalante off Rte. 12, allows an opportunity to explore the park's fascinating collection of petrified wood along a 1 mi. nature trail. ($14. Showers, drinking water, flush toilets.)

DRIVING AND FOUR-WHEELING

Travelers just passing through the Escalante area en route to national parks east and west have a variety of options for getting a brief glimpse of the Monument's wild beauty. Tracing the picturesque slickrock hills between Boulder and Escalante, scenic **Rte. 12** is arguably one of the Southwest's most spectacular stretches of highway. The views are both immediate and transcendent as the road crests and plunges among sculpted sandstone rises, skating atop a narrow ridge before descending into the tranquil farming community of Boulder. Over the 40min. needed to complete this 28 mi. drive, the imagination receives enough provocation to inspire a summer's worth of enchantment.

Another route between Boulder and Escalante, the **Hell's Backbone Rd.** climbs high into the Dixie National Forest for spectacular views of the Death Hollow area and the colorful Escalante slickrock. The well-maintained and graded dirt road can accommodate any vehicle. As magnificent as the views along the 45 mi. route may be, don't miss Rte. 12 between Boulder and Escalante to see them.

Starting from Boulder, the paved 40 mi., one-way ◼**Burr Trail Road** descends into a spectacular red-walled gulch before emerging onto the Circle Cliffs and a breathtaking series of red, white, purple, yellow, and orange dunes. From there it continues east toward the looming monuments of Capitol Reef National Park. The paved surface ends at the park boundary, and though two-wheel-drive vehicles should not descend the switchbacks into Capitol Reef, a picnic table with a view awaits a few miles down the gravel road. For those willing to make an early start, the morning light brings the red rocks and rainbow dunes to life.

If passing through Escalante around lunchtime, picnic among the sculpted natural statues at **Devil's Garden.** Splendid slickrock formations and bizarre hoodoos await travelers here, 13 mi. down the **Hole-in-the-Rock Rd.** While the road surface alternates between gravel washboard, sand, dried mud, and slickrock, the first half is generally passable to most cars. Picnickers with high-clearance four-wheel-drive vehicles and a bit more time to kill can travel the 57 mi. length of the road to Lake Powell in order to marvel at the original Mormon wagon trail as it descends down a sheer, 600 ft. face to the lake.

Traveling the 50 mi. between Cannondale and Rte. 89, the popular **Cottonwood Canyon Rd.** cuts through the **Cockscomb,** a remarkable fissure in the earth's crust delineated by sawtooth edges. Though often passable to two-wheel-drive vehicles, the road surface is treacherous and marked by large sandy patches. Inquire at the Cannondale Visitors Center or the Paria Contact Station for road conditions.

Several other, more remote, **four-wheel-drive roads** criss-cross the monument, providing a day's or several days' worth of pristine desert scenery. Check at the Interagency Office for info on traveling the Monument's backcountry roads.

The area just south of **Cannondale** contains several other easily accessible parks and outdoor experiences. At the northern tip of the Cottonwood Canyon Road, 9 mi. south of Cannondale and Rte. 12, **Kodachrome Basin State Park** (☎ 800-322-3770) preserves the unique, solidified spires of ancient geysers. Seventeen miles south of Cannondale along a passable stretch of the Cottonwood Canyon Rd. stands **Grosvenor Arch,** a rare and impressive double span.

PARIA CANYON WILDERNESS   ☎ 435

South of Grand Staircase-Escalante National Monument, the Paria River cuts through a wild region of petrified sand dunes to create a gallery of slickrock canyons and buttes. Eons of wind and water erosion have sculpted elegant, sensuous, otherworldly formations such as **The Wave.**

For info on the wilderness, permits, camp fees, and weather forecasts or to fill up on drinking water, visit the **Paria Contact Station,** near the Cottonwood Canyon Rd. turnoff 30min. west of Lake Powell on U.S. 89. (Open Mar.-Nov. daily 8:30am-4:30pm.) The swirling slickrock patterns in the **Coyote Buttes** area draw more eager visitors than resources can support, prompting the BLM to place strict limitations on daily use. Only 20 people are allowed to make the 3 mi. trek to **The Wave** each day. Ten **permits** ($5 per person per day) are made available at the Paria Contact Station at 9am the morning before the proposed hike; the other 10 may be reserved 6 months in advance on the Paria web site (https://paria.az.blm.gov). Additional hikes in the wilderness include the 16 mi. journey through narrow **Buckskin Gulch,** said to be the longest slot-canyon in the world, and the serene, 38 mi. trek through the **Paria Canyon** itself. Come prepared with plenty of water and sunscreen.

Two miles past the contact station on a gravel road lies **White House Campground** and **Trailhead ❶.** Walk-in sites ($5) have pit toilets, fire pits, and water. The trailhead serves as the northernmost access to the Paria Canyon Wilderness Area.

Just west of the contact station at MM 21/22, the friendly, hospitable proprietors of **Paria Outpost Restaurant and Outfitters** (☎ 928-691-1047; www.paria.com) make visitors feel at home. The Outpost and Outfitters provide guide services to both Glen Canyon and Grand Staircase-Escalante National Monument, as well as hiker shuttle services, a charming room for rent ($40), and an endless Western-style buffet that draws locals from Page on Friday and Saturday (served 5-8pm; $12). Down the dirt road at the ◪**Paria Canyon Guest Ranch ❶,** a hip, remodeled farm welcomes a young and international crowd. The ranch entertains its guests with trail rides ($20 per hr.), a climbing wall/adventure course, and a clubhouse with two turntables and 1000 LPs. On summer nights, European teenagers traveling across the country throb to techno beats in this surreal wood-panelled lounge. (☎ 689-0398; www.pariacampground.com. Guest showers $1, non-guests $2. Dorms $12; campsites $15 per vehicle. Private room available.)

CAPITOL REEF   ☎ 435

What do you get when you cross rock formations that strangely resemble the Capitol in Washington with rock cliffs that impeded the travel of Mormon pioneers? A strangely un-apt name for this stunning youngest national park in the state, which lies in the center of southern Utah's string of park gems but remains less congested than most of the others. A geologist's fantasy and the park's feature attraction, the hundred-mile Waterpocket Fold, with its rocky peaks and pinnacles, bisects its 378 square miles and presents visitors with millions of years of stratified natural history. Many of the settlers who gave the Reef its name chose to put down roots in the fertile soil along Fremont River, planting a variety of fruit trees in the midst of these geological wonders. The town that sprang up here was aptly named

AT A GLANCE: CAPITOL REEF NATIONAL PARK

AREA: 241,904 acres.	**GATEWAY TOWNS:** Torrey, Caineville.
FEATURES: Waterpocket Fold, Fremont River.	**CAMPING:** Fruita Campground $10; free permit required for backcountry camping, and camping at Cedar Mesa and Cathedral Valley.
HIGHLIGHTS: Scenic drive, backcountry hiking, fruit picking at the Fruita orchard.	
	FEES: Entrance free; scenic drive $4.

"Fruita." Today, the spot serves as the home for the park's Visitors Center and main campground, and over 100 years later, visitors still enjoy the fruits of their predecessors' labors.

✳ ORIENTATION

The middle link in the Fab Five chain of national parks, east of Zion and Bryce Canyon and west of Arches and Canyonlands, Capitol Reef is unreachable by train or bus. The closest Amtrak and Greyhound stops are in **Green River.** For a fee, **Wild Hare Expeditions** (see p. 316) will provide a shuttle between Richfield and the park.

The park extends over 50 mi. north to south, but on average is no more than 10 mi. wide. **Rte. 24,** the main route through the park, crosses at one of the wider portions, providing access to the Visitors Center, campground, and scenic drive in Fruita as well as a number of sights and trailheads. In addition, a number of secondary roads, including the **Scenic Drive, Notom-Bullfrog Rd.,** and **Burr Trail Rd.,** offer more secluded experiences of this incredible area.

⚡ PRACTICAL INFORMATION

The **Visitors Center,** on Rte. 24, 11 mi. east of Torrey and 19 mi. west of Caineville, is equipped with free brochures on trails, info on daily activities, and plenty of maps for sale. (☎ 425-3791. Open June-Aug. daily 8am-6pm; Sept.-May 8am-4:30pm.) For more info, contact the Superintendent, Capitol Reef National Park, Torrey, UT 84775, or call 425-3791. Other services include: **weather and road conditions,** ☎ 425-3791; **Wayne County Medical Clinic,** 128 S. 300 W (☎ 425-3744), 19 mi.

 WHEN TO GO. With low humidity all year, there is no truly bad time to visit Capitol Reef. The summer months can see highs in the upper 90s, with significantly cooler evenings, and the spring and fall are temperate, with highs averaging in the 60s. Beware of thunderstorms in July and August—flash flooding may accompany them.

west of the Visitors Center in downtown Bicknell; and the **post office,** 222 E. Main (☎ 425-3488; open M-F 7:30am-1:30pm, Sa 7:30-11:30am). **ZIP code:** 84775.

🏠🍴 ACCOMMODATIONS AND FOOD

Torrey, a sleepy town 11 mi. west of the Visitors Center on Rte. 24, is home to the nearest lodging and restaurants to Capitol Reef. The friendly ⬛**Sandcreek Hostel ●,** 54 Rte. 24, features an espresso and smoothie bar, organic produce and local crafts, and remarkably inexpensive accommodations. A single dorm room houses eight comfy beds, a minifridge, and a microwave. There are also 12 tent sites, 12 hookups, and two rustic cabins that can sleep up to four people. (☎ 425-3577.

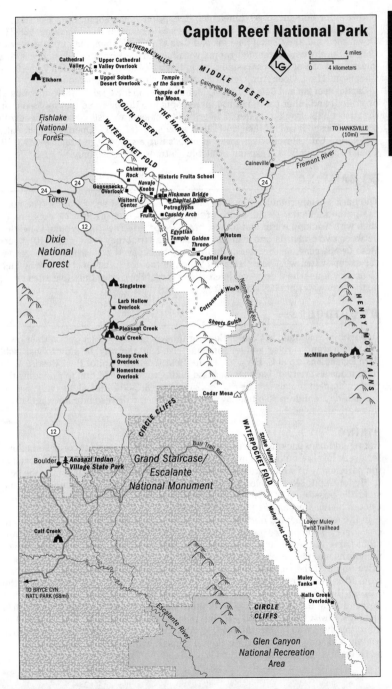

Capitol Reef National Park

0   4 miles
0   4 kilometers

TO HANKSVILLE
(10mi)

CATHEDRAL VALLEY

MIDDLE DESERT

Cathedral
Valley
Elkhorn

Upper Cathedral
Valley Overlook
Upper South
Desert Overlook

Temple
of the Sun
Temple of
the Moon

Caineville Wash Rd.

Fishlake
National
Forest

SOUTH DESERT

THE HARTNET

WATERPOCKET FOLD

Caineville

Fremont River

Chimney
Rock

Historic Frulta School

24

24

Goosenecks
Overlook

Navajo
Knobs

Hickman Bridge

Torrey

Visitors
Center

Capital Dome
Petroglyphs

12

Frulta

Cassidy Arch

Egyptian
Temple

Golden
Throne

Notom

Dixie
National
Forest

Capitol Gorge

Scenic Drive

Notom-Bullfrog Rd.

HENRY MOUNTAINS

Singletree

Larb Hollow
Overlook

Cottonwood Wash

Pleasant Creek
Oak Creek

Sheets Gulch

Steep Creek
Overlook
Homestead
Overlook

McMillan Springs

Cedar Mesa

12

CIRCLE CLIFFS

WATERPOCKET FOLD

Strike Valley

Boulder

Anasazi Indian
Village State Park

Burr Trail Rd.

Grand Staircase/
Escalante
National Monument

Muley Twist Canyon

Lower Muley
Twist Trailhead

Calf Creek

Muley
Tanks

Halls Creek
Overlook

TO BRYCE CYN.
NAT'L PARK (68mi)

Escalante River

CIRCLE
CLIFFS

Glen Canyon
National Recreation
Area

Showers for non-guests $3. Linens $2. Reception 7:30am-8pm. Check-out 11am. Open Apr. to mid-Oct. Dorms $10, tent sites $10, hookups $15-18, cabins $28-34.) Down the road, the **Capitol Reef Inn and Cafe ❷**, 360 W. Main, puts up guests with flair in Southwestern themed rooms with handmade furniture, plus access to a jacuzzi and one of the best restaurants in town (☎425-3271. Reception 7am-10pm. Check-out 11am. Open Apr.-Oct. Rooms $40, each additional person $4.)

Capitol Reef Inn and Cafe ❷, 360 W. Main, dishes up local rainbow trout (smoked or grilled) and other fresh, natural ingredients in a dining room that looks out on the russet hills. Don't miss the $7.75 grilled trout sandwich served on a bagel with cream cheese, or one of their $8-11 lush salads. (☎425-3271. Open Apr.-Oct. daily 7am-9pm.) Greasier offerings await at **Brink's Burgers ❶**, 163 E. Main. (☎425-3710. Open daily 11am-9pm. Take-out available. Entrees $2-5. Cash only.)

📷 CAMPING

The park's campgrounds offer sites on a first come, first served basis. The main campground, **Fruita**, 1¼ mi. south of the Visitors Center off Rte. 24, contains 71 sites with drinking water and toilets, but no showers. The campground is nestled between two orchards, and visitors can eat all the fruit they want (sites $10). **Cedar Mesa Campground,** on the Notom-Bullfrog Rd. (half paved, accessible by passenger car except when wet), and **Cathedral Valley,** in the north (accessible only by high clearance four-wheel-drive vehicle or by a long hike), have only five sites each; neither has water but hey, they're free.

🏔 OUTDOORS

Opportunities abound in Capitol Reef for those who want to set out on their own, but if you want to relax and let someone else lead the way, be sure to visit **Wild Hare Expeditions**, 2600 E. Hwy. 24, in the Best Western Capitol Reef Resort. Wild Hare leads a variety of backpacking and hiking tours, in addition to providing the best equipment rentals in the area. (☎425-3999 or 888-304-4273. Hours vary. $40-50 per half-day, children $35; full-day $60-75/$50. Scenic drives and four-wheel-drive tours are also available.)

HIKING

Hiking and backpacking possibilities in the park abound, and there is something for every level of outdoorsman. Bicycling is allowed only on established roads in the park, many of which are pretty sandy, so sticking to foot is generally the best tactic for Capitol Reef exploration. On all hikes, be aware of the weather and consider the possibility of flash floods. **Water** is available in the park at the Visitors Center, picnic area, and Fruita Campground.

In the less frequented northern and southern sections of the park, all hikes are considered backcountry travel. Be sure to get a **free backcountry permit** for all overnight trips. In the north, Cathedral Valley features an incredible moonscape of monoliths and pinnacles. A four-wheel drive, high-clearance vehicle is needed to drive on all of the roads here, but you can hike either on the roads or overland from Rte. 24 and enjoy the solitude of the remotest region of park. Along the Notom-Bullfrog Rd., a number of strenuous hikes head up the washes that descend from the Waterpocket Fold. **Burro Wash, Cottonwood Wash, Sheets Gulch,** and **Muley Twist Canyon** are all exciting possibilities for both day hikes as well as more involved forays into the backcountry. Some of these washes may require wading and some scrambling. Be sure to consult with a park ranger before diving in. Good hikes in close proximity to Rte. 24 and the Visitors Center include:

Chimney Rock Trail (3.5 mi. loop, 3-4hr.). This moderate loop trail departs from a turn-off on the north side of Rte. 24 at the west entry of the park, and climbs a set of switch-backs to an upper loop trail that traverses cross-sections of Capitol Reef's unique geology. Great views of Chimney Rock and panoramas of the Waterpocket Fold. 600 ft. elevation gain. Hikeable year-round, except when very wet.

Rim Overlook and Navajo Knobs Trail (4.5-9 mi. round-trip, entire route 4-8 hr.). This hike, one of the more challenging maintained routes in the park, departs from the Hickman Bridge parking area and climbs to the canyon rim above the Fremont River. Huge domes of the reef tower over the trail, while views of the valley below reward upward trekkers. The vista from the Rim Overlook at 2.25 mi. is fantastic, and from Navajo Knobs (4.5 mi.) you'll have a 360-degree panorama. 1600 ft. elevation gain. Treacherous when wet.

Frying Pan Trail (5 mi. one-way, 4-5hr.). The trailhead for this hike, as well as for the Cohab Canyon Trail, sits across from the Hickman Bridge parking lot, 2 mi. east of the Visitors Center. This moderately strenuous trail parallels a portion of the Waterpocket Fold atop Capitol Reef, and makes a good one-way trip requiring a two-car shuttle, although it can be combined with the Grand Wash Trail for a loop (including a portion of the highway). A short 0.5 mi. spur heads out to the inconspicuous but lovely Cassidy Arch. May also be hiked south to north from the Grand Wash parking area. 1000 ft. elevation gain. Exposed to wind and weather, especially in the winter.

DRIVING

While a full understanding of the remarkable land here requires a hike or two, the Reef's haunting landforms can also be appreciated from the seat of your car on the 20mi. **Scenic Drive,** a 1hr. round-trip jaunt through red and white sedimentary cliffs and hoodoos along paved and improved dirt roads. The route cuts through a wide range of sedimentary layers as it progresses south, giving a more tangible sense of the geological forces that shaped the land. The drive features spur roads to Grand Wash and Capitol Gorge, two of the more narrow and windy canyons that cut through the Waterpocket Fold, as well as a number of access points for rewarding day hikes and backpacking trips. Along Rte. 24, you can ponder the bathroom-sized **Fruita Schoolhouse** built by Mormon settlers, 1000-year-old petroglyphs etched on the stone walls of the canyon by Fremont Indians, and Behunin, the homestead of an early pioneer. In addition to these sites, the road also provides its fair share of sights. Chimney Rock and the Castle are two of the more abstruse sandstone formations along the route, and both may be explored up close via hiking trails. **Capitol Dome,** the parks namesake, can also been seen from the highway.

For a more in-depth experience of the Waterpocket Fold, more involved excursions on the **Notom-Bullfrog** and **Burr Trail Rd.** are necessary. The Notom-Bullfrog

GARDEN OF EATIN' Intrepid Mormon settlers must have known that Brigham Young had found the Promised Land when they emerged out of the deserts of southern Utah and stumbled across the bountiful **orchards** of their brethren homesteaders in **Fruita,** on the Fremont River. Cherry, apricot, peach, and apple trees were first planted by pioneers in the 1880s and provided sustenance for this small town, which was rarely home to more than ten families. Today, a two-person orchard crew maintains the 2700 trees in Capitol Reef solely for the enjoyment of park visitors. The cherry harvest kicks things off in early June, followed by apricots (late June to mid-July) and peaches and pears (Aug. and early Sept.), and finishes off with apples (Sept. to mid-Oct.). While in the orchards, you are welcome to eat as much ripe fruit as you want, but cash is necessary to take some home. Either way, you're likely to enjoy solitude in the orchards, with the company of only a deer or two, if you're lucky.

Rd. parallels the fold for almost 30 mi. before its intersection with the Burr Trail Rd. Trailheads for a number of good day hikes and backcountry explorations are found along the road. In good weather, cars should have no trouble negotiating the road. When wet, however, the bentonite clay transforms Dr. Jeckyll to Mr. Hyde and can be impassable even by four-wheel-drive vehicles. Many travelers do not follow the road all the way to Bullfrog Marina on Lake Powell, and instead take the Burr Trail Rd. west to Boulder on Rte. 12 (130 mi. loop; allow a full day). This is the one route that climbs the Waterpocket Fold, and the trip passes through both Capitol Reef and the adjacent, desolate **Grand Staircase/Escalante National Monument** (see p. 308). The **ferry service** at Bullfrog Marina shuttles cars and people 3.1 mi. across Lake Powell to Hall's Crossing on Rte. 276 (☎684-3000. 27min. trip. mid-May to mid-Sept. 8am-7pm; mid-Sept. to May 8am-3pm and 5-7pm. $12 cars, $5 motorcycle, $3 pedestrian/bike.)

ROCK CLIMBING

A great deal of excellent rock climbing also exists in the park. Climbs require the placing of your own protection and often a good deal of route finding, so they aren't for beginners, but for those hard-core wall rats passing through, Capitol Reef's soft sandstone provides a nice vertical stopover. Consult a park ranger and detailed guidebook before setting out.

SOUTHEASTERN UTAH

This less-traveled corner of Utah boasts a few of the state's more unknown wonders, including Valley of the Gods, Natural Bridges, and the spine-tingling Moki Dugway drive, interspersed with a few small towns that make for little more than places to sleep and fill up the gas tank. These off-the-beaten track destinations make for a nice detour from the crowds at the Fab Five chain of Southern Utah national parks, the cultural isolation of the Navajo Nation to the south, or the hell-bent recreational spirit of Southwest Colorado.

BLANDING   ☎435

The agricultural town of **Blanding**, 45 mi. northwest of Hovenweep (see p. 349), 47 mi. east of Natural Bridges (see p. 321), and 73 mi. northeast of Monument Valley (p. 128), is something of a rarity in this part of the world with broad, tree-lined streets and lots of green lawns. It makes a good stop from Moab and the parks to the north on the way to the Four Corners and can serve as a base for exploring the region as well. Unlike many of its neighbors, the town features the full gamut of services. The nearest **buses,** though, run through Green River on I-70. The new **Visitors Center** on U.S. 191 at the northern edge of town provides helpful info about the surrounding area and hosts a small pioneer museum. (☎678-3662. Open M-Sa 8am-8pm.) Archaeological enthusiasts will delight in **Edge of the Cedars State Park,** 660 W. 400 N, home to reconstructed Ancestral Puebloan ruins and an informative museum featuring a large array of pottery and baskets. (☎678-2238. Open mid-May to mid-Sept. daily 8am-7pm; mid-Sept. to mid-May 9am-5pm. Museum and ruins $2, vehicles $5.) The **San Juan County Multi-Agency Visitors Center,** 21 mi. north on U.S. 191 in Monticello, can provide useful resources for exploring the outdoors of southeastern Utah, and can direct questions to the nearby **Forest Service regional office.** (☎587-3235. Open Apr.-Sept. M-F 8am-5pm, Sa-Su 10am-5pm; Oct.-Mar. M-F 8am-5pm.) You can do a wash at the **Blanding Laundromat,** 225 E. 100 N. (☎678-2786. Open M-Sa 8am-10pm, Su 8am-8pm.) Other services include: **police,** 62 E. 200 S (☎678-2334, after hours 678-2916); **San Juan Hospital,** 364 W. 1st St. in Monticello (☎587-2116), 21 mi. north on U.S. 191; **San Juan Pharmacy,** 67 S. Main (☎678-2781;

open M-Th and Sa 9am-7pm, F 9am-6pm; window closes at 1pm); **free Internet access** at the **San Juan County Library**, 25 W. 300 S (☎ 678-2335; open M-Th noon-7pm, F 2-6pm, Sa 10am-2pm); and the **post office**, 90 N. Main (☎ 678-2627; open M-F 8am-4:30pm, Sa 8am-noon). **ZIP code:** 84511.

Nine miles north of town on U.S. 191, surrounded by and affording great views of the Manti-La Sal National Forest, is the **Devil's Canyon Campground ❶** (33 sites; water, pit toilets, and picnic tables; $10). The **Blanding Sunset Inn ❷**, 88 W. Center St., has basic, phoneless rooms for about as cheap as they come, and friendly management. (☎ 678-3323. Check-out 11am. Singles $25; doubles $30-33. Slightly cheaper Mar-Apr. Closed Dec.-Feb.) The **Cliff Palace Motel ❷**, 132 S. Main, must have been posh when it was built in the 1955, but time has taken its toll. (☎ 678-2264 or 800-553-8093. Reception 4-11pm. Check-out 11am. Singles $29; doubles $38; lower in winter.) Unfortunately, Blanding doesn't have as many dining options as it does motels. For sandwich lunches ($5-7), burgers and salads ($5.50-8), and hearty dinners ($9-16), try the **Homestead Steakhouse ❹**, 121 E. Center St. (☎ 678-3456. Open M-F 11am-9:30pm, Sa-Su 4:30-9:30pm.) A better bet for meals is to head north 21 mi. to Monticello. The **MD Ranch Cookhouse ❷**, 380 S. Main in Monticello, serves up hearty breakfasts ($3-8), affordable lunches ($5.25 specials), and dinners with all the fixings ($8-13), all in a friendly atmosphere. (☎ 587-3299. Open daily 8am-2pm and 5-10pm.) **Mesa Java ❶**, 516 N. Main, is the only place in the area where you can get a real cappuccino. (☎ 587-2601. Open daily 7am-5pm.)

VALLEY OF THE GODS

This amazing wonderland of rock probably served as a sandbox or testing ground for young gods gearing up for the more grandiose work of carving out Monument Valley. The towers are not as tall as those of their more famous southern neighbor, and the buttes, with their red crumbling sides, seem a little rougher, hewn with less precision. However, for all the quirks of these little siblings, Valley of the Gods surpasses Monument Valley in terms of its solitude and exploratory potential.

An incredible 17 mi. drive departs from U.S. 163, about two thirds of the way between the towns of Bluff and Mexican Hat, and runs right through the valley, emerging on Rte. 261 at the base of the **Moki Dugway** (see below), about 6 mi. west of the intersection of 163 and 261. The dirt track is generally passable by all cars, but watch for loose rock and rough sections across washes, and don't attempt the drive if the route is wet. The drive only takes about 1hr., but be sure to allow time for jaunts away from the car. You'll feel like you're the only person for miles, and nothing is "off-limits," a freedom you won't enjoy in Monument Valley.

Although no services lie along this remote route, travelers interested in spending a heavenly night or two in these godly stomping grounds might consider splurging on a stay at the **Valley of the Gods Bed and Breakfast.** The friendly owners of this charming 1930s homestead treat guests to lavish lodging in four exquisitely decorated rooms with private bathrooms featuring stone-laid showers and offer a full breakfast, and an unbeatable location flanked on all sides by rock and sky. (☎ 970-749-1164; www.valleyofthegods.cjb.net. Singles $85; doubles $100-110. Located ½ mi. from Rte. 361 on Valley of the Gods Rd.)

On your way back to U.S. 163, be sure to check out the wild geology of **Goose-neck State Park.** About 1 mi. west of the intersection of Rte. 261 and 163, a road leads about 4 mi. south to this remarkable lookout over the San Juan River. In the deepest and most dramatic example of an entrenched meander in the United States, the river wends its way over 6 mi. while only traveling a little over 1 mi. as the crow flies. The rock exposed by the river's relentless carving 1000 ft. below the lookout is some of the oldest in the country.

Southeastern Utah

MOKI DUGWAY AND MULEY POINT

Ascending the treacherous switchbacks through the sandy red dirt of the Moki Dugway, you feel like the modern day Orpheus on his long climb from Hades—any look back and all will be lost. The desolate Rte. 261 winds south from Rte. 95 and Natural Bridges National Monument, climbing into the San Juan River Valley and off of the Cedar Mesa, but this is no ordinary descent, even for the perilous West. Most of the 34 mi. road is solid asphalt, but a 3 mi. stretch dropping 1100 ft. down the sandstone side of Cedar Mesa remains unpaved. This incredible section teeters over spine-tingling drop-offs and negotiates 5 m.p.h. hairpin turns while providing glorious views of the San Juan River and Monument Valley. Drivers must maintain a constant balance between sights and safety.

Immediately at the top of the dugway on the left-hand side of the road is the unmarked, unpaved turnoff for Muley Point, which handles the seemingly impossible mission of providing even more astounding vistas. This overlook hangs on the edge of Cedar Mesa at the end of a 5 mi. road, lying within **Glen Canyon National Recreation Area.** The panorama visible from the point encompasses the **Henry Mountains** and **Glen Canyon** to the west, the **San Juan River** and **Monument Valley** to the south, and **Sleeping Ute Mountain** and the western tip of the Rockies to the east. Except when wet, the graded, mostly level road is easily passable by any vehicle that already made it up onto the mesa.

GRAND GULCH PRIMITIVE AREA

This 52 mi. stretch of wild land from the top of Cedar Mesa to the banks of the San Juan River features the largest concentration of **Ancestral Puebloan ruins** and artifacts in Utah. These archaeological attractions, as well as the scenery and desolation of Grand Gulch, make it a popular destination for backpackers. The **Kane Gulch Ranger Station,** on Rte. 261 4 mi. south of the intersection with Rte. 95, provides permits and area info. (Open Mar. to mid-June and Sept.-Oct. irregular hours; best chance at catching them 8am-noon. Day-use permits $2, overnight $5, weekly $7.) The spring and fall are the best times to visit; during the summer, temperatures frequently exceed 100°F. **Grand Gulch,** home to some of the most well-preserved remains, is 4 mi. from the ranger station and makes for a good day hike. For more info, call the San Juan Resource Area BLM Office in Monticello (☎587-1532).

NATURAL BRIDGES NAT'L MONUMENT

Forty miles from the nearest town and 25 mi. from such luxuries as gas, the remote Natural Bridges National Monument is a relatively tourist-free destination, though much more crowded than it was in the days when prospectors wandered this land in search of gold, or when early inhabitants etched petroglyphs and handprints on the sandstone at the canyon bottom. The first federally protected land in Utah, the national monument boasts three of the world's largest natural bridges, each spanning between 180 and 268 feet, produced by geological uplift and the erosive action of water. While most visitors confine themselves to the road on the canyon rim, the only way to really appreciate the size and shape of these natural wonders is to take the plunge and view them from underneath.

⊞ ⊠ ORIENTATION AND PRACTICAL INFORMATION. With the closest **Greyhound** and **Amtrak** stations several hours north in Green River, a **car** or a lucky hitch is essential to get to Natural Bridges. The entrance road to the monument, **Rte. 275,** departs from Rte. 95 35 mi. northwest of Blanding and 45 mi. southeast of Hite on Lake Powell, and can be reached from almost every direction. The nearest gas is 25 mi. west at Fry Canyon, and much more expensive than in surrounding towns. The park's paved, 9 mi. long one-way loop, the **Bridge View Drive,** passes the overlooks and trailheads to each of the three major bridges.

The **Visitors Center,** 4½ mi. along Rte. 275, offers a slide show and some interesting exhibits, and is the only spot where you can fill up on **water.** (☎692-1234. Open Mar.-Oct. daily 8am-6pm; Nov.-Feb. 8am-5pm. Weekly park entrance $6 per vehicle, $3 per hiker or biker. National Parks Passes accepted.) For weather and road conditions, call 800-492-2400. For more info, write the Superintendent, Natural Bridges National Monument, Box 1, Lake Powell, UT 84533.

You can sleep under the stars at the **Natural Bridges Campground ❶,** less than 1 mi. west of the Visitors Center on the park road. Thirteen shaded sites set amid piñon pines accommodate up to nine people each and include grills and picnic tables, but no water. (First come, first served. $10.) Free camping is available on

BLM land along a gravel road that begins at the intersection of Rte. 95 and Rte. 261, 6 mi. from the Visitors Center. The sites are flat and shaded but have no facilities.

☑ ◪ SIGHTS AND HIKES. All three bridges are spectacular and each displays unique and striking features. Through one of nature's remarkably educative coincidences, each bridge represents a stage in a bridge's typical erosive progression. **Kachina,** still thick and bulky but eroding rapidly, is a youngster; **Sipapu,** with its long, curving span is middle-aged; and **Owachomo,** exhilaratingly thin, is an old-timer. Each is visible from overlooks along the park drive, but can be more intimately explored via short trails that drop beneath the canyon rim.

Hearty hikers desiring to escape the crowds while visiting each of the three bridges delight in the **trail** that follows the floors of **White** and **Armstrong Canyons.** An 8.6 mi. loop completed by a trail network across the mesa top can be begun at any of the three major parking areas, but park officials recommend taking the Sipapu trail since the ascent from Owachomo Bridge is easier. The trail itself, unmaintained but easy to track, follows the canyon floor for the 6 mi. separating Sipapu and Owachomo. About 1 mi. south of Sipapu Bridge, the Horsecollar Ruins sit tucked into the western canyon wall and are accessible by a short scramble. South of Kachina Bridge the trail rises out of the canyon, skirting an impassable dry waterfall. The loop can be shortened to 5.5 mi. to include only two bridges, but once you've dropped into the canyon you won't want to leave short of the third.

Visitors shorter on time or looking for the challenge of hiking down and out of the canyon multiple times can take advantage of the shorter trails leading from parking areas to each of the bridges. The 1.2 mi. round-trip **Sipapu Bridge Trail** drops 500 ft. to the floor of **White Canyon.** The trail is moderately strenuous and requires hikers to negotiate a number of ladders while making their way down the sandstone walls of the canyon. The next major stop on the drive is the **Horsecollar Ruin Overlook,** a 0.6 mi. trail with little elevation change, which heads out to the canyon's edge above well-preserved Ancestral Puebloan dwellings. The **Kachina Bridge Trail** descends 650 ft. over 0.75 mi. to the valley floor for impressive views of the massive Kachina as well as some petroglyphs. The trail includes some difficult sections with steel handrails. The **Owachomo Bridge Trail** is the easiest in the park, descending 180 ft. over 0.2 mi. to end beneath this svelte formation.

COLORADO

With the world's largest hot springs, Ancestral Puebloan ruins standing watch in barren desert, high-speed gondolas flying up forested mountains, extreme skiing, and raging rivers, southwestern Colorado offers a diverse travel experience unified by the truly wild country found around every corner and behind every bend.Bounded by Pagosa Springs in the east and Grand Junction to the north, this rectangle of mountains, canyons, forests, and deserts is home to two national parks and the vast Uncompahgre and San Juan National Forests, which provide an outdoorsman's dream come true. Whether bombing down uncrowded ski slopes at Purgatory and Telluride or tearing up whitewater on the Animas and Gunnison Rivers, travelers are sure to find challenges that push their skills and strength to the limit. The San Juan Mountains are home to several of Colorado's 14,000 ft. peaks, and the San Juan Skyway, blazing a path straight through the mountains, offers access to myriad hiking and biking trails, including the 500-mile Colorado Trail running between Durango and Denver.

Amid the untamed wilderness characteristic of the region, signs of civilization remind travelers of the cultures that have made their home in southwestern Colorado for thousands of years. The Ancestral Puebloan cliff dwellings at Mesa Verde and the mesa-top ruins at nearby Hovenweep attest to the ancient human presence in this part of the world. More recent history is evoked by the steam railroad that still runs between Durango and Silverton, as well as mines that dot the Unaweep/Tabeguache Scenic Byway—remnants of an era when the dream of striking it rich brought optimistic souls to the region.

Finally, the communities of southwestern Colorado stand as evidence of the population's relationship with the great outdoors. From fans at Telluride's myriad music festivals to ranchers herding cattle across vast alpine expanses, interaction with the natural world is vital to everyday life. For travelers yearning to discover themselves in the woods, the wilds of southwest Colorado beckon.

✎ HIGHLIGHTS OF SOUTHWESTERN COLORADO

SKIING. Rivaling Salt Lake as ski capital of the Southwest, **Purgatory** (p. 340), **Telluride** (p. 342), and newly opened **Silverton** (p. 336) offer access to crisp powder.

RUINS. Cliff dwellings at **Mesa Verde** (p. 344) delight the eye and boggle the mind.

OURAY. Pleasant hot springs meet extreme ice climbing in this small town, the "Switzerland of America" (p. 341).

SAN JUAN RANGE

Ask Coloradans about their favorite mountain retreats, and they'll most likely name a peak, lake, stream, or town in the San Juan Range of southwestern Colorado. Durango is an ideal base camp for forays into these mountains, and northeast of town, the Weminuche Wilderness tempts the hardy backpacker with vast expanses of rugged terrain where sweeping vistas stretch for miles. Moreover, the San Juans are loaded with campgrounds and hostels, making them one of the more economical places to visit in the Southwest.

CRESTED BUTTE ☎970

In the heart of the Rockies far from any interstate, the historic coal mining town of Crested Butte was left alone by commercial developers to evolve at its own pace. The result is a place where laid-back residents pay more attention to trail and snow conditions than fattening up on the flow of tourists. A mecca for mountain bikers and site of the Extreme Ski Championships, Crested Butte is perfectly situated for forays into the pristine wilderness spreading out in three directions from town. This self-proclaimed "Wildflower Capital of Colorado" delightfully defies the commercial mold of ski towns like Aspen and Vail.

⎧ TRANSPORTATION

A car is essential in getting to Crested Butte, but a hindrance once there. **Mountain Express buses** circulate, offering free rides across town and up to the ski village at Mt. Crested Butte. Rides every 10 minutes (☎349-7318).

✴ ⁊ ORIENTATION AND PRACTICAL INFORMATION

Crested Butte lies at the dead end of Rte. 135, 28 miles from Gunnison. Its streets form a grid bisected by a creek which sometimes interrupts car access. **Highway 135** carries visitors to the main intersection, referred to locals as "the 4-way stop" (although it's not the only one). A left turn brings one on to **Elk Avenue,** the site of most of the action in town.

Tourist Office: Located in the large building on the right at the main intersection of Elk Ave. and Rte 135, the **Chamber of Commerce** (☎800-215-2226; www.crestedbutte-chamber.com) provides useful information and maps. Open year-round daily 9am-5pm.

Bank: Also at the main four-way stop sits the **Community First Bank** (☎349-6606) with its **24hr. ATM** (also located at Mt. Crested Butte). Open M-Th 9am-5pm, F 9am-6pm.

Post office: 221 Elk Ave. (☎349-5568). Open M-F 7:30am-4:30pm. **ZIP code:** 81224.

Police: ☎349-5231.

Road Conditions: ☎245-8800.

Internet Access: 30 min. free at **Old Rock Community Library**, 507 Maroon Ave. (☎349-6535). Take the first right after the four-way stop and look for the old schoolhouse with the bell tower. Open M, W, F 10am-6pm; Tu, Th 10am-7pm; Sa 10am-2pm.

Laundry: Coin-operated machines are available to the public at the **Crested Butte International Hostel and Lodge**.

Outdoor Equipment: ▨**The Alpineer** (☎349-5210), located on the left just before the four-way stop coming into town, is stocked with an unparalleled selection of outdoor gear and a full bike shop. The knowledgeable staff can clue you into the best hikes and rides in the area. Lucky mid-June visitors hit the jackpot at the annual Father's Day Sale. Open 9am-6pm June to mid-Sept. and Dec. to mid-Apr., 10am-5pm otherwise.

Medical Services: Available at the **Ore Bucket Building** at the corner of Maroon Ave. and Gothic Rd. (☎349-0321).

⌂ ⌂ ACCOMMODATIONS AND CAMPING

Completely devoid of chains, Crested Butte sleeps visitors in quirky B&Bs and a fantastic hostel. Campers will delight in the glut of free, spacious tent sites.

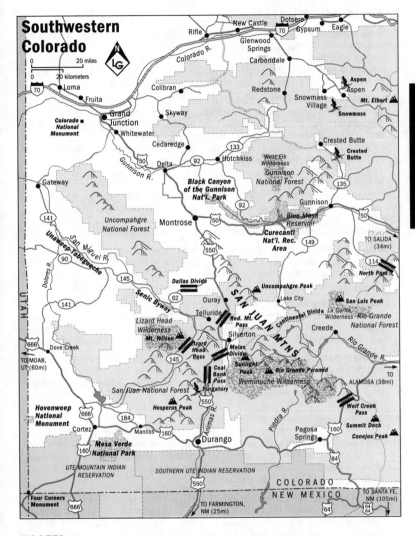

Southwestern
Colorado

HOSTEL

■ **Crested Butte International Hostel and Lodge,** 615 Teocalli Ave. (☎349-0588 or 888-389-0588; hostel@crestedbutte.net), two blocks north of the four-way stop, treats travellers to a tidy stay in gorgeous modern facilities. Its huge kitchen and bright common area make it an ideal base for exploring the area. No curfew or lock-out. Breakfast available, $1-5. Lock rental $2. **Showers** for non-guests $5. Coin-op **laundry.** Rates rise during ski season. Group discounts. Roomy 4-6 bed dorms $22 ($20 for multiple-night guests), doubles $55-65. Spacious third-floor apartment (sleeps up to 6) $115-160. ❶

COLORADO

BED AND BREAKFASTS

Purple Mountain Lodge, 714 Gothic Ave. (☎349-5888 or 800-759-9066; www.purple-mountain.com) puts up guests in high style on the east side of town. The rooms rival Martha Stewart in decor and your favorite sweatshirt in comfort. Rooms range from $75-98, with a family suite sleeping 4-6 available for $150. Rates decline unofficially off-season (spring, fall). Full breakfast included, kitchen available. ❺

The Claim Jumper, 704 Whiterock Rd. (☎349-6471; www.visitcrestedbutte.com/claim-jumper). The proprietor, Jerry, has comprehensively outfitted all seven themed rooms to a remarkable level of detail. For a real treat, try Jack's Cabin with its sunroom and outdoor patio—just remember how to open the secret doors to get into the room and access the TV/VCR! All guests enjoy private bathrooms and an indoor hot tub, as well as a hearty breakfast. Rooms range $99-139, with discounts in the off-season. ❺

CAMPING

The relaxed atmosphere of Crested Butte spells plenty of free camping opportunities for those willing to venture down dirt roads and up mountain passes. In addition to the sites listed below, traditional campgrounds with full facilities line **Cement Creek Rd.** and **Taylor Canyon Rd.,** south of town off Rte. 135.

Oh-Be-Joyful, located 5-6 mi. from the town center, doesn't disappoint with its brookside location and pit toilets. Take the first left as you drive north out of town onto Slate River Rd. and continue until you see the sign for Oh-Be-Joyful. Take the hairpin turn to the left to the water, or continue to higher sites if the road looks too rough. Free. ❶

Lake Irwin Campground (☎877-444-6777), a rough 9 mi. drive west of town, rewards guests with heavenly views from the alpine lake at over 10,000 ft. From the west end of Whiterock Ave., follow Kebler Pass Rd. until it forks. Take the left side and follow the signs to the campsite. $12 per vehicle and tent/camper, $6 per extra tent/camper. ❶

Paradise Divide, a 30 mi. trek up dirt roads to a saddle at 11,000 ft. provides seclusion to the world-weary. Follow directions for Oh-Be-Joyful, above, but continue further along Slate River Rd. until the old townsite of Pittsburg. Go right at the fork and then straightish at the intersection. Primitive sites, free. ❶

⬛ FOOD

Crested Butte sports more eateries than its size would suggest, so travellers have no trouble fueling up before or after a day on the trail. **Clark's Market,** located in the plaza on Rte. 135 at the sound end of town, sells groceries. (☎349-6492. Open daily 8am-9pm; until 10pm during busy seasons.)

Pitas in Paradise, 214 Elk Ave. (☎349-0897), a self-proclaimed "Mediterranean Cafe with Soul," wows diners with its delicious $5 gyros, $3.75 salads, and $3 smoothies. Watch your meal being made at the counter or sit down to wait for it in the backyard. Open daily 7-11am for breakfast ($1-4) and 11am-10pm for lunch and dinner. ❶

The Secret Stash, 21 Elk Ave. (☎349-6245), all the way at the west end of town, operates one of the highest coffee roasters in the world. With a menu ranging from eclectic pizzas ($8-17) to salads and wraps ($3.50-8) to grilled wings (10 for $7), this hip joint aims to please, and succeeds. Sip a soy latte in the side garden or on the vast second floor, where one might mistake the cushy couches, mood lighting, wall tapestries, and acoustic guitar for a hippie's living room. Open M-Sa 11am-11pm. Happy hour runs from 4:20-6:20pm featuring $1.50 beers and slices and $4 forties. ❸

Paradise Cafe (☎349-6233) bustles with business, contrary to its island theme. This Crested Butte staple fills bellies with hearty breakfasts and lunches (specials $5-7). Sit in or outdoors at the Paradise, located at Elk Ave. at 3rd in The Company Store building. Open daily 7am-3pm. ❶

Soupcon (☎349-5448) tempts the palate with a gourmet French menu including fois gras and game such as elk and duck in an intimate setting in an alley off 2nd St. behind Kochevar's Bar. Entrees $18-36. Open daily June-Sept. and Dec. to mid-Apr. for dinner. Reservations recommended; seatings at 6 and 8pm. ❺

■♫ NIGHTLIFE AND ENTERTAINMENT

Crested Butte is stocked with extreme sports types, but true to the town's frontier roots, they still get their drink on at saloons. **Kochevar's Bar and Saloon** (est. 1899) at 127 Elk Ave. is still in the family after over a century, and although gambling here is no longer legal it still sports several pool tables and the relics of its days as a gaming hall. (☎349-6745. Happy hour 3-7pm, Tu open mic night, live music during the summer. Open daily 11:30am-2am.) Those hungry for late-night munchies fill the booths at **The Last Steep Bar and Grill,** where $4-7 appetizers and $6-8 specials satisfy. (☎349-7007. Open and Su-Th 11am-11pm, F-Sa 11am-midnight.)

It's not tough to land in Crested Butte during some sort of festival, especially in the summer. Most notable are **Fat Tire Bike Week** in late June and the renown **Wildflower Festival** in mid-July. The **4th of July** festivities and the early-August **Festival for the Arts** are also local favorites. Throughout the summer and winter, local talent and touring companies grace the stage at the **Center for the Arts** (☎349-7487), located just south of the town park on Rte. 135.

▲ OUTDOOR ACTIVITIES

MOUNTAIN BIKING
Crested Butte claims to be one of the places this sport originated, and with the rugged trails lacing the area it's not surprising. The **Mountain Bike Hall of Fame,** located in the **Crested Butte Mountain Heritage Museum** at Sopris Ave. and 2nd St. (☎349-1880), features many locals including the beloved restaurateur at Donita's. Bikes can be rented at **The Alpineer** (see p. 324) and multiple locations around town. Guides can be hired from **Pioneer Mt. Bike Guide Service.** (☎349-551. Half-day $50 for 1, $40 each for 2, and $30 each for 3 and more; full day including lunch $80/70/60; multi-day trips $125 per day).

Beginner Ride: Peanut Lake, 3 mi. From Crested Butte, follow Gothic Rd. north for ¼mi. to Butte Ave. Turn left and continue to Peanut Lake and Mine. Return in reverse.

Intermediate Ride: Poverty Gulch, 20 mi. From Crested Butte, follow Gothic Rd. north for ½mi. to Slate River Rd. (FS 734). After 7 mi., turn left onto FS 734.2A and climb towards Cascade Mt. for 2 mi. until hitting trail #404. Take a right and ride or hike to the stunning view at the top. Return in reverse.

Advanced Ride: Trail #401, 24 mi. Ride north from Crested Butte on Rte. 135 through Mt. Crested Butte to Schofield Pass. Turn right onto trail #401 and climb along Mt. Belleview to the boundary of the Maroon Bells-Snowmass Wilderness Area. After descending to Schofield Pass Rd., continue on trail #401 to a 4WD road. Turn right, then left onto Highway 135. Head south back to Crested Butte.

SKIING
Three miles north of town, **Crested Butte Mt. Resort,** 12 Snowmass Rd., takes skiers to "the extreme limits" and offers over 800 acres of bowl skiing. Many of the other 85 runs are less spine-tingling, but the panoramic views are equally inspiring.

(☎800-544-8448. Open mid-Dec. to mid-Apr. Day passes around $50; ages 65-69 half-price; over 70 free; children 5-16 pay the numerical value of their age.)

HIKING

Just about any Crested Butte resident will gladly clue visitors into gorgeous hikes of all levels, many starting right at the edge of town. From the Nordic Center in town, **Green Lake** is a favorite destination for a picnic (6 mi. round trip). The **Upper Loop** and **Peanut Lake** are bike trails friendly to hikers as well.

FISHING

The Gunnison River Basin delights fly-fishermen with its wild trout. Much of the **East River** and its tributary **Taylor River** are public; access them from Rte. 135 and Taylor Canyon Rd. **Dragonfly Anglers,** a shop and guide service based at 307 Elk Ave. in Crested Butte, sells and rents gear and runs expert-led trips. (☎349-1228 or 800-491-3079; www.dragonflyanglers.com. Walk/wade trips: half-day $160 for 1, $210 for 2; full day $200/265. Float trips: half-day $230/265, full-day $255/295.)

DURANGO   ☎970

In its heyday, Durango was one of the main railroad junctions in the Southwest. Walking down the town's main thoroughfare today, it is easy to see that Durango remains a crossroads. Dreadlocked, hemp-clad youths share the sidewalks with weathered ranchers in ten-gallon hats and stiff Wranglers, and toned, brazen mountain bikers rub shoulders in the bars with camera-toting tourists. What brings all these folks together are their experiences in the great stretches of wilderness that engulf the town. Whether you choose to enjoy the flora, rope doggies at the rodeo, bike the San Juans, or ride the narrow gauge railroad, you're bound to spend a good chunk of your time in southwestern Colorado's great outdoors.

▐ TRANSPORTATION

Flights: Durango/La Plata County Airport, 1000 Airport Rd. (☎247-8143), 14 mi. southeast of downtown along U.S. 160. Flights to Durango can be quite expensive, so flying into regional hubs such as Denver or Phoenix might make more sense.

Buses: Greyhound, 275 E. 8th Ave. (☎259-2755). Runs 1-2 times per day to: **Albuquerque** (5hr., $42-45); **Denver** (11½hr., $60-64); **Grand Junction** (5hr., $35-37). Station open M-F 7:30am-noon and 3:30-5pm, Sa 7:30am-noon, Su and holidays 7:30-10am.

Public Transportation: The Durango Lift (☎259-5438) provides trolley service up and down Main Ave. every 20min. Memorial Day-Labor Day daily 6am-10pm; call about off-season service. Fare 50¢.

Taxis: Durango Transportation (☎259-4818). $2 per mi. plus $2 per person.

Car Rental: Rent-A-Wreck, 21698 W. U.S. 160 (☎259-5858 or 800-682-5858). Starting at $20 per day.

✦ ▐ ORIENTATION AND PRACTICAL INFORMATION

The largest town in southwestern Colorado, Durango lies alongside the Animas River at the intersection of **U.S. 160** and **U.S. 550.** Generally, you can count on streets running perpendicular to avenues, but try not to get thrown off by the fact that **Main Ave.** is always called "Main St." The other central drag, **Camino Del Río,** forks from Main Ave. at **14th St.** and heads diagonally for several blocks, parallel to the river. Main Ave., with its trading posts in Victorian downtown (between 5th and 14th St.) and motels on its northern stretch, coddles bus-loads of tourists, while Camino Del Río, with supermarkets and hardware stores, caters to locals.

Visitor Info: Durango Area Chamber Resort Association, 111 S. Camino del Río (☎247-0312 or 800-525-8855; www.durango.org), on the southeast side of town at Santa Rita Park along Rte. 160. Offers info on accommodations, food, sights, and the outdoors, with the added bonus of a free phone for local calls. Open M-Sa 8am-5:30pm (M-F until 6pm in summer), Su 10am-4pm. For outdoors info, inquire at the staffed **Forest Service Desk** at the Visitors Center (☎385-1210) or visit the **San Juan Public Lands Center,** 15 Burnett Ct. (☎247-4874), in the Durango Tech Center on U.S. 160 W. Open Apr. to mid-Dec. daily 8am-5pm; mid-Dec. to Mar. 8am-4:30pm.

Equipment Rentals: Southwest Adventures, 1205 Camino Del Río (☎259-0370 or 800-642-5389). Rents mountain bikes ($6 hourly, $25-40 daily), and climbing and backpacking gear. Runs guided tours (hiking from $55, mountaineering from $190, and mountain biking $30-90) and climbing lessons ($18 per hr.). Open daily 8am-6pm.

Laundromat: King Center Laundry, 1127 Camino Del Río (☎259-2060), provides self-service facilities. Open daily 7am-9pm.

Weather Info: ☎264-6397. **Road Conditions:** ☎264-5555.

Police: 990 E. 2nd Ave. (☎385-2900).

Pharmacy: Wal-Mart, 1155 S. Camino Del Río (☎259-8788). Open M-F 8am-8pm, Sa 8am-6pm, Su 10am-4pm.

Medical Services: Mercy Medical Center, 375 E. Park Ave. (☎247-4311).

Internet Access: Free and wheelchair accessible at the **Durango Public Library,** 1188 E. 2nd Ave. (☎385-2970). Open M-W 9am-9pm, Th-Su 9am-5:30pm; June-Aug. closed on Su.

Post Office: 222 W. 8th St. (☎247-3434). Open M-F 8am-5:30pm, Sa 9am-1pm. **ZIP code:** 81301.

ACCOMMODATIONS

Durango Hostel, 543 E. 2nd Ave. (☎247-9905). One block up the hill from downtown. Located near the heart of downtown, this hostel serves as a focal point for Durango's young backpacking crowd with its simple beds in a converted two-story home. Linens provided. Kitchen and campfire. 3-night max. stay. Check-in 7-10am and 5-10pm. Check-out 10am. No lockout. No curfew. 3-5 bed dorms $20. ❶

Alpine Motel, 3515 Main Ave. (☎247-4042 or 800-818-4042). The friendly managers' attention to detail makes the Alpine one of the best budget accommodations in Durango. Rooms are spotless and some include microfridges and microwaves. Right by lift to downtown. Reception 8am-10pm. Check-in and check-out flexible. Singles mid-May to mid-Sept. $42-68, mid Sept. to mid-May $28-32; doubles $58-84/$38-42. ❸

Spanish Trails Inn & Suites, 3141 Main Ave., (☎247-4173; www.spanishtrails.com) across from City Market. Behind the adobe exterior by the noisy road, immaculate rooms with great bathrooms and kitchenettes await. Check-out 10:30am. Check-in about 3pm, but flexible. Rooms start at $39, two-room suites from $69. ❷

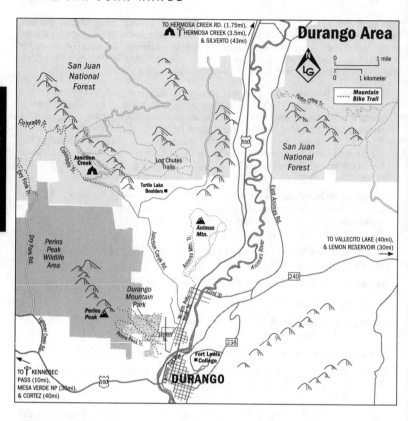

CAMPING

■ **Junction Creek Campground,** Forest Rd. 171 (☎247-4874). From Main Ave. turn west on 25th St. (Junction Creek Rd.), which becomes Forest Rd. 171 after 4 mi.; turn off to left at signpost 1 mi. past national forest entrance. Basic sites and facilities, breathtaking location on a forested mountainside above Junction Creek. The **Log Chutes Trails** run in the vicinity of the campground, and make for some low-key hiking and biking. 34 sites. 14-night max. stay. Open year-round, but expect snow Dec.-Mar. $12 per vehicle, each additional person $6. 6 mi. farther up Forest Rd. 171 (a ¼ mi. past Animas Overlook), free dispersed camping is allowed along the roadside. ❶

Hermosa Creek Campground, Country Rd. 201. Drive 10 mi. north of Durango on U.S. 550 to Hermosa Creek Road on left; immediate right on Country Rd. 201; after 3.9 mi., turn right. This primitive campground has only pit toilets and no defined sites, but its location deep in the woods above Hermosa Creek means you'll only share it with the cows. The **Hermosa Trail,** which provides access to vast tracks of roadless land, begins a few hundred feet up the road from the campground. For the more adventurous, numerous turnouts and spurs on the road up provide good crash sites. 14-night max. stay. Open May-Oct., depending on snow. Free. ❶

◘ FOOD

While some of Durango's eateries pander to the monied train crowd, several quality affordable places exist as well. The frugal can pick up groceries at City Market's two locations: Main Ave. (corner of 32nd St.) and Camino Del Rio near 7th St. (both open daily 6am-midnight). Organic goodies can be had at **Nature's Oasis,** 1123 Camino Del Río (☎247-1988; open M-Sa 8am-9pm, Su 8am-7pm; M-Sa 8am-8pm in winter). Pick up fresh produce on Saturdays from 8am-noon at the **Durango Farmers' Market** in the First National Bank parking lot.

Johnny McGuire's Deli, 552 Main Ave. (☎259-8816). Choose among more than 25 sandwiches, all made with fresh-baked bread (regular $5, footlong $10), and you'll go away satisfied. The Free Iron Willy and the 4:20 Vegan are some local favorites, but whatever you pick will cure a case of the munchies. Take-out and delivery available. Open daily M-Sa 7am-7:30pm, Su 7am-6pm. Cash only. ❷

Skinny's Grill, 1017 Main Ave. (☎382-2500). The best vegetarian place in town, Skinny's is also a bargain with nothing on the menu (including meat and fish dishes) costing more than $10. You'll enjoy large portions of such Southwestern treats as Deep Dish Spinach Enchiladas ($7.50) or Fajitas ($8.50) in a bright, low-key atmosphere. Don't pass up the award-winning desserts. Take-out is available, but you'll miss the lively waitstaff. Open Su-Th 11:30am-9pm, F-Sa 11:30am-10pm. ❷

Steaming Bean Coffee Co., 915 Main Ave., at 9th St. (☎385-7901). You can find any liquid creation ($1-4) that your cosmopolitan palate could desire in this popular hangout, as well as sandwiches ($5), wraps ($3), and light breakfast items ($1-2). Open M-Th 6:30am-9pm, F-Sa 6:30am-10pm, Su 7am-8pm. ❶

Carver Brewing Co., 1022 Main Ave. (☎259-2545), between 10th and 11th St. This local hang out, famous for its pancakes and hospitality, serves delicious fresh-baked bread and breakfast specials ($3-7) such as Southwest Benedict. Dinner, however, is a pricier proposition. Take-out available. Open M-F 6:30am-10pm, Su 6:30am-1pm. ❸

▣ ♫ NIGHTLIFE AND ENTERTAINMENT

The ski-lodge atmosphere and frequent live music at **The Summit,** 600 Main Ave. near the train station, attracts the college crowd for good rowdy fun. (☎247-2324. Open daily 4pm-2am.) On Saturday, check out ladies' night at **Steamworks Brewing Co.,** 801 E. 2nd Ave. With a DJ spinning, this bar gets hoppin', and you can enjoy the great beers, brewed on the premises. (☎259-9200. Open daily 11am-2am.) One of the best **Victorian-style melodramas** in the US—full of high-flying vocals and tap dancing—takes place at the **Strater Hotel and Diamond Circle Theater** at 7th St. and Main Ave. (☎247-3400. June-Sept. M-Sa. Doors open at 7:30pm, curtain at 8pm. Tickets $19, under 12 $14.) Fort Lewis College hosts concerts and shows year round at its **Community Concert Hall.** (☎247-7657; www.durangoconcerts.com.)

◉ SIGHTS

More of a tourist attraction than a means of transportation, the **Durango and Silverton Narrow Gauge Train,** 479 Main St., runs up the Animas River Valley to the historic mining town of Silverton. Old-fashioned, 100% coal-fed locomotives wheeze through the San Juans, making a 2hr. stop in Silverton before returning to Durango. It may be cheaper and more comfortable to drive the route yourself, but you'll miss out on a piece of living history that has been in continuous operation since 1881. The train also offers excellent access to the Weminuche Wilderness, dropping off and picking up backpackers at various scenic points; call for more info on this service and on monthly special events. (☎247-2733; www.durangotrain.com. Office open June to mid-Aug. daily 6am-8pm; mid-Aug. to Oct. 7am-7pm; Nov.-Apr. 8am-5pm; May 7am-7pm. Morning trains from Durango and afternoon trains from Silverton; 9hr. including stop, layover day optional; $60 mid-June to mid-Aug., $55 Sept. to early Oct., ages 5-11 $30/$27.50.)

The **Durango Pro Rodeo Series,** at the LaPlata County Fairgrounds at 25th St. and Main Ave., moseys into town every summer. Saddling up on Tuesday and Wednesday nights, the action starts at 7:30pm with a barbecue at 6pm. (☎247-2790. Mid-June to Aug. $12, under 12 $6.) On U.S. 550 north at the edge of town, **Trimble Hot Springs** allow visitors to soak in two hot pools and one regular one with a great view of Missionary Ridge (of 2002 fire fame) for $8.

🏔 OUTDOOR ACTIVITIES

Durango is surrounded by the **San Juan National Forest,** a diverse area for all kinds of outdoor pursuits. The **USFS headquarters** in Durango, at 15 Burnett Ct. off U.S. 160 W, provides info on hiking, backpacking, biking, mountaineering, and skiing in the forest. (☎247-4874. Open Apr. to mid Dec. daily 8am-5pm, mid-Dec. to Mar. 8am-4:30pm.) Pay them a visit, especially if you're planning a trip into the massive Weminuche Wilderness, northeast of Durango. **Southwest Adventures,** 1205 Camino Del Río, provides guided hiking, backpacking, mountain biking, and rock climbing in the San Juans. (☎259-0370 or 800-642-5389; www.mtnguide.net.)

DAY HIKING

With the San Juan Mountains on all sides, trails around Durango abound, providing the opportunity for leisurely walks as well as intense ascents. The **Colorado Trail,** which covers 474 mi. of Rockies, starts in Durango on its way to Denver, and parts of this trek may make for interesting day hikes. The town also provides access to many of the highest peaks in the contiguous US. Although it is hard to go wrong hiking in this area, here are some of your best bets:

Animas City Mountain (6 mi. round-trip, 3-4hr.). From Main Ave. take 32nd St. west to W. 4th Ave. Turn right on W. 4th Ave. and follow it to the end to reach the trailhead. This easy and popular hike to the high points on Animas Mountain offers spectacular views of the Animas River Valley and Durango, as well as the chance to see elk and deer. Elevation gain 1800 ft. Hikeable year-round, snow-free Apr.-Nov.

Haflin Creek Trail (7 mi. round-trip, 5-6hr.). From Main Ave. take 32nd St. east and turn left on E. Animas Rd.; 5 mi. up on the right is a sign for the trailhead. This moderate hike cuts into the deep woods of Animas Valley and ascends over 3000 ft. through several climatic zones, providing clear views of the valley and the La Platas to the west. Hikeable year-round, snow-free Apr.-Nov.

Perins Peak (5 mi. round-trip, 3½-4½hr.). From Main Ave. take 22nd St. west-bound, which soon becomes Montview Pkwy.; after 1 block, turn right on Leyden St. Follow it to the end and head west up the drainage past the last house. This difficult hike to the summit of Perins Peak requires a fair deal of bushwhacking and scrambling and rewards the hearty hiker with panoramic vistas above the tree line. There is a trail only for the lower half of the hike, which leaves the initial drainage and climbs the western valley wall after about 0.5 mi. Elevation gain 1700 ft. Advisable May-Sept.; the trail may be difficult to find at other times of the year.

BACKPACKING

The **Weminuche Wilderness** to the northeast of Durango lies in the heart of the San Juan Mountains, straddling 50 mi. of the Continental Divide. With an average elevation of 10,000 ft., the area offers some of the highest, most remote backcountry travel in the continental US. The closest access is from trailheads near Lemon Reservoir and Vallecito Lake. Much of the wilderness is above the treeline, in sensitive alpine tundra. Numerous streams and creeks criss-cross the wilderness, and while some backcountry travelers swear by the water, without some sort of treatment (iodine or filter) you'll be tempting the giardia gods. Campfires are generally allowed (except in the vicinity of lakes) but are to be avoided in alpine and high-use areas. No permits required. The Colorado Trail (see p. 332), beginning west of Durango, provides an opportunity for fantastic extended trips.

MOUNTAIN BIKING

While mountain biking may have gotten its start in northern California, the sport came into its own in Durango. Many of the town's inhabitants are world-class riders, and the web of trails that surround the town hub are geared toward a range of bikers, presenting an exhilarating challenge to beginners and experts alike. Bikes are available at **Hassle Free Sports,** 2615 Main Ave., but you must have a driver's license and major credit card. (☎259-3874 or 800-835-3800. Open summer M-Sa 9:30am-6pm, Su 9am-5pm; winter daily 7:30am-7pm; spring and fall M-Sa 8:30am-6pm. Half-day $16, full-day $25. Full suspension $24/35. Ski rental packages $16-27 per day.) **Southwest Adventures** (see p. 329) provides shuttles to popular mountain biking locations, rents bikes for $6 an hour or $25-40 daily, and operates bike tours for $30-90.

Dry Fork (9 mi. round-trip, 1-2hr.). Take U.S. 160 west 3.5 mi. from Durango to Lightner Creek Rd. (County Rd. 207); turn right and follow this paved road 1 mi. to County Rd. 208; follow the dirt road 2 mi. to a fork, bear right, and continue for 1 mi. to the Dry Creek trailhead to the left. This moderate ride along a loop of singletrack cuts uphill and downhill through the thick woods of the Perins Peak Wildlife Area, and includes a portion of the Colorado Trail. Elevation gain 1200 ft. Recommended May-Oct.

Around Perins Peak (18 mi. round-trip, 2-3hr.). This ride may be started right in Durango from anywhere on Main Ave. From Main Ave. head west on 25th St. for 3.5 mi., over the San Juan National Forest boundary, before turning left on the Colorado Trail. This advanced loop is a favorite of local riders and incorporates a portion of the Dry Creek ride listed above. The ride climbs a series of steep switchbacks, then rewards with scintillating downhill singletrack, and offers some awesome views. Route combines single-track and road. Elevation gain 1500 ft. Recommended May-Oct.

Kennebec Pass (34 mi. one-way, 5-7hr.). This ride requires a drop-off or shuttle, or else it becomes a 50 mi. loop. Drive west of Durango on U.S. 160, and turn right after 10 mi. on Country Rd. 124; after 4 mi. the beginning of the ride coincides with the transition to dirt road. This expert ride cuts into the La Plata Mountains and includes 20 mi. of rugged Colorado Trail. A mountain biking classic and one hell of a trip. Elevation gain 4500 ft. Recommended July-Sept.

FLY FISHING

The many streams and rivers around Durango are renowned world-wide for their excellent fishing. The Animas, which runs through the city, is open to public access, as are the Piedra and San Juan rivers a short drive away. Whether you're a seasoned expert or a bumbling gumshoe, stop by **Duranglers** on Main Ave. between 9th and 10th St. (☎385-4081 or 888-347-4346; www.duranglers.com. Open mid-May to Aug. M-Sa 7am-8pm, Su 9am-5pm mid-May to Aug.; Sept. to mid-May M-Sa 8am-6pm, Su 10am-4pm.) This fly shop has the largest selection in the region and sets up trips with extremely knowledgeable and experienced guides. (Half-day trips from $195, full-day from $235. Price for groups of 1 or 2 people.)

ROCK CLIMBING

Though Durango is not a destination for serious climbers, many different levels and types of climbing are accessible from Durango. Climbing is best from May to October. There is a good deal of excellent bouldering for less experienced climbers. The best nearby bouldering is at the **Turtle Lake Boulders,** where both beginners and experts find great problems. From Main Ave., take 25th St./Junction Creek Rd.; bear right on County Rd. 205; pass Chapman Lake and you'll see the sandstone boulders. **Animas City Rock Gym,** 1111 Camino Del Río (☎259-5700; www.climbacr.com), offers guides and extensive instruction for all abilities.

RIVER RUNNING

The Animas River offers everything from family trips on placid Class II rapids to intense Class V battles, in easy reach of Durango. If the prospect of rafting out in the wilderness appeals to you, the rapids of the Piedra River beckon. **Flexible Flyers,** 2344 County Rd. 225, offers the cheapest trips in town. (☎247-4628 or 800-346-7741. Trips daily 9am-5pm. 2hr.; $20, under 15 $14. Reservations recommended.) The largest outfitter in the area, **Mild to Wild Rafting,** 701 Main Ave. (booth) or 1111 Camino Del Rio (office), runs trips on major southwestern Colorado rivers. (☎247-4789 or 800-567-6745. Open daily 8am-8pm. Half-day mild trips $41, full-day mild trips $65; children $32/55. Full-day intense trips $105. Reservations recommended.)

SKIING

Durango Mountain Resort (see p. 340), better known as **Purgatory,** 30min. north on U.S. 550, hosts skiers of all levels.

SILVERTON   ☎970

Silverton's old Town Hall and rickety county jail/museum are constant reminders of the town's heyday as a mining center, where silver was extracted by the ton. Silverton's mountains draw thrill seekers of all types, who cross paths with the rough-and-tumble locals along the town's ragged gravel roads and in its wind-beaten establishments. The Alpine Loop, an incredible jeep road that traverses the Rockies, as well as many other four-wheel-drive trails, are accessible from the town, and the area boasts some of the most extreme hiking and skiing in Colorado.

⚐ PRACTICAL INFORMATION. The **Durango & Silverton Narrow Gauge Railroad,** depot at 10th and Animas St., platform at 12th and Blair St., sends trains daily to Durango (see **Durango: Sights,** p. 331). **Greyhound** (☎259-2755) stops at Teki's Place at 11th and Greene St. on its way between Durango and Montrose. Passengers can board here and then pay for tickets to either destination. Buses go to **Durango** (1hr., 7:30am) and **Montrose** (1½hr., 9:30am). Silverton's main thoroughfare, Greene St., runs from U.S. 550 through town.

The **Silverton Chamber of Commerce Visitors Center,** 414 Greene St. at the junction of U.S. 550 and Highway 110, provides info about accommodations, food, sights, and the outdoors in Silverton and its environs. (☎387-5654 or 800-752-4494; www.silverton.org. Open June-Sept. daily 9am-6pm, Oct.-May 10am-4pm.) **ATM** access available at **Citizens State Bank,** 1218 Greene St. **Outdoor World,** 1234 Greene

St., has a basic selection of outdoor equipment. (☎387-5628. Open daily June-Aug. 8am-8pm; Oct.-May 10am-4pm.) Laundry is at **Wash Tub**, 10th and Greene St. (open daily 8am-8pm). Other services include: **weather and road conditions** (☎877-315-7623); **emergency** (☎387-5531); **medical services** at 1450 Greene St. (☎387-5354); **free Internet access**, Silverton Public Library, 11th and Reese St. (☎387-5770; open Tu-Th 11am-8pm, F-Sa 10am-5pm); and the **post office**, 139 W. 12th St. (☎387-5402; open M-F 8:30-4:30, Sa 11am-1pm). **ZIP code:** 81433.

🏠🍴 ACCOMMODATIONS AND FOOD. The Silverton Hostel ❶, 1025 Blair St., offers cheap lodging year-round in clean and simple quarters with a colorful kitchen, all steps away from the owner's pottery studio. (☎387-0115 or 888-276-0088. Reception 8-11am and 4-10pm. Check-out noon. Dorms $12, in winter $10; private rooms $32-42/$25-30. Public showers $3.50. Reservations recommended late June-Aug. and holidays.) Guests at the 100-year-old **Teller House Hotel ❹** experience the respectable side of Silverton in its heyday, in high-ceilinged Victorian rooms hosted by two cousins native to the city. Its convenient location at 1250 Greene St. and full breakfast seal the deal. (☎387-5423 or 800-342-4338; mid-May to Sept. $64-69, Oct. to mid-May $49 without breakfast.) The 26 sites at **South Mineral Campground ❶**, 4.5 mi. down County Rd. 7/Forest Rd. 585, off U.S. 550 2 mi. west of Silverton, are tucked away along Mineral Creek in the heart of the San Juans. Free dispersed camping is permitted in primitive sites along the road leading up to the campground. (14-night max. stay. Open May-Sept. $12 per vehicle.)

🍽Rocky Mountain Funnel Cakes ❶, 1249 Greene St., is unquestionably the place for tasty, inexpensive down-home cooking in Silverton. Try the Mexican Funnel Cake or a delectable dessert concoction with hot fudge and raspberry sauce, and don't forget to pinpoint your hometown on the wall map and peruse the vast selection of used books for sale. Those lucky enough to be in town on a Thursday morning can enjoy the bonus treat of fresh donuts. (☎387-5450. Open Sept.-May daily 10am-7:30pm; June-Aug. 10am-9pm. Cash only.) Situated at number 1067 on "notorious" Blair St., **Avalanche Coffeehouse ❶** serves up lighter fare including soup, sandwiches, and town gossip in a cozy little cottage atmosphere. (Soup and salad $5. Open Tu-Sa 8am-3:30pm, Su 10am-3pm.) For a more upscale experience, head to **Handlebars Food & Saloon ❷**, 117 13th St. (just off Greene). Scores of animal eyes peer down from the walls as locals enjoy lunch specials ($7-10) by day and cold brews by night. Anyone sporting a handlebar moustache gets their Polaroid shot posted around the bar. (☎387-5395. Open May-Oct. daily 10:30am-10pm; saloon open daily 10:30am-2am.) Limited groceries are available at **TNT Market** next to the laundromat on Greene St. (☎387-5341. Open M-Sa 7:30am-9pm, Su 8am-8pm.)

📷🎵 SIGHTS AND ENTERTAINMENT. Next to the courthouse at the east end of Greene St., the **San Juan County Historical Society Museum** inhabits the 100-year-old county jail. Exhibits range from ancient outdoor equipment to a restored miners' boarding house accessed through a tunnel. (☎387-5838. Open late May to mid-Sept. 9am-5pm, mid-Sept. to mid-Oct. 10am-3pm. $3.50.) Just east of the museum, Route 110 forms the southern base of the scenic **Alpine Loop.** Crossing the high country between Silverton, Ouray, and Lake City, four-wheel-drive vehicles are recommended for those wishing to tackle the entire loop. About 12 mi. northeast of Silverton on Rte. 110, the ghost town of **Animas Forks,** can be reached easily by passenger car in the warm months. Go at dusk to avoid crowds and catch the site at its eeriest. For a live experience, attend the **Miners Union Theatre** at Greene and 11th St. in town. (☎387-5337 or 800-752-4494. $10.) Every year in late June, the **Silverton Jubilee Folk Music Festival** hits the streets with rootsy flair. (www.silvertonfestivals.com. One-day tickets from $30.)

COLORADO

COLORADO

🎿 **OUTDOOR ACTIVITIES.** The area surrounding Silverton presents excellent hiking options. **Ice Lakes** is a moderate 7 mi. round-trip climb. The trail begins opposite the **South Mineral Campground,** 8 mi. west of Silverton. (2400 ft. elevation gain. Accessible June-Sept.) **Highland Mary Lakes** is a moderately difficult 6 mi. round-trip hike above the treeline to a group of large alpine lakes. To get to the trailhead, follow Rte. 110 northeast of town for 4¼ mi.; turn right on Cunningham Gulch and continue 4 mi. to the head of the canyon. Be careful—the trail is easy to lose above treeline. (1650 ft. elevation gain. Accessible June-Sept.)

There are two distinct skiing options in Silverton. The town-run **Kendall Mountain** offers one lift on winter weekends for $6. Contact **City Hall** (☎387-5522) for info. At the other end of the spectrum, the lift for **Silverton Mountain Ski Area** (☎387-5706; www.silvertonmountain.com) provides access to some of Colorado's most extreme backcountry skiing in winter and unparalleled summertime views of the San Juans. (Lift $15 in summer, guided skiing $99 per day, unguided permit $30.)

TELLURIDE   ☎970

Site of the first bank Butch Cassidy ever robbed (the San Miguel), Telluride was very much a town of the Old West. Locals believe that their city's name derives from a contraction of "to hell you ride," a likely warning given to travelers to the once hell-bent city. Things have quieted down a bit in the last few years—outlaw celebrities have been replaced with film celebrities, and six-shooter guns with cinnamon buns. Skiers, hikers, and vacationers come to Telluride to pump gold and silver into the mountains, and the town can also claim the most festivals per capita of any ZIP code in the US. During the summer and fall, Telluride is inundated by outsiders every few weeks, a schedule that allows just enough time for the community to catch its breath before the next onslaught. Still, a small-town feeling prevails—rocking chairs sit outside brightly painted, wood-shingled houses, and dogs lounge on storefront porches.

🚌 TRANSPORTATION

The town is most easily and economically accessible by car, via **Rte. 145** from the north or south. The **Telluride Airport,** 1500 Last Dollar Rd. (☎728-5313), charges a pretty penny for planes from Denver, Phoenix, Houston, Chicago, Dallas, and Newark ($250-500), and the nearest bus station is **Greyhound** (☎249-6673) in Montrose, 65 mi. away. **Budget Rent-A-Car** has a location at the airport (☎728-4642).

Getting around the town itself is fairly easy. The public bus line, called the **Galloping Goose,** runs the length of town on a regular basis, and out to the towns of Placerville and Norwood several times daily. (☎728-5700. May-Nov. every 20min. 7:30am-6pm, Dec.-Apr. every 10min. 7am-midnight. Town loop free, outlying towns $1-2.) A **gondola** runs from downtown to Mountain Village. (☎728-8888. Runs 7am-midnight. Free.) **Taxi** service from **Mountain Limo** serves the western slope. (☎728-9606 or 888-546-6894. Airport fare $8.)

✳ 🛈 ORIENTATION AND PRACTICAL INFORMATION

Telluride sits on a short spur of Rte. 145, 127 mi. southeast of Grand Junction and 71 mi. northeast of Cortez, in a box canyon nestled among high peaks. The main drag, **Colorado Ave.,** runs perpendicular to a series of streets bearing the names of trees. Fabulous **Mountain Village,** primarily a residential area, sits on the mountainside 2 mi. above town, accessible from Telluride by car via Rte. 145 south or the gondola which departs from **San Juan St.** on the south edge of town.

Visitor Information: Telluride Visitor Information Center, 666 W. Colorado Ave. (☎ 728-4431 or 888-288-7360), upstairs from Clark's Market, immediately on the right as you enter downtown. Office open M-Sa 9am-7pm, Su noon-5pm.

Equipment Rental: Downtown Telluride seems to have a gear store on every corner, and several of them rent mountain bikes. One, **Paragon Ski & Sports,** 217 W. Colorado Ave. (☎ 728-4525), combines bikes, skis, and outdoor equipment under one roof. Open daily 9am-7pm, in ski season 8:30am-9pm. Bikes from $16 per half-day, $28 per day; skis and boots $20 per day.

Laundromat: Washateria, 107 W. Columbia Ave. (☎ 728-4360). Open daily 8am-9pm.

Weather Conditions: ☎ 240-4900, ext. 9901. **Ski Conditions:** ☎ 728-7425. **Road Conditions:** ☎ 249-9363.

Police: 160 S. Fir St. (☎ 728-3818). **Rape Crisis Hotline:** ☎ 728-5660.

Medical Services: Telluride Medical Center, 500 W. Pacific Ave. (☎ 728-3848).

Pharmacy: Sunshine Pharmacy, 236 W. Colorado Ave. (☎ 728-3601). Open daily 9am-9pm.

Internet: Wilkinson Public Library, 100 W. Pacific St. (☎ 728-4519), offers **free** Internet access, a phone for free local calls, and a beautiful place to read and relax. Open M-Th 10am-8pm, F-Sa 10am-6pm, Su noon-5pm.

Free Box: A Telluride tradition. People drop off stuff they no longer want and take stuff that they do. On the corner of Pine and Colorado.

Post Office: 150 S. Willow St. (☎ 728-3900). Open M-F 9am-5pm, Sa 10am-noon. **ZIP code:** 81435. Those in search of tickets and camping passes on big festival weekends might get lucky asking around outside the post office, near the entrance to Town Park.

ACCOMMODATIONS AND CAMPING

If you're visiting Telluride during a festival, bring a sleeping bag; the cost of a bed is outrageous, and many open public spaces are morphed into temporary tent cities ($40-90 for up to 6 days).

Telluride Town Park Campground (☎ 728-2173), east of downtown along Colorado Ave. Telluride offers affordable camping within walking distance from downtown. Particularly nice are the 5 primitive sites, which lie along Bear Creek removed from the road. Coin-operated showers $1.50; water, bathrooms, and access to the full range of facilities in the park (tennis and basketball courts, playing fields, pool ($3), kids fishing pond). 46 sites. 7-night max. stay. Open mid-May to mid-Oct., except the week of the Bluegrass Festival. Reception open M-Tu 8am-5pm, W-F 8am-8pm, Sa-Su 8am-4pm. $12 per vehicle; $10 primitive sites. ●

Oak Street Inn, 134 N. Oak St. (☎ 728-3383). Offers cozy, if sparsely appointed rooms for the lowest rates in town. Centrally located near the ski lift and downtown and sporting a sauna. Reception 8-10am and 3-10pm. Check-in 4pm. Check-out 11am. Reserve ahead for festivals and holidays. Singles $42, with private bath $66; doubles $58/$66; rooms around $20 more during Christmas and bluegrass and film festivals. ❸

New Sheridan Hotel, 231 W. Colorado Ave. (☎ 728-4351 or 800-200-1891). William Jennings Bryan delivered his historic "Cross of Gold" speech from the front balcony of the hotel, and if you can afford it, the luxurious rooms, complimentary gourmet breakfast, free Internet, and roof-top hot tubs make it worth your while. Reception 24hr. Check-in 2pm. Check-out 11am. Rooms with shared bathroom from $90, approximately double during big festivals. ❺

Matterhorn (☎ 728-4211), 12 mi. south of town on Rte. 145. This campground provides a little distance from the hubbub of Telluride at the edge of the vast Uncompahgre National Forest. 28 sites with access to water, showers, and toilets. 7-night max. stay. Open late-May to Sept. $12 per vehicle. Public showers $3. ❶

Priest Lake Campgrounds (☎ 728-4211), 14 mi. south of Telluride, and **Alta Lakes Campgrounds,** 18 mi. south, offer free campsites with primitive facilities. ❶

🔲 FOOD

Groceries are available at several small markets in town, including **Clark's** downstairs from the Visitors Center on Colorado Ave. at the west end of town (open daily 8am-9pm), but true to Telluride tradition, prices are through the roof. Stock up before arriving or be prepared to shell out for cuisine a cut above the American average. The little **hot dog stand** located on Colorado Ave. across from Elk Park grills up fat dogs that won't thin your wallet, with heaps of tasty toppings ($2-3).

■ **Baked in Telluride,** 127 S. Fir St. (☎ 728-4775). This mellow bakery has enough rich coffee, delicious pastries, pizza, sandwiches, and bagels to get you through a hungry weekend. The apple fritters ($2) are rightly famous and nightly dinner specials ($7-8) might be the best (and only) deal in town. Open daily 5:30am-10pm. ❶

Deli Downstairs, 217 W. Colorado Ave. (☎ 728-4004). This subterranean nook feels like a food stand at a Grateful Dead show crossed with a New York City neighborhood deli. Energizing sandwiches ($3.50-7) and homemade veggie burgers ($5) keep young patrons boogying and biking for hours. Open daily 10am-midnight. Cash only. ❶

Magic Market, 115 W. Colorado Ave. (☎ 728-8789). Grab a quick breakfast (buffet style, $7 per lb.) or lunch ($3-7) at this basement gem, or stock up on organic food products for your own creations. Lots of tasty vegetarian and vegan choices, especially salads. Open M-F 8am-8pm, Sa-Su 9am-5pm. ❶

Fat Alley Barbeque, 122 S. Oak St. (☎ 728-3985). The wooden benches and long tables are reminiscent of the sawdust saloons of yore, but Telluride's miners never ate BBQ ($5-17) like this. Telluride's large transplanted Southern population swears by the Carolina Pork sandwich and the sweet potato fries. Sides $2-5. Take-out available. Open daily 11am-10pm. ❸

🔲 🔲 NIGHTLIFE AND ENTERTAINMENT

Telluride may have a new-age air by day, but its bars still rollick with old-fashioned fun by night. Jiving with Telluride's hip, **Fly Me to the Moon Saloon,** 132 E. Colorado Ave., shines with some of the area's freshest musical talent, and thrills groovers with its spring-loaded dance floor. Jam bands like Leftover Salmon and The String Cheese Incident have played many a free show here. (☎ 728-6666. $1-5 cover. Open daily 9pm-2:30am. Cash only.) The lively **Last Dollar Saloon,** 100 E. Colorado, is a favorite among locals, who affectionately refer to it as "the buck." With the juke box blaring and darts flying, its not hard to see why. (☎ 728-4800. Open daily 11:30am-2am. Beer $2.75-3.75. Cash only.) The **New Sheridan Bar,** 231 W. Colorado Ave., (☎ 728-3911. Open daily 3pm-2am.) and the **Roma Bar & Cafe,** 133 E. Colorado, (☎ 728-3669. Open daily 11:30am-3pm and 5pm-2am. Dinner until 10pm.) are great places to end the evening.

Given that only 1900 people live in Telluride, the sheer number of festivals in the town seems staggering. For general festival info, contact the **Telluride Visitors Center** (☎ 728-4431 or 888-288-7360). Gala events occur throughout the summer and fall, from the quirky **Mushroom Festival** (late August), to the multi-sport challenge of the **360° Adventure** (mid-July) and, of course, the renowned **Bluegrass Festival.** (☎800-624-2422; www.planetbluegrass.com. 3rd weekend in June. Tickets $55 per day, 4-day pass $155.) One weekend in July is actually designated "Nothing Festival" to give locals a break from the onslaught of visitors and special events. The **Telluride International Film Festival** premiers some of the hippest independent flicks; *The Crying Game* and *The Piano* were both unveiled here. (☎728-4401. First weekend in Sept.) Telluride also hosts a **Jazz Celebration** during the first weekend of August (☎728-7009) and a **Blues & Brews Festival** (☎728-8037) during the third weekend in September. For some festivals, volunteering to usher or perform other tasks can result in free admission. Throughout the year a number of concerts and performances go up at the **Sheridan Opera House,** 110 N. Oak St. (☎728-6363).

▚ OUTDOOR ACTIVITIES

Sandwiched in the San Juans between the Mount Sneffels, the Lizard Head Wilderness and the Uncompahgre National Forest, biking, hiking, and backpacking abound. Ghost towns and alpine lakes tucked away to the south wow visitors. For a relaxed Rocky Mountain high, take the **free gondola** to San Sophia station.

HIKING

Jud Wiebe Trail (2.7 mi. loop, 1½-2hr.). This local favorite begins and ends in downtown Telluride, at the north end of Aspen St. and on Tomboy Rd. off Oak St. Of moderate difficulty, it carries hikers up 1200 ft. into the aspens in the shadow of Mt. Emma to marvel at magnificent views of town and the valley in just a few miles.

Bear Creek (4-5 mi. round-trip, 2-3hr.). S. Pine St. ends at the trailhead. This easy hike up Bear Creek Canyon passes the remnants of old mining operations as well as some good bouldering spots before reaching Bear Creek Falls. 1050 ft. elevation gain. Recommended Apr.-Nov. guide available at local bookstores.

Bridal Veil Falls (3.5 mi. round-trip, 2-3hr.). Trail begins at the east end of the Rte. 145 spur (Colorado Ave.). This moderate hike climbs 1200 ft. along a switchbacking jeep trail to the waterfall visible from almost anywhere in Telluride. At 365 ft., Bridal Veil is the highest waterfall in Colorado. Recommended May-Nov.

Sneffels Highline Trail (13 mi. round-trip, 6-10hr.). Trailhead at the end of N. Aspen St. (same as Jud Weibe). This difficult hike ascends 3600 ft. into the mountains to the north of Telluride. The loop trail affords spectacular views of the San Miguel Valley and the surrounding mountains. Recommended June-Oct.

MOUNTAIN BIKING

Good mountain biking trails include the **Mill Creek Trail** and **Deep Creek Trail** (starting at Jud Wiebe trailhead, 6.5 mi. one-way/18 mi. loop) west of town, which climb into the northern mountains, and the **Telluride Trail** south of town, which ascends the ski mountain and bombs back down (access from base or use gondola, contact ski area for details at 728-7538). The intense **Wasatch Trail** southeast of town makes for a technical all-day outing (begins at Bear Creek trailhead on S. Pine St.).

FLY FISHING, RAFTING, AND JEEPING

Telluride's rivers and dirt roads are a virtual playground for anglers, floaters, and drivers. Much of the San Miguel and Dolores Rivers is open to public fishing. Stop by **Telluride Angler,** a full service fly outfitter at 121 W. Colorado Ave., for advice or to schedule a trip (☎728-6230 or 800-831-6230. Wade trips from $185 per half-day/ $245 full-day. Best deal with two people.) At the same location, **Telluride Outside** runs whitewater raft trips, jeep tours, and mountain bike trips (all from $65).

More a runway to the mountains and clouds than a terrestrial highway, the San Juan Skyway soars across the rooftop of the Rockies. Winding its way through San Juan and Uncompahgre National Forests, Old West mountain towns, and Native American ruins, the byway passes a remarkably wide range of southwestern Colorado's splendors. Reaching altitudes up to 11,000 feet, with breathtaking views of snowy peaks and verdant valleys, the San Juan Skyway is widely considered one of America's most beautiful drives. Travelers in this area inevitably drive at least parts of it as they head to destinations such as Telluride, Durango, and Mesa Verde. Several exhilarating unpaved mountain passes depart the main road and promise extreme off-road adventure for experienced four-wheel-drivers. A hard-core cadre of cyclists embarks on the **"Death Ride"** every June near the full moon, attempting to complete the 236 mi. loop in a single day. Many sections of the skyway skirt steep drop-offs and involve driving curvy mountain roads. Call the San Juan (☎970-247-4874) or Uncompahgre (☎970-874-6600) National Forests to check road conditions or to inquire about driving the skyway.

TIME: 5-7hr. driving time

DISTANCE: 236 mi.

SEASON: year-round

A loop road, piggy-backing on Rte. 550, 62, 145, and 160, the skyway voyage can be started from anywhere along the loop, at towns such as Durango, Ridgway, or Cortez. Beginning in Durango, the skyway heads north along Rte. **550 N (Million Dollar Highway),** climbing into the San Juan Mountains, and paralleling the Animas River.

1 DURANGO MOUNTAIN RESORT. 27 mi. north of Durango along the pastoral glacial valley of the Animas River, the **Durango Mountain Resort,** known popularly as **Purgatory,** offers outdoor adventures in any season. Skiers will enjoy 11 lifts, including a high-speed, six-person super chair serving 75 trails (25% beginner, 50% intermediate, 25% advanced) and 1200 skiable acres with a 2029 ft. vertical drop. (☎800-979-9742. Annual snowfall 260 in. Open late Nov. to early Apr. 9am-4pm. $34-48, under 12 $17-29.) When the heat is on, travelers can trade in their skis for a sled and test out the alpine slide or take a chairlift ride to access over 50 mi. of mountain bike trails. (Open mid-June to Aug. daily 10am-6pm. Slide ride $8; mountain bike lift $5, all day $15.)

2 MOLAS PASS AND MOLAS LAKE. 15 mi. farther north on Rte. 550, the road peaks on the way to Silverton at Molas Pass (10,910 ft.). Breathe deep; researchers have allegedly documented the cleanest air in the United States in Molas. Here, on its way to Denver, the **Colorado Trail** crosses U.S. 550. The trail may be picked up at the pass or 1 mi. east at Little Molas Lake. **Molas Lake Campground ❶,** at the lake, 1¼ mi. north of the pass on U.S. 550, offers visitors 58 tent and RV sites ($14), cabins ($25), canoe rentals ($5 per hr.), horseback riding ($20 per hr.), showers, and picnic tables. (☎970-749-9254 or 800-846-2177. Open mid-May to Oct. 8am-8pm.) The Molas Trail begins at the lake and after 4 mi. connects with the Elk Creek Trail, a popular access trail to the Weminuche Wilderness. On the other side of 550, a turnoff down a bumpy road treats visitors to the relative alpine solitude of **Little Molas Lake ❶,** where primitive campsites are free.

3 SILVERTON. Falling to 9310 ft., the road enters this easy-going town. Savvy drivers plan to avoid the two-hour mid-day rush of tourists that pour off the narrow-gauge railroad to luncheon, shop and gawk. (See p. 334)

4 RED MOUNTAIN PASS. Here the drive reaches its highest point at 11,018 ft. This stretch of road between Silverton and Ouray, called the "Million Dollar Highway" in reference both to its scenic splendor and mining yield, is one of the most avalanche-prone regions in Colorado. The snow shed a few miles outside of Ouray protects the road from the deadly **Riverside Chute,** one of 59 avalanche chutes along 550 between Ouray and Coal Bank Pass (south of Molas). This section of the drive also showcases stellar 14,000 ft. mountain peaks and defunct mines. The small and difficult to reach area around Red Mountain Pass once held over 200 inhabitants in six now-abandoned towns. In 1991, the Reclamation Act shut down most of the mines, but you can still see remnants in the most unlikely places.

⑤ OURAY. The skyway next arrives in Ouray, the "Switzerland of America." With fabulous views and hedonistic hot springs, this town is a relaxing stop for the weary. Indulge at one of the preponderant chocolate and ice cream shops, or soak at the public hot springs pool along the main road near the Visitors Center. (Open June-Aug. 10am-10pm, Sept.-May noon-9pm. $7.50, shower alone $2)

Ouray also features the world's only **Ice Park**, on Camp Bird Mine Rd. (☎326-4061; www.ourayicepark.com; free), with some of the best ice climbing anywhere. The season runs from mid-December to mid March, with an ice festival in mid-January. Area guides include **Above Ouray Ice & Tower Rock Climbing School,** 450 Main St. (☎325-4879 or 888-345-9061; www.towerguides.com) and **San Juan Mountain Guides,** (☎325-4925; www.ouray-climbing.com). In the summer, the ice walls turn into waterfalls at **Box Canyon Park.** (☎325-4464. Open daily 8am-dusk. $2.50, ages 5-12 $1.)

⑥ TELLURIDE. This spectacular, self-consciously chic community awaits travelers along Rte. 145. From the **Lizard Head Pass** and its access to the desolate **Lizard Head Wilderness,** the skyway runs along the Taylor Mesa through the quiet towns of Rico, Stoner, and Dolores. Rte. 145 connects with Rte. 160 between **Cortez** and **Mesa Verde National Park.** (see p. 336.)

⑦ MESA VERDE NATIONAL PARK. Stunning **Ancestral Puebloan ruins** stand in this national park on top of a high plateau off Rte. 160. Moving east along Rte. 160, the skyway cuts through Mancos and finally returns to Durango. (see p. 344)

SKIING

Telluride Mountain (☎ 888-605-2579; www.telluride-ski.com) is one of the premier American ski resorts. With 16 lifts (9 high speed), over 1750 skiable acres, and 3500 ft. of vertical drop, the mountain offers some of the most extreme skiing and snowboarding in Colorado without extreme crowding. The season generally runs from late November to mid-April, with 309 in. of annual snowfall blanketing 66 trails (25% beginner, 36% intermediate, 39% advanced). Even self-proclaimed atheists can be spied praying before hitting the "Spiral Stairs" and the "Plunge," two of the Rockies' most gut-wrenching double black diamond runs. (☎ 866-287-5015. Nov. 26 to Dec. 20 and Mar. 31 to Apr. 6 full-day $51, half-day $40, children $29/$23; Jan. 6 to Feb. 13 and Feb. 24 to Mar. 30 $65/$51/$36/$28; Dec. 21 to Jan. 5 amd Feb. 14 to Feb. 23 $68/$54/$39/$31. Lifts open 8:45am-4pm.) For an even more intense experience, **Telluride Helitrax** (☎ 728-2062 or 800-831-6230; www.helitrax.com) offers Colorado's only heli-skiing. **Paragon Ski and Sport,** 217 W. Colorado Ave., rents bikes in summer and skis in winter. (☎ 728-4525. Open daily 9am-8pm, in ski season 8:30am-9pm. Bikes from $16 per half-day/$28 per day; skis and boots $20 per day.)

PAGOSA SPRINGS   ☎ 970

The Ute people—the first to discover the waters of Pagosa—believed that the springs were a gift from a divine source. Today, the town's Chamber of Commerce would be hard pressed to disagree. Pagosa Springs, some of the world's hottest and largest, bubble from the San Juan Mountains 60 miles east of Durango on Rte. 160, and draw visitors from around the globe. At the same time, the mountains and forests surrounding town have their own appeal, and Pagosa Springs (pop. 1900) makes a fine base for excursions into the heights of the Rockies.

■ ▶ **ORIENTATION AND PRACTICAL INFORMATION.** Pagosa Springs lies just west of the junction of U.S. 160 and U.S. 84 on the banks of the San Juan River. **U.S. 160** is the main thoroughfare through town. West of downtown, a series of strip malls line the highway for several miles. In the heart of town, **Hot Springs Blvd.** runs perpendicular to U.S. 160. Pagosa Springs is accessible by car via U.S. 160. The nearest airport and bus station are in Durango. The **Mountain Express** bus line, used mostly by locals, provides transportation along the highway and throughout downtown. (☎ 264-2250. M-F about every 1½hr. 6:30am-7:50pm. 50¢.)

The **Pagosa Springs Area Chamber of Commerce,** 402 San Juan St. (just of Hot Springs Blvd.), provides info on accommodations, food, and sights. (☎ 264-2360 or 800-252-2204; www.pagosaspringschamber.com. Open M-F 8am-6pm, Sa-Su 9am-5pm May-Oct., Nov.-Apr. Sa-Su 10am-2pm.) The **San Juan Ranger Station,** 180 Pagosa St., offers a host of outdoors info. (☎ 264-2268. Open M-F 7:30am-5:30pm, Sa 9am-12:30pm and 1-3pm.) **Juan's Mountain Sports,** 155 Hot Springs Blvd., has a selection of outdoor equipment and **rents bikes** at $15 for 4 hrs. or $25 for a full day. (☎ 264-4730 or 800-955-0273. Open June-Sept. M-F 9am-6pm, Sa-Su 10am-4pm; Oct.-May daily 7:30am-6pm.) Services include: **Piedra Laundromat,** 120 Piedra Rd. (☎ 731-4000); **Weather/Road Conditions,** ☎ 264-5555; **City Market Pharmacy,** several miles west of downtown at 63 N. Pagosa Blvd. (☎ 731-6000; market open daily 6am-10pm; pharmacist M-F 9am-7pm, Sa 9am-6pm); and **Mercy Home Health and Hospice,** 35 Mary Fisher Clinic (☎ 731-9190), near the City Market. **Free Internet access** at the Sisson Library, 811 San Juan St. at the corner of 8th St. (☎ 264-2209. Open M-W 8:30am-6pm, Th 8:30am-7:30pm, F 8:30am-5pm, Sa 9am-3pm.)

Post Office: 250 Hot Springs Blvd. (☎264-5440; open M-F 7:30am-5:30pm, Sa 9am-2pm). **ZIP code:** 81147.

⌐⌐ ACCOMMODATIONS AND FOOD. Pinewood Inn ❸, 157 Pagosa St., four blocks from downtown, rents 25 wood-paneled rooms with cable TVs and phones, several with kitchens. (☎264-5715 or 888-655-7463. Reception 7:30am-11pm. Check-in 2pm. Check-out 11am. Singles $35-48; doubles $55-80.) **East Fork Campground ❶,** East Fork Rd., is a quiet little spot 11 mi. east of Pagosa Springs offering many shaded, rarely crowded sites with toilets and water faucets. (☎264-2268. 14-night max. stay. $8 per vehicle. Open May-Sept.)

Daylight Donuts & Cafe ❶, 2151 W. Rte. 160, dishes out big portions of classic breakfast and lunch fare for just $3-5.50. (☎731-4050. Open daily 6am-2pm.) **Harmony Works ❶,** 145 Hot Springs Blvd., sells organic food and serves some interesting vegetarian and vegan options ($1-5) for breakfast, lunch and dinner. (☎264-6633. Open May-Sept. M-Th 8am-9pm, F-Sa 8am-10pm, Su 8am-8pm; Oct.-Apr. M-Th 8am-8pm, F-Sa 8am-9pm, Su 8am-7pm.)

◙ ⚑ SIGHTS AND OUTDOORS. Follow the sulfur smell to **The Springs,** 157 Hot Springs Blvd., right beside the Chamber of Commerce, where 15 different outdoor pools ranging from 89° to 114°F are available "to relax the body and refresh the spirit." (☎264-2284 or 800-225-0934. Open daily 7am-1am. $12 per person.) Across the street at **The Spa,** hot spring water is pumped into indoor mineral baths. Access to an outdoor pool and hot tub are also included in admission (☎264-5910. $8. Open M-F 1-10pm, Sa-Su 8am-10pm. Pool closed every other W for cleaning.) **Chimney Rock Archaeological Area,** 17 mi. west of Pagosa Springs on U.S. 160 and Rte. 151 S, is a national Historical Site containing the ruins of a high-mesa Ancestral Puebloan village, where over 200 undisturbed structures have been found in a 6 sq. mi. area. (☎883-5359; www.chimneyrockco.org. Open daily mid-May to late Sept. 9am-4pm. 2½hr. tours leave at 9:30, 10:30am, 1, and 2pm. $5, ages 5-11 $2.)

There is plenty of **hiking** around Pagosa Springs as well as easy access to the **Continental Divide Trail** from Wolf Creek Pass and the Weminuche Wilderness for longer **backpacking** trips. Some good treks near town include the **Cimarrona Creek Trail,** northwest of Pagosa Springs near the Cimarrona Campground, the **Quartz Lake Trail,** east of town off U.S. 84, and the **Anderson Trail,** which skirts Pagosa Peak north of town and includes the shorter trek to **Fourmile Falls.** Visit the **ranger station,** 180 Pagosa St. (☎264-2268), for more info, or pick up a guide to area hikes at the Chamber of Commerce office (see above).

Many excellent **mountain bike** trails criss-cross the area. The **Willow Draw** 18 mi. loop can be begun anywhere in downtown Pagosa Springs. From U.S. 160, head south on U.S. 84 to Mill Creek Rd. and follow the doubletrack dirt road across Mill Creek after the 3rd cattleguard. This intermediate ride offers a sense of seclusion while staying close to town. (700 ft. elevation gain. Recommended June-Oct.) To get to the 8 mi. round-trip **Chris Mountain Trail,** turn north on Piedra Rd. from U.S. 160 and follow it for about 6 mi.; turn left on FS 629 and follow it 4½ mi. north through the woods to the "Steep and Narrow Road" sign. This doubletrack ascent presents a variety of challenging terrain that will test technical skills. (800 ft. elevation gain. Recommended June-Sept.)

Wolf Creek Ski Area, 20 mi. east of Pagosa, claims to have the most snow in Colorado, and offers nice access to glades and bowls. Six lifts service over 1500 acres and 1600 ft. of vertical drop. (☎264-5639 or 800-754-9653; www.wolfcreekski.com. Adult full day lift ticket $42, rental $13.)

MESA VERDE NATIONAL PARK ☎970

Some of the most elaborate Pueblo dwellings found today, millennium-old sky-scrapers or, more appropriately, rockscrapers, draw the largest crowds. Fourteen hundred years ago, Native American tribes began to cultivate the relatively wet valleys of the area now known as Mesa Verde National Park. In the centuries that followed, these people—today called the Ancestral Puebloan, and formerly the Navajo term, Anasazi, or "ancient enemies"—constructed a series of expansive cliff dwellings beneath the overhanging sandstone shelves surrounding the mesa. Then, around 1275 AD, 700 years after their ancestors arrived, the Pueblo people abruptly left behind the dwellings whose eerie and stark beauty now captures the imaginations of thousands of marvelling visitors. Over 600 more years elapsed before local rangers chasing stray cattle stumbled upon the magnificent ruins of Cliff Palace in 1888. Established in 1906, Mesa Verde National Park was the first, and remains the only, national park set aside exclusively for archaeological remains. Ravaged by wildfires in the summer of 2000, parts of the park are marked by charred trees whose black silhouettes lend to the now-recovering mesa's flavor of eternity. Mesa Verde is not for the snap-a-shot-and-go tourist; the best sites require a bit of physical effort to reach.

AT A GLANCE: MESA VERDE NATIONAL PARK

AREA: 52,000 acres.	**GATEWAY TOWNS:** Cortez (p. 347), Mancos, Durango (p. 328).
FEATURES: Chapin and Wetherill Mesas.	
HIGHLIGHTS: Camping at Morefield Campground, wandering around the cliff dwellings at Chapin Mesa.	**CAMPING:** Morefield Campground $20.
	FEES: Weekly pass for vehicles $10, pedestrian or bike $5.

✈ ⁊ ORIENTATION AND PRACTICAL INFORMATION

The park's sole entrance lies at its north end, ½ mi. from a well-marked exit for the park off U.S. 160, 10 mi. east of **Cortez** (see p. 347) and 8 mi. west of **Mancos**. The park's main road runs 21 mi. from the entrance station to Chapin Mesa and the park headquarters. Fifteen miles in on the main road, a branch road heads out 12 mi. to Wetherill Mesa.

Car or bicycle is the best way to travel through the park. Nevertheless, there are a few other options for intra-park transport. **Aramark Mesa Verde** offers daily bus tours of the park. (☎529-4421 or 800-449-2288; www.visitmesaverde.com. Runs Mid-Apr. to mid-Oct. Half-day tours $32-34, under 12 $21-23; full-day $53/$41.) A **tram** runs on Wetherill Mesa from the parking lot at the ranger station. (Runs May-Sept., 30min. ride every 30min., 9:30am-4pm. Free.) **Gas** is available only at More-field Village, 4 mi. from the park entrance. Trailers and towed vehicles are not allowed past Morefield Campground; park in the lot just before the entrance station. Much of the park is wheelchair accessible.

Several facilities within the park are equipped to aid visitors at various hours and times of the year. The **Far View Visitors Center,** 15 mi. in on the main road, offers plenty of helpful info on the park and is also the only place to buy tickets ($2.25) for guided tours. (☎529-5036. Open mid-Apr. to mid-Oct. daily 8am-5pm, some-times extended to 5:30 in high season.) When the Visitors Center is closed during the winter, head to the **Chapin Mesa Archaeological Museum.** (☎529-4631. Open June-Sept. daily 8am-6:30pm; Oct.-May 8am-5pm.) In the summer if you arrive in the evening, the **Morefield Ranger Station** (☎529-4465) at Morefield Village is open from 5-8:30pm. Basic camping supplies and groceries are available at the **Morefield**

WHEN TO GO. Snowy and icy conditions often render Mesa Verde an undesirable winter destination. Summer temperatures can reach the 90s, and afternoon thunderstorms are likely in July and August. The best times to visit Mesa Verde are the late spring and early fall, when the weather tends to be fairly reliable and not too hot.

Village General Store. (☎565-2133. Open mid-Apr. to mid-Oct. daily 7am-9pm.) Public **showers** are offered at Morefield Village, as well as coin-operated laundry machines and a gas station. (☎565-2407. Open mid-Apr. to mid-Oct. 7am-9pm.) For **weather conditions,** call 529-4461; for **road conditions,** 529-4465. For non-emergencies, contact the **Chief Ranger's Office** (☎529-4469). There is a **post office** on Chapin Mesa by the park headquarters and museum. (☎529-4554. Open M-F 9am-4:30pm, Sa 10am-1:45pm.)

ACCOMMODATIONS AND FOOD

Lodging in the park is pricey. Rooms at Mesa Verde's only motel-style accommodation, the **Far View Lodge ❺,** are costly and not particularly interesting. (☎592-4422 or 800-449-2288. June-Aug. $100+, Apr.-May and Sept.-Oct. $80.) Even the park's **Morefield Campground ❷,** 4 mi. from the entrance station, hikes up the cost of liv-

Mesa Verde National Park

ing, but with 452 beautiful, secluded sites equipped with running water and toilets, it might be worth it. Public showers and laundry are available at Morefield Village. (☎564-1675 or 800-449-2288. Reception 7am-9pm. Check-out 11am. Open Apr. to mid-Oct. Tent sites $20, RVs $26.) Outside the park, affordable overnight options abound in nearby **Cortez** (see p. 347), as well as grocery stores and eateries.

☉ SIGHTS

A good starting point, the **Far View Visitors Center** is a 15 mi. drive from the entrance gate off Rte. 160. A comprehensive visitors guide and tour tickets are available here, as well as the attention of friendly park rangers. (☎529-4465. Open in summer daily 8am-5:30pm.) At the Visitors Center, two roads diverge in what *might* be called a wood. One of the roads heads to **Chapin Mesa**, which features the largest number of cliff dwellings, and the other runs to **Wetherill Mesa**.

The **Chapin Mesa Archaeological Museum**, along the first loop of the Chapin branch (before the dwellings), provides an overview of the Ancestral Puebloan lifestyle, and is a good place to start before exploring the mesa. (☎529-4631. Open daily 8am-6:30pm; Oct.-May 8am-5pm. Rangers lead **tours** of the cliff dwellings at Cliff Palace and Balcony House, each lasting about 1hr., departing every 30min. $2.25 tickets must be purchased at Visitors Center.) Tours of the spectacular **Cliff Palace** (Apr.-Oct. daily 9am-6:30pm) explore the largest cliff dwelling in North America, with over 200 preserved rooms, some of which are a few stories up and preserve plaster decorations in their interiors. The ticket-less can only view the ruins from an overlook along the road. The impressive **Balcony House** is a 40-room dwelling 600 ft. above the floor of Soda Canyon; entrance requires climbing several ladders and squeezing through a tunnel. (Open mid-May to mid-Oct. daily 9am-5:30pm. Tickets required.) In addition, a few self-guided tours of sites are accessible from Chapin Mesa. **Spruce Tree House** is Mesa Verde's third-largest and most well-preserved cliff dwelling and features a reconstructed *kiva*. This is the only dwelling open from November to March, when it is part of a guided tour leaving from the museum. (Trail ½ mi. Open late May to early Sept. daily 8:30am-6:30pm, Apr.-May and Sept. to mid-Oct. 9am-6:30pm, mid-Oct. to early Nov. and Mar. 9am-5pm. Tours Nov.-Feb. daily 10am, 1, and 3:30pm.) About ½ mi. north of the museum on the road to Far View, the **Cedar Tree Tower** and **Farming Terraces Trail** give a sense of what work was like on the mesa top. (½ mi. Open daily 8am-sunset.) Three miles farther down the road and 2 mi. from the Visitors Center, the **Far View Sites** are comprised of five mesa-top villages. (Trail 0.8 mi. Open daily 8am-sunset.) A more low-key approach to seeing the Chapin Mesa is the self-guided **Mesa Top Loop Rd.**, passing a chronological progression of ruins from the 6th to the 13th century. (6 mi. Open daily 8am-sunset.)

The long drive out to Wetherill Mesa illustrates the various stages of regeneration occurring in the forest, which has suffered not only the Pony Fire of 2000, but multiple other wildfires over the past century. From the ranger station, 1½hr. tours of sprawling **Long House,** composed of 150 rooms and 21 *kivas*, include a tram ride that passes a number of sites. (Open late May to early Sept. daily 10am-5pm. Tickets required for tour but not for tram.) **Step House,** also located on Wetherill Mesa, features a well-preserved set of prehistoric stairs as well as pictographs. (Open late May to early Oct. daily 10am-5pm.) On both mesas, walks in the early morning tend to be less crowded and cooler.

▨ HIKING

In addition to the guided and self-guided tours through many of the sites, there are some good day hikes around the park, although none would challenge an experi-

WILD FIRE During the summer of 2000, two tremendous forest fires ripped through Mesa Verde National Park leaving a charred, apocalyptic landscape in their wake. The Bircher Fire, which began on July 20, burned 6000 acres in its first two days, and then blew out of control, consuming more than 23,000 acres before the last flame was doused over a week later. The effects of the inferno are easily recognized in the barren hills surrounding the stretch of the park road after Morefield Village. However, Mesa Verde was far from done playing with fire. On August 4, the first day the park was open after the Bircher affair, the Pony Fire raged out of control on the western edge of the park. The blaze soon reached Wetherill Mesa and consumed the park's day-use facilities there. The mesa has been ravaged by fire a number of times over the last century and the drive to Wetherill clearly illustrates the stages of regeneration occurring in the forest. Despite the structural losses, thankfully there were no losses of life. More than 1000 firefighters from 28 states combatted these infernos. During the height of the Bircher Fire, over 3000 eggs, 250 lbs. of bacon, and 250 gallons of coffee were consumed by the crews. And that was just for breakfast...

enced hiker. Most of these trails are much less frequented than the rest of the park and make for a good respite from the crowds. Staying on established trails is critical to the preservation of Mesa Verde's archaeological remains.

The trails on Chapin Mesa require hikers to register at the Chief Ranger's Office before setting out. **Petroglyph Point Trail** begins from the Spruce Tree House Trail and ends near the museum. This 2.8 mi. round-trip hike affords good views of the Spruce and Navajo canyons as well as a few petroglyphs. **Spruce Canyon Trail** begins from the Spruce Tree House Trail and ends at the Chapin Mesa picnic area. This 2.1 mi. hike follows the bottom of Spruce Canyon before climbing to the mesa top, giving hikers the chance to experience the range of Mesa Verde environments.

None of the three trails leading from Morefield Campground require permits. **Prater Ridge Trail,** by far the most challenging in the park, begins and ends at the western side of the Morefield Campground. The 7.8 mile trail, composed of two loops (2.5 and 4 miles) which can be done independently of each other for a shorter hike, climbs the east side of Prater Ridge through a few different types of vegetation, and on a clear day provides incredible views of Montezuma Valley to the west and the La Platas to the east. Mule deer and birds flourish on Prater Ridge despite the apocalyptic appearance of trees charred in the Bircher Fire of 2000. **Knife Edge Trail** begins in the northwest corner of Morefield Campground and ends at the Montezuma Valley Overlook or may be followed back to its start. A 3 mi. round-trip, this hike follows an old road along the mesa top and presents great views of Montezuma Valley, particularly striking around sunset. **Point Lookout Trail** begins and ends at the parking lot in the northern tip of Morefield Campground. This 2.3 mi. hike, which switchbacks up the side of Point Lookout and offers good views of the Montezuma and Mancos Valleys, is a great spot to watch the sunrise.

CORTEZ   ☎970

Recently named one of the top ten pit stops in America, Cortez lives up to this title, for better or for worse, with the gusto of a Southwestern ranching community. The motels and service stations lining U.S. 160 abut the great pasture lands of Montezuma Valley as evidence to the fact that most of today's cowboys are less likely to be coiling a braided lasso than the hose of a gas pump.

■■ **ORIENTATION AND PRACTICAL INFORMATION.** Cortez is 40 mi. north of Shiprock, NM and 46 mi. west of Durango at the junction of U.S. 160 and U.S.

COLORADO

666. These two highways represent the town's main thoroughfare, called Main St. downtown and Broadway on the stretch headed south. The **Cortez Municipal Airport** (☎800-872-7245), 2 mi. south on U.S. 160/666, offers prohibitively expensive flights from Denver and Farmington, NM. Getting to Cortez requires the use of a car; the nearest train (Gallup, NM) and bus (Durango) stops are many miles away. **Save-A-Buck Taxi** (☎749-5009) does run throughout town, from 9:30am-2am.

Visitor information is available at the **Colorado Welcome Center and Cortez Chamber of Commerce**, 928 E. Main St. (☎565-3414. Open daily 8am-6pm late May to early Sept., 8am-5pm the rest of the year.) 10 mi. north in Dolores, the **Mancos-Dolores District Ranger Station**, 100 N. 6th St., provides lots of info on the outdoors. (☎882-7296. Open Apr.-Oct. daily 8am-5pm, Nov.-Mar. 8am-3pm.) Other services include: **Plaza Laundry**, 1419 E. Main (☎565-8467; open daily 8am-8pm); **Weather and Road Conditions**, ☎565-4511; **police**, 601 N. Mildred Rd. (☎565-8441); and **Southwest Memorial Hospital**, 1311 N. Mildred Rd. (☎565-6666). Free **Internet access** is available at the **Cortez Public Library**, two blocks north of U.S. 160 at 202 N. Park on the corner of E. Montezuma Ave. (☎565-8117. Open June-Aug. M-Th 9am-7pm, F 9am-4pm, Sa 10am-4pm; Sept.-May M-Th 9am-8pm, F 9am-4pm, Sa 10am-4pm.) **Post office**: 35 S. Beech St. (☎565-3181; open M-F 9am-5pm, Sa 11am-1pm). **ZIP code**: 81321.

▐▪▐▌ ACCOMMODATIONS AND FOOD. Cortez has no dearth of motel and fast-food options. The **Ute Mountain Motel ❷**, 531 S. Broadway, a blast from the 70s with shag carpeting and veneer furniture, has cheap beds. (☎565-8507. Reception 8am-11pm. Check-out 11am. Singles $26-32; doubles $30-42.) The friendly owners of the **Sand Canyon Inn ❸**, 301 W. Main St., keep the place immaculately clean and give it a little spunk. (☎565-8562. Reception open 24hr. Check-out 11am. Singles $36-51, doubles $44-65.) **McPhee Campground ❶**, 13 mi. north of Cortez on Rte. 184, offers 64 quiet sites above McPhee Reservoir looking out on Montezuma Valley. The campground is part of a well-marked recreation area west of the Rte. 145/184 intersection. (☎800-280-2267 or 877-444-6777. Showers $2. 30-night max. stay. Check-out noon. Open May-Oct. Tent sites $10-12.)

▧**Francisca's ❷**, 125 E. Main St., is a popular spot for Mexican food, and rightfully so. The white wicker gazebos are perfect for savoring large portions of fresh, original dishes, all for $5-9. (☎565-4093. Take-out available. Open Tu, W, Sa 4-10pm; Th-F 11am-10pm. No reservations.) The attached **cantina** (☎564-1880) features unique nightly drink specials ($3.50-7.50) and a $3 appetizer menu. Another good bet right down the street, the **Main Street Brewery and Restaurant ❷** at 21 E. Main, sports its own Bavarian brewmaster and some great beers ($2-4), as well as innovative pub creations ($6-12) like the $9 Bratwurst Burrito. (☎564-9112. Take-out available. Open daily 4pm-midnight.)

◪ SIGHTS. Visitors fresh from or en route to ancient ruins will find ample illumination of indigenous culture both millennia-old and modern. 10 mi. north of Cortez at 27501 Rte. 184, the **Anasazi Heritage Center's** large, expert exhibits enhance appreciation for the ancient inhabitants of the four corners region and the processes used to excavate their ruins. (☎882-4811. Open daily 9am-5pm Mar.-Oct., 9am-4pm Nov.-Feb. $3). In town just off Main at 25 N. Market St., the **Cortez Cultural Center and Museum** highlights the work of local artists and features drama and dance programs on summer evenings. (☎565-1151; www.cortezculturalcenter.org. Open M-Sa 10am-9pm June-Aug., 10am-5pm Sept.-May. Free.)

▟▌ OUTDOOR ACTIVITIES. Though not as charismatic as Durango, Cortez offers quite a lot to do in the outdoors. The region combines Moab's slickrock with Durango's mountains, making for great **mountain biking.** To the north and east of town, a number of rides climb logging roads and single track into the foothills of the La Platas near the towns of Stoner and Mancos. West of Cortez, there are several rides that traverse the rock desert mesa tops or follow the course of the Dolores River. Access roads to a number of the sites at **Hovenweep National Monument** (see p. 281) also make for some excellent rides. The San Juan National Forest **Ranger Station** in Dolores, 100 N. 6th St. (☎882-7296), and **Kokopelli Bike and Board**, 30 W. Main St., are good resources. (Kokopelli: ☎565-4408 or 800-565-6736. Open M-Sa 10am-6pm. Bikes $25 per day.) The **Dolores River,** a little-traveled waterway, offers fierce whitewater and great cultural sites. **Wilderness Aware** (☎800-462-7238) and **Rocky Mountain Adventures** (☎800-568-6808) both offer extended rafting trips. The recently designated **Canyons of the Ancients National Monument** covers 164,000 acres of canyon country north and west of Cortez which await exploration by avid hikers and ruins-seekers. The 6 mi. loop hike at **Sand Canyon**, accessible on the G Rd. on the way to Hovenweep, passes several serene cliff dwellings. The ruins at **Painted Hand** and **Lowry** are also worth a peek. Contact the **BLM** at the Anasazi Heritage Center (☎882-4811).

HOVENWEEP NATIONAL MONUMENT ☎970

Hovenweep, from the Ute meaning "deserted valley," was aptly named by pioneer photographer William Jackson in 1874, and today it remains one of the emptiest regions in the US. Those who have made the trip to this strip of land spanning the border between Utah and Colorado since its founding in 1923 have been treated to national park solitude (not always an oxymoron), and get to explore the six groups of Pueblo ruins, dating back more than 1000 years, that still hang precipitously from canyon tops around the monument.

■🚩 **ORIENTATION AND PRACTICAL INFORMATION.** Desolate roads usher visitors to Hovenweep. From Utah or Arizona, follow U.S. 191 to its junction with Rte. 262 E (14 mi. south of Blanding, 11 mi. north of Bluff). After about 30 mi., watch for signs to the monument. From Cortez, CO, go south on U.S. 160/666 to G Rd.; follow the signs to Hovenweep. The **Visitors Center** is accessible from both the Utah and Colorado sides. (☎562-4282 or 435-692-1234. Open daily 8am-6pm, off-season 8am-5pm, except when the ranger is out on patrol. $3 per person, $6 per car; National Parks Passes accepted.) For more info, contact the Superintendent, Hovenweep National Monument, McElmo Rte., Cortez, CO 81321 (☎970-562-4282). There is no gasoline or food at the monument. Aneth, 20 mi. south, is the closest spot for these amenities. The **Hovenweep Campground ❶**, a few hundred yards after the Visitors Center, offers 30 scenic sites ($10) with shaded picnic tables. Water and toilets are available, though campers must carry out all of their trash.

🏔 **OUTDOOR ACTIVITIES.** The most well-preserved and impressive remains, **Square Tower Ruins,** lie footsteps away from the Visitors Center. The 2 mi. round-trip **Square Tower Loop Trail** winds around **Little Ruin Canyon**, accessing **Hovenweep Castle** and the **Twin Towers**. A short spur trail, the 0.5 mi. **Tower Point Loop**, accesses the ruins of a tower perched over the canyon. Both of these walks are relatively easy and give a good sense of the Pueblo ruins in a short amount of time. The canyon overlook is wheelchair friendly. For the more archaeologically inclined, or those looking for a more serious hike, the outlying sites—**Cajon** in Utah and **Holly, Horseshoe & Hackberry**, and **Cutthroat Castle** in Colorado—are isolated and provide more of a challenge to reach. A 4 mi. canyon-bottom trail runs one-way between the campground and the Holly, Horseshoe & Hackberry ruins. All sites are accessible via dirt roads; a high-clearance four-wheel-drive vehicle is highly recommended. Directions to the outlying sites are provided at the Visitors Center.

The ideal way to explore the monument, however, is by **bike.** A couple rides are particularly worth trying. The **Horseshoe Ruins Trail** is a moderate 10 mi. round-trip loop along some great double and single-track, beginning 4 mi. north of the Visitors Center, at the Holly, Horseshoe & Hackberry turnoff. (500 ft. elevation gain. Best in spring and fall.) The **Cutthroat Castle Ruins Ride** begins 9 mi. northwest of the Visitors Center, and covers some of the same ground as the Horseshoe ride, but in a much longer loop. The 20 mi. round-trip trail is marked with sign posts and offers access to the Cutthroat Castle Ruins while affording some real desert solitude. Bring lots of water. (700 ft. elevation gain. Best in spring and fall.)

WEST CENTRAL PLATEAU

After spending days marveling at the Front Range of the Rockies, many tourists access Interstate 70 and propel themselves west at dizzying speeds, bypassing all of western Colorado, capturing only fleeting, auto-glass-distorted vistas. Paying homage to Grand Junction's self-proclaimed centrality, said travelers might purchase a night's lodging before continuing west to Moab, Salt Lake City, southern Utah, or the Grand Canyon. These road-slaves don't know what they're missing. Featuring two spectacular canyons, a heavily forested mesa with beautiful lakes and campgrounds, and a city with an acclaimed hostel and diverse food options, it won't hurt you to get out of your car and spend a couple of days exploring this region's relatively unknown attractions.

GRAND JUNCTION   ☎970

Grand Junction gets its name from its seat at the junction of the Colorado and Gunnison Rivers and the conjunction-junction of the Río Grande and Denver Railroads. Today, the name aptly describes Grand Junction's role as a transportation hub for the masses heading to southern Utah and the Colorado Rockies. While the city doesn't have the reputation of some Colorado hot spots, a unique mix of cowboys and computers makes it worth a closer look if you've got time to spare.

F **TRANSPORTATION. Walker Field,** 2828 Walker Field Dr., is the biggest airport in Western Colorado. Major airlines all fly to nearby hubs including Salt Lake City, Phoenix, and Denver. **Amtrak,** 339 S. 1st St. (☎241-2733), heads daily to Denver (8hr., $49-85) and Salt Lake City (7hr., $45-77). **Greyhound,** 230 S. 5th St. (☎242-6012), runs to Denver (5½hr., 5 per day, $35-37); Durango (5hr., 1 per day, $35-37); Las Vegas (11hr., 3 per day, $65-69); and Salt Lake City (6hr., 1 per day, $46-49). **Grand Valley Transit** offers buses throughout the area. (☎256-7433. M-F 5:45am-7:15pm, Su 8:45am-6:15pm. 50¢.) Taxi service is provided by **Sunshine Taxi** (☎245-8294). All the usual suspects for **car rental** are at the airport, including Thrifty (☎243-6626) and Budget (☎244-9155).

7 **PRACTICAL INFORMATION.** The **Grand Junction Visitors Bureau,** 740 Horizon Dr., Exit 31 off I-70, behind the Taco Bell, supplies high-quality city maps and allows visitors to check email briefly free of charge. (☎244-1480 or 800-962-2547. Open May to Sept. daily 8:30am-8pm; Oct. to Apr. 8:30am-5pm.) For outdoor info head to the **Bureau of Land Management,** 2815 H. Rd. (☎244-3000. Open M-F 7:30am-

4:30pm.) For outdoor equipment you can't beat **REI**, 644 North Ave. (☎254-8970. Open M-F 10am-8pm, Sa 10am-6pm, Su 11am-5pm.) Other services include: **Orchard Mesa Laundromat**, 757½ U.S. 50 (☎245-3203; open daily 7am-11pm); **weather conditions**, ☎243-0914; **road conditions**, ☎245-8800; **police**, 625 Ute Ave (☎242-6707); **domestic violence line**, ☎241-6704; and the **Community Hospital**, 2021 N. 12th St. (☎242-0920). **Internet access** is available at the Mesa County Library, 530 Grand Ave. (☎243-4442. Open M-Th 9am-9pm, F-Sa 9am-5pm. Sept.-May also open on Su 1-5pm). **Post Office**: 241 N. 4th St. (☎244-3400. Open M-F 7:45am-5:15pm, Sa 10am-1:30pm.) **ZIP code**: 81501.

▐▌ ACCOMMODATIONS AND FOOD. The lovely and historic **Hotel Melrose ❶**, 337 Colorado Ave., between 3rd and 4th St., beds travelers in the heart of the city. In addition to dorms, meticulously decorated private rooms are available. (☎242-9636 or 800-430-4555; www.hotelmelrose.com. Reception 9am-1pm and 4-10pm; call if arrival time will not coincide. Check-out 11am. Dorms $20; singles $35, with private bath $50; doubles from $65. Reduced rates off-season.) **Daniel's Motel ❷**, 333 North Ave., offers clean rooms close to downtown, some with kitchenettes. (☎243-1084. Check-out 10am. Singles $30-45; doubles $45-55.) In addition to a couple of RV parks close to town, camping is available at **Fruita State Park ❶**, 10 mi. west of downtown, off I-70 from Exit 19. (☎800-678-2267. 80 sites. Showers and hookups. $10-16. Entrance fee $4 per day.) Also, check out **Colorado National Monument** (see p. 351), and the BLM's free **Rabbit Valley ❶**, west of Fruita near I-70 (no water or facilities).

Ying Thai ❷, south of downtown at 757 U.S. 50, offers the best Thai for hundreds of miles in a homey setting. (☎245-4866. Open Tu-F 11am-2pm and 5-9pm, Sa 5-9pm. Lunch $6, dinner $9-15.) Massive, mouth-watering breakfasts ($4-8) are the specialty at the friendly and hopping **Crystal Cafe ❶**, 314 Main St., but the hot lunches ($5.50-7) and decadent baked goods don't fall short either. (☎242-8843. Open M-F 7am-1:45pm, Sa 8am-noon. Bakery open until 3pm on weekdays.) **Rockslide Restaurant and Brew Pub ❷**, 401 S. Main St., joins the avalanche of micro-breweries blanketing the nation, and serves as a Grand Junction nightlife fixture. The Big Bear Stout comes in an $8.50 half-gallon growler. (☎245-2111. Half-price appetizers M-F 4-6pm. Open daily 10am-midnight.) Lying between Denver and Salt Lake City, Grand Junction draws bands who refuse to drive 500 mi. between gigs; check local listings for concerts.

▐▌ OUTDOOR ACTIVITIES. Mountain bike trails near Grand Junction thrill riders with mountain views on rugged terrain characteristic of the Colorado Plateau. Several excellent routes begin just a couple of miles from downtown. The **Roller Coaster**, a moderate 8.2 mi. loop, can be reached by driving north on Horizon Drive from the airport to H Rd. Another trailhead 2 mi. southwest of town offers several options for loops with less ATV traffic and more challenging terrain. **Andy's Loop** (6.6 mi.), the **Gunny Loop** (10.3 mi.), and **The Ribbon** (12.8 mi.) also leave from the parking lot on Monument Rd. To reach these strenuous rides, take Exit 26 off I-70 and follow U.S. 6/50 to Broadway (Rte. 340) over the river to Monument Road. Turn left and continue 2.2 mi. to the parking area on the left.

COLORADO NATIONAL MONUMENT ☎970

Sitting on the outskirts of Grand Junction, Colorado National Monument is a 32 square mile sculpture of steep cliff faces, canyon walls, and obelisk-like spires wrought by the forces of gravity, wind, and water. The monument serves as a playground for climbers, bikers, and hikers from the local area, and an appetite-whet-

COLORADO

ting experience for travelers en route to the more thrilling destinations of Arches, Canyonlands, or the Rockies. The monument was established in 1911, largely due to the efforts and antics of one man, John Otto, who blazed most of the trails still used today and badgered the government to protect this wonderland of rock.

⑦ PRACTICAL INFORMATION. A car or bike is essential to explore the Colorado National Monument. Entrances lie at the east end, 4 mi. from Grand Junction on Monument Rd., and along Rte. 340 on the west end near Fruita (Exit 19 off I-70). The 23-mi. **Rim Rock Drive** runs along the edge of red canyons across the mesa top between the two entrances, providing views of awe-inspiring rock monoliths, the Book Cliffs, Grand Mesa, and the city of Grand Junction.

Check in at the monument's headquarters and **Visitors Center,** 4 mi. east of the western entrance, for info about ranger-led programs as well as a general orientation. (☎858-3617. Open June-Sept. daily 8am-6pm; Oct.-May 9am-5pm. Entrance fee $5 per vehicle, $3 per cyclist or hiker.) Both **Fruita** and **Grand Junction** provide a full range of services including equipment outfitters, ATMs, grocery stores, medical services, and post offices. For **weather and road conditions,** call 245-8800. **Water** is available at the Visitors Center, **Saddlehorn Campground,** and Devil's Kitchen Picnic Area, near the eastern entrance.

⑦ CAMPING. Saddlehorn Campground ❶, ½ mi. north of the Visitors Center, offers 50 beautiful sites on the mesa's edge, and never fills up. Sites include tables and grills. Summertime ranger programs occur nightly at the nearby amphitheater. (☎858-3617. Water and bathrooms, but no showers. Open year-round. $10.) **Backcountry camping** is free and allowed anywhere more than ¼ mi. from roads and 100 yards from trails. A free, required permit is available at the Visitors Center.

⑦ HIKING. Although Rim Rock Drive provides breathtaking views, the trails that criss-cross the monument are the only way to fully appreciate the scope and scale of this canyon country. Unlike some of the other parks in the Southwest, Colorado National Monument allows off-trail backcountry hiking for those travelers in search of respite from roads and crowds.

For those with limited time in the park, there are a number of short walks that whisk hikers away from the road and immerse them in the terrain. The 0.5 mi. round-trip **Window Rock Trail** leaves from a trailhead on the campground road and offers expansive vistas through piñon-juniper woodland over the Grand Valley, and views of Monument Canyon, Wedding Canyon, and many of the monument's major rock formations. The 1.5 mi. **Devil's Kitchen Trail** begins off the park drive just past the east entrance, and drops into No Thoroughfare Canyon and Devil's Kitchen, a natural grotto surrounded by enormous upright boulders.

There are a number of options for longer hikes in the monument. Most of these trails are fairly primitive and marked with cairns. The **Serpents Trail** follows "the Crookedest Road in the World," so named when it served as part of the main road to the high country during the first half of the 20th century. The moderately difficult 1.3 mi. route climbs more than 50 switchbacks from the trailhead, just beyond the Devils Kitchen Picnic Area, before rejoining Rim Rock Drive just north of the tunnel. (1000 ft. elevation change. 1.3 mi. with shuttle, 2.5 mi. round-trip.) The moderately strenuous 6 mi. **Monument Canyon Trail** is one of the park's most popular because it allows hikers to view many of the of the eerie, skeletal rock formations up close. The trail descends 600 ft. from the mesa top to the canyon floor and then wanders amid the giant rocks, including Independence Monument, Kissing Couple, and the Coke Ovens, until it emerges on Rte. 340 (Broadway/Redlands Rd.). A two-car shuttle conveniently allows for the trail to be done in one direction (downhill), but round-trip hikers enjoy the formations from multiple angles and can turn around whenever they fancy (ranging between 6 and 12 mi.) Find the trailhead along Rim Rock Drive, southwest of the Monument Canyon View. The **Ute Canyon Trail** begins along Rim Rock Drive, just southeast of the Fallen Rock Overlook. This challenging 14 mi. round-trip hike follows a maintained trail off the plateau and into the narrow Ute Canyon. An undeveloped route then traces the canyon streambed through cottonwoods and willows with views of a few arches. It may be combined with the Liberty Cap Trail for an interesting roundtrip. The **No Thoroughfare Trail** begins near Devils Kitchen and follows the Devils Kitchen Trail at its start. This strenuous 17 mi. out-and-back route accesses the most remote portion of the monument as it follows the streambed that cut No Thoroughfare Canyon, which features several cascading waterfalls during spring run-off. This hike makes for a good overnight trip.

UNAWEEP CANYON

The spectacular **Unaweep/Tabeguache Scenic and Historic Byway** winds its way 133 mi. through the heart of the Uncompahgre Plateau and some of the most varied terrain in Colorado. This drive follows Rte. 141 and 145 in the extreme western part of the state from **Whitewater** in the north (near Grand Junction) to **Placerville** on the San Juan Skyway in the south. Following the red rock canyons of the Dolores and San Miguel Rivers as they make their way westward to eventually join the Colorado, the road passes the remains of prehistoric Native American cultures as well as long abandoned mining operations.

One of the most striking sections of this drive is its northern end, as the highway passes beneath the towering gray cliffs of the canyon. The streams that eroded the canyon cut through typical Colorado Plateau sedimentary layers to expose underlying igneous and metamorphic rocks. Additionally, Unaweep is the only canyon in the world with a divide in the middle and streams running out of both ends.

This geologist's wonderland is fittingly a **rock climber's** as well. 25 mi. of beautiful granite make up the walls of the canyon with crags, boulders, and cracks. There are routes of every level of difficulty, rating from 5.5 to 5.13, and of every length from multi-pitch spine-tinglers to one-move bouldering problems. Unlike many choice climbing locales across the nation, Unaweep is virtually unknown among all but local climbers. The opportunities for outdoor recreation don't end with climbing, however; possibilities for **hiking, backpacking, and mountain biking** on BLM land and in the **Uncompahgre National Forest** abound. Be sure to respect property rights, particularly in Unaweep Canyon, where some of the land leading to climbing routes is privately owned. **Divide Road** (USFS), which leaves the northern section of the byway and traverses the Uncompahgre Plateau, provides access to hiking and biking trails as well as some choice sites for **free primitive camping**. Passenger cars can navigate the early miles, but high-clearance four-wheel drive vehicles are recommended for most of this alternative route across the plateau.

The byway may be driven in 3-5hr. depending on stops made along the way, and is a good alternate route between Grand Junction and points south, particularly for those headed to Telluride, Cortez, or Durango. The northern end of the byway is about 15 mi. south of Grand Junction off of U.S. 50. The southern end of the byway leaves Rte. 62 in Placerville. For more info, contact the Bureau of Land Management, 2815 H Rd., Grand Junction, CO 81506 (☎ 244-3000) or the U.S. Forest Service, Main St., Norwood, CO 81423 (☎ 327-4261).

GRAND MESA

Covered in a fine coat of aspen and spruce, the largest flattop mountain in the world rises over 6000 feet from the floor of Grand Valley with such grandeur and might that it seems the Rockies' final proclamation against the flat, barren deserts that lie to the west. Formed over millions of years by lava flows, glaciers, and the erosional forces of the Gunnison and Colorado Rivers, Grand Mesa today is sanctuary to a variety of plants and animals that thrive in this remote landscape of alpine forests, lakes, and lively streams. Outdoor enthusiasts also find the area exceptionally hospitable to hiking, biking, skiing, and fishing.

The **Grand Mesa Scenic Byway (Rte. 65)** traverses 63 mi. between I-70 in the north and Cedaredge in the south, climbing to over 10,000 ft. before winding across the mesa top. Overlooking Ward Lake on highway 65, the **Grand Mesa Visitors Center** supplies a wealth of information on outdoor activities (☎856-4153. Open late May to mid-Oct. 9am-5pm). A number of forest service campgrounds dot the landscape at heights between 8500 and 10,300 ft., providing cool, shady respite from the heat down below. **Ward Lake ❶**, **Little Bear ❶**, and **Cobbett Lake ❶** sit beside the highway in shady groves and provide quiet sites most amenable to tent campers desiring a base for exploration or a relaxing night's rest. (☎800-280-2267. 14-night max. stay. $12 per night.) Bring groceries, or sit down to home-cooked meals at **Spruce Lodge Resort and Restaurant ❸** on Forest Service Road 121 near the Visitors Center, where cabins that sleep up to 6 are available for $100-170 per week. (☎856-6240. Open 8am-10pm. Breakfast and lunch $5-8, dinner from $8.) On a clear day, astounding views surround **Land's End Overlook** at the end of a 12 mi. spur road off the byway. Panoramas of hundreds of miles of terrain, including the San Juan Mountains to the south and Utah's canyon country to the west turn jaws slack.

Powderhorn Ski Resort, 35 mi. east of Grand Junction on Grand Mesa, is small by Colorado standards, but it offers good deals and a less crowded counterpart to some of its glitzier neighbors. The mountain has four lifts accessing 510 acres of terrain, 80% intermediate or higher, with a base elevation of 8200 ft., a summit of 9850 ft., and 1650 ft. of vertical drop. Although the season only runs from December to March, Powderhorn receives over 250 in. of powder annually. (☎268-5700. Open Dec.-Mar. daily 9am-4pm. Ski rentals $15, snowboards $25. Full-day lift tickets $35, college students $28, ages 55-69 and 7-18 $25, over 70 and under 6 free.)

BLACK CANYON ☎970

Native American parents used to tell their children that the light-colored strands of rock streaking through the walls of the Black Canyon were the hair of a blond woman, and that if they got too close to the edge they would get tangled in it and fall. The edge of Black Canyon of the Gunnison National Park is indeed a staggering place, literally; watch for those trembling knees. The Gunnison River slowly gouged out the 53-mile canyon, crafting a steep 2500-foot gorge that claims the honor of having the greatest combination of depth, steepness, and narrowness of any canyon in North America. It's no wonder that Black Canyon wasn't fully explored until 1901, by a pair of brave souls on an air mattress. The Empire State Building, if placed at the bottom of the river, would reach barely halfway up the canyon walls. The youngest national park in the county, christened by President Clinton in the fall of 1999, Black Canyon has seen increased visitation over the last couple of years, but it is still possible to enjoy the terrain in relative solitude, especially for those willing to get on hands and knees and explore the inner canyon.

🛈 **PRACTICAL INFORMATION.** The Black Canyon lies 15 mi. east of the town of **Montrose**. The **South Rim** is easily accessible via a 6 mi. drive off U.S. 50 at the end of Highway 347 ($7 per car, $4 walk-in or motorcycle. National Parks Passes accepted); the wilder **North Rim** can only be reached by an 80 mi. detour around the canyon followed by a gravel road from Crawford off Rte. 92. This road is closed in winter. **Greyhound** (☎249-6673) shuttles once a day between Montrose and the **Gunnison County Airport**, 711 Río Grande (☎641-0060), and will drop you off on U.S. 50, 6 mi. from the canyon ($12). **Gisdho Shuttles** conducts tours of the Black Canyon and Grand Mesa from Grand Junction. The price includes entrance fees. (☎800-430-4555. 10-11hr. May-Oct. W and Sa. $39.) A **Visitors Center** sits on the South Rim full of information on history, geology, and hiking. Free **permits** for inner-canyon treks can be filled out here. (☎249-1914, ext. 23. Open daily 8am-6pm May-Oct.; Nov.-Apr. 8:30am-4pm.) **Water** is available here and at the campgrounds. The **North Rim Ranger Station** also provides **permits** and advice (open sporadically). Most services are in Montrose. **Cimarron Creek**, 317 E. Main St., caters to your backcountry needs. (☎249-0408. Open M-F 9am-5:30pm, Sa 9am-4pm.) Other services include: **weather and road conditions**, ☎249-9363; **police**, 435 S. 1st St. (☎252-5200); **crisis line**, ☎626-3777; **Montrose Memorial Hospital**, 800 S. 3rd St. (☎249-2211). There is free **Internet access** at Montrose Public Library, 320 S. 2nd St. (☎249-9656. Open M-Th 10am-8pm, F 10am-6pm, Sa 10am-5pm, Su 1-5pm.) **Post office**: 321 S. 1st St. (☎249-6654. Open M-F 8am-5pm, Sa 10am-noon.) **ZIP code**: 81401.

ACCOMMODATIONS AND FOOD. At the canyon, the **South Rim Campground** has 102 well-designed sites with pit toilets, charcoal grills, water, and some with paved wheelchair access. (Tent sites $10, full hookup $15). The **North Rim Campground**, a quarter mi. past the ranger station, offers more space, rarely fills, and is popular with climbers. (13 sites; water and toilets. $10.) Many inexpensive motels line Main St./U.S. 50 in downtown Montrose. At **Western Motel ❸**, 1200 E. Main St., a pool, hot tub, and continental breakfast make the clean, basic rooms a deal. (☎249-3481 or 800-445-7301. Reception 24hr. Check-out 10am. Singles from $45 in summer, $35 in winter; doubles and family units, which sleep 6, available.) The prices at **Traveler's B&B Inn ❷**, 502 S. 1st St., can't be beat in Montrose. Despite the name, no breakfast is served. (☎249-3472. Singles $32, with private bath $34-36; doubles $42.) **Nay-Mex Tacos ❶**, 489 W. Main St., serves up tasty Mexican cuisine that's easy on the wallet. (Open M-F 11am-9pm, Sa-Su 9am-9pm. Tacos $1.25; tostadas $3.) For tasty sandwiches ($4.50) and delightful omelettes ($5.50), head for the **Daily Bread Bakery and Cafe ❶**, 346 Main St. (☎249-8444. Open M-Sa 6am-3pm.)

OUTDOOR ACTIVITIES. The spectacular 8 mi. **South Rim Drive** traces the edge of the canyon, and boasts jaw-dropping vistas including the spectacular **Chasm View**, where you can peer 2300 ft. down the highest cliff in Colorado and across to the streaked **Painted Wall**. A little farther along, between the **Painted Wall** and Cedar **Point Overlooks**, a well-worn path leads to **Marmot Rocks**, which offer excellent **bouldering**. A detailed guide is available at the Visitors Center. Not surprising, the sheer walls of the Black Canyon make for a **rock climbing paradise**. This terrain is not for beginners or the faint at heart. Climbers must register at the Visitors Center. Several guide services have applied for permission to lead trips in the canyon; call the Visitors Center for current details. A couple of hiking routes skirt the edge of canyon, and provide a more in-depth experience than the straight-forward overlooks can offer. On the South Rim, the moderate 2 mi. round-trip **Oak Flat Loop Trail** begins near the Visitors Center and gives a good sense of the terrain below the rim. On the North Rim, the moderate 7 mi. round-trip **North Vista Trail**, which begins at the North Rim Ranger Station, provides terrific scenic panoramas such as **Exclamation Point** (3 mi. roundtrip) as well as some of the best inner-canyon views. When it comes down to it, however, dropping over the edge of the canyon and reaching the roaring **river** is where it's really at. From the South Rim, you can scramble down the popular **Gunnison Route**, which drops 1800 ft. over 1 mi. Allow about an hour for the treacherous descent, and even longer for the climb out. Or, if you're feeling

COLORADO

LIKE A CHICKEN WITH ITS HEAD CUT OFF

Clutching the bird in one hand, the farmer in faded dungarees picks up the wood handle of the gleaming axe. He holds the chicken firmly against the worn chopping block and with one clean, smooth motion, brings the blade slicing down across the rough, golden skin of its scrawny neck. Blood spurts across his bare forearm as he releases the mass of twitching feathers and flailing feet. In a second, the beast is on its feet and races around the farmyard—for two years! When Mike, **The Headless Chicken,** was beheaded in Fruita, Colorado, sometime in the middle of the last century, things didn't go exactly as planned. Rather than falling to the ground, dead as a doornail after a run-in with a farmer's axe, Mike managed to survive for more than two years. His amazed owners fed him with a medicine dropper and Mike toured the country to rave reviews. Today all that remains of Mike's legend are the tales told by Fruita old-timers and a piece of sculpture in downtown Fruita, depicting the illustrious Mike in full stride.

courageous, tackle the much more difficult **Tomichi** or **Warner Routes**, which make good overnight hikes. From the North Rim, **S.O.B., Long,** and **Slide Draws** cascade over the edge and serve as day hikes to the canyon floor. A free **wilderness permit** (from the South Rim Visitors Center or North Rim Ranger Station) is required for inner-canyon routes. Bring at least one gallon of **water** per person per day. In the canyon, unimproved campsites are dispersed on a beach along the river.

NEW
MEXICO

New Mexico can fulfill any outdoors fantasy. Skiers find fluffy powder and steep terrain around Taos, and hikers can choose anything from a one-mile jaunt around the rim of Capulin Volcano to a week-long trek in the Gila Wilderness. Mountain bikers traverse the trails of Lincoln National Forest, Carson National Forest and the Sandía Mountains, and water rats can find endless entertainment kayaking and rafting on the Río Grande Wild and Scenic River.

Outdoor adventures find their counterpart in the art museums and galleries of Santa Fe, the nightclubs of Albuquerque, and the pueblos of northern New Mexico. With a rich cultural mosaic of Mexican, Native American, and European influence, historical and geological discovery is a never-ending process in New Mexico, and travelers would be remiss not to tap into this rich past. After all is said and done, save some time to wander across white sand dunes, or relax in the warmth of natural hot springs. This land of enchantment has something for everyone.

◼ HIGHLIGHTS OF NEW MEXICO

ARCHAEOLOGY. Climb up 140 ft. of stairs and ladders to the Ceremonial Cave *kiva*, tucked into a cliff at **Bandelier National Monument** (p. 375). Hike between great Ancestral Puebloan houses at **Chaco Culture National Historical Park** (p. 396).

OUTBACK. Spend a week or two backpacking amongst some of the most remote wilderness in the country, the **Gila Wilderness** (p. 408).

HIGH ROAD. Explore the churches, pueblos, and Spanish farming villages, and drink the **holy dirt of Chimayo** along this popular drive from Santa Fe to Taos (p. 380).

ALBUQUERQUE. Hit the town for the best nightlife in New Mexico (p. 362).

ALBUQUERQUE   ☎ 505

Albuquerque is the crossroads of the Southwest. Anyone traveling north to Denver, south to Mexico, east to Texas, or west to California passes through this commercial hub. But Albuquerque is also a place full of history and culture, with many ethnic restaurants and offbeat galleries, quirky cafes, and raging nightclubs. Route 66 may no longer appear on any maps, but it's still alive and kicking here. Most residents still refer to Central Avenue as Route 66, and visitors can feel the energy flowing from this mythic highway—shops, restaurants, and bars on the thoroughfare emit an energy not found anywhere else in the state. The University of New Mexico is responsible for the town's young demographic, while the Hispanic, Native American, and gay and lesbian communities chip in cultural vibrancy and diversity. Downtown Albuquerque may lack East Coast urban sophistication, but it has a cosmopolitan feel of its own, deriving from its unique juxtaposition of students, cowboys, bankers, and government employees. From historic Old Town to modern museums, ancient petroglyphs to towering mountains, travelers will be surprised at how much there is to see and do in New Mexico's largest city.

◧ TRANSPORTATION

Flights: Albuquerque International, 2200 Sunport Blvd. SE (☎842-4366), south of downtown. Take bus #50 from 5th St. and Central Ave., or pick it up along Yale Blvd. **Airport Shuttle** (☎765-1234) shuttles to the city ($12, 2nd person $5). Open 24hr.

Trains: Amtrak, 214 1st St. SW (☎842-9650). 1 train per day to: **Flagstaff** (5hr., $59-106); **Kansas City** (17hr., $116-207); **Los Angeles** (16hr., $67-120); Santa Fe (1hr. to Lamy, $16; 20min. shuttle to Santa Fe, $14). Reservations required. Open daily 10am-5:30pm.

Buses: Greyhound (☎243-4435) and **TNM&O Coaches,** 300 2nd St. Both run buses from 3 blocks south of Central Ave. to: **Denver** (10hr., 5 per day, $64); **Flagstaff** (6hr., 5 per day, $41); **Los Angeles** (18hr., 7 per day, $76); **Phoenix** (10hr., 5 per day, $43); **Santa Fe** (1½hr., 4 per day, $12.60). Station open 24hr.

Public Transit: Sun-Tran Transit, 601 Yale Blvd. SE (☎843-9200; office open M-F 8am-6pm, Sa 8am-noon). Pick up maps at Visitors Centers, the transit office, or the main library. Most buses run M-Sa 6:30am-8:30pm and leave from Central Ave. and 5th St. Bus #66 runs the length of Central Ave. 75¢, seniors and ages 5-18 25¢. Request free transfers from driver.

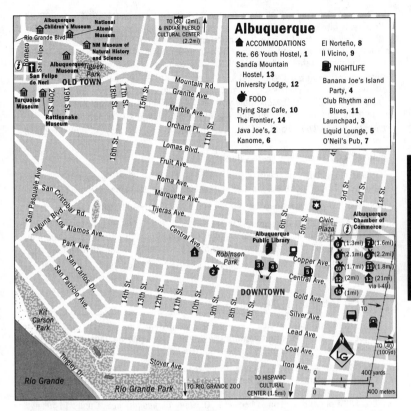

Albuquerque

🏠 ACCOMMODATIONS
Rte. 66 Youth Hostel, 1
Sandía Mountain
Hostel, 13
University Lodge, 12

🍴 FOOD
Flying Star Cafe, 10
The Frontier, 14
Java Joe's, 2
Kanome, 6

El Norteño, 8
Il Vicino, 9

🍸 NIGHTLIFE
Banana Joe's Island
Party, 4
Club Rhythm and
Blues, 11
Launchpad, 3
Liquid Lounge, 5
O'Neil's Pub, 7

Taxis: Albuquerque Cab, ☎ 883-4888.

Car Rental: Rent-a-Wreck, 504 Yale Blvd. SE (☎ 232-7552 or 800-247-9556). Cars starting from $20 per day with 150 free mi.; 20¢ per additional mi.; starting at $120 per week. Insurance $11 per day, $70 per week. Must be 21+ with credit card or $250-500 cash deposit; under age 25 surcharge $3 per day. Open M-F 8am-5:30pm, Sa 8am-4pm, Su 11am-2pm. Reservations recommended. **Enterprise Rent-a-Car** (☎ 800-736-8222) has 18 locations in Albuquerque, including the airport. 21+ with license and major credit card. Rentals start at $30 per day. Most offices open M-F 9am-5pm.

✈ 🛈 ORIENTATION AND PRACTICAL INFORMATION

Central Ave. (Rte. 66), is still the main thoroughfare of Albuquerque, running through all the city's major neighborhoods. Central Ave. (east-west) and **I-25** (north-south) divide Albuquerque into four quadrants. All downtown addresses come with a quadrant designation: NE, NW, SE, or SW. The adobe campus of the **University of New Mexico (UNM)** spreads along Central Ave. from University Ave. to Carlisle St. **Nob Hill,** the area of Central Ave. around Carlisle St., features coffee shops, bookstores, used CD stores, and art galleries. The revitalized **downtown** lies on Central Ave. between 10th St. and Broadway. Historic **Old Town Plaza** sits between San Felipe, North Plaza, South Plaza, and Romero, off Central Ave.

Visitor Info: Albuquerque Visitors Center, 401 2nd St. NW (☎842-9918 or 800-284-2282), 3 blocks north of Central Ave. in the Convention Center. Open M-F 9am-5pm. Recorded info 24hr. **Old Town Visitors Center,** 303 Romano St. NW (☎243-3215), in the shopping plaza west of the church. Open Apr.-Oct. daily 9am-5pm; Nov.-Mar. 9:30am-4:30pm. Airport **info booth** open Su-F 9:30am-8pm, Sa 9:30am-4:30pm.

Outdoor Equipment: 2320 Central Ave. SE (☎268-4876) sells camping and rock-climbing equipment, as well as kayaks and canoes. Open M-F 10am-6pm, Sa 9am-5pm, Su noon-5pm. **REI,** 1550 Mercantile Ave. (☎247-1191), at the Montano exit off I-25. Open M-F 9am-9pm, Sa 9am-7pm, Su 10am-6pm. Offers gear for sale and rent.

Laundry: Wash Tub Laundry, 1105 Central Ave. NW. Open daily 6:30am-11pm. Last wash 9:30pm.

Police: 5408 2nd St. NW (☎761-8800), at Montano.

Hotlines: Rape Crisis Center, 1025 Hermosa SE (☎266-7711). Center open M-F 8am-noon and 1-5pm, hotline 24hr. **Gay and Lesbian Information Line,** ☎891-3647. 24hr.

Hospital: Presbyterian Hospital, 1100 Central Ave. SE (☎841-1234), just east of I-25.

Internet Access: UNM Zimmerman Library (☎277-5761), at the heart of campus. Open fall and spring semesters M-Th 8am-midnight, F 8am-9pm, Sa 9am-6pm, Su 10am-midnight; in summer M-Th 8am-9pm, F 8am-5pm, Sa 10am-5pm, Su 10am-9pm.

Post Office: 1135 Broadway NE, at Mountain St. (☎346-8044). Open M-F 7:30am-6pm. **ZIP code:** 87101.

▐ ACCOMMODATIONS

Cheap motels line **Central Ave.,** even near downtown. Though many of them are worth their price, be sure to evaluate the motel before paying. During the October **balloon festival** (see **Sights,** p. 361), rooms are scarce, so call ahead for reservations.

▨ **Route 66 Youth Hostel,** 1012 Central Ave. SW (☎247-1813), at 10th St. Get your kicks at this friendly hostel. Located between downtown and Old Town, it offers a down-home feel. Dorm and private rooms are simple but clean. Key deposit $5. Reception daily 7:30-10:30am and 4-11pm. Check-out 10:30am. Chores required. Dorms $14; singles with shared bath $20; doubles $25; 2-bed doubles with private bath $30. ❶

▨ **Sandía Mountain Hostel,** 12234 Rte. 14 N (☎281-4117), in nearby Cedar Crest. Take I-40 E to Exit 175 and go 4 mi. north on Rte. 14. Call ahead and the owners will pick you up in Albuquerque. Only 10 mi. from the Sandía Ski Area, this large wooden building makes a great ski chateau. Comfortable living room with fireplace, kitchen, and a family of resident donkeys. Sandía hiking and mountain-biking trails are just across the street. Linen $1. Coin-op laundry. Wheelchair accessible. Dorms $12; private cabins $30. ❶

University Lodge, 3711 Central Ave. NE (☎266-7663). About a 15min. walk from campus in the historic and cool Nob Hill district. Unusually cozy rooms with cable TV, A/C, free local calls, and access to a pool. Reception 24hr. Check-out 11am. Singles in summer $33, in winter $28; doubles $37/$33. AAA and AARP discounts. ❷

Coronado Campground (☎980-8256), about 15 mi. north of Albuquerque. Take I-25 to Exit 242 and follow the signs. A pleasant campground on the banks of the Río Grande. Adobe shelters offer a respite from the heat. Toilets, showers, and water available. Office open daily 8am-5pm; see host to check in after hours. Tent sites $8, with water and electric $18. Remote shelters $11. Open W-M 8:30am-5pm. ❶

Turquoise Trail Campground and RV Park (☎281-2005). Take I-40 East from downtown to Exit 175 and go 4 mi. north on Rte. 14. A large campground up in the Sandía Mountains with trails leading up into the Cibola National Forest. Tent sites are shaded by trees. Showers and laundry available. Office open daily noon-8pm. Tent sites $11, each additional person $2; 4-person cabins $26. ❶

☐ FOOD

A diverse ethnic community, a lot of hungry interstate travelers, and one big load of green chiles render Albuquerque surprisingly tasty. The area around **UNM** is the best bet for inexpensive eateries. A bit farther east, the hip neighborhood of **Nob Hill** is a haven for yuppie fare, including avocado sandwiches and iced cappuccino.

■ **Java Joe's,** 906 Park Ave. SW (☎765-1514), 1 block south of Central Ave., and 2 blocks from the Rte. 66 Hostel. This lively restaurant with a laid-back atmosphere has hearty wraps ($5), sandwiches ($5.50), salads ($4-5), and great breakfast burritos ($3). Lots of vegetarian dishes and occasional live music. Open daily 6:30am-3:30pm. ❶

El Norteño, 6416 Zuni (☎256-1431), at California, is family-run and renowned as the most authentic and varied Mexican food in town. Shrimp roasted with garlic is a treat, and their extensive repertoire runs from chicken *mole* ($8) to *caldo de res* (a beef stew) to beef tongue ($7-9). Open daily 8:30am-9pm. ❷

Flying Star Cafe, 3416 Central Ave. SE (☎255-6633). This cafe soars beyond Starbucks to offer lattes, fancy pastries, and hearty lunches and dinners. An artsy crowd reads magazines and eats portabello mushroom sandwiches and Saigon wraps (both $7). Open Su-Th 6am 11:30pm, F-Sa 6am to midnight. ❷

Il Vicino, 3403 Central Ave. NE (☎266-7855), is possibly the best budget Italian in the country. No foolin'. Combinatoric pizzas ($6-8), calzones ($7-8), and lasagna for $7.25. Open Su-Th 11am-11pm, F-Sa 11am-midnight. ❷

The Frontier, 2400 Central Ave. SE (☎266-0550). If it's 3am and an insatiable appetite for some sort of ground beef product has you pressing hard on the accelerator, you'll wind up here. College kids, a friendly staff, lively-to-the-wee-hours atmosphere, and good eats. Remarkable breakfast burritos $3, green chile stew $2, burgers $2-3, sweet rolls $1. Open 24hr. ❶

Kanome, 3128 Central Ave. SE (☎265-7773), defies all conventional eating logic. No Albuquerque visit should miss this unique pan-Asian Tex-Mex fusion restaurant: the Ginger shrimp with scallion pancakes ($14) and the won ton nachos with slivered duck ($8) are must-haves. Open Tu-Th 5pm-10pm, F-Sa 5pm-11pm, Su 5pm-10pm. ❸

☐ SIGHTS

OLD TOWN. When the railroad cut through Albuquerque in the 19th century, it missed Old Town by almost 2 mi. As downtown grew around the railroad, Old Town remained untouched until the 1950s, when the city realized that it had a tourist magnet right under its nose. Just north of Central Ave. and east of Río Grande Blvd., the adobe plaza today looks remarkably as it did over 100 years ago, save for ubiquitous restaurants, gift shops, and jewelry vendors. Old Town is an architectural marvel and a stroll through it is worthwhile. **Walking tours** of Old Town meet at the Museum of Albuquerque. *(1hr. Tu-Su 11am. Free with admission.)* On the north side of the plaza, the **San Felipe de Neri Church,** dating back to 1793, has stood the test of time. *(Open daily 9am-5pm, accompanying museum open M-Sa 10am-4pm; Su mass in English 7 and 10:15am, in Spanish 8:30am.)* A posse of museums and attractions surrounds the plaza. To the northeast, the **Albuquerque Museum** showcases New Mexican art and history. The comprehensive exhibit on the Conquistadors and Spanish colonial rule is a must-see for anyone interested in history. *(2000 Mountain Rd. NW. ☎ 243-7255. Open Tu-Su 9am-5pm. $3, seniors and children $1. Wheelchair accessible.)* Tours of the Sculpture Garden are available Tu-F at 10am: free with admission. The museum also offers tours of the historic Casa San Ysidro in Corrales, NM. *(☎ 898-3915 for reservations.)* Across the street from the museum, Spike and Alberta, two statuesque dinosaurs, greet tourists outside the kid-friendly **New Mexico Museum of Natural History and Science.** Inside, interactive exhibits take visitors through the history of life on earth. The museum features a five-story dynatheater, planetarium, and simulated ride through outer space. *(1801 Mountain Rd. NW. ☎ 841-2802. Open daily 9am-5pm, closed M in Sept. $5, seniors $4, children $2; combination Dynamax theater ticket $10/$8/$4.)* No visit to Old Town would be complete without seeing the **Rattlesnake Museum,** which lies just south of the plaza. With over 30 species from the deadly mojave to the tiny pygmy, this is the largest collection of live rattlesnakes in the world. *(202 San Felipe NW. ☎ 242-6569. Open M-Sa 10am-6pm, Su 1-5pm. $2.50, seniors $2, 17 and under $1.50.)*

UNIVERSITY MUSEUMS. The University of New Mexico has a couple of museums on campus that are worth a quick visit. The **University Art Museum** features changing exhibits that focus on 20th-century New Mexican paintings and photography. *(☎ 277-4001. Near the corner of Central Ave. and Cornel St. Open Tu-F 9am-4pm. Free.)* The **Maxwell Museum of Anthropology** has excellent exhibits on the culture and ancient history of Native American settlement in the Southwest. *(☎ 277-5963. On University Blvd., just north of MLK Blvd. Open Tu-F 9am-4pm, Sa 10am-4pm. Free.)*

CULTURAL ATTRACTIONS. The **Indian Pueblo Cultural Center** provides a good introduction to the history and culture of the 19 Indian Pueblos of New Mexico. The center includes a museum, store, and restaurant. *(2401 12th St. NW. ☎ 843-7270. Take bus #36 from downtown. Museum open daily 9am-4:30pm. Art demonstrations Sa-Su 10am-3pm, Native American dances Sa-Su 11am and 2pm. $4, seniors $3, students $1.)* The brand-new **Hispanic Cultural Center** has an excellent art museum with exhibits that explore folk-art and surreal representations of Hispanic social and cultural life in America. *(1701 4th St. SW, on the corner of Bridge St. Open Tu-Su 10am-5pm. $3, seniors $2, under 16 free.)*

OTHER ATTRACTIONS. The **Albuquerque Aquarium and Botanic Garden** is on Central Ave., just west of Old Town. The aquarium features marine life from the Gulf of Mexico and has a 285,000 gallon shark tank. The Botanic Garden features desert plants and a butterfly conservancy. *(2601 Central Ave SW. ☎ 764-6200. Open Sept.-May M-Su 9am-5pm, June-Aug. M-F 9am-5pm, Sa-Su 9am-6pm. $5, children and seniors $3.)* The **Río Grande Zoo** has animals from around the world. *(903 10th St. SW. Open M-F 9am-5pm, Sa-Su 9am-6pm. $7, children and seniors $3.)* The **National Atomic Museum,** 1905 Mountain Rd. across from the **Albuquerque Museum,** tells the story of US nuclear weapons from Little Boy and Fat Man, the atomic bombs dropped on Hiroshima and Nagasaki, to the more sophisticated weapons of the cold war. *Ten Seconds that Shook the World,* a documentary on the making of the atomic bomb, shows on the hour. *(☎ 284-3243. Museum open daily 9am-5pm. $4, seniors and children $3.)*

NIGHTLIFE AND ENTERTAINMENT

If you're looking for a change from honky-tonk bars, Albuquerque will be an oasis. Hopping with interesting bars, jamming nightclubs, art film houses, and a large university, Albuquerque has quicker blood in its veins. Check flyers posted around the university area for live music shows or pick up a copy of *Alibi*, the free local weekly. During the first week of October, hundreds of aeronauts take flight in colorful hot-air balloons during the **balloon festival**. Even the most grounded of land-lubbers will enjoy the week's barbecues and musical events.

Most nightlife huddles on and near Central Ave., downtown and near the university; Nob Hill establishments tend to be the most gay-friendly. The offbeat **Guild Cinema**, 3405 Central Ave. NE, runs independent and foreign films. (☎255-1848. Open M-Th at 4:30 and 7pm, F-Su at 2, 4:30, and 7pm.)

Banana Joe's Island Party, 610 Central Ave. SW (☎244-0024), is the largest club in Albuquerque. With 6 bars, a tropical outdoor patio, a performance hall, and 1 big dance floor, Banana Joe's delivers nightlife to the masses. Nightly live music ranges from reggae to flamenco. DJ downstairs Th-Sa. Happy hour daily 5-8pm. 21+ Cover Th-Sa $5. Open Tu-Su 5pm-2am.

Club Rhythm and Blues, 3523 Central Ave. NE (☎256-0849). Great live music M-Sa with a crowd that's not afraid to get up and dance. World beat M, open mic Tu, Latin W, Jazz Th, and blues F-Sa. 21+. Cover M $3, W-Th $5, F-Sa $7. Open M-Sa 8pm-2am.

O'Neil's Pub, 3211 Central Ave. NE (☎256-0564), in Nob Hill. This friendly neighborhood pub has 16 beers on tap, Guinness included, as well as the famous Parrot Rum Punch ($4.25, happy hour $2.75). The pub also serves great hamburgers and sandwiches to its loyal crowd. Live music Sa 10pm-1am, Celtic tunes Su 5-8pm. 21+ unless accompanied by parent. No cover. Open M-Sa 11am-2am, Su 11am-midnight. Happy hour daily 4-7pm and 10pm-1am.

Launchpad, 618 Central Ave. SW, (☎764-8887) has concerts every night, featuring everything from reggae to roots to metal to indie rock. Cover varies. Open M-Sa 6pm-2am, Su 6pm-midnight).

Liquid Lounge, 405 Central Ave. NW (☎843-7299), is one of Albuquerque's up-and-coming, trendy bars. This swanky joint has Internet access for your laptop and live DJs. (Open M-F 11am-2am, Sa 4pm-2am.)

THE SANDÍA MOUNTAINS

Rising a mile above Albuquerque to the northeast, the crest of the Sandía Mountains is visible from just about anywhere in the city. The Spanish gave these mountains the name *sandía* (watermelon) because of the pink color they turn at sunset. The mountains' accessibility draws hordes of hikers, bikers, and rock climbers from spring through fall, while skiers and snowboarders descend on these snowy peaks in winter months.

HIKING

The Sandía Mountains offer hikes for all ages and abilities, but don't always provide solitude. Because of easy access from neighboring Albuquerque, the peaks are overrun by locals and tourists alike in the spring, summer, and fall. At least the 37,232-acre Sandía Mountain Wilderness allows a brief respite from cars and bikers. To avoid trampling this heavily used mountain range, stick to the trails.

Sandía Man Cave Trail (0.5 mi., 15min.). To reach the trail, drive halfway up Rte. 536 towards the Sandía Crest and turn right onto Rte. 165 at the Balsam Glade Picnic Area. The parking lot is on the right after 5 mi. Evidence of prehistoric humans has been discovered in the cave at trail's end. Bring a flashlight if you intend to explore the cave.

La Luz Trail (7.5 mi. one-way). This trail, which climbs the Sandía Crest, begins at the Juan Tabo Picnic Area. From Exit 167 on I-40, drive north on Tramway Blvd. 9.8 mi. to Forest Rd. 333. From the trailhead, stay on Trail 137 for 7 mi. and turn left onto Trail

84, which leads to the crest. Despite the length and difficulty of this trail, it is one of the most heavily used in New Mexico, so try to avoid going on summer weekends. It can also be very hot in the late afternoon. Rather than hiking the full 15 mi. round-trip, hikers can drive or take the tram (see p. 364) to eliminate one leg of the journey.

10-K Trail (6.5 mi round-trip, 3-5hr.). The trail begins along Rte. 536, 11.6 mi. from the junction with Rte. 14, at a well-marked parking lot. Follow the diamond trail markers along Spring Trail 147 3 mi. to an intersection with the 10-K trail. This trail eventually intersects with 130N, the North Crest trail: head north on this up the mountain if you've got some juice left. The trail continues further 2 mi. down the mountain.

North Crest Trail (12 mi. one-way, 1-2 days). This route makes for a pleasant backpacking trip through the Sandía Wilderness. From Albuquerque take I-25 N to Exit 242. Turn right after the ramp, drive east 4.9 mi. and turn right onto Tunnel Spring Rd. The road ends after 1.5 mi. From Tunnel Spring, the Sandía Crest Trail (#130) follows the ridge of the Sandía Mountains, offering great views all along the way. After about 12 mi. the trail reaches the Sandía Crest Recreation Area. Day hikers can arrange for a car pickup here; backpackers set up camp in the wilderness and return the way they came.

MOUNTAIN BIKING

The Sandía Mountains have excellent mountain biking trails. Warm up on the moderately easy **Foothills Trail** (7 mi.), which skirts along the bottom of the mountains, just east of the city. The trail starts at the Elena Gallegos Picnic Area, off Tramway Blvd. The most popular place for biking is at the **Sandía Peak Ski Area**, 6 mi. up Rte. 536 on the way to Sandía Crest. Bikers can take their bikes up the chairlift and then ride down on 35 mi. of mountain trails and rollers, covering all skill levels. (☎242-9133. Chairlifts run June-Aug. Sa-Su 10am-4pm. Full-day lift ticket $14, single ride $8. Bike rentals at the summit $38 per day. Helmets required.)

ROCK CLIMBING

The Sandía Mountains are blessed with thousands of feet of hard, granite cliffs, perfect for rock climbing. Many routes are accessible from the recreation area at the end of Rte. 536. There are also some good climbs along the foothills of the Sandías, near the Juan Tabo Picnic Area. The best spot for sport bolt climbing is along **Palomas Peak.** The parking area is at the concrete blocks along Rte. 165 between Mile 15 and 14, 3 mi. north of the Capulin Spring Picnic Area on Rte. 536. Albuquerque also boasts the **Stone Age Climbing Gym,** 4201 Yale Ave. NE. (☎341-2016. Open M-F noon-10pm, Sa 1-9pm, Su 1-6pm. $11 per day.)

SKIING

Sandía Peak Ski Area (see **Mountain Biking,** above), only 30min. from downtown, is a serviceable ski area for those who can't escape north to Taos or south to Ruidoso. Six lifts service 25 short trails (35% beginner; 55% intermediate; 10% advanced) on 200 skiable acres. The summit (10,378 ft.) tops a vertical drop of 1700 ft. (☎242-9133. Snowboards allowed. Annual snowfall 125 in. Open mid-Dec. to mid-Mar. daily 9am-4pm. Full-day $39, half-day $28, ages 13-20 $32, under 13 and seniors $28.) There are also excellent cross-country skiing trails in the **Cibola National Forest.** The North Crest and 10-K trails are popular with skiers.

SCENIC VIEWS

There are two ways to ascend Sandía Crest without breaking a sweat: the **Sandía Peak Aerial Tramway,** up Tramway Rd. from I-25 (Exit 234) or Tramway Blvd. from I-40 (Exit 167). The world's longest aerial tramway, it travels 2.7 mi. up the west face of Sandía Peak to a height of 10,378 ft. The view from the top overlooks Albuquerque and the Río Grande Valley—a 11,000 sq. mi. panorama. The ascent is especially striking at sunset. (☎856-6419. Open June-Aug. and during the Balloon Festival daily 9am-10pm; Sept.-May Th-Tu 9am-8pm, W 5-8pm. During ski season Th-Tu 9am-8pm, W noon-8pm. $14, children $10.)

One can also drive to the top of **Sandía Crest** (10,678 ft.). Winding through lovely forests of piñon and ponderosa pines, oaks, and spruce, the 12 mi. drive is unforgettable. To reach the road, take I-40 E to Exit 175, turn north onto Rte. 14, and turn west after 6 mi. onto Rte. 536. A ranger station greets visitors at the top, as do views of Albuquerque and the Cibola National Forest. A dazzling 1.8 mi. **ridge hike** connects the crest with the top of the tram. (☎248-0190. Open June to mid-Oct. Th-Su 10am-4pm. $3 per vehicle parking fee.)

⊞ DAYTRIPS FROM ALBUQUERQUE

PETROGLYPH NATIONAL MONUMENT. Located at the edge of suburbia on Albuquerque's west side, this national monument features more than 20,000 images etched into lava rocks between 1300 and 1680 by Pueblo Indians and Spanish settlers. The park encompasses much of the 17 mi. West Mesa, a ridge of black basalt boulders that formed as a result of volcanic activity 130,000 years ago. The most easily accessible petroglyphs can be found via three short trails at **Boca Negra Canyon**, 2 mi. north of the Visitors Center. The **Rinconada Canyon Trail,** 1 mi. south of the Visitors Center, has more intricate rock art and is an easy 2.5 mi. desert hike along the base of the West Mesa. To see the nearby volcanoes, take Exit 149 off I-40 and follow Paseo del Volcán to a dirt road. The volcanoes are 4.8 mi. north of the exit. To reach the park itself, take I-40 to Unser Blvd. (Exit 154) and follow signs for the park. (☎899-0205. Park open daily 8am-5pm. Admission to Boca Negra Canyon M-F $1, Sa-Su $2; National Parks passes accepted.)

MANZANO MOUNTAINS. The Manzano Mountains southeast of Albuquerque were formed in the same geologic upheavals as the Sandías to the north. The range reaches heights of 10,000 ft. and contains lush forests of ponderosa pine, birch, oak, maple, and aspen. *Manzano* is Spanish for "apple"—when Spanish explorers came in the 1700s, they found apple trees, a plant not native to North America. In all likelihood, the apples had been obtained by Native Americans by trading with other Spaniards. Despite their proximity to Albuquerque, the Manzanos receive little use, so campers and hikers can expect to find themselves alone with nature.

The quiet town of **Mountainair** serves as the gateway to the Manzano Mountains. To reach the town, take I-40 E to Exit 175, drive 30 mi. south on Rte. 337, turn right onto Rte. 55 and continue 24 mi. into town. The **Forest Ranger District Office** in Mountainair sells topo maps and is a helpful resource for hiking and camping info. (☎847-2990. Open M-F 8am-4:30pm.) There are six developed campgrounds in the Manzano Mountain region of the **Cibola National Forest** as well as another campground operated by Manzano Mountains State Park. Thirty miles south of Tijeras off Rte. 337, the free **Tajique Campground** is less than 1hr. from Albuquerque and has vault toilets but no drinking water. **Red Canyon Campground,** 15 mi. northwest of Mountainair, has vault toilets and drinking water (sites $7). The **Manzano Mountains State Park,** 13 mi. northeast of Mountainair, has the most facilities with flush toilets, running water, and RV sites. (☎847-2820. Tent sites $8, full hookups $14.)

The 37,000-acre **Manzano Wilderness** has some wonderful hiking trails. To access the **Red Canyon Loop** (7.5 mi. round-trip, 4-6hr.), take Rte. 55 north to Manzano and go 6 mi. on Forest Rd. 253 to Red Canyon Campground. Trail 189 climbs through the forest for 3 mi. and reaches a junction with Trail 170. Take Trail 170 for 1 mi.

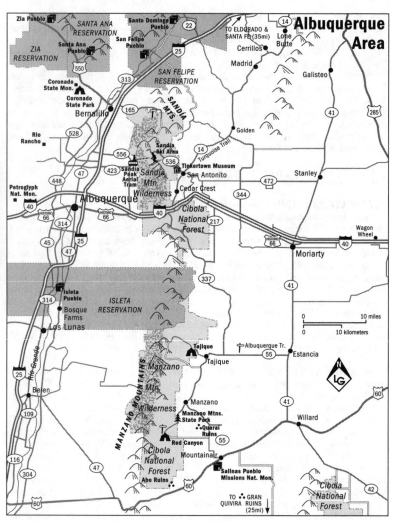

until the trail ends. Here you can go west off the trail for a few hundred yards to the 10,003 ft. summit of Gallo Peak. From this vantage point, you can see nearly 100 mi. of the Río Grande Valley and the Jemez, Sandía, and San Mateo Mountains. Back on the trail for 0.5 mi., Trail 170 meets Trail 89 in a large meadow. Trail 89 returns to the trailhead through Red Canyon, passing two seasonal waterfalls. The **Albuquerque Trail** (2 mi. one-way) is an easier hike through a grove of maple trees that turn brilliant colors in late October. The trail begins at a marked sign, 6.9 mi. east of the tiny town of Tajique along Forest Rd. 55.

Also in Mountain air is the main office for the **Salinas Pueblo Missions National Monument.** At the time of the Spanish colonization in the 17th century, the Salinas Valley had a thriving Native American population. Catholic priests forced the natives to convert to Christianity and build massive stone churches. Harsh treatment by the Spanish, disease, and Apache raids led to the abandonment of these villages by the 1670s. The pueblo ruins are well worth the drive from Albuquerque. Begin by watching the 15min. video at the **Visitors Center,** 201 W. Broadway, in Mountainair. (☎847-2585. Open Jan.-Aug. daily 8am-6pm; Sept.-May 8am-5pm.) The ruins are in three locations: **Gran Quivira** (☎847-2290), the largest site, is 25 mi. south of Mountainair on Rte. 55; **Abo** (☎847-2400) is 9 mi. west of Mountainair on U.S. 60; and **Quarai** (☎847-2290) is 8 mi. north of Mountainair on Rte. 55. (All 3 sites open June-Aug. daily 9am-7pm; Sept.-May 9am-5pm. Admission free.)

ROUTE 14: THE TURQUOISE TRAIL TO SANTA FE ☎505

The scenic and historic **Turquoise Trail** extends along Rte. 14 between Albuquerque and Sante Fe. Miners once harvested copious amounts of turquoise, gold, silver, and coal from the surrounding area, but the town suffered greatly during the Great Depression. Six miles north of I-40 and Exit 175 on Rte. 14 is the turnoff for Sandía Crest and the unique **Tinkertown Museum** (see **"Stuff,"** below).

Following the highway another 26 mi. north on Rte. 14 brings you into the former coal-mining town of **Madrid** (*MA-drid*). In 1898, the town had one of the state's first electric power plants, and during the 1940s, the town's coal mines supplied operations in Los Alamos. Today, hippie refugees populate the town, cranking out offbeat art instead of minerals. **The Old Coal Mine Museum,** 2846 Rte. 14, has an interesting collection of relics from the days when Madrid was a booming coal town. (☎438-3780. Open daily 9:30am-5:30pm. $3, children $1.) The locally-revered **Mine Shaft Tavern,** next to the museum, busts out the self-proclaimed "best burgers west of the Mississippi." (☎473-0743. Food served M, Tu, Th 11am-4pm; F-Su 11am-8pm. W Special dinners 5-7pm. Bar open M-Th 11am-11pm, F-Sa 11am-2am, Su 11am-midnight. Live music W 6-9pm, F 9pm-1am, Sa 2-6pm and 9pm-1am, Su 2-6pm.) If you need a pick-me-up on the road, **Java Junction,** 2855 Rte. 14, in the middle of town, offers lattes ($2.60), mochas ($3.10), as well as a selection of coffee-themed T-shirts and a one-room B&B upstairs. (☎438-2772. Open 7:30am-6pm.)

Three miles past Madrid towards Santa Fe is the ghost town of **Cerrillos.** In the 1880s this town, with 21 saloons and four hotels, was nearly chosen to be the capital of New Mexico. The 83-year-old **Cerrillos Bar,** at Main St. and 1st St., hasn't changed a bit since the town's peak. (Open daily 10am-9pm.) Farther north on Rte. 14 is an area of strange rock formations known as the **Garden of the Gods.** The Turquoise Trail ends 19 mi. north of Cerrillos at I-40, just south of Santa Fe.

SANTA FE ☎505

You're much more likely to encounter khaki-clad tourists than conquistadors in Santa Fe today; nonetheless, it is still possible to find places with character and authenticity in the cracks. Traditional adobe buildings adorn narrow streets that wind and curve, and, unlike in any other city in the Southwest, walking is still a viable means of transportation. Founded by the Spanish in 1608, Santa Fe is the second-oldest city in the US and the only state capital to serve under the administrations of three countries. Lying at the convergence of the Santa Fe Trail, an old trading route running from Missouri, and the Camino Real ("Royal Road"), which originates in Mexico City, Santa Fe has always been a place of commerce and bustle. These days, art is the trade of choice, with Native Americans, native New Mexicans, and exiled New Yorkers all hawking their wares on the streets and in the galleries surrounding the Central Plaza. In recent years, Santa Fe's popularity has

NEW MEXICO

NEW MEXICO

Santa Fe

🏠🏕 ACCOMMODATIONS
Black Canyon, **1**
Hyde State Park, **2**
Rancheros
  de Santa Fe, **17**
Silver Saddle Motel, **16**
Thunderbird Inn, **15**

🍎 FOOD
Cafe Oasis, **13**
Carlo's Gospel Cafe, **4**
El Farol, **14**
Tia Sophia's, **8**
The Shed, **7**

🍸 NIGHTLIFE
Catamount Bar & Grill, **9**
Cowgirl Hall of Fame, **10**
Paramount, **12**

🏛 MUSEUMS
Georgia O'Keeffe
  Museum, **3**
Institute of American
  Indian Arts, **11**
Museum of Fine Arts, **5**
Musuem of Indian Arts &
  Culture, **19**
Museum of International
  Folk Art, **18**
Palace of the Governors, **6**

skyrocketed, leading to an influx of gated communities, ritzy restaurants, and Californian millionaires. As a result, Santa Fe can be expensive, but the fabulous art museums, traditional churches, and mountain trails make it a worthwhile stop.

📠 TRANSPORTATION

Buses: Greyhound, 858 St. Michael's Dr. (☎471-0008). To: **Albuquerque** (1½hr., 4 per day, $12.60); **Denver** (8-10hr., 4 per day, $59); **Taos** (1½hr., 2 per day, $15.75). Open M-F 7am-5:30pm and 7:30-9:45pm, Sa-Su 7-9am, 12:30-1:30pm, 3:30-5pm, and 7:30-9:30pm.

Trains: Amtrak's nearest station is in Lamy (☎466-4511), 18 mi. south on U.S. 285. 1 train daily to: **Albuquerque** (1hr., $20); **Flagstaff** (7hr., $63-113); **Kansas City** (17hr., $108-192); **Los Angeles** (18½hr., $71-127). Call 982-8829 in advance for a shuttle to Santa Fe ($14). Open daily 9:30am-6:30pm.

Public Transit: Santa Fe Trails (☎955-2001) runs 9 downtown bus routes (M-F 6am-10pm, Sa 8am-8pm). Most bus routes start at the downtown Sheridan Transit Center, 1 block from the plaza between Marcy St. and Palace Ave. Buses #21-24 go down Cerrillos Rd., #10 goes to the museums on Camino Lejo, #5 goes to the Greyhound station. 50¢, ages 6-12 25¢; day pass $1. **Sandía Shuttle Express** (☎474-5696 or 888-775-

5696) runs to the Albuquerque airport (10 per day, $23) from downtown hotels. Reserve at least 1 day in advance. Open M-F 7am-6pm, Sa-Su 7am-5pm.

Car Rental: Enterprise Rent-a-Car, 2641 Cerrillos Rd. (☎473-3600). $45 per day, $240 per week. Must be 21+ with driver's license and major credit card. Open M-F 8am-6pm, Sa 9am-noon. **Advantage Rent-a-Car,** 1907 St. Michael's Dr. $35 per day, $175 per week. $15 per day surcharge for ages 21-24. Open M-F 7:30am-6pm, Sa 8am-4pm.

Bike Rental: Sun Mountain Bike Co., 2 locations at 107 Washington Ave, 1 block north of the Plaza, and 905 St. Francis Dr. (☎820-2902). Rentals for 1 day $28, extended rental $15 per day. Open daily 9am-5pm.

Taxis: Capital City Taxi, ☎438-0000.

✦ 🛈 ORIENTATION AND PRACTICAL INFORMATION

Santa Fe, abutting the Sangre de Cristo Mountains, stands at an elevation of 7000 ft., 58 mi. northeast of Albuquerque on I-25. The streets of downtown Santa Fe seem to wend and wander without rhyme or reason. It is helpful to think of Santa Fe as a wagon wheel, with the Plaza in the center and roads leading outwards like spokes. **Paseo de Peralta** forms a loop around the downtown area, and the main roads leading out towards I-25 are Cerrillos Rd., St. Francis Dr., and Old Santa Fe Trail. Except for the museums southeast of the city center, most upscale restaurants and sights in Santa Fe cluster within a few blocks of the **downtown plaza** and inside the loop formed by the **Paseo de Peralta.** Narrow streets make driving troublesome; park your car and pound the pavement. You'll find **parking lots** behind Santa Fe Village, near Sena Plaza, and one block east of the Federal Courthouse near the plaza, while metered spaces (2hr. maximum) line the streets south of the plaza. Parking is also available along the streets near the galleries on Canyon Rd.

Visitor Information: Visitors Information Center, 491 Old Santa Fe Trail (☎875-7400 or 800-545-2040). Open daily 8am-6:30pm; off-season 8am-5pm. **Santa Fe Convention and Visitors Bureau,** 201 W. Marcy St. (☎800-777-2489 or 955-6200). Open M-F 8am-5pm. **Info booth,** at the northwest corner of the plaza, next to the First National Bank. Open mid-May to Aug. daily 9:30am-4:30pm.

Equipment Rental: Wild Mountain Outfitters, 541 W. Cordova Rd. (☎986-1152), has the largest selection of hiking, camping and climbing gear in Santa Fe. Open M-Sa 9am-7pm, Su 10am-5pm. **Sangre de Cristo Mountain Works,** 328 S. Guadalupe St. (☎984-8221), rents tents and backpacks to prospective campers. Open M-F 10am-7pm, Sa 10am-6pm, Su noon-5pm.

Hotlines: Rape Abuse (☎986-9111), on-call 24hr. **Gay and Lesbian Information Line,** ☎891-3647.

Police: 2515 Camino Entrada (☎955-5033).

Hospital: St. Vincent Hospital, 455 St. Michael's Dr. (☎983-3361).

Laundry: Adobe Laundromat, 411 W. Water St. (☎982-9063). Open daily 6:30am-9pm. Last wash 8pm.

Internet Access: Santa Fe Public Library, 145 Washington Ave. (☎955-6781), 1 block northeast of the Plaza. Open M-Th 10am-9pm, F-Sa 10am-6pm, Su 1-5pm.

Post Office: 120 S. Federal Pl. (☎988-6351), next to the courthouse. Open M-F 7:30am-5:45pm, Sa 9am-1pm. **ZIP code:** 87501.

ACCOMMODATIONS AND CAMPING

Hotels in Santa Fe tend toward the expensive side. As early as May, they become swamped with requests for rooms during **Indian Market** (3rd week of Aug.) and **Fiesta de Santa Fe** (2nd weekend of Sept.). Make reservations early or plan to sleep in your car. In general, the motels along **Cerrillos Rd.** have the best prices, but even these places run $40-60 per night. For budget travelers, nearby camping is pleasant even during the summer and is much easier on the wallet. Two popular sites for free primitive camping are **Big Tesuque ❶** and **Ski Basin Campgrounds ❶** on national forest land. These campgrounds are both off Rte. 475 up toward the Ski Basin and have pit toilets.

Thunderbird Inn, 1821 Cerrillos Rd. (☎983-4397). Slightly farther from town than the hostel, but an excellent value (for Santa Fe, anyway). Large rooms, some with fridge and microwave, all with A/C and cable TV. Reception 24hr. Summer singles $50-55; doubles $55-60; winter $39-44/$44-49. ❸

Silver Saddle Motel, 2810 Cerrillos Rd. (☎471-7663). Beautiful adobe motel rooms decorated with cowboy paraphernalia have A/C and cable TV. Reception 6am-11:30pm. Summer singles $67, winter $45; doubles $72/$50. ❹

Rancheros de Santa Fe, 736 Old Las Vegas Hwy. (☎466-3482). Take I-25 N to Exit 290, turn left and make an immediate right onto Old Las Vegas Highway. Big, friendly campground with 23 acres of land, swimming pool, laundry, groceries, and nightly movies. Tent sites in a secluded wooded area with fire pits and nearby showers. Sites $19, full hookups $30; 2-bed rustic cabins $40. ❷

Hyde State Park Campground (☎983-7175), 8 mi. from Santa Fe on Rte. 475, has over 50 sites in the forest with water, pit toilets, fire rings, and shelters. Tent sites $10, hookups $14. No reservations for tent sites. ❶

Black Canyon Campground, (☎753-7331; reservations 877-444-6777) 7 mi. from Santa Fe on Rte. 475, is run by the Santa Fe National Forest. Sites in the pine forest have pit toilets, water, and grills. No hookups. Tent sites $9. Reservations accepted. ❶

FOOD

Spicy Mexican food served on blue corn tortillas is a Santa Fe staple. Bistros near the plaza dish up savory chiles to tourists, businessmen, and local artists, but most run $20 an entree. Cheaper alternatives lie south of the plaza on Cerrillos and on Guadalupe St. Wandering down side streets uncovers smaller Mexican restaurants where the locals eat; grill carts in the plaza can sell you fragrant fajitas ($3) and fresh lemonade ($1). **Albertson's,** 199 Paseo de Paralta, ½ mi. northwest of the plaza in the De Vargas Mall, is the closest supermarket to downtown. (☎988-2804. Open daily 6am-midnight.) The **Santa Fe Farmers' Market** (☎983-4098), at the Rail-yard near the intersection of Guadalupe St. and Paseo de Peralta, has fresh fruits and vegetables. (Open late Apr. to early Nov. Tu, Sa 7am-noon. Call to inquire about indoor winter location and hours.) If you just can't get enough of New Mexican cuisine, consider taking a 2½hr. cooking class at the **Santa Fe School of Cooking,** 116 W. San Francisco St. (☎983-7540. Courses $40-60.)

Tia Sophia's, 210 W. San Francisco St. (☎983-9880). It looks and feels like a diner (the servers are quick and curt), but the food is exceptional. The most popular item is the Atrisco plate ($6)—chile stew, cheese enchilada, beans, *posole,* and a *sopapilla.* Arrive before noon for the fastest service. Open M-Sa 7am-2pm. ❶

■ **Cafe Oasis,** 526 Galisteo St. (☎983-9599), at Paseo de Peralta. All the food is organic at this laid-back restaurant that feels like a hippie commune. The collection of dining rooms includes the Tahitian Tea Room, the Mystic Room, the Victorian Room, the Mushroom and an outdoor patio garden lit with torches and lanterns at night. Creative dishes range from veggie enchiladas ($10) to *Samari* stir-fry ($13). Breakfast served all the time. Live music nightly. Open M-W 10am-midnight, Th-F 10am-2am, Sa 9am-2am, Su 9am-midnight. ❸

The Shed, 113½ E. Palace Ave. (☎982-9030), up the street from the plaza, feels like an open garden, even in the enclosed section. Lots of vegetarian dishes including quesadillas ($6) and excellent blue corn burritos ($8.50). Meat-eaters will enjoy the amazing chicken enchilada verde ($9). Lunch M-Sa 11am-2:30pm, dinner M-Sa 5:30-9pm. ❷

Carlo's Gospel Cafe, 125 Lincoln St. #117 inside the mall (☎983-1841). A popular spot with locals, Carlo's is pure temptation with devilishly stacked sandwiches ($5 and up) and biblically-rich pies. Open M-Sa 11am-3pm. ❷

El Farol, 808 Canyon Rd. (☎983-9912). This upscale Spanish bistro has a bar with nightly live music and spectacular tapas. Flamenco shows W 7 and 9pm. Cover W-Th $5, F-Sa $7. Open M-F 11am-1:30am, Sa 10am-1:30am, Su 10am-11:30pm. Live music starts at 8:30pm. ❹

◉ OLD-STYLE SIGHTS

The grassy **Plaza de Santa Fe** is a good starting point for exploring the museums, sanctuaries, and galleries of the city. Since 1609, the plaza has been the site of religious ceremonies, military gatherings, markets, cockfights, and public punishments—now it holds ritzy shops and loitering tourists. Historic **walking tours** leave from the blue doors of the Palace of the Governors on Lincoln St. (May-Oct., M-Sa 10:15am. $10.) **Fiesta Tours** offers 75min. open-air van tours from the corner of Lincoln St. and Palace Ave. (☎983-1570. 3-6 per day. $7, children $4.)

MNM MUSEUMS. Sante Fe is home to six world-class and imaginative museums. Four are run by **The Museum of New Mexico.** They all hold the same hours and charge the same admission. A worthwhile four-day pass ($15) includes admission to all four museums; it can be purchased at any of them. (☎827-6463. Open Tu-Su 10am-5pm; single visit $7, under 17 free. The 2 downtown museums—Fine Arts and Palace of the Governors—are both free on F 5-8pm.) Inhabiting a large adobe building on the northwest corner of the plaza the **Museum of Fine Arts** dazzles visitors with the works of major Southwestern artists, as well as contemporary exhibits of often controversial American art. (107 W. Palace Ave. ☎476-5072. Open daily 10am-5pm) The **Palace of the Governors,** on the north side of the plaza, is the oldest public building in the US and was the seat of seven successive governments after its construction in 1610. The *haciendas* palace is now a museum with exhibits on Native American, Southwestern, and New Mexican history, with an interesting exhibit on Jewish Pioneers. (107 W. Palace Ave. ☎476-5100.) The most unique museums in town are 2½ mi. south of the Plaza on Old Santa Fe Trail. The fascinating **Museum of International Folk Art,** houses the Girard Collection, which includes over 10,000 handmade dolls, doll houses, and other toys from around the world. The miniature village scenes are straight out of a fairy tale. Other galleries hold changing ethnographic exhibits. (706 Camino Lejo. ☎476-1200.) Next door, the **Museum of American Indian Arts and Culture** displays Native American photos and artifacts. (710 Camino Lejo. ☎476-1250.)

OTHER PLAZA MUSEUMS. While the two other Sante Fe museums have no affiliation with the Museum of New Mexico, they are just as worthwhile. The popular

Georgia O'Keeffe Museum attracts the masses with O'Keeffe's famous—and famously suggestive—flower paintings, as well as some of her more abstract works. Spanning her entire life, the museum's collection demonstrates the artist's versatility. *(217 Johnson St. ☎ 946-1017. Open daily 10am-5pm. $8, under 17 and students with ID free; F 5-8pm free. Audio tour $5.)* The **Institute of American Indian Arts Museum,** downtown, houses an extensive collection of contemporary Indian art with an intense political edge. *(108 Cathedral Place. ☎ 983-8900. Open M-Sa 9am-5pm, Su noon-5pm. $4, students and seniors $2, under 16 free.)* The round **New Mexico State Capitol** was built in 1966 in the form of the Zia sun symbol. The House and Senate galleries are open to the public, and the building also contains an impressive art collection. *(☎ 986-4589. 5 blocks south of the Plaza on Old Santa Fe Rd. Open M-F 7am-7pm; June-Aug. Sa 8am-5pm. Free tours M-F 10am and 2pm.)*

CHURCHES. Santa Fe's Catholic roots are evident in the Romanesque **St. Francis Cathedral,** built from 1869 to 1886 under the direction of Archbishop Lamy (the central figure of Willa Cather's *Death Comes to the Archbishop*), to bring Catholicism to the "ungodly" westerners. The cathedral's architecture is especially striking against the New Mexican desert. *(213 Cathedral Pl. ☎ 982-5619. One block east of the Plaza on San Francisco St. Open daily 7:30am-5:30pm.)* The **Loretto Chapel** was the first Gothic building west of the Mississippi River. The church is famous for its "miraculous" spiral staircase; see **"Stairway to Heaven,"** below. *(207 Old Santa Fe Trail. ☎ 982-0092. 2 blocks south of the Cathedral. Open M-Sa 9am-6pm, Su 10:30am-5pm. $2.50, seniors and children $2.)* About five blocks southeast of the plaza lies the **San Miguel Mission,** at DeVargas St. and the Old Santa Fe Trail. Built in 1610 by the Tlaxcalan Indians, the mission is the oldest functioning church in the US. Also in the church is the San Jose Bell, made in Spain in 1356 and the oldest bell in the US. *(☎ 983-3974. Open M-Sa 9am-5pm, Su 10am-4pm; may close earlier in winter. $1.)*

GALLERIES. Santa Fe's most successful artists live and sell their work along Canyon Rd. To reach their galleries, depart the Plaza on San Francisco Dr., take a left on Alameda St., a right on Paseo de Peralta, and a left on Canyon Rd. Extending for about 1 mi., the road is lined on both sides by galleries displaying all types of art, as well a number of indoor/outdoor cafes. Most galleries are open from 10am until 5pm. At the **Hahn Ross Gallery,** the art is hip, enjoyable, and way out of your price range. *(409 Canyon Rd. ☎ 984-8434. Open daily 10am-5pm.)* **Off the Wall** vends offbeat jewelry, pottery, clocks, and sculpture, with a coffee bar out back. *(616 Canyon Rd. ☎ 983-8337. Open daily 10am-5pm.)*

A BIT OF CLASS. Strange verse and distinguished acting invade the city each summer when **Shakespeare in Sante Fe** raises its curtain. The festival shows plays in an open-air theater on the St. John's College campus from late June to late August. *(Shows run F-Su 7:30pm. Number of shows per week varies so call to check the schedule. Reserved seating tickets $15-32; lawn seating is free, though a $5 donation is requested. Tickets available at show, or call 982-2910.)* The **Santa Fe Opera,** on Opera Dr. 7 mi. north of Santa Fe on Rte. 84/285, performs outdoors against a mountain backdrop. Nights are cool; bring a blanket. *(☎ 800-280-4654 or 877-999-7499. July W, F; Aug. M-Sa. Performances begin 8-9pm. Tickets $20-200, rush standing-room tickets $8-15; 50% student discount on same-day reserved seats. The box office is at the opera house; call or drop by the day of the show for specific prices and availability.)* The **Santa Fe Chamber Music Festival** celebrates the works of great Baroque, Classical, Romantic, and 20th-century composers in the **St. Francis Auditorium of the Museum of Fine Arts** and the **Lensic Theater.** *(Info ☎ 983-2075, tickets 982-1890. Mid-July to mid-Aug. Tickets $16-40, students $10.)*

FESTIVALS. Santa Fe is home to two of the US's largest festivals. In August, the nation's largest and most impressive **Indian Market** floods the plaza (Aug. 23-24,

STAIRWAY TO HEAVEN In 1873, under the guidance of Bishop Lamy and the Loretto Sisters, French and Italian masons began construction of a beautiful Gothic church in the heart of Santa Fe. After the building was finished, the sisters realized they had a problem: there wasn't room to build a staircase to the choir loft. Many carpenters tried, but each declared the task impossible. Rather than give up, the Loretto Sisters did what nuns do best—they prayed. According to legend, a gray-haired man appeared at the convent with a donkey and a tool chest. Using only a hammer, a saw, and a T-square, the carpenter built a wooden spiral staircase that made two 360° turns with no supporting pole in the center. When the sisters went to pay the man, he had vanished. Over the past 125 years, architects and structural engineers have been unable to explain how the staircase supports itself, and many agree that the wood is not from New Mexico. Some say the mysterious carpenter was St. Joseph himself.

2003). The **Southwestern Association for Indian Arts** (☎983-5220) has more info. Don Diego de Vargas's peaceful reconquest of New Mexico in 1692 marked the end of the 12-year Pueblo Rebellion, now celebrated in the three-day **Fiesta de Santa Fe** (☎988-7575). Held in early September, festivities begin with the burning of the *Zozobra* and include street dancing, processions, and political satires. The *New Mexican* publishes a guide and a schedule of the fiesta's events.

NIGHTLIFE AND ENTERTAINMENT

The bars in Santa Fe attract an eclectic mixture of tourists, artists, bums, and millionaires. Here you can walk into a bar and sit between a Wall Street investment banker and the sculptor who crafted the metal cross worn by the Pope. Nightlife in Santa Fe tends to be more mellow than in Albuquerque. The ▨ **Cowgirl Hall of Fame,** 319 S. Guadalupe St., has live music hoe-downs that range from bluegrass to country. BBQ, Mexican food, and burgers served all evening, with midnight food specials. Ranch breakfast served weekend mornings. 12 microbrews on tap. (☎982-2565. Happy hour 3-6pm and midnight-1am; Cowgirl Margaritas $3.50. 21+ after midnight. Cover varies, but is never more than $3. Open M-F 11am-2am, Sa 8:30am-2am, Su 8:30am-midnight.) **Paramount,** 331 Sandoval St., is the only dance club in Santa Fe. Everyone in town shows up for trash disco Wednesdays. (☎982-8999. Dance Sa, live music Tu, Th, Su. 21+. Cover $5-7, Sa $5-20. Open M-Sa 9pm-2am, Su 9pm-midnight.) **Bar B,** in back, has a futuristic setting and live music most nights. Cover $2-7. (☎982-8999. Open M-Sa 5pm-2am, Su 5pm-midnight.) **Catamount Bar and Grill,** 125 E. Water St., has a restaurant/bar downstairs and a large pool hall upstairs with outdoor balcony. (☎988-7222. Tu 10¢ wings and $2 pints. F-Sa Live music. 21+ after 9pm. No cover. Open M-Sa 11am-2am, Su noon-midnight.)

OUTDOOR ACTIVITIES

There's a reason that *Outside Magazine* is headquartered in Santa Fe. The nearby **Sangre de Cristo Mountains** reach heights of over 12,000 ft. and offer countless opportunities for hikers, bikers, skiers, and snowboarders. The **Pecos** and **Río Grande** rivers make great playgrounds for kayakers, rafters, and canoers. Before heading into the wilderness, stop by the **Public Lands Information Center,** 1474 Rodeo Rd., near the intersection of St. Francis Rd. and I-25, to pick up maps, guides, and friendly advice. (☎438-7542. Open M-F 8am-5pm.) The Sierra Club Guide to *Day Hikes in the Santa Fe Area* and the Falcon Guide to *Best Easy Day Hikes in Santa Fe* are good purchases for those planning to spend a few days hiking in the area.

NEW MEXICO

HIKING

The closest trailheads to downtown Santa Fe are along Rte. 475 (Artist Rd.) on the way to the Santa Fe Ski Area. The **Tesuque Creek Trail** is an easy 4 mi. loop through the forest that leads to a flowing stream. The trail begins 10 mi. northeast of Santa Fe on Rte. 475. Look for a parking area on the left just across from a small brown sign that says "leaving Hyde State Park." Take Trail 150 for 1.5 mi. and turn left at the intersection with Trail 254. The trail follows the stream for about 1 mi. before reaching the turnoff for Trail 182, which leads back to the trailhead.

Near the end of Rte. 475 and the Santa Fe Ski Area, are trailheads that lead up into the 223,000 acre **Pecos Wilderness.** For more info on extended backpacking trips in the Wilderness Area, see p. 376. For those in search of a day hike near Santa Fe, several trips lead into the adjacent **Santa Fe National Forest** from Artist Rd. A strenuous full-day climb to the top of 12,622 ft. **Santa Fe Baldy** (14 mi. round-trip) affords an amazing vista of the Pecos Wilderness Area to the north and east. The trailhead is marked on the left side of the road, 15 mi. northeast of Santa Fe on Rte. 475. Follow Trail 254 for 4.5 mi., then turn left on Trail 251 which leads up to the summit. Another good, strenuous hike is 12,000 ft. **Tesuque Peak** (12 mi. round-trip). The trail begins at the Aspen Vista Picnic Area, 13 mi. from Santa Fe on Rte. 475. From the parking area, the trail follows Forest Rd. 150 to the summit.

One of New Mexico's most beautiful hikes, **Kasha-Katuwe Tent Rocks National Monument** has two short trails that wind through spectacular slot canyons towering over a hundred feet straight up. The slot canyon trail continues up the mesa: the view at top is worth triple the exertion. To reach the trailhead from Santa Fe, take I-25 S to Exit 264. Turn right onto Rte. 16; go 8 mi. and turn right onto Rte. 22. To stay on Rte. 22, make a left into Cochiti Pueblo and then turn right onto Forest Rd. 266. The parking area is 5 mi. from the turnoff. (☎ 761-8700. Vehicles $5.)

BIKING

Sun Mountain Bike Co. has two locations in Santa Fe that rent bikes (see p. 368) and offer guided tours ($60 per day). Craig Martin's *Santa Fe Area Mountain Bike Trails* ($12) has detailed listings of 34 mountain bike trails in the area. The **Santa Fe Rail Trail** (12.6 mi. one-way) is the most popular local ride, following the tracks between Santa Fe and Lamy. To reach the trailhead from downtown Santa Fe, drive south on St. Francis Dr. and turn right onto Old Agua Fria Rd. The dirt parking area is on the left just past the railroad tracks. Many bikers choose to ride the steep, 17 mi. **Rte. 475** between Santa Fe and the ski area. For a more challenging backcountry ride, consider climbing Forest Rd. 150 to the top of **Tesuque Peak** (see hiking, above). The uphill portion of the trail is very hard work, but the downhill return trip is fun, fun, fun. For more on biking in the Los Alamos area, see p. 379.

SKIING

Only 16 mi. northeast of downtown, **Ski Sante Fe** heats up the winters. Located in the towering Sangre De Cristo Mountains on Rte. 475, the ski area operates six lifts, including four chairs and two surface lifts, servicing 43 trails (20% beginner; 40% intermediate; 40% advanced) on 600 acres of terrain with a 1650 ft. vertical drop. (☎ 982-4429. Snowboards welcome. Annual snowfall 225 in. Open late Nov. to early Apr. 9am-4pm. Lift tickets: full-day $43, teens $36, children and seniors $28. Rental packages start at $18.)

RIVER RUNNING

While the Río Grande does not actually flow through Santa Fe, there are a few out-fitters in town that run rafting trips. **Santa Fe Rafting,** 1000 Cerrillos Rd. (☎ 988-4914 or 800-467-7238) and **New Wave Rafting Co.,** 103 E. Water St. (☎800-984-1444 or 984-1444) both offer guided half-day to three-day trips on rapids ranging from Class I to IV (both companies half-day $40-50; full day $70-$80).

🢒 DAYTRIPS FROM SANTA FE

BANDELIER NATIONAL MONUMENT. Bandelier, 40 mi. northwest of Santa Fe off Rte. 502 on Rte. 4, features the remains of spectacular cliff dwellings, stone houses, and ceremonial *kivas,* amid some of the most awe-inspiring scenery in New Mexico. The Ancestral Puebloan ancestors of today's Pueblo Indians inhabited this area between the 12th and 16th centuries. They lived in small villages of stone and mud houses and farmed the fertile soil along the canyon floors. The **Visitors Center,** 3 mi. into the park at the bottom of **Frijoles Canyon,** has an archaeological museum and shows a short video. (☎672-3861, ext. 517. Open June-Aug. daily 8am-6pm; Sept. to late Oct. daily 9am-5:30pm; late Oct. to late Mar. 8am-4:30pm; late Mar.-May 9am-5:30pm.) Just past the main entrance, **Juniper Campground ❶** offers the only developed camping in the park, with water and toilets (sites $10). Get a free permit at the Visitors Center for **backcountry camping ❶.** Water is available year-round in Capulin Canyon, Upper Alamo Canyon, and Frijoles Canyon, making these popular spots to camp.

Bandelier encompasses 33,000 acres of wilderness with over 70 mi. of backcountry trails. All visitors to the park should start by hiking the 1.2 mi. **Main Loop Trail** to see the **cliff dwellings** and the ruins of the Tyuonyi Pueblo. Part of the trail is wheelchair accessible, but reaching the dwellings requires climbing narrow stairs. Those with more time should continue ½ mi. past the Main Loop Trail to the **Ceremonial Cave,** a *kiva* carved into a natural alcove, high above the canyon floor.

More aggressive hikers will find what they want in Bandelier. **Frijoles Falls** (5 mi. round-trip), begins at the Visitors Center parking lot and follows the Frijoles Creek downstream 2.5 mi. to the Río Grande. Upper Frijoles Falls, dropping 80 ft., is 1.5 mi. from the trailhead. The **Tsankawi Trail** (1½ mi. round-trip), is in a different area of Bandelier from the Visitors Center. To reach the trail, turn right when leaving the park and follow Rte. 4 for 11 mi. until you see a parking area on the right. The trail meanders along the top of a mesa and passes unexcavated cliff dwellings, pueblo ruins, and petroglyphs. A multi-day backpacking trip, **Yapashi Ruin and Painted Cave** (22 mi. round-trip), leads into the heart of the Bandelier wilderness, climbing mesas and passing the unexcavated Yapashi Pueblo and the beautiful Painted Cave.

PECOS NATIONAL HISTORICAL PARK. Before the time of the Spanish conquest, over 2000 natives lived in high-rise adobe complexes at this site. They grew corn, beans, and squash, traded extensively with nomadic Plains Indians, and partook in highly ritualized religious ceremonies in underground rooms called *kivas.* Franciscan priests who arrived at the beginning of the 17th century forced the natives to abandon their *kivas* and embrace Catholicism. Today, visitors can take an easy 1 mi. walk through the ruins of the pueblo and its Spanish mission church. Two reconstructed *kivas* are open to the public and provide a first-hand look at ceremonial life in the pueblo. The park is 25 mi. southeast of Santa Fe. From the city, take I-25 N to Exit 299; drive east on Rte. 50, go right at the only intersection in Pecos, and drive 2 mi. south on Rte. 63. (Open June-Aug. daily 8am-6pm; Sept.-May 8am-5pm. Entrance $3, under 17 free. National Parks passes accepted.) The **Visitors Center** (☎757-6032) has a small museum and a 10min. video.

NEW MEXICO

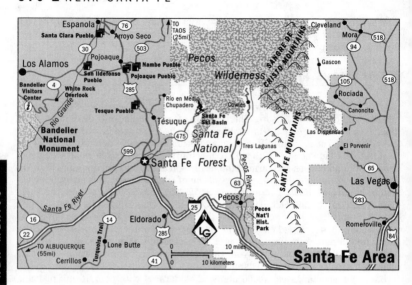

Santa Fe Area

NEAR SANTA FE

While Santa Fe is a must-see destination for travelers in New Mexico, offering countless galleries, restaurants, and old churches, don't be surprised to find yourself anxious for a getaway from the pricey glamour of this artsy city. When such a feeling strikes, you're in luck. Not far from Santa Fe, you can find hiking and solitude in the Pecos Wilderness, old-town history in Las Vegas, nuclear secrets in Los Alamos, and a quick taste of pueblos and old villages on the High Road to Taos.

PECOS WILDERNESS AREA   ☎505

The Pecos Wilderness protects 233,667 acres of high country in the heart of the Sangre de Cristo Mountains, punctuated by the second highest peak in New Mexico, 13,103-foot Truchas Peak. Winters are long and snowy, but from late spring to early autumn this is an ideal spot for backcountry hiking. The upper Pecos River is the premier trout-fishing area in the Southwest, so don't be surprised to find campgrounds crowded with Texan fishermen. Once you get a few miles into the backcountry, you'll find yourself alone amid beautiful mountains, forests, and rivers.

⚑ PRACTICAL INFORMATION. There are two main access roads into the Pecos Wilderness: **Rte. 475** from **Santa Fe** and **Rte. 63** from **Pecos,** 28 mi. southeast of Santa Fe. The trails along Rte. 475 tend to be more crowded because of their proximity to a major city. Prime fishing spots are located along Rte. 63 north of Pecos. Before heading into the Wilderness stop by the **Pecos Ranger District Office,** on Rte. 63 just south of Rte. 50, to pick up large topo maps ($7) and free descriptive trail handouts. (☎757-6121. Open June-Aug. M-Sa 8am-5pm; Sept.-May M-F 8am-4:30pm.) More info on the Pecos Wilderness is available at the **Public Lands Information Center** in Santa Fe (see p. 373). For fly-fishing equipment and guiding service, head to **Pecos River Outfitters,** on Rte. 63 in Pecos, south of Rte. 50. (☎757-2270 or 877-583-1265. Fishing packages $18 per day; full-day fly fishing clinic $175. Men-

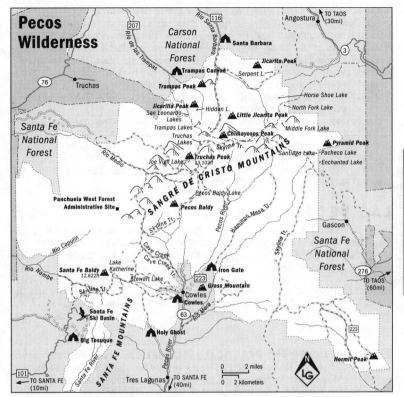

Pecos Wilderness

Carson National Forest

Rio 116
Rio Santa Barbara
Rio de las Trampas
207

Angostura
TO TAOS (30mi)

Santa Barbara

76
Truchas

Trampas Canyon
Trampas Peak

Jicarita Peak
Serpent L.

3

Jicarilla Peak
San Leonardo Lakes
Trampas Lakes
Truchas Lakes

Hidden L.

Little Jicarita Peak

Horse Shoe Lake
North Fork Lake
Middle Fork Lake

Chimayosos Peak

Santa Fe National Forest

Pyramid Peak
Pacheco Lake
Enchanted Lake

Rio Medio

SANGRE DE CRISTO MOUNTAINS

Skyline Tr.

Joe Vigil Lake

Truchas Peak 13,102ft

Santiago Lake

Panchuela West Forest Administrative Site ■

Pecos Baldy Lake

Pecos Baldy

Skyline Tr.

Hamilton Mesa Tr.

Pecos River

Gascon

Rio Capulin

Cave Creek
Cave Creek

Skyline Tr.

Santa Fe National Forest

276
TO TAOS (60mi)

Rio Nambe

Santa Fe Baldy 12,622ft

Lake Katherine

Stewart Lake

Iron Gate

223

Grass Mountain

SANTA FE MOUNTAINS

Cowles
Cowles

63

Rio Mora

223

Santa Fe Ski Basin

Big Tesuque

Holy Ghost

Pecos River

Hermit Peak

101
← TO SANTA FE (10mi)

Santa Fe River

Tres Lagunas

TO SANTA FE (40mi)

0   2 miles
0   2 kilometers

N

LG

tion *Let's Go* for a discount on guided trips.) For required **fishing licenses** and groceries, stop by **Adelo's Town and Country,** at Rte. 63 and Rte. 50. (☎757-8565. Open M-Sa 9am-7pm, Su 9am-2pm. 1-day license $14, 5-day license $22.)

🏕 **CAMPING.** . There are **National Forest Campgrounds ❶** along both Rte. 475 and Rte. 63. Campsites are available only on a first come, first served basis. **Field Tract ❶,** 10 mi. north of Pecos, is the only campground with flush toilets ($8). **Holy Ghost ❶, Cowles ❶** and **Iron Gate ❶** have trailheads that lead into the wilderness area. Backcountry camping inside the park is free and permits are not required.

🥾 **HIKING AND BACKPACKING.** Though the Pecos remains a pocket of designated wilderness, the crowds that tread the area's trails every summer are not insignificant. Good stewardship and **Leave No Trace** hiking and camping techniques (see p. 60) are required to keep the wilderness from showing the ill effects of recreational traffic. The main way to travel the Wilderness is by foot, though horses are allowed on most trails. The remote wilderness lends itself more to overnight camping than day hiking, but there are a few options for ambitious day hikers. The **Cave Creek Trail** (6-10 mi. round-trip) follows a tributary of the Pecos River through thick conifer forest. To reach the trailhead, drive north 20 mi. from Pecos; turn left at Cowles and cross the water. Go right at Panchuela Rd. and follow it to the Panchuela Trailhead. Trail 288 follows the Panchuela Creek 1.5 mi. to an intersection with Cave Creek. Turn left and follow Cave Creek to a series of caves where the creek flows underground. For a shorter hike turn around after the caves; otherwise, the trail continues 2 mi. up a steep incline. The grassy-meadowed 10,000 ft. **Hamilton Mesa** (3-10 mi. one-way) is accessible from a trailhead at Iron Gate Campground by Trail 249. The road to Iron Gate, about 30 mi. from Pecos on Rte. 63, requires a high-clearance vehicle. Those with cars can park at Jack's Creek Campground and hike 3 mi. up to Iron Gate, though this makes for a long day hike. Trail 249 leads 1.5 mi. to the mesa and another 8.5 mi. to Pecos Falls. The top of Hamilton Mesa offers great views of the high Sangre de Cristos.

Backpacking trails abound in this large wilderness area. One of the most popular is the **Skyline Trail** (50 mi.), which makes a large loop around the highest terrain of the Wilderness. The Skyline Trail passes some of the most scenic spots in northern New Mexico, including **Truchas Peaks** and the Truchas Basin. Many trails intersect this large loop, including the Santa Fe Baldy Trail (#254) from Rte. 475 near Ski Santa Fe, the Cave Creek Trail (#288).

LAS VEGAS   ☎ 505

While its Nevada counterpart revels in the glitzy, fast-paced here-and-now, *this* Las Vegas lingers in its forgotten days of glory. The arrival of the railroad in 1879 brought an influx of white settlers to what was once a small Spanish town. By 1900, Las Vegas had become the largest city in the New Mexico Territory, and it boasted the first telephone, trolley car, and Jewish synagogue in New Mexico. However, prosperity was short-lived. The construction of new rail lines and the Great Depression put an end to Las Vegas's fame. What remains today is a town frozen in time, with nine historic districts and 900 buildings on the National Register of Historic Places.

■⁊ **ORIENTATION AND PRACTICAL INFORMATION.** Located 64 mi. east of Santa Fe on I-25, Las Vegas is situated on the border between the Great Plains and the Rocky Mountains. To the east, flat grasslands stretch to the horizon, while Sangre de Cristos Mountains rise to the west. Motels and chain restaurants line Grand Ave., parallel to I-25, while more interesting restaurants and shops can be found a few blocks west on Douglas St., or near the old Plaza on Bridge St. **Amtrak** (☎800-872-7245), at the corner of Railroad Ave. and Lincoln St., has one train daily to Albuquerque and one to Chicago. **Greyhound,** 611 Mills Ave. in the Mail and Parcels store (☎425-8689), offers bus service to Albuquerque (2½hr., 2 per day, $23) and Denver (7hr., 2 per day, $60). Visitor info can be found at the **Las Vegas Welcome Center,** 501 S. Grand St. (☎454-4101. Open M-F 9am-noon and 1-5pm; June-Aug. Sa-Su 9am-5pm.) The **Santa Fe National Forest Las Vegas Ranger District Office,** 1926 7th St., has info about hiking and camping in the Sangre de Cristos Mountains. (☎425-3534. Open M-F 8am-noon and 1-5pm.)

⌐⌐ **ACCOMMODATIONS AND FOOD.** Budget motels can be found all along Grand Ave. between I-25 Exits 343 and 347. The **Town House Motel ❷,** 1215 N. Grand Ave., has clean, comfortable rooms. (☎425-6717. Singles $36; doubles $45.) Next door, the **Sunshine Motel ❷,** 1201 N. Grand Ave. (☎425-3506), offers pleasant rooms at similar prices. (Singles $28; doubles $38.) **Storrie Lake State Park ❶,** 3½ mi. north of Las Vegas on Rte. 518, has campsites with flush toilets and showers. (☎425-7278. Primitive sites $8, developed sites $10, w/ electric $14.) **El Porvenir Campground ❶,** 17 mi. northwest of Las Vegas in the Santa Fe National Forest, sits on a beautiful spot along a stream. (☎425-3534. Drinking water and vault toilets. $8 per night.)

NEW MEXICO

Estella's Cafe ❶, 148 Bridge St., is a local institution that has been serving Mexican food for over 50 years. It has often been rated one of the best Mexican restaurants in New Mexico. (☎454-0048. Open M-W 11am-3pm, Th-Sa 11am-8pm. Entrees $4-7.) **Charlie's Spic and Span Bakery and Cafe ❶,** 715 Douglas Ave., serves breakfast all day. (☎426-1921. Open M-Sa 6:30am-5:30pm, Su 7am-3pm.)

🏔 OUTDOOR ACTIVITIES. Storrie Lake State Park is a summer playground for boating, waterskiing, and swimming. (Open daily 6am-8:30pm. Vehicles $4.) The Las Vegas National Wildlife Refuge, 1½ mi. east of Las Vegas on Rte. 104, then 4 mi. south on Rte. 281, is a haven for birdwatchers. Hawks, ducks, and songbirds inhabit these marshlands during the spring and summer. Migrating shorebirds, geese, and bald eagles rest here from late fall to early spring. (☎425-3581. Open daily sunrise to sunset, Visitors Center open daily 8am-4:30pm. Free.) The El Porvenir Campground provides access to a host of hiking trails in the Santa Fe Forest and the Pecos Wilderness. The Hermit Peak Trail (#223) is a strenuous 9.5 mi. round-trip climb to the top of the 10,160 ft. mountain. From the summit, you can see where the Great Plains meet the Rocky Mountains. For a multi-day backpacking trip, follow Trail 247 from the Porvenir Campground through a scenic canyon and up into the Pecos Wilderness. Visit the Santa Fe National Forest Office in Las Vegas for maps and descriptions of nearby trails.

LOS ALAMOS ☎505

Known only as the mysterious P.O. Box 1663 during the heyday of the Manhattan Project, Los Alamos is no longer the nation's biggest secret. With the infamous distinction of being the birthplace of the atomic bomb, Los Alamos now attracts visitors with its natural beauty and outdoor activities.

Overlooking the Río Grande Valley, Los Alamos hovers above the Pueblo and Bayo Canyons on finger-like mesas, 35 mi. northwest of Sante Fe. **Los Alamos Visitors Center** is on Central Ave. just west of 15th St. (☎662-8105. Open M-F 9am-5pm, Sa 9am-4pm, Su 10am-3pm.) In town, the **Bradbury Science Museum,** at 15th St. and Central, explains the history of the Los Alamos National Laboratory and its endeavors with videos and hands-on exhibits. (☎667-4444. Open Tu-F 9am-5pm, Sa-M 1-5pm. Free.) The **Los Alamos Historical Museum,** at 20th and Central, has exhibits on what life was like for residents in this "secret city" during WWII. (☎662-4493. Open June-Aug. M-Sa 9:30am-4:30pm, Su 11am-5pm; Sept.-May M-Sa 10am-4:30pm, Su 1-4pm. Free.) Not to be missed in Los Alamos is the 🖪**Black Hole,** 4015 Arkansas St., a store that sells all the junk the laboratory doesn't want anymore, including 50-year-old calculators, fiber-optic cables, flow gauges, time-mark generators, optical comparators, and other technological flotsam. Leave with your very own $2 atomic bomb detonator cable. (☎662-5053. Open M-Sa 10am-5pm.)

The Jemez Mountains and the mesas around Los Alamos are overflowing with great views and outdoor opportunities. For a cheap, easy thrill, the view from the **White Rock Overlook** will knock your socks off. To reach this spot, take Rte. 4 to White Rock, NM; turn at the Conoco and immediately turn left onto Meadow Ln. Overlook Rd. is on the left after 1 mi. The **Valles Caldera,** a giant crater west of Los Alamos, was formed a million years ago when a huge volcano collapsed on itself. For a view of the caldera, go southwest 6 mi. from Los Alamos on Rte. 501, then turn right and go another 8 mi. on the winding Rte. 4. Nearly the entire caldera is encompassed in the **Valles Caldera National Preserve,** a recent addition to the national park system.

The Visitors Center has a free pamphlet on 50 hikes in the Los Alamos area. In May 2000, the devastating **Cerro Grande Fire** burned 48,000 acres of forest and left

431 families homeless. Because of damage to the forest, many trails have been closed; call the **US Forest Service Office,** 475 20th St., Suite B (☎667-5120), before setting off on a hike through the charred mountains behind Los Alamos. For a short hike with awesome views, try the **Blue Dot Trail,** which descends 1 mi. from the White Rock Overlook to the Río Grande. Twenty-five miles west of Los Alamos on Rte. 4, **Jemez Falls** and **McCauley Hot Spring** are excellent hiking destinations.

The mesas around Los Alamos offer biking and climbing opportunities. To rent a bike or purchase a map of local trails ($5), head to **D.O.M.E.,** 3801 Arkansas St., a biking and climbing outfitter. (☎661-3663. Open Tu-F 9am-6pm, Sa 10am-3pm. Mountain bikes $25 per day, $40 per 4-day weekend.) The 30 mi. road loop from Los Alamos to White Rock and Bandelier is a popular paved ride. **Pajarito Ski Area** has some excellent technical mountain biking. For area rock climbing info, contact the **Mountaineer Group** (☎665-0604). The cliffs below the White Rock Overlook have bolt routes that range from 5.8 to 5.12+. Another good spot for climbing is along Rte. 502 just east of the intersection with Rte. 4.

NORTHEASTERN NEW MEXICO

Whether you're looking for an artist colony, a piece of living history, extreme skiing, hiking, or a taste of the Wild West, northeastern New Mexico has got it. The galleries and pueblos of Taos are the most touristed destinations of the region, but travelers would be remiss not to explore the hidden towns along the Enchanted Circle, hike the state's tallest mountain, relive wild shoot-outs in Cimarron, or wander the rim of the Capulin Volcano.

TAOS   ☎505

Before 1955, Taos was a remote artist colony in the Sangre de Cristo Mountains. When the ski valley opened and the thrill-seekers trickled in, they soon realized that the area also boasted the best whitewater rafting in New Mexico, as well as some excellent hiking, mountain biking, and rock climbing. By the 1970s, Taos had become a paradise for New-Age hippies, struggling artists, and extreme athletes, and the deluge of tourists wasn't far behind. Today, Taos has managed to balance a ski resort culture with a Bohemian pace and lifestyle without losing any of its sunflower charm. Visitors who come to Taos to enjoy the natural beauty of the region and the company of locals will be pleasantly rewarded. To make the most of your time in Taos, spend a few days hiking in the Wheeler Peak Wilderness, biking through Carson National Forest, or taking a dip in the Hondo hot springs. Or, head a few miles north to the village of Arroyo Seco, where locals practice yoga in the morning, hike in the afternoon, and discuss their favorite movies over coffee at the Casa Vaca Cafe.

▀ TRANSPORTATION

The only intercity transport is offered by **Greyhound,** 1213A Gusdorf St. (☎758-1144), which sends two buses daily to Albuquerque (3hr., $23), Denver (7½hr., $60), and Santa Fe (1½hr.; $17). The local bus service, the **Chile Line,** runs every 15-30min. along Paseo del Pueblo from Ranchos de Taos, south of town, to and from the pueblo. In ski season, a bus runs from the center of Taos to the Ski Valley every 2½hr. (☎751-4459. Daily 7am-7pm. 50¢, ski shuttle $5.) **Taxi** service is offered by **Faust's Transportation** (☎758-3410) daily until 8:30pm. Car rentals are

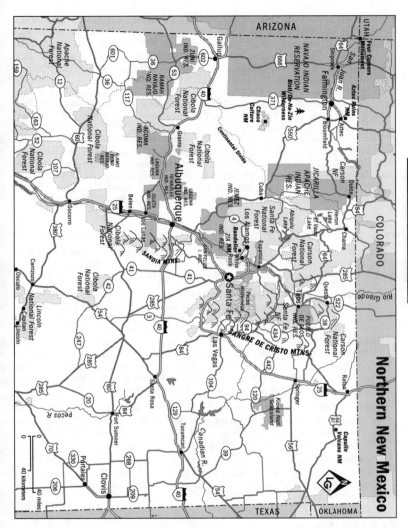

available at **Enterprise,** 1137 Paseo del Pueblo Sur. (☎737-0514. Open M-F 8am-6pm, Sa 9am-3pm, Su noon-6pm. Must be 21+, surcharge for drivers 21-24. $43 per day, $200 per week.)

ORIENTATION AND PRACTICAL INFORMATION

Taos is located 79 mi. north of Santa Fe, between the dramatic Río Grande Gorge and the mighty Wheeler Peak. **Paseo del Pueblo** (Rte. 68) is the main north-south thoroughfare in town, dubbed "Paseo del Pueblo Norte" north of the central plaza, and "Paseo del Pueblo Sur" south. Be aware that traffic on Paseo del Pueblo can be extremely heavy during the summer and the ski season. Drivers should park on **Camino de la Placita,** a block west of the plaza, or at meters on side streets. Several miles north on Paseo del Pueblo Norte, there is an important intersection: a right turn onto Rte. 150 leads to Arroyo Seco and Arroyo Hondo; straight onto Rte. 522 is the beginning of the Enchanted Circle; and a left turn onto Rte. 64 West leads to the Río Grande Gorge Bridge and the earthships beyond it.

Visitor info is available at the **Chamber of Commerce,** 1139 Paseo del Pueblo Sur, 2 mi. south of town at the junction of Rte. 68 and Paseo del Cañon. (☎758-3873 or 800-732-8267. Open daily 9am-5pm.) The **Carson National Forest Office,** 208 Cruz Alta Rd., has free info on camping and hiking. (☎758-6200. Open M-F 8am-4:30pm.) Services include: **Pinch Penny Wash-O-Mat,** 823 Paseo del Pueblo Norte (☎758-1265; open M-Sa 7am-8pm, Su 7am-5pm); **police,** 107 Civic Plaza Dr. (☎758-2216); **Holy Cross Hospital,** 1397 Weimer Rd. (☎758-8883); **Internet access** ($1 per 30min.) at the **public library,** 402 Camino de la Placita (☎758-3063; open M noon-6pm, Tu-Th 10am-7pm, F 10am-6pm, Sa 10am-5pm); **post office,** 318 Paseo Del Pueblo Norte, ¼ mi. north of the plaza (☎758-2081; open M-F 8am-5pm). **ZIP code:** 87571.

ACCOMMODATIONS

Tourism is big business in Taos, which means that a room costs big bucks. Expect to pay upwards of $60 for a simple motel room. Camping and hostelling are much more economical options for those willing to stay a few miles outside of town.

The Abominable Snowmansion Hostel (HI-AYH) (☎776-8298), 8 mi. north of Taos in the village of Arroyo Seco. Located on the road to Taos Ski Valley only 9 mi. from the mountain, this hostel is packed with skiers all winter and is accessible by public transportation only during the ski season. Tepees and tent camping are available in the backyard during the summer. The hostel has 2 kitchens (one only open during summer), a pool table, and a fireplace in the common room. Reception 8am-noon and 4-10pm. Reservations recommended. Mid-Apr. to mid-Nov. dorms $15, non-members $17; dorm tepees $15/$17; private doubles $38-42; tent sites $12. Mid-Nov. to mid-Apr. dorms (breakfast included) $22, weekly $120; private rooms $40-52. ❶

Budget Host Motel, 1798 Paseo del Pueblo Sur (☎758-2524 or 800-323-6009), 3¼ mi. south of the Plaza. The least expensive motel in Taos, with large, clean rooms and free continental breakfast. A/C, TV, free local calls. Singles $43-54, doubles $49-61. 10% discount for AAA senior, and veteran. ❸

Indian Hills Inn, 233 Paseo del Pueblo Sur (☎758-4293), 2 blocks south of the Plaza. This is the most affordable motel within walking distance of downtown. Cozy rooms have fireplaces, as well as A/C and cable TV. Rooms range from $45 in low season to $59-99 during the summer and ski months. ❹

CAMPING

Considering the price of lodging in Taos, sleeping under the stars is a particularly appealing option. The **Orilla Verde Recreation Area ❶,** 15 mi. south of Taos on Rte. 68, has five campgrounds in the scenic **Río Grande Gorge ❶.** (☎751-4899 or 758-8851. Water and toilets available. Sites $7.) The **Carson National Forest ❶** has three campgrounds to the east of Taos on Rte. 64. Tent sites are adjacent to a stream and are surrounded by tall pines. The closest, **Las Petacas,** is 4 mi. east of Taos and has vault toilets but no drinking water. **Capulin Campground ❶,** 7 mi. east of Taos, and **La Sombra ❶,** 1 mi. farther, both have water and vault toilets. For more info, contact the Carson National Forest Office in Taos (☎758-6200; sites $12.50). Campgrounds on the road to Taos Ski Valley are free, but have no facilities.

THE HIGH ROAD

3 CHIMAYO. Five miles past Nambe Pueblo, turn left on **Juan Medina Rd.** (County Rd. 98) to get to Chimayo (see p. 380). At the end of Juan Medina Rd. turn right onto Rte. 76. For a side trip to **Santa Cruz Lake Recreation Area ❶**, turn right after 2 mi. and follow the signs to the lake. The BLM-managed recreation area has fishing, boating, hiking trails, and camping. (☎ 758-8851. Day use $5 per vehicle, camping $7.)

> **TIME:** 2-3hr. driving time
>
> **DISTANCE:** 70 mi.
>
> **SEASON:** year-round

4 TRUCHAS. The farming village of Truchas is 8 mi. up Rte. 76 from Chimayo. Though the highway curves left, drive through the town to see the picturesque farms, meadows, and old houses, as well as Truchas Peak (13,103 ft.), and other high peaks of the Pecos Wilderness. Robert Redford filmed *The Milagro Beanfield War* (1987) in this village.

5 LAS TRAMPAS. Eight miles past Truchas in the tiny hamlet of Las Trampas is the **San José de Gracia Church,** one of the finest Spanish Colonial churches in New Mexico. One mile past it, the 8 mi. Forest Rd. 207 leads to the free **Trampas Campground.** From here, two 12 mi. round-trip trails lead into the Pecos Wilderness, Trail 30 leading to the San Leonard Lakes, and Trail 31 heading for Trampas Lakes. Five miles farther along Rte. 76, turn left on Rte. 75 and then right after ½ mi. for a short detour to the **Picuris Pueblo.**

6 PICURIS PUEBLO. Hidden in a valley of the Sangre de Cristo Mountains, Picuris Pueblo is the most highly elevated and geographically isolated of New Mexico's pueblos, and the people of Picuris will tell you that they were the last tribe to be "discovered" by the Spaniards. The museum was closed for renovations in summer 2001 but is scheduled to reopen by summer 2002. Pueblo residents celebrate the annual **San Lorenzo Feast Day** (Aug. 9-10) with dances, foot races, and church services. (☎ 587-2519 or 587-2957. Open daily 8am-5pm. Self-guided tour $3 per person, $5 with photo permit.)

Turn east onto Rte. 75 to continue toward Taos. The turnoff for Rte. 73 leads to **Hodges Campground** and **Santa Barbara Campground** in the **Carson National Forest.** Santa Barbara Campground serves as a trailhead for hikes into the northern Pecos Wilderness. **Carson Forest Camino Real Ranger District,** 15160 Rte. 75, just north of the turn in Penasco, sells maps and provides info on hiking and camping in the Carson National Forest. (Open M-F 8am-4:30pm.)

7 FINISHING UP. Past Penasco, Rte. 75 passes through the village of **Vadito.** Just past Vadito, Rte. 518 intersects with 75; turn left to continue to Taos, or continue on Rte. 75 for 6 mi. for a quick side-trip to check out the rustic **Sipapu Ski Area** (☎ 587-2240). The **Amole Cross Country Ski Area** (☎ 758-6200) sits 1½ mi. north of the junction of Rte. 518. 18 mi. farther, Rte. 518 meets Rte. 68 in **Ranchos de Taos.** Turn left and drive ¼ mi. to get to the San Francisco de Asis Church. This striking structure is one of the US's most photographed churches and has been immortalized by Georgia O'Keeffe and Ansel Adams. (☎ 758-2754. Church open M-Sa 9am-4pm.)

C
v
fe

chile omelette ($5) for breakfast, or choose from a wide variety of sandwiches ($6) for lunch. Open daily 7am-6pm. ❶

Sheva Cafe, 812B Paseo del Pueblo Norte (☎737-9290), has a wonderful selection of vegetarian Middle Eastern dishes including falafel ($4.50) and *borekas* ($3). Occasionally your hummus will be accompanied by trippy experimental live music. (Open Su-Th 11am-3pm, 5-10pm, F 7:30am-4pm). ❶

Taos Pizza Outback, 712 Paseo del Pueblo Norte (☎758-3112), 1 mi. north of the plaza. This pizza joint has an old gas pump and an outdoor seating area. Listen to good ol' rock 'n' roll music while munching on a giant slice of pizza ($2.75) or calzone ($8). Open June-Sept. daily 11am-10pm; Oct.-May Su-Th 11am-9pm, F-Sa 11am-10pm. ❶

Michael's Kitchen, 304 Paseo del Pueblo Norte (☎758-4178). A rustic eatery with the best all-day breakfast in town ($3-7). Lunch and dinner menus offer $5-7 sandwiches, $7 burritos, and $9-14 steaks. Open daily 7am-8:30pm. ❷

🎵 NIGHTLIFE

The **Alley Cantina,** one block north of the Plaza at 121 Teresina Ln., inside the oldest building in Taos, is the most lively nightspot in town. This friendly bar has a pool table, couches, and an outdoor patio. Watch out for the ghost of **Governor Bent's Daughter.** (☎758-2121. Live music W-S nights. 21+. Cover $3-5. Open M-Sa 11:30am-1am, Su 11:30am-11pm.) **Caffe Tazza,** 122 Kit Carson Rd., has live music three nights a week, open mic Wednesday 7-9pm, and poetry and prose readings most Friday nights 7-9pm. (☎758-8706. Open daily 7am-8pm, later if there's music.)

👁 SIGHTS

ART MUSEUMS. For such a small town, Taos has a surprising number of high-quality art museums. The **Harwood Museum** houses works by early and mid-20th-century local artists, including a gallery of minimalist painter Agnes Martin, as well as a large collection of Hispanic Art including a striking Día de los Muertos (Day of the Dead) piece. *(238 Ledoux St. ☎758-9826. Open Tu-Sa 10am-5pm, Su noon-5pm. $5.)* The **Millicent Rogers Museum** has an extravagant collection of Indian jewelry, textiles, pottery, and Apache baskets once belonging to Millicent Rogers, a glamour queen and socialite. *(4 mi. north of the Plaza on Rte. 64, turn left at the sign. ☎758-2462. Open Apr.-Oct. daily 10am-5pm; Nov.-Mar. Tu-Su 10am-5pm.)*

HISTORIC SITES. Mythic mountain man **Kit Carson** used Taos as a base for his many expeditions out on the frontier. The house where Carson and his wife lived between 1843 and 1868 has been preserved as a museum full of guns, saddles, and depictions of the life of rocky mountain fur trappers. *(113 Kit Carson Rd., one block east of the plaza. ☎758-4741. Open daily 9am-5pm. $5, children $3.)* The **Governor Bent Museum,** in the house where Charles Bent was murdered during the 1847 uprising, displays many of Bent's personal belongings, Americana from the period, and an eight-legged lamb that could keep Wes Craven awake at night. *(117 Bent St. ☎758-2376. Open daily 10am-5pm. $2, children $1.)*

The **Martinez Hacienda,** 2 mi. southwest of the plaza on Ranchitos Rd., is one of the few surviving Spanish Colonial mansions in the United States. Built in 1804, this fortress-like adobe structure was home to the prosperous Martinez family and served as the headquarters of a large farming and ranching operation. The restored 21-room hacienda features excellent exhibits on life in the northernmost reaches of the Spanish Empire. *(2 mi. south of downtown on Ranchos Rd. ☎758-1000. Open Apr.-Oct. daily 9am-5pm; Nov.-Mar. 10am-4pm. $5, children $3.)*

ARTS AND CRAFTS. Taos ranks second only to Santa Fe as a center of South-western Art. Galleries clustered around the Plaza and Kit Carson Rd. include the **Lumina Gallery and Sculpture Garden,** which is more captivating than any art museum in town. Set in a stunning adobe home with five acres of rolling grassy lawn, gardens, and fountains, the cutting-edge contemporary paintings and sculptures here are captivating. Of the many arts-and-crafts shops in town, **Taos Drums** is the most unique. Local craftsmen here make wooden drums in the traditional Native American style, and performers including Fleetwood Mac and Pearl Jam have made use of their wares. Take a free tour of the workshop and bang the largest drum in New Mexico, or attend one of the drum classes offered several times a week for $10. *(On Rte. 68, 5 mi. south of the Taos Plaza, look for the giant tepees. ☎ 800-424-3786. Open M-Sa 9am-5pm, Su 11am-6pm.)*

TAOS PUEBLO. The five-story adobe homes of this pueblo are between 700 and 1000 years old, making it the oldest continuously inhabited settlement in the US. Taos Pueblo was named a UNESCO world heritage site in 1992, and is the only pueblo in Northern New Mexico where the inhabitants still live traditionally, without electricity or running water. Guided tours are offered daily May through September, and visitors are able to take self-guided tours all day. Highlights of the Pueblo include the **San Geronimo Church,** the ruins of the old church and cemetery, the adobe houses, and the *kivas.* The **San Geronimo Feast Days** (Sept. 29-30) and the annual **powwow** (2nd weekend in July) are the most popular events of the year. *(¾ mi. north of the Plaza, bear right at the intersection and continue another 2 mi. to the Pueblo. Chileworks Buses stop at the Pueblo every 30min.-1hr. ☎ 758-1028. Open May-Sept. M-Sa 8am-4:30pm, Su 8:30am-4:30pm; Oct.-Apr. M-Sa 8am-4pm, Su 8:30am-4pm. $10, seniors $8, students $3, 12 and under free. Camera permit $10, video cameras $20.)*

OTHER SIGHTS. The **Río Grande Gorge Bridge** spans the gorge 500 ft. above the river. From Taos, drive north 3 mi., then turn left and follow Rte. 64 about 7 mi. to the bridge. For the best experience, get out of your car and walk across. There are a number of natural hot springs along the Río Grande near Taos. One of the most popular is the **Stagecoach Hot Springs**, at the bottom of the Río Grande Gorge. From Taos, drive north 3 mi. and take Rte. 64 W towards the Gorge Bridge. After passing the airport turn right onto Tune Rd. After 5 mi., go left at the second fork and follow this road to the gorge's edge where you can park. The springs are a steep 0.8 mi. hike down into the gorge. The **Hondo Hot Springs** are located in Arroyo Hondo's portion of the gorge. Take the Arroyo Seco-Arroyo Hondo Rd. on the side of the Abominable Snowmansion hostel. At Rte. 522, turn right over the bridge, and once over, take the immediate left. Follow this road to its end and turn left over a small bridge. Take this dirt road up to a fork in the road: turn right down into the gorge, over the John Dunne bridge and to the parking lot. The trail down to the springs is shorter and less strenuous. *Clothing is optional in both of these hot springs.*

◤ OUTDOOR ACTIVITIES

Between skiing, rafting, hiking, biking, and rock climbing, Taos offers outdoor activities year round. Due to the popularity of the **Taos Ski Valley,** Taos is the only town in New Mexico that is more crowded in the winter than in the summer.

HIKING

Wheeler Peak/#90 (15 mi. round-trip, 1-2 days). At 13,161 ft., Wheeler Peak is the highest point in New Mexico. The trailhead to this very strenuous hike is well-marked at the main Taos Ski Valley parking lot; the trail goes northeast for the first 2 mi. and then turns south towards Wheeler Peak at Bull-of-the-Woods Pasture. Thunderstorms are common near the summit and can be very dangerous—to avoid getting caught, start hiking as early in the day as possible. As the trek is easiest as an overnight, consider camping in the forested valley 5 mi. from the trailhead.

Williams Lake/#62 (4 mi. round-trip, 3-5hr.). This short, moderate hike to an 11,000 ft. glacial cirque is an excellent half-day hike into the Wheeler Peak Wilderness. To reach the trailhead, drive to the Taos Ski Valley and turn south on Twining Rd. (it's off to the left in the parking lot). Follow the signs to the Bavarian Lodge and park at the marked trailhead. Williams Lake affords great views of Wheeler Peak and the surrounding mountains. *The air on this trail is extremely thin: bring plenty of water and take you time on the ascent.*

Devisadero/#108 (5 mi. round-trip, 2-3 hr.). This is the ideal hike for someone who wants to get out into the woods without driving far from the town of Taos. The trail begins 3 mi. east of town on Rte. 64, across the highway from the El Nogal Picnic Area. The strenuous 5 mi. loop leads to the top of Devisadero Peak, offering excellent views of Taos, the Río Grande Gorge, and the surrounding area.

Italianos Canyon/#59 (7.4 mi. round-trip, 4-6 hr.). This strenuous trail leads to the summit of 12,115 ft. Lobo Peak, offering great views of the Wheeler Peak Wilderness and the Río Grande Valley. The trailhead is located along the road to the Taos Ski Valley (Rte. 150), 3 mi. east of Upper Cuchilla Campground.

MOUNTAIN BIKING

The Taos area offers some of the finest mountain biking in New Mexico. For bike rentals, visit **Gearing Up,** 129 Paseo del Pueblo Sur (☎751-0365; open daily 9:30am-6pm; bikes $35 per day, $90 per 5 days), or **Native Sons Adventures,** 1033A Paseo del Pueblo Sur (☎758-9342 or 800-753-7559; open daily 7am-7pm; bikes $20-30 per day, $15 per day for longer rentals).

The best biking around Taos is in the Camino Real Ranger District, to the southeast of town. There are many popular trails along Rte. 518 including **La Cueva** and **Policarpo Canyon.** The strenuous 27 mi. **South Boundary Trail** (#164) is cited as one of the top ten rides in the Southwest. To reach the start of the trail, take Rte. 64 east toward Angel Fire and turn south on Rte. 434, then turn right onto County Rd. B-1. The **West Rim Trail** is an easy one-way 9 mi. ride along the rim of the Río Grande Gorge, with great views of the river below and the Sangre de Cristos to the east. The trail begins at the west side of the Río Grande Gorge Bridge on Rte. 64.

ROCK CLIMBING

Both **Mudd-n-Flood,** 134 Bent St. (☎751-9100), and **Taos Mountain Outfitters,** 114 South Plaza (☎758-9292), offer climbing gear and friendly advice. **Mountain Skills** (☎776-2222) has guided climbing trips. The best spot for top-rope climbing is **Dead Cholla,** on the west rim of the Río Grande Gorge. Sport and traditional climbs of 5.7 to 5.12 are also plentiful at Dead Cholla. **John's Wall,** in Arroyo Hondo, offers sport and traditional climbs in the 5.8 to 5.11 range. Farther from Taos, the granite rocks in back of the water tower in **Tres Piedras** have great climbs, for bouldering and sport climbing. Another popular spot a little farther from Taos is the **Questa Dome,** north of Arroyo Hondo in Questa, which has great granite bouldering.

SKIING

Taos Ski Valley (☎776-2291), located 18 mi. north of town on Rte. 150, is the premier downhill ski destination in New Mexico and the brainchild of Swiss-born Ernie Blake, who chose this site in 1955 after an extensive aerial search to find the "perfect" mountain. His friends complained that the terrain was too difficult for American skiers, but Blake was confident that people could learn to ski these steeps with the right instruction. Over the years, Taos's **Ernie Blake Ski School** has consistently been ranked as one of the top ski schools in the country.

Taos is an extreme skier's delight—51% of the trails are most difficult, compared with 24% beginner and 25% intermediate. Receiving 312 in. of snow annually, the mountain boasts 898 skiable acres, 72 trails, a vertical drop of 2612 ft. serviced by lifts, and a 3274 ft. vertical drop for those willing to hike to the top of Kachina Peak. In the summer, sightseers can ride the ski lift for a view of the Wheeler Peak Wilderness. (24hr. snow report ☎776-2916. Nov. 22 to Apr. 7 9am-4pm; $47, ages 13-17 $37, 12 and under $28. Summer Th-Su 10am-4:30pm; $6, children $4.)

Nearby ski areas **Red River** and **Angel Fire** offer more intermediate terrain than Taos Ski Valley (see p. 390, p. 390). There are also many places to go **cross-country skiing** near Taos, including the **Amole Cross-Country Ski Area,** 17 mi. south of Taos on Rte. 518, and the **Enchanted Forest Cross-Country Ski Area** (☎754-2374 or 800-966-9381), 3 mi. east of Red River, the only full-service cross-country facility nearby, with 26km of groomed trails.

RIVER RUNNING

The dramatic **Río Grande Gorge** extends 78 mi. through northern New Mexico and into Colorado. This section of river is administered by the BLM as a **Wild and Scenic River** and it offers the best whitewater rafting and kayaking in New Mexico. Many rafting outfitters operate out of Taos. **Los Ríos River Runners** (☎776-8854 or 800-544-1181), **Far Flung Adventures** (☎758-2628 or 800-359-2627), and **Native Sons Adventures** (☎758-9342 or 800-753-7559) all offer a range of guided half-day ($40-50) and full-day ($80-110) rafting trips, including the popular 15 mi. Class IV **Taos Box** and the 11 mi. **Lower Gorge,** which offers Class II-IV rapids. Kayakers may want to visit the **Río Grande Gorge Visitors Center,** 15 mi. south of Taos on Rte. 68, to get info on river conditions, as well as a helpful mile-by-mile guide ($15) to the Río Grande Gorge. (☎751-4889. Open Apr.-Oct. daily 8:30am-5pm.) The **Orilla Verde Recreation Area,** inside the Río Grande Gorge 15 mi. south of Taos on Rte. 68, has river access for boaters, a hiking trail, and five campgrounds along the Río Grande. (☎751-4899. Sites $7.) A popular two-day river trip incorporates Taos Box and the Lower Gorge, with a night of camping at Orilla Verde.

RED RIVER   ☎505

Red River attempts to recreate an Old West ambience, but the buildings are merely false facades that pander to the Disneyfied visions of vacationers. What redeems Red River, however, is its dramatic setting in a high mountain valley and the many available outdoor activities. Shops, restaurants and accommodations line Rte. 38 and High St., one block to the north. Tourist info is available at the **Red River Chamber of Commerce,** on Rte. 38 in the middle of town. (☎800-348-6444. Open daily 8am-5pm.) Accommodations in Red River are pricey, but **River Ranch ❶** (☎754-2293), west of town on Rte. 38, is a reasonable option, offering tent sites ($16) and cozy cabins in the summer ($61+). There are five Forest Service campgrounds (☎586-0520) on Rte. 38 between Red River and Questa. More upscale rustic lodging is available throughout Red River. Call **Alpine Lodge** (☎800-252-2333) or **Pioneer Lodge** (☎800-542-0154) for reservations well in advance of ski season.

The **Red River Ski Area,** with 183 skiable acres, 58 trails, and a vertical drop of 1600 ft. (32% beginner; 38% intermediate; 30% advanced), is a good mountain for families. (☎754-2223. Open Thanksgiving to Easter daily 9am-4pm. Full-day lift tickets $43, ages 13-19 $38, seniors and children $29.) Three and a half miles east of Red River on Rte. 38, **Enchanted Forest** (☎754-2374 or 800-966-9381) is the largest cross-country ski area and snowshoe area in Northern New Mexico. For a unique

Rte. 522, Rte. 38, and U.S. 64 form a loop that circles Wheeler Peak and other peaks of the Sangre De Cristos, offering endless opportunities for hiking and camping amid beautiful views and hidden towns. Seeing the snow-capped Sangre de Cristos in winter is particularly breathtaking. The circle itself takes about 2½ hours, but allow a full day to explore the many sites and activities along the route.

TIME: 2-3hr. driving time

DISTANCE: 82 mi.

SEASON: year-round

Three miles north of town, a right turn leads to the Taos Ski Valley and a left turn leads to the **Río Grande Gorge Bridge.** Five miles farther, Rte. 522 passes through the small village of **Arroyo Hondo.** A left turn just after the bridge in town leads to the John Dunn Bridge, where rafters and kayakers put in their boats to run the Class IV **Taos Box** (see river running, p. 389).

1 D.H. LAWRENCE MEMORIAL. Three miles north of Río Hondo, turn right at the sign for San Cristobol and go straight on the dirt road for 5 mi. to reach the memorial. While Lawrence aficionados will get a kick out of it, the lay public will tend more toward head-scratching at this peculiar memorial. (☎776-2245. Open daily 8am-5pm. Free.)

2 QUESTA. Nine miles north of the D.H. Lawrence Ranch and 3 mi. north of the **Red River State Trout Hatchery,** where the state of New Mexico raises over 500,000 trout each year for stocking in lakes and rivers, sits Questa. This unassuming town near the confluence of the Red River and the Río Grande grew up around a large Molybdenum mine. The **El Seville Restaurant ❶,** at the intersection of Rte. 522 and Rte. 38, is a family-run restaurant with the finest Mexican food along the Enchanted Circle, famous for its delicious sopapillas. (☎586-0300. Open daily 7am-8pm. Dishes $4-7.) The **Carson National Forest Questa Ranger Station,** on Rte. 38, 1½ mi. east of the Rte. 522 intersection, has info on hiking and camping in the northern section of the Carson National Forest (☎586-0520, open M-F 8am-4:30pm). Questa serves as an entryway to the remote **Latir Peak Wilderness** of the Carson National Forest. To reach the wilderness, take Forest Rd. 134 NE from Questa to the Cabresto Lake Campground. From here, trails lead to Baldy Mountain, Heart Lake, and Latir Peak. Heart Lake makes an excellent spot for overnight backcountry camping. For more info, contact the Questa Ranger District.

3 WILD RIVERS NATIONAL RECREATION AREA. This rarely utilized park, 15 mi. northeast of Questa, has some of the most dramatic scenery in northern New Mexico. The **Chawalauna Overlook** provides views of the 800 ft. Río Grande Gorge, and **Junta Point** looks out over the confluence of the Red River and the Río Grande. The park has five campgrounds with sites along the rim of the Gorge, all with drinking water and vault toilets (sites $7). Excellent short hikes leading down into the Gorge include La Junta and Big Arsenic Springs. Backcountry camping ($5) is permitted at designated shelters inside the gorge. (For more info, call BLM Taos at 758-8851. Day use hours 6am-10pm. Day use $3 per vehicle.)

4 RED RIVER. Continuing east of Questa on Rte. 38, one begins to understand why this drive has been named the "Enchanted Circle." The highway weaves between pine-covered mountains, offering views of multi-colored cliffs and the Red River. Seven miles east of Questa, an enormous molybdenum mine is visible on the left side of the highway. The tourist-dominated village of Red River is just a few miles past the mine (see p. 389).

5 ELIZABETHTOWN. Leaving Red River, Rte. 38 climbs to Bobcat Pass (9820 ft.), the highest point on the Enchanted Circle. Eight miles out of Red River, the forest gives way to green meadows and one can see the rocky top of Baldy Mountain (12,400 ft.) on the left side of the road, and the snow-covered Wheeler Peak (13,161 ft.) to the right. The ghost town of Elizabethtown is 12 mi. southeast of Red River. Follow the signs to the **Elizabethtown Museum** to learn about the history of the town through photographs, mining tools, and a documentary video. (☎377-3420. Open June-Aug. daily 10am-5pm. Free.)

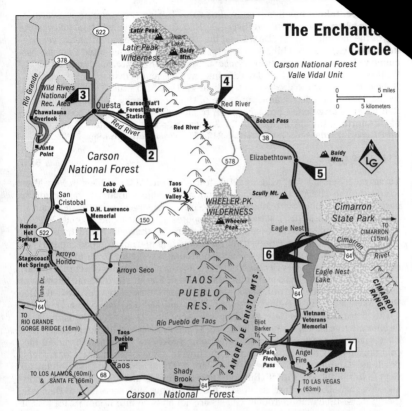

The Enchant..
Circle

🆕 EAGLE'S NEST. A few miles past Elizabethtown is the quiet town of Eagle's Nest. The main attraction is the large **Eagle's Nest Lake,** popular with fishermen year round. Turn left on Rte. 64 to go to **Cimarron Canyon State Park,** and the hiking and camping therein (see p. 392). Otherwise, turn right on Rte. 64 toward Taos.

🆕 ANGEL FIRE. Eight and a half miles south of Eagle's Nest sits the **Vietnam Veterans National Monument.** (☎377-6900. Visitors Center open daily 9am-7pm, chapel always open. Free.) South of the monument, Rte. 434 leads to the **Angel Fire Ski Resort,** with 68 trails on 445 acres of terrain with a vertical drop of 2077 ft., as well as over 11 mi. of cross-country ski trails. The **New Mexico Championship Mountain Bike Race** is held here every June; in the summer, bikers can take their bikes up the chairlift ($7), or run a dual slalom course. (☎377-6401. Open Dec. 14 to Mar. 24 9am-4pm. Full-day lift tickets $43, teens $35, children and seniors $27; cross-country skiing $7 per day.)

West of Angel Fire, Rte. 64 climbs into the mountains again and enters the Carson National Forest. There are four campgrounds and numerous trailheads along the road. Beginning 1.5 mi. west of the Angel Fire turnoff, **Eliot Barker Trail,** a moderately strenuous 10 mi. round-trip hike, offers views of Angel Fire and the Wheeler Peak Wilderness. Just past the Eliot Barker Trail, Rte. 64 ascends to the 9100 ft. **Palo Flechado Pass.**

adlamp snowshoe tour. During the summer, a swarm of
d on Red River. The Red River Ski area will take bikes to the
or $9. Be warned that the trails on the mountain are very dif-
ced bikers should try the trails at the Enchanted Forest cross-
d the nearby **Pioneer Canyon Trail. New Mexico Adventure Co.,** 217
kes (half-day $25, full-day $35) and provides a free shuttle to
the cross-country ski area. They also offer $25 3hr. **jeep tours.**
daily 8am-7pm.) One of the more wacky outdoor activities in
-**Golf,** a cross between frisbee and golf. The free course is two
blocks ~~~~ Rte. 38 on Mallette Rd. **Sitzmark's Sports,** 416 W. Rte. 38, rents disks
for $7 and sells them for $9-21. (☎800-843-7547. Open daily 8am-8pm.)

CIMARRON ☎ 505

Cimarron is Spanish for "wild," and this town was one of the wildest in New Mexico during the late 19th century. The land surrounding Cimarron was originally part of the 1.7 million acre Maxwell Land Grant, the largest private land grant in the US. During the 1870s, a series of land disputes led to the Colfax County War, an intense period of shootings, hangings, and murders, that was finally quashed by the arrival of US Cavalry troops from Ft. Union. Life in Cimarron has calmed considerably over the past hundred years, and today this sleepy town of 900 people relies on tourists and Boy Scouts to prevent it from slipping into obscurity. Cimarron sits 54 mi. east of Taos and 41 mi. southwest of Raton. The **Cimarron Chamber of Commerce,** on the corner of Lincoln Ave. and Rte. 64, distributes info. (☎376-2417. Open May-Oct. daily 9am-6pm; Nov.-Apr. M-Tu and Th-Sa 8:30am-5:30pm.)

The historic **St. James Hotel ❺,** on the corner of Rte. 21 and 17th St., is the most fascinating tourist attraction in Cimarron. This hotel was run by Henry Lambert, a Frenchman who served as personal chef to both General Grant and President Lincoln during the Civil War. Lambert's hotel hosted a motley assortment of traders, ranchers, gamblers, and robbers. Jesse James, Wyatt Earp, and Doc Holiday all slept in this hotel, and Buffalo Bill and Annie Oakley planned their Wild West show here. Twenty-six men were shot dead in this building and, according to the staff, their ghosts still haunt the rooms. Guests are not allowed into Room 18, for fear of the angry ghost named TJ. The exquisitely decorated, antique Victorian rooms at the St. James are pricey at $90-120 per night. Annex rooms $60-100. But even if you can't afford to stay here, be sure to take a free self-guided tour. (☎376-2664. 7-11am complimentary continental breakfast served.) **Johnson's Cabins ❸,** 161 W. 13th St., rents two-person cabins on the Cimarron River with a full kitchen and bath. There are only three cabins, so reserve in advance. (☎376-2210. $45.) **Camping** is available at **Cimarron Canyon State Park ❶,** 12 mi. west of Cimarron on U.S. 64. (☎377-6271. Campsites with flush toilets and sink $10.) Food options are scarce in Cimarron, but the **Coffee Shop ❶** in the St. James Hotel serves tasty sandwiches ($4-7) and Mexican dishes ($6-7) daily 7am-9pm.

The four-story **Old Mill Museum,** on 17th St. one block west of Rte. 21, was built as a grist mill in 1864. The eclectic collection includes the original grinding equipment, Kit Carson's saddle, a T-Rex footprint, an ancient roulette wheel, and phonographs. (Open June-Aug. M-W and F-Sa 9am-5pm, Su 1-5pm; Sept. and May Sa 9am-5pm, Su 1-5pm.) The headquarters of the 130,000 acre **Philmont Boy Scout Ranch** is 4 mi. south of Cimarron on Rte. 21. The land was given to the Boy Scouts in 1941 by Oklahoma oilman Waite Phillips. The Scouts conduct daily tours of Phillips's mansion, the **Villa Philmonte,** throughout the summer. (☎376-2281. Tours June-Aug. daily 8am-5pm every ½hr. $4 donation requested.) The Boy Scouts also operate the **Kit Carson Museum,** 7 mi. south of Philmont Headquarters on Rte. 21, an 1850 hacienda on the Santa Fe Trail, where Kit Carson lived for four years. (Open daily June 1-Aug. 22 8am-5pm. Free.) **Cimarron Canyon State Park** (☎377-6271), 15 mi. west of Cimarron on U.S. 64, encompasses a scenic 8 mi. stretch of the Cimarron River. The park offers four campgrounds along the river ($10) with running water and flush toilets. The 7 mi. round-trip **Clear Creek Canyon Trail** follows a tributary of the River up the side of the canyon, passing four waterfalls and offering views of the Sangre de Cristo Mountains to the north and south.

RATON   ☎505

This gateway town on the Colorado border is basically used as a pit stop for travelers between Denver and Albuquerque. Just north of town, the Raton Mountain Pass was once the most treacherous stretch of the Santa Fe Trail. Raton makes a good base for exploring the wonders of Capulin Volcano and Sugarite Canyon.

Raton is only 8 mi. south of the Colorado border on I-25. **Amtrak**, 201 1st St., stops in Raton at a 100-year-old adobe station, sending one train daily to Albuquerque and to Chicago (open daily 9:30am-6:30pm). **Greyhound**, 419 Clayton Rd. (☎445-9071), has bus service from Raton to Albuquerque (5hr., 3 per day, $38) and Denver (5hr., 3 per day, $37). The **Raton Visitors Center,** 100 Clayton Rd., has free maps and info. (☎445-2761. Open June-Aug. daily 7am-7pm; Sept.-May 8am-5pm.)

El Portal Hotel ❸, 101 N. 3rd St., was built in 1900 and its lobby is covered with murals painted in the 1930s by the WPA. Beautifully decorated antique rooms have cable TV and bathtubs with "feet." (☎445-3631 or 888-362-7345. Singles and doubles $44-59.) Reasonably priced motels line 2nd St. and Clayton Rd., clustering around Exit 451 on I-25. The **Oasis Restaurant and Motel ❸,** 1445 South 2nd St., is your next best option for a room. An adjacent restaurant serves up soups and burgers like it's going out of style. (☎445-2221. Singles $39; doubles $53.) **Sugarite Canyon State Park ❶,** 10 mi. northeast of Raton, has campsites ($10).

Sugarite Canyon State Park, 6 mi. northeast of town, has 15 mi. of hiking trails that traverse the dramatic **Little Horse Mesa** and the remains of a once-prosperous coal mining operation. Within the park, **Soda Pocket Campground ❶** has water and vault toilets, in a forested area with great views of the mesas. (☎445-5607. Visitors Center open daily 8am-5pm, often closed in winter. Day use $4 per car, campsites $10.)

CAPULIN VOLCANO NATIONAL MONUMENT

The grassy plains of northeastern New Mexico are interrupted by the mountains and mesas of the 8000 square mile Raton-Clayton Volcanic Field, which has been sporadically active over the past nine million years. Capulin Volcano, which erupted around 60,000 years ago, is one of the most recent eruptions in the field. Although the eruption lasted only a few years, in that time volcanic rock fragments accumulated to form a symmetrical cinder cone rising 1400 feet above the surrounding plains. After the eruption ended, soil accumulated on the surface of the mountain, and today the volcano is covered by grass, pine, juniper, and many shrubs. Deer, rodents, hummingbirds, and snakes all inhabit this ecosystem.

At the base of the mountain, the **Visitors Center** shows a 10min. introductory video. From here, a 2 mi. drive leads to the top of the cinder cone. A 1 mi. hike circles the rim of the crater, and a 0.2 mi. hike leads down into the center of the crater. From the highest point on the rim trail, you can see four states. To get to the volcano, drive 30 mi. east of Raton, and 3 mi. north of the village of Capulin on Rte. 325. (☎278-2201. Open summer Su-Th 7:30am-6:30pm, F-Sa 7:30am-sunset, winter 8am-4:30pm daily. $5 per vehicle.)

NORTHWESTERN NEW MEXICO

Offering a chunk of the Navajo Nation, the Bisti Badlands, ancient indigenous dwellings at Chaco Canyon, and unique lava formations at El Malpais, northwestern New Mexico has much more to offer than the stretch of Rte. 66 that too-often simply shuttles travelers between the Petrified Forest and Santa Fe. Stray from the highway to explore the area's diverse landscape and cultural offerings.

CHAMA   ☎505

Just south of the Colorado border, Chama seems to have been skipped over by the sweeping homogenization of American culture. And yet no one seems to care. The Cumbres & Toltec Scenic Railroad still chugs northeast to Antonito, Colorado, as though stuck in some forgotten era, and the largely Hispanic population concerns itself with tending local cattle herds and sheep flocks rather than tourists.

■■ **🛈 ORIENTATION AND PRACTICAL INFORMATION.** U.S. 84/64 runs north from Santa Fe, skirting Chama a few miles south of downtown before heading west toward Farmington and Pagosa Springs. Rte. 17 forms the main drag downtown, Terrace Avenue, running parallel to the river and the train tracks.

A car is a must in Chama. The closest bus line runs through Espanola, 95 mi. away. The **New Mexico Welcome Center,** 2372 Rte. 17, sits at the intersection with U.S. 84/64. (☎756-2235. Open June-Oct. daily 8am-6pm; Oct.-May 8am-5pm.) The **Chama Valley Chamber of Commerce,** 463 Terrace Ave. in the Cumbres Mall building, offers local info. (☎756-2306 or 800-477-0149; www.chamavalley.com. Open M,W,F, 8am-noon, Tu, Th 1-5pm.) Other services include: **Speed Queen Laundromat,** 400 Pine Ave. (☎756-2782; open M-Sa 8am-8pm); **weather and road conditions** (☎800-432-4269); **police** (☎756-2319); **pharmacy:** Río Drugs of Chama, 587 Terrace Ave. (☎756-2131; open M-F 9am-6pm, Sa 9am-5pm). **Medical Services: La Clínica del Pueblo** (☎588-7252, 12 mi. south on U.S. 84); **post office,** 199 5th St. (☎756-2240; open M-F 8am-4:30pm, Sa 10am-noon). **ZIP code:** 87520.

🛏🍴 ACCOMMODATIONS AND FOOD. The **Y Motel ❷,** 2450 Rte. 84/64, isn't pretty, but the rooms are clean and it's inexpensive. (☎756-2166. Reception 24hr. Check-in 2pm. Check-out 11am. Singles $30; doubles $37.) With the benefits of its convenient location downtown and a complementary continental breakfast, the recently redecorated rooms at **Chama Station Inn ❸** are also a deal. (☎756-2315; www.chamastationinn.com. Singles $54; doubles $66; deluxe rooms $75.) The chainlink fence and barbed wire around **Río Chama RV Campground ❶,** two blocks north of the railroad depot on Rte. 17, are a little disconcerting, but the 13 sites are grassy and equipped with electricity, flush toilets, and showers. (☎756-2303; Reception 8am-8pm. Check-out 11am. $12 per tent.)

Inexpensive meals can be had all over Chama. With sandwiches for $3-5, and entrees for $7-8, **Viva Vera's Mexican Kitchen ❷,** 2202 Rte. 17, is the place to go for cheap Mexican food. (☎756-2557. Open daily 7am-8pm.) **High Country Restaurant & Saloon ❸,** 2289 Rte. 17, serves up the best steaks and trout in town (lunches $5-9, dinner $9-19), and you can't go wrong with the burgers, which are $6-7. (☎756-2384. Open daily 11am-10pm, bar open later.)

◧ SIGHTS. The **Cumbres & Toltec Scenic Railroad,** on Rte. 17 in downtown Chama, is a steam locomotive that runs 64 mi. between Chama and Antonito, Colorado. The train crosses the highest railroad summit in the West at Cumbres Pass and steams across a number of dizzying trestles before continuing through tunnels

FOUR CORNERS **New Mexico, Arizona, Utah,** and **Colorado** meet at a neat intersection about 40 mi. northwest of **Shiprock, NM,** on the Navajo Reservation. **Four Corners** epitomizes American ideas about land; these state borders were drawn along scientifically determined lines of longitude and latitude, disregarding natural or cultural boundaries. There's little to see; nonetheless, a large number of people veer off the highway to marvel at the geo-political anomaly. At the very least, getting down on all fours to put a limb in each state is a good story for a cocktail party. *(Open May-Aug. daily 7am-8pm; Sept.-Apr. 8am-5pm. $2.)*

above the Toltec Gorge. The ride takes about 6½hr., including a stop for lunch in the ghost town of Osier. Shuttle buses are provided for return transportation. For free, pick up a pamphlet detailing the trainyard's history in a walking tour. (☎756-2151 or 888-286-2737; www.cumbrestoltec.com. Trains depart daily late May to late Oct. Tickets $29-60 regular, up to $99 in the parlour car; children under 12 $15-30.) The **Monastery of Christ in the Desert,** Forest Service Road 151, is a Benedictine Monastery standing deep in the colorful Río Chama canyon. Forty miles south of Chama on U.S. 84, take Forest Rd. 151 for 13 mi. Twenty-seven monks are cloistered in this electricity-free, self-sustaining locale, and there is a guesthouse for visitors interested in silence and prayer. (www.christdesert.org. Guests welcome daily 8:45am-6pm.)

In the winter, Chama is known for its cross-country skiing, particularly in the Cumbres Pass meadows. Every Presidents Day Weekend the town hosts the **Chile Classic,** the largest ski race in New Mexico. Operators maintaining overnight yurts for rent include **Southwest Nordic Center** (☎758-4761) and **Cumbres Nordic Adventures** (☎888-660-9878). Call the **Chama Ski Service** (☎756-2492) for more info.

FARMINGTON ☎505

A large part of the labor force in this busy town is employed in the local mines and powerplants, and the long days of hard toilin' flow into nights of hard drinkin' for locals. For travelers, after a day exploring the land and cultures of the Four Corners, Farmington is a good place to get a good night's rest, but not to do much else.

■ 🛿 **ORIENTATION AND PRACTICAL INFORMATION.** Just west of downtown, U.S. 64 swings right and, heading southeast, splits into Broadway and Bloomfield Hwy. after it crosses the Animas River. Getting its start from the curve in 64, Main St. (U.S. 516) bears left and heads northwest through downtown. Main and Broadway serve as Farmington's chief commercial strips. Farmington boasts the **Four Corners Regional Airport,** 1300 W. Navajo St. (☎599-1395), which offers flights to Phoenix and Denver, as well as all major New Mexican cities. Regional bus service is provided by **TNM&O Coaches,** 101 E. Animas St. (☎325-1009), with daily buses running to Durango ($15) and Albuquerque ($28.35).

Visitor info is available at the **Farmington Convention and Visitors Bureau,** 3041 E. Main St., a brand new building with a few galleries displaying the works of local painters and a small museum detailing Farmington's history, as well as info about the town and outdoor activities in the area. (☎326-7602. Open M-F 8am-6pm in summer (museum open Sa as well), M-F 9am-5pm in winter.) **7-2-11** runs laundromats open from 7am-11pm in town at 4200 E. Main St. (☎325-0945), and 1800 E. Murray Dr. (☎325-0925). Other services include: **police,** 900 Municipal Dr. (☎334-6622); **San Juan Regional Medical Center,** 801 W. Maple St. (☎325-5011); **Internet** at the **Farmington Public Library,** 100 W. Broadway (☎599-1270; open M-Th 9am-6pm,

F-Sa 9am-5pm); and the **post office,** 2301 E. 20th St. (☎325-5047; open M-F 8:30am-5:30pm, Sa 10am-1pm). **ZIP code:** 87401.

📷📷 **ACCOMMODATIONS AND FOOD.** The **Sage Motel ❷,** 301 Airport Dr., offers clean rooms with microwaves and fridges for rock-bottom prices. (☎325-7501. Reception 24hr. Check-out 11am. Singles $25; doubles $32; triples $40; quads with 2 bathrooms and a kitchenette $50.) Right next door, the **Journey Inn ❷,** 317 Airport Dr., also offers a good, cheap night's sleep. (☎325-3548. Singles $2; doubles $35.) Tenters can set up near the heart of downtown for a pittance at **Mom and Pop RV Park ❶,** 901 Illinois Ave (off Murray at the southeast end of town). You'll be camping in a cramped suburban wasteland, but hey, the fee includes showers. (☎327-3200. Reception 8am-10pm. 5 tent sites $7, 34 RV sites $16.)

Farmington does not offer much for the sophisticated palate, but a few places offer inexpensive dining options. **El Charro ❷,** 737 W. Main St., is a friendly little nook serving Mexican food for $5-8. (☎327-2464. Take-out available. Open M-Sa 8am-9pm, Su 9am-5pm.) **Sonya's Cookin' USA ❷,** 2001 Bloomfield Hwy., is a popular breakfast spot among locals. Big portions of standard American fare for not-so-big portions of standard American dough. (☎327-3526. Open M-Sa 6am-9pm, Su 9am-7pm. Entrees $3-11.)

📷 **OUTDOOR ACTIVITIES.** Serving more as a base for exploration than a site of its own, Farmington particularly provides a jumping-off point for mountain biking in the surrounding hills. The **Glade Mountain Bike Trails** northeast of downtown Farmington, off Main St., offer some fast singletrack with more than its share of bumps and jumps. The **Piñon Mesa Trails** off La Plata Hwy. present a lot of fast downhill, as well as the steep climbs that come with that luxury. **Cottonwood Cycles,** 4370 E. Main St. (☎326-0429; open M-F 1-6pm, Sa 9am-5pm), and **Havens Bikes and Boards,** 2017 E. Main St. (☎327-1727), both are good sources of more info.

CHACO CULTURE NATIONAL HISTORICAL PARK ☎ 505

Sun-scorched Chaco Canyon served as the first great settlement of the Ancestral Puebloans. The ruins here, which date from the ninth century, are among the most well-preserved in the Southwest. The skill and craftsmanship with which Chacoans built the monumental masonry buildings that lie at the floor of the canyon has played a critical role in their preservation. They planned the multiple stories of these enormous structures before the first brick was laid, and positioned their "great houses" in accordance with solar and lunar patterns. The most celebrated of these ancient works of "public architecture" is Pueblo Bonito, a massive D-shaped structure with many interior *kivas* and two plazas.

The Chacoans did not limit the scope of their expertise to a single valley: through trade and communication within a vast region of the present-day Southwest and Mexico, they spread their ideas and culture. The historical and cultural sacredness of Chaco Canyon was recognized in 1987, when it was designated a World Heritage Site. Today Chaco is revered by visitors from around the world who venture out into the desert, as well as by the Hopi, Navajo, and Puebloan peoples who consider the canyon part of their sacred homeland.

📷📷 **ORIENTATION AND PRACTICAL INFORMATION.** Chaco Canyon lies 92 mi. northeast of Gallup. From the north, take Rte. 44/550 to County Rd. 7900 (3 mi. east of **Nageezi** and 50 mi. west of **Cuba**), and follow the road for 21 mi., 16 of which are unpaved. From the south, take Rte. 9 from **Crownpoint** (home of the nearest ATM and grocery store) 36 mi. east to the marked park turnoff in Pueblo Pintado;

turn north onto unpaved Rte. 46 for 10 mi.; turn left on County Rd. 7900 for 7 mi.; turn left onto unpaved County Rd. 7950 and follow it 16 mi. to the park entrance. You can also take Rte. 57 straight north from Rte. 9 into the park.

Car is the only practical means by which to reach Chaco Canyon. *None of these roads are paved: pick-up trucks and high-clearance vehicles with four-wheel drive are recommended. There is no gas in the park, and gas stations en route are few and far between.* The nearest gas station is 21 mi. from the entrance on Rte. 44/550. If it has recently rained, the unpaved roads may be impassable. Call the park (☎ 786-7014) in advance to inquire about the conditions or call 888-386-7637 for more general weather and road info.

The **Visitors Center,** at the east end of the park, has an excellent museum that exhibits Ancestral Puebloan art and architecture. Pay the entrance fee and stock up on water here. All the ruins have interpretive brochures at their sites that can be purchased for 50-75¢. (☎ 786-7014. Open June-Aug. daily 8am-6pm; Sept.-May 8am-5pm. $8 per vehicle.) In case of an emergency, call 786-7060. The nearest post office is in Nageezi, 25 mi. northeast of the park.

⚐ CAMPING. The **Gallo Campground ❶,** a little more than 1 mi. from the Visitors Center, offers serene desert camping for $10 per site; register at the campground. The 48 sites have access to tables, fireplaces, and central toilets. For those bedding down at the park, star-gazing is offered at the observatory, open to visitors four nights a week (call ahead for available nights). The most accessible inexpensive lodgings are in Farmington, 75 mi. north.

◪ SIGHTS. The largest pueblos are accessible from the main loop road. Although there are only five primary pull-outs on this 9 mi. road, several hours or an entire day should be dedicated to seeing the sites. The first of the six major Chacoan cultural sites, **Una Vida,** is accessed via a trail beginning at the Visitors Center. Most of the site is unexcavated, providing a good glimpse at what the other ruins must have been like before the archaeologists got their hands on them. There are also some excellent petroglyphs on the canyon wall above the site. The first site on the loop road is **Hungo Pavi,** where relatively small-scale ruins serve as an introduction for the monumental "great houses" to come. The second set of ruins is **Chetro Ketl,** which ups the ante with its raised plaza and vast *kiva,* a circular prayer room used in religious rituals. Nearby **Pueblo Bonito** is the canyon's largest pueblo; it was once four stories high and contained more than 600 rooms. **Pueblo del Arroyo,** built relatively quickly toward the end of the Chacoan ascendancy, is the next site. Finally, on the south side of the canyon, **Casa Rinconada** features a "Great *Kiva,*" one of the largest in the Southwest.

◪ HIKING. The opportunities for backcountry hiking in the park abound, and several excellent trails lead to more remote ruins. All the treks are hikeable year-round. Stay on designated trails, and be sure to snag a free backcountry permit from the Visitors Center before heading out. The **Wijiji Trail** explores a great house built around 1100 AD. Starting at the Wijiji parking area 1 mi. east of the Visitors Center, this easy hike makes for a 3 mi. round-trip. The moderately difficult 5.4 mi. round-trip **Pueblo Alto Trail** offers stunning overlook views of Pueblo Bonito and the other great houses, as well as exploring feats of Chacoan engineering on the mesa top (elevation gain 250 ft.). The **Peñasco Blanco Trail** is the longest trail in the park, heading deep into Chaco Canyon and providing a perspective on the many cultures who have lived and traveled here. The trail ends at the unexcavated great house, Peñasco Blanco. The trailhead is located at the Pueblo del Arroyo parking area. (6.4 mi. round-trip. Elevation gain 150 ft.) Finally, the **South Mesa**

Trail climbs high above the canyon onto South Mesa from the trailhead at the Casa Rinconada parking area, and explores another great house, Tsin Kletzin. The entire trail affords spectacular panoramas of the canyon and San Juan Basin. (4.1 mi. round-trip. Elevation gain 450 ft.)

GALLUP   ☎ 505

Gallup, located at the intersection of I-40 and U.S. 666, falls into the unfortunate class of Western cities that seem to have been built too quickly, filling their cultural void with an empty supermarket-and-styrofoam-cup modernity. However, Gallup's proximity to the Petrified Forest National Park (see p. 119), the Navajo Reservation (see p. 122), Chaco Culture National Historic Park (see p. 396), and the El Morro and El Malpais National Monuments (see p. 399) somewhat redeems it for travelers. Gallup is also a good base for exploring the Four Corners region.

◪ **PRACTICAL INFORMATION. Gallup Municipal Airport** offers flights daily to Denver and other New Mexico cities on **Mesa Airlines** (☎722-5404 or 800-235-9292). **Amtrak,** 201 E. Rte. 66 (☎800-872-7245), chugs two trains through Gallup daily. (Eastbound train departs 8:51am; westbound train departs 7:55pm.) **Greyhound,** 201 E. Rte. 66 (☎863-3761), runs to **Albuquerque** (2½hr., 4 per day, $21), and **Flagstaff** (4hr., 4 per day, $38). Another good option is the **Navajo Transit System,** 201 E. Rte. 66., which sends buses a few times daily all over the Navajo Nation. (☎928-729-4115. Call for more info.) **Luna's Taxi** (☎722-9777) services the Gallup area. **Price King Rent-a-Car,** 2000 S. 2nd St., offers vehicles from $30 per day.

You can visit the **Gallup Visitors Center,** 701 Montoya Blvd., just off Rte. 66, for info on all of New Mexico. (☎863-4909 or 800-242-4282; www.gallupnm.org. Open daily 8am-5pm, June-Aug. 8am-6pm) Other services include: **Pronto Laundry,** 2422 E. Rte. 66 (☎863-2207); **Weather and Road Conditions:** ☎863-3811; **Police:** 451 State Rd. 564 (☎722-2231); **Crisis Line:** ☎800-721-7273; and **Rehoboth McKinley Christian Hospital,** 1901 Red Rock Dr. (☎863-7000). Free **Internet access** is available at the **Octavia Fellin Library,** 115 W. Hill St. (☎863-1291. Open M-Th 9am-8pm, F-Sa 10am-6pm.) **Post office:** 950 W. Aztec. (☎722-5265. Open M-F 8:30am-5pm, Sa 10am-1:30pm.) **ZIP code:** 87301.

▐◘ **ACCOMMODATIONS AND FOOD. Old Rte. 66,** which runs parallel to I-40 through downtown, is lined with dirt-cheap motels, often with the emphasis on the dirt. The best place to stay in town, hands down, is **El Rancho Hotel and Motel ❸,** 1000 E. Rte. 66, which is a step up in price from most other options, but a leap in quality. The who's-who of the silver screen all stayed here once (John Wayne, Jack Benny, Kirk Douglas) and had a room named after him or her. (☎863-9311. Reception 24hr. Check-in 2pm. Check-out 12pm. Singles $47; doubles $55.) One of the best spots for those watching their bottom line is the **Blue Spruce Lodge ❷,** 119 E. Rte. 66, with clean, well-maintained rooms. (☎863-5211. Reception 8am-11pm. Check-out 11am. Singles $24; doubles $26.) You can pitch a tent in the shadow of red sandstone cliffs at **Red Rock State Park Campground ❶,** Rte. 566, which offers access to hiking 5 mi. east of town off Rte. 66. (☎863-1329. 142 sites with showers and hookups. Tent sites $10, hookups $14.)

In addition to the usual fast-food suspects, a number of diners and cafes line both sides of I-40. **Earl's Restaurant ❷,** 1400 E. Rte. 66, has been around since 1947, and the food and prices show why. (☎863-4201. Open M-Sa 6am-9:30pm, Su 7am-9pm. Entrees $4-10.) **The Ranch Kitchen ❷,** 3001 W. Rte 66, has filling breakfasts, sandwiches and burgers ($5-7) and steaks. (Open in summer 7am-10pm, in winter

7am-9pm). **Panz Alegra ❷,** 1201 E. Rte. 66, is an upscale spot with good deals on Mexican dishes ($7-10), as well as steaks. (☎722-7229. Open M -Th 11am-10pm, F-Sa 11am-11pm.) **Wild Sage People's Market,** 610 E. Pershing, offers a good selection of organic foods in bulk quantities; a nice respite from the rest of Gallup. (☎863-5383. Open Tu, W, F 3:30-7pm, Sa 10am-6pm.)

EL MORRO NATIONAL MONUMENT ☎505

Drawn by a nearby spring while traveling through what is now New Mexico, Native Americans, Spanish explorers, and Anglo pioneers left their inscriptions on a giant sandstone bluff. **Inscription Rock,** its signatures dating back to 1605, has been the center piece of El Morro National Monument since its founding in 1906. The monument is located just west of the Continental Divide on Rte. 53, 42 mi. west of Grants and 56 mi. southeast of Gallup. The **Visitors Center** includes a small museum and warnings against emulating the graffiti of old. (☎783-4226. Open June-Aug. daily 8am-7pm; off-season 9am-5pm. $3, under 17 free.) The small, tranquil **El Morro Campground ❶** has running water, primitive toilets, and is rarely full. (9 sites, 1 wheelchair accessible. Open year-round. $5 per site.)

The monument offers two hiking options. The 0.5 mi. wheelchair-accessible **Inscription Trail** winds past the rock and neighboring spring, providing excellent views of the signatures and neighboring petroglyphs. The 2 mi. **Mesa Top Trail** continues on, climbing 200 ft. to the top of the rock before skirting the edges of two ancient pueblos. The entire trail is well-marked and affords impressive panoramas of the entire region. Trails close 1hr. before the Visitors Center.

EL MALPAIS NATIONAL MONUMENT ☎505

Home to a spectacle of converging lava flows and sandstone mesas, this 15 year-old national monument and its associated BLM land feature some of the Southwest's most unique and varied terrain, from miles of lava tubes to one of New Mexico's largest natural arches. Despite its spectacular landscape, the monument does not receive the traffic of some of its neighbors, making it a perfect spot to escape the crowds and head into some true wilderness.

◪ ▨ ORIENTATION AND PRACTICAL INFORMATION. Rte. 53 runs along the western side of the monument, while Rte. 117 borders the eastern side. Both roads are the means of accessing the trailheads, and are themselves excellent ways to see the diverse landscape. In addition, Rte. 42 runs into the monument's belly, but because it is unmaintained, a high-clearance vehicle is recommended.

A number of Visitors Centers are located throughout El Malpais and serve as invaluable resources for would-be explorers. Off I-40 at Exit 85, the **Northwest New Mexico Visitors Center** sits at the northern part of the monument and is the best place to begin the venture. (☎876-2783. Open May-Sept. daily 9am-6pm; Oct.-Apr. 8am-5pm.) The park service's **El Malpais Information Center** (☎783-4774) is 23 mi. south of I-40 on Rte. 53, while the **Bureau of Land Management's Ranger Station** (☎280-2918) is on Rte. 117, 9 mi. south of I-40 off Exit 89. (Both open daily 8:30am-4:30pm.) There is now one established campground at **The Narrows ❶,** which has five free sites with vault toilets. It is located off Rte. 117, and there is no water or electricity. **Backcountry camping ❶** is free in designated spots in the Big Tubes and El Calderon areas. Obtaining a permit at one of the Visitors Centers is recommended. For more info, contact any of the Visitors Centers or write the National Park Service, 123 E. Roosevelt, Grants, NM 87020.

NEW MEXICO

◪ **SIGHTS.** Rte. 117 runs by the most accessible wonders of the monument. The wheelchair-accessible **Sandstone Bluffs Overlook,** 10 mi. south of I-40 and 1 mi. south of the Visitors Center, offers panoramic vistas of the El Malpais lava flows and the surrounding landscape. Seven miles farther south, **La Ventana Natural Arch** is the largest of New Mexico's readily accessible natural arches. Less than 1 mi. farther along, Rte. 117 enters **The Narrows,** where lava flowed to the base of 500 ft. tall sandstone cliffs thousands of years ago.

◪ **HIKING.** The **Narrows Rim Trail** provides excellent access to the landscape around the Narrows. The 6 mi. roundtrip trail begins at the southern end of The Narrows, 21 mi. from I-40, and scrambles to the top of the rim, where spectacular views of the lava flows and La Ventana Natural Arch greet you.

Rte. 53 offers access to the heart of the monument's lava flows via a number of good hiking trails. The **Zuni-Acoma Trail,** 16 mi. south of I-40, traces an ancient Puebloan trade route across four of the area's major lava flows and is part of the Continental Divide Trail. The strenuous hike is a 15 mi. round-trip or 7.5 mi. one-way to Rte. 117. Four miles farther down Rte. 53, the **El Calderon Area** provides access to a relatively old lava flow and volcanic cinder cone. An easy 3 mi. loop passes by **Junction Cave,** sink holes, and trenches amid vegetation resilient enough to make the lava flow its home.

◪ **OTHER OUTDOOR ACTIVITIES.** The **Big Tubes Area,** on the Big Tubes Rd., 4.5 mi. after the turnoff from Rte. 42, encompasses 17 mi. of lava tubes as well as a marked trail to two caves open to the general public, **Big Skylight** and **Four Windows.** Be sure to speak with a ranger about the necessary precautions of caving before setting out. Farther south off of Rte. 42, the 36 mi. **Chain of Craters Backcountry Byway** passes along a rift lined with 30 cinder cones, and necessitates a high-clearance vehicle. The **West Malpais Wilderness** and **Hole-in-The-Wall** offer the most remote backcountry experiences in the area. Hole-in-the-Wall is an island of ponderosa pines surrounded by a sea of lava, and many species have adapted to the unique conditions here. East of Rte. 117, opportunities for backcountry hiking and camping abound in the Cebolla Wilderness.

SOUTHWESTERN NEW MEXICO

With some of the most remote wilderness in all of the Southwest, southwestern New Mexico offers a backcountry hiker's wonderland with miles of untraveled land. While many towns in the region are mostly residential areas, the outdoors opportunities and history make up for it. Hiking in the Gilas, rejuvenating yourself at the mineral baths of Truth or Consequences, and rejoining civilization in the historic town of Mesilla are just a few of the reasons to pull over.

TRUTH OR CONSEQUENCES   ☎505

In 1950, Ralph Edwards' popular radio game show, "Truth or Consequences," celebrated its tenth anniversary by renaming this small town, formerly Hot Springs, NM, in its honor. Every year on the first weekend of May, residents celebrate the name change with a fiesta. Events include parades, rodeos, art displays, country music, high-energy drum circles, and canoe races. Today, T or C (pronounced "tee-er-see") is a slow-paced, one-traffic-light town of 7500 people. As its maiden name suggests, the town was a tourist attraction prior to the publicity stunt. Mineral baths provide the mythic fountains of youth and an ex-drifter, down-home spirit is its consequence.

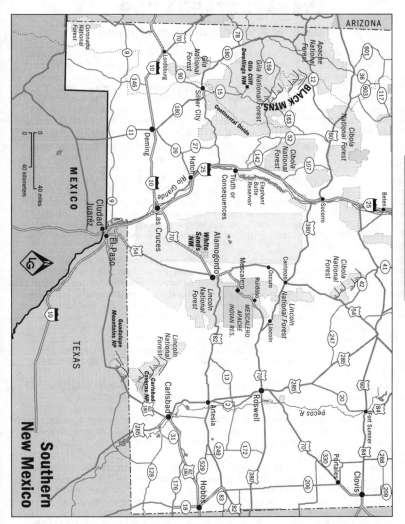

■ 🛈 ORIENTATION AND PRACTICAL INFORMATION. T or C sits approximately 150 mi. south of Albuquerque on I-25. **Buses** depart and arrive from C.W.'s Premium Water and Ice, 8 Date St. **Greyhound,** in cooperation with **TNM&O Coaches** (☎894-3649), runs two coaches daily from Albuquerque (3hr., $31.50) and one from El Paso (2hr., $26.50). The **Chamber of Commerce,** 201 S. Foch St., has free maps and brochures about area accommodations and attractions. (☎894-3536. Open M-F 9am-5:30pm, Sa 9am-1pm.) Other services include: **24hr. ATM,** 509 Broadway, at the Bank of the Southwest; **Davis Fleck Pharmacy,** 500 Broadway (☎894-3055; open M-F 9am-6pm, Sa 9am-3pm); **hospital,** 800 E. 9th Ave. (☎894-2111); **police,** 401 McAdoo (☎894-1185, after hours 894-7111); **free Internet access,**

ANASAZI STARGAZING
The Case for Ancient Astronomy at Chaco

On July 4, 1054, a seemingly new object appeared in the constellation: Taurus, an object so bright that it could be seen during the day for almost a month. A star in Taurus had gone supernova; the explosion created the famous Crab nebula and pulsar. The only known written record of this event comes from the Sung-Shih, the dynastic records of the Sung Dynasty of China; why no European or Middle Eastern chronicle mentions the 1054 supernova remains a mystery. Nearly as mysterious is whether the supernova was also observed and recorded by the Ancestral Pueblo peoples (also referred to as Anasazi Indians), who inhabited Chaco Canyon in the middle of the 11th century.

From the mid-9th to the mid-12th century, Chaco Canyon was the political, economic, and ceremonial center of a "Chacoan world" that encompassed the Chaco Plateau and the San Juan Basin, and is now referred to as the Four Corners area. An irrigation system helped support an estimated population of between 2000 and 5000 people in the arid desert in and around Chaco, and more than 400 miles of roads linked the Canyon to 75 smaller settlements. Copious archaeological evidence, including macaw skeletons and seashells, suggests that trade contacts came from as far as Mexico. However, the great civilization centered on Chaco Canyon did not have a written language, and this is one major reason the question of whether the supernova was recorded at Chaco has remained unresolved.

The proposed records of the supernova in the American Southwest are rock art, making them often difficult to date and interpret. At Chaco, the ceiling of a cave near Penasco Blanco, one of the Canyon's "great houses," contains a pictograph, or pigment painted onto the rock face, of a moon-like crescent and a star; pictographs of a human hand and the sun are also nearby. Just before dawn on July 5, 1054, the new supernova and a crescent moon would have appeared, very near each other, in the sky over Chaco Canyon. This fact, combined with the overall rarity of crescents in Southwestern rock art, has led some scholars to consider the pictograph a record of the 1054 supernova. Yet the identification is almost impossible to confirm. Any given rock-art site contains pictographs that span centuries, and it is often difficult to establish which pictographs were created at the same time.

Chaco Canyon has a number of sites with less ambiguous connections to specific astronomical phenomena, particularly solar solstices and equinoxes. Some of the niches in the Great *Kiva* at Casa Rinconada may be aligned to be illuminated at the summer solstice, and at least three different spots on the mesa top—near Wijiji, Pueblo Bonito, and Casa Rinconada—have been identified as possible solstice markers or solstice-observing stations. *Kivas* are circular ceremonial structures, usually built into the ground and accessed via a ladder through the roof.

Near the top of Fajada Butte, a 135m rock tower near the southern entrance to the Canyon, is Chaco's "sun dagger," an arrangement of three enormous sloping stone slabs and two petroglyphs that marked both solstices and equinoxes. Near noon on the summer solstice, a moving "dagger" of sunlight bisects the larger, spiral petroglyph, while on the winter solstice, two daggers of light frame the same spiral; on the equinoxes, a smaller dagger of light bisects the snake petroglyph. The light show was discovered in 1977, and now the site is visited only once a year to monitor its condition. Recently, the National Park Service established a small observatory at the Chaco Canyon Visitors Center to take advantage of the same dark skies observed by the Ancestral Pueblo peoples who built the great houses of Chaco.

__Claudia Cyganowski__ graduated from Harvard University with a degree in Astronomy. She has participated in archaeological field research in Southwestern Colorado and Copán, Honduras, and has researched the significance of astronomy and the calendar in classic Maya society, the Zapotec hieroglyphic writing system, and other archaeological topics.

325 Library Ln. (☎894-3027), at the public library, and **post office,** 300 Main St., in the middle of town (open M-F 9am-3pm), or 1507 N. Date St. (open 8:30am-5pm). **ZIP code:** 87901.

Γ ACCOMMODATIONS. ▓**Riverbend Hot Springs Hostel (HI-AYH) ❶,** 100 Austin St., can be reached from I-25. Take Exit 79, turn right, and continue 1½ mi. to a traffic light. Turn left at the light, then immediately turn right onto Cedar St. and follow it down to the river and the blue building at the road's bend. Use of on-site mineral baths and a meditation cove are free for guests. Riverbend is reason enough to stop in T or C—many travelers plan to spend a night and end up staying a week. (☎894-6183; www.nmhotsprings.com. Kitchen and laundry. Reception open 8am-10pm, call ahead for late-night arrivals. Tepees or dorms $14, non-members $16; private rooms $30-48; tent site $10, non-members $12.) The **Charles Motel and Spa ❷,** 601 Broadway, offers simple and clean accommodations. The large rooms have kitchenettes, A/C, and cable TV. There are also mineral baths on the premises. (☎894-7154 or 800-317-4518; www.charlessspa.com. Singles $30, with kitchenette $35; doubles $39; rooftop suites $45.) **Campsites** at the nearby **Elephant Butte Lake State Park ❶** have access to restrooms and cold showers. (Primitive sites $8; developed sites with showers $10; with electricity $14.)

❏ FOOD. Nearly all of T or C's restaurants are as easy on the wallet as the baths are on the body. For groceries, try **Bullock's,** at the corner of Broadway and Post. (☎894-6622. Open M-Sa 7:30am-8pm, Su 8am-7pm.) **La Hacienda ❷,** 1615 S. Broadway, is well worth the drive out of the center of town. *Arroz con pollo* ($7), and breakfast *chorizo con huevos* ($5) make this the best Mexican food around. (Open Tu-Sa 11-9pm Su 11-8pm.) The popular **La Cocina ❷,** 1 Lake Way Dr. (look for the "Hot Stuff" sign above N. Date St.), also pleases with huge portions of Mexican and New Mexican food, including chimichangas ($7). A Carrizozo cherry cider ($1.50) will slake your thirst. (☎894-6499. Open daily 10:30am-10pm.) **Hot Springs Bakery Cafe ❷,** 313 Broadway, located in a stucco turquoise building, has an outdoor patio and cactus garden. Pizzas go for $7-14. (☎894-5555. Open Tu-Sa 8am-3pm.) **Bar-B-Que on Broadway ❷,** 308 Broadway, serves plentiful breakfast specials (starting at $2.50) and hearty lunch entrees ($5-8), as well as local buzz. (☎894-7047. Open M-Sa 7am-4pm.)

☒ NIGHTLIFE. Raymond's Lounge, 912 N. Date St., next to the Circle K, is T or C's rock'n' roll bar. (☎894-4057. Free pool Th night. Draft beers $1.50. Open M-Sa 11am-2am, Su noon-midnight.) The **Pine Nut Saloon,** 700 E. 3rd Ave., just up the road towards Elephant Butte, is a vintage Western saloon adorned with photos of John Wayne. (☎894-2714. Karaoke Th and live music on weekends.) **The Dam Site,** just past the **Elephant Butte Dam** on Rte. 51, is a bar and grille with an outdoor patio, offering spectacular views of the lake and surrounding mountains. (☎894-2073. Live music Sa afternoon Easter to Labor Day. Dinner entrees $7-19, drafts $2.50. Open Su-Th 11am-9pm, F-Sa 11am-10pm; bar open F-Sa until midnight.)

◨ ⚘ SIGHTS AND OUTDOORS. T or C's **mineral baths** are the town's main attraction; locals claim that they heal virtually everything. The only outdoor tubs are located at the **Riverbend Hostel,** where four co-ed tubs (bathing suits must be worn) abut the Río Grande. Access to the baths is $6 per hr. for the public (10am-7pm), but complimentary for hostel guests (7am-10am and 7pm-10pm).

Five miles north of T or C (take Date St. north until a sign for Elephant Butte; turn right onto 181 and follow the signs), **Elephant Butte Lake State Park** features New Mexico's largest lake. A public works project dammed up the Río Grande in 1916 after the resolution of a major water rights dispute between the US and Mexico. The resulting lake is named after the elephantine rock formation at its southern end. The park offers sandy beaches for swimming and a marina for boating. (Cars $4, bikes and pedestrians free.) **Sports Adventure,** on the lake at the end of Long Point Rd., rents jet skis. (☎ 744-5557 or 888-736-8420. Rentals start at $35 per 30min.) The marina at the **Dam Site** rents motorized boats of all kinds. (☎ 894-2041. Must be 18+ and have a valid driver's license to rent. Motorboats $20 per hr., pontoon boats $30 per hr., ski boats $45 per hr.) There is a **Visitors Center** at the entrance to the park with a small museum on the natural history of the area. (☎ 877-664-7787. Open M-F 7:30am-4pm, Sa-Su 7:30am-10pm.) An easy 1.6 mi. nature trail begins in the parking lot just past the Visitors Center.

■ **DAYTRIP FROM TRUTH OR CONSEQUENCES: BOSQUE DEL APACHE NATIONAL WILDLIFE REFUGE.** Damming the Río Grande in the early decades of the 20th century destroyed the wetlands that were once winter feeding grounds for migratory waterfowl. In 1939, Franklin Roosevelt created Bosque del Apache in an effort to recreate these lost wetlands. At the end of every summer, 7000 acres of land are flooded to provide a fertile resting ground for 20,000 sandhill cranes, 30,000 snowgeese, and countless other waterfowl. The peak season for bird-watching is November through February, and the best times of day are sunrise and sunset. During the **Festival of the Cranes,** which is held every November, over 5000 bird-watchers descend on the Refuge to attend talks and embark on tours. To reach the Refuge, take I-25 to Exit 124 (at San Marcial) and go north on Rte. 1 for 8 mi. (Open 1 hr. before sunrise to 1 hr. after sunset. $3 per car.)

A 15 mi. **auto loop** takes visitors past the prime bird-viewing locations. The loop also makes an excellent bike trail. Within the wildlife refuge are a number of hiking trails, ranging from easy to strenuous. The **Canyon Trail** is a moderately difficult 2.5 mi. hike through the northern tip of the Chihuahuan Desert. It begins by winding through a dry river bed and passes a natural rock arch on its way to an overlook with a view of the Río Grande and the refuge wetlands. The **Chupadera Trail** is the most challenging hike in the refuge. A 9.7 mi. round-trip, it leads to the summit of 6195 ft. Chupadera Peak, which stands nearly 2000 ft. above the valley floor. Three and a half miles from the trailhead, the trail enters a stunning red canyon created by volcanic activity. From the summit, you can see the northern shore of Elephant Butte Lake to the south, White Sands Missile Range to the east, and the town of Socorro to the north. The **Visitors Center** offers detailed brochures with maps for all hikes within the park. (☎ 835-1828; www.friendsofthebosque.org. Open M-F 7:30am-4pm, Sa-Su 8am-4:30pm.)

Eight miles north of the Wildlife Refuge along Rte. 1 lies the attractive, small village of **San Antonio.** The **Owl Bar and Cafe ❶,** at the main intersection in town, is notable for its famous green chile hamburgers ($3) and its old wooden bar, once owned by Conrad Hilton, the town's most famous resident. (☎ 835-9946. Open M-Sa 8am-9:30pm.) A couple blocks south of the Owl on 4th St. is a beautiful **adobe church** with blue and yellow glass windows. Three and a half miles farther south of San Antonio on Rte. 1 is the **Bosque Birdwatchers RV Park ❶.** (☎ 835-1366. Tent sites $10, with electricity $12; for 2 people $12/$14.)

LAS CRUCES   ☎ 505

The second largest city in New Mexico, Las Cruces is situated in the fertile Río Grande Valley, 32 miles north of El Paso and the Mexican border. No one knows exactly how the town got its name. Some say the name comes from the crosses erected in the area to commemorate the deaths of traders traveling north to Santa Fe along the Camino Real and those townspeople killed during Apache raids. Others claim that it is a Spanish translation of "the crossroads," because in the 18th century, this site marked the intersection of the north-south Camino Real with the east-west Butterfield Trail. Today, Las Cruces marks the intersection of I-25 and I-10. There isn't much to do in Las Cruces itself, but historic Mesilla, just three miles southwest of downtown, has interesting shops, restaurants, and a thriving art community. The rugged Organ Mountains, towering over the city to the east, offer recreational opportunities, including hiking, mountain biking, and camping.

■ ▰ ORIENTATION AND PRACTICAL INFORMATION. Most of the city lies within the frame of **I-25** to the east and **I-10** to the south. East to west, the major north-south streets are Telshor Blvd. (I-25), Main St., and Valley Dr. Lohman Ave. runs east-west through the heart of the city, while University Ave. forms the southern boundary, leads east to the Organ Mountains, and is the easiest route to the historical Mesilla plaza. **Greyhound,** 490A N. Valley Dr. (☎524-8518), on the west side of the city, sends buses to El Paso (45min., $9) and Albuquerque (6½hr., $37). Buses operated by **Road Runner Transit** (☎541-2500) service the Las Cruces area. There are 8-9 routes; adults 50¢, children 25¢. The **Convention and Visitors Bureau,** 211 N. Water St. (☎541-2444), boasts a staff with maps, brochures. Other services include: **police,** 217 E. Picacho Ave. (non-emergency ☎526-0795); **Memorial Medical Center** (☎522-8641), on Telshor Ave. at University Ave.; and the **post office,** 201 E. Las Cruces Ave. (☎524-2841). **ZIP code:** 88001.

▰ ▰ ACCOMMODATIONS AND CAMPING. There are many cheap motels on Picacho Ave. to the west of Valley Dr., within walking distance of the bus station. *However, this area is not very safe at night, so be careful when walking alone.* Other motels are clustered around the exits from I-10 and I-25. The ▨**Lundeen Inn of the Arts Bed and Breakfast ❹,** 618 S. Alameda Blvd., one block west of Main St., is worth the premium price. This beautifully decorated, 100-year-old adobe mansion serves as both a guest house and an art gallery. The spacious rooms are named after area artists, and each has a private bath, A/C, cable TV, and a minifridge. Reservations absolutely necessary. (☎526-3327; www.innoft-hearts.com. Reception 8am-10pm. Singles $58-64; doubles $75-85; suites with kitchen $85-105. Discounts for AAA, AARP, and students.) For a cheaper room, **Day's End Lodge ❷,** 755 N. Valley Dr., just a couple blocks from the bus station, offers simple accommodations with A/C, heating, and cable TV. (☎524-7753. Singles $25, doubles $28-33.) If you are looking for a scenic place to pitch your tent, drive east on Rte. 70 for about 15 mi. and turn left on Aguirre Spring Road to reach the **Aguirre Spring National Recreation Area ❶,** on the eastern side of the Organ Mountains. (☎525-4300. Entrance gate open mid-Apr. to mid-Oct. 8am-8pm, mid-Oct. to mid-Apr. 8am-6pm. Bathroom facilities available. $3 per vehicle.)

▱ FOOD. The food in Las Cruces revolves around fast-food and chain restaurants, but there are a slew of interesting places to dine in nearby Mesilla. **La Posta ❷,** 2410 Calle de San Albino one block from Mesilla plaza, is a favorite among camera-toting tourists and Billy the Kid, Kit Carson, Douglas MacArthur, and Pancho Villa before them. (☎524-3524. Open Su-Th 11am-9pm, F-Sa 11am-9:30pm.) You may want to check out **El Comedor ❷,** 2190 Avenida de Mesilla. Understated and plentiful, the menu includes traditional Mexican stew for $7. (Open M-Th 8am-8pm, F-Sa 8am-9pm, Su 9am-3pm.)

▨ ▰ SIGHTS AND OUTDOORS. Though Las Cruces is the demographic center of the area, Mesilla, only 3 mi. away, is the cultural center. When the US acquired the land in 1854 with the Gadsden Purchase, Mesilla became an important stop for traders and travelers on the route between San Antonio and San Francisco. By the 1880s the town was as wild as any other in the West; it was in Mesilla that Billy the

FROM THE ROAD

THE APPENDIX

Riverbend is a magnet for eccentricity and a knotted yarn. My first night there might've been directed by a New Age crystallogist obsessed with Billy Bob Thornton. Over my head four geckos fought for flies on the hostel's wall, and after swallowing, bobbed their heads to the Red Hot Chilli Peppers' "Give It Away." I still felt dizzy from over two thousand miles of driving cast over four days and the 103-degree dunk in the hot springs hadn't cured me. I pulled up a chair to the circle, pet the guard dog, and eavesdropped on a few stories as my head spun. What I can recall (now jumbled and remixed) sounds a bit like this: "I found me an English girl and I'm gonna marry her...I once made out on Harvard's campus just to spite them, I think he was just horny...I had a pet iguana named Scab 'cause he always used to stick his nose in ashtrays and burned it permanently; he liked to hang out on my ceiling fan and when I'd come home and flip the switch, he'd get flung across the room... MacGyver or the Professor on *Gilligan's Island?*...I find stone much more forgiving....My aunt thought she was Anastasia....it's a shame that insects can fly and have sex at the same time because they can't even appreciate it."

All scored to some guy's cover of Beck's "Cyanide Breathmint," the yipping of a young pup named Magnolia, and an Argentinian woman imitating the howling of monkeys she heard over her hammock in the rainforest.

(continued on next page)

Kid was tried for murder and sentenced to hang in 1881. Today Mesilla looks much the same as it did in the 1880s, and most of the adobe buildings around the central plaza date back 150 years. On the plaza, the **Visitors Center**, 2348 Ave. de Mesilla, shows a short video on the town's history. (☎647-9698. Open daily 9:30am-4:30pm.) Presiding over the plaza is the majestic **San Albino Church** (☎526-9349), originally built in 1855. On Nov. 2-3, residents recognize All Saints Day with the Día de Los Muertos (Day of the Dead) Celebration by putting up tables on the plaza with pictures of their deceased relatives and their favorite culinary dishes.

The **Organ Mountains** to the east of Las Cruces offer great opportunities for hiking, mountain biking, and rock climbing. On the western slope of the Organ Mountains, Dripping Springs and La Cueva, both easy, 1 mi. hikes, are accessible by Dripping Springs Rd. The **Dripping Springs Trail** leads to the ruins of a resort and the "weeping wall" at Dripping Springs. The **La Cueva Trail** leads to an archaeological site that is associated with the ancient Mogollon culture. For more info, check at the **A.B. Cox Visitors Center** (☎522-1219; open daily until sundown). The entrance gate to the park closes every day at sunset. On the eastern slope of the **Organ Mountains, Aguirre Springs** is farther from Las Cruces, but the hiking is more challenging. The **Baylor Pass Trail** is a 6 mi. hike to the top of 5500 ft. Baylor Pass. From the top, one can see Las Cruces and the Río Grande Valley to the west and White Sands National Monument to the east.

SILVER CITY   ☎505

In its heyday, Silver City was a raw, wild place. It spawned the famous outlaw Billy the Kid—brown historical markers scattered around town point out the sites of his home, his school, his first bank robbery, and his first jailbreak. Unfortunately, buildings dating from Billy's Wild West days are few; an 1890s mudslide swept away most of downtown Silver City, producing the trench that downtown Big Ditch Park commemorates. The current downtown dates from the turn of the century and contains some stately buildings, but Silver City's attraction for most visitors is its distance from civilization and proximity to the undisturbed wilderness of Gila National Forest.

■ ☑ ORIENTATION AND PRACTICAL INFORMATION. Silver City is about 50 mi. off I-10 and can easily be reached by state roads. Rte. 90 links the city with **Lordsburg** on I-10 near the Arizona border, U.S. 180 stretches from **Deming** on I-10 through Silver City to northeastern Arizona, and Rte. 152 leads east to

Truth or Consequences. **U.S. 180 (Silver Heights Blvd.)** and **Rte. 90 (Hudson St.)** make up the backbone of the city's street grid. Around the center of town, College Ave. bisects Hudson St. and leads to the **University of Western New Mexico.** A few blocks south, Broadway runs parallel to College Ave. and leads through downtown. One block west of the main drag, Bullard St. contains galleries, health food stores, New Age herb shops, cafes, and various services. **Enterprise Rent-A-Car** has an office at 1455 U.S. 180 E. (☎534-0000. 21+ with credit card and valid driver's license. Open M-F 8:30 am-6pm.) **Silver Stage Lines** (☎800-522-0162) has bus service twice daily to Silver City from the El Paso airport (round-trip $59). **Las Cruces Shuttle Service** (☎800-288-1784) offers daily trips to: Deming (3 per day; $25 one-way, $35 roundtrip, additional person $15); El Paso (3 per day, $38/$60/$25); and Las Cruces (3 per day, $33/$50/$20). Both services pick up passengers from the corner of N. Bullard St. and Broadway. The **Chamber of Commerce/Visitors Center,** 201 N. Hudson St., is near the intersection with Broadway. (☎538-3785. Open M-Sa 9am-5pm, Su noon-4pm.) Other services include: **Laundryland,** 407 N. Hudson St. (☎538-2631; open daily 7:30am-9:30pm); **free Internet access** (1 hr. max.; signup in advance) at the public library, 515 W. College Ave. (☎538-3672; open M, Th 9am-8pm, Tu-W 9am-6pm, F 9am-5, Sa 9am-10); and the **post office,** 500 N. Hudson St. (☎538-2831; open M-F 8:30am-5pm, Sa 10am-noon). **ZIP code:** 88061.

⌐☐ ACCOMMODATIONS AND FOOD. Unfortunately, since the closure of the Carter House Hostel, Silver City accommodations begin in the $30 range. A half-block from Bullard St., ❧**Palace Hotel ❸,** 106 W. Broadway, has beautiful antique-styled rooms that hail from 1882, but only five of them are at the cheap end of the spectrum, and reservations are absolutely necessary in the summer. (☎388-1811. Small rooms $35, doubles $47, additional person $5; suites $57.) Chain motels and other inexpensive lodgings flank U.S. 180 on the east side of town. Bring a phonograph and you're set. Two solid options are the **Copper Manor Motel ❷,** 710 Silver Heights Blvd. (☎538-5392 or 800-853-2916) and the **Drifter Motel and Cocktail Lounge ❷** 711 Silver Heights Blvd. (Motel: ☎800-853-2916. Rooms $36-52. Lounge: ☎538-2916. Live music F-Sa. Open daily 5pm-1:30am.) For chow, the tourist favorite **Jalisco Cafe ❷,** 100 S. Bullard St., at Spring St. in the heart of downtown, serves heaping portions of spicy Mexican food with a unique jalapeño guacamole. (☎388-2060. Open M-Th 11am-8:30pm, F 11am-9pm, Sa 11am-8:30pm. Meals $5-8.) **Olde World Bakery and Cafe ❶,** at the corner of Bullard and

(continued from previous page)

The Río Grande glints; a three-legged cat an English guest has dubbed Tripod hops by; and the last enchilada beds down. Either I'm at the center of the world or its appendix.

Still can't shake the dizziness, and the cabin murals are pulsing in the corner of my headache. I wouldn't be able to sleep even if I could find my cabin, and my ears are fighting each other to listen to two monologues: one on the edibility of dog, the other on repairing the woodwork of old folk guitars. Zero to NM in four days and the only language I know fluently is melting down in the heat. New York summers are hardly such punishment on the body (well, it's only your second day out here). I find my cabin, my bed. If I remember any part of this in the morning, I'll think I swallowed a Jefferson Airplane record.

—Jonathan Sherman

Broadway, is by far the best spot for breakfast or lunch in Silver City. Danishes ($1.50), stacked cold cut and vegetarian sandwiches for $5-6. (☎534-9372. Open M-Sa 7am-5pm. Outdoor seating too.)

🅖 🅜 **SIGHTS AND OUTDOORS.** For a view of the Wild West, try the **Billy the Kid Historical Walk.** It starts at the corner of Hudson St. and Broadway; follow the arrows to take the walk.

Silver City houses the headquarters for the **Gila National Forest;** the main forestry station is on the 32nd Bypass Rd. off U.S. 180 east of town. The station provides excellent maps of the forest and its wilderness areas, as well as having info on various outdoor activities in the region. (☎388-8201. Open M-F 8am-4:30pm.) Its proximity to the national forest makes Silver City the base for a variety of outfitting operations. The **Gila Hike and Bike Shop,** 103 E. College Ave., rents mountain bikes and cross-country skis for exploring Gila and the surrounding foothills, repairs bikes, sells outdoor equipment, and provides maps of the area. (☎388-3222. Open M-F 9am-5:30pm, Sa 9am-5pm, Su 10am-4pm. Bike rentals first day $20, 2nd day $15, 3rd day $10, each additional day $5; cross-country skis $12 per day.) **Continental Divide Tours,** run by one of the Hike and Bike boys, runs van, hiking, and biking tours in the Gila area. (☎534-2953. 4hr. tour $50, full-day $110.)

GILA NATIONAL FOREST ☎505

The Gila National Forest encompasses hundreds of miles of hiking trails through mountains, canyons, and forests. This area includes more wilderness than any other national forest in the Southwest. Rugged, mountainous terrain makes it ideal for extended and intense backpacking trips.

🔢 PRACTICAL INFORMATION

Three **ranger stations** serve the Gila National Forest one in **Silver City** (see p. 406), one near **Mimbres** along Rte. 35, and another northwest of Silver City along U.S. 180 near **Glenwood.** The Silver City ranger station is the regional headquarters, offering offers recreational info and maps pertaining to the entire area.

Dispersed camping is permitted without permit or restriction anywhere in the forest—the only exception may be sensitive areas of the designated wilderness, where seasonal limitations may take effect. Ask rangers for details. More accessible than the vast tracts of wilderness, there are several maintained campgrounds in the area. Thirty-eight miles north of Silver City, 4 mi. south of the Cliff Dwellings Visitors Center, the free **Grapevine ❶** and **Forks Campgrounds ❶** provide toilets, although there are no designated sites. A scant ¼ mi. from the Visitors Center, the **Scorpion Campground ❶** features more services (water and toilets in summer, picnic tables, and grills) at the same low price.

🔯 HIKING AND BACKPACKING

Gila National Forest is truly colossal and singular in that the entire forest is in one contiguous chunk. As a result, the trails are as close to infinite as can be had outside of Siberia. The only limits to **backpacking** trips in the forest are your creativity and stamina. A brief glance at a topo map will get your mind swimming with ideas for a week-long escape. There are very few established routes, though consulting with a park ranger might give you a way to narrow down the possibilities. Horses are allowed on most trails. A number of popular trailheads lie along the length of

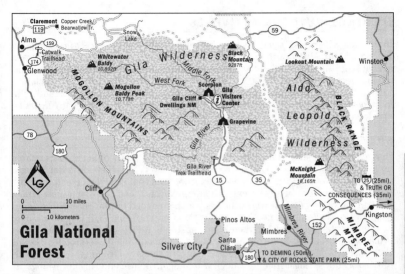

Forest Rd. 15 to the Cliff Dwellings. Many of these trailheads offer both day hiking and backpacking alternatives. Some of the **day hiking** opportunities in the Gilas are a bit more established. The following hikes will give you a good place to start.

The Gila River Trek (17 mi. round-trip, 1 *long* day or 2). Beginning at the Sapillo Trailhead, just south of the junction with Rte. 35, this trail crosses canyon country for its first leg before following the Gila River north and east 10 mi. to link up with Forest Rd. 15 near Grapevine Campground. The first part follows Spring Canyon Trail (#247). The initial ascent is a short climb and after approximately 5 mi. of hiking that is mostly dropping in elevation, the trail hits the Gila River. The final 10 mi. are along the river, which provides a reliable water source year-round. This hike is scenic but not strenuous.

The Catwalk Trail (18 mi., another *long* day or 3). This loop begins at the Whitewater Picnic Area near Glenwood. Reaching the trailhead involves a 60 mi. drive from Silver City along U.S. 180 N; signs mark the turnoff clearly. The first length of this trail crosses into Whitewater Canyon in an intriguing way; a remnant of the mining industry, a steel-grate catwalk is suspended along the side of the Canyon above the rushing creek; steep cliff faces rise on either side. Even for those unwilling to walk the full hike, this first section merits a quick stroll. Boulders inside the canyon, accessible from either end of the catwalk, make for good bouldering. Cross over the catwalk (less than 1 mi.) and follow Trail 207. It continues to trace Whitewater Canyon and does not ascend or descend significantly. After 5 mi., Winn Canyon branches south and Trail 179 follows it for 1.5 mi. to Spider Saddle, an intersection of several trails. Take Trail 181 farther south (which is strenuous as it leaves one canyon to enter another) and begin the return via 8 mi. of the South Fork Trail (#212), hugging the south fork of Whitewater Canyon. The recreation area requires a $3 parking fee and officially closes at 6pm. Leave a note on your dash giving an approximate time of return to avoid being ticketed.

Mimbres River Trail (28 mi., 2 or 3 nights). Take Rte. 35 to Forest Rd. 150. Go 8 mi. and park at the Continental Divide Trail parking lot. Enter the wilderness at the sign for the Mimbres River Trail. The first leg is 13 mi. up the Mimbres river to the Diamond Peak Lookout Tower. The return is 13 mi. along the Continental Divide Trail. Water is available only on the first segment of the trail.

⚠ OTHER OUTDOOR ACTIVITIES

In the vast wilderness, which sees little tourist traffic, many types of recreational fix can be had. Much of the area is designated wilderness, but not all—the trails available for mountain biking are fewer but still plentiful. **Rock climbing** is permitted in select parts of the forest, and many of the canyons make for good **bouldering.** Remember, the canyon floors do not make for good falling. Use caution and common sense at all times. If you intend to use tackle or gear on the canyon walls, check with the rangers for seasonal or territorial restrictions.

HOT SPRINGS

Due to the active subterranean geology of the area, a variety of hot springs bubble up in the Gila Wilderness. One of the easiest to find is the **Middle Fork Hot Springs.** Conveniently located 1 mi. up the well-marked trail that stretches north from the National Monument Visitors Center, it's popular and sees consistent use. **Jordan Hot Springs,** more of a lukewarm springs, can be reached on the Middle Fork Trail from TJ Corral Trailhead north of the Visitors Center. From TJ, it is a 4.5 mi. hike overland to the Gila River and then 1.5 mi. upstream for a total of 6 mi. The Canyon is narrow at points and fills up quickly and suddenly during flash flooding. *Do not enter the canyon in such conditions.* Rangers can give directions to other, out-of-the-way hot springs. **Warning:** Check with rangers before entering hot springs, as they are inhabited by an amoeba fatal to humans. There's a one out of a million chance of this happening, but one should still check with authorities first.

MOUNTAIN BIKING

Much of the Gila National Forest, including almost all of the area around the Gila Cliff Dwellings, is designated wilderness and, as such, is off-limits to mechanized vehicles, including mountain bikes. That said, there is great biking in the area. The area around Glenwood, north of Silver City on U.S. 180, falls outside the wilderness designation, and thus accommodates bikers.

    Copper Creek/Bearwallow Trail (10 mi. round-trip). Following Forest Rd. 119 from Claremont to Bearwallow Park, this trail is not a loop, but rather an out-and-back trip. To reach the beginning, head north of Glenwood approximately 7½ mi. to Forest Rd. 119. Turn right and drive 10 mi. to Claremont, where you switch from 4 wheels to 2. Stick to 119 to stay on track; the roads are well marked, so this shouldn't be difficult. The trail gains nearly 3000 ft. along its course, and passes not just through forests and canyons, but also through abandoned, turn-of-the-century mining ruins. Seasonal creek beds pass the road, but Turkey Springs, near the middle of the ride, is the only reliable water source. The area is mostly abandoned during the summer, but is a popular hunting locale during the fall. In those months, be careful and wear orange.

GILA CLIFF DWELLINGS NATIONAL MONUMENT   ☎ 505

The mysterious Gila Cliff Dwellings National Monument preserves over 40 stone and timber rooms carved into the cliff's natural caves by the Mogollon tribe during the late 1200s. About a dozen families lived here for about 20 years, farming on the mesa top and along the river. During the early 1300s, however, the Mogollon abandoned their homes for reasons unknown, leaving the dwellings as their only trace.

    From Silver City, the Cliff Dwellings are reached via 44 mi. on **Forest Rd. 15** through Piños Altos. From San Lorenzo, **Rte. 35** leads 26 mi. and ends 19 mi. south of the monument at an intersection with Forest Rd. 15. Though both roads are narrow and winding, Forest Rd. 15 is somewhat steeper and more difficult. Both roads require 2hr. for safe passage. Road conditions can be impassable in winter; pay close attention to the weather and the road surface.

The **Visitors Center,** at the end of Rte. 15, shows an informative film and sells various maps of the Gila National Forest. (☎536-9461. Open daily 8am-6pm, off-season 8am-4:30pm.) The picturesque 1 mi. round-trip **hike** to the dwellings begins past the Upper Scorpion Campground, and rangers occasionally give short interpretive tours through the cliffs. A trail guide (50¢) can be purchased at the trailhead or Visitors Center. (Dwellings open daily 8am-6pm; off-season 9am-4pm. Entrance fee $3, under 12 free.) A variety of commercial cabins, campgrounds, and recreation sites are sporadically distributed along Rte. 35; **services,** such as groceries and gas stations, are much more expensive than in Silver City.

The nearest accommodations can be found at the comfy **Grey Feathers Lodge ❸,** 20 mi. south at the intersection of Forest Rd. 15 and Rte. 35. Drawing as many as 4000 hummingbirds on certain summer weekends, the lodge is a perfect place to relax and bird-watch. (☎536-3206. Singles $45; doubles $50.) The adjoining **cafe ❶** outfits travelers with sandwiches ($3-7) and ice cream ($1.25 per scoop).

SOUTHEASTERN NEW MEXICO

White sands, ponderosa pines, caves, aliens, and the atomic bomb add up to form one of the most idiosyncratic pockets of the Southwest. Some of the country's most enigmatic history, as well as outdoors opportunities in the Lincoln National Forest, Sacramento Mountains, and Tulorosa Basin, make this region one that appeals to a wide variety of travelers. Be prepared for the uncanny.

ALAMOGORDO   ☎505

Alamogordo is Spanish for "fat poplar," a fitting description for this rapidly growing community of 30,000. Much as the area's poplar trees suck up water flowing down from the Sacramento Mountains, Alamogordo gorges itself on the region's military bases. As a tourist destination, the city has little charm, but many visitors pass through or spend a night on the way to White Sands National Monument and other area attractions.

■■ **ORIENTATION AND PRACTICAL INFORMATION.** Alamogordo lies 86 mi. north of El Paso (see p. 426) on U.S. 54 and just 16 mi. west of the mountain town of Cloudcroft (see p. 413). White Sands Blvd. (U.S. 70/54) and 10th St. are the main avenues of commerce. **Greyhound,** 601 N. White Sands Blvd. (☎437-3050), in cooperation with **TNM&O Coaches,** has service to Albuquerque (5hr.; 2 per day; $36) and El Paso (1hr.; 3 per day; $14). The **Visitors Center** offers standard info at 1301 N. White Sands Blvd. (☎437-6120; open M-F 8am-5pm, Sa-Su 9am-5pm). The **Lincoln National Forest Office,** 1101 New York Ave., is a great resource for planning a hiking or camping trip in the Sacramento Mountains. (☎434-7200. Open M-F 7:30am-4:30pm.) **Outdoor Adventures,** 1516 10th St., rents bikes and offers advice on where to ride in the area. (☎434-1920. Open M-F 10am-6pm, Sa 10am-5pm. Bikes $20-25 per day.) Other services include: the **police,** 700 Virginia Ave. (☎439-4300); **Gerald Champion Regional Medical Center,** 2669 Scenic Dr. (☎439-6100); **free Internet access** at the public library, 920 Oregon Ave. (☎439-4140; open M-Th 10am-8pm, F 10am-5pm, Sa 11am-5pm, Su 1-5pm); and **post office,** 930 E. 12th St. (☎443-8186). **ZIP code:** 88310.

■■ **ACCOMMODATIONS AND FOOD.** The **Alamo Inn ❷,** 1450 N. White Sands Blvd., is one of the many budget motels lining White Sands Blvd. (U.S. 70). Plain rooms have cable TV, A/C, and access to an outdoor pool. (☎437-1000. Singles $26; doubles $35.) **Oliver Lee State Park ❶**, 10 mi. south of town on U.S. 54, has excellent camping facilities with clean showers (tents sites $10; hookups $14). There are two nearby hostels: The **Mountain Park Hostel ❶**(see p. 414), 12 mi. east in Cloudcroft, and the **High Desert Hostel Ranch ❶** (see p. 415), 40 mi. north in Oscuro.

Dave's Pizza, 415 S. White Sands Blvd., is a family-run Italian restaurant with good, homemade pasta ($6-9) and pizza. (☎437-2505. Open M-Th 11am-10pm, F-Sa 11am-midnight.) For Mexican food, try **Maximinos ❶**, 2300 N. White Sands Blvd. Breakfast burritos start at $2.25 and popular chicken *mole* goes for $5.50. (☎443-6102. Open Tu-Sa 8am-2pm and 5-9pm, Su 8am-3pm.) **Keg's Sports Bar,** 817 Scenic Dr., is the popular night spot in town. (☎434-5654. Karaoke W-Th and Sa. DJ plays popular music F. Open M-Th 4pm-midnight, F-Sa 4pm-1:30am.)

🄶 **SIGHTS.** In addition to its contributions to the space program, this region of the country is known for its pivotal role in the development of weapons of mass destruction. Sixty-five miles northwest of Alamogordo, the Trinity Site was the site of the world's first atomic bomb detonation on July 16, 1945. The heat of the explosion caused the desert sand to melt and form a green glass called Trinitite. Part of the original trinitite has been preserved, but otherwise the area is now barren. The Alamogordo Chamber of Commerce organizes two tours annually to the site, on the first Saturday of April and October. (☎437-6120 or 800-826-0294. Call ahead for reservations.) Located 34 mi. west of Alamogordo on Rte. 70, the White Sands Missile Range runs a small museum and outdoor exhibit of missiles. (Open M-F 8am-4pm, Sa-Su 10am-3pm. Free. Driver's license, proof of insurance, and car registration are required to enter the military base.)

WHITE SANDS NAT'L MONUMENT ☎505

The giant sandbox of White Sands evokes nostalgia for playground days. Situated in the Tularosa Basin between the Sacramento and San Andres Mountains, the world's largest dunes formed as rainwater flushed gypsum from the nearby peaks and into Lake Lucero. As desert heat evaporated the lake, the gypsum crystals were left behind and now form the blindingly white sand dunes. These drifts of fine sand create an arctic tundra look, but don't be fooled: the midday sun assaults the shadeless with a light and heat that can be unbearable. Trekking or rolling through the dunes provides hours of mindless fun or mindful soul-searching; the sand is particularly awe-inspiring at sunset.

🄴🄽 **ORIENTATION AND PRACTICAL INFORMATION.** White Sands lies on Rte. 70, 15 mi. southwest of Alamogordo and 52 mi. northeast of Las Cruces. Rte. 70 is prone to closures due to missile testing at the nearby military base. Delays can run up to 1hr.; call 479-9199 to check the status of Rte. 70 closures. The **Visitors Center** has a small museum with an introductory video and a gift shop. (☎479-6124. Park open June-Aug. daily 7am-10pm, last entrance 9pm; Sept.-May 7am-sunset. Visitors Center open June-Aug. daily 8am-7pm; Sept.-May 8am-5pm. Park admission $3, under 16 free.) The nearest **grocery store, ATM, post office, hospital,** and **Internet access** are in Alamogordo. In an **emergency,** call 479-9199. For more info visit the park web site (www.nps.gov/whsa) or write to the Superintendent, White Sands National Monument, P.O. Box 1086, Holloman AFB, NM 88330.

🄿 **CAMPING.** The only way to spend the night inside the park is to camp at one of the **backcountry campsites ❶.** The ten sites ($3 per person in addition to the park entry fee) are available on a first come, first served basis and have no water or toilet facilities; they are not accessible by road and require up to a 2 mi. hike through the sand dunes. Campers must register in person at the Visitors Center and be in their sites before dark. Campfires are prohibited, but stoves are allowed. Sleeping amid the white dunes can be a rewarding experience, but plan ahead, because sites fill up early on full-moon nights. Occasionally, the sites are closed due to Missile Range launches (900 per year).

The closest **campgrounds** with amenities are at **Oliver Lee State Park ❶** (see p. 411) and **Aguirre Springs ❶** (see p. 405). The park does not offer roofed accommodation. Affordable hostels are found in Oscuro (see p. 415) and Cloudcroft (see p. 413). Motels and restaurants abound in Alamogordo (see p. 411).

◙ ▮ SIGHTS AND OUTDOORS. The 8 mi. **Dunes Drive** is a good way to begin a visit to White Sands. However, to really experience the uniqueness of the monument, you must get out of your car and take a walk across the dunes. Off-trail hiking is permitted anywhere in the eastern section of the park. Anyone considering a backcountry hike should bring a compass and map; it is quite easy to get lost in the vast sea of seemingly uniform gypsum dunes.

The only **wheelchair-accessible trail** in the park is the **Interdune Boardwalk,** an easy ¼ mi. walk above the sand. The best hike in the park is the **Alkali Flat Trail,** a moderately strenuous 4.6 mi. loop through the heart of the dunes to the parched, salty lakebed of Lake Otero. The trail is marked by white posts with orange reflective tape. *Do not hike the trail in strong winds, when blowing sand reduces visibility and makes it very easy to lose the trail. Bring lots of water and protect yourself from the intense sunlight.*

There is a free guided **sunset stroll** every evening (call ahead), and on summer nights, a park ranger gives an **evening talk** on various topics (June-Aug. 8:30pm). On **full moon nights** in the summer, the park stays open late (until 11pm, last entrance 10pm), and a guest speaker offers his two cents. A **star talk** takes place most Fridays during the summer at 8:30pm. During the **Perseid Meteor Shower** (usually the 2nd week of Aug.), the park remains open until midnight.

CLOUDCROFT   ☎ 505

At 9000 ft. in the Sacramento Mountains, it is easy to forget that you are still in New Mexico and not the Pacific Northwest. The Ponderosa Pines that blanket the mountainsides were big business for loggers 100 years ago; today, with the timber industry gone to the real Pacific Northwest, the vast Lincoln National Forest protects the trees so hikers, bikers, and campers can enjoy the spectacular scenery. Due to its high elevation, temperatures are always cool in Cloudcroft, making for comfortable summers and white, snowy winters. The town's temperament is as agreeable as its climate; despite an influx of summer tourists, Cloudcroft's 750 year-round residents maintain a friendly atmosphere.

▰ ▯ ORIENTATION AND PRACTICAL INFORMATION. Cloudcroft is 16 mi. east of Alamogordo on U.S. 82. Most of the town's shops and restaurants are either along James Canyon Hwy. (U.S. 82), or Burro St., one block to the north. There is **no public transportation.** The **Chamber of Commerce,** 1001 James Canyon Hwy., sets visitors straight inside a log cabin. (☎ 682-2733. Open M-Sa 10am-5pm.) The **Lincoln National Forest Office,** 61 Curley Place, just across U.S. 82 from the gas station, is a great resource for info about hiking and camping in the area. (☎ 682-2551. Open June-Aug. M-Sa 7:30am-4:30pm; Sept.-May M-F 7:30am-4:30pm.) The nearest **laundry** is at the **High Rolls General Store** (☎ 682-2955), 5 mi. west of town along U.S. 82.

Other services include: the **police,** 201 Burro Ave. (☎682-2101); **free Internet access** at the public library, 90 Swallow Pl. (☎682-1111); and the **post office,** 20 Curlew Pl. (☎682-2431; open M-F 8:30am-5pm, Sa 9:30-11:30am). **ZIP code:** 88317.

■ ■ ACCOMMODATIONS AND CAMPING. There are quite a few options for lodging in Cloudcroft. The premier budget accommodation in town is the new **Cloudcroft Mountain Park Hostel ❶,** 1049 U.S. 82, 5 mi. west of town between mile markers 10 and 11. This hostel stands on 27 acres adjacent to Lincoln National Forest and has a living room, kitchen, and a large front porch. Pets are allowed, and there are free pickups from the Alamogordo bus station. *This hostel is still under construction: check with the Visitors Center to see if it's open.* (☎682-0555. Wheelchair accessible. Dorms $17; private rooms $34.) The **Alta Vista Motel ❸,** 1605 James Canyon Hwy., has the cheapest motel-style rooms in town. (☎682-2221; www.cloudcroft-motel.com. Rooms $50 year-round. Reservations accepted by email.) Another option, attractive mainly to families and groups, is to rent wood cabins in the forest outside of town. These cabins generally come with fireplaces, TV, and full kitchens and run about $60-100 for occupancy by two to eight people. Rates are highest in summer and during the ski season; reservations are advised, especially during peak season.

If you have a tent, camping under the tall pines of **Lincoln National Forest** is not to be missed. The six national forest campgrounds within a 4 mi. radius of Cloudcroft offer drinking water and pit toilets, but do not accommodate RVs. **Silver, Saddle ❶,** and **Apache ❶,** 3 mi. north on Rte. 244 from U.S. 82, are popular because they have access to showers (sites $11). The other three campgrounds are **Pines ❶** (on Rte. 244, 1 mi. north of U.S. 82; sites $8), **Sleepy Grass ❶** (1½ mi. east of Cloudcroft on U.S. 82; sites $9), and **Deerhead ❶** (2 mi. south of town on U.S. 130; sites $9). All campgrounds are generally open mid-May to mid-October. **Backcountry camping ❶** is free in the national forest. **Bluff Springs ❶,** on Río Penasco Rd., is one of the more trafficked sites because it sits next to a stream and a waterfall. Directions are complicated, so inquire at the Forest Office for more info.

■ FOOD. There are only a few restaurants in Cloudcroft. The friendly **Western Bar and Cafe ❸,** on Burro St., is a popular dive, and serves the best breakfast in town. At night, this place turns into the town's main watering hole. The steak Diane ($11) is fantastic. (☎682-2445. Open daily 6am-9pm; bar open M-Sa 9am-2am, Su noon-midnight. Cowboy karaoke on alternate W and Sa. Pool tables. Breakfast special $3-5, dinner entrees $6-11. Cash only.) The **Cookshack ❷,** on U.S. 82 in the center of town, is a great spot for a quick lunch or dinner. (☎682-9920. Open daily 11am-7pm. BBQ Plate $6.50. Cash only.) To get basic food supplies head to the **Mountain Top Mercantile and Grocery,** 105 James Canyon Hwy. (☎682-2777. Open daily 7am-8pm.)

■ OUTDOORS. With miles of hiking trails, dozens of mountain bike routes, challenging rock climbing, and even downhill skiing, the Sacramento Mountains have plenty to offer any outdoorsman. The Lincoln National Forest Office in town is a good place to get your bearings before heading off into the wilderness.

The numerous hiking trails in the mountains around Cloudcroft could keep an energetic hiker busy for months. For a complete list of hikes in the Lincoln National Forest purchase the *Lincoln National Forest Trail Guide* at the Forest Office in Cloudcroft ($15). The **Osha Trail** (2.6 mi. round-trip), begins 1 mi. west of Cloudcroft off U.S. 82 and offers views of White Sands, the Tularosa Basin, and the village of Cloudcroft. Another easy day hike is the **Cloud-Climbing Rail Trail** (2.2 mi. round-trip), a jaunt that passes two large railroad trestles. The trailhead is on U.S.

82 at the western side of town in the Trestle Recreation Area. For an extended backpacking trip, the best trail in the area is the 22 mi.

The **mountain biking** near Cloudcroft is hailed as some of the best and most challenging in the region. All Lincoln National Forest trails are open to bikes. **High Altitude Outfitters,** on Burro St. in Cloudcroft, sells bike equipment and gives advice on area trails. (☎682-1229. Open June-Sept. daily 10am-6pm; Oct.-May W-M 10am-5pm.) Bikers have to share the Rim Trail, but it is still the most popular area route for riding. The Forest Service has maps of other interesting trails.

Rock climbers scale the cliff next to the U.S. 82 tunnel, 6 mi. west of town. For beginners and those eager to learn, **Leroy Lewis** (☎430-2987) is a local climbing instructor who takes climbers of all skill levels for half-day and full-day trips.

TULAROSA VALLEY/U.S. 54   ☎505

The Tularosa Valley, a wide expanse of desert, dunes, fractured lava flows, and plains, stretches between the San Andres Mountains to the west and the Sacramento Mountains to the east. Because of its bleakness and flat terrain, the military requisitioned much of the valley in the form of White Sands Missile Range and, to the south, Fort Bliss. The eastern side of the valley nestles along the foothills of the Sacramento Mountains and traces the path of U.S. 54.

THREE RIVERS PETROGLYPHS AND ENVIRONS. The highway affords access to several cultural and geological sites, as well an out-of-the-way hostel on its 60 mi. between **Alamogordo** and **Carrizozo.** Thirty miles north of Alamogordo and 17 mi. north of Tularosa, **Three Rivers Petroglyphs** represents one of the largest displays of rock art sites in the Southwest. Over 21,000 carvings can be found here. The art was left by the Jornada Mogollon Indians who lived in the area 1000 years ago. The petroglyphs are accessible via a 1 mi. trail that ascends a small rocky ridge. An interpretive pamphlet, available at the trailhead, explains some of the more distinctive designs. The **BLM ❶** permits camping on the gravel parking lot; facilities include water and toilets. (☎525-4300. Park open sunrise-sunset. Visitors Center open daily 9am-4pm. Admission $2; camping $2.)

Eight miles past Three Rivers Petroglyphs on Forest Rd. 579 is the **Three Rivers Campground ❶** in Lincoln National Forest. Sites ($8) have pit toilets and potable water. The **Three Rivers Trail** starts at the campsite and climbs 4000 ft. into the **White Mountain Wilderness Area** in the Lincoln National Forest. The strenuous hike (6 mi. one-way) follows a stream most of the way and offers great views of Sierra Blanca, White Sands, and the Malpais Lava Flow. Many do this hike as part of a **backpacking** trip through the White Mountain Wilderness. Contact the Lincoln National Forest offices in Alamogordo (☎434-7200) or Ruidoso (☎257-4095) for more info.

OSCURO. The ◪**High Desert Hostel Ranch ❶,** the most unique accommodation in southern New Mexico, sprawls 15 mi. south of Carrizozo. The 86-year-old orange adobe ranch house is comfortable and friendly, offering weary travelers a peaceful respite from life on the road. The ranch's 240 acres come complete with an orchard, an organic vegetable garden, plenty of land for hiking, and stunning sunsets behind the mountains. Guests enjoy access to all the food in the kitchen and a vast living room with TV. The hostel is in the tiny hamlet of Oscuro, a flag stop on the **Greyhound** route from El Paso to Albuquerque ($24 one-way from either city; one per day from Albuquerque and two from El Paso); call ahead for a free pickup. The hostel is 1 mi. east down a dirt road from the 108 mi. marker on U.S. 54; follow the signs. (☎648-4007. Free laundry. Dorm beds $14; private doubles $27; triples $32. Cash or traveler's checks only.)

CARRIZOZO, VALLEY OF FIRES, AND ENVIRONS. Fifteen miles north of the hostel is the quaint town of **Carrizozo.** Offering coffee and sandwiches, **Carrizozo Joe's,** 113 Central Ave., also peddles the area's only public **Internet access.** (☎648-5637. Open M 7am-6pm, Tu-W 7am-2pm, Th-F 7am-6pm, Sa 8am-3pm.) **Sierra Blanca Brewing Co.,** 503 12th St., offers free tours and tastings, a great way to while time away. (☎648-6606. Open M-F 9am-4pm.) **Sturges Market,** on U.S. 54, sells the town's only groceries. (☎648-2125. Open M-Sa 8:30am-7pm.)

The old gold-mining village of **White Oaks,** 5 mi. north of Carrizozo on U.S. 54 and 8 mi. east on Rte. 349, used to be the second largest town in New Mexico; now it's a ghost town with 24 residents. The main reason to stop in White Oaks is to visit the 120-year-old **White Oaks Saloon** with its infamous "No Scum Allowed" sign out front. (☎648-9915. Open M, W-Sa 10am-9pm, Su noon-9pm. Beer $2.25.)

A volcanic eruption 1500 years ago caused lava to flow south into the Tularosa Basin, covering over 125 sq. mi. To see the fractured lava beds, visit the **Valley of Fires Recreation Area,** 4 mi. west of Carrizozo on U.S. 380. The 0.7 mi. **Malpais Nature Trail** allows visitors to tread the volcanic terrain. The park has a **campground** with showers. Sites offer no shade but have great views of the valley. (☎648-2241. Park open 24hr. Visitors Center open daily 8am-4pm. Vehicles $5, bikes or pedestrians $3. Camping: primitive sites $5, developed sites $7, full hookups $12.)

RUIDOSO ☎505

During the summer months and then again in ski season, a West Texas twang is audible in the streets of Ruidoso, the premier summer and winter resort destination in southern New Mexico. In the summer, thousands of tourists, mostly Texans, flock here to fritter away their money at the casinos and the racetrack. In the winter, nearby Ski Apache, an impressive low-latitude ski area, is the major draw. Though it is even possible to escape to the woods during the summer, the peaceful spring and fall months offer an even quieter opportunity to explore the trail system of the Lincoln National Forest and the White Mountain Wilderness.

■♦🖪 **ORIENTATION AND PRACTICAL INFORMATION.** Ruidoso sits at 7000 ft. in the Sacramento Mountains, 46 mi. northeast of Alamogordo (see p. 411) and 75 mi. west of Roswell (see p. 419). Everything in the town sprawls. Sudderth Dr. (Rte. 48) is the town's main thoroughfare. U.S. 70 passes east of downtown and leads to Ruidoso Downs. **Greyhound,** 138 Service Rd. (☎257-2660), sends buses to **Alamogordo** (1hr.; 3 per day; $10) and **Albuquerque** (6hr.; 2 per day; $40). The **Chamber of Commerce,** 720 Sudderth Dr., doles out the requisite visitor info. (☎257-7395 or 800-253-2255. Open M 9am-5pm, Tu-Th 8:30am-5pm, F 8:30am-4:30pm, Sa 9am-3pm; May-Aug. additionally Su 9am-1pm.) For more info on the greater Sacramento Mountains area, check out the informative **Billy the Kid Scenic Byway Visitors Center,** 841 U.S. 70 W, next to the racetrack. (☎378-5318. Open daily 10am-4pm.) The **Lincoln National Forest Smokey Bear Ranger Station,** 901 Mechem Dr., has the area's outdoors info. (☎257-4095. Open June-Aug. M-Sa 7:30am-4:30pm; Sept.-May M-F 7:30am-4:30pm.) Other services include: **Becker's Mountain Laundry,** 721 Mechem Dr. (☎257-7667; open M-Sa 7:30am-8pm, Su 8am-5pm); the **police,** 1085 Mechem Dr. (☎258-7365); **Lincoln County Medical Center,** 211 Sudderth Dr. (☎257-8200; open M, W, Th 9am-6pm; Tu 9am-7pm; F 9am-5pm; Sa 11am-3pm); and the **post office,** 1090 Mechem Dr. (☎257-7120). **ZIP code:** 88345.

🛏 **ACCOMMODATIONS.** Because of nearby hostels in Oscuro (see p. 415) and Cloudcroft (see p. 413), many budget travelers eschew overnight visits to Ruidoso. Motels clustered around the intersection of U.S. 70 and Rte. 48 offer rooms for $40-

WILLIAM H. BONNEY, CHILD PRODIGY

Lawrence G. Murphy owned the one and only general store in Lincoln in the 1870s. When John Tunstall and Alexander McSween opened a rival store in 1878, Murphy got angry, and his assistant James Dolan had Tunstall killed. One of Tunstall's men, William H. Bonney, vowed to get revenge. Bonney (a.k.a. Billy the Kid) rounded up a group of men called the Regulators, and they wreaked havoc on Lincoln, killing Tunstall's assassins along with Sheriff Bill Brady, a friend of Dolan's. Dolan's men fought back, burning McSween's house and killing McSween and three Regulators who sought to escape the fire. Billy the Kid escaped and spent the next two years on the run. The new sheriff in Lincoln, Pat Garrett, finally caught Billy in nearby Ft. Sumner, and Billy was subsequently put on trial in Mesilla for killing Sheriff Brady. The judge sentenced him to hang, and he was in jail awaiting execution in Lincoln when he made his famous escape. Less than three months later, on July 14, 1881, Pat Garret caught up with Billy again, and this time did not give the slippery Kid a chance. Garret shot him dead.

70, but most motels jack up prices between June and August. It is not impossible for this town to completely sell out on a busy weekend like July 4th. The **Apache Motel ❷**, 344 Sudderth Dr., is the best buy in town, with large, comfortable rooms, many with futons and fully-equipped kitchens. (☎ 257-2986 or 800-426-0616. Singles $35-40; doubles $40-56.) The **Nob Hill Lodge ❸**, on U.S. 70, west of Rte. 48, across from the Super 8, has old rooms with worn furniture, but every room has cable TV, A/C, and a view of Sierra Blanca Peak. (☎ 257-9212. Singles $30-55; doubles $40-65. 10% student discount Sept.-May.) The invading Texans rent cabins and so can you, although it's only a good deal if you have a family or large group. Expect to pay $50-120 per night for a cabin with a fireplace, TV, and full kitchen. For the real woodsman's experience there are a number of national forest campgrounds northwest of Ruidoso with pit toilets and no running water. **South Fork ❶** is the only campground with drinking water and flush toilets (sites $10). To reach South Fork, drive north 11 mi. on Rte. 48; turn left and follow Forest Rd. 107 for 5 mi. Call the Smokey Bear Ranger Station (see **Practical Information**, p. 416) for info on other campsites. Campgrounds are generally open May to October.

🍴🌙 **FOOD AND NIGHTLIFE.** Restaurants are everywhere in Ruidoso, with the highest density on Sudderth Dr. in the downtown area between Mechem Dr. and Paradise Canyon Rd. The laid-back **Lincoln Country Grill ❷**, 2717 Sudderth Dr., serves up its famous Billy the Kid Burger for $7. (☎ 257-7669. Open daily 7am-9pm.) Vegetarians stampede to the **Terraza Camanario ❷**, 1611 Sudderth Dr., which has the most authentic Mexican food in town. (☎ 257-4227. Enchiladas $6; Mexican steaks $7-8.) The twenty-something crowd spends their evenings at **Farley's**, 1200 Mechem St., which offers pool, video games, and 16 beers on tap. (☎ 258-5676. Open M-Th 11:30am-midnight, F-Sa 11:30am-1am, Su 11am-11:30pm. Beers $2.25-3.50.) **Quarters Restaurant and Nightclub**, 2535 Sudderth Dr., is as authentic as Ruidoso gets: solid steaks and tunes. (☎ 257-9535. Live classic rock W-Su and blues Su afternoon. Open M-Sa 11am-2am, Su noon-midnight.)

🔳 **SIGHTS.** Much of Ruidoso's summer activity revolves around wagering money. **Ruidoso Downs**, 4½ mi. east of town, is one of America's top horseracing venues. The All-American Futurity is the biggest paying quarterhorse race in the country, giving out $2.2 million annually. (☎ 378-4431. Races June-Aug. Open Th-Su.; Th-F races start at 3:30pm, Sa-Su 1pm. Free.) The **Hubbard Museum of the American West**, next to Ruidoso Downs, is affiliated with the Smithsonian and has exhibits on chuckwagons, stagecoaches, saddles, guns, and Native American crafts. The building also houses the Ruidoso Downs Hall of Fame. (☎378-4142. Open daily 10am-5pm. $6, seniors $5, children $2.)

🏔 OUTDOOR ACTIVITIES. During the winter, skiing is king. Eighteen miles northwest of Ruidoso, **Ski Apache,** on the side of Sierra Blanca Peak is southern New Mexico's best ski area. Eleven lifts, including New Mexico's only gondola, serve 55 trails (20% beginner; 35% intermediate; 45% advanced) on 750 skiable acres. The base of the mountain is a whopping 8000 ft. above sea level, and the top of the highest lift reaches 11,500 ft. (☎336-4356, 24hr. snow report 257-9001; www.skiapache.com. Open late Nov. to early Apr. 8:45am-4pm. Snowboards welcome. Annual snowfall 185 in. Full day $43, half day $30; under 13 $28/$20.)

The Lincoln National Forest around Ruidoso is one of the most beautiful areas of the Sacramento Mountains, and during the summer, hiking is a great way to escape the racing and gambling crowds. Beginning at the entrance to Ski Apache, the 6 mi. round-trip hike up **Lookout Mountain** (11,600 ft.) leads to the highest point in the national forest. Take Trail 15 0.5 mi. to Trail 25; turn left and then turn left again on Trail 78, which leads to the top of Lookout Mountain. Hikers can turn around or continue south on an unmarked trail 1.3 mi. to the 12,000 ft. summit of **Sierra Blanca** in the Mescalero Indian Reservation. On a clear day, you can see all the way to the Gila Mountains in the west and the Sangre de Cristo Mountains to the north. The 21.1 mi. **Crest Trail** is an unforgettable backcountry hiking route into the heart of the White Mountain Wilderness. To reach the trailhead, drive north on Rte. 48; turn left and go 1 mi. on the road to Ski Apache. Turn right on Forest Rd. 117 and follow it 5½ mi. until you see a sign that says "hiker."

For a great view of the Sacramento Mountains that doesn't involve much hiking, drive to the **Monjeau Lookout,** a granite fire tower built in the 1930s by the Civilian Conservation Corps. To visit the lookout, drive north from Ruidoso and turn left on Rte. 532; after 1 mi., turn right onto Forest Rd. 117 and follow it for 6 mi. **Mountain biking** is popular on the trails of the national forest, but is not allowed on the trails of the White Mountain Wilderness Area. The 3 mi. **Perk Canyon Trail** is a favorite with locals. From the traffic circle in Ruidoso take Upper Canyon Rd. 1 mi. to Ebarb St., turn right and then left onto Perk Canyon Rd. **High Altitude Outfitters,** 2316 Sudderth Dr. (☎257-0120), rents mountain bikes.

🏙 DAYTRIP FROM RUIDOSO: LINCOLN. On April 28, 1881, Billy the Kid made one of the most famous jailbreaks in history from the Lincoln County Courthouse. While in the outhouse, he picked up a pistol, came out, and killed one of his guards. Billy then managed to run to the arsenal, find a shotgun, and kill his other guard, before fleeing town on a horse. The bullet hole from Billy's gun is still in the wall at the bottom of the staircase.

Little has changed in Lincoln (northeast of Ruidoso on U.S. 380) since the days of Billy the Kid and the infamous "Lincoln County War." The town's buildings have not been Disney-fied, making Lincoln one of the best preserved Wild West towns in New Mexico. The **Lincoln Visitors Center,** on the east side of town, has a comprehensive museum and shows a video about the Lincoln County War. (☎653-4025. Open daily 8:30am-4pm.) Buildings open to the public include the Courthouse, Dr. Wood's House, the Tunstall Store, and the Montano Store. The buildings are essentially museums, preserving the Lincoln of yore. (Open daily 8am-4:30pm. Admission to each building $3.50, all 5 buildings $6.)

The small town of **Capitan,** 12 mi. west of Lincoln on U.S. 380, is famous for being the "birthplace" of Smokey the Bear. On May 9, 1950, a fire crew found a badly burnt black bear cub clinging to a tree in the Capitan region of Lincoln

National Forest. After healing, Smokey moved to the National Zoo in Washington, where he became the poster-bear for preventing forest fires. When he died in 1976, his body was returned to Capitan for burial. **Smokey Bear Historical Park** has a small museum telling the story of America's most famous bear. Next door, a park houses Smokey's gravesite. (☎354-2748. Open daily 9am-5pm. $1, children 50¢.) But don't just stop for Smokey: every July 4th weekend, the annual Old West Ranch Rodeo and Smokey Bear Stampede is held out at the fairgrounds. If you want to grab lunch on the way, **Downtown Deli ❶,** 101 Lincoln, is just down the street; try a Piquante chicken with cucumber dill sauce, Asian slaw, and chipotle *aioli* for $5. (354-0407; Open M-Tu 11am-3pm, W-Sa 11am-3pm and 5pm-9pm.)

ROSWELL   ☎505

With giant inflatable Martians advertising used cars, streetlights donning painted-on pointy eyes, and flying saucers adorning fast-food signs, one thing is certain: aliens *have* invaded Roswell. Located 76 miles north of Carlsbad, Roswell is a celebration of extra-terrestrial life and the mania that accompanies it. The fascination began in July 1947, when an alien spacecraft reportedly plummeted to the earth near the dusty town. The official Army press release reported that the military had recovered pieces of some form of "flying saucer," but a retraction arrived the next day—the mysterious wreckage, the brass claimed, was actually a harmless weather balloon. Everyone admits that something crashed in the desert northwest of Roswell on that fateful night some 50 years ago. Was the initial Army admission just a poor choice of words by some PR hack or a crack in an elaborate cover-up?

■■🛈 **ORIENTATION AND PRACTICAL INFORMATION.** Aside from its extra-terrestrial peculiarities, Roswell is a fairly normal town. The intersection of 2nd St. (Rte. 70/380) and Main St. (Rte. 285) is the sun around which the Roswell solar system orbits. To reach Roswell from Albuquerque, head 89 mi. south on I-25 to San Antonio, then 153 mi. east on U.S. 380. **Greyhound,** 1100 N. Virginia Ave. (☎622-2510), in conjunction with TNM&O, runs buses to Albuquerque (4hr.; 2 per day Tu-Sa, 1 on Su; $33) and El Paso (4½hr.; 3 per day; $41 M-Th, $43 F-Su). **Pecos Trails Transit,** 515 N. Main St., runs buses all over town. (☎624-6766. M-F 6am-10:30pm, Sa 7:10am-10pm, Su 10:30am-7pm. 75¢, students 50¢, seniors 35¢.) The cheery and helpful **Visitors Center** is at 426 N. Main St. (☎624-0889 or 623-5695. Open M-F 8:30am-5:30pm, Sa-Su 10am-3pm.) Laundry machines adorn **L&W Kwick Wash,** 211 S. Union Ave (☎627-8257). The **public library,** 301 N. Pennsylvania Ave., has **free Internet access.** (Open M-Tu 9am-9pm, W-Sa 9am-6pm, Su 2pm-6pm.) The **post office** occupies 415 N. Pennsylvania Ave. (☎623-7232. Open M-F 7:30am-5:30pm, Sa 8am-noon.) **ZIP code:** 88202.

🛏🍴 **ACCOMMODATIONS AND FOOD.** Main St. and 2nd St. are both lined with budget motels, but the chain motels that have settled on Main St. north of downtown tend to be pricier than the options on 2nd St. The **Budget Inn West ❷,** 2200 W. 2nd St., has newly remodeled rooms with A/C, telephones, and refrigerators. (☎623-3811 or 800-806-7030. Singles $27-37; doubles $32-48. Reservations recommended.) **The Belmont Motel ❷,** 2100 W. 2nd St., has clean, newly refurnished rooms with fridge, cable TVs, and A/C. (☎623-4522. Singles $20-$27l; doubles $30-39. **Bottomless Lakes State Park ❶** has camping along the shores of seven beautiful natural lakes. To reach the park, drive 12 mi. east on Rte. 380, then 5 mi. south on Rte. 409. (☎624-6058. Tent sites $10, full hookups $18.)

Fast-food restaurants are as prevalent in Roswell as allusions to alien life, and they are concentrated along N. Main St. and W. 2nd St. Side streets are home to

CLASSIFY YOUR CLOSE ENCOUNTERS Most

people are familiar with Steven Spielberg's movie *Close Encounters of the Third Kind.* But did you know that there are other kinds of close encounters as well?

Close Encounter of the First Kind: a UFO is spotted within 150 yards.

Close Encounter of the Second Kind: physical evidence of a UFO is found.

Close Encounter of the Third Kind: a UFO is spotted with visible occupants inside.

Close Encounter of the Fourth Kind: a human is abducted by aliens.

Close Encounter of the Fifth Kind: communication between humans and aliens.

less commercial budget eateries. **Albertson's Supermarket** is at 1110 S. Main St. (☎623-9300). Just around the corner from the UFO Museum, the **Crash Down Diner ❶**, 106 W. 1st St., is an out-of-this-world-themed restaurant. Try a Starchild burrito creation ($5.75), a "hungry alien" sub ($3-5), or an "unidentified" burger ($4). A giant alien mural covers the wall, and even the salt and pepper shakers are shaped like aliens. (☎627-5533. Open M-Sa 8am-6pm, Su 8am-6pm.) **Martin's Capitol Cafe ❶**, 110 W. 4th St., delights with tasty Mexican dishes at down-to-earth prices. The gigantic burritos (starting at $3.50) with red or green salsa scream "take me to your stomach." (☎624-2111. Open M-Sa 6am-8:30pm.) **Peppers Bar and Grill ❷**, 500 N. Main St., serves American and Mexican food indoors and on an outdoor patio. (☎623-1700. Live music Apr.-Oct. F-Sa, DJ spinning on the patio W. Dining room open M-Sa 11am-10pm, bar open 11am-midnight.)

🔘 📺 **SIGHTS AND ENTERTAINMENT.** Believer or skeptic, most visitors will find the alien side of Roswell entertaining, if not enlightening. During the first week of July, the **UFO Festival** commemorates the anniversary of the alleged encounter, drawing thousands for live music, an alien costume contest, and a 5km "Alien Chase" race. With a plastic flying saucer above its storefront, the popular **International UFO Museum and Research Center,** 114 N. Main St., dedicates itself to telling the story of what happened near Roswell in 1947. Exhibits feature testimonials and newspaper clippings about the 1947 incident, as well as features on alien sightings around the world. Some remain skeptical of its scholarly credentials, but the museum's backers say the reading rooms and archives are academically legitimate. (☎625-9495. Open daily 9am-5pm. Free. Audio tour $1.) The truly curious will want to see the crash site itself. Long-time Roswell resident **Bruce Roads** (☎622-0628) gives private tours in his four-wheel-drive Suburban. Take a tour to the Ragsdale impact site (3½hr.; $75) or the Corona debris site (6hr.; $150). Remember that 24hr. notice is required for tours.

If you can tear yourself away from the alien mania, the **Roswell Museum and Art Center,** 100 W. 11th St., houses a superb art museum that showcases works by area artists Peter Hurd and Henriette Wyeth. The museum also features the laboratory of Robert Goddard, the Roswell resident who invented the liquid fuel rocket. The center has a **planetarium** running shows frequently during the summer. (☎624-6744. Museum open M-Sa 9am-5pm, Su 1-5pm; free. Planetarium shows Th-Sa nights in summer, one week per month in the winter; $3.)

To cool off on a hot summer day, head to **Bottomless Lakes State Park,** 12 mi. east of Roswell on U.S. 380. The seven lakes in the park formed when underground caves collapsed and filled with water. Swimming is allowed only at Lea Lake at the southern end of the park. (☎624-6058. Visitors Center open June-Aug. daily 9am-6pm; Sept.-May 8am-5pm.)

CARLSBAD CAVERNS   ☎505

In 1898, Jim White, a 16-year-old Texan cowboy, thought he saw smoke coming from the top of a hill while riding through southern New Mexico. When he got closer he realized that what he thought was smoke was actually millions of bats emerging from a fissure in the ground. With a kerosene lantern and a ball of string, White began the first thorough exploration of the cave. What he found beneath the earth's surface was nothing short of spectacular: underground rooms, delicate stone draperies, natural sculptures, and millions of stalagmites and stalactites.

The limestone rock that composes the outer walls of the caverns are the lithofied remains of the same Capitan Reef that forms the spine of the Guadalupe Mountains. Beginning several million years ago, rainwater seeped through cracks in the reef, slowly dissolving the limestone. Meanwhile, oil and gas deposits below the reef leaked hydrogen sulfide gas upwards. When the hydrogen sulfide met the rainwater, highly corrosive sulfuric acid formed. This acid ate through huge amounts of limestone rock to create the vast chambers of Carlsbad Caverns.

While Jim White may have been the first white man to explore the caves, he was certainly not the last. By 1923, colonies of tourists clung to the walls to see the newest national monument, and by the end of the decade, an "underground lunch-room," elevator, and electric lighting all had been added to the main cave. Today, over 1000 light bulbs and 19 miles of wires help illuminate the cave's features for its 600,000 annual visitors. The developed Carlsbad Cavern is the main tourist attraction, but some of the other 93 caves in the park are more spectacular and remote. The largest in the park, Lechuguilla Cave, is off limits to the general public, but several other undeveloped caves are accessible by ranger-guided tours.

AT A GLANCE: CARLSBAD CAVERNS NATIONAL PARK

AREA: 46,427 acres.

FEATURES: The Big Room, King's Palace, Slaughter Canyon, Lechuguilla Cave.

HIGHLIGHTS: Touring the self-guided Big Room, climbing through Lower Cave, exploring rugged Slaughter Canyon Cave.

GATEWAYS: White's City, Carlsbad (p. 424).

CAMPING: No developed campgrounds. Backcountry permits are free.

FEES AND RESERVATIONS: No park entrance fee. Big Room entrance $6. Other cave tours $8-20. Reservations highly recommended (see p. 422).

■ ⁊ ORIENTATION AND PRACTICAL INFORMATION

The closest town to the park is **White's City,** on U.S. 62/180, 20 mi. southwest of Carlsbad, 6 mi. from the park Visitors Center. Flash floods occasionally close the roads; call the park for road conditions. **El Paso, TX** (see p. 426) is the nearest major city, 150 mi. west past **Guadalupe Mountains National Park** (see p. 433).

The borders of the park include the subterranean limestone chasms, but above ground large canyons lead up towards the crest of the Guadalupe Range. The park itself has north and south entrances. The northern entrance lies just west of White's City and leads to the main cavern system and the Walnut Canyon Desert Drive. The southern entrance is accessible by Rte. 418 and leads to Slaughter Canyon Cave, Yucca Canyon, and North Slaughter Canyon Trail.

Greyhound, in cooperation with **TNM&O Coaches** (☎887-1108), runs two buses per day between El Paso ($32) and will make a flag stop at White's City. **Carlsbad Caverns Visitors Center** has trail maps and tour info. (☎785-2232. Open daily 8am-7pm; late Aug. to May 8am-5:30pm. Entrance fee $6.) Make reservations by phone

NEW MEXICO

WHEN TO GO. The main attraction of the park is the elaborate cave system, which remains about 56°F all year. Above ground, the weather heats up in the summer to temperatures over 100°F. Most visitors flock to the caves in the summer for the natural air conditioning. To avoid the crowds, visit during the mild fall.

through the **Guided Tour Reservation Hotline** (☎800-967-2283) or on the web (www.reservations.nps.gov). White's City, just outside the park on U.S. 62/180, provides most major services: **laundry, gas station, grocery store,** and **ATM.** In an **emergency,** call 785-2232. White's City's **post office,** 23 Carlsbad Caverns Hwy., resides next to the Best Western gift shop. (☎785-2220. Open M-F 8am-noon and 12:30-4:30pm, Sa 8am-noon.) **ZIP code:** 88268.

ACCOMMODATIONS

Cheap motels and chain hotels abound in Carlsbad (see p. 424). Sleep closer to the park at **White's City Resort RV Park ❷,** outside the park entrance, which has water, showers, and a pool. (☎785-2291 or 800-228-3767. Tent sites with full hookup $20. Register in the Best Western lobby.) Though the national park doesn't have an established campground, Guadalupe Mountains National Park, 32 mi. south on U.S. 62/180 has nice sites ($8). **Backcountry camping ❶** in the wilderness of Carlsbad Caverns National Park is free; get a permit at the Visitors Center.

SUBTERRANEAN ACTIVITIES

There are two ways to get down into the **Big Room:** walking a steep 1.3 mi. through the **natural entrance** or taking the **elevator** down 75 stories. The natural entrance route is spectacular and should only be skipped by visitors short on time or hesitant to walk down such a steep slope. Walking down into the cave from the natural entrance, one will see the cave just as the early explorers did. Once inside the cave, the self-guided Big Room is the main attraction. Most of this 1 mi. walk is wheelchair accessible. The Big Room is over 600,000 sq. ft., the size of 14 football fields. Inside this room are many fascinating cave formations including **Rock of Ages, Bottomless Pit, Painted Grotto,** and **Giant Dome.** (Natural entrance open June to mid-Aug. daily 8:30am-3:30pm, mid-Aug. to May 8:30am-2pm. Big room open June to mid-Aug. daily 8:30am-5pm, mid-Aug. to May 8:30am-3:30pm. Admission $6, age 6-15 $3. Audio tour $3.)

The caverns adjacent to the Big Room are only accessible by ranger-guided tour. Call the toll-free hotline for reservations. The most frequently offered tour, the **King's Palace Tour,** passes through four of the cave's lowest rooms and some of the most awesome anomalies. (1½hr. tours every hr. 9-11am and 1-3pm. $8, Golden Age Passport holders and ages 6-15 $4. Advance reservations required.) Other guided tours in the Big Room include a lantern tour though the **Left Hand Tunnel** (daily; $7) and a climbing tour of the **Lower Cave** (M-F; $20).

Tours of the undeveloped **Slaughter Canyon Cave** offer a more rugged spelunking experience. A reliable car is required to get there, as there's no public transportation, and the parking lot is 23 mi. down Rte. 418, an unpaved road, several miles south of the main entrance to the park on U.S. 62/180. The cave entrance is a steep, strenuous 0.5 mi. from the lot. Ranger-led tours (bring a flashlight) traverse difficult and slippery terrain; there are no paved trails or handrails. (2hr. tours; June-Aug. twice daily, Sept.-May Sa-Su only. $15, Golden Age Passport holders and ages 6-15 $7.50. Call the Visitors Center as least 2 days ahead to reserve.) Tours of **Hall of the White Giant** and **Spider Cave** require crawling and climbing through tight passages.

SPELEOTHEM? I HARDLY KNOW THEM!

"Speleothem" is the scientific term for a cave formation. As water seeps through the limestone above the cave, it dissolves the mineral calcite. When the water drips through a crack in the cave's ceiling, it deposits the calcite to form stalactites, stalagmites and other speleothems. Two factors that influence speleothem formation are temperature and pH levels. When the above-ground temperature rises, organic matter decays faster, increasing the level of carbon dioxide in the soil. When more carbon dioxide is present, the water in the soil becomes more acidic, dissolving more calcite and depositing it in the cave. After heavy rains, more water penetrates the cave and speleothems grow faster. Formations in Carlsbad Caverns include:

Stalactite: a formation that hangs from the cave's ceiling. Formed as water deposits calcite before dripping to the floor. Remember: stalactites hold "tight" to the ceiling.

Stalagmite: a formation that grows from the floor of the cave. Formed when water deposits calcite after dripping from the ceiling, these formations "might" grow to meet the stalactite.

Soda Straw: a tube on the ceiling of a cave, about the diameter of a soda straw. As water drips through a pore, it deposits a ring of calcite, leaving hollow center.

Drapery: a wavy pattern resembling curtains, deposited by water flowing along the slanted ceiling of a cave.

Popcorn: clusters of calcite balls that build up on the wall of a flooded cave and resemble popcorn kernels.

Let's Go does not recommend these tours for claustrophobes. (☎800-967-2283. Tours 4hr. 1 per week. $20. Call at least a month in advance to reserve.)

Visitors can also explore some of the park's caves on their own. Free permits are available by mail one month in advance. For a permit application write: Superintendent, Carlsbad Caverns National Park, 3225 National Parks Highway, Carlsbad NM, 88220; or call 505-785-2232, ext. 363 or 368 and leave your name, address, and phone number. Vertical caves such as **Chimney Cave** and **Christmas Tree Cave** require spelunking equipment. **Ogle Cave** involves a fun rappel, but because of the fragile environment, visitors to Ogle Cave need a ranger guide and must pay $15 per person. **Goat Cave, Lake Cave,** and **Corkscrew Cave** are horizontal caves and require no special equipment or technical training.

Plan your visit for late afternoon to catch the magnificent **bat flight.** The ritual, during which hungry bats storm out of the cave at a rate of 6000 per minute is preceded by a ranger talk. (Daily May-Oct. just before sunset.)

⚠ OUTDOOR ACTIVITIES

Opportunities for driving, hiking, biking, and camping abound. The park offers a 9.5 mi. **scenic drive** through the Chihuahuan Desert. An interpretive brochure (available at the Visitors Center) explains the vegetation and scenery along the route. This trail is also good for **mountain biking.** For those less mechanically inclined, the park includes 33,125 acres of designated federal wilderness. **Hiking** trails are rarely used, making Carlsbad Caverns a great spot to find solitude on the trail. The **Rattlesnake Canyon Trail** (6 mi. round-trip) makes for a fun day hike. The trail begins at marker #9 of the Desert Loop Scenic Drive and descends into Rattlesnake Canyon. For an overnight backpacking trip, consider hiking the **Yucca Canyon Trail** or the **Guadalupe Ridge Trail.** The Yucca Canyon Trail is a strenuous 11 mi. hike one-way up to a ridge in the Guadalupe Mountains; the Guadalupe Ridge Trail is a strenuous 11.3 mi. hike one-way to Putnam Cabin on the northwest boundary of the national park. Hikers often use this trail as the last leg of a week-long backpacking trip from Guadalupe Mountains National Park to Carlsbad Caverns (see p. 433). Hiking and backcountry camping require free permits from the Visitors Center. Bring lots of water; there are no reliable water sources in the backcountry.

CARLSBAD   ☎ 505

In 1899, townsfolk decided to name their agricultural settlement Carlsbad after the Karlsbad Spa in Czechoslovakia, hoping to attract tourists to the area's natural springs. In a weird twist of fate, the splendors of Carlsbad Caverns became widely known in the 1920s, and tourists flocked here to see the caves. Carlsbad itself is a fairly dull city of 25,000, but it makes a good base for exploring the area. Folks from all over the world descend on Carlsbad each year at the end of September for the International Bat Festival.

ORIENTATION AND PRACTICAL INFORMATION. Carlsbad stands at the intersection of U.S. 62/180 and U.S. 285, 166 mi. northeast of El Paso, TX and 278 mi. southeast of Albuquerque. Canal St. is the main downtown thoroughfare. South of downtown, Canal St. becomes National Parks Hwy. (U.S. 62/180). **Carlsbad City Air Terminal** (☎887-1500), south of downtown on U.S. 62/180, offers flights to Albuquerque on Mesa Airlines. The **Greyhound Station**, 1000 S. Canyon (☎887-1108; open M-F 7:30-11:30am and 1:30-4pm, Sa 8:30-10am), has service to El Paso (3hr., 2 per day, $32) and Albuquerque (6hr., 2 per day, $46). The **Chamber of Commerce**, 302 S. Canal, has basic tourist info. (☎887-6516. Open M-F 8am-5pm, Sa 9am-4pm.) The **National Park Service Information Center**, 3225 National Parks Hwy., has a plethora of brochures and other resources on nearby parks. (☎885-5554. Open June-Aug. daily 8am-4:30pm, Sept.-May M-F 8am-4:30pm.) Services include: **Clean Corner Coin and Laundry,** 521 S. Canal St. (☎885-1183; open daily 7am-9pm; last wash 8pm); **police station,** 405 S. Halagueno St. (☎885-2111); and **Carlsbad Medical Center,** 2430 W. Pierce St. (☎887-4100). The **public library,** 101 S. Halagueno St., has **free Internet access.** (☎885-6776. Open M-Th 10am-8pm, F-Sa 10am-6pm, Su 2-6pm.) **24hr. ATM:** 111 N. Canal St. The **post office** is at 301 N. Canyon St. (☎885-5717). **ZIP code:** 88220.

ACCOMMODATIONS AND FOOD. A slew of budget motels line U.S. 62/180 south of downtown. The **Stage Coach Inn ❷,** 1819 S. Canal St., is the nicest of the lot with an outdoor pool, indoor jacuzzi, and laundry. Comfortable, clean rooms have A/C, cable, and refrigerators. (☎887-1148. Singles $40; doubles $47. 15% AAA and AARP discount.) For a cheaper room, try the **Park View Motel ❷,** 401 E. Greene St., just across the Greene St. Bridge on the right. Clean, cinderblock rooms have A/C, cable, microwave, and refrigerator, with a swimming pool outside. (☎885-3117. Singles $22; doubles $29.) The **Carlsbad RV Park and Campground ❷,** 4301 National Parks Hwy. (☎888-885-6333), 4 mi. south of town, has two wooden camping cabins with a full-size bed, two bunk beds, and A/C ($30; linen not provided). Tepees ($22) and low-privacy tent camping ($14.50) are also available. All guests have access to showers and a swimming pool.

Food options in Carlsbad are pretty decent. The **No Whiner Diner ❷,** 1801 S. Canal St., is a vital institution in Carlsbad, complete with a whiners' room. The food is standard diner fare. (☎234-2815. Open Tu-Th 11am-2pm, 5-8:30pm; F0Sa 11am-2pm, 5-9pm. Burgers $5.25, pasta $7-9, chicken-fried steak $8.) For down-home Western barbecue, check out **Red Chimney BBQ ❷,** 817 N. Canal St. Dinners ($7-8) come complete with meat (turkey, chicken, spare ribs, or pork), beans, bread, and salad. (☎885-8744. Open M-F 11am-2pm, 4:30-8:30pm.) **Albertson's Supermarket,** 808

N. Canal, makes a good stop before heading off for a day trip. (☎885-2161. Open daily 6am-11pm.)

◎ ⚠ SIGHTS AND OUTDOORS. The Carlsbad Museum and Art Center, 418 W. Fox St. right next to the library, houses a collection of New Mexican art and artifacts. Highlights include pueblo pottery, paintings by the Taos Ten, and an 1858 Wells Fargo Stagecoach. (☎887-0276. Open M-Sa 10am-5pm. Free.) The **Waste Isolation Pilot Plant,** 4021 National Parks Hwy, 40 mi. east of Carlsbad, is a deep repository for long-term disposal of radioactive waste. Curious visitors can travel ½ mi. underground to tour the disposal facilities. If you are pressed for time or risk-averse, visit the info center and learn all about nuclear waste. (☎800-336-9477. Open M-Th 7am-4pm, F 7am-3:30pm. Call a month in advance to schedule a tour.) If you think the desert is ugly and barren, a trip to the beautifully maintained **Living Desert Zoo and Botanical Garden,** 4 mi. north of Carlsbad on U.S. 285, will set you straight. The 1.3 mi. walking tour takes visitors through different desert environments and offers great views of Carlsbad and environs. Flora and fauna include many types of cacti, and javelinas, deer, mountain lions, and numerous desert birds populate the park. (☎887-5516. Open June-Aug. 8am-8pm, last entry 6:30pm; Sept.-May 9am-5pm, last entry 3:30pm. $4, children $2.)

Outdoor activities abound in the Carlsbad area. Before heading up into the mountains (or down into the caves) stop by **Guadalupe Mountain Outfitters,** 216 S. Canal St., to purchase camping, hiking, climbing and caving gear. The store is also a great resource for info on rock climbing in the area. (☎888-844-9492. Open W-Su 10am-6pm.) Mountain bikers should stop by **The Bike Doc,** 304 W. Orchard Ln., for maps and guides to area trails. (☎887-7280. Open Tu-F 10am-6pm, Sa 9am-5pm.)

Sitting Bull Falls, 42 mi. west of Carlsbad, offers a pleasant respite from the desert sun. From Carlsbad, drive north 12 mi. on U.S. 285, turn left onto Rte. 137, and after 23 mi. turn right onto Forest Rd. 276. Most people come just to bathe in the cold spring water at the foot of the waterfall, which is at the end of the road. There are 16 mi. of hiking trails in this area of Lincoln National Forest. **The Bowl,** above the parking lot, is a popular **rock climbing** spot. More info on climbing is available at **Guadalupe Mountain Outfitters** in Carlsbad. A 1 mi. hike along Trail 68a (Sitting Bull Falls Trail) leads to **The Grotto,** a natural spring with a deep pool alongside a rocky cave. A popular 10 mi. loop, including the Sitting Bulls Falls Trail and the Overlook Trail, takes hikers past a few different mountain springs. Primitive camping along the trail is free with permission from the on-duty ranger. Remember to take lots of water and wear pants for protection against prickly cacti. This is mountain lion country, so exercise caution. Free maps and hiking info are available in Room 159 of the Carlsbad Federal Building, 114 S. Halegueno St. (☎885-4181. Gates open daily 8am-7pm. $5 per vehicle.)

TEXAS

Hundreds of miles from Dallas's Trinity River and even farther from the rolling hills and bright lights of Austin, West Texas offers a look at a sincere, unpolished side of the Lone Star State. Populated by prickly-pears and yuccas, rattlesnakes and mountain lions, the desert plains and jagged mountains of West Texas suggest that much of the land remains untamed. Moreover, the region is a summertime pressure cooker, with temperatures reaching and occasionally exceeding 110°F.

The outdoors of West Texas are a playground for savvy enthusiasts and novices alike. Big Bend National Park is a haven for bikers and backpackers, while the Guadalupe Mountains draw climbers from across the country. In the northern portion of the region, the Panhandle, visitors are treated to an unspoiled view of American history and culture.

DESERT LOWLANDS

Expansive Big Bend National Park, the crown jewel of southern West Texas, offers excellent hiking, biking, and kayaking, yet the campgrounds and trails remain quiet most of the year. Beyond Big Bend, West Texas boasts backpacking in the remote Guadalupe Mountains, bouldering and climbing at Hueco Tanks, and biking through Chihuahuan scrub in the Franklin Mountains. For those inclined to urban surroundings, El Paso offers plenty of excitement and easy access to fun south of the border.

▨ HIGHLIGHTS OF WEST TEXAS

MCKITTRICK CANYON. In the **Guadalupe Mountains** (p. 433), this canyon fosters lush vegetation, which turns a particularly striking red in November.

HIKING IN BIG BEND. In summer, the **Chisos Mountains** (p. 444) provide premium vistas at relatively mild temperatures. In winter, the Río Grande affords riverside hiking.

EL PASO   ☎ 915

The largest of the US border towns, El Paso boomed in the 17th century as a stopover on an important east-west wagon route that followed the Río Grande through "the pass" *(el paso)* between the Rocky Mountains and the Sierra Madre. Today, the El Paso-Ciudad Juárez metropolitan area has nearly three million inhabitants, a number that keeps growing due to an increase in the cross-border enterprises fueled by NAFTA. Nearly everyone in El Paso speaks Spanish, and the majority of are of Mexican ancestry. After dark, activity leaves the center of town, migrating toward the suburbs and south of the border to raucous Ciudad Juárez.

▮ TRANSPORTATION

Flights: El Paso International Airport (☎ 780-4700), 10 mi. northeast of downtown. Sun Metro bus #33 runs to the city center. Major airlines offer flights, including **American** (☎ 800-433-7300), **Delta** (☎ 800-221-1212), and **Southwest** (☎ 800-435-9792).

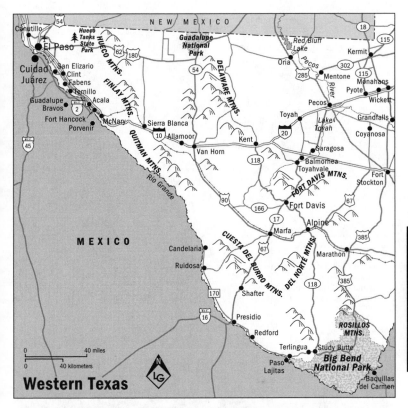

Western Texas

Trains: Union Train Depot, 700 San Francisco St. (☎545-2247), 2 blocks west of the civic center complex. **Amtrak** runs trains to **Tucson** (6hr., 3 per week, $57-100) and **San Antonio** (12½hr., 3 per week, $86-151).

Buses: Greyhound, 200 W. San Antonio (☎532-2365), near the Civic Center, has daily service to: **Albuquerque** (5½hr., 3 per day, $38); **Tucson** (6hr., 6 per day, $35); **Dallas** (12hr., 7 per day, $60); **Los Angeles** (16hr., 6 per day, $45). **El Paso-LA Bus Lines,** 720 Oregon St. (☎532-4061), on the corner of 6th Ave, is significantly cheaper than Greyhound and offers service to major destinations in the Southwest. To: **Albuquerque** (4hr., 3 per day, $20); **Las Vegas** (1 per day, $45); **Phoenix** (4 per day, $35).

Public Transportation: Sun Metro (☎533-3333) leaves from San Jacinto Plaza and other locations. $1, students 50¢.

Taxis: Checker Cab, ☎532-2626.

Car Rental: Budget (☎778-5287), with locations at 4024 N. Mesa and the airport. **Enterprise** (☎779-2260), also at the airport.

◼ ▐ ORIENTATION AND PRACTICAL INFORMATION

San Jacinto Plaza, at the corner of Main and Oregon, is the heart of El Paso. **I-10** runs east-west and **U.S. 54** into the city from the north. El Paso is divided east-west

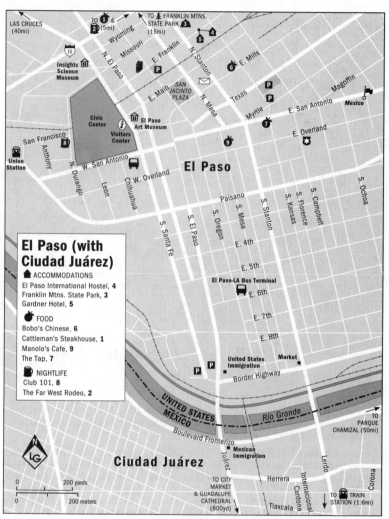

El Paso (with Ciudad Juárez)

🏠 ACCOMMODATIONS
El Paso International Hostel, **4**
Franklin Mtns. State Park, **3**
Gardner Hotel, **5**

🍎 FOOD
Bobo's Chinese, **6**
Cattleman's Steakhouse, **1**
Manolo's Cafe, **9**
The Tap, **7**

🎵 NIGHTLIFE
Club 101, **8**
The Far West Rodeo, **2**

by Santa Fe Ave. and north-south by San Antonio Ave. **Warning:** *Tourists should be wary of the streets between San Antonio and the border late at night.*

Visitor Information: 1 Civic Center Plaza (☎ 544-0062; www.visitelpaso.com), at Santa Fe and Mills. Visitors can purchase tickets here for the **Border Jumper Trolley** (☎ 544-0061). 30min. of parking ($3) is available in the Convention Center parking lot, directly underneath the Visitors Center. Open daily 8am-5pm.

Mexican Consulate: 910 E. San Antonio (☎ 533-3644), on the corner of Virginia. Dispenses tourist cards. Open M-F 8:15am-3pm.

CROSSING THE BORDER. The easiest way to cross the border is to walk. Take the north-south #8 or 10 green trolley operated by Sun Metro to the Santa Fe Bridge, the last stop before the trolley turns around (every 20min.; M-F 6:15am-8:30pm, Sa 7:45am-8:45pm, Su 8:45am-7:55pm; 25¢). Do not confuse the green trolley with the more expensive Border Jumper Trolley. Two pedestrian and motor roads cross the Río Grande: **El Paso Ave.**, a crowded, one-way street, and **Stanton Ave.**, a parallel road lined with stores and restaurants. Walk to the right side of the Stanton Bridge and pay the 25¢ fee to cross. Daytrippers, including foreign travelers with multi-entry visas, should be prepared to flash their documents of citizenship. US citizens need proof of citizenship or a driver's license. Non-US citizens must have either an I-94 form or a passport. If you are planning to venture more than 22km into Mexico's interior, you need a **tourist card.** Get one at the immigration office, to your right as you enter Ciudad Juárez.

To re-enter the US, cross the Santa Fe Bridge near the large *"Feliz Viaje"* sign. Be ready to answer questions posed by border guards and to show a valid visa or proof of citizenship. Once in El Paso, wait at the bus stop on the right-hand sidewalk just across from the bridge. The north-south bus runs M-F 6:15am-8:45pm, Sa 7:40am-8:45pm, and Su 8:45am-7:45pm. Either the #8 or the 10 bus will return you to downtown El Paso. If **driving** to and from Mexico, note that vehicles are charged $1.25 each way and may require a permit.

Currency Exchange: Valuta, 301 E. Paisano (☎544-1152), at Mesa St., is open 24hr. Conveniently near the border and also open 24hr. **Melek,** 306 E. Paisano (☎532-4283), next to Valuta. Most of the banks in the downtown area have **24hr. ATMs**.

Police: 200 Campbell St. (☎577-5000).

Hospital: Providence Memorial Hospital, 2001 N. Oregon St. (☎577-6011).

Internet access: The **public library,** 501 N. Oregon St. (☎543-5433), has free access. Open M-Th 8:30am-8:30pm, F-Sa 8:30am-5:30pm, Su 1-5pm.

Post office: 219 E. Mills (☎532-8824), between Mesa and Stanton. Open M-F 8:30am-5pm, Sa 8:30am-noon. **ZIP code:** 79901.

ACCOMMODATIONS AND CAMPING

El Paso offers safer, more appealing places to stay than Ciudad Juárez. Several good budget hotels can be found downtown, near Main St. and San Jacinto Square.

El Paso International Hostel, 311 E. Franklin (☎532-3661), between Stanton and Kansas in the Gardner Hotel. From the bus station walk up Santa Fe and turn right on Franklin. From San Jacinto Park, walk 2 blocks north to Franklin, turn right, and head east 1½ blocks. Located in the 80-year-old Gardner Hotel, the best budget accommodation in El Paso takes great pride in meeting the needs of backpackers. Dorms only open to guests with HI, HA, ISIC or student ID (also to teachers with ID). Visitors occupy clean 4-bed single-sex rooms, a full kitchen, and a large lounge with cable TV. Self-service laundry. Check-out 10am. Dorms $15, HA Members $14. Sheets $2. Towels 50¢. ❶

Gardner Hotel, 311 E. Franklin (☎532-3661, www.gardnerhotel.com). Built in the 1920s, this is the oldest continually operating hotel in El Paso. Make calls from a wooden phone booth and ride in an elevator with a metal screen door. John Dillinger stayed here in 1934. All rooms have A/C and cable TV. Singles with shared bath $25; doubles with shared bath $37; private baths start at $48. ❷

TEXAS

TEXAS TEA
A Voyage into the Crude Heart of Texas

Anyone driving through Texas will see it sooner or later—a field of cattle happily grazing in the shadow of a big steel well that is rhythmically pumping oil. The cattle, like all Texans, recognize that oil is a fact of life here. Its impact can be seen everywhere: vast refineries light up the night skies all over the state; skyscrapers purchased by oil money tower over Houston, Dallas, and San Antonio; and 150,000 wells pump sweet crude out of the ground and into the cars of Americans everywhere.

The modern oil industry was launched in 1901 by a gusher in East Texas on a hill called Spindletop. Frantic drilling exhausted the well within three years, but its immense output inspired confidence that there was enough oil to fuel an entire industrial economy. Spindletop drilling gave birth to future global oil giants like Texaco, Gulf, Mobil, and Humble Oil (now Exxon). It also inaugurated a cycle of boom and bust that has continued in Texas to this day. "Wildcatters" scoured the state, looking for the next gusher. They found them all over, resulting in the explosive growth of cities such as Wichita Falls, Amarillo, Odessa, and El Paso. Huge refineries and petrochemical plants sprung up along the Gulf of Mexico near Houston and Beaumont. Today, Texas produces more crude oil than any other state (1.2 million barrels per day), it has the largest proven reserves (5.3 billion barrels), and it has 25 percent of the nation's refining capacity. It also leads the nation in petroleum consumption, at 133 million gallons per day—there is no reason to conserve in Texas.

Texas in 1900 was a sparsely populated frontier land of farmers, ranchers, and real estate speculators, but oil money changed all that. High-paying jobs and the chance to strike it rich beckoned people from throughout the century, and today Texas is the second most populous state in the country, with three of America's biggest cities: Houston (4th), Dallas (8th), and San Antonio (9th). Wealthy philanthropists and healthy state oil revenues helped build thriving cultural and academic institutions. Oil money also fueled a culture of excess, exemplified by the phrase, "Everything is bigger in Texas." To get a feel for this, catch some reruns of the TV show *Dallas*, or drive through the River Oaks neighborhood in Houston.

There are two sides to a boom and bust cycle, however, and Texas has seen its share of busts. The dozen or so price shocks that have hit the industry over the last century have always resulted in waves of bankruptcies and abandoned mortgages. When OPEC flooded the market in the mid-80s, the resulting price drop put an end to the days of *Dallas*. Wells that were profitable at $30 per barrel became hopeless at $15, so entire operations were abandoned.

The impact of the Texas oil industry extends beyond the banks of the Sabine and the Río Grande. President George Bush Sr., a New Englander-turned-Texas oilman, launched a powerful military invasion to liberate the Kuwaiti oil fields. His son George W. Bush also got his start in the oil business, and Vice President Dick Cheney was CEO of Halliburton, the Dallas-based oil services leviathan. Some observers suggest that these ties may have influenced the Bush administration's enthusiasm for oil drilling in the Arctic National Wildlife Refuge, the administration's continuing lack of enthusiasm for the Kyoto Global Warming Treaty, and the handling of corporate mis-management scandals.

While Texas has grown fat off the oil industry, the reality is that it won't last forever; reserves have been declining for decades, and no one expects the early-80s boom days to return. With characteristic gumption, Texans have diversified their economy. Dallas and Austin have emerged as technology centers, and Houston has managed to expand its "downstream" energy business by refining cheaper foreign oil. Whether Texas can survive the inevitable collapse of its biggest industry, however, remains to be seen.

Ryan Hackney was the Editor of Let's Go: Ireland 1996 and a Researcher-Writer for Ireland 1995 and Ecuador 1997. He now lives in Texas, where he is pursuing a career as a novelist.

Franklin Mountains State Park (☎566-6441). Drive west on I-10 to the Trans-Mountain Road exit; the park entrance is on the left just before the road climbs into the mountains. *Because of the campground's proximity to the city, campers should guard belongings carefully and take safety precautions.* Sites are primitive; no water or electricity. Reservations recommended. Tent sites $8; park entrance fee $3. ●

Hueco Tanks State Historical Park (☎849-6684), 32 mi. east of El Paso. Offers camping 7 days a week. Water and showers; no charcoal or wood fires. Call to reserve a site. Campers must arrive at the park by 6pm. Tent sites $10; entrance fee $4 per person. For more info on Hueco Tanks, see p. 433. ●

◘ FOOD

There's no shortage of good Mexican food in El Paso, and prices are generally cheap. If it's a burger you crave, El Paso's fast food joints cluster around Stanton and Texas. Be aware that many downtown restaurants close on the weekends.

The Tap Bar and Restaurant, 408 E. San Antonio (☎532-1848), is dimly lit but it has excellent Mexican food. Don't mind the mirrored walls or the waitresses' skimpy dresses. Just enjoy the tasty burritos ($1.75-4), enchiladas ($4.25), and grilled shrimp in garlic ($9). Open M-Sa 7am-2am, Su noon-2am. ●

Manolo's Cafe, 122 S. Mesa (☎532-7661), between Overland and San Antonio, offers cheap food in a spartan setting. *Menudo* ($2), burritos ($1), and generous lunch specials ($4) are standard fare. Open M-Sa 7am-5pm, Su 7:30am-3pm. ●

Bobo's Chinese, 313 Mills (☎533-6116), between Kansas and Stanton. $5 all-you-can-eat buffet. Dishes $5-6. Open M-Sa 11am-7:30pm. ●

Cattleman's Steakhouse, located on the grounds of the Indian Cliffs Ranch. Take I-10 east to Exit 49, go north 5 mi. (☎915-544-3200). This place is considered El Paso's finest in steak. A bit of a drive (around 35min.) is all that separates you from famous steaks and other Southwestern favorites. For a splurge, try the 2 lb. T-bone steak at $27 or settle for one of their other selections at around $19. Open M-F 5-10pm, Sa noon-10pm, and Su noon-9pm. ❺

◪ NIGHTLIFE

Most nightlife seekers follow the younger drinking age across the border to Ciudad Juárez. Still, there remain several viable options north of the Río Grande. **Club 101,** 500 San Francisco, is El Paso's oldest club, drawing a vibrant crowd with its three dance floors and changing party scene. (☎544-2101. W-F 18+, Sa 21+. Cover $5. Open W-Sa 9pm-3am.) **Far West Rodeo,** 1225 Airway Blvd., the largest nightclub in El Paso, is a Western entertainment complex accommodating up to 6000 cowboys, urban cowboys, and just plain city slickers at any given time. Test your strength and balance on the mechanical bull for $2. (☎772-9378. Concerts weekly. 18+. Cover $5. Sports bar open daily 11am-2am.)

◙ SIGHTS

Most visitors are either stopping on the long drive through the desert or heading south to Ciudad Juárez. For a whirlwind tour, hop aboard the Border Jumper Trolleys, departing from the tourist office. Historic **San Jacinto Plaza** swarms with daily activity and affords an opportunity to rest on a shaded bench. To take in a view of the Río Grande Valley, head northwest of downtown along Stanton and make a right turn on Rim Rd. (which becomes Scenic Dr.) to reach **Murchison Park,** at the

TEXAS

base of the ridge. The Park offers a commanding vista of El Paso, Ciudad Juárez, and the Sierra Madre Mountains that is particularly impressive at night. The **El Paso Museum of Art,** 1 Arts Festival Plaza, with over 5000 works of art and a recently renovated building, is one of the largest art museums in the Southwest. Particularly impressive are the holdings of 19th- to 20th-century Southwestern art and 18th- to 19th-century Mexican colonial art. (☎532-1707. Open Tu-Sa 9am-5pm, Su noon-5pm. Free.) Sixteen miles west of El Paso off I-10 and on Rte. 28, at a small airport in Santa Teresa, NM stands the **War Eagles Air Museum,** which displays 29 historic aircraft, mostly from WWII and the Korean War. (☎505-589-2000. Open Tu-Su 10am-4pm. $5, seniors $4, students and children free.)

⚠ OUTDOOR ACTIVITIES

North of downtown El Paso, **Franklin Mountains State Park** covers 24,000 acres, making it the largest urban wilderness park in the US. Flora include Yucca, Pincushion Cactus, and the Barrel Cactus. Mule deer and mountain lions are among the park's diverse fauna. The **Visitors Center** is located in McKelligon Canyon on the east side of the Franklin Mountains. To reach the Visitors Center from downtown, take Scenic Dr. east and turn left onto Alabama St. The canyon and Visitors Center are a couple miles down on the left. (☎566-6441. Open M-F 8am-8pm during summer.) The Tom Mays section of the park is accessible only from the west side of the Franklin Mountains. Activities in this section of the park include hiking, mountain biking, and rock climbing. In the summer, the park is *very hot*, and any physical activity should be accompanied by the frequent consumption of water. (Park open June-Sept. daily 8am-8pm; Oct.-May 8am-5pm. $3 entrance fee.)

HIKING

Beginning from Sneed's Cory, **West Cottonwood Spring** is a moderate 1.6 mi. round-trip hike leading to a spring with an amazing view of the valley. Also from Sneed's Cory, the **North Mt. Franklin Trail** is a difficult 9 mi. round-trip to the top of 7200 ft. Mt. Franklin. Allot at least 5hr. for the trek. The **Aztec Caves Trail,** a steep 1.3 mi. round-trip, takes about 2hr. To reach the trailhead, take the second right after the fee station. One of the easier hikes in the park is **Upper Sunset,** a 1.2 mi. walk along the western edge of the mountain, with benches along the way to sit and admire the view. The trail begins just after the fee station on the left side of the road.

MOUNTAIN BIKING

Biking in the park caters to intermediate and advanced riders. A number of loop trails vary in length up to 16 mi. For equipment rentals and trail info, call or visit **Crazy Cat Cyclery,** 2625 N. Mesa (☎577-9666; open M-Sa 10am-8pm, Su 10am-6pm).

ROCK CLIMBING

Make the first right after the fee station to reach **Sneed's Cory,** the primary site in the park for **rock climbing.** A diagram of routes and boulder problems with their difficulty ratings is available from the ranger station. A premier bouldering and climbing location in the vicinity is **Hueco Tanks State Historical Park** (see p. 433).

OTHER ACTIVITIES

In the Franklin Mountains, the **Wyler Aerial Tramway,** northeast of downtown on the corner of Alabama St. and McKinley Ave., takes visitors to the top of 5632 ft. Ranger Peak. The third tramway of its kind in the US, it was built in 1960 to service TV and radio antennas. On a clear day, you can see 7000 sq. mi. from the top—all the way to the Guadalupe Mountains and Ruidoso, NM. (☎562-9899. Open M and Th-F noon-6pm, Sa-Su noon-9pm. Ticket sales stop one hour before closing time.

$7, children $4.) The truly gutsy should consider a trip to **Skydive El Paso,** next to the War Eagles Museum in Santa Teresa, NM. (☎505-589-4506. Skydives Sa-Su. Training starts at exactly 7:30am. Dives $135 per person.)

HUECO TANKS STATE HISTORICAL PARK   ☎915

This out-of-the-way site features unique geological formations and great rock climbing opportunities. The park's name is actually redundant. *Hueco* is the Spanish word for "natural rock basin that stores water," a meaning only faintly echoed in the English equivalent, "tank." The park's outcrops formed when magma intruded into older sedimentary layers over 34 million years ago. After overlaying sedimentary rocks eroded, the resistant igneous rock, syenite, remained, forming the *huecos* and bubbly rock mountains that rise 300 ft. from the desert floor.

The Jornada Mogollon tribe inhabited this area around 1150 AD, and their artistic efforts are responsible for many of the pictographs seen on rocks in the park. The pictographs include over 200 masks, the largest collection in North America. After the disappearance of the Mogollon Indians, other tribes, including the Apache, Kiowa, and Tigua, settled briefly in the area and added to the collection. These tribes valued the rocks for the precious water they stored, and the site remains sacred to Native Americans today.

Hueco Tanks is a **rock climber's paradise.** There are climbs of all difficulty levels, and the park is known as one of the best bouldering sites in the world. Technical climbers should purchase John Sherman's book, *Hueco Tanks Climbing and Bouldering Guide,* available in El Paso bookstores and at rock climbing outfitters nationwide. A great resource for people interested in technical climbing is the **Hueco Rock Ranch,** located just outside the park grounds. Knowledgeable staff will customize a day of rock climbing to meet the visitor's individual needs. Rock Ranch staff have access to all areas of Hueco Tanks, including those closed to the general public. Call ahead to reserve guides. The Rock Ranch also offers camping with showers for $5 per person. (☎855-0142; www.routfitters.com. Bouldering $20 per person per day, multi-pitch $110, top rope $60.)

The challenging scramble to the top of **North Mountain** is a rewarding venture that requires only a modicum of cardiovascular fitness and no technical rock-climbing accessories. Those who reach the summit will see a wide variety of desert flora and fauna. Moreover, the view from the top is quite spectacular.

To get to Hueco Tanks from El Paso, take U.S. 62 east from El Paso for 24 mi. Turn left at the spaceship, and continue another 8 mi. to the park entrance. The state park consists of three mountains. The North Mountain is open to the public for climbing and hiking, but no more than 70 people may be on the mountain at once. *Once the limit is reached, the park closes its gates and no one else can enter the park until someone leaves.* Because of this restriction, visitors should call the **state parks department** (☎512-389-8900) to reserve a spot before coming to the park. This is particularly important for visits during weekends and holidays. Visitors are allowed on the **West Mountain** and **East Mountain** on guided tours only. (Park office and tours ☎849-6684. Park open Oct.-Apr. daily 8am-6pm; May-Sept. M-Th 8am-6pm, F-Su 7am-7pm. Tours June-Aug. W-Su 9am and 11am; Sept.-May W-Su 10am and 2pm. Tours often available during the week for visitors who call at least 10 days prior to visiting; subject to guide availability. Access $4; children free.)

GUADALUPE MOUNTAINS   ☎915

The Guadalupe Mountains are the highest and most remote of the major West Texas ranges. The peaks are remnants of the ancient Capitan reef that formed 225 million years ago along the edge of a vast inland sea and covered much of what is now western Texas and southeastern New Mexico. After the sea receded, the reef

T E X A S

AT A GLANCE: GUADALUPE MOUNTAINS NATIONAL PARK	
AREA: 86,190 acres.	**GATEWAYS:** White's City; Carlsbad (p. 424).
FEATURES: El Capitán, Guadalupe Peak, McKittrick Canyon, "The Bowl."	
	CAMPING: Park campgrounds $8; free permit required for backcountry camping.
HIGHLIGHTS: Hiking to the "Top of Texas," visiting the beautiful McKittrick Canyon, seeing Williams Ranch.	**FEES AND RESERVATIONS:** No entrance fee.

was buried under layers of sediment until major block faulting and erosion excavated and exposed the petrified remains 26 million years ago.

Mescalero Apaches inhabited this land for three centuries until they were forcibly relocated to reservations in 1880. Upon their departure, ranching was taken up by a group of hardy latter-day pioneers, who barely eked out a living. In 1921, wealthy oil geologist Wallace Pratt took a fancy to the area. He bought up large tracts of land, which he eventually deeded to the government for the establishment of a national park. A long time in the making, the park finally opened in 1972.

Guadalupe Mountains National Park accommodates a particularly wide variety of flora and fauna. Drivers can glimpse the park's most dramatic sights from U.S. 62/180: **El Capitan**, a 2000 ft. high limestone cliff, and **Guadalupe Peak,** the highest point in Texas at 8749 feet. Nonetheless, Guadalupe Mountains is a true wilderness; there are no roads that penetrate the center of the park. The only way to truly appreciate the magnificence of these mountains is to get out of the car and hit the trails. *Anyone hiking alone should let someone know her/his destination and expected time of return.*

ORIENTATION AND PRACTICAL INFORMATION

The Guadalupe Mountains lie on the interior of the park, and there are only three park entrances accessible by car. In the southwestern portion of the park, **Pine Springs** is the main entrance and contains park headquarters, a Visitors Center, and a campground. **McKittrick Canyon** lies only a few miles farther on U.S. 62/180. The **Dog Canyon** campground on the north side of the park is 2hr. by car from Pine Canyon, accessible via Rte.137 from Carlsbad, NM.

The park lies 110 mi. east of El Paso (see p. 426) and 55 mi. south of Carlsbad, NM (see p. 424) on U.S. 62/180. **TNM&O Coaches** (☎505-887-1108) may stop at Pine Springs on its route between Carlsbad, NM (2½hr., $26) and El Paso if you call ahead and ask the driver nicely. The **Pine Springs** (☎828-3251; open daily June-Aug. 8am-6pm, Sept.-May 8am-4:30pm) and **McKittrick Canyon** (open Apr.-Oct. 8am-6pm; Nov.-Mar. 8am-4:30pm) **Visitors Centers** have park info and permits. For additional info, check the web site (www.nps.gov/gumo), call the Visitors Center, or write to Guadalupe Mountains National Park, HC 60, Box 400, Salt Flat, TX 79847.

There are very few services within the park itself. **Gas** is available at the **Nickel Creek Cafe,** 5 mi. north of Pine Springs. (☎828-3295. Open M-Sa 7am-2pm and 6pm-9pm. Cash only.) **White's City, NM,** 35 mi. northeast on U.S. 62/180, has the nearest post office, ATM, laundry, and 24hr. gas station.

ACCOMMODATIONS AND FOOD

The park's two simple campgrounds, **Pine Springs ❶,** just past park headquarters, and **Dog Canyon ❶,** at the north end of the park, have water and restrooms but no hookups or showers. Wood and charcoal fires are not allowed. (☎828-3251. Tent sites $8. Reservations for groups only.) Dog Canyon is accessible via Rte. 137 from Carlsbad, NM (72 mi.), or by a full-day hike from Pine Springs. After hours info is

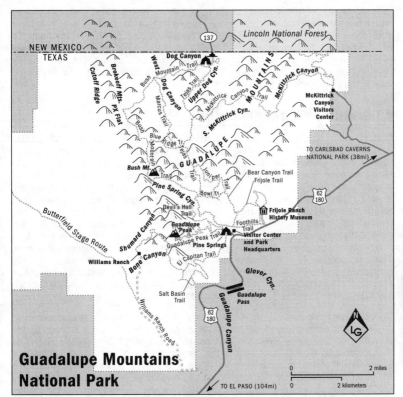

Guadalupe Mountains National Park

TEXAS

posted on the bulletin board. Free **backcountry camping** permits are available at the Visitors Center. None of the 10 backcountry sites in the park has water or toilets. Backpackers should carry at least one gallon of water per day and pack out all trash.

The park's lack of development is attractive to backpackers, but it creates some inconveniences. **Nickel Creek Cafe ❶**, 5 mi. north of Pine Springs, is the only restaurant near the park. The friendly owner serves Mexican food ($3-5), burgers ($4), and beer. (☎828-3295. Open M-Sa 7am-2pm and 6-9pm. Cash only.) White's City, 35 mi. north of Pine Springs, offers a handful of restaurants and a small **grocery store** (open May-Sept. daily 7am-10pm; Oct.-Apr. 7am-8pm). For more restaurants and the nearest supermarket, visitors must travel 65 mi. north to Carlsbad.

👁 SIGHTS

The remote Guadalupe Mountains were the home to many late 19th- and early 20th-century ranching efforts. The still-standing ranch buildings are the only nearby

 WHEN TO GO. Most people visit this park in the spring or fall when temperatures are moderate. Leaf-peepers make a cameo during late October and early November. Snow can stick to the highest peaks in the winter, and summers bring oppressive heat to the surrounding desert plains.

sights. Just up U.S. 62/180 from Pine Springs is **Frijole Ranch,** a restored ranch house with a history museum inside. Hours vary depending on the availability of volunteer staff. The only road into the interior of the park is a 7.3 mi. dirt road that begins 8.3 mi. west of Pine Springs on U.S. 62/180 and leads to the **Williams Ranch** at the base of a 3000 ft. cliff on the west side of the Guadalupe Mountains. The road is only open to high-clearance, four-wheel-drive vehicles. Visitors must get the key to the gate at the Pine Springs Visitors Center.

HIKING AND BACKPACKING

With 80 mi. of established trails and low visitation figures, Guadalupe Mountains National Park is a hiker's paradise. Most trails in the park begin at the Pine Springs Campground. Backpackers have plenty of options for multi-day hiking trips. Trekking from Pine Springs to the McKittrick Canyon Visitors Center is an arduous 20 mi., two- to three-day hike. Another interesting backpacking route follows the Tejas Trail from Pine Springs all the way to the Dog Canyon Campground and then return via the **Bush Mountain Trail.** The 24 mi. loop goes through the heart of the Guadalupe Mountains and includes the summit of Bush Mountain (8368 ft.), the second highest peak in Texas. Free backcountry camping permits are required.

Dehydration and weather are the most important safety concerns for hikers. There are no reliable water sources in the backcountry; hikers must pack in plenty of the wet stuff. When in the high country, hikers should watch the weather closely. Strong winds often blow through the Guadalupes; take a windbreaker on any hike and be careful at high elevations if the wind is really gusting.

Guadalupe Peak (8.4 mi. round-trip, 6-9hr.), at 8749 ft., is the highest mountain in Texas, and many people hike this trail as an ego-booster. The climb is tough on the lungs, but the trail is well marked. From the Pine Springs Campground, the route ascends quickly and affords views of the Permian Basin to the east. At the summit is a monument erected in 1958 to commemorate the 100th anniversary of the first transcontinental mail route, which passed through Pine Springs. From the top, the expansive Chihuahuan Desert stretches to the east, south, and west. White splotches to the southwest are salt flats, and on a clear day the Davis Mountains are visible 125 mi. to the southeast. Hikers should be prepared for strong winds at the top.

Devil's Hall (4.2 mi. round-trip, 3-5hr.), a moderate hike, the trail starts at Pine Springs, begins by winding through the Chihuahuan Desert, and drops down into a dry stream bed after about 1 mi. Maples, oaks, and pines surround and shelter the stream bed. The trail leads to a series of rocky steps known as the Hiker's Staircase and ends between the vertical stone walls of Devil's Hall.

Smith Spring Trail (2.3 mi. round-trip, 1-2hr.), a short, easy trail is a good choice for those with limited time in the park. The trail begins at the Frijole Ranch House, the first permanent building in the park. Bearing east, the trail passes Manzanita Spring, where the US cavalry destroyed a large cache of Mescalero Apache food and clothing in 1878. The trail terminates at Smith Spring, a favorite watering spot for area wildlife, especially around sunrise and sunset.

McKittrick Canyon (2.3-10.9 mi. one-way). The canyon lures hikers with the lush vegetation growing alongside McKittrick Stream. During the last two weeks of Oct. and the first week of Nov., people drive hundreds of miles to see the maple leaves turn brilliant shades of red. From the McKittrick Canyon parking lot, the spectacular scenery requires at least a 2 mi. jaunt up the trail. Wallace Pratt's cabin stands 2.3 mi. from the trailhead, and the most beautiful section of the canyon lies beyond the cabin. Day hikers should consider hiking to the Grotto Picnic Area, 3.4 mi. from the parking lot. Backpack-

HIKING PARK TO PARK. If the idea of jumping back in the car to drive from Guadalupe Mountains National Park to Carlsbad Caverns (see p. 421) doesn't suit you, don your pack and spend five days to a week hiking the 60 mi. stretch along the spine of the Guadalupe Mountains. The trip can be completed in either direction and is most pleasant in the spring or fall. *The route lacks any reliable water sources, and strong winds and heavy thunderstorms are constant threats.* Contact either national park for more info and trail conditions.

ers will probably stop at the backcountry campsite 7.4 mi. from the trailhead. The trail can be hiked all the way to Dog Canyon (2 days) or Pine Springs (3-4 days).

The Bowl Loop (9 mi. round-trip, 8-10hr.). This route offers hikers a great opportunity to see the flora and fauna of the Guadalupe high country. Visitors will be surprised to find a dense, coniferous forest full of deer and elk, remnants of an earlier time when much of western Texas was blanketed in trees, not desert. From Pine Springs Campground, start on the Tejas Trail, then take the Bowl Trail to the summit of 8368 ft. Hunter Peak. The impressive view from the summit stretches in all directions. Continue down the mountain on the Bear Canyon Trail and then Frijole Trail. Many visitors choose to do this hike as an overnight, sleeping at the Pine Top campsite, about 4 mi. up the trail.

ALPINE ☎ 915

Alpine is the seat of Brewster County, the largest and most sparsely populated county in Texas. While there is little to see in the town itself, it makes a great stop-over en route to Big Bend National Park (see p. 440). Labor Day weekend brings tourists in for the Alpine Balloon Rally and the nearby Marfa Lights Festival.

Alpine lies at the junction of U.S. 90 and Rte. 118. Most of the town's accommodations and restaurants are along U.S. 90, which splits into Holland Ave. and Ave. E in the downtown area. The **Amtrak** station (☎800-872-7245), at the highway junction, runs trains to El Paso (5hr., 3 per week, $40-73) and San Antonio (8hr., 3 per week, $64-113). **Greyhound**, 601 East Ave. E (☎837-5302), runs buses to El Paso (3hr., 1 per day, $36) and San Antonio (9hr., 3 per day, $54). **Alpine Auto Rental,** 414 E. Holland, next to the Sonic, will rent cars for a trip to Big Bend. (☎837-3463. 21+ with valid driver's license and proof of insurance. From $36 per day, 10¢ per mi.) Tourist info is available at the **Chamber of Commerce,** 106 N. 3rd St. (☎837-2326). **Police station:** 309 W. Sul Ross (☎837-3486). **Medical Services: Big Bend Medical Center,** 2600 N. Rte. 118 (☎915-837-3447). The public library, 203 N. 7th St., has **free Internet access.** (☎837-2621. Open M 9:30am-8pm, Tu-F 9:30am-5:30pm, Sa 10am-1pm.) **Post office:** 901 W. Holland, M-F 8am-4pm, Sa 10am-1pm. **ZIP code:** 79830.

A glut of cheap motels is located east of downtown on Rte. 90 near Sul Ross State University. The nicest budget accommodations in town are at the **Antelope Lodge ❷,** 2310 W. Rte. 90, 2 mi. west of Rte. 118. Each room occupies half of a small cottage and has a kitchenette, A/C, cable TV, and desert art on the wall. (☎837-2451 or 800-880-8106; www.antelopelodge.com. Singles and doubles start at $35.) The cheapest rooms in town are at **Motel Bien Venido ❷,** 809 E. Holland Ave., two blocks west of the university. The rooms are a bit run-down, but they have A/C, cable, and private baths. (☎837-3454; Singles $28; doubles $34.) The **Woodward Ranch ❶,** 16 mi. south of Alpine on Rte. 118 (☎364-2271), has primitive campsites along a mountain stream with oak trees ($10; no bathroom facilities), or less scenic sites with bathrooms and showers ($15). Stop at the **Food Basket,** 104 N. 2nd St. (☎837-3295), to stock up on food before heading to Big Bend. **Penny's Diner ❶,** 2407 E. Holland, east of downtown on Rte. 90 by the Oak Tree

TEXAS

THE MYSTERIOUS MARFA LIGHTS In 1883, a cowboy named Robert Ellison was camping west of Alpine when he saw strange lights in the distance. He first thought that they were Apache fires, but upon further investigation he concluded that they were not man-made. Since that day, many people have searched for the source of these persistent lights but no one has conclusively determined their origin. They take many forms: dividing into separate balls of light, moving up and down, and flickering on and off. Individuals have even claimed to have been chased by the lights. Many theories have been proposed to explain this mysterious phenomenon, but not one has been accepted as accurate.

The lights come out almost every night. There is a public viewing area 9 mi. east of Marfa on the south side of U.S. 90. Look toward Chinati Peak along the southwestern horizon. The **Apache Trading Post,** 2701 W. Rte. 90, 2 mi. west of Alpine, continuously shows a short video on the lights. (*Open M-Sa 9am-6pm, Su 1-6pm. Video free.*)

Inn, is a great spot to tank up before or after a long drive. The sandwiches ($4-5), burgers ($5), or big salads ($5.25) are tasty options, and breakfast is served all day. (☎837-5711. Open 24hr.)

Sul Ross State University is the main fixture of Alpine. The school is known for its rodeo team, one of the best in the nation. The university also hosts an annual **Cowboy Poetry Festival.** The festival includes three days of recitations by cowboys and cowgirls, along with a rodeo, music, and Western cooking. Also at the university, on the first floor of Lawrence Hall, is **Museum of the Big Bend,** a small museum with exhibits on the history and art of the Big Bend region of Texas. Every April the museum shows a special cowboy art exhibit. (☎837-8143; open Tu-Sa 9am-5pm, Su 1-5pm.) At night, the **Railroad Blues,** 504 W. Holland Ave., is the place to hang your hat in Alpine. With 118 brands of beer from 80 countries, 33 types of wine, and a special house sangria, you can pick your poison. Live music Friday and Saturday nights ranges from rock to reggae. (☎837-3103. 21+. F-Sa cover $5-7. Open M-F 4pm-midnight, Sa 4pm-1am.)

FORT DAVIS AND THE DAVIS MOUNTAINS ☎915

Life is quiet in Fort Davis. Somehow, this town of 1400 has managed to eschew traffic lights, chain motels, franchise restaurants, and even numbered street addresses. Instead, wooden buildings adorn downtown's main drag and tall tales bordering on Old West mythology are told in the town's lazy, mom-and-pop establishments. The highest town in Texas at 5000 ft., Fort Davis lies at the foot of the scenic Davis Mountains. Renowned for wonderful stargazing opportunities, this rounded range offers a greener, gentler alternative to the rugged desert peaks of Big Bend and the Guadalupe Mountains.

🖪🖬 ORIENTATION AND PRACTICAL INFORMATION. The town is in the Davis Mountains at the junction of Rte. 17 and 118. The roads merge to form the main street of the town and then diverge again south of the courthouse. Tourist info is available at the **Chamber of Commerce,** on the south side of town on Rte. 17, just after the highways split. (☎426-3015. Open M-F 9am-5pm.) The public library, in the center of town just behind the Limpia Hotel, has **free Internet access.** (☎426-3802; open M-F noon-6pm.) The closest **medical facility** is Big Bend Regional Medical Center in Alpine. The **post office** is at Memorial Square. **ZIP code:** 79734.

🖪🖸 ACCOMMODATIONS AND FOOD. Private rooms in Fort Davis are pricier than in larger towns nearby. Camping is more economical, and the mountain scenery beats wallpaper. The best place to pitch your tent is in nearby **Davis Mountains State Park ❶**, 5 mi. north of town. (☎426-3337. Primitive sites $6, water and showers $8; entrance fee $2.) The **Stone Village Motel ❸**, on Rte. 118 halfway between the courthouse and the Fort, has the cheapest rooms in town, with A/C, heat, and cable TV. (☎426-3941 or 800-649-8487. Singles $51; doubles $57.) The old town **Drugstore ❶**, on Rte. 118 at the center of town, serves large, thick milkshakes ($3), and a hearty breakfast special is only $5. (☎426-3118. Open daily 8am-4pm.) **Pops Grill ❶**, Hwy. 17 near the vet clinic, serves great burgers ($3.30) and offers takeout. (☎426-3195. Open daily 9am-9pm.) For groceries, try **Baeza's Thriftway** (☎426-3812), on Rte. 118 across from the fort.

◙ SIGHTS. In town, the **Fort Davis National Historic Site** incorporates the restored buildings of the original 19th-century fort, named after Jefferson Davis. The **Visitors Center** has a video and summer history programs. (☎426-3224. Open June-Aug. daily 8am-6pm; Sept.-May 8am-5pm. $3, children free.) Operated by the University of Texas, the **McDonald Observatory,** 17 mi. north of Fort Davis on Rte. 118, is the most publicly accessible research observatory in the world. Every year, 120,000 visitors are tallied, and a new Visitors Center was finished in 2002 to accommodate the traffic. Visitors can view images of the sun through a filtered telescope and take daily tours of the facility. The most popular program at the observatory is the **Star Party.** Every Tuesday, Friday, and Saturday evening visitors look through telescopes to see star clusters, planets, and far-away galaxies. (☎426-3640 or 877-984-7227; mcdonaldobservatory.org. Check web site for updated schedule; hours seasonal. Visitors Center open daily 9am-5pm. Guided tours $4, children $3, family $10. Star Party $5/$4/$15.) At the end of a bumpy dirt road 4 mi. south of town on Rte. 118, the **Chihuahuan Desert Research Institute** promotes the scientific and public understanding of the geology, flora, and fauna of the Chihuahua Desert.

⚑ OUTDOOR ACTIVITIES. High up in the scenic mountains, 5 mi. north of town on Rte. 118, **Davis Mountains State Park** offers an abundance of wildlife, miles of hiking trails, amazing scenic vistas, and a great campground. Wildlife in the park include javelinas, grey foxes, and ring-tail cats. Mule deer are abundant and tend to dart across the roads, so *be careful when driving,* especially at night. A 3 mi. scenic drive takes visitors to the highest point in the park with a great view of the Davis Mountains. The **Fort Davis Trail** is a moderate 4.5 mi. oneway hike that begins behind the interpretive center and leads over the mountains to the Fort Davis National Historic Site. Hikers will need to pay an entrance fee at the Historic Site. The **Limpia Canyon Trail** is the most challenging hike in the park. The trail is 6.5 mi. one-way and takes hikers through a canyon and up to a scenic lookout, 600 ft. above the valley floor. There are six primitive campsites near the top of the trail with no water or bathroom facilities. Campers should reserve a site in advance and must check in with the park office before beginning the hike and again upon returning. For more info about recreation in the park, contact the park office. (☎426-3337. Open daily 8am-5pm. Entrance fee $3, seniors $2, children free.) A 75 mi. **scenic drive** loop along Rte. 118 and Rte. 166 takes tourists through the entire Davis Mountain Range. From the town of Ft. Davis, drive north on Rte. 118. At 6791 ft., the point where the highway passes the McDonald Observatory is the highest elevation on the Texas Highway system. Thirteen miles past the Observatory turn left at the intersection onto Rte. 166. Sawtooth Peak and then Mt. Livermore (the second-highest peak in Texas) will be visible on the left as the road leads south. To return to town, continue along Rte. 166 and turn left on Rte. 17.

FROM THE ROAD

EIGHT-LEGGED FREAK

I think it first really hit that I was far away from a Tower Records or a CVS when I tried to get my change out of the motel's pay phone and retrieved two legs. "Push for Coins" should have read "Push for Dead Black Widow Spider" (I pulled out the rest of the body): had it been alive, I imagine I would've screamed like a seven-year-old Whitney Houston. No, it was earlier than that. The day I drove into Study Butte, outside Big Bend, I nearly ran over a red licorice shoelace about three feet long: I later learned it was a non-venomous coachwhip. I was to be tested night after night by like-minded suicidal furries hell-bent on painting my right front tire: a full-scale coordinated carnivalesque game of Don't-Whack-a-Mole. Five roadside jackrabbits who had lost everything in the stock market chose this method of death but met with no success. With any luck, my swerving convinced them not only to reinvest themselves in the Chisos Mountains skyline but to reinvest in telecommunications and office furniture. At least the javelinas (black peccaries) give you fair warning. They run out a full fifteen yards ahead and in threes, giving you ample time to avoid trimming their backsides.

Yes, the circle of life is a bloody wonder: out here, it can be more of a hexagram than a circle. The bugs that fly past your ears in Big Bend and at the Guadalupe Mountains sound like loud FM static and if challenged, could probably benchpress a toaster

(continued on next page)

BIG BEND NATIONAL PARK ☎ 915

Early Spanish travelers called the region *el despoblado*, the unpopulated land. However, evidence suggests that Native American tribes inhabited this land as early as 8500 BC and as late as the 18th century, when the Mescalero Apaches displaced the Chisos Indians. Interest in the area grew at the onset of the 20th century when valuable mineral deposits were discovered, and a number of mining operations opened in the park. In the 1920s, though, a hot springs resort opened near Boquillas Canyon and established Big Bend as a tourist attraction. It was purchased by private landholders and then donated to the federal government in 1944 as Big Bend National Park.

Today, the park's remote location in western Texas and the scarcity of nearby tourist facilities help keep visitors to a minimum. About 265,000 visitors came to Big Bend last year, most of whom flocked to the Chisos Mountains and the Río Grande. Off the beaten path, vast expanses of empty desert basins and mountain ranges lure the intrepid traveler searching for untrammeled ground.

AT A GLANCE: BIG BEND NATIONAL PARK

AREA: 801,163 acres.

FEATURES: Río Grande, Chisos Mountains, Sierra del Carmen.

HIGHLIGHTS: Hiking on the South Rim Trail in the Chisos Mountains, rafting the Santa Eleña Canyon, cruising the Ross Maxwell Scenic Drive.

GATEWAY TOWNS: Alpine (p. 437), Terlingua, Marathon, Study Butte.

CAMPING: Park campgrounds $8; free permit required for backcountry camping.

FEES: Weekly entrance pass for vehicles $10; pedestrian, bike, or motorcycle $5; yearly pass $20.

■ ORIENTATION

There are three developed areas in the park: Río Grande Village in the south, the Chisos Basin in the center of the park, and the Castolon/Santa Eleña Canyon area in the southwest. The best hiking is found in the Chisos Mountains. The other two locations are on the Río Grande and cater more to those viewing or running the river. Much of the rest of the park is wilderness, dominated by flat Chihuahuan Desert and volcanic mountain ranges.

▐ TRANSPORTATION

There is no transportation service into or around the park. **Amtrak** offers trains to Alpine (see p. 437), 103 mi. north of the park entrance. **Car rentals** are also available there. Three roads lead south from U.S. 90 into the park: from Marfa, U.S. 67 to Rte. 170; from Alpine, Rte. 118; from Marathon, U.S. 385. The fastest route to the park headquarters is via U.S. 385. There are two **gas stations** within the park, one at **Panther Junction** (☎477-2294; open Sept.-Mar. daily 7am-7pm; Apr.-Aug. 8am-6pm; 24 hr. credit card service), next to the park headquarters, and one at **Río Grande Village** (☎477-2293; open Mar.-May daily 9am-8pm; June-Feb. 9am-6pm). The **Study Butte Store** also sells gas. (Open 24 hr., credit cards only.

WHEN TO GO. Due to the oppressive summer heat, peak visitation of the park occurs during spring break and winter holidays, but there really isn't a bad time to visit Big Bend. In the summer months, areas along the river are unbearably hot—hikers will find more pleasant temperatures in the Chisos Mountains. In the winter, when the mountain climate is cold and blustery, the temperature in the lowlands along the Río Grande is more comfortable. The best season for rafting is the fall, when river levels tend to be highest, though flash floods can render the river impassable. June to October is the rainy season at Big Bend; bring raingear during these months. Thunderstorms can roll in quickly, so keep an eye to the sky to avoid lightning danger, especially in the mountains.

▐ PRACTICAL INFORMATION

Visitor information: The park web site (www.nps.gov/bibe) is a great resource for planning a trip to Big Bend. For more info, write the Superintendent, Big Bend National Park, P.O. Box 129, Big Bend National Park, TX 79834.

Park Headquarters (☎477-2251), at Panther Junction, 26 mi. south of the northern park boundary. Open daily 8am-6pm.

Visitors Centers located at: **Persimmon Gap,** where U.S. 385 enters the park (☎477-2393; open daily 8am-5pm); **Chisos Basin** (☎477-2264; open daily 9am-4:30pm); and **Río Grande Village** (☎477-2271). A **ranger station** (☎477-2225) is located at Castolon. The Río Grande Village Visitors Center and the Castolon Ranger Station are usually closed June-Oct.

(continued from previous page)

oven. Texas insects aren't so much living organisms as abstract ideas like annihilation, desperation, and desire (her name is June).

Some are sapphire blue and appear to be fashioned out of blown glass; others are clearly pure titanium and recall scenes from *Critters 4*. Still others have filed applications to be included in the mollusk family, and one insect I had coffee with has started a ska band called St. Vincent and the Grenadines. Still you need to stay in harmony with your natural surroundings: fear the beetle, die by the beetle. Repeat after me: as I walk through the valley of the shadow of Guadalupe, I shall fear nothing on four legs. The scorpions are nothing you'd tickle under the chin, but admire it for its own relentless force. If your spirit is at ease, foraging deer walk three feet to your side in the Chisos Basin, mother and child, no questions asked. Even the hawks wheeling in the blue sky over Boquillas Canyon will pose for photos you'll need to title "Hawk and Moon." Some will even be kind enough to ask you to dinner: declining the offer requires ducking.
—Jonathan Sherman

Groceries: Stores selling food and camping supplies are located near all three camp-grounds: **Río Grande Village** (☎477-2293; open daily 9am-5pm); **Chisos Basin** (☎477-2291; open daily 9am-7pm); and **Castolon** (☎477-2222; open daily 10am-6pm). For a larger selection of food go to the **Study Butte Store** (☎371-2231), on Rte. 118, about 1 mi. from the western park entrance. Open daily 7am-9pm.

Money: The nearest ATM is at the **Quicksilver Branch Bank and ATM** (☎371-2211), 1 mi. outside the park in Study Butte. The Lodge, restaurant, stores, and gas stations in the park all accept credit cards, but camping fees must be paid with cash.

Laundry: The only laundry facilities in the park are at the store in Río Grande Village. Open daily 9am-5pm.

Emergency: ☎477-2251, then press 9. If no answer, dial 911.

Medical Services: The closest medical facility is the **Big Bend Family Health Center** (☎371-2661), 2 mi. west of Study Butte on Rte. 170.

Post office: Main office (☎477-2238) in Panther Junction, next to Park Headquarters. Open M-F 8am-4pm. Chisos Basin office is inside the grocery store. Open M-Sa 9am-5pm. Post office accepts general delivery mail addressed to visitor's name, Big Bend National Park, TX. There is another post office in Study Butte next to the bank. **ZIP code:** 79834.

ACCOMMODATIONS

The expensive **Chisos Mountains Lodge ❹,** in the Chisos Basin, 10 mi. from park headquarters, offers the only motel-style shelter within the park. Reservations are a must for high season; the lodge is often booked a year in advance. (☎477-2291; www.chisosmountainslodge.com. Singles $78; doubles $84, additional person $10.) The lodge contains the only **restaurant ❷** in the park, serving three square meals a day. (Open daily 7-10am, 11:30am-4pm, and 5:30-8pm. Breakfast buffet $6.75, lunch sandwiches $4-8, dinner entrees $6-15.) Just west of the park lies Ter-lingua, a mellowed-out, historic ghost town (the name is from the Spanish for "three languages"), Lajitas, and Study Butte, two sand-swept hamlets with a few restaurants and motels. The closest budget motel to the park, the **Chisos Mining Co. Motel ❷,** on Rte. 170, ¾ mi. west of the junction with Rte. 118, provides clean rooms with A/C and an offbeat atmosphere. Life out at this gateway to Big Bend is welcoming enough to skip staying in the Basin. (☎371-2254. Singles $37; doubles $47; 5-6 person cabins with kitchenettes $60.)

CAMPING

The three developed campsites within the park do not take reservations and are run on a first-come, first-served basis. During Thanksgiving, Christmas, March, and April the campgrounds fill early; call park headquarters (☎477-2251) to inquire about availability. The **Chisos Basin Campground ❶,** at 5400 ft., has 65 sites with running water and flush toilets and stays cooler than the other campgrounds in the summer. The **Río Grande Village Campground ❶** has 100 sites near the only showers in the park. Flush toilets and water are also available. The more primitive **Cotton-wood Campground ❶** has pit toilets and prohibits generators. Stays at all developed campgrounds are limited to 14 days; visitors wishing to stay longer must receive special permission from campground personnel. Wood and ground fires are pro-hibited. Tent sites $8. The **RV park ❶** at Río Grande Village has 25 full hookups ($14.50 for up to two people; $1 per additional person).

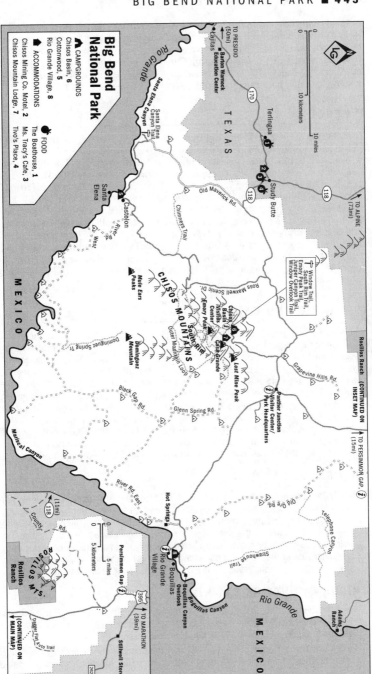

Big Bend National Park

▲ CAMPGROUNDS
Chisos Basin, 6
Cottonwood, 5
Rio Grande Village, 8

◆ ACCOMMODATIONS
Chisos Mining Co. Motel, 2
Chisos Mountain Lodge, 7

🍴 FOOD
The Boathouse, 1
Ms. Tracy's Cafe, 3
Tivo's Place, 4

TEXAS

Backcountry camping in the park is free but requires a permit from one of the Visitors Centers. Nearly all areas of the park are open to backcountry camping. A number of backcountry sites are accessible by paved roads, and many more are reached only by dirt roads requiring four-wheel drive. Sites in the Chisos Mountains have pit toilets. Backcountry campsites have no water; plan ahead and bring water. Consult a park ranger before setting off on an overnight trip.

▐ FOOD

Restaurants are scarce in the Big Bend area, though there are some options near Terlingua and Lajitas. **Ms. Tracy's Cafe ❶,** on Rte. 118 just south of the intersection with Rte. 170, has outdoor seating and decorative cacti. Ms. Tracy serves eggs, hamburgers, and burritos and a number of vegetarian entrees. (☎371-2888. Open Oct.-May 7am-9:30pm; June 7am-2pm; July-Sept. 7am-5pm.) **Tivo's ❷,** off Rte. 170 in Terlingua is popular for its Mexican fare, priced at around $6-8. (☎371-2133. Open M-F 11am-2pm, 5pm-9:30pm, Sa 11am-2pm sometimes, Su 5pm-9:30pm.) Off Rte. 170 in Terlingua, 7 mi. from the park entrance, the lively **Starlight Theater Bar and Grill ❷** has healthy portions of Tex-Mex ($3-9) and live music on weekends. (☎371-2326. Food served daily 5:30-10pm; bar open Su-F 5pm-midnight, Sa 5pm-1am. Indoor pool: no joke.) **The Boathouse ❸,** in Terlingua's historic ghost town, has a gourmet chef, nightly specials ($8-13), and the Zenternet cafe ($2 per 15 min. of Internet access).

▐ HIKING AND BACKPACKING

There are 200 miles of hiking trails in the park, ranging from 30min. nature walks to extended backpacking trips. Park rangers at the Visitors Centers are happy to suggest hikes and sights; the *Hiker's Guide to Big Bend* ($2), available at Panther Junction, is a good investment. Those hiking in the Chisos Mountains should purchase the topographical *Chisos Mountains Trail Map* for $1 at the Visitors Center. The number one safety hazard in the park is dehydration; *always carry at least a gallon of water per person per full day of desert hiking. Also, anyone hiking alone should let someone know his/her destination and expected time of return.* Sneakers can be worn on very short hikes, but hiking boots are absolutely crucial for more strenuous hikes. When hiking or backcountry camping, be sure to pack out all trash and bury all human waste 6 in. below ground.

RÍO GRANDE DAY HIKE

Santa Eleña Canyon (1.7 mi. round-trip, 1½hr.). Starting at a trailhead at the end of the Ross Maxwell Scenic Drive, this spectacular trail takes hikers through a 1500 ft. high limestone canyon carved by the Río Grande. The trail begins by crossing Terlingua Creek; most of the year the water is shallow and hikers can easily wade across. *Do not attempt this hike after heavy rains when the water is high and the current is strong.* On the other side of the creek the trail climbs to a view of the canyon, slopes down to the river's edge, and continues along the canyon floor before ending at a rock wall.

CHISOS MOUNTAINS DAY HIKES

Window View (0.3 mi, 20min.). A short, paved loop from the Chisos Basin parking lot with benches along the way. Watching the sun set through the Window is must for all visitors to Big Bend National Park. Wheelchair accessible.

Lost Mine Trail (4.8 mi. round-trip, 3-4hr.). This moderately strenuous hike that goes into the Chisos Mountains begins at Panther Pass (*not* Junction), which is located at

Mile 5 of the road that leads up into the Chisos Basin. The trail passes below Casa Grande and climbs 1100 ft. to a vantage point high above Juniper Canyon. Those pressed for time or sapped of energy can hike to the impressive Juniper Canyon Overlook, 1 mi. from the trailhead.

Window Trail (5.2 mi. round-trip, 3-4hr.). From the Chisos Basin parking lot, this popular hike leads down from the Chisos Lodge to a U-shaped rock formation known as the Window. The trail follows the natural drainage of the basin and passes a wide variety of desert flora and colorful rock formations. In rainy months the Window becomes a 200 ft. waterfall. A side trail toward Oak Spring, 0.3 mi. from the Window, has great views down into the desert and up toward the Chisos. During the hot summer, the best time to hike this trail is in the early morning. Some people begin this hike next to site #52 in the Basin Campground to shave 1.2 mi. off the round-trip distance.

South Rim (13-14.5 mi. round-trip, 6-10hr.). The South Rim of the Chisos Mountains, 2500 ft. above the Chihuahuan Desert, offers the most impressive views in Big Bend National Park. On a clear day, you can see the Río Grande winding its way through the Chihuahuan Desert, mountain peaks in Mexico nearly 50 mi. to the south, Santa Elena Canyon 20 mi. to the west, and the Sierra del Carmen Mountains 30 mi. to the east. There are 2 trails from the Chisos Basin parking lot that lead to the South Rim, Laguna Meadow (6.5 mi. one-way), and Pinnacles Trail (6.4 mi. one-way). Most hikers ascend the mild Laguna Meadow trail and come down the steeper Pinnacles Trail. Once at the South Rim, hikers may wish to add the 3.3 mi. East Rim loop for views of the eastern section of the park (closed Feb. 1-Jul. 15 for peregrine falcon nesting season). The descent on the Pinnacles Trail follows a series of stagnant rainwater pools through the high woodlands of Boot Canyon and offers scenic overlooks of Casa Grande and the Chisos Basin. For those who choose to do the South Rim as an overnight hike, primitive campsites with pit toilets are located along the trail.

Emory Peak (4.5 mi. one-way, 5-8hr.). At 7825 ft., this is the highest mountain in the park, and one of the highest in Texas. From the Basin Trailhead in the parking lot take the Pinnacles Trail 3.5 mi. to the Emory Peak Trail. The summit is a mile from this junction, and reaching it requires scrambling up a sheer rock wall. *Be very careful climbing up the rocks: serious accidents have occurred here.* Dedicated hikers will be rewarded with a 360-degree view from the top. Emory Peak also can be combined with a hike to South Rim for a 15 mi. round-trip.

BACKPACKING

Big Bend offers numerous backpacking opportunities to those willing to rough it in the desert. One of the more popular multi-day hikes is the **Outer Mountain Loop** (31.6 mi., at least 3 days; includes the **Dodson Trail** among others). This trail offers a great diversity of scenery, from the woodlands of the High Chisos Complex to the scrub and cacti of the Chihuahuan Desert. It begins at the Basin trailhead, climbing up to Emory Peak and the South Rim, then loops around and travels through the desert below South Rim (these are side-trips). All backcountry camping requires a permit, available at any park Visitors Center. **Desert Sports** and **Big Bend River Tours** (see below) each offer day and overnight guided hiking trips.

RIVER RUNNING

The Río Grande can be much better appreciated by taking a trip down the river. The National Park Service has jurisdiction over the entire 118 mi. of river along the southern boundary of the park, as well as an additional 127 mi. downstream of the park known as the **Río Grande Wild and Scenic River**. Until 1899, these 245 mi. of the

TEXAS

Río Grande were considered impassable to boats. An 1852 surveying expedition floated an unmanned boat through Santa Elena Canyon, only to find splintered pieces of wood at the other end. Today, because of extensive damming, only those with the necessary knowledge and experience can navigate the river.

There are three main river canyons within the park boundaries. Near the western end of the park, **Santa Elena Canyon** is a 20 mi., one-to-three-day trip with a 7 mi. stretch where the river is confined by 1500 ft. limestone walls. Two miles into this canyon is the Rock Slide, a Class IV rapid when the water level is high. **Mariscal Canyon** is a 10 mi., one-day trip through 1400 ft. canyon walls. The rapids within this canyon are Class II-III. **Boquillas Canyon,** along the eastern edge of the park, is a two- to three-day, 33 mi. journey through 1200 ft. walls. The rapids here do not exceed Class II, making Boquillas a good choice for rafters with less experience. Another easy, one-day trip is **Colorado Canyon,** in **Big Bend Ranch State Park** (see p. 447), upstream of the national park. The **Lower Canyons,** downstream of the Big Bend, wind through 137 mi. of rugged desert and deep canyons. Floating the Lower Canyons can take five to ten days depending on how far one ventures.

There are three options for river trips: bring your own equipment, rent equipment from an outfitter, or go on a guided trip. Those tackling the river on their own must obtain a permit from the Visitors Centers at Persimmon Gap, Panther Junction, or Río Grande Village. Boaters should buy the detailed river guide available at park headquarters. Inflatable rafts are much safer than canoes because they bounce off rocks and canyon walls. In Terlingua, **Desert Sports** (☎371-2727 or 888-989-6900; www.desertsportstx.com) rents rafts and canoes starting at $40 per day. Guided tours start at $125 for a daytrip. In Terlingua off Hwy. 170, **Big Bend River Tours** (☎371-3033 or 800-545-4240; www.bigbendriver-tours.com) rents canoes ($45 per day) and inflatable kayaks ($35 per day). Guided trips available: half-day $62, full day $130. Both offer **shuttle services** to pick people up downriver.

For those without river experience, a guided trip is the safest option and generally runs $100 per person per day. Desert Sports, Big Bend River Tours, and **Texas River and Jeep Expeditions and Far-Flung Adventures** (☎371-2633 or 800-839-7238; www.farflung.com/tx), in Terlingua, offer single- and multi-day canoe and kayak trips through the park's canyons (also specialty trips with area chefs and musicians; call well in advance for reservations). For each of these guided trips, a minimum of two people is required to start a separate scheduled trip.

■ OTHER ACTIVITIES

MOUNTAIN BIKING

Bikes are allowed on all roads in the park, both paved and unpaved. **Old Ore Rd.** (26 mi. one-way, 4-6hr.) is perhaps the best ride in the park. Start at the Dagger Flat Auto Trail, halfway between Persimmon Gap and Panther Junction; from here the trip is mostly downhill. The road is rough but the views are spectacular with the Chisos Range to the west and the Sierra del Carmen to the east. Another good route is **Glenn Springs Rd.** to **River Rd.** (25 mi., 3-4hr.) starting about 6 mi. south of Panther Junction and ending up near Río Grande Village. For a smoother ride, consider biking the **Ross Maxwell Scenic Drive** and **Old Maverick Rd. Loop** (56 mi. round-trip, 5-6hr.). All but 13 mi. of this loop are paved, and bikers can stop at Santa Elena Canyon. **Desert Sports** (see above) rents mountain bikes for $25 per day.

ARABIAN NIGHTS IN TEXAS? In the 1850s, Secretary of War Jefferson Davis initiated a novel experiment to determine whether camels might be practical for military use in the American West. In 1859, topographers William H. Echols and Edward L. Hartz led 24 camels across Texas and into the Big Bend Region. The camels were able to carry more weight and cover 50% more territory each day than a horse or mule. With the Civil War, the program was abandoned. It's too bad. Imagine the Lone Ranger riding off into the sunset on a camel.

ROCK CLIMBING

Although the mountains and canyons of Big Bend have plenty of exposed rock faces, much of the rock is sedimentary and too soft for climbing. Nonetheless, the park offers a few decent rock-climbing spots. Many climbers frequent **Indian Head,** on the northwest border of the park, 6 mi. northeast of Terlingua. Another spot is the top of the **Lost Mine Trail,** which offers 5.8 and 5.9+ pitches. For the location and ratings of climbing problems, pick up a copy of *A Climber's Guide to Big Bend,* available at Park Headquarters. Hand-drills are allowed only with approval of the superintendent. Only white chalk with oil-based additives may be used.

SCENIC DRIVING

There are only five paved roads in the park. Of these, the best sight-seeing is along the **Ross Maxwell Scenic Drive,** a 30 mi. paved route from the western edge of the Chisos Mountains that leads down to the Río Grande and Santa Eleña Canyon. The 8 mi. drive that winds its way up into the **Chisos Basin** is also quite rewarding. However, the most spectacular drives in the park are unimproved, only accessible to four-wheel-drive jeeps and trucks. **River Rd.,** a 51 mi., 6-8hr. drive, skirts along the Río Grande from Castolon to the Río Grande Village. Another good drive is the 26 mi. **Old Ore Rd.,** which travels along the western edge of the Sierra del Caballo Muerto. Those interested in driving the backroads of Big Bend should purchase the guide to backcountry roads at the Visitors Center for $2. For visitors without their own four-wheel-drive vehicle, Big Bend River Tours (see p. 445) offers backcountry jeep tours ($65 per person for a half day).

BIG BEND RANCH STATE PARK ☎ 915

This 400-square-mile state park adjoins the National Park and was a private ranch until the state of Texas bought the land in 1988. Today, the state operates the ranch as a state park. The rarely visited park includes mountains, waterfalls, vast stretches of Chihuahuan Desert, and the Río Grande. The **Barton Warnock Education Center,** 1 mi. east of Lajitas on Rte. 170, has an excellent interpretive exhibit on the geology and natural history of the Big Bend region and a sizeable desert garden. The Visitors Center sells multi-use permits ($6) for hiking, camping, and river access. (☎ 424-3327. Open daily 8am-4:30pm. Exhibit $3, children $1.50.)

The most accessible hiking trails in the park begin from Rte. 170. The **Closed Canyon Trail,** 1.4 mi., winds through the walls of a narrow canyon carved by a tributary of the Río Grande. The **Rancherias Canyon Trail** leads 4.8 mi. along the canyon floor to 70 ft. Rancherias Falls. The **Rancherias Trail** is a 19 mi., three-day backpacking trail into the canyon country of the Bofecillos Mountains. There are three primitive camping areas with pit toilets located along Rte. 170. Campers must obtain a backcountry permit from the Warnock Education Center.

Ranch headquarters at Sauceda, in the park interior, is at the end of a 29 mi. gravel road. Visitors can stay at the historic **Ranch House** (☎ 229-3416) in private rooms ($40 per person) or bunks ($15 per person) in the hunting lodge. Reservations for rooms and meals are essential. The road to Sauceda makes a great mountain bike ride, and there are many hiking trails that begin near park headquarters.

Within the confines of the state park, the 50 mi. **El Camino del Río Scenic Drive** follows Rte. 170 along the Río Grande from Lajitas to Presidio. Named by *National Geographic* as one of the prettiest drives in the US, the road winds through mountains, canyons, desert, and farmland. Allow 1½hr. to drive the route, plus additional time for stops. Five miles from Lajitas is the **Contrabando movie set,** the set of many Westerns, including the 1984 movie *Uphill all the Way* with Roy Clark, Glen Campbell, Mell Tillis, and Burl Ives. Thirteen miles from Lajitas, the road climbs a large hill with a 15% grade. This is a popular spot to watch sunrise and sunset. Looking east from the top of the hill one can see the Chisos Mountains more than 30 mi. away. Six miles west of the hill is a parking area for the **Closed Canyon Trail.** This 1.4 mi. round-trip hike within the confines of the park follows a dry river bed through the narrow walls of a large canyon.

INDEX

458 ■ INDEX

MAP INDEX

MAP LEGEND

Park	**Water**	**Beach**
✚ Hospital	✈ Airport	🏨 Hotel/Hostel	14 Forest Road
🚓 Police	🚌 Bus Station	⛺ Camping	207 State Road
✉ Post Office	🚆 Train Station	🍎 Food	56 U.S. Road
ⓘ Visitor Information	P Parking	🍷 Nightlife	70 Interstate Highway
Border Crossing	M Metro Station	Primitive Campsite	Freeway
Embassy/Consulate	Church	Shelter	Paved Road
▪ Site or Service	Mission	Ranger Station	Unpaved Road
🖥 Internet	Pueblo	Mountains	4-Wheel Drive Road
🏛 Museum	Ruins	Butte	Trail
📕 Library	Ski Area	Pass	The Let's Go compass always points NORTH
Pedestrian Zone	Trailhead	Waterfall	

466